THE INTERNATIONAL LIBRARY OF ESSAYS ON AVIATION POLICY AND MANAGEMENT

THE INTERNATIONAL LIBRARY OF ESSAYS ON AVIATION POLICY AND MANAGEMENT

Edited by

LUCY BUDD AND STEPHEN ISON
De Montfort University, Leicester

Volume VI
Aviation Design and Innovation

Routledge
Taylor & Francis Group

LONDON AND NEW YORK

First published 2020
by Routledge
2 Park Square, Milton Park, Abingdon, Oxon OX14 4RN

and by Routledge
52 Vanderbilt Avenue, New York, NY 10017

Routledge is an imprint of the Taylor & Francis Group, an informa business

British Library Cataloguing-in-Publication Data
A catalogue record for this book is available from the British Library

Library of Congress Cataloging-in-Publication Data
A catalog record has been requested for this book

ISBN: 978-0-367-28136-6 (set)
ISBN: 978-1-4724-5160-6 (volume VI)

Typeset in Times New Roman
by codeMantra

Publisher's Note
References within each chapter are as they appear in the original complete work

Contents

Part III Alternative fuels

Part IV Business Model Innovation

Acknowledgments

The Publishers would like to thank the following for permission to reprint their material:

Elsevier for permission to reprint Amedeo R. Odoni and Richard de Neufville, 'Passenger Terminal Design', *Transportation Research Part A*, 26A, 1, 1992, 27–35.

Elsevier for permission to reprint Alexandre G. de Barros and S. C. Wirasinghe, 'Optimal Terminal Configurations for New Large Aircraft Operations', *Transportation Research Part A*, 37, 2003, 315–331.

Taylor & Francis for permission to reprint Richard de Neufville, 'Low-Cost Airports for Low-Cost Airlines: Flexible Design to Manage the Risks', *Transportation Planning and Technology*, 31, 1, 2008, 35–68.

Elsevier for permission to reprint Peter Forsyth, 'The Impacts of Emerging Aviation Trends on Airport Infrastructure', *Journal of Air Transport Management*, 13, 2007, 45–52.

Elsevier for permission to reprint Alan MacPherson and David Pritchard, 'The International Decentralisation of US Commercial Aircraft Production: Implications for US Employment and Trade', *Futures*, 35, 2003, 221–238.

Taylor & Francis for permission to reprint Jorge Niosi and Majlinda Zhegu, 'Aerospace Clusters: Local or Global Knowledge Spillovers?', *Industry and Innovation*, 12, 1, 2005, 5–29.

Elsevier for permission to reprint John M. C. King, 'The Airbus 380 and Boeing 787: A Role in the Recovery of the Airline Transport Market', *Journal of Air Transport Management*, 13, 2007, 16–22.

Elsevier for permission to reprint Alexander Z. Ibsen, 'The Politics of Airplane Production: The Emergence of Two Technological Frames in the Competition between Boeing and Airbus', *Technology in Society*, 31, 2009, 342–349.

Elsevier for permission to reprint Emma Nygren, Kjell Aleklett and Mikael Höök, 'Aviation Fuel and Future Oil Production Scenarios', *Energy Policy*, 37, 2009, 4003–4010.

Elsevier for permission to reprint Per Gegg, Lucy Budd and Stephen Ison, 'The Market Development of Aviation Biofuel: Drivers and Constraints', *Journal of Air Transport Management*, 39, 2014, 34–40.

Elsevier for permission to reprint Thushara K. Hari, Zahira Yaakob and Narayana N. Binitha, 'Aviation Biofuel from Renewable Resources: Routes, Opportunities and Challenges', *Renewable and Sustainable Energy Reviews*, 42, 2015, 1234–1244.

Elsevier for permission to reprint Niven Winchester, Robert Malina, Mark D. Staples and Steven R. H. Barrett, 'The Impact of Advanced Biofuels on Aviation Emissions and Operations in the U.S.', *Energy Economics*, 49, 2015, 482–491.

Elsevier for permission to reprint Marina Kousoulidou and Laura Lonza, 'Biofuels in Aviation: Fuel Demand and CO_2 Emissions Evolution in Europe Toward 2030', *Transportation Research Part D*, 46, 2016, 166–181.

Elsevier for permission to reprint Graham Francis, Ian Humphreys, Stephen Ison and Michelle Aicken, 'Where Next for Low Cost Airlines? A Spatial and Temporal Comparative Study', *Journal of Transport Geography*, 14, 2006, 83–94.

Elsevier for permission to reprint David Gillen and Alicja Gados, 'Airlines Within Airlines: Assessing the Vulnerabilities of Mixing Business Models', *Research in Transportation Economics*, 24, 2008, 25–35.

Elsevier for permission to reprint Richard Klophaus, Roland Conrady and Frank Fichert, 'Low Cost Carriers Going Hybrid: Evidence from Europe', *Journal of Air Transport Management*, 23, 2012, 54–58.

Elsevier for permission to reprint Sascha Albers, Benjamin Kock and Christine Ruff, 'Strategic Alliances between Airlines and Airports—Theoretical Assessment and Practical Evidence', *Journal of Air Transport Management*, 11, 2005, 49–58.

Elsevier for permission to reprint Peter Forsyth, Hans-Martin Niemeier and Hartmut Wolf, 'Airport Alliances and Mergers – Structural Change in the Airport Industry?', *Journal of Air Transport Management*, 17, 2011, 49–56.

Taylor & Francis for permission to reprint Donald McNeill, 'The Airport Hotel as Business Space', *Geografiska Annaler. Series B, Human Geography*, 91, 3, 2009, 219–228.

Elsevier for permission to reprint Michael B. Charles, Paul Barnes, Neal Ryan and Julia Clayton, 'Airport Futures: Towards a Critique of the Aerotropolis Model', *Futures*, 39, 2007, 1009–1028.

Disclaimer

The publishers have made every effort to contact authors/copyright holders of works reprinted in the *International Library of Essays on Aviation Policy and Management*. This has not been possible in every case, however, and we would welcome correspondence from those individuals/companies whom we have been unable to trace.

Introduction

Lucy Budd and Stephen Ison

Introduction to *the International Library of Essays on Aviation Policy and Management*

This collection comprises 6 distinct but interrelated volumes that contain previously published academic essays that collectively address important issues in international civil aviation policy and management. Despite air transport's relatively short presence in world history, it has evolved into one of the world's most significant modes of international and long-distance mobility that facilitates the routine transnational movement of billions of passengers and millions of tonnes of highly valuable freight annually. Understanding the policy and management implications of this rapidly developing transport mode has been considered by disciplines as diverse as civil engineering and the social sciences, and tens of thousands of essays, both empirical and theoretical, have been published in the field. In this collection, we limit ourselves to essays published in the English language; while we do not (and cannot) claim to be comprehensive, the aim of this collection is to present essays which showcase significant and thought-provoking essays that have sought to stimulate debate in this diverse and dynamic field of academic inquiry.

The collection comprises 6 volumes, each covering a different aspect of aviation policy and management. The collection seeks to provide useful insight into key areas of aviation that are of interest both to academics and practitioners worldwide. The choice of essays is necessarily subjective; however, every effort has been made to be as inclusive and informative as possible by drawing on a wide range of disciplinary perspectives and journal titles. Given the diversity of the empirical, theoretical and disciplinary approaches that have been applied to the study of aviation, this is no straightforward task and is inherently problematic and subjective. We appreciate that not every reader will agree with our selection and may have his or her own opinion concerning which essays should have been included or excluded. Nevertheless, it is our intention that this collection will act as a foundation from which readers can make their own further forays into the academic research base surrounding aviation.

The 6 volumes have been configured and presented as follows:

Volume 1 addresses aspects of *Aviation Law and Regulation*. This volume sets the scene for the legal and regulatory operation of international civil aviation from the earliest days to the present. It contains 4 Parts and 18 essays that cover aviation law, regulation and deregulation, competition and contestability and open skies.

Volume 2 *Aviation Planning and Operations* comprises 25 essays with Parts covering forecasting, infrastructure planning and provision, capacity, scheduling, safety and security, disruption management and resilience.

Volume 3 *Aviation Business Strategy* comprises 26 essays that cover market structure, revenue cost and pricing, mergers and acquisitions, global airline alliances and marketing and customer loyalty.

Volume 4, which focuses on *Aviation Performance and Productivity*, includes Parts relating to privatisation and commercialisation, efficiency, service delivery and service quality, human resources and industrial relations. This volume comprises 26 essays.

Volume 5 *Aviation Social and Economic Impacts* contains 26 essays divided into 5 Parts, namely airports and economic development, airports, logistics and supply chains, air transport and tourism, air transport in remote regions and environmental externalities.

Volume 6 *Aviation Design and Innovation* comprises 20 essays presented in 4 Parts – airport design and sustainability, aircraft design and manufacturing, alternative fuels and business model innovation.

Introduction to Volume 6 *Aviation Design and Innovation*

The 20 essays in this volume are presented in 4 Parts.

Part I Airport Design and Sustainability

In order to facilitate the safe, efficient and cost-effective exchange of passengers and cargo between ground and sky, airports require the provision of adequate runways, aircraft-manoeuvring areas, cargo sheds and passenger-processing facilities. Airports are capital-intensive facilities, and planning errors that result in the over- or under-provision of capacity are both costly and problematic to rectify. The first essay in this part examines the procedures that are used to size the spaces afforded to different passenger activities in the terminal. In it, Odoni and de Neufville (1992) note the need to develop flexible designs that optimise the efficient use of space under a broad range of operational conditions.

The design of passenger terminal buildings is influenced not only by levels of demand, the commercial requirements of airlines and tenant companies, the availability of investment funds and political influence but also by the aircraft that will be using the facility both now and in the future. Indeed, the introduction of the first generation of passenger jets in the 1950s and higher-capacity wide-bodied aircraft in the late 1960s required not only the expansion of gate areas and passenger-processing facilities but also the introduction of new technologies such as the travelator, the baggage reclaim carousel and the airbridge. The introduction of the A380 'Super Jumbo' into passenger service in 2007 similarly demanded a reconfiguration of the airports it serves. The second essay in this part, by de Barros and Wirasinghe (2003), analyses the options for accommodating a new generation of large aircraft.

While large aircraft generally require a lengthy turn around period between flights and the extensive provision of expensive fixed ground support infrastructure, low-cost carriers pursue a business model based on very short turnarounds and minimal use of airport infrastructure assets such as airbridges. One of the main challenges facing airport operators is how to accommodate the diverse and dynamic requirements of different operators. In the third essay in this part, de Neufville (2008) proposes a flexible design strategy to deal with this uncertainty and to enable airports to effectively respond to changes in type, needs and the location of traffic. The final essay in this part, by Forsyth (2007), explores the likely impacts of new and emerging aviation trends on airport infrastructure.

Part II Aircraft Design and Manufacturing

The essays in Part II of this volume collectively address issues of aircraft design and manufacture. Traditionally, aircraft were made and manufactured by small companies within one country but as costs have increased and technology has become more sophisticated, a relatively small number of manufacturers, which are supported by international supply chains, have come to dominate the commercial aircraft market. MacPherson and Pritchard (2003) examine the role of industrial offset agreements in the global decentralisation of the production of US commercial aircraft and discuss the economic implications of this spatial reconfiguration for US aerospace employees. Despite the decentralisation of supply chains, final airframe assembly occurs in a select few major aerospace assemblies such as those in Seattle, Toulouse and Hamburg. Niosi and Zhegu (2005) analyse some of these aerospace clusters and note the role of anchor tenants in creating large highly skilled local labour markets.

One of the most interesting recent developments in large aircraft manufacturing has been the difference in the approaches adopted by Boeing and Airbus. Airbus developed the A380 'Super Jumbo' to serve high demand routes between major hubs, whereas Boeing developed the B787 'Dreamliner' to serve the so-called 'long and lean' point-to-point routes. The penultimate essay in this part, by King (2007), examines the role of the A380 and B787 in the evolving air transport market. As well as offering different products to fit their respective corporate forecasts of future air traffic demand, Airbus and Boeing have also pursued different flightdeck philosophies and it is this aspect of their business models that is explored in the final essay in this part. Ibsen (2009) employs economic models of technological innovation and sociological approaches to the study of organisations to examine why Boeing pilots are allowed ultimate command of their aircraft, while Airbus obliges pilots of its aircraft to surrender this authority to the flight computers.

Part III Alternative fuels

Until recently, the majority of aviation jet fuels were derived from crude oil. However, concerns about future oil supply and energy security combined with the need to improve aviation's environmental performance and sustainability have driven the development of alternative fuel sources. The first essay, by Nygren, Aleklett and Höök (2009), examines the impact of future oil production scenarios on the industry and notes the challenges of replacing the current fuel supply with alternatives. Biofuel – that is fuel derived from biological feedstocks – offers one potential solution. Gegg, Budd and Ison (2014) examine the market development of aviation biofuel and identify a number of drivers and constraints to uptake. The routes, opportunities and challenges of obtaining aviation biofuel from different renewable sources is the focus of the essay by Hari, Yaakob and Binitha (2015).

One of the most compelling drivers for the use of biofuels in aviation is the potential environmental benefits they afford in terms of improved sustainability. In the final two essays in this part Winchester, Malina, Staples and Barrett (2015) examine the impact of advanced biofuel use on US aviation emissions and operations, while Kousoulidou and Lonza (2016) examine the situation in Europe and report on the current global supply potential and production capacity.

Part IV Business Model Innovation

The final 7 essays in this volume address business model innovation in the airline and airport sector. One of the most important innovations in the airline sector has been the advent of the low-cost model as this has led to innovations in products, service, network offering and the competitive response of airports and incumbent airlines. The first essay, by Francis, Humphreys, Ison and Aicken (2006), analyses the temporal and spatial evolution of low-cost carriers around the world and considers patterns of future growth. In order to respond to the threat, low-cost carriers posed to their operation, and to protect their market share in key markets a number of full-service operators and, to a lesser extent, charter airlines, established their own in-house low-cost carriers. Examples of these 'carriers within carriers' include British Airways/Go, bmi/bmibaby, United/Ted, Delta/Song, SAS/Snowflake, Lufthansa/Germanwings, Air India/Air India Express and Thomson/Thomsonfly. However, as Gillen and Gados (2008) note in the second essay in this part, mixing business models is not always a straightforward process and can leave the incumbent carrier very vulnerable. Indeed, as they note, running a full-service and a low-cost brand is fraught with challenges and many low-cost brands have been reabsorbed into the parent carrier or sold off to other companies.

Interestingly, however, while full-service operators sought to adopt elements of the low-cost business model by eliminating free in-flight food and charging for hold baggage, some low-cost operators have started to incorporate elements of full-service operation (such as frequent flyer programmes and priority boarding) into their product portfolio. Klophaus, Conrady and Fichert (2012) examine the evidence from Europe of low-cost airlines 'going hybrid', and their research indicates that the short-haul airline business models in the continent are converging.

Further business model innovation can be seen in the ways in which airlines and airports collaborate. Initially formed in response to regulatory restrictions governing foreign ownership, strategic airline alliances such as STAR, oneworld and Skyteam have become very familiar aspects of full-service operations that aim to give customers a seamless global service and access to far more destinations than any one member alone could serve. Other, smaller, alliances have also been formed between cargo operators, regional airlines and aircraft maintenance organisations. However, despite such developments, there are relatively few examples of vertical integration in the airline–airport business or examples of strategic alliances between airports and airlines. The essay, by Albers, Kock and Ruff (2005), uses the alliance between Lufthansa and Munich airport to explore the issue of strategic airline and airport alliances and suggests that such alliances may become increasingly important as processes of liberalisation, competition and globalisation intensify.

While much research has been conducted into strategic airline alliances, the-emergence of multi-airport multinational companies has not gone unnoticed. The essay, by Forsyth, Niemeier and Wolf (2011), identifies the factors that have driven the emergence of multinational multi-airport companies and discusses the implications of them for competition and competition policy. As well as meeting the mobility needs of airline users and passengers, policies of liberalisation, commercialisation and privatisation have meant that airports have become commercial entities which, out of necessity, derive an increasing proportion of their revenues from non-aeronautical sources. The essay, by McNeill (2009), explores the evolution of airport hotels from mere lodgings to luxury five-star resort hotels and conference facilities. This seemingly 'urban' development which, combined with the construction of business parks, office facilities and industrial units on airport peripheries, led some commentators to remark on the apparent formation of 'airport cities' has resulted in the publication of a corpus of work on what has been termed the 'aerotropolis' (Kasarda and Lindsay, 2011). The final essay in this volume, by Charles, Barnes, Ryan and Clayton (2007), provides a critique of the aerotropolis model and the likely role of airports and aviation within an increasingly complex global future.

Conclusion

Over 6 volumes, this collection has presented 141 essays concerning various carefully selected aspects of aviation policy and management from which a number of important aspects are apparent. The first is the sheer diversity of disciplinary approaches and philosophical, theoretical and empirical perspectives that have been employed in respect to aviation. The other is the spatial distribution of authors – although voices from certain world regions have for too long been (and in some cases remain) absent, there is a growing number of essays that concern aviation in regions other then North America and Europe. Such diversity enriches and informs the discipline and will hopefully act as a platform for further empirical investigation, which will inform future aviation policy, planning and management of aviation worldwide for the benefit of both the users of the air transport product and the prevention of harm (though better management of noise, land use, airport development and emissions) to non-users alike.

Reference

Kasarda J D and Lindsay G (2011) *Aerotropolis: the way we'll live next*, Allen Lane, London.

Part I:

Airport Design and Sustainability

1

PASSENGER TERMINAL DESIGN

AMEDEO R. ODONI and RICHARD DE NEUFVILLE

Abstract — The standard procedures for sizing the spaces for passenger activities in airport terminals are unsatisfactory in that they easily lead to expensive errors. The essential difficulty lies in the nature of the process, and in particular with the several formulas which specify the area per passenger in different parts of the building. The process and these formulas are insensitive both to the variations in the operational characteristics of terminals and to the overall variability in the level and nature of the traffic. This paper presents practical procedures for incorporating such considerations into terminal design, based both on theory and on experience internationally at major airports. The approach builds upon detailed consideration of the sequences of flows of the passengers, their likely dwell-time in each facility, and their psychological response to the configuration of the spaces. The overall objective is to create flexible designs that use space efficiently under the broad range of conditions that may prevail. It entails an iterative process of exploring the response of design options to different patterns of loads. This approach invites computerized models of the performance of terminals with spreadsheet-like capability to answer "what-if" questions rapidly.

INTRODUCTION

Passenger terminals at airports are very expensive, both absolutely and per gate for aircraft. As of 1990, for example, the new International Terminal Building (ITB) for Sydney will cost about US $200 million, or $25 million per gate; the central terminal for the new Milano/Malpensa airport about $500 million or $17 million per nose-in gate. The cost of fully fitted out space in airport terminals is easily $2000 per sq.m. (about $200 per sq ft).

Mistakes are correspondingly costly. For example, the simple, avoidable errors in the original design of the interior spaces for the Air France Terminal at Paris/Roissy (de Neufville and Grillot, 1982) had an estimated price tag of around $75 million in 1990 terms.

Overdesign, either as a simple expedient for avoiding future congestion or for the aesthetic of open spaces, can also be most expensive. For example, the decision to make the central corridor of the 180 m. long corridor of finger pier of the new two-level Sydney ITB 12m wide, instead of a feasible 6m, implied an extra capital cost of about US $4 million.

Cost-effective, efficient design of passenger terminals is thus important, especially in view of the number of new facilities projected. Unfortunately, the standard design procedures for airport terminals are based on handbook formulas insensitive to the realities of each situation. These crude approaches cannot be considered adequate to the task. Worse, it is our observation that the formulas are easy to misunderstand and thus frequently misapplied.

A more scientific approach is required, one that incorporates a realistic appreciation of the dynamics and behavior of sequences of queues, the psychology of crowds in such situations, and the ways airport users truly allocate the time they spend in passenger terminals. The design process should also recognize that, as we experience deregulation, the elimination of frontier controls, and new airline organizations, the actual levels and needs of future traffic may be quite different from those now anticipated.

To develop this approach, this paper examines the nature of the current design process and identifies the three elements most in need of improvement. It then proposes how each of these elements could be handled better, and concludes by integrating these suggestions into an outline of a comprehensive design process for passenger terminals.

The terms *processing facilities* (e.g. ticket counters, check-in counters, security controls, passport controls, baggage carousels, customs counters, etc.), *holding areas* (e.g. lobbies, atria, gate lounges, etc.) and *passageways* (e.g. corridors, escalators, moving sidewalks, etc.) will be used below to refer to servers or spaces where passengers and other airport users, respectively, are processed or served, wait or spend time voluntarily, and travel on foot while in the terminal. Holding areas also include ancillary facilities and concessions.

TYPICAL DESIGN PROCESS

A more or less standard process has evolved over the years for the design of passenger terminals at airports. It consists of four steps:

1. Forecasting traffic levels for peak hours;
2. Specification of level-of-service standards;
3. Flow analysis and determination of server and space requirements; and
4. Configuration of servers and space.

The review of these steps provides the basis for understanding why and how the current design process should be changed.

Forecasting of traffic levels at peak hours

The objective of this exercise is to produce highly detailed, peak-hour demand scenarios for the design day many years ahead. These figures provide the basis for the actual design. It is a most speculative enterprise.

This forecasting process normally first estimates aggregate traffic for the "target year" for which a new, expanded or modified terminal is being designed. This aggregate forecast, in turn, is converted into a further estimate of traffic for the "design day," normally taken to be the 30th or 40th busiest day of the year, or something such as the "average weekday of the peak month." This is usually done using a set of "conversion factors," partly based on historical data. Note that the target year is arbitrary, generally a round number; and that the use of conversion factors assumes that the pattern of traffic over twenty years or so is predictable, contrary to our current experience.

Alternatively, design exercises frequently develop hour-by-hour traffic scenarios for the design day, down to the level of a specific schedule of flights, for which assumptions must be made concerning the type of aircraft involved, their origin or destination, load factors, percentage of transfer or transit passengers, etc. In truth, this can be done, at a reasonable level of expected accuracy, for periods of several years in highly regulated environments (as in much of Western Europe until now) or, at best, for a couple of years in more dynamic environments, such as the one in the United States. It is clear, however, that the forecast of a schedule for fifteen or twenty years hence is close to divination, no matter what the country or the regulatory environment.

Forecasts are in any case demonstrably inaccurate. This has been repeatedly shown by retrospective analyses comparing forecasts to what actually occurred (U.S. Office of Technology Assessment, 1982; Ascher, 1978; de Neufville, 1976). The 6 year forecasts of the U.S. Federal Aviation Administration (FAA) have been, over the years, over 15–20 percent different from reality about half the time. Figure 1 illustrates the situation for aggregate national forecasts. The 11 year forecast for 1981, as an example, overestimated the actual number of flight services by about 145% and the 7 year forecast by 70%. (To update Fig. 1, we note that actual total flight services in 1989 were 45 million, far fewer than predicted in the late 1970s.) The situation usually gets worse for more detailed predictions, as one moves to individual airports and then to subsections of the airport activities. In any event, limited confidence should be placed in the detailed forecasts usually generated by the standard design process for airport terminal buildings.

Specification of level-of-service standards

The objective here is to specify explicitly level-of-service (LOS) standards for waiting times and space allocation (i.e. the number of square meters per space occupant) at the processing facilities, the holding areas, and the passageways of the terminal. These standards provide the basis for translating the forecasts into an architectural program.

To specify the LOS standards, the designer must work closely with the airport owner or operator. Higher standards imply more space and cost, and these have to be made compatible with the financial objectives of the owner or operator of the terminal. The level of detail at which the step is carried out varies greatly from airport to airport, and the results may also be very different.

The LOS for space are usually defined in terms of "space conversion factors" giving the appropriate space per simultaneous occupant. The best-known and most widely used factors are listed in Table 1. These were originally developed by Transport Canada during the early 1970s, and subsequently adopted jointly by the International Air Transport Association (IATA) and the Airport Associations Coordinating Council (AACC), (AACC/IATA, 1981). As can be seen, the factors span a considerable range, from the LOS = A (best) to LOS = E (worst). A number of other organizations, such as British Airports, Aeroports de Paris, and the Australian Department of Housing and Construction (1985) have developed their own space conversion factors (see Ashford, 1988). These are all usually single-valued for any specific activity, and roughly in the same range as those in Table 1.

Similar factors have been developed for persons flowing through passageways or corridors (Fruin, 1971; Benz, 1986). They are stated in terms of passengers per foot width per minute (PFM), with typical values of around 12 (LOS = C) and 16 (LOS = D).

While the specific values of the space conversion factors can certainly be disputed, there is little doubt about the soundness of the general principle of allocating space in proportion to the number of persons who are *simultaneously* in any particular part of the terminal. In practice, however, the application of this principle has been characterized by widespread misinterpretation and lack of insight.

The concept of *dwell time* (the amount of time spent in a particular area), is central to determining the number of *simultaneous* occupants. For instance, if the flow of passengers through a lobby is relatively uniform over time at a rate of 900 per hour, and if dwell time is 20 minutes or 1/3 of an hour, then the number of people in the lobby at any time is 900 × 1/3 = 300. Thus, space needs to be provided for 300 people, not 900. While this should be obvious, it is surprising how often it is misunderstood. A most common mistake in practice is to disregard dwell time altogether and use the number of peak hour

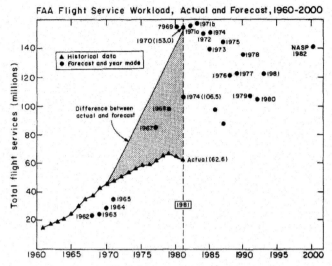

Fig. 1. Example of wide discrepancy between forecast and reality.
(Source: U.S. Office of Technology Assessment, 1982).

passengers for the design day (often known as "typical peak hour passengers" or TPHP) as the number of simultaneous occupants. In our case, this error would result in the provision of three times as much space as needed.

It would seem that much of this confusion stems from a set of guidelines ("FAA standards," see FAA, 1969) issued a generation ago, which specified space requirements in terms of area per TPHP (see Ashford and Wright [1984] and Horonjeff and McKelvey [1983] for details). For example, these guidelines recommend a total of 24.2 m² per TPHP for a domestic terminal, with 1.0 m² allocated to the ticket lobby, 3.3 m² to customs, etc.

Clearly, the "FAA standards" were originally developed for a specific set of conditions regarding how long typical domestic or international passengers spend in the terminal, what percentage of them go through the ticket lobby and use the ticket counters, what type of customs procedures are in effect, etc. Given the major changes that have taken place in airport operations over two decades, the FAA standards are probably inapplicable today, even for the medium-size U.S. airports for which they were developed. An improved design process for airport terminals thus needs to focus attention on the time passengers *actually* spend in a space, or their dwell time.

A further problem with these standards is that they assume that the space provided for an activity will be useful, no matter how or where it is provided. Implicit in the formula is the idea that the occupants of a space somehow disperse to make use of an entire area. People are not gasses, however, and unfortunately no such physical law exists for them. The fact is that people tend to congregate in specific places either because of a focus of attention, such as an information booth or an open check-in counter; or because they perceive such points in the terminal to be convenient (e.g. the mouth of the baggage chute or the check-in counters immediately in front of the entrance of the terminal). Thus, it easily and quite predictably happens that a terminal with enough space by the above LOS criteria, in fact has a number of significant problem areas which make the building feel, and thus be, inadequate.

Flow analysis and determination of server and space requirement

There are essentially three ways that have been used to analyze the flows and determine the amount of space and the number of servers required:

Table 1. Level of service standards (sq.m. per occupant)
(Source: AACC/IATA, 1981)

Sub-System	Level of Service Category				
	A	B	C	D	E
Holding with Bags:					
Check-in	1.6	1.4	1.2	1.0	0.8
Bag Claim Area					
Holding w/o Bags:					
Holdroom	1.4	1.2	1.0	0.8	0.6
Pre-Inspection					
Wait/Circulate	2.7	2.3	1.9	1.5	1.0

1. Formal applications of queueing theory;
2. Graphical analyses using cumulative diagrams; and
3. Detailed computer simulations.

The formal applications of classical, steady-state queueing theory (e.g. Lee, 1966) have not proven particularly effective for design. This is because the processing facilities in airports are essentially never in steady-state; they are almost always undergoing some kind of dynamic change. Furthermore, the queues are often undisciplined. The only exceptions that we are aware of — and where steady-state queueing formulae do prove useful — are cases in which: either (a) parallel processing facilities are shared by a number of airlines, and roughly constant rates of demand at high server utilization levels are thus achieved for significant periods of time — as, for example, at common check-in areas encountered at many European airports; or (b) facilities are quite underutilized — a situation which is of limited interest, anyway.

Graphical analyses of the cumulative arrivals and service (Newell, 1971) have proven most effective in analyzing and designing quite specific elements of the terminal such as departure lounges (Horonjeff and Paullin, 1969) or ticket-counters (de Neufville and Grillot, 1982). This approach presumes that the pattern of loads is known: they are thus best for the redesign of a particular space within an existing structure. This approach does not tie in very well to the process of designing a complete terminal, since each major alternative is likely to change the pattern of flows into a particular activity area and the flows into individual processing facilities are interdependent in often complicated ways.

Simulations provide the means — in principle at least — for investigating the flows throughout an entire building. So far, however, they have been generally unsuccessful as support tools for the design of airport terminals, primarily because the available computer programs (a) lag seriously behind the state-of-the-art in simulation and are often virtually impossible to use and (b) do not really match the needs of the design process. They require extensive reprogramming to fit with any specific configuration of a terminal, take a long time to process any particular run, and require that detailed hour-by-hour forecasts be available for every run (McKelvey, 1989). A typical program is ALSIM (Airport Landside Simulation) which was developed during the mid-1970's and is publicly available through the FAA. A designer would be extremely lucky to get this kind of simulation to model more than a handful of possible scenarios.

Configuration of servers and space

The final design attempts to integrate the above steps. What happens in practice is that the design team takes a specific level of flows for a peak hour associated with a particular schedule, associates these with level-of-service standards for space, and then fits them into an architectural concept. The characteristics of the peak hours are, in fact, typically driven by the arrivals and departures of some group of widebody aircraft (e.g. several Boeing 747-400's). Thus, the design of the terminal is strongly attuned to the specifics of the assumed schedule.

The result is a design that will perform well (if none of the usual mistakes have been made) for that particular scenario. The problem is that neither the client nor the designer has any real idea how the design would perform under the wide range of alternative scenarios that may well occur, and has no way to evaluate the performance of the proposed design against that of alternative designs that may be more "robust" under change.

Good design should do more than arrive at a feasible solution for a single scenario. It should define solutions that will perform well over the range of possible circumstances, and that can be demonstrated to be preferred to others. This is what we should seek to achieve.

PROPOSED DESIGN PROCESS

An improved design process for passenger terminals would both address the specific analytic issues indicated above, and provide for the capability to assess the performance of any design over the range of circumstances it may encounter. Below we propose a number of steps in this direction.

Forecasting

Since the future traffic is so uncertain both as to level and its nature, what justification is there to postulate a single scenario at great effort? The cost effectiveness of this exercise must be very low since the cost of demand forecasting studies is often high and the value and credibility of the result limited.

It makes more sense to concentrate professional effort in investigating the implications and effects of the uncertainties. Thus the design effort should create a set of scenarios, with plausible ranges both for the levels of traffic and for key parameters that affect the design. It would, for example, want to consider a wide range of transfer rates, e.g. from 30 to 60%, since these are known both to change and to have a major effect on the design of a terminal (de Neufville and Rusconi-Clerici, 1978). Likewise, one could investigate the effect of changes in customs and security procedures, in check-in processing of passengers, etc. (Airports in EEC countries in Europe are about to undergo a momentous change of this type, as intra-EEC flights will probably be treated as domestic flights after 1993.) A few airport planning studies do, in fact, already use scenarios with broad estimates of traffic; so far, however, these are exceptional.

The values of the parameters and the levels of traffic would be *nominated* for each scenario — obviously after careful study and consideration. When the object is to define the performance of a system over a range of circumstances, it is not necessary to define whether any particular one is most likely. In nominating the values, only a rudimentary effort to justify each one of them is necessary. This approach thus does away with the very detailed, hour-by-hour speculations about what might happen a generation hence.

Specification of level of service standards and determination of space requirements

This process would proceed as now, with two exceptions. It would focus attention on the matter of the dwell time, and it would also specifically investigate the possibility that concentrations of traffic at "hot spots" would degrade the overall performance of the terminal. We begin with a discussion of the much-neglected subject of dwell times.

A principal determinant of dwell times, especially in the case of spaces used by departing passengers, is the amount of "discretionary" (or "slack") time that airport users spend in the various parts of the terminal. Let:

T = the time interval between a particular departing passenger's arrival at the airport terminal and the time when she boards her flight

T_{wi} = the total amount of time that same passenger spends waiting in queue and being served/processed at processing facility i

T_{pj} = the amount of time the passenger spends moving through passageway j

If the passenger in question is processed at I processing facilities and has to move through J passageways, then,

$$T_s = T - \sum_{i=1}^{I} T_{wi} - \sum_{j=1}^{J} T_{pj} \qquad (1)$$

= the passenger's total slack time

This total slack time, T_s, is in turn allocated among the various holding areas of the terminal, according to the passenger's preferences or judgement. For instance, an international passenger with 50 minutes of slack time, may decide to spend 10 of these minutes in the departures lobby prior to check-in (possibly saying goodbyes to relatives and friends), 20 minutes in the duty-free shopping area and 20 minutes at the gate departure lounge assigned to her flight. In general, if T_s is allocated among K holding areas, then

$$T_s = \sum_{k=1}^{K} T_{sk} = \sum_{k=1}^{K} f_k T_s \qquad (2)$$

where T_{sk} is the amount of slack time spent in holding area k and f_k is the fraction of T_s allocated by the passenger to holding area k, i.e. $\sum_{k=1}^{K} f_k = 1$.

Clearly the "loading" (number of simultaneous occupants) of any particular part of the airport terminal and, therefore, the amount of space to be allocated to each part depends directly on the values of

T_s and of the fractions f_k ($k = 1, 2, \ldots, K$). In fact, the importance of T_s and T_{sk} as determinants of space requirements is often **much greater** than of T_w ($= \sum_{i=1}^{I} T_{wi}$) and of T_p ($= \sum_{j=1}^{J} T_{pj}$) the amounts of time passengers spend being processed, waiting to be processed, and moving through passageways. For instance, it is well known that many departing international passengers arrive at the airport two or more hours prior to their scheduled departure time and typically experience values of T_w and T_p which add to less than 30 minutes. Thus, T_s often accounts for 75% or more of the time such passengers spend at the terminal. Yet, the existing literature on airport terminal design hardly ever discusses slack time and most publicly available surveys contain very little information or data on how passengers allocate their slack time, i.e. on the values of the f_k (see Dunlay and Park, 1978).

While we have referred only to departing passengers so far, an entirely analogous discussion could focus on transfer and transit passengers, their processing, slack times and space allocation needs. For arriving, trip-terminating passengers, however, the concept of slack time is far less important as these passengers typically try to leave the airport terminal as early as possible, i.e. spend very little time there beyond that needed for processing (immigration, baggage claim, customs, meeting welcomers) and for traversing the arrival complex's passageways and holding areas. Shorter dwell times are, in fact, the principal reason why the part of airport terminals allocated to arriving passengers requires considerably less space than that for departing passengers. (But note that for welcomers waiting for arriving passengers, the amount of slack time available and the question of where this time is spent are again important in determining space requirements.)

Reducing dwell times

One of the observations resulting from the remarks in the last section is that the need for large passenger terminal areas and the attendant construction and operating costs can be moderated to a considerable extent by reducing total dwell times and, especially, their "slack" time component.

There are two principal ways of achieving this effect: Consider Fig. 2 that depicts a typical probability density function for random variable T, the dwell times associated with the departing (trip-originating) passengers on a particular flight. We are primarily interested in $E[T]$, the expectation of T.

There are some well-understood differences among the observed values of $E[T]$ for various types of flights at any given airport (e.g. flights scheduled to depart very early in the morning have a smaller $E[T]$ than those scheduled for later in the day, international flights have longer $E[T]$ than domestic ones, etc.). However, we shall focus our attention here on the underlying factors that affect $E[T]$ for any individual flight (e.g. a long-range domestic flight leaving at noon).

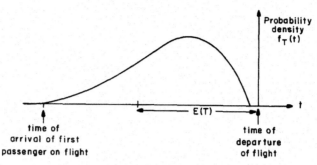

Fig. 2. Probability density function for dwell time T of a specific flight.

First, $E[T]$, for any flight, is affected by passenger perceptions regarding the amount of processing times, T_w (including waiting) and passageway travel time, T_p, that they will face at the terminal. Given the high stake people have in not missing their flights, these perceptions must necessarily take into consideration both the expected value and the variability of T_p and T_w. For example, a plausible normative behavioral model might postulate that each departing passenger will select a T large enough to ensure a probability of 95% or better of "making the flight." One could then argue that, for the ensemble of passengers departing on the flight in question, $E[T]$ should be at least as large as a quantity such as

$$t_o \cong \hat{E}[T_w] + \hat{E}[T_p] + c_1\hat{\sigma}(T_w) + c_2\hat{\sigma}(T_p) \quad (3)$$

where $\sigma(X)$ denotes the standard deviation of X, c_1 and c_2 are constants of the order of 2.0 or 3.0 and we have used the "hat" symbol to indicate that we are dealing not with the true values of $E[T_w]$, $E[T_p]$, etc., but with their perceived and/or anticipated values when each passenger makes his/her decision on the target time for arriving at the terminal. Clearly, the perceived/anticipated quantities $\hat{E}[T_w]$, $\hat{\sigma}(T_w)$, $\hat{E}[T_p]$ and $\hat{\sigma}(T_p)$ will be strongly influenced by the worst previous experiences of the passengers involved, the anecdotes they have heard from acquaintances and the information that airlines and airport authorities provide to prospective airport users. Thus, the "hatted" quantities are likely to be high-side estimates of the corresponding true ("unhatted") values.

Combining (3) with the above observations, we can now write:

$$\begin{aligned}
E[T_s] &\cong E[T] - E[T_w] - E[T_p] \\
&\geq t_o - E[T_w] - E[T_p] \\
&= [\hat{E}(T_w) - E(T_w)] + [\hat{E}(T_p) - E(T_p)] \\
&\quad + c_1 \cdot \hat{\sigma}(T_w) + c_2 \cdot \hat{\sigma}(T_p) \quad (4)
\end{aligned}$$

(Note that in the preceding paragraph we argued that

the two quantities in brackets on the right-hand-side of [4] are positive, in practice.) It follows from (4) that $E[T_s]$ and the resulting pressure for additional passenger terminal space can be reduced by: (a) bringing the expected processing and passageway travel times anticipated by the passengers ($\hat{E}[T_w]$ and $\hat{E}[T_p]$) as much as possible in line with the true values ($E[T_w]$ and $E[T_p]$); and/or (b) reducing as much as possible the variability of service times and travel times within the terminal—and making sure that the airport users become aware of these reductions. Thus a combination of efforts toward improving the reliability of service times and travel times and toward educating/informing the public can offer significant benefits in terms of reducing or alleviating space requirements.

A second, perhaps surprising, way to achieve a similar effect is by reducing the variability of ground access times to the airport! The following example, based loosely on the situation at Boston's Logan International Airport, will help explain this point: Suppose a departing passenger wishes to arrive at the airport terminal about 30 minutes prior to her domestic flight's scheduled departure time, so she will have ample time to be processed and arrive at the flight's departure gate. Average travel time from the downtown area where she works to the airport is 20 minutes. However, due to frequent and unpredictable traffic breakdowns, the standard deviation of this travel time is large, about 15 minutes. To account for this variability the traveler, therefore, decides to allow a total of 50 minutes for the trip to the airport, leaving her place of work 80 minutes before flight departure time. Since the expected travel time to the airport is known to be 20 minutes, this means that, on the average, the traveler will be at the airport 60 minutes before departure time, instead of the desired 30. She pays a penalty of 30 minutes on the average, as a "hedge" against the variability of ground access time. This same penalty is also paid by the airport in having to accommodate an additional 30 "person-minutes." Her airport dwell time—and the "loading" she imposes on the terminal's facilities, mostly in the form of additional "slack" time—could be reduced, up to a point, in direct proportion to any reductions in the standard deviation of ground access time.

An added benefit of reduced dwell times is that lower LOS standards (i.e. space conversion factors) can be tolerated by airport users for short periods of time. For example, passengers in a departure gate lounge may accept LOS = D (0.8 sq.m. per simultaneous occupant) when the peak loading of the lounge lasts for 15 minutes or less, but may be unhappy if these conditions persist longer.

Operators of shuttle-type services have long known that it is possible to serve very large numbers of annual passengers from very small terminals (e.g. at New York/La Guardia) by: requiring very limited processing of these passengers at the terminal; ensuring short dwell times through frequent and reliably on-time service; and tolerating low LOS standards for short periods of time, just before each flight's boarding time.

Recent developments

A number of recent developments have tended to increase dwell times and have, therefore, had an adverse effect on airport terminal space requirements.

Foremost among those is the increased emphasis on airport security procedures—especially for international flights—and the attendant need for departing passengers to be at the terminal well in advance of their flight departure times. Most carriers between the United States and Britain now require passengers to present themselves for check-in at least two hours in advance. Airport terminals at New York/Kennedy and London/Heathrow have been affected particularly strongly and adversely by this change.

In response to concerns about airport security, a number of West European Civil Aviation Authorities have been mandating in recent years that new passenger terminals be designed so that arriving and departing passengers not come in contact at any areas/facilities beyond the points where departing passengers pass security checks. This means, for instance, that the type of common finger-pier concourses on which both arriving and departing passengers walk to/from the terminal's gates at most airports in the United States are not permissible. Instead, arriving and departing passengers would typically move at two different floor levels of finger-piers. While this new requirement should not have any obvious effect on dwell times, it will certainly increase space requirements of airport terminals.

The dramatic growth in airfield and ATC delays which has been experienced in the United States, West Europe, East Asia, and Australia in recent years is also having an adverse effect on airport terminal dwell times and consequent space requirements. To see why, it is sufficient to note that if in Fig. 2 the actual flight departure time is moved to the right, relative to the scheduled departure time (as a result of the aircraft's late arrival at the airport of interest) then $E[T]$ will increase by an amount equal to the delay of the departure. In fact, these delays increase the "loading" of terminals in the worst possible way, since by the scheduled departure time all departing passengers are at the airport.

Finally, it should be noted that several airports, especially in West Europe, have themselves tended to encourage longer dwell times through the provision of extensive shopping areas, restaurants, etc. within airport terminals. This has been particularly true of international terminals, where many Airport Authorities have reaped rich financial rewards from such ancillary facilities located in duty-free areas. This practice is not a "one-way" street: it requires a careful balancing of the financial objectives of the airport owner or operator against the need for gigantic terminals that it implies and the large expenditure it entails. As noted earlier, this balancing should be discussed in depth with the responsible airport authorities during Step 2 of what we called the standard airport terminal design process.

Analysis of traffic concentrations

Traffic concentrations that degrade the performance of a terminal arise routinely. These "hot spots" then make the overall facility appear inadequate and, in effect, cause premature obsolescence or failure of the terminal. For example, the Air France terminal at Paris/Roissy had been intended to serve 10 aircraft operations per gate per day. However, because of the way passengers naturally tended to cluster around the check-in counters as soon as these counters opened to process a flight, blockage of the passage of other passengers through the terminal regularly occurred and the number of daily operations per gate had to be reduced to about six. The failure to anticipate this "hot spot," in a terminal for which there was sufficient overall area per occupant on average, forced the construction of a new terminal many years ahead of schedule (de Neufville and Grillot, 1982).

The analysis for traffic concentrations is quite simple. The key element is that the designers should put themselves in the shoes of the users of the terminal (Sommer, 1974). Patterns are then usually quite easy to anticipate, and avoid. People, for example, naturally cluster around information booths, the first queues in front of them in any set of parallel queues, the mouth of the baggage chute, telephone banks, etc. These facilities should thus not be sited where they could cause bottlenecks. Most particularly, they should not be placed at the areas of maximum traffic in a corridor, as they so often are (de Neufville and Grillot, 1982), unless the design makes special provision for the presence of these facilities and their queues, e.g. by widening of the space, visual cues and other information, etc.

Flow analysis

A computer model is virtually a necessity for exploring the performance of a complex system such as an airport terminal under a wide range of circumstances. But not just any kind of model will do. As a tool for the design of a system that should be evaluated for scenarios that can only be guessed at, the computer model of the flows should have three characteristics.

First, the model must be flexible. It must permit reconfiguration of the spaces, and thus of the patterns of flows, without complex reprogramming. It must allow the design team to ask "what if" questions readily. In this aspect it should be rather like a modern "spreadsheet," which any reasonably computer-literate professional can use.

Second, the model must be fast. It must be able — within the time allowed for decisions — to estimate and help evaluate performance under all the combinations of conditions that might reasonably arise, and this number rapidly becomes quite large. For example, if one wishes to consider the performance of the terminal for three levels of possible loads, with three possible transfer rates and, say two different possible customs and two check-in routines, there are 36 possibilities to investigate — for each design alternative. Note that the time available for analyzing alternate designs is frequently quite short in practice. Once the decision-makers decide to proceed with a project, the schedule typically moves quickly. For example, the process for redesigning the configuration of the airport terminals at Boston to accommodate a major tunnel and interchange (the cross-harbor tunnel or "CHART" study) lasted about 6 months. As another example, all the basic design decisions for the new International Terminal Building for Sydney were fixed within a couple of months of the beginning of the project.

Finally, however, the model need not be enormously precise. If we can only hope to guess at the level of traffic to within 30% (and that would be good compared to the general record over a twenty year life of a terminal building), it is meaningless to try for extreme detail in the analysis itself. The designer cannot hope, given the uncertainty of the traffic, to obtain an accurate assessment of the performance of a terminal in absolute terms. The information that is truly useful will indicate the *relative* performance of alternative designs, and their ability to meet the range of possible loads.

These requirements argue for a new kind of "simulation" model for airport terminals, almost totally different from the simulation models of fifteen years ago. It would be flexible, not rigid; fast, not slow; approximate, not fine-detail. Fortunately, it would seem that programming and computer advances now make this possible.

The proposed "mini-simulation" models can be made flexible through the use of object-oriented programming (OOP), a programming style which modularizes classes of objects, and thus permits rapid redefinition and reconfiguration. Speed is possible both through the improved hardware now available, and the smaller amount of data that needs to be handled once one recognizes that aggregate analyses suffice.

These new models will be most useful for the overall, conceptual design of passenger terminals. They will allow the planners and owners to evaluate the relative means of alternative configurations, and to determine which solution most appropriately balances cost, performance, and flexibility over the long term. The current inability to analyze alternative concepts under various loads, with the time available for deciding on a design, means that it is impossible to define the best design. This deficiency leads to inefficiencies and higher costs; this is the motivation for the proposed "mini-simulation" models.

CONCLUSION

We have argued for the need to overhaul in major ways several components of the standard process for the design of airport passenger terminals. Instead of demand forecasts focusing on what is supposedly the single most likely flight schedule for the "design day," one should aim for the identification of a set of plausible alternative scenarios encompassing a broad range of future operating conditions and demand sizes and characteristics. In estimating space requirements, dwell times are crucial, with "discretionary" or "slack" time being a particularly important component. Dwell times can be influenced by the airport operator's actions and so can the spatial distribution and concentration of airport users within the terminal. Intelligent planning in these respects can yield large savings in capital and operating costs.

Currently available quantitative tools to support the design process are inadequate for exploring the relative performance of several alternative designs/configurations of the terminal under a large number of plausible scenarios. A new generation of flexible, fast, and approximate computer-based models is needed for this purpose and seems feasible under the current state-of-the-art.

Most important, in the face of massive uncertainty the overall objective should be to create flexible designs that use space efficiently and perform well under a broad range of conditions.

Acknowledgements — The encouragement and support of Larry Kiernan of the U.S. Federal Aviation Administration and of Zale Anis of the U.S. Transportation Systems Center have stimulated much of our recent thinking about airport terminal design. We also thank Frank McKelvey for sharing his review of landside simulations with us, Matthew Coogan for his perspective on the design process and the time available for decision, John Pararas for his insights into modern simulation programming, Gordon Newell for his pioneering analyses of truly practical queueing systems, and the editors for their interest and suggestions.

REFERENCES

AACC/IATA (1981) *Guidelines for Airport Capacity/Demand Management*, Geneva, Switzerland.
Ascher, W. (1978) *Forecasting, An Appraisal for Policy-Makers and Planners*. Johns Hopkins University Press, Baltimore, MD.

Ashford, N. (1988) Level of service design concept for airport passenger terminals – a European view. *Transportation Planning and Technology*, **12**, 5–21.

Ashford, N. and Wright, P. H. (1984) *Airport Engineering* (2nd Edition). John Wiley and Sons, New York, NY.

Australian Department of Housing and Construction (1985) *Airport Terminal Planning Manual*. Canberra, A.C.T.

Benz, G. P. (1986) *Pedestrian Time-Space Concept – A New Approach to the Planning and Design of Pedestrian Facilities*. Parsons, Brinckerhoff, Quade and Douglas, New York, NY.

de Neufville, R. (1976) *Airport Systems Planning: A Critical Look at the Methods and Experience*. Macmillan and MIT Press, London, England, and Cambridge, MA.

de Neufville, R. (1990) Successful siting of airports. *ASCE Journal of Transportation Engineering*, **116**, 37–48.

de Neufville, R. and Grillot, M. (1982) Design of pedestrian space in airport terminals. *ASCE Transportation Engineering Journal*, **108**, 87–101.

de Neufville, R. and Rusconi-Clerici, I. (1978) Designing airport terminals for transfer passengers. *ASCE Journal of Transportation Engineering*, **104**, 775–787.

Dunlay, W. J. and Park, C. H. (1978) Tandem-queue algorithm for airport user flow. *ASCE Transportation Engineering Journal*, **104**, 131–149.

Fruin, J. J. (1971) *Pedestrian Planning and Design*. Metropolitan Association of Urban Designers and Environmental Planners, New York, NY.

Horonjeff, R. and McKelvey, F. (1983) *Planning and Design of Airports*. McGraw-Hill, New York, NY.

Horonjeff, R. and Paullin, R. H. (1969) Sizing of departure lounges in airport buildings. *ASCE Transportation Engineering Journal*, **95**, 267–278.

IATA (1989) *Airport Terminal Reference Manual*. 7th edition, Montreal, Canada.

Lee, A. M. (1966) *Applied Queueing Theory*. Macmillan, London and St. Martin's Press, New York, NY.

McKelvey, F. X. (1989) A review of airport terminal system simulation models. Report to the US Transportation Systems Center (unpublished).

Newell, G. F. (1971) *Applications of Queueing Theory*. Barnes and Noble, Boston, MA and Chapman and Hall, London, England.

Sommer, R. (1974). *Tight Spaces: Hard Architecture and How to Humanize It*. Prentice Hall, Englewood Cliff, NJ.

US Federal Aviation Administration (1969) *Aviation Demand and Airport Facility Requirement Forecasts for Median Air Transportation Hubs Through 1980*. Washington, DC.

US Office of Technology Assessment (1982) *Airport and Air Traffic Control Systems*. US Congress, Washington, DC.

2

Optimal terminal configurations for new large aircraft operations

Alexandre G. de Barros, S.C. Wirasinghe

Abstract

This paper analyses passenger terminal configurations for accommodating new large aircraft (NLA) operations. NLA are new aircraft developments larger than the Boeing 747, of which the Airbus A380, scheduled to enter service in 2006, is the most prominent example. The analysis is performed individually for a single pier, several types of pier–satellites, and a set of remote parallel piers connected by an automated people mover (APM). In all cases, the best location for the NLA gate positions is sought, using analytical models. The overall disutility of walking and riding APM is taken as the criterion for optimality.
© 2003 Elsevier Science Ltd. All rights reserved.

Keywords: New large aircraft; Terminal configuration; Passenger walking distance; Passenger disutility

1. Introduction

Terminal configuration refers, in general, to the way aircraft gate positions are arranged at the terminal. The choice of the terminal configuration is usually the next step after evaluating the number of gates. The configuration is comprised of a combination of the terminal *concept* and *geometry*. Terminal *concept* refers to the general physical and functional shape of the terminal buildings. Horonjeff and McKelvey (1994) and Ashford and Wright (1992) have divided the existing terminal concepts into four groups: (1) linear; (2) pier or finger; (3) satellite; (4) transporter. These terminal concepts could be combined as made necessary by physical constraints and operational needs. Practically all existing airports fit in one or more of these categories. Once the

316   *A.G. de Barros, S.C. Wirasinghe / Transportation Research Part A 37 (2003) 315–331*

terminal concept is chosen, then it is time to set its *geometry*, which is defined as the set of parameters that give the final shape of the terminal. As an example, if the terminal is to be built as a set of parallel piers, its geometry can be defined as the number of piers, the length of each pier, and the spacing between them.

The introduction of larger aircraft known as new large aircraft (NLA) (Barros and Wirasinghe, 1998) will influence the terminal configuration in two ways. Existing airports may adapt to NLA operations by either converting existing gates to NLA ones, or building a new terminal or satellite. The former would be preferred should the number of NLA operations be small and if it does not imply significant restrictions to airside operations. In many cases, however, new terminals are built for mixed operations of NLA and conventional jets (CJ). In those cases, the best terminal configuration should be chosen among the options available.

This paper will analyse the gate arrangement for a terminal designed to accommodate one or more NLA. It is assumed that the number and size of gates of each type—and consequently the terminal dimensions—have been previously determined. The objective of this work is to determine, for each configuration studied, where in the terminal the NLA gates should be located. Three of the most popular configurations will be analysed: a single-pier, a pier–satellite and a parallel-pier terminal with automated people mover (APM). The first case attempts to solve the problem of an airline-owned pier, where it is predetermined which pier of a multiple-pier terminal the NLA must be parked at. Pier–satellites are very interesting due to the possibility of using a significant part of the satellite section as a single departure lounge for the NLA. The third case is an analysis of a configuration that has become very popular in the last decade and where the NLA could be located at any pier.

Although security has become the main concern of terminal design after the terrorist attacks of September 2001, passenger comfort is still important as it is a critical component of the utility of travelling. A good terminal design should offer a high level of passenger comfort while satisfying heightened security standards. Thus this paper focuses on passenger comfort, assuming all current and future security standards can be met with the configuration selected.

The criterion used in this work to choose the best terminal configuration is the mean walking distance for NLA passengers. Several studies have used this approach for terminal configuration analysis (Wirasinghe et al., 1987; Wirasinghe and Vandebona, 1988; Robusté, 1991; Robusté and Daganzo, 1991; Bandara and Wirasinghe, 1992; Wirasinghe and Bandara, 1992; de Neufville et al., 2002). Walking could actually be measured in terms of either distance or time. Walking time is chosen when it must be compared with other passenger inconveniences such as standing and riding moving belts or APM. Modal choice models such as the one described by Kumarage and Wirasinghe (1990) for Atlanta Hartsfield Airport favour walking time over distance. In this work, walking distance will be used when only walking is taken into account, while the *disutility* of walking—which can be measured as time—will be preferred when a comparison with APM riding is necessary.

2. Single-pier terminals

The case of single-pier terminals has been studied in Barros and Wirasinghe (2000). The study was based on the overall average passenger walking distance. A critical assumption is that for one

A.G. de Barros, S.C. Wirasinghe / Transportation Research Part A 37 (2003) 315–331   317

or two NLA positions, the location of those will not significantly influence the average walking distance of other aircraft passengers. In that case, the location of the NLA gate(s) can be done so as to minimise the NLA passenger walking distance only, provided that no airside constraints prevent this. It is also assumed that hub transfers are uniformly distributed along the length of the pier.

The average walking distances are calculated separately for each of the following three groups of passengers:

(a) *Originating/terminating/non-hub transfers (OTNH):* Comprised of those passengers who are required to report to the main building for processing and must therefore walk between the aircraft and the pier entrance;
(b) *CJ hub transfers:* Connecting passengers who are not required to report to the main building and may therefore walk directly between the NLA and CJ gates;
(c) *NLA transfers:* Passengers who arrive and leave on an NLA and are not required to report to the main building.

The overall mean walking distance for all passenger types is the weighted average of the individual passenger groups' averages:

$$W = p_{\mathrm{T}} W_{\mathrm{T}} + p_{\mathrm{N}} W_{\mathrm{N}} + (1 - p_{\mathrm{T}} - p_{\mathrm{N}}) W_{\mathrm{O}}, \tag{1}$$

where W_i is the mean walking distance for passenger set i; p_{N}, p_{T}, proportion of NLA passengers who are hub transfers connecting to another NLA and to a CJ, respectively; $i = \{\mathrm{T}, \mathrm{N}, \mathrm{O}\}$; O, OTNH passengers; T, hub transfers to CJ gates; N, hub transfers to NLA gates.

The passenger walking distances W_i are dependent on the location of the NLA gates. The objective is to find the optimal location of those gates that minimises the overall mean walking distance W given in Eq. (1), by setting its derivative to zero. This analysis was done for two cases: one NLA gate only, and two NLA gates. For more than two NLA gates, a discrete approach was taken.

2.1. Pier configurations for one NLA gate

The pier entrance is usually located at either end of the pier or at the pier centre. The former is the case of pier-finger terminals, whereas the latter is more common in remote piers with underground access to the terminal block. Fig. 1 shows a schematic of a pier terminal, with the two possible locations for the pier entrance.

Atlanta Hartsfield, Denver International and the new Northwest Airlines terminal at Detroit are examples of pier terminals with the entrance located at the pier centre. OTNH passengers have to pass through the pier centre, whereas hub transfers can move directly between the NLA and the CJ. In either case, the mean walking distance will be minimal when the NLA gate is located as close as possible to the pier centre.

Pier-finger terminals like Calgary International Airport and remote piers like Orlando are connected to the terminal block through an entrance located at one end of the pier. Hub transfers are still able to walk directly between the NLA and the CJ. OTNH passengers, however, must move between the NLA and the end of the pier. In this case, the mean walking distance for hub

318   *A.G. de Barros, S.C. Wirasinghe / Transportation Research Part A 37 (2003) 315–331*

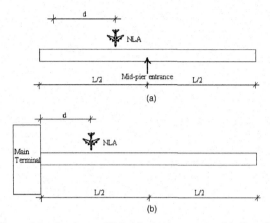

Fig. 1. Pier configuration for one NLA: (a) mid-pier entrance, (b) pier-end entrance.

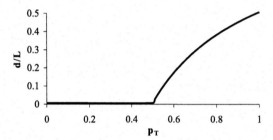

Fig. 2. Optimal NLA gate location for the pier-end entrance case.

transfers, W_T, will depend on the distance d between the NLA gate and the pier entrance, as illustrated in Fig. 1. Setting the derivative of W with respect to d to zero, we find the optimal location of the NLA gate along the terminal. Fig. 2 summarises the optimal location of the NLA gate as a proportion of the terminal length, L, and as a function of the proportion of transfers, p_T.

2.2. Pier configurations for two NLA gates

Two NLA gates can be placed on opposite sides of the pier, facing each other as illustrated in Fig. 3a, or could be offset such that there is a distance S along the pier axis between the two positions, as shown in Fig. 3b. In the case of the former, the problem is similar to the one with only one NLA gate and the same equations and results apply. In the latter case, the distance S is assumed to be not smaller than a minimum S_{min} which must be no less than the sum of the NLA wingspan and the minimum wing-tip-to-wing-tip distance.

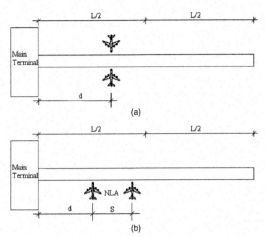

Fig. 3. Pier configuration for two NLA gates: (a) on opposite sides of the pier; (b) on the same side of the pier, offset by a distance S.

It is assumed that the number of passengers and the proportions of transfers will be the same for both NLA positions. Other than that, the same assumptions made for the case of one NLA gate will be made for two. The problem then is to find the values of d and S that minimise the overall passenger walking distance.

The formula for the overall walking distance can be found by evaluating W_T, W_O and W_N and substituting in Eq. (1). The pair (d, S) that minimises W is found by analysing the gradient of W with respect to (d, S). Such analysis is performed in Barros and Wirasinghe (2000), and finds that in the case of two NLA gates on one side of the pier and pier-end entrance, the optimal solution requires the two NLA gates to be separated by the minimum distance S_{min}. The NLA gate closer to the entrance should either be at the pier end or at a distance d' from the main building. For a given ratio S_{min}/L, a coefficient α is used such that $d' = \alpha L$ can be plotted as function of the proportions p_N and p_T. As an example, Fig. 4 shows a graph for $S_{min}/L = 0.05$. Similar figures can be developed for other values of S_{min}/L.

In the case of mid-pier entrance, Barros and Wirasinghe show that the optimal solution is to have both gates symmetrically located near the pier centre, separated by the minimum distance S_{min}.

2.3. Pier configurations for three or more NLA

The assumption that the mean walking distance for non-NLA passengers is not significantly affected by the location of the NLA gates holds well for a very small number of NLA positions. However, for a higher number of NLA, this effect may be significant. In addition, the error introduced by the continuous approach is also increased due to the presence of gates of considerably different sizes handling different numbers of passengers. In this case, a discrete approach becomes

320   A.G. de Barros, S.C. Wirasinghe / Transportation Research Part A 37 (2003) 315–331

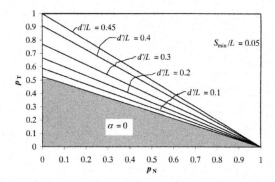

Fig. 4. Isometric curves for the location of the NLA gates.

necessary. Barros and Wirasinghe (2000) report on the use of a discrete model, where the walking distances are evaluated individually for each pair of gates and averaged by the proportions of passenger movements between all gate pairs.

3. Pier–satellite terminals

Pier–satellite terminals feature a pier that serves both as a boarding area, with aircraft parking at its faces, and as a connector between the terminal block at one end of the pier and a satellite terminal located at the other end.

The analyses done in this section will be based on the same definitions and assumptions made for the pier terminal case. However, as pier–satellites are usually attached to the terminal block, only the case of entrance through the pier end will be considered.

3.1. Description of the pier–satellite types

The greatest advantage of a circular pier–satellite for NLA operations is the existence of a very large departure lounge at the satellite section, which is usually of common use for all gates at the satellite section. If the size of the departure lounge is a constraint at the pier section, then the NLA could be parked at the satellite section and take advantage of the departure lounge commonality.

Fig. 5 shows the configuration of a circular pier–satellite terminal for one NLA position. The pier section has a useful length L_1, whereas $2L_2$ is the useful perimeter of the circular satellite. At the junction of the pier and the satellite portions, an extra clearance must be kept where no aircraft can be parked due to manoeuvring constraints. Thus a section of the pier of length y_1 cannot be used for aircraft docking, neither can a section $2y_2$ of the satellite perimeter. Under these circumstances, the useful perimeter of the satellite section is

$$L_2 = \pi R - y_2, \tag{2}$$

where R is the radius of the circular satellite section.

A.G. de Barros, S.C. Wirasinghe / Transportation Research Part A 37 (2003) 315–331   321

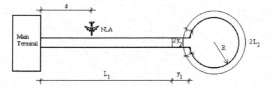

Fig. 5. Circular pier–satellite configuration for one NLA gate.

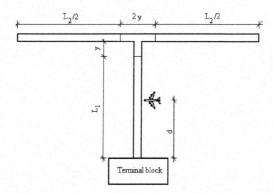

Fig. 6. T-shaped pier–satellite configuration for one NLA gate.

The configuration of a T-shaped pier–satellite is shown in Fig. 6. In a T-shaped configuration, the terminal consists of two piers: one is the main concourse, with one end attached to the terminal building and the other to the centre of the satellite section. This main concourse has a useful length L_1 and must keep a clearance y_T of the satellite section. Each arm of the satellite section has a useful length L_2. Both arms must keep a clearance y_T of the main concourse on the inner face; however, aircraft can be parked all along the outer face of the satellite.

The Y-shaped pier–satellite can be considered a special case of the T-shaped one where the angles between the arms and the main concourse are not 90°, and aircraft cannot be parked near the junctions. Fig. 7 illustrates this configuration. In our study, the angles are assumed to be 120°, and the satellite arms to be of the equal length.

3.2. Evaluation of walking distances

The three types of pier–satellite terminals in this study have in common a main concourse to which a satellite is attached. Defining $2L_3$ as the total terminal frontage length available for aircraft parking at the satellite section, it follows that

$$L_3 = \begin{cases} L_2, & \text{circular and Y-shaped satellites;} \\ L_2 + y, & \text{T-shaped pier–satellite.} \end{cases} \tag{3}$$

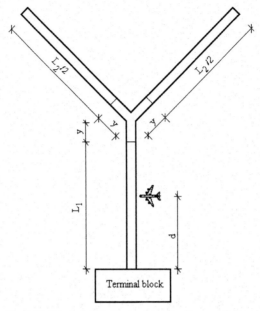

Fig. 7. Y-shaped pier–satellite configuration for one NLA gate.

For the calculation of the walking distances, in addition to the assumptions made for the pier terminal case, we will further assume that passengers going to or from a gate within the circular satellite must pass through the satellite centre. Therefore, if the NLA gate is located at the pier section, then the mean walking distance for all NLA passengers will be

$$W = p_T \left[\frac{d^2 + (L_1 - d)^2 + (L_1 - d + y_1 + 2R)2L_3}{2(L_1 + L_3)} \right] + (1 - p_T)d, \tag{4}$$

$$W = p_T \left[\frac{d^2 + (L_1 - d)^2 + 2\left(L_1 - d + \frac{L_3 + 7y}{4}\right)(L_3 - y) + 2\left(L_1 - d + \frac{3y}{2}\right)y}{2(L_1 + L_3)} \right] + (1 - p_T)d, \tag{5}$$

$$W = p_T \left[\frac{d^2 + (L_1 - d)^2 + 2(L_1 - d + 2y + L_3/4)L_3}{2(L_1 + L_3)} \right] + (1 - p_T)d \tag{6}$$

for a circular, T-shaped and Y-shaped pier–satellite, respectively.

Differentiating W with respect to d and comparing it to zero, we find that the optimal location for the NLA gate within the concourse section is

$$d' = \begin{cases} L_1, & p_T \geqslant 0.5(1 + L_1/L_3) \text{ and } L_3 \geqslant L_1; \\ 0, & p_T < 0.5; \\ (L_1 + L_3)\left(1 - \frac{1}{2p_T}\right), & \text{otherwise} \end{cases} \qquad (7)$$

for all pier–satellite types. The optimal location for the NLA gate is illustrated in Fig. 8. It can be seen that the optimal location within the concourse changes more rapidly towards the satellite section with p_T as the ratio L_3/L_1 increases.

So far, we have studied the location of the NLA gate restrained to within the pier section. In order to determine whether the NLA gate should be at the main concourse or at the satellite section, we must compare the walking distances yielded by each location. In the case of a circular satellite, any position within the satellite section will yield the same mean walking distance. As to T- and Y-shaped pier–satellites, the minimum walking distance will occur when the NLA gate is located as close as possible to the junction with the main concourse. By comparing the walking distances for NLA gates located at the pier and satellite sections, one can determine the conditions under which the mean walking distance will be greater if the NLA gate is positioned within the main concourse instead of at the satellite section. In this case, the best location for the NLA gate would be at the satellite section—anywhere within the circular satellite or as close as possible to the junction at a T- or Y-shaped pier–satellite. Table 1 shows these conditions for each pier–satellite type.

3.3. More than one NLA gate

At many airports, two or more NLA gates must be provided to meet the demand. In that case, it is possible to draw some conclusions from the analyses done for one NLA gate and for single piers. Two NLA gates could be placed on opposite sides of the main concourse or of one of the satellite arms, at the same distance from the terminal block. In that case, the results of the one-gate analysis still apply. An exception is made for passengers who transfer directly between the two NLA gates, who must be subtracted from the total passengers for the computation of p_T. This is due to the fact that transfers between NLA have a negligible walking distance (the width of the pier).

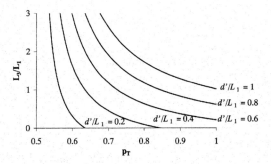

Fig. 8. Optimal location of the NLA gate within the concourse section.

Table 1
Conditions for the location of the NLA gate at the satellite section

Pier–satellite type	Conditions for $W^{CONC} > W^{SAT}$ (optimal location at the satellite section)
Circular	$L_3 > L_1$ $p_T > (1 + L_1/L_3)/2$ $y_1 > \dfrac{4p_T[L_1+L_3(1-p_T)]\left(L_3-2\frac{L_3-y_2}{\pi}\right)-(L_1+L_3)^2}{4p_T[L_1+L_3(1-2p_T)]}$
T-shaped	$L_3 \gtrless L_1$ $p_T > (1 + L_1/L_3)/2$
Y-shaped	$L_3 > 2L_1$ $p_T > (1 + L_1/L_3)/3$

The location of three or more NLA gates will have a greater impact on the walking distance of non-NLA passengers. Therefore, it cannot be determined analytically for a general case. However, from the analyses performed so far, it is possible to infer that the gates should be clustered at the main concourse near the terminal block, if the proportion of OTNH passengers is high, or near the concourse–satellite junction, if that proportion is low. In the case of a circular satellite, it may be preferable to park all NLAs at the satellite, to take advantage of the common lounge provided by this configuration.

4. Parallel-pier terminal configuration

Parallel-pier terminals became very popular in the 80's and 90's. Not only does this configuration provide shorter walking distances for hub operations; it also allows for easy expansion of each individual pier and for the construction of other piers as demand makes it necessary. However, this configuration usually requires the use of underground APM to connect the piers and the terminal block. These APM systems are very costly and also impose a certain level of disutility to the passenger, although this disutility is supposedly much lower than that of walking. Denver International (DIA) and Atlanta Hartsfield are the most prominent examples of this type of terminal configuration with the use of APMs.

With the exclusive-use policy adopted in most North American airports, airlines usually own one or more piers and have exclusive rights over those facilities—e.g. Denver's concourse B, which is exclusively operated by United Airlines. In this case, the location of NLA gates may be restricted to those piers managed and controlled by the airport authority. If an airline wishes to operate its own NLA at its own terminal, the location of the NLA gates can be done using the methodology described earlier in this paper for a single pier. The same is valid for the cases where an international pier is provided—e.g. concourse A at Denver and concourse E at Atlanta—and one wishes to provide one or more NLA gate positions for international flights. These exclusive pier use policies are, however, very inefficient as every pier must be designed for its own peak hour. Peak hours for different operations may not be concurrent, however, which means that while one pier is fully occupied at a given time, the others may have a large amount of idle resources. Steinert and Moore (1993) suggest that terminals be designed for joint use by several airlines, for both international and domestic passengers. The new terminal at London Stansted is

A.G. de Barros, S.C. Wirasinghe / Transportation Research Part A 37 (2003) 315–331 325

an example of parallel-pier configuration with common gate usage policy. In this case, the NLA gates can be located at any piers and the impact on the terminal performance parameters such as walking distance and baggage handling requires a unique model to determine the best location of those gates, as well as the best overall geometry of the terminal.

4.1. Optimal location—basics and assumptions

4.1.1. Terminal configuration

Fig. 9 shows the generic configuration of a parallel-pier terminal. The pier extended from the terminal block is numbered 0 and is assumed to have aircraft parking on the external face only. The remote piers are numbered 1–n from the closest to the terminal block to the farthest and can accommodate aircraft on both faces. It is also assumed that the centres of the piers are aligned.

4.1.2. APM system

All APM stations are assumed to be similar and located at the pier centres. The distances between the pier stations are assumed to be the same whereas the distance between pier 1 and the terminal block can be different. The passenger capacity of the vehicles and the frequency of service are known and remain constant for the duration of the terminal's life span.

4.1.3. Types of passengers

Passengers are divided into two categories: originating/terminating and transfers. Originating/terminating passengers initiate or terminate their flight at the airport; therefore they move in one direction only between the NLA gate and the terminal block. For terminating passengers, their movement consists of: (a) walk from the NLA gate to the APM station; (b) ride the APM to the terminal block; (c) walk through the terminal block. Originating passengers will take the same steps in the opposite direction.

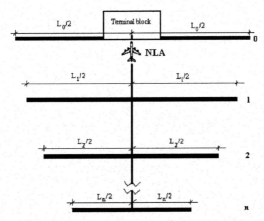

Fig. 9. NLA gate at the middle of the pier attached to the terminal block.

326   *A.G. de Barros, S.C. Wirasinghe / Transportation Research Part A 37 (2003) 315–331*

The proportion of transfers with respect to total passengers, p_T is assumed to be known. Transfers are further subdivided into two subcategories: hub and non-hub transfers. Hub transfers move directly between the NLA gate and their arrival/departure gate, whereas non-hub transfers must pass through the terminal block for further processing. The proportion of hub transfers with respect to the total number of transfers, q, is also assumed to be known.

The movement of non-hub transfers consists of the following (the NLA gate could be either the arrival or the departure one): (a) walk from the arrival gate to the APM station; (b) ride the APM to the terminal block; (c) walk through the terminal block; (d) ride the APM to their departure pier; (e) walk from the APM station to their departure gate.

Finally, hub transfers, if transferring to another gate at the same pier, just have to walk directly from their arrival gate to their departure gate. Those transferring to a flight parked at another pier take the following steps: (a) walk from the arrival gate to the APM station; (b) ride the APM to their departure pier; (c) walk from the APM station to their departure gate.

4.1.4. Disutility of passenger movement

The disutility of passenger movement is comprised of three elements: walking, riding the APM, and access to the APM. The disutility of walking can be assumed to be proportional to the distance walked. In the same way, the disutility of riding the APM is proportional to the distance ridden. The disutility of access to the APM comprises all extra walking, changes of levels, and waiting associated with the process of boarding and unboarding the APM at the station. This disutility can be considered constant for those passengers who use the APM system (Wirasinghe and Bandara, 1992). All the mean disutilities in the objective function are a function of the pier i where the NLA gate is located. The pier i is the decision variable in the problem. We will determine i such that the total mean disutility of passenger movement is minimised.

The objective function is to minimise the mean disutility of passenger movement, including walking and riding the APM. This objective function is similar to the one presented by Bandara and Wirasinghe (1992) and can be written as

$$\min W = (1 - p_T)W_O + p_T[qW_H + (1 - q)W_{NH}], \tag{8}$$

where W is mean disutility of passenger movement for all passenger types; W_O the mean disutility of passenger movement for originating/terminating passengers; W_H the mean disutility of passenger movement for hub transfers; W_{NH} the mean disutility of passenger movement for non-hub transfers.

The expressions for each disutility type depend on the number of NLA gates under consideration and on whether they will be located at the pier centre or at the pier end.

4.2. One NLA gate

The location of a single NLA gate in a parallel-pier terminal consists of determining both the pier and the point within the pier where the NLA gate should be located. With respect to the pier where the NLA gate will be located, it has been shown earlier in this paper that, if no airside constraints prevent this, the best location is in the middle of the pier, as close as possible to the pier entrance. If airside constraints exist—such as insufficient inter-pier lane width—then the

A.G. de Barros, S.C. Wirasinghe / Transportation Research Part A 37 (2003) 315–331   327

NLA should be parked at the end of the pier. Given the airside constraints, the problem is then reduced to choosing which of the piers should accommodate the NLA gate.

4.2.1. No airside constraints—NLA gate at the pier centre

In the case of one NLA gate located at the middle of the pier, the walking of passengers from the NLA gate to the APM station is negligible. Clearly the mean walking distance from the APM station to the other aircraft gates—and to the terminal block—is independent of the pier where the NLA gate is located. Therefore, the location of this NLA gate will be based on the disutility of using the APM system.

Originating/terminating passengers must ride the APM between the pier where the NLA gate is and the terminal block. For these passengers, the NLA gate should be positioned as close as possible to the terminal block. Non-hub transfers must move to and from the terminal block. The part of the movement between the CJ gate and the terminal block does not depend on the NLA gate location; the part comprising the movement between the terminal block and the NLA gate is similar to the case of originating/terminating passengers. Therefore, the disutility of these passengers will be minimised when the NLA is near the terminal block. Only hub transfers, who move directly from their origin pier to their destination one, will benefit from locating the NLA at an intermediate pier. The best location for the NLA gate is hence dependent of the total proportion of hub transfers, $p_T q$.

Should there be no hub transfers, it is clear that the NLA gate location that minimises the disutility of using the APM system is at or near the terminal block. Fig. 9 shows this solution for a terminal where the NLA is allowed to park at the terminal block. Conversely, if all NLA passengers are hub transfers, the middle pier is preferred. The conclusion is that only when the total proportion of hub transfers $p_T q$ is very high should the NLA gate be located somewhere other than at or close to the terminal block pier.

4.2.2. Airside constraints—NLA gate at the pier end

Airside constraints, such as the spacing available between piers, may restrict NLA operations to the pier end. This solution may even be the best when other factors are counted in, like the possibility of parking at 45° to allow for two NLA to park at the pier end and the widening of the pier at the end to provide a larger departure lounge.

If, due to any of the factors mentioned above, the NLA gate must be located at the pier end, then all NLA passengers must walk between the end of the pier and the APM station, i.e. half the length of that pier. An exception is made for the hub transfers within the pier—who can walk directly between the NLA and the CJ gates. Therefore, the optimal location of the NLA gate will be a balance between walking and APM riding disutilities.

Wirasinghe and Bandara (1992) showed that the best geometry for a parallel-pier terminal with APM is with the length of the piers increasing towards the terminal block. In a terminal with such configuration, the best location for the NLA will depend on the walking/APM riding disutility ratio. If this ratio is high, the NLA should be parked at the end of the shortest pier—as illustrated in Fig. 10, for this will provide the lowest disutility of walking for all passengers. For a low walking/APM disutility ratio, OTNH passengers will be best served when the NLA gate is close to terminal block, whereas hub transfers would have the lowest mean disutility when the NLA gate is at an intermediate pier. The best overall location in this case will therefore be near the terminal for

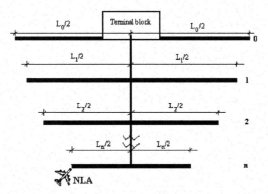

Fig. 10. NLA at the end of the shortest pier.

a low proportion of hub transfers, and moving towards the middle pier for higher proportions of hub movements.

4.3. Two or more NLA gates

4.3.1. NLA allowed at the pier centre

It has been shown that, if NLA are allowed at the pier centre, then one single NLA gate should be positioned at the centre of one of the piers closer to the terminal block. For more than one NLA, it seems clear that they should always be clustered around the centre of one or more piers. Besides providing minimum disutility for passengers, this solution will also minimise passenger walking/baggage transfer between NLA. The size of each NLA cluster will depend mainly on the walking/APM riding disutility ratio.

For two NLA only, the solution found for one NLA could be easily adapted for two. At the terminal block pier, two NLA could be put side by side at the pier centre. At a remote pier, these two aircraft could be parked on opposite faces of the pier. Up to four NLA can be parked this way at the centre of a remote pier.

For one pier, as the number of NLA increases, so does the walking/baggage handling distance between the NLA farther away from the centre and the APM station. This distance increases to a point where the increment in the walking disutility—with respect to the disutility yielded by parking the NLA at the pier middle—exceeds the increment in the disutility of APM riding that would be yielded by parking this NLA at the next remote pier, moving away from the terminal block. In this case, those NLA should be parked at or near the centre of the next remote pier, initiating a new cluster at that pier. As the number of NLA increases, the clusters tend to form a triangle as shown in Fig. 11, with the size of the clusters increasing towards the terminal block. The actual form of that cluster triangle will depend on the ratio of walking to APM riding disutilities. The lower that ratio, the larger the clusters located closer to the terminal block. Fig. 11 shows different arrangements for 10 NLA gates at a terminal with a terminal block pier and three remote piers. In Fig. 11(a), the high walking/APM riding disutility ratio causes the NLA to be

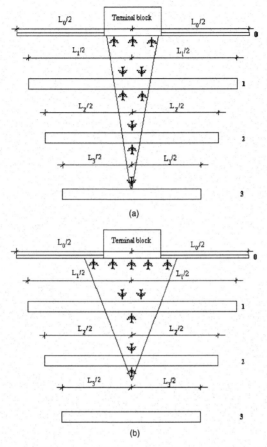

(a)

(b)

Fig. 11. NLA gate locations for different ratios of walking to APM riding disutilities: (a) high ratio, (b) low ratio.

more scarcely distributed among the piers. In Fig. 11(b), the low ratio allows the NLA to be more concentrated near the terminal block.

5. Summary and conclusions

5.1. Single pier

For piers with only one or two NLA positions, the approximation of the problem to a continuous distribution of passengers along the pier provides an accurate, easy to understand insight

330 *A.G. de Barros, S.C. Wirasinghe / Transportation Research Part A 37 (2003) 315–331*

to the problem of locating those gates in the pier. Four basic scenarios were studied using this approach, combining the location of the pier entrance—at one of the pier ends or at the pier centre—and the number of NLA positions—one or two.

In the case of either a sole NLA gate or two gates facing each other and entrance at the pier centre, the best location is as close as possible to the pier centre. If the pier entrance is located at one end of the pier, the best location will vary according to the proportion of passengers who are hub transfers. However, regardless of the proportion of transfers, the NLA gate position should be located in the same pier half as the entrance.

For two NLA gates positioned on the same side of the pier, it has been shown that they should be located side by side at the pier centre, if that is where the entrance is. On the other hand, if the pier entrance is located at one of the pier ends, then the best location for the NLA gates will depend on the proportions of hub transfers and on the minimum separation between those gates, as they should also be put side by side.

5.2. Pier–satellite

For pier–satellites it has been shown that, just like in the case of a single pier, the NLA gate should be located as close as possible to the terminal block if the proportion of passengers who must walk to or from the terminal block is above 50%. If more than 50% of the NLA passengers are allowed to walk directly between the NLA gate and another gate within the terminal, then the best location for the NLA gate will depend on the actual proportion of transfers and on the relative lengths of the main concourse and of the satellite. If the main concourse airside frontage is longer than that found at the satellite section, then the minimum walking distance will occur when the NLA gate is located at the main concourse. Only if the satellite airside frontage is longer than that of the main concourse and with a very high rate of transfers should the NLA be parked at the satellite section.

In the case of more than two NLA gates, it can be inferred from the analysis done for one gate that those gates should be clustered near the terminal block for a low rate of hub transfers, and at or near the satellite section for a high rate. A circular satellite provides a very large common departure lounge and thus it may be preferable to park the NLA at the satellite in the case.

5.3. Parallel-pier terminal

Parallel remote piers may pose a severe constraint to NLA operations due to possible lack of sufficient clearance in-between the piers. If that is the case, then the NLA gates should be positioned at the end of the shortest piers, as allowed by the airside constraints.

If the distance between piers allows NLA to be parked near the centre of the pier, then the NLA positions should be clustered at the centres of piers, with the size of the clusters resembling a triangle. The shape of the triangle will depend on the disutility ratio between walking and APM riding—the greater that ratio, the smaller the base of the triangle.

Acknowledgements

This research was supported in part by the Natural Sciences and Engineering Research Council of Canada and by CNPq, an agency of the Brazilian government dedicated to scientific and technologic development.

References

Ashford, N., Wright, P.H., 1992. Airport Engineering, third ed. John Wiley and Sons, New York.

Bandara, S., Wirasinghe, S.C., 1992. Walking distance minimisation for airport terminal configurations. Transportation Research A 26, 59–74.

Barros, A.G., Wirasinghe, S.C., 1998. Issues regarding the compatibility of airports and proposed large and high speed aircraft. In: McNerney, M.T. (Ed.), Airport Facilities—Innovations for the Next Century. ASCE, Reston, VA, USA, pp. 77–94.

Barros, A.G., Wirasinghe, S.C., 2000. Location of new large aircraft gate positions in pier terminals. In: Nambisan, S.S. (Ed.), The 2020 Vision of Air Transportation: Emerging Issues and Innovative Solutions. ASCE, Reston, VA, USA, pp. 198–213.

de Neufville, R., de Barros, A.G., Belin, S., 2002. Optimal configurations of airport passenger buildings for travelers. Journal of Transportation Engineering 121, 211–217.

Horonjeff, R., McKelvey, F.X., 1994. Planning and Design of Airports, fourth ed. McGraw-Hill, New York, NY, USA.

Kumarage, A.S., Wirasinghe, S.C., 1990. Multinomial mode choice models for Atlanta airport passenger movement. Journal of Advanced Transportation 24, 87–98.

Robusté, F., 1991. Centralized hub-terminal geometric concepts: I. Walking distance. Journal of Transportation Engineering 117, 143–158.

Robusté, F., Daganzo, C.F., 1991. Centralized hub-terminal geometric concepts: II. Baggage and extensions. Journal of Transportation Engineering 117, 159–177.

Steinert, R., Moore, A., 1993. Designing for efficiency in joint-use passenger terminals. Airport Forum June, 40–42.

Wirasinghe, S.C., Bandara, S., 1992. Planning of parallel pier airport terminals with automated people mover systems under constrained conditions. In: Transportation Research Record 1373. National Research Council, Washington, DC, pp. 35–45.

Wirasinghe, S.C., Bandara, S., Vandebona, U., 1987. Airport terminal geometries for minimal walking distances. In: Gartner, N.H., Wilson, H.M. (Eds.), Transportation and Traffic Theory. Elsevier, New York, pp. 483–502.

Wirasinghe, S.C., Vandebona, U., 1988. Passenger walking distance distribution in single and dual concourse centralized airport terminals. In: Transportation Research Record 1147. National Research Council, Washington, DC, pp. 40–45.

3

Low-Cost Airports for Low-Cost Airlines: Flexible Design to Manage the Risks

RICHARD DE NEUFVILLE

ABSTRACT Airport planning is shifting from the traditional pattern – driven by long-term point forecasts, high standards, and established clients – to that of recognizing great forecast uncertainty, many standards and changeable clients. This is a consequence of economic deregulation of aviation and the rise of low-cost airlines.

Low-cost airlines are becoming significant factors in airport planning. Their requirements differ from those of 'legacy' carriers. They drive the development of secondary airports and cheaper airport terminals. They catalyze 'low-cost airports' around the 'legacy main airports' built for the 'legacy airlines'.

This paper proposes a flexible design strategy to deal with the uncertainty of this dynamic. This differs significantly from traditional airport master planning. It builds flexibility into the design, to enable airports to adjust to changes in the type, needs and location of traffic. The case of Portugal illustrates the current risks, and indicates how flexible design could manage uncertainties and maximize expected value.

KEY WORDS: Airport planning; low-cost carriers; airport terminals; risk management; flexible design; Portugal

36   *Richard de Neufville*

Introduction

This paper argues that a paradigm shift is taking place in airport planning, away from the traditional pattern driven by long-term point forecasts, high standards, and established clients, toward one that recognizes great uncertainty in forecasts, a broad range of standards, and the potential for a rapidly changing client base.

After a brief review of the traditional airport planning process, this paper makes the case for a paradigm shift in airport planning, from a focus on traditional airlines to one that considers the needs, practices, and volatility of low-cost airlines. The new approach recognizes great uncertainty in the type, location and level of investments in airport infrastructure. This paper proposes a process of flexible design for dealing with these uncertainties. Its key element involves the use of real options that permit airport owners to adjust their facilities easily to changes in the location and needs of air transport. It illustrates this approach through a discussion of the prospective aviation future for Portugal.

Traditional Airport Planning

During the second half of the 20th century, the practice of airport planning adopted standard procedures attuned to the needs of the dominant airlines – those now known as the 'legacy carriers'. These procedures were encoded into long-lasting, slowly evolving manuals such as those of the International Air Transport Association (2004) and other entities, as de Neufville and Odoni (2003) describe.

The standard paradigm was compatible with the regulatory regimes and business models that prevailed during most of this period. It reflected the then prevailing reality that:

- organizational change occurred slowly, given the consistency and slowness of the regulatory process, and airports could count on decade-long relationships with their airline customers;
- changes in airlines, through mergers (e.g. BOAC and BEA into British Airways) or changes in route structures were of little consequence for airports, as one airline would simply substitute for another to serve the travel market;
- standards for the quantity and quality of the space in airport buildings were high, given the IATA and other definitions of appropriate practice; and
- technological changes (such as the introduction of the Boeing 747) could be easily anticipated because of their long lead times.

Low-Cost Airports for Low-Cost Airlines   37

The traditional practice of airport planning and design reflected a fairly static view of the industry. Granted, the actual levels of traffic could be volatile, suffering slow-downs or benefiting from expansionary bursts, but airport practitioners came to understand these variations as fluctuations around long-term trends, which they could cope with by delaying or accelerating the delivery of airport facilities.

Argument for Paradigm Shift

As the basis for the change in airport planning, this paper presents and defends the hypothesis that the ascendancy of low-cost airlines entails increased expansion of the network of low-cost airports, and of low-cost airport facilities in general. The proposition is simple, and might appear obvious, but leads to a paradigm shift in the concept of airport development.

Airport planners and investors need to recognize the effect of low-cost airlines. It implies a downward shift in standards, and acceptance of the volatility of these carriers. Established airport organizations and professionals find this new order difficult to accept. To many it is degrading, beneath their standards, to deal with the low-cost carriers. The trend runs counter to the practice of the past generation that has committed to massive, multi-billion Euro investments in hub airports featuring spectacular edifices by signature architects (de Neufville, 2006).

This hypothesis involves propositions concerning the timing, location, and business proposition of low-cost airports. It implies that in general but with exceptions:

- The development of low-cost airports and airport facilities is largely catalyzed by the expansion of low-cost airlines, in the sense that the low-cost airlines come first, and the low-cost airports (and low-cost facilities) mostly come afterwards.
- Low-cost airports largely develop in competition with major airports, either as secondary airports in a metropolitan multi-airport system, or as destinations that bypass the use of a centralized metropolitan hub.
- The business model for low-cost airports is distinct from that of the traditional major airports. Mirroring the difference between low-cost and legacy airlines, low-cost airports emphasize profitability through operational efficiency and minimal frills.

Extensive worldwide data support these points.

The proposition that the growth of low-cost airlines leads to the development of low-cost airports and airport facilities has important

38   *Richard de Neufville*

consequences for airport planning, and for policy and investment in airport infrastructure. To the extent that one believes that inexpensive, mass air transport is either inevitable or socially desirable, the proposition has consequences for how and where:

- governments should develop and promote airport infrastructure;
- private investors should allocate their investments in airport facilities; and
- thus for the role, objectives and criteria of success for airport planning.

In general, the implication is that policy makers and investors should focus more attention on the development of airport facilities serving low-cost carriers, both at the legacy and low-cost airports, and correspondingly be careful about the long-term future for multi-billion Euro facilities constructed along traditional lines. This thought contradicts the main line of on-going discussions, obviously dominated by the existing large airports, their spokesmen, and associated professionals who promote the development of expensive main airports.

Hypothesis in Detail

Background. Economics teaches that oligopolies enable their members to extract extraordinary profits from consumers. Furthermore, organizational studies indicate that the stakeholders in the enterprise tend to share the oligopoly benefits. Conversely, economics teaches that lower-cost producers compete away and eventually eliminate oligopolies and oligopoly profits. It also gives us to understand that the pressure on the front-line competitors to lower costs is transmitted to the providers of all their factors of production. That is, competition between 'legacy' and 'low-cost' airlines leads to competition between 'legacy' and 'low-cost' airports.

The history of airline competition after economic deregulation is an epitome of these standard economic teachings. In detail:

1. For the first half-century of the airline industry, governments protected it economically in a variety of ways. Regulatory regimes created barriers to entry into the business and particular markets. Cartels pervaded the enterprise. For example, in Australia, governmental regulation compelled the two domestic airlines (Australian and Ansett at the time) to buy the same equipment, operate the same routes on virtually the same schedules, and correspondingly divide the market. Elsewhere pooling arrangements as between Spain and France, both limited capacity in their shared markets, and divided the profits between the airlines allowed to fly the routes. In short, the

Low-Cost Airports for Low-Cost Airlines 39

regulatory environment created a 'cost-plus' environment aimed at insuring airline success.

2. In this context, airline employees obtained extraordinary wages and working conditions compared to workers of comparable skills in other sectors. Salary levels were higher, hours of work shorter, and retirement benefits more generous than in other industries – as the subsequent history demonstrates.

3. Correspondingly, airports serving the main airlines and national hubs obtained access to large amounts of cheap capital that they used to construct monumental structures, often among the most expensive architectural expressions in a metropolitan region. The recent passenger buildings at Bangkok/Suvarnabhumi, Hong Kong/Chep Lak Kok, Madrid/Barajas, San Francisco/International, and Shanghai/Pudong illustrate this pattern. London/Heathrow Terminal 5, costing around €6.5 billion (US$9.6 billion), represents the ultimate in this kind of expense.

4. Economic deregulation has been changing this picture. In the United States, price competition since 1978 has forced the legacy airlines to cut back drastically on their costs. This phenomenon has been propagating to Australia, Canada, Europe, and Asia.

5. Pressure on the airlines has in turn forced the employees of the legacy airlines to forego their comparatively generous terms of employment. As airlines faced bankruptcy and disappearance, employees confronted the choice of losing the airline and their jobs, or lowering their pay packages. Thus, wages at North American legacy carriers have dropped by about a third in real terms, working hours have lengthened, and jobs have enlarged. For example, at Northwest Airlines (NWA) the pilots agreed to cut their pay by 15% in 2004, and a further 24% in 2006, for a total overall reduction of 35% (Fedor, 2006). Machinists and ramp workers took a 26% and then a further 11.5% pay cut, as well as foregoing about 2 weeks of annual vacation. Flight attendants likewise took an additional 21% pay cut and accepted work rule changes, such as participating in the cleaning of the aircraft cabin (Jorgenson, 2006).

6. Similarly, legacy airlines have been cutting back on airport expenses, for example, by not moving into expensive facilities built for them (Swissair did not move into the new satellite at Zürich, and Lufthansa declined to move into the €1 billion (US$ 1.5 billion) Terminal 2 at Frankfurt/Main); or by cutting back substantially on the design of facilities, as American did at New York/Kennedy (DMJM Aviation, 2005).

Hypothesis in detail. The hypothesis is that the ascendancy of low-cost airlines entails an increased importance and expansion of low-cost

40   *Richard de Neufville*

airports and airport facilities. Specifically, as the low-cost airlines come to represent a sizeable fraction of the market:

- They catalyze the development of low-cost airports and airport facilities, both in the major metropolitan areas and throughout the regions.
- The low-cost airports compete with the traditional major 'legacy' airports, both locally in metropolitan areas and through a network of services connecting these facilities.
- In contrast with the traditional airports, low-cost airports will not have expensive buildings, and will focus on efficiency, and sparse commercial areas.

Low-cost airlines catalyze the development of low-cost airports. Because these carriers focus on cost competitiveness, they deliberately seek out and create opportunities for low-cost airports. This does not imply that they either build or invest heavily in these facilities. It means that they take advantage of the availability of the large number of existing under-used runways left over from an earlier technological era or obsolete military needs. The low-cost airlines then negotiate mutually beneficial arrangements with the local authorities under which the airlines create jobs and promote business and tourist opportunities for the region, and the local authorities organize the airport on advantageous terms for the low-cost airlines. These deals have often been win–win arrangements for both parties. Indeed, they follow the pattern for airport development that prevailed for most of the last century: national governments and local communities world-wide have provided capital for airport facilities at favorable interest rates or fiscal conditions. In the United States, for instance, airport facilities are largely financed by a combination of grants from the national treasury and by tax-free (i.e. subsidized) private bonds. Elsewhere, a traditional practice has been for governments to build the airports from tax resources.

Low-cost airports compete with major airports in three major ways:

1. Most obviously, as secondary airports in a metropolitan multi-airport system, they provide alternatives to the major hubs. These low-cost airports may be more convenient to some customers (as London/Stansted is to travelers from Cambridge and the Northeast of London); cheaper to users (as by lower parking charges); and provide access to a less expensive range of services.
2. In a larger sense, they compete with the larger hubs because they offer opportunities to bypass these hubs. Thus, Londoners interested in going to the South of Spain can now go on Ryanair directly to Jerez, and avoid passing through Madrid as they would ordinarily

Low-Cost Airports for Low-Cost Airlines 41

have had to do on a legacy airline, such as Iberia. Likewise, they can get to Carcassonne directly and avoid travel through Paris or Toulouse; or reach the Algarve by flying to Faro and avoiding Portugal's premier airport at Lisbon.

3. Moreover, the low-cost airlines and airports jointly form parallel networks that compete against the routes of the legacy airlines and the major hubs. Thus, Ryanair provides service between London, Brussels, Frankfurt, and Barcelona – using the low-cost airports of Stansted, Charleroi, Hahn, and Girona. Similarly in North America, Southwest serves Boston, Washington, and Miami – using Providence, Baltimore, and Fort Lauderdale.

Finally, the business model for low-cost airports is distinct from that of the traditional major airports. Mirroring the difference between low-cost and legacy airlines, low-cost airports emphasize economy through operational efficiency and minimal frills:

1. Most obviously, they avoid grandiose buildings by signature architects and others. They favor simple designs that, as one architectural critic put it, 'have the charm of a high school gymnasium'. The contrast at Singapore between the new Terminal 3 and the low-cost terminal built around the corner illustrates this point. The low-cost terminal is a cinder block and metal truss arrangement, built at about 1/10th the cost per passenger of capacity as the resplendent Terminal 3 built concurrently.

2. The interior spaces of low-cost airport buildings reflect the performance standards of the low-cost airlines. They have lower service levels in terms of space per person, and overall higher annual capacity per square meter of space, associated with lower dwell times of passengers due to fast turnarounds of the aircraft. Because the total space required per passenger is directly related to the average time people stay in a space, that is, the dwell time, the faster an airline turns its aircraft, the faster travelers use the gate, and the less space per person is required (de Neufville & Odoni, 2003). They also emphasize common hold rooms to minimize the overall space allocated to this function. The common practice, outside of the United States, has been to build separate hold rooms for each gate. It is more economical to provide common hold rooms, so that the space provided can be used more intensively. This practice reduces the total space required by up to 50% (de Neufville & Belin, 2002).

3. Low-cost airports will not create large amounts of expensive commercial space, even though retail activities can be important sources of revenue, as Francis *et al.* (2003) document. Building and operating commercial space on airports is particularly costly.

Security measures and general difficulty and delays of access multiply construction costs. Likewise, it is expensive to pass commercial items and staff through security – which is where they mostly have to be, to appeal to passengers. In short, the economic rationale for building airport terminals as shopping arcades is not clear. It is one thing to stuff an otherwise empty space with shops, as has been widely done in the existing terminals at main hub airports, for example, at London/Heathrow. It is quite another to spend around €6.5 billion (US$9.6 billion) on Terminal 5 at Heathrow, much of which is designed around multiple shopping floors.

As the overall hypothesis exists in a social context, its manifestations do not follow mechanically. Exceptions to the general rule occur. Moreover, the units of analysis are to some degree ambivalent. The definition of a low-cost airline is not unique. How should one classify jetBlue, for example, which acts like Southwest and easyJet in many ways, but offers amenities not found on other low-cost airlines (such as individual television screens)? The correctness of the hypothesis depends on the overall trends, and it is in this light that we should look at the evidence.

Evidence

Unit of analysis. As the hypothesis centers on low-cost airlines, it is necessary to be clear about the definition of this concept, at least in this context. As Gillen and Lall (2004) highlighted, low-cost airlines come in a variety of forms. For example, Southwest, Ryanair and easyJet each have distinct approaches to their business. However, because the argument in this paper rests on the economic reality that producers with the lowest costs ultimately define the market, the definition of 'low-cost airlines' centers on the airlines' actual costs of production, for example, per seat-mile.

Current data in the United States appear to define low-cost airlines reasonably clearly. As Figure 1 shows, there is a division between the legacy airlines that have seat-mile costs in the range of US15 cents, and the others whose costs are about 40% lower. This kind of data demarcates the low-cost airlines. Comparable data on other low-cost airlines are not available. However, from industry and other sources it is reasonably clear that easyJet, Ryanair, GOL, AirAsia, Westjet and others can confidently be placed in the low-cost category.

In thinking about this issue, it is important to recognize that an airline that offers low fares is not necessarily a low-cost airline in the sense of being a low-cost producer, which is the sense used in this paper. For a customer, low price = low cost. From that perspective, US

Low-Cost Airports for Low-Cost Airlines   43

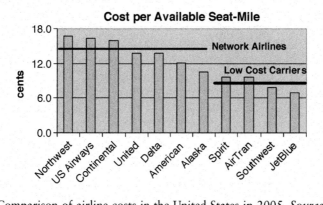

Figure 1. Comparison of airline costs in the United States in 2005. *Source*: US FAA, Bureau of Transportation Statistics (2007a)

Airways has been cited as a 'low-cost airline' (Wikipedia, 2007a), even though its costs have been among the highest, as Figure 1 indicates. However, from the perspective of an economic analysis, there is a big difference between low-cost and high-cost producers. Furthermore, from economics we know that producers in a market ultimately need to match the going price for a given quality, so that the price charged is not an appropriate way to identify low-cost producers.

Ascendancy of low-cost airlines. Low-cost carriers now drive much of the future of air travel. This fact may surprise casual observers. Most of us know that the low-cost airlines are newcomers compared to the legacy carriers, many of which have proudly commemorated their 75th anniversaries. From our travels through leading airports, we can recall the showcase terminal buildings associated with these traditional carriers. Many memories can combine to imprint us with the continuing importance of the legacy carriers. Yet, the fact is that by 2005 well over 50% of the revenue passenger-miles in the United States consisted of traffic of the low-cost carriers or traditional airlines that were matching their fares (Morrison & Winston, 2005). In particular, Southwest Airlines has been by far the largest domestic carrier in the United States since 2004. In 2006 it had 96.3 million emplanements, about 30% more than the next largest (American, at 76.3) and about 50% more than the third largest domestic carrier (Delta, at 63.4) (US Federal Aviation Administration, Bureau of Transportation Statistics, 2007a).

Similar stories are emerging elsewhere. In Canada, the low-cost Westjet has been humming along while one of the two legacy carriers went bankrupt (Canadian), merged with the other legacy carrier, Air Canada, which also went bankrupt. In Europe, Ryanair and easyJet have grown rapidly and rank among the strongest passenger airlines in

44   *Richard de Neufville*

Table 1. Market capitalizations of leading airlines (US$ billion) as of 2 January 2007

Airline	Market cap	Airline type	Went bankrupt?
UPS	80.5	Integrated freight	
Fedex	33.4	Integrated freight	
Ryanair	12.6	Low-cost	
Lufthansa	12.3		
Southwest	12.1	Low-cost	
British Airways	11.8		
Air France	11.3		
Singapore	8.2		
American	6.5		
GOL	5.6	Low-cost	
EasyJet	5.1	Low-cost	
United	4.9		Yes
US Airways	4.7		Yes
Continental	3.7		Yes
Iberia	3.3		
JetBlue	2.5	Low-cost	
Virgin Blue	2.0	Low-cost	
Air Canada	1.9		Yes
Alaska	1.6		
Westjet	1.4	Low-cost	
Air Tran	1.1	Low-cost	
AirAsia	1.0	Low-cost	
Japan Airlines	0.6		
Allegiant	0.5	Low-cost	
Northwest	0.4		Yes
Delta	0.3		Yes
Hawaiian	0.2		

Source: finance.yahoo.com and industry estimates. US$10 billion:€6.8 billion.

the world, as Table 1 shows. In total, the various low-cost European airlines already account for around 1/3 of all traffic in the European Union. Likewise, in Brazil, GOL has overtaken the national flag carrier, Varig, which has collapsed economically and passed from the largest airline in South America to the number 4 in Brazil (Wikipedia, 2007b). In Asia finally, AirAsia, Lion Air, and Jetstar – each new since 2001 – already carried 6% of that traffic by 2004 (International Air Transport Association, 2005).

The rise of the integrated freight airlines, such as UPS, Fedex, and DHL, is further eclipsing the legacy carriers and the legacy hub airports with which they are associated. Fedex has more major jet aircraft than Lufthansa, British Airways or Air France, and UPS is in the same league (International Air Transport Association, 2005). Fedex and UPS have

Low-Cost Airports for Low-Cost Airlines   45

seized the lion's share of the market for profitable air cargo. Most importantly, these innovative carriers preferentially (although not exclusively) use secondary airports in metropolitan areas. Thus in North America, beyond their main hubs at the second tier airports of Memphis and Louisville, Fedex and UPS have hubs at such airports as Chicago/Rockport, Los Angeles/Ontario, San Francisco/Oakland, and Toronto/Hamilton. The integrated freight airlines are developing their own networks of services independent of those of the legacy carriers and airports.

The market capitalizations of the low-cost and innovative carriers underscore their rise compared to the legacy carriers. The 'market cap' equals the product of the number of shares in the company times the market price per share. This standard financial measure thus takes into account the current situation and future prospects of a business. It is the investors' valuation of a company, indicating their willingness to provide it with capital (such as aircraft and terminal buildings). Equally, it represents the financial power of a company, which can use its shares to buy or otherwise acquire assets. Conversely, when an airline is bankrupt and thus has no significant market cap, it has very little financial power, even though it may have its name painted on many aircraft. Table 1 shows that the financial power of the low-cost carriers is comparable if not superior to that of the legacy carriers. Ryanair, for example, is more valuable than British Airways. Southwest has twice the value of the next US carriers, American and United.

The market capitalization is a better measure of the strength of an airline than more traditional measures, such as fleet size. The reality is that airlines largely do not own the aircraft with their logos – they lease them. The largest owner of commercial aircraft is International Lease Finance (2007) which at the end of 2006 owned 823 Boeing and Airbus aircraft – more than the combined fleets of Air France, British Airways and Lufthansa (Wayne, 2007). Table 2 illustrates this in another way: Southwest, the company with the largest market cap in the United States, is buying many new aircraft and has the youngest fleet compared with its biggest rivals.

Table 2. Southwest compared to nearest rivals for US domestic traffic

Airline	Domestic traffic (millions, 2006)	Average aircraft age (years)	Fleet size 2006	Fleet size 2007	Change (%)
Southwest	96.3	9.8	445	491	+10
American	76.3	14.1	699	672	−3
Delta	63.4	13.3	434	428	−3

Sources: Airfleets.net (2007), US FAA (2007a).

46   *Richard de Neufville*

Table 3. Low-cost airports whose development was catalyzed by low-cost airlines

Metropolitan region	Secondary airport	Low-cost airline	Pre-low-cost traffic
Barcelona	Girona	Ryanair	Insignificant
Boston	Providence	Southwest	Half
Boston	Manchester, NH	Southwest	Half
Brussels	Charleroi	Ryanair	Insignificant
Budapest	Balaton	Ryanair	Insignificant
Copenhagen	Malmo, Sweden	Ryanair	Half
Dallas/Fort Worth	Love	Southwest	Insignificant
Frankfurt	Hahn	Ryanair	Insignificant
Glasgow	Prestwick	Ryanair	Insignificant
Hamburg	Lübeck	Ryanair	Half
Houston/Galveston	Hobby	Southwest	Almost all SW
London	Stansted	Ryanair	One-third
London	Luton	EasyJet	Half
Los Angeles	Long Beach	jetBlue	Half
Manchester (UK)	Liverpool	EasyJet	Insignificant
Manila	Clark	AirAsia	Insignificant
Melbourne (Australia)	Avalon	Jetstar	Insignificant
Miami	Fort Lauderdale	Southwest	Half
Milan	Orio al Serio	Ryanair	Insignificant
New York	Islip	Southwest	Insignificant
Orlando	Sanford	Allegiant	Insignificant
Oslo	Torp	Ryanair	Insignificant
Paris	Beauvais	Ryanair	Insignificant
Rome	Ciampino	easyJet, Ryanair	Insignificant
San Francisco	Oakland	Southwest	Two-Thirds
Stockholm	Skvasta Vasteras	Ryanair	Insignificant
Vancouver	Abbotsford	Westjet	Insignificant
Venice	Treviso	Ryanair	Insignificant
Vienna	Bratislava, Slovakia	Ryanair	Half

Source: de Neufville Multi-Airport Systems database.

Development of low-cost airports. The record shows that the low-cost airlines have been major drivers of the development of low-cost airports. Table 3 gives details. Ryanair has been the impetus behind the development of Barcelona/Girona, Brussels/Charleroi, Frankfurt/Hahn, London/Stansted, and others (Beck, 2007; Garriga, 2003, 2004). Likewise, easyJet has led the growth of Manchester/Liverpool and London/Luton. In the United States, the phenomenon has been known as the 'Southwest effect', as that airline has energized the doubling and tripling of traffic at airports, such as Boston/Manchester, Boston/

Low-Cost Airports for Low-Cost Airlines   47

Providence and Miami/Fort Lauderdale. In Asia, Asia Air has been promoting Manila/Clark and Jetstar in Australia created Melbourne/ Avalon from virtually nothing into an international gateway with service to Indonesia, Japan, Thailand and Vietnam (Jetstar, 2007). Overall, the low-cost airlines have catalyzed the widespread development of multi-airport systems in metropolitan areas. These used to be confined to metropolitan areas with over 10 million departing passengers a year (de Neufville, 1995), but now are a feature of many smaller areas – such as Budapest, Oslo, Stockholm, Venice, and other metropolitan regions.

Note that the cost of developing a low-cost airport is minimal – in contrast to that of a new or expanded traditional major airport (such as Madrid/Barajas, Miami/International, Paris/de Gaulle, Tokyo/Narita, etc.) that easily cost €3 billion (US$4.4 billion) or more. Low-cost airports have almost been free, due to the fact that obsolete military and other airfields are plentiful. These have provided the runways and basic facilities for many of the airports listed in Table 3. In any case, regional authorities have been glad to supply the modest supplemental facilities needed for passenger services, in exchange for the jobs the low-cost airlines create and the passengers they bring to the area. The possibilities are far from exhausted. Portugal provides a case in point: It has a sizeable military field at Beja, which the central government and local authorities wish to convert to a low-cost airport for about €30 million (US$44.4 million) (Câmara de Comercio Luso-Britânica [British-Portuguese Chamber of Commerce], 2007).

Low-cost carriers like to use low-cost, secondary airports for two reasons. Most obviously, they appreciate the low charges. Perhaps more importantly, however, they like the smaller airports because these are relatively uncongested and thus free from ground and air traffic control delays, as Table 4 indicates, and Warnock-Smith and Potter (2005) document in detail. Lack of congestion, together with work rules that permit fast turnaround times at the gate, enable low-cost airlines to increase the flying time and thus the productivity of their aircraft, and thus lower their operating costs significantly. Low-cost airlines choose secondary airports because they are generally integral to their efficiency.

The combination of quick turnaround times and use of secondary airports with low delays leads to significant cost advantages for the low-cost airlines. This fact needs to be stressed as many observers appear not to appreciate the applicable economies. The box presented in Figure 2 provides an illustration of how this works. This crude analysis does not specify many operational details such as the maintenance required after specified hours of flying. It does, however,

48   *Richard de Neufville*

Table 4. Secondary airports in metropolitan areas enabling less aircraft delays

Primary airport in metropolitan region	Secondary airports	Flights with delays >15 minutes (%)
Boston/Logan		33
	Manchester, NH	25
	Providence, RI	26
Dallas/Fort Worth		30
	Love	23
Los Angeles/International		25
	Burbank	20
	Ontario	18
	Wayne/Santa Ana	21
San Francisco/International		27
	Oakland	19
	San Jose	18

Source: US FAA, Bureau of Transportation Statistics (2007b).

indicate the kind of productivity airlines can achieve by cutting their turnaround times and congestion delays.

Low-cost airlines emphasize the use of low-cost airports when these are available. Conversely, they tend to avoid legacy hub airports, even

---

Sample Comparison of Flight Hours/Day Achieved by Legacy and Low-Cost Carriers

Both carriers fly between cities 1.5 hours apart, over about a 17 hour day (6 am to 11 pm)

Assume 30 minutes delay at congested airports, 20 minutes at less congested airports.

Turn-around time not needed at start of day.

A) Legacy Carrier flying between congested airports, with 1 hour turn-around time

Time per leg = flight time + turn-around time + allowance for delays = 1.5 + 1 + 0.5 = 3 hours

Round trips per day = 17 / 6 => 3   (allowing for no turn-around at start and end).

B) Low-Cost Carrier flying between less congested airports, with 0.5 hour turn-around

Time per leg = 1 + 0.5 + 0.33 = 1.83 hours

Round Trips per day = 17 / 3.67 => 5 (allowing for no turn-around at start and end.)

Comparative Advantage of Low-Cost Carrier:\

Productivity increase of Aircraft (Capital employed) = + 67 %

Decrease in Capital Cost per Passenger = 40%

Figure 2. Comparison of flight hours/day achieved by legacy and low-cost carriers

Low-Cost Airports for Low-Cost Airlines   49

though they serve some of them. Thus Southwest, by far the larger carrier of passengers in the United States (US Federal Aviation Administration, Bureau of Transportation Statistics, 2007a), as of 2007 does not provide service to half the top 10 busiest US airports (Atlanta, Chicago/O'Hare, Houston/Bush, Minneapolis/St.Paul, and New York/Kennedy) nor to obvious destinations such as Boston/Logan, New York/Newark-Liberty and Miami/International.

Competition with hub airports. Low-cost secondary airports in a metropolitan area compete with the traditional main ports. As the low-cost carriers expand along with these low-cost airports, they contribute to reducing the market share of the legacy airports as Table 5 illustrates. The impact of this competition on specific routes (such as Dublin–Brussels served by Ryanair), can be very strong, as Barrett (2004) showed. Of course, other factors contribute to the changes in market share, such as changing demographics and congestion at the legacy airport. These particular two factors cannot, however, be considered important for the examples in Table 5, as each of the cited primary airports has ample capacity to absorb the traffic at the emerging low-cost airport, and as their demographics have not changed substantially in the decade under consideration.

The point is that competition now exists between the low-cost and the legacy airports, in a way it did not when the low-cost carriers were marginal. Many legacy airports have lost their previous virtual monopolies. This fact has to motivate their management – more than they would otherwise be inclined – to build facilities that will be more competitive with low-cost airports.

More subtly, the low-cost airlines and innovative freight carriers are establishing parallel networks that bypass the traditional main airports (de Neufville, 2005). This is strikingly evident in Europe, where many low-cost carriers make a point of serving major metropolitan areas through secondary airports. Thus, the Ryanair network comprises

Table 5. Example market share drops for primary airports associated with rise of low-cost carriers

Metropolitan region	Primary airport	Market share (%) in	
		1994	2004
Boston	Logan	90	72
Brussels	Zaventam	99	90
Miami	International	69	56
San Francisco	International	68	58

Source: de Neufville Multi-Airport Systems database drawn from various reports.

London/Stansted, Barcelona/Girona, Brussels/Charleroi, Frankfurt/ Hahn, Rome/Ciampino, Stockholm/Skvasta, and so on. The situation in the United States is similar as Southwest serves Boston/Providence, Dallas/Love, Houston/Hobby, Miami/Fort Lauderdale, and Washington/Baltimore.

Moreover, the low-cost carriers compete with the main airports when they fly directly from major metropolitan areas (such as London) to secondary airports, thus bypassing the hub airports that have traditionally provided connections to secondary areas. Thus when Ryanair serves Carcassonne direct from London/Stansted, it not only competes with flights that might go direct from London/Heathrow, but also those that might provide service through Paris.

Overall, we are witnessing the development of parallel air transport networks. On the one hand there are the legacy carriers, largely attached to their hub or legacy airports. On the other hand, there are the low-cost carriers, which have been promoting the definition of low-cost airports. This low-cost network is complemented in North America by a network of Fedex and UPS low-cost airports, such as Chicago/Rockford, Los Angeles/Ontario, and San Francisco/Oakland.

Business model for low-cost airports. Low-cost airlines generally aim to cut frills. They do not intend to pay for architectural showcases and gateway projects, and the associated high airport charges, it they can avoid them. According to the head of Ryanair, their top three airport requirements are: low airport charges, fast turnaround times, and single-story airport terminals (Barrett, 2004). Thus the Ryanair wing of the London/Stansted airport is a one-story structure that passengers walk to – in sharp contrast to the expensive multi-level buildings, designed by a signature architect (Sir Norman Foster), that travelers on other airlines have to access using an expensive special-purpose train.

When low-cost carriers have the opportunity to define their passenger facilities, they make them simple and sparse, with a minimum of commercial facilities. They do not use the traditional industry design standards. The terminals for Ryanair at Frankfurt/ Hahn (Beck, 2007); easyJet at Manchester/Liverpool; jetBlue at Los Angeles/Long Beach, Jetstar at Melbourne/Avalon, and AirAsia at Kuala Lumpur all demonstrate this fact. At Singapore, an airport known for its excellent retail opportunities, it is remarkable that their low-cost terminal has few shops.

Low-cost airlines often apply design standards deeply different from those generally used in traditional passenger facilities, such as those of the International Air Transport Association (2004) and de Neufville and Odoni (2003). They use space more intensively, planning on higher densities of passengers per unit of area, and using shared hold rooms instead individual gate lounges. They also process passengers quicker, with turnaround times of around 30 minutes instead of the more standard hour. For example, at Boston/Logan jetBlue manages to process about 0.5 million passengers/gate, compared to its competitor Delta which manages only about half as many. This means that jetBlue needs fewer gates for a given number of flights. The net result is that low-cost airlines often require around half the space per passenger as the legacy airlines (de Neufville, 2006).

Their approach gives the low-cost carriers a tremendous financial advantage compared to the legacy carriers that must operate out of, and consequently pay for, grandiose monuments. The airlines operating out of Terminal 5 at London/Heathrow will be carrying a substantial handicap, compared to their low-cost competitors. The cost of this building (by the signature architect Lord Richard Rogers) is already over €6.5 billion (US$9.6 billion). Its annual cost for amortization and operation will be on the order of about €20 (US$30) per passenger. This kind of burden is difficult for low-cost airlines, and they generally avoid such costs. As low-cost airlines continue to expand at the expense of the legacy carriers, so will the low-cost airports at the expense of the legacy airports.

Greater Forecast Uncertainty

The economic deregulation of the air transport industry has driven both the rise of the low-cost carriers and a significant increase in the forecast uncertainty. The collapse of limiting regulatory regimes and bi-lateral conventions has removed the bureaucratic brakes to rapid changes. The concurrent rise of the low-cost carriers, with new visions of how and where to operate airlines, has changed the nature of the business. The situation now is that:

- Changes occur quickly once the regulatory brakes are off, as de Neufville and Barber (1991) demonstrated.
- Changes in airlines can matter tremendously – when one company's business model fails, its services may not be replaced – witness the cases of TWA, US Airways, Sabena, and Swissair, with the collapse of traffic at St. Louis, Pittsburgh, Brussels and Zürich.
- Alternative service standards are appearing, so that what was designed for one airline may be incompatible with the business needs of replacements, as happened at Baltimore (de Neufville & Odoni, 2003) and more recently at Boston/Logan where the facilities built for the legacy airline Delta are not being taken up by the competitor (jetBlue) that has taken much of their traffic.

- Low-cost carriers routinely experiment with alternative, non-traditional destinations.

Airport planners thus now have to confront far greater uncertainty than ever before. Previously, they mainly worried about how fast traffic might grow, and when to time the development of facilities. Now they have to also pay attention to three key questions:

- where might the traffic grow, at main, secondary or regional airports?
- will there be abrupt and long-lasting breaks in traffic, as can occur when an airline fails? and
- what kind of facilities might future customers need? Airport developers can no longer assume that a facility can be re-branded for another airline. Low-cost carriers have repeatedly demonstrated their reluctance to use facilities designed for legacy airlines (as at Boston, Brussels, Hamburg, London/Stansted, San Francisco/International, and Zürich).

Consequences for Airport Planning, Design, and Management

The traditional paradigm of airport planning is threatened. The established pattern has been driven by long-term forecasts, based on established long-term clients, and aimed at a common appreciation and desire for high standards. These premises are no longer an obvious basis for investing and developing in airports.

Demand forecasts for any airport must be considered to be much more uncertain than before. In addition to the accustomed variability in the rates of growth due to economic cycles, we first add the market volatility associated with absence of the dampening effects of economic regulation, and further add on the great uncertainties of an industry in the midst of extensive change:

- Major airport users may disappear. As has happened extensively in North America, many legacy carriers will merge with others or go out of business. In Europe, the national airlines of Belgium and Switzerland (Sabena and Swissair) have vanished – causing great traffic decreases at Brussels and Zürich. The Dutch national airline merged with Air France. The national carrier of Brazil, Varig, has practically disappeared. Many more can be expected to vanish, with consequent impacts on their current airport bases.
- The distribution and patterns of traffic may change. Low-cost carriers may divert traffic to secondary metropolitan airports, as they have done in most of the airports listed in Table 3, or in a nation – as they have done in Portugal by building traffic at Faro and Porto.

- Different design standards may apply. The airline clientele may reject facilities provided, leaving them underutilized and possibly unprofitable, as Ryanair has done in Porto.

Airport developers thus face much greater risks of investing in the wrong place, in the wrong way, at the wrong time. They now need a planning and development process that allows them to recognize explicitly the uncertainties that threaten the planned developments and investments, and develop ways to respond easily to the many different scenarios that might develop. This is the essence of the paradigmatic shift in airport planning.

The change in paradigm has physical consequences. It is shifting the concepts about appropriate investments in airport infrastructure away from monumental airport facilities and main ports, built according to the conventional space and other standards, toward increased use of simpler facilities located at secondary airports with facilities using much less generous standards for space and expense.

What experience and practice has taught airport planners over the past half-century may no longer be fully acceptable. A new class of clients has arisen, and they are demanding and obtaining different kinds of facilities and locations. Political and business leaders concerned with airport planning and development need to think carefully and cautiously about future investments. Good airport planning, design, and management are not what they used to be.

Process for Flexible Design

The essence of a flexible design process is to put in place arrangements that enable the airport owners to respond easily and effectively to the range of scenarios that might occur. From a design perspective, flexibility consists of technical features that enable the owners to change, easily and inexpensively, the configuration of their facility to meet new needs.

Vancouver airport provides a good example of flexible design. To cope with the shifting numbers of travelers who require different processing procedures (Canadian, transborder to the United States, and other International traffic), the Vancouver terminal is basically a large open hall divided by interior glass panels into spaces that can be connected in different ways by escalators and passages. The airport can thus easily adjust to short- and long-term shifts of traffic through the building. In the short run, operators open and close doors between various sectors. In the long run, they can displace panels.

Because of the way traditional airport planning practice has focused on fixed, point forecasts of traffic, flexible designs for airports have not been common. If you believe you know what the future requires, there is no need to plan for any adaptation to future conditions. The experience of Baltimore provides an example of how this traditional lack of recognition of uncertainty can lead to difficulties. In that case, the airport created an international terminal for US Airways based on long-term forecasts of its need. However, when the low-cost carrier Southwest drove US Airways to abandon its Baltimore hub, the airport could not transform the terminal to serve domestic passengers. The airport had to spend over US$100 million (€68 million) to create a new facility to fulfill the needs of Southwest (de Neufville & Odoni, 2003). If the airport had not relied on long-term forecasts and had instead recognized the possible scenarios, they could have avoided this loss.

Flexible designs incorporate capabilities to adjust easily to different scenarios. They create 'real options', similar to financial options (such as puts and calls) that give their owners the 'right, but not an obligation, to take an action, now or in the future.' Specifically, flexible designs involve real options 'in' projects, that is, capabilities to adjust that are due to technical elements built into the design itself (Wang & de Neufville, 2006). These require careful crafting and preparation. For example, a real option to convert a terminal from international to domestic use involves both technical foresight (such as that implemented in Vancouver) and political steps, to gain governmental and airline acceptance. In this sense, flexible designs involve 'complex options' (McConnell, 2007).

Design for flexibility is usefully compared to playing chess. The skillful practitioner will think through many scenarios, anticipate possible responses, and make moves that both deal with different threats and exploit opportunities. This is the kind of thinking involved in the new paradigm of airport planning, which is developing in response to the changes in the nature of the air transport system being brought about by the rise of low-cost airlines and the concurrent emergence of low-cost airports and airport facilities. In a nutshell, planners and investors need to adopt a flexible, evolutionary approach to the development of their airport infrastructure.

Steps of Process

A flexible design process consists of three basic elements:

• *Recognition of the range of uncertainty.* The reality of a wide variation of possible outcomes, from the least favorable to the most advantageous, is what motivates the development of plans both to mitigate downside difficulties, and to take advantage of the upside opportunities;

Low-Cost Airports for Low-Cost Airlines   55

- *Definition of flexible design opportunities.* These enable the system owners to adjust their facilities easily to the actual future situations. Flexible design involves the ability to reconfigure the facilities to meet different technical or market developments; and
- *Analysis of the development strategies.* Identifies the strategies that could be used to exploit these design opportunities, and the selection of the initial, the 'inaugural' airport plan that provides the best starting basis for future expansions and reconfigurations.

A detailed worked-out example of this process, with supporting spreadsheets, is available on the web from de Neufville *et al.* (2006).

The flexible design process is deeply different from traditional airport planning and design (de Neufville & Odoni, 2003). The traditional process starts with the definition of the most likely forecast – and as a practical matter ignores the considerable uncertainties that lie ahead for the following decades, then defines a single Master Plan for the development of the airport facilities (and does not contemplate any substantial deviations to adapt to industry changes) and finally commits to this Master Plan, both conceptually and physically.

The traditional design process has led to many embarrassments for airport owners, where they lacked the flexibility to adapt the design to actual conditions, and thus suffered severe financial and operational difficulties, as at:

- Bangkok, where the inability to adjust to low-cost and other industry developments stalled the opening of the new airport for 2 years, thus increasing the capitalized cost of the facility by 25% or more. The author has been a consultant to the Bangkok airport project for over a decade, and has observed that the widespread explanations that attribute the situation to technical difficulties mask the deep-seated conflicts over transport policy and the airline–airport competition, and are designed to save face and avoid embarrassment, rather than portray the root causes;
- Frankfurt, where the €1 billion (US$1.5 billion) Terminal 2 is under-used because it could not be adapted to the hubbing needs of Lufthansa (for which the building had been intended);
- Kansas City, whose design likewise could not adapt to needs of its main client, TWA, which thus subsequently moved its corporate base to another city (St. Louis), thus creating huge financial difficulties for Kansas City; and
- Pittsburgh, where the design failed to account for the possibility that hubbing operations might disappear, and thus placed the airport and its owners under great financial stress when US Airways shifted its hub operations to Philadelphia.

Such failures of the traditional design motivate the use of a flexible design process that can adapt to the situations that could exist.

Recognition of uncertainty. Forecasts are 'always wrong', in that the actual level of traffic that occurs in 5, 10 or 20 years is routinely far from what is predicted, both as to the level and type of traffic. This has been extensively documented (de Neufville & Odoni, 2003). The differences between actual and forecast traffic occur because 'trend-breakers' inevitably worsen the usual swings in economic cycles. These sudden shifts in traffic patterns may be:

- Economic/Financial (airline bankruptcy, such as Sabena, Swissair, Northwest Airlines, or Air Canada);
- Industrial (airline merger, such as American and TWA, or Air France and KLM);
- Political (the opening of China to world trade and the boom of cheap tourism in Asia);
- Technical (such as the Geographic Positioning Systems (GPS) that reduce the cost of air traffic control and ground radars); and
- Other, as with terrorism, war, and the price of fuel.

The major long-term reconfiguration of the air transport industry, associated with the development of low-cost carriers, is now added to this standard list of classes of uncertainties. As many industry observers stress, the future of low-cost carriers is uncertain (Dennis, 2004; Williams, 2007). Many ventures have disappeared, such as Peoples Express, Canada 3000, and Buzz. Investors and planners need to confront and deal proactively with these risks.

In the deregulated era of low-cost airlines, leaders also need to recognize that any airport investment may be strongly affected by competitive forces far beyond their control. They should now, as never before, anticipate the possibility of large and sudden changes in traffic, as when a low-cost carrier decides to develop a market and triples traffic in a few years (the 'Southwest effect', widely experienced in the United States) or when a legacy carrier closes a hub and traffic drops dramatically in a year (as happened in Brussels with Sabena, in Zürich with Swissair, St. Louis with TWA and American, and in Pittsburgh with US Airways). Airports now need to be considered as part of a system. Any airport planning exercise that focuses only on the local situation, and fails to confront the role of the airport in its larger context, must be considered to be deficient. As Graham (2004) indicates, airport owners and managers need to consider and develop strategies to gain and maintain competitive advantage.

Low-Cost Airports for Low-Cost Airlines   57

Definition of flexible design opportunities. Managers of airport systems need to be careful about committing to single major projects conceived along traditional lines. Given the great uncertainty about the future of air transport, they could easily find themselves spending billions on projects that turn out to have been misguided. Thus, Thailand decided to build Bangkok/Suvarnabhumi airport without thinking through the role of Bangkok in the market for low-cost tourism, and the needs of low-cost carriers. Yet now the low-fare airlines want to stay at the old (but inexpensive and convenient) Bangkok/Don Muang, and the international carriers serving that market need to be near their partners. Thus, they have been reluctant to move. This conflict contributed to the delayed opening of the new airport, and continues to be a major political and economic embarrassment to the owners. It is not an experience anyone wants to repeat.

A flexible approach to the development of major infrastructure is needed in these circumstances. Flexible designs can take many forms. For example, political leaders and investors can:

- commit to a site for a major airport, think through how they could implement it, and yet only decide to invest in a small 'Inaugural airport'. Such a facility would establish the political and technical reality of the airport, without committing it to be a supplemental or replacement hub, or a secondary or low-cost facility.
- simultaneously create both traditional and low-cost facilities at a new airport, to appeal to the range of possible customers. Doing this is very different – in concept and in cost – from a commitment to a traditional design around a single architectural statement (as originally at Bangkok/Suvarnabhumi, Kansas/City, Kuala Lumpur, London/Stansted, Paris/de Gaulle and elsewhere).
- select an airport layout that easily enables different futures. They would learn from London/Stansted and Munich Terminal 1, whose designs locked in on configurations that were both difficult to alter and ill-suited to current traffic. They would not commit to a development that could not easily morph into the range of configurations that future traffic might need.
- insist that architects develop flexible spaces that can easily accommodate both short- and long-term fluctuations in traffic, as they did attractively and effectively at Vancouver.

Leaders should also anticipate the possibility that low-cost carriers and others will stimulate the demand for distributed airport infrastructure consisting of many smaller airports in contrast to one or more national facilities. They should thus manage the development of their portfolio of airports, retaining the option to develop facilities according to the type of traffic that actually emerges. Investments in smaller airports that have not yet fully established themselves can be risky – but investments in large airports have also proven themselves to be risky, and involve far greater amounts of capital. Efforts should, for example, go into establishing and preserving sites and traffic corridors, the preparation of low-cost passenger facilities, and investments in technical support facilities for air traffic control, refueling, etc. Compared to the billions required to establish a major new hub, such investments are cheap, and might provide good provision against future needs. For example, in Portugal the adaptation of the Beja military field into a possible civilian airport is projected to cost about 1% of the anticipated totally new airport for Lisbon. This might be regarded as cheap insurance.

Overall, a key part of the flexible design process lies in the identification of design solutions that minimize irrevocable commitments that may be premature, and that simultaneously provide easy pathways to the development of the range of facilities that might actually be needed in the future.

Analysis of development strategies. The final part of the design for flexibility is to think through how alternative initial designs could adapt to future circumstances. Managers need to consider what they could do, how the future might turn out, and how they might correspondingly respond. This process is conceptually similar to how chess or bridge players think through their moves.

Professionally, this process plays on two major planes: the physical and the financial. The airport owners and managers need to know that they will be able to accommodate the buildings, aircraft, access modes and other facilities in a reasonable sequence. Equally, they need to know the financial consequences in terms of costs and revenues.

Standard analytic tools can help designers think through the possible combinations of possible outcomes and responses. Most are computerized and can be quickly learned and used. Two deserve particular attention:

- Decision Analysis, which is a process for systematically organizing the sequences of possible design decisions, the range of possible developments, and subsequent further decisions. This process was central to the original strategy for the development of Sydney's airport facilities as it entered privatization (de Neufville, 1991).
- Simulation of spreadsheet *pro forma* financial statements, a well-used process for developing useful measures such as the Expected Net Present Value (ENPV), the Value at Risk and Gain, the Minimum and Maximum results, the Initial Capital Expenditures, and Return on Investment (Hassan *et al.*, 2005).

Low-Cost Airports for Low-Cost Airlines 59

The outcome of the process is a decision concerning the initial development, together with a strategy of how the facility will be further developed as circumstances unfold and the nature of the air transportation market becomes clear. Conceptually, this is similar to what a good chess player has in mind when making each move.

Portugal as an Example

The on-going situation in Portugal illustrates the issues discussed. The push to develop a new major airport for the capital, accelerating since 2005, gives local color to the planning, policy, and investment questions indicated above.

Background. Portugal has traditionally been served by national airlines, TAP and Portugalia (merged in 2006), and international airlines focused on the main hub at Lisbon/Portela. This facility, situated close to central Lisbon with flight paths directly over densely inhabited areas, is clearly limited in its potential expansion. Since around 1990, there has correspondingly been pressure to define a site for a major new airport. In the late 1990s, the Government selected the Ota site and commissioned the Aéroports de Paris to prepare a Master Plan for the development of this old military air base. Their conventional result featured a multi-level terminal building with air bridges to all aircraft according to the highest traditional standards. It had no obvious provision for low-cost carriers or flexibility in the overall configuration or the interior arrangements, and no strategy for alternative developments according to how air transport traffic might evolve in Portugal or Europe. The preliminary cost estimates of this fixed plan exceed €3 billion (US$4.4.billion) (ACI World and Momberger Airport Information, 2005).

In January 2007, the Government of Portugal reaffirmed its intention of developing a second airport (AFX News, 2007). It also confirmed its plan to privatize the national airport company, Aeroportos de Portugal (ANA), and to require the successful consortium to develop the new airport.

Recognition of uncertainty. Since the plans for the €3 billion airport for Lisbon emerged a decade ago, the air transport situation has changed dramatically – both in Europe and Portugal. The low-cost airlines have developed strongly. The mid-size national airlines (such as Olympic, Sabena, Swissair, and TAP, the Portuguese flag airline) have struggled financially and required substantial subsidies to stay alive (European Commission 2000). Their future is unclear. Experience in North America, Brazil, and Europe indicates that some of them may disappear through merger or bankruptcy.

60   *Richard de Neufville*

Meanwhile, the low-cost carriers have become important partici-pants in Portuguese air transport. For example, easyJet is competing vigorously with TAP at its hub in Lisbon and Ryanair is undermining the position of TAP at Porto. Both airlines provide frequent direct service to the popular Portuguese tourist destination of Faro in the Algarve – which TAP mostly serves with indirect flights via Lisbon. The outcome of this competitive struggle is not clear. From experience elsewhere, it is possible that the low-cost carriers may come to dominate intra-European air traffic for Portugal.

The low-cost airlines have not developed a secondary low-cost airport around Lisbon – in any case there have been no airfield opportunities to do so. However, this might change if local military airfields were opened for civilian use, and as additional airport capacity is inaugurated in the Lisbon area. In this connection, the Portuguese Government announced in early 2007 that it was promoting the use of the Beja military base for commercial purposes (Câmara de Comercio Luso-Britânica [British-Portuguese Chamber of Commerce], 2007). As this site is around 200 km from Lisbon, it does not appear to offer realistic prospects for a second airport for Lisbon. Other opportunities exist, however.

In any case, the low-cost airlines are demonstrating their desire and need for low-cost airport facilities. Thus at the Porto airport, which features elegant facilities up to the best standards, Ryanair avoids the air bridges and has its passengers walk to their flights. Its business model demands inexpensive efficient service, and it would look for similar facilities at a new airport.

Prospective investors in the new airport thus face considerable risk. While air traffic to Portugal has been growing steadily so there appears to be an evident need for additional airport facilities, there is considerable uncertainly about the future of the airline industry for Portugal. Thus:

- The national airline, TAP, which would appear to be the obvious main tenant of a new airport, is in a difficult financial situation, and may not be able to afford expensive new facilities when they are provided. Toronto faced with a similar situation when its national carrier, Air Canada, went bankrupt at the time of the move into the new elegant facilities conceived by the signature architect Moshe Safdie.
- The rapidly rising low-cost carriers have demonstrated their reluc-tance to serve expensive facilities, either avoiding the area entirely, or insisting on using low-cost facilities at the airport, as Ryanair does at Porto.

Low-Cost Airports for Low-Cost Airlines 61

- The future of the low-cost airlines is volatile, not only in terms of their overall health, but most particularly in terms of what areas they will choose to serve. They have no intrinsic loyalty to Portugal, and can easily redeploy their services if regulations or economic conditions become unfavorable. They might also bankrupt TAP and become the dominant European carriers for the country, as Southwest is for the United States.
- The long-term growth in air traffic is subject to many unknowns such as fuel prices, carbon taxes, general economic conditions, and the effect of low-cost airlines.

In short, future traffic and revenues from a major new airport are highly uncertain.

For the sake of specificity, the example analysis uses numbers to illustrate the process for analyzing a flexible design. These numbers are entirely speculative, and are not intended as a realistic investigation. Thus the analysis assumes

- a 50:50 possibility that low-cost carriers become dominant for Portugal over the coming decade. This scenario would parallel the situation that has occurred in the United States, Canada, and Brazil, where Southwest, Westjet, and GOL have become major domestic transporters;
- three alternate scenarios for traffic growth over the following decade, that it could be High (7%/year), Medium (4%/year) or Low (2%/year). Roughly, this represents the spread from traffic doubling every decade, to merely about 50% growth in 20 years. This range approximates long-term trends at airports worldwide comparable to Lisbon.

Definition of flexible design opportunities. Flexible designs could be created for the new airport along many of the lines identified in the previous corresponding section. The case example focuses on three ways to design the passenger terminal buildings, the standard inflexible Master Plan and two alternatives. Of course, many more configurations could be investigated, indeed should be before investing €1 billion (US$1.5 billion) or more in a modern new terminal.

A conventional Master Plan design, as suggested by the Aéroports de Paris, involves a high-standard structure built along traditional lines. It would feature multiple levels, ample spaces, superior finishes, and loading bridges for all aircraft – and would cost in the range of €1.2 billion (US$1.8 billion). As indicated by experience in Toronto, London/Stansted and elsewhere, such a building would not easily serve low-cost carriers. It may be considered an inflexible alternative.

At the other end of the spectrum, a low-cost passenger building could be built, along the lines that are now being implemented at Frankfurt/ Hahn. It would be a one-level building with tight spaces, adequate finishes and no loading bridges. It would cost about 10 to 20% of the standard structure; say a nominal €200 million (US$300 million). In the short run, it would not easily be organized to serve traditional airlines. In the longer run, however, conventional facilities could be implemented. This may also be considered an inflexible design.

As a compromise, one could design a half-sized standard building supplemented by low-cost facilities and featuring bus services to remotely parked aircraft. This solution could fulfill the immediate needs of both standard and low-cost airlines. It would also be suitable, with proper disposition of the first phase, for easy expansion emphasizing either traditional or low-cost carriers, depending on how traffic evolved. The cost of this flexible facility might be €700 million (US$1036 million).

Analysis of development strategies. A Decision Analysis is an appropriate first-cut way to consider the best strategy for a situation in which there are several distinct uncertainties. Numerous textbooks describe the mechanics of Decision Analysis, for example, de Neufville (1990).

The illustrative analysis is inspired by Chambers (2007). His thesis considers two stages. The first covers the short-term future during the expansion of the low-cost carriers, and second the long-term growth of air transport in Portugal. The two-stage analysis is complex, because it considers the many ways the airport could be developed for each of the outcomes of the first phase. To illustrate the approach, this case presents only a first stage analysis.

The analysis requires estimates of the outcomes from the decisions, for example, in terms of ENPV of the investments. A *pro forma* spreadsheet showing traffic, revenues, and expenses conveniently develops these numbers. The case uses the data shown in Table 6. Given three possible configurations and two possible developments (in terms of which airlines dominate after the next 10 years), there are six possible outcomes.

The following justifies the relative numbers used to calculate the Net Present Values (NPV):

- If the standard expensive terminal were built, and if the traditional airlines continue to dominate, it is assumed that the revenues after 10 years will recover the cost of the building (NPV = 1200). However, if low-cost carriers dominate and do not choose to use the expensive building, the revenues are much lower, as experienced in past years by Kansas City, Kuala Lumpur, Manila, Osaka/Kansai, and Washington/ Dulles (NPV = 300).

Low-Cost Airports for Low-Cost Airlines   63

Table 6. Decision Analysis for hypothetical first stage of airport development

	Terminal type	Dominant airlines	Revenues (NPV €M)	Expected value (EV €M)
Build which terminal?	**Standard** Cost = 1200 €M	Traditional	1200	
				−450
		Low-cost	300	
	All low-cost Cost = 200 €M	Traditional	150	
				−25
		Low-cost	300	
	Flexible mixed Cost = 700 €M	Traditional	1000	
				50
		Low-cost	500	

Note: Assumes 50:50 probability of whether traditional or low-cost airlines dominate at end of period. Revenues assumed for example purposes and do not represent any specific design.

- If the all low-cost terminal were implemented, it would recover its costs if the low-cost carriers dominate (NPV = 300). Conversely, it would not make much if they did not (NPV = 150). However, its overall losses could not be great, as its costs are low.
- If the flexible terminal is designed, it would perform adequately in either case. It would not do as well as the standard design if the traditional airlines dominate (NPV = 1000), but would perform better than the low-cost terminal even if they dominate, since it would provide good service to the traditional airlines (NPV = 500).

These data are illustrative, not based on detailed analysis of the situation or of specific designs.

The Decision Analysis calculates the average of each of the possible choices, and recommends the design with the higher expected value (EV). In this case, the preferred choice would be the flexible design (EV = 50), as Table 6 indicates. Note also that the flexible design, by providing 'insurance' by being adaptable to the circumstances that develop, provides superior performance across many important criteria (Hassan *et al.*, 2005). The flexible design reduces both the 'value at risk', that is, the maximum loss, and the original investment or 'CAPEX' (Table 7).

This recommendation of a flexible solution is fairly standard, since flexible designs have the advantage of performing reasonably well over a range of situations – in contrast to inflexible designs that work well for the situations for which they were designed, but poorly when other scenarios prevail. As a general rule, a Decision Analysis recognizes the

64   *Richard de Neufville*

Table 7. Comparison of hypothetical flexible and standard designs

Criterion	Design choice		Which better?
	Standard	Flexible mixed	
Expected value	−450	50	Flexible
Capital invested	1200	700	Flexible
Maximum loss	−900	−200	Flexible
Range of risk	900	500	Flexible

merit of an adaptable strategy of development that proceeds according to what the future brings – instead of a Master Plan that designs for a fixed concept of the future and does not allow for alternative possibilities. Walker *et al.* (2001) provide an extended general description of adaptive policies.

The best strategy over the two stages would depend on both the future structure of the airline industry (does TAP flourish or not?) but also on the rate of growth. The overall recommendation strategy would then be of the form:

- If TAP flourishes and traffic growth is high, build high-standard extensions to the flexible terminal as needed. However, if growth is low, only invest marginally.
- If the low-cost carriers dominate, develop the site to their requirements.

Note that the strategy recommended involves the use of designs that easily accommodate alternative developments. A properly flexible approach requires more than staging a plan over time. If an inflexible design is chosen at the beginning, it is difficult – if not financially impossible – to 'stage' into a completely different arrangement. The history of Kansas City and Munich Terminal 1 provide two of many examples of this. Both facilities were designed around the 'gate arrival concept' suitable for origin–destination traffic. These proved inappropriate for the hubbing traffic that developed. As these designs could not be re-configured to what was needed, the airports suffered. Kansas City lost its prime tenant, TWA. Munich had to commission a brand new facility to serve the traffic of their prime tenant, Lufthansa.

Conclusions

The paradigm of airport planning and design is changing. It is shifting from the traditional pattern driven by long-term point forecasts, high

Low-Cost Airports for Low-Cost Airlines 65

standards, and established clients; to one that recognizes great uncertainty in forecasts, a broad range of standards, and the potential for a rapidly changing client base. This is an extended consequence of economic deregulation of air transport, and of the rise of low-cost airlines.

Low-cost airlines are becoming significant drivers of airport planning. Their requirements differ from those of the 'legacy' carriers. They focus on cost and handle passengers differently. Now that they are sizeable participants in the air transport industry, they influence airport design. They are central to the proliferation of secondary airports and are propelling the development of cheaper airport terminals. They are thus catalyzing 'low-cost airports' for low-cost carriers around the 'legacy main airports' built to serve the 'legacy airlines'. Consistent with economic theory, the competition between the legacy and low-cost airlines is extending to their major factors of production, that is, the airports and airport facilities.

The uncertain outcome of this dynamic poses substantial strategic issues. Airport planners, investors, and managers need to develop strategies that will enable them to avoid over commitments that are financially risky, and position them to take advantage of opportunities as they develop. They thus need to adopt a flexible approach to airport analysis and design.

The proposed flexible design strategy deals with this reality. It differs significantly from traditional airport Master Planning. Its core element is to build flexibility into the design, to enable airport owners to adjust facilities easily to changes in the type, needs, and location of traffic. The case of Portugal illustrates the current risks in airport development, and suggests how a flexible design process could develop a strategy that manages uncertainties and maximizes Expected Value.

Acknowledgements

The Government of Portugal, through its long-term contract with the MIT Engineering Systems Division, provided financial support. The author is also indebted to: Regine Weston, Weston-Wong associates; Dr. Lloyd McCoomb, Greater Toronto Airport Authority; Craig Coy, formerly of the Massachusetts Port Authority (Massport); Professors José Viegas of the Instituto Superior Técnico and Álvaro Costa of the Universidade do Porto in Portugal; colleagues at the University of Amsterdam; Professor Warren Walker at the Delft University of Technology; and local airport managers at Bangkok/Suvarnabhumi, Lisbon/Portela, London/Heathrow Terminal 5, San Francisco/International, Singapore, and Toronto/Pearson. Finally, I appreciate the frank and helpful comments of anonymous reviewers.

66   Richard de Neufville

References

ACI World and Momberger Airport Information (2005) *Airport Development News*. Available at: http://www.airports.org/aci/aci/file/ADN%20-%20Momberger/ACI-ADN%20Dec%20 2005.pdf (accessed 3 June 2007).

AFX News (2007) *Portugal Government to Fully Privatise ANA Airports Authority*, 30 January. Available at: http://www.finanznachrichten.de/nachrichten-2007-01/artikel-7661191.asp (accessed 3 June 2007).

Airfleets.net (2007) *Database on Aircraft Fleets*. Available at: http://www.airfleets.net/home/ (accessed 3 June 2007).

Barrett, S. (2004) How do the demands for airport services differ between full-service carriers and low-cost carriers? *Journal of Air Transport Management*, 10, pp. 33–39.

Beck, P. (2007) Planning of secondary airports in the era of low cost airlines – the case of Frankfurt-Hahn, in: *Airneth Conference*, 12 April, Den Haag. Available at: http://www.airneth.nl/document.php?page=271&parentType=1&parentId=19 (accessed 3 June 2007).

Câmara de Comercio Luso-Britânica [British-Portuguese Chamber of Commerce] (2007), *Beja Airport*. Available at: http://www.bpcc.pt/airports.asp#ancora13 (accessed 3 June 2007).

Chambers, R.-D. (2007) Tackling uncertainty in airport design: A real options approach, Master of Science Thesis, MIT Technology and Policy Program, Cambridge, MA. Available at: http://ardent.mit.edu/real_options/Real_Options_Papers/ (accessed 3 June 2007).

Dennis, P. (2004) *Can the European low-cost airline boom continue? Implications for regional airports*, European Regional Science Association (ERSA) Conference Paper ersa04p571. Available at: http://ideas.repec.org/p/wiw/wiwrsa/ersa04p571.html (accessed 3 June 2007).

DMJM Aviation (2005) *American Airlines Terminal, John F. Kennedy International Airport*. Available at: http://www.dmjmhm.aecom.com/MarketsandServices/4028/index.jsp (accessed 3 June 2007).

European Commission (2000) *Assunto: Auxilio estatal (N336/2000) – Notificação da primeira fase da reprvatização da empresa Transportes Aéreos Portugueses*, Brussels. Available at: http://ec.europa.eu/community_law/state_aids/transports-2000/n336-00.pdf (accessed 3 June 2007).

Fedor, L. (2006) *NWA Pilots Seek to Sell Bankruptcy Claim Early*, LexisNexis, 26 November. Available at: http://airportbusiness.com/article/article.jsp?siteSection=1&id=9034 (accessed 3 June 2007).

Francis, G., Fidato, A. & Humphreys, I. (2003) Airport–airline interaction: The impact of low-cost carriers on two European airports, *Journal of Air Transport Management*, 9, pp. 267–273.

Garriga, J. (2003) Airport dynamics – Towards airport systems, in: *Airport Regions Conference*, Barcelona: DVA associats.

Garriga, J. (2004) Low-cost, a regional affair – A winner business model, new catalysts for airport regions, in: *Airport Regions Conference*, Barcelona: DVA associats.

Gillen, D. & Lall, A. (2004) Competitive advantage of low-cost carriers: Some implications for airports, *Journal of Air Transport Management*, 10, pp. 41–50.

Graham, A. (2004) *Airport Strategies to Gain Competitive Advantage*. Available at: http://www.garsonline.de/Downloads/Slots%20Competition%20Benchmarking/04119-graham.pdf (accessed 3 June 2007).

Hassan, R., de Weck, O., Hastings, D., de Neufville, R. & McKinnon, D. (2005) Value-at-risk analysis for real options in complex engineered systems, in: *IEEE Conference on Large Scale Infrastructures*, Vol. 4, October, Hawaii, pp. 3697–3704, digital object identifier 10.1109/

Low-Cost Airports for Low-Cost Airlines   67

ICSMC.2005.1571721. Available at: http://ardent.mit.edu/real_options/Real_opts_papers/ Hassan_deN_IEEE_SMC_2005_final1.pdf (accessed 3 June 2007).

International Air Transport Association (2004) *Airport Development Reference Manual* (9th edn) (Montreal: International Air Transport Association).

International Air Transport Association (2005) *World Air Transport Statistics* (Montreal: International Air Transport Association).

International Lease Finance (2007) Available at: http://www.ilfc.com/introduction.htm (accessed 3 June 2007).

Jetstar (2007) *Our Company*. Available at: http://www.jetstar.com/about-us/our-company-43. html (accessed 3 June 2007).

Jorgenson, R. (2006) *Machinists Union Reaches Tentative Agreement with Northwest Airlines*, 25 May. Available at: http://www.wsws.org/articles.2006.may2006/nwa-m25.shtml

McConnell, J. (2007) A life-cycle flexibility framework for designing, evaluating and managing complex real options, PhD Dissertation, MIT Engineering Systems Division, Cambridge, MA.

Morrison, S. & Winston, C. (2005) *What's Wrong with the Airline Industry? Diagnosis and Possible Cures*, Statement to the US Congress Subcommittee on Aviation, 28 September, Washington DC. Available at: http://www.economics.neu.edu/morrison/research/ (accessed 3 June 2007).

de Neufville, R. (1990) *Applied Systems Analysis* (New York, NY: McGraw-Hill). Available at: http://ardent.mit.edu/ (accessed 3 June 2007).

de Neufville, R. (1991) Strategic planning for airport capacity: An appreciation of Australia's process for Sydney, *Australian Planner*, 29(4), pp. 174–180.

de Neufville, R. (1995) Management of multi-airport systems: A development strategy, *Journal of Air Transport Management*, 2(2), pp. 99–110. Available at: http://ardent.mit.edu/airports/ ASP_papers/mas.atm1.pdf (accessed 3 June 2007).

de Neufville, R. (2005) The future of secondary airports: Nodes in a parallel air transport network? http://ardent.mit.edu/airports/ASP_Papers/ English version of 'Le devenir des aéroports secondaires: bases d'un réseau parallèle de transport aérien?' *Cahiers Scientifiques du Transport*, 47, pp. 11–38.

de Neufville, R. (2006) Accommodating low cost airlines at main airports. Transportation Research Board presentation, http://ardent.mit.edu/airports/ASP_papers/ summarized in *International Airport Review*, 10(1), pp. 62–65.

de Neufville, R. & Barber, J. (1991) Deregulation induced volatility of airport traffic, *Transportation Planning and Technology*, 16(2), pp. 117–128.

de Neufville, R. & Belin, S. (2002) Airport passenger buildings: Efficiency through shared-use of facilities, *ASCE Journal of Transportation Engineering*, 127(3), pp. 201–210.

de Neufville, R. & Odoni, A. (2003) *Airport Systems Planning, Design, and Management* (New York, NY: McGraw-Hill).

de Neufville, R., Scholtes, S. & Wang, T. (2006) Valuing options by spreadsheet: Parking garage case example, *ASCE Journal of Infrastructure Systems*, 12(2), pp. 107–111. Available at: http://ardent.mit.edu/real_options/Common_course_materials/papers.html (accessed 3 June 2007).

US Federal Aviation Administration, Bureau of Transportation Statistics (2005) *Third Quarter 2005 Airline Financial Data*, Washington DC. Available at: http://www.bts.gov/press_ releases/2005/bts058_05/html/bts058_05.html (accessed 3 June 2007).

US Federal Aviation Administration, Bureau of Transportation Statistics (2007a) *2006 Airline Traffic Data*, Table 9, Top 10 US Airlines, Washington DC. Available at: http://www.bts.gov/ press_releases/2007/bts012_07/html/bts012_07.html#table_09 (accessed 3 June 2007).

68   *Richard de Neufville*

US Federal Aviation Administration, Bureau of Transportation Statistics (2007b) *TranStats Airline On-Time Statistics and Delays Causes*, Washington DC. Available at: http://www.transtats. bts.gov/ (accessed 3 June 2007).

Walker, W., Adnan Rahman, S. & Cave, J. (2001) Adaptive policies, policy analysis, and policymaking, *European Journal of Operational Research*, 128(2), pp. 282–289.

Wang, T. & de Neufville, R. (2006) Identification of real options 'in' projects, in: *16th Annual International Symposium of the International Council on Systems Engineering (INCOSE)*, July, Orlando, FL. Available at: http://ardent.mit.edu/real_options/Real_Opts_papers/ Identification%20of%20Real%20Option%20in%20INCOSE.pdf (accessed 3 June 2007).

Warnock-Smith, D. & Potter, A. (2005) An exploratory study into airport choice factors for European low-cost airlines, *Journal of Air Transport Management*, 11, pp. 388–392.

Wayne, L. (2007) The real owner of all those planes, *New York Times*, 10 May, C1-ff.

Wikipedia (2007a) *US Airways*. Available at: http://en.wikipedia.org/wiki/US_Airways (accessed 3 June 2007).

Wikipedia (2007b) *Varig*. Available at: http://en.wikipedia.org/wiki/Varig (accessed 3 June 2007).

Williams, A. (2007) Competitive volatility and structural change in the international low cost carrier markets: A discussion on the basic causes and probable outcomes, *Singapore Journal of Aviation Management*, in press.

4

The impacts of emerging aviation trends on airport infrastructure

Peter Forsyth

Abstract

The demands on airport infrastructure around the world are both growing and changing. This paper explores what problems these changing demands imply for airports, and how they are coping with them. Growth in demand imposes a problem of allocation of scarce capacity in the short run—how well mechanisms such as the slot system are coping with them is explored. In the long term, increases in capacity are warranted, and how the emerging ownership and regulatory environments for airports will handle these is examined. Changes in patterns of demand will come from new business models, such as low-cost carriers and from new aircraft types, such as the Airbus A380—the implications of these for airports of these are considered. Finally, the issue of airport cost efficiency, and how ownership and regulatory environment impact on it, is examined.
© 2006 Elsevier Ltd. All rights reserved.

Keywords: Airport congestion; Airport slot allocation; Airport peak pricing; Airport regulation; Incentive regulation; Airport investment

1. Introduction

Airport infrastructure around the world has to cope with a range of changing demands. One of these is the growth in air traffic which has been taking place for the last 4 or so years (though this growth is now being muted by the fuel price increases and the consequent impact on air travel). In addition, there have been changes in the patterns of the demands put on the airport infrastructure, coming about from changes in airline business models, such as the growth in low-cost carriers (LCCs) and from new aircraft types. New aircraft such as the Airbus A380 and Boeing 787 are due to come into service, and they will have implications for the pattern of airport use.

The problems which are posed for airports, and how they can cope with changes in the level and patterns of demand, are explored in this paper. The problems are general, affecting airports worldwide, but a European emphasis is adopted here. Most of the important changes which are affecting airports are present in Europe. Europe is a region which faces considerable constraints on airport expansion, and thus the issues of allocation of scarce capacity are particularly relevant. In addition, there is considerable change in the institutional environment of airports, with privatisation

and regulation, taking place in Europe—these changes will have implications for how changes in demand are handled.

The paper concentrates on five main themes:

- the short run problem—recovery and the allocation of airport capacity;
- the long run problem—recovery, growth and investment;
- new business models and their impacts on the demand/capacity balance;
- new aircraft technologies and their impact on the demand/capacity balance;
- improving airport efficiency and reducing cost levels.

2. The short run problem—demand recovery and the allocation of airport capacity

In the short run, it is difficult to expand airport capacity, and thus as the recovery in demand develops, there is the problem of ensuring that existing capacity is utilised most efficiently. This leads us to focus in on the capacity allocation devices in place. The two most important of these are:

- the slot system, in place at most busy airports outside the US; and
- the structure of airport prices.

46   *P. Forsyth / Journal of Air Transport Management 13 (2007) 45–52*

The slot system has a major advantage along with a significant limitation. The advantage is that it enables demand for the airport to be kept within capacity at an acceptable price in terms of delays. The disadvantage is that available slots are not allocated as efficiently as they could be.

As demand grows and runway capacity remains unchanged at an airport, congestion will develop. The great merit of the slot system is that it restricts effective use of busy airports to a level which can be handled with an acceptable level of delay. Delays arise for several reasons, such as poor weather, but delays resulting to airport capacity restrictions can be kept moderate with an effective slot system. The slot system limits the number of flights which are permitted to use the airport at busy times. Where slot systems are not in place, as is the case for most US airports, delays can become very large. The efficacy of the slot system in avoiding delays tends to be taken on trust—empirical studies are not easy to come by. However, there is evidence that the system does make a difference. Some slot prices are very high—for example, slot pairs at London Heathrow have exchanged for £10 m. This is an indication that slots are performing a substantial rationing function—if slots were replaced by delays as the rationing device at Heathrow, the costs of the delays would be very large. Slot systems need not always work well in avoiding delays—authorities have to set slot limits at the right level. There is little evaluation of how well authorities have been in setting slot limits. Overall, however, the evidence is that most slot systems work well in avoiding costly delays.

It is likely that slot systems will be able to cope as demand for airport capacity rises. As demand grows, slot limits will be either constant or can increase only slowly, in the absence of substantial capacity increases. Airlines have to adapt to the shortage of slots. They may be able to use off peak slots, they may be able to schedule larger aircraft into slot constrained airports, and they may have some scope to use alternative airports. Delays are kept at moderate levels as demand for airport capacity increases—this contrasts with increasing delays in non-slot constrained airports, such as those in the US. Slots become more valuable, and this means that the costs of misallocation of slots become greater. The delay lessening function of slots works effectively but the slot allocation problem becomes a more important one.

It would be possible to use prices to ration scarce airport capacity. Thus far, this has rarely been done, except occasionally to handle peaks. Higher prices would ration demand to be closer to capacity, though the effects on actual throughput would be less certain than slot limits. However, the real difficulty with prices is that rationing prices could be very high, and airport profits would be correspondingly high. Most airports are required by government owners or regulators to keep revenues close to costs. A slot system enables capacity to be rationed tolerably efficiently, while at the same time keeping prices down. If there is to be regulation which seeks to keep prices close to costs, there has to also be slot rationing, or delays.

The efficiency with which the limited available capacity at the busy airports is allocated depends on the slot allocation system, and also the airports' pricing structures.

The primary criticism of slots is that there is no guarantee that they will be allocated efficiently, to the airlines with the greatest willingness to pay for them (Bass, 2003; Humphreys, 2003; Starkie, 2003). The grandfathering of slots, and the limits on slot trading in Europe, lend credence to these criticisms. It is difficult for new airlines to obtain slots at busy airports even if they are prepared to pay for them. The slot-controlled airports have become the preserve of the legacy airlines—LCCs have difficulties in accessing them, even when they would be willing to pay the price. The lack of adequate slots makes it difficult for new airlines to enter with viable schedules, and it keeps the innovators out.

Legacy airlines do well out of the slot system, since they possess most of the slots at busy airports. Thus, they have preferential access to the airports in demand, and gain assets of considerable value. The access to slots is an important competitive advantage they have over LCCs, since they can charge a premium for using the preferred airports which LCCs can only access with difficulty, perhaps by buying a slots (if available). Some airlines, like British Airways and Lufthansa have high proportions of the slots at very desirable airports such as London Heathrow and Frankfurt. A desirable aspect of this is that these airlines have a strong incentive to allocate the slots internally as effectively as possible, though they also have the scope to hoard slots, if they chose to do this. Airlines with substantial slot endowments are in something of a quandary. While they might gain from reforms such as more open trading of slots, they are reluctant to advocate change in a system under which they do very well.

Thus, the key problem with the slot system concerns how well slots are allocated. Some reforms are relatively straightforward. These include promoting more open trading of slots. For some time, the development of a slot market has been prevented in Europe, though grey markets have developed, and markets have emerged for the busy UK airports (NERA, 2004). More open trading need not work perfectly—it would still be possible for airlines to hoard slots. However, it should be possible to achieve more efficient allocation of slots without imposing substantial costs on any airlines. There are suggestions for more active promotion of trading, though these would involve some costs on some airlines (NERA, 2004). Slot auctions are a less likely reform if only because they would involve major shifts in the slot rents away from the airlines.

Overall, there is some pressure for slot reform, though it is muted. Legacy airlines are not pressing for change, though some airlines which do not have substantial slot endowments, including LCCs, would like to see change. Airports do not have a major stake in change, except to the extent that their non-aeronautical revenues will increase if

P. Forsyth / Journal of Air Transport Management 13 (2007) 45–52   47

they manage to increase the passenger throughput by increasing average aircraft size. The authorities who oversee the slot system have been slow to reform the system, though the EU looks set to remove the prohibitions on trading which have prevented a market from developing.

The slot allocation system is not the only mechanism affecting how well scarce airport capacity is allocated. Airport charging structures also affect how efficiently scarce capacity is allocated to airlines. Most busy airports have price structures which became obsolete in the 1960s, when excess capacity ceased to be the rule. The price charged depends solely or primarily on the weight of the aircraft or the number of passengers—even though there is little or no cost justification for this structure. This structure is tolerably efficient when there is a problem of recovering costs at minimum cost in terms of reduced output (Morrison, 1982). However, it encourages the use of the airport by inefficiently small aircraft—airlines do not have strong incentive to rationalise small feeder flights. There are some exceptions, such as BAA's London Airports, which have price structures which are more in line with the reality of excess demand rather than excess capacity. Airports also make very little use of peak/off peak pricing differentials to improve the allocation of traffic over the day.

Pricing structures are in the hands of the airports, though they are influenced by the airlines. Airports often have little incentive to change their price structures even if they are performing poorly. Publicly owned airports which are simply required to cover costs, or privately owned airports which are regulated to keep revenues at cost, will not gain from implementing a price structure which makes better use of their capacity. Airports which are subjected to incentive regulation, such as well-designed price caps, can have an incentive to price more efficiently, but these airports are in a distinct minority. On the other side, airlines oppose airport pricing reforms. In particular, they have strongly opposed peak pricing (see IATA, 2000). While this may appear slightly surprising, given that airlines use peak pricing extensively themselves, the workings of the slot system are such that airlines will lose if airports introduce peak pricing. This is because they will suffer a loss of profits when peak prices are raised, and slot values fall, but they will be forced by competition to pass on the benefit of lower off peak prices. With airline opposition, and little interest on the part of most airports, there is little likelihood of airport pricing reform.

For some airports, it is inadequate terminal capacity which is the problem. Terminal capacity also can be rationed by slots or prices—often administrative means are used to even out the flow of passengers or limit the overall throughput. However, terminals are different from runways in two important respects. The capacity constraints in terminals are less rigid, since it is usually possible to squeeze more passengers through at a cost in terms of crowding and congestion. Also, the timescale of terminal expansion (Heathrow Terminal 5 excluded) is usually much less than that for runway expansion. New runways usually provoke more opposition from nearby residents than extensions to terminals do.

One of the more pressing issues involving passenger processing concerns security. This is not so much a problem which arises because of a growth of demand—rather it comes about because of the tightening of security over recent years—but demand growth makes the problem more acute. Increased security poses a number of issues, ranging from who should pay for it to how it can be achieved most effectively at airports. Enhanced security involves additional labour, additional equipment and increased terminal space. Labour and equipment can be provided relatively simply at a cost. However, at some airports, the provision of space for the enhanced security can be a problem—most were designed without current security levels in mind. Apart from these space problems, these extra security requirements should not create serious problems for airports to cope with additional traffic. As with other functions such as passport control, customs and quarantine, delays can be kept low if adequate facilities are provided, though, this cannot be done costlessly.

Most airports can cope adequately in the short term with demand increases. The slot system works well in keeping throughput at practical capacity, and thus limiting the growth of delays as demand grows. However, as slots become more valuable, the costs of inefficient allocation of slots grow. This is compounded by the inefficient pricing structures at virtually all busy airports, which encourage the use of the airport by small rather than large aircraft, and do not encourage effective use of off peak capacity.

3. The long run problem—recovery, growth and investment

If the recovery is sustained, it will add to the need for more airport capacity. Even if it is not, existing capacity bottlenecks will need to be addressed by investment. Adding to airport capacity is notoriously difficult—environmental factors mean that airports are often refused permission for major developments, such as new runways, and adding to capacity on constrained sites can be a very slow and expensive process, as the London Heathrow Terminal 5 illustrates.

Decisions about investments in additional capacity are partly made by governments. However, increasingly, with corporatisation or privatisation of airports, decisions are being made by the airports themselves, though influenced by the regulators. The underlying concern is whether the institutional and ownership arrangements under which airports operate will get investment right.

- too little investment means congestion, or suppressed demand (and what capacity there is available may not be well allocated by a rigid slot system and an obsolete pricing structure);
- too much investment, with cost recovery, leads to airports which are unnecessarily expensive to use.

The older model of publicly owned airports relied heavily on public owners and managers acting in the public interest, by carefully assessing the need for extra capacity and then providing it if was warranted. While there are examples of good practice (in the past, UK evaluations of the need for additional London capacity), practice often fell short of the ideal.

The model to which many or most countries are moving towards now is that of privately owned, but regulated, airports. Much depends on the incentives faced by the airport owners, and on the content of regulation.

Regulation often takes the form of cost plus regulation. This is especially so for several of the newly privatised airports in Europe (Gillen and Niemeier, 2006). The regulator seeks to keep prices at, or just above, cost. In such an environment, there is limited pressure for careful scrutiny of investments. If anything, it can lead to excessive investment, as the Averch and Johnson effect demonstrates (see Armstrong et al., 1994; Ch. 3). If an airport makes an investment in additional capacity, regardless of whether it is needed, its regulated asset base will increase. It will then be permitted by the regulator to increase its prices. The airport may seek to invest excessively to increase its asset base and thereby total profit.

There is a particular danger of this happening with airports. Because airports possess market power, it is easy for them to increase charges. Excessive investment in capacity, or in quality, can easily be funded. Furthermore, airports are enterprises which are likely to come under strong pressure to invest or over-invest. Governments still see airports and especially terminals as prestige invest-ments. Governments are also keen to ensure that airport capacity is more than adequate, so as to attract more traffic—airports are seen by many governments as a stimulus to economic activity. Thus, governments will induce airports to have too much rather than too little or just enough capacity.

While the majority of airports are now subject to cost plus regulation, some are subjected to (at least approxima-tions of) incentive regulation. Incentive regulation pays little attention to the airport's own cost levels and seeks to set prices more by benchmarks. Such an airport could have a tendency to under invest (Helm and Thompson, 1991). If it makes an investment in improving quality, or in extra capacity (which could be expensive for an airport on a constrained site), it will increase its asset base, but it will not be permitted to increase its prices. Thus, such an airport will tend not to make many investments, and will tend to sweat its assets. Regulators do recognise this, and they build in investment incentive mechanisms. For example, the Civil Aviation Authority (CAA) in the UK allows BAA to increase its charges at London Heathrow when it achieves specified investment targets (Civil Aviation Authority, 2003). This resolves the investment issue, but it does give very large discretion to the regulator. It also becomes critical for the regulator to get it right, by involving itself in careful scrutiny of the airport's capital expenditure plans,

and perhaps by undertaking its own analyses. In addition, airports and regulators will game each other, seeking to advance their own objectives. Airports will threaten to withhold investment unless they are granted a higher regulated price. Regulators will be under pressure to grant higher prices that they believe are warranted so as to ensure that the investment goes ahead. On the other hand, regulated airports may mistrust regulators, whom they see as trying to keep prices unrealistically low. Investments in airports are often for the very long term, yet regulators can commit to a price path only for a short period, say 5 years (Hendriks and Andrew, 2004). Regulation of investment has become a major, perhaps the major, problem for regulation of infrastructure industries—it is becoming a critical problem with airports.

Some of the newer airport owners, such as Macquarie Airports (Brussels, Copenhagen and Sydney airports) and Infratil (Luebeck), are keener in their search for profits than older groups, which were content with being passive investors in infrastructure (and arguably, BAA has become more aggressive of late, and especially after the recent takeover by Ferrovial). Such airports have different incentives when it comes to investment. They will only invest if it is profitable to do so—and this will depend very much on how the regulator handles investment. It is very difficult for regulators to set prices which simultaneously keep profits to an "acceptable" level and induce the right amount of investment.

Some of these issues can be resolved by alternative ownership structures. If airlines owned their terminals, they have strong incentives to get the level of investment right. There can be competition policy issues which arise when large airlines own all the terminals, though this situation can usually be avoided. Long term contracts between airlines and airports—or possibly third party owners of terminals—can also contribute (see Graham, 2004, on US experience; Klenk, 2004, on Frankfurt). Terminals are likely to pose fewer problems for investment than runways because they can be built in smaller stages and they pose fewer environmental problems.

Another factor which makes the efficient resolution of investment issues difficult is the fact that the users of capacity, the airlines, have effective control of scarce capacity, through their access to slots. Busy airports are difficult to operate from, and scarce capacity poses problems for airlines. However, slots at busy airports are highly valuable, since they restrict the ability of airlines to add capacity and compete. If there is ample capacity, the more flights which are operated will reduce margins on existing flights, to the point that slots lose all their value. Thus, even though it may be in the public interest for more capacity to be provided, airlines with a substantial investment in slots (which would fall in value when capacity is increased) would be, at best, ambivalent about pressing for more capacity.

Even in an environment of private, but regulated, airports, governments will still have a major role in

P. Forsyth / Journal of Air Transport Management 13 (2007) 45–52 49

assessing and approving large airport investments. Governments, possibly working through planning authorities or environmental regulators, will need to make trade offs between the benefits of additional airport capacity and the environmental costs which this might impose. These costs, from additional noise or emissions, are becoming better quantified, and to an extent, more accurately costed. Ideally, the costs and benefits of additional airport capacity will be evaluated using cost–benefit criteria.

The conflicts between objectives become very clear when the siting of additional capacity is an issue. Additional capacity may be warranted, but it need not be at the existing airport. The current airport may be operating on a constrained site, and further expansion may be difficult for environmental reasons. New airports can be built on less constrained sites, or secondary airports can be expanded. Almost invariably these solutions will be less convenient and less preferred than expansion at the main airport. Thus, the British government has chosen not to expand London Heathrow, but to give priority to the expansion of London Stansted, a much less preferred airport.

While governments make such decisions, they need to be implemented by the privately owned airport, working within a framework set by the regulator. This poses issues for the regulator. Is it its task to promote efficiency, or should it promote government policy, by taking into account other objectives, including the reduction of environmental costs, which the government is emphasising (this issue is touched upon in Civil Aviation Authority, 2006)? To what extent should a regulator create incentives for the private airport to make investments now which may not be warranted, on commercial grounds, for some time to come? For example, should it permit a cross subsidy from a busy, profitable airport to fund an investment at a more remote airport, which is unprofitable because it is being made ahead of time (Starkie, 2004)?

Overall, airports have not always responded to the need for additional capacity by providing it when it is needed—this is due to the constraints they operate under. The new ownership and regulatory environments give airports more flexibility to invest, subject to overall planning controls imposed by governments, though regulators arguably have the greatest influence on investment. There is a danger that the regulatory system will promote excessive investment in some directions, and that the pressure for the most valuable capacity expansions will be muted and less effective than it might be.

4. New business models and their impacts on the demand/capacity balance

The aviation market has probably adjusted to the impacts of airline strategic alliances, which were the major change of the previous decade. It has yet to adjust to the full implications of the boom in LCCs. LCCs continue to gain market share in the short haul markets, though in some cases they may be approaching their long term share (in the US?). They are now beginning to enter long haul markets—there are LCC flights from Asia to Australia, and the Qantas owned LCC Jetstar is beginning to operate long haul routes (it has Boeing 787 aircraft on order). It has yet to be seen how successful the LCC model is for long haul. The LCCs are having a serious impact on the legacy carriers, which will need to respond carefully (perhaps by operating lower cost services). Here, we are interested mainly on their implications for the use of airport capacity.

LCCs target budget conscious travellers, who are prepared to use less convenient airports if this saves them money. Thus, the LCCs have made a point of flying to and from less convenient, but cheaper, secondary airports (Lawton, 2002; Doganis, 2006). To a degree, this has been a case of making a virtue out of necessity, since they would have had difficulty in obtaining adequate slots to operate from busy airports. (If slots were more readily available, albeit at a price, some LCCs which target business travellers might be prepared to pay for them and use busy major airports). LCCs also make extensive use of those major airports which have spare capacity. It is likely that long haul LCCs will also be prepared to use secondary airports.

To the extent that this is so, it is putting less pressure on the demand for the busy capacity constrained airports. The growth that the LCCs stimulate may be handled through secondary airports, and though the use of the less busy major airports. In addition, to the extent that the LCCs are winning market share from the established airlines, they may be lowering the demand for capacity at the major airports. If long haul LCCs succeed, this may increase the substitution process away from the major airports, since it will lessen their importance as hubs to some degree.

In countries such as the UK and Germany, there seems to be a stream of secondary airports entering and seeking to gain a share of the market. One issue concerns how viable these secondary airports are. Currently, they have the advantage of lower charges (for aeronautical use and for car parking), which attracts the LCCs. However, it is not clear how sustainable this advantage is. They face lower land prices, and major airports' construction costs can be high because of restricted sites. They also may be more efficient (See Section 6 below). Many airports which serve LCCs are very small, and would be unable to take any advantage of economies of scale. Some are recipients of substantial local subsidies—it is not obvious that they would be such strong competitors without these subsidies.

Where the secondary airports handle traffic which would be difficult to accommodate at busy major airports, they serve a useful function—though subsidies would not be needed for them to succeed in doing this. On the other hand, where they simply use subsidies to finance lower charges to win traffic from major city centre airports with spare capacity, they will result in a locational misallocation of traffic. Local authorities may be prepared to subsidise

50   *P. Forsyth / Journal of Air Transport Management 13 (2007) 45–52*

their airports because they believe that attracting more traffic at them will stimulate the local economy. While it may be in a local authority's interest to do this, it need not be efficient for the nation as a whole, since this results in a shifting, not necessarily an overall increase, in economic activity (Forsyth, 2006).

The major airports can, and do, respond by offering price schedules which effectively charge LCCs less than incumbent airlines. Some are building new low cost terminals, designed to appeal to the LCCs but not the legacy carriers. Where the major airports succeed in holding traffic which is inexpensive to handle, such policies can be efficient. However, if they set charges to LCCs below cost, to retain their business, this can lead to an inefficient allocation of traffic between airports. They might do this if they are publicly owned, and only subjected to a cost recovery requirement, or if they are subject to poorly designed regulation such as a price cap on average revenue per passenger. An airport which is subject to an average revenue cap, set at a level above marginal cost, will be prepared to cross subsidise a user which pays less than the marginal cost of service, to increase its revenue base, thus over-expanding its output.

Even when the price to the LCC is not below marginal cost, and the discount offered to it leads to the LCC choosing the major airport, this can create inefficiencies at the airline level. This creates a competitive imbalance at the airline level, where one airline is cross subsidising another with which it is attempting to compete.

Thus, the increased use of secondary airports, along with spare capacity at major airports, does help solve the airport capacity problem in the short term. In the long term, though, this need not be a particularly efficient solution. The LCCs are using the airports which have available capacity, and the airports which are cheap. The LCCs might still prefer to use a busy major airport if it had the capacity, even at a higher price, and it might be efficient to expand this capacity. In addition, to an extent the LCCs are going to the airports which are subsidised. It may be more efficient to expand capacity at the busy airports than subsidise airlines to use airports which are less convenient. Subsidies to secondary airports, and cross subsidies given by some major airports with spare capacity will affect current airport usage patterns, but they do not provide accurate signals for where investment in capacity for the longer term is warranted.

5. New aircraft technologies and their impact on the demand/capacity balance

The introduction of the Airbus A380 will have significant impacts on many larger airports. There will be costs in accommodating it, by widening the runway and by building specialised gates at terminals—in some cases (Melbourne) these costs are modest (less than US $50 m), though in other cases (London Heathrow and Los Angeles) the costs will be considerable (several hundred US $m).

One issue concerns who will pay these costs—will it be the airlines which schedule the A380, and gain the advantage of its lower costs, or will the costs be spread over all users of the airport (Forsyth, 2005)? Once the costs are sunk, the extra costs of handling the A380 need not be any higher than those for any other type of aircraft. To this extent, it would seem efficient to not levy any special charge for it. However, in the long term, it is desirable to set the right signals for airlines to use the A380 only when it is cost efficient to do so, taking into account the costs of airport modifications. If no charge is levied, the airlines will not take these into account, and will use the aircraft to an excessive extent.

Another issue concerns whether airports will make careful assessments of the worth of investing to accommodate the A380—some airports may be unrealistically optimistic about their chances of attracting services using the A380, and having A380 capability may be a prestige issue for some airports and regions. As noted before, in the ownership and regulatory environment that many airports operate in, it is easy for airports to make investments which are not warranted since they are able to simply pass on the costs to the users. Thus there is a risk of excessive investment by airports in preparing for the introduction of the A380.

The impact of the new aircraft on airports depends on their costs per passenger kilometre as compared to those of alternative aircraft, larger and smaller. The new aircraft will have lower per passenger kilometre costs, but just how much lower these are will determine their impact. They will impact on the patterns of use of airports, especially on the balance of hubs and non-hubs.

The introduction of the A380 will impact on the demand/capacity balance at airports in two ways. To the extent that the A380 replaces services by smaller aircraft (two services using the A380 replacing three services using the Boeing 747or 777 aircraft) it will ease the pressure on busy airports. If the A380 is able to achieve large cost savings relative to smaller aircraft, airlines will move back towards hub and spoke operations. If airlines have difficulties in filling the A380 in early days, they will drop fares, and this will make hub based operations more attractive, at least for a time—however, the slower than anticipated delivery of the A380 will mitigate this problem. In both cases, there will then be more feeder flights and demand for busy hub airports will increase, not decrease (it should be noted that not all hubs are busy, and some airports with capacity problems are not hubs). The balance of these effects is difficult to predict. The hub creation effects of the A380 is not likely to be nearly as great as that of the Boeing 747 when it was introduced, because the latter aircraft was very much larger than the alternative aircraft. The impact of the A380 will be larger if the stretched version is introduced, with lower per passenger kilometre costs.

The Boeing 787 will tend to have the reverse effects on hubs than the A380. To the extent that it is smaller and cost

P. Forsyth / Journal of Air Transport Management 13 (2007) 45–52   51

efficient, it will make direct services relatively competitive. However, if it is very cost efficient, it may be used to replace larger aircraft at busy airports, thus adding to the number of flights.

The two aircraft will be introduced at about the same time, and they will tend to counteract each other. The greater number of Boeing 787s on order suggests that the hub bypassing effects of this aircraft may be dominant.

If scarce capacity at airports were efficiently allocated, by slot trading and price structures, the impacts of the A380 and the Boeing 787 on the airport demand/capacity balance would not be of much public significance. Airlines will take into account the advantages of the A380 in economising slot use, since it is they that will gain from having more slots available for other flights. While capacity at busy airports around the world is far from efficiently allocated—slots are imperfectly allocated and price structures encourage small aircraft to use busy airports, it not clear whether shifting flights to or from hubs would be desirable on efficiency grounds.

6. Improving airport efficiency and reducing cost levels

Airport benchmarking studies are clearly indicating that there are substantial variations amongst airports in their productivity and the level of their charges (ATRS, 2005). While there are difficulties in standardising for different output mixes and achieving comparisons of like with like, it is clear that many airports in Europe and some in Asia are relatively high cost. To some degree this may due to cost factors beyond the control of the airports—for example, the need to operate on a very constrained site. Nevertheless, there is likely to be scope for many airports to lower their costs.

Cost reduction has not been a priority for many airports. This is true for publicly owned airports, but also so for private regulated airports which are subject to cost plus regulation (as most of them are). The effects of private ownership on costs are also muted since often privatisation is only partial. Airports have become more commercial, and they have exploited their non-aviation revenue sources more effectively. Where this is combined with single till regulation it can lead to reductions in charges. This happened in the early years of BAA's privatisation.

Much will depend on how well the moves towards private ownership and regulation work. Newly privatised airports which have simple ownership structures and shareholder focussed owners, can be expected to give greater priority to cost control than before, though they are also likely to wish to make what use they can of their market power. Thus, the benefits of cost reductions will not be passed on to airlines and their passengers unless regulators require this to happen. Where airports are not directly regulated, as in Australia and New Zealand, airlines have been very critical of the pricing policies of some airports (Productivity Commission, 2006), and IATA

has been critical of several European airports (Bisignani, 2006). If regulators keep costs down, however, they risk destroying the incentives for cost reduction. It has yet to be seen how well the new regulatory arrangements for airports will work—designing regulation which keeps prices down, yet gives effective incentives to minimise costs and make adequate investments is a complex challenge. Many jurisdictions have avoided this challenge and simply opted for cost-based regulation.

The success of secondary airports, especially in Europe, might be due in part to inefficiencies in the major airports with which they are competing. These airports do appear to have cost advantages, even after taking out the effects of subsidies. They may be able to offer the LCCs lower charges because they are more efficient than the major airports, in spite of not being to achieve scale economies. Competition from secondary airports can have the positive effect of stimulating the major airports to improve their productive efficiency. If the major airports are able to improve their efficiency, they will be able to lessen their loss of traffic to the secondary airports. This will be particularly important for those major airports which do have spare capacity, and it will result in a more efficient overall allocation of traffic between airports. Competition can improve efficiency if it is not too distorted by subsidies and cross subsidies.

7. Conclusions

Increasing demand and changing patterns of demand pose an adjustment problem for airports. Increasing demand puts pressure on facilities, which cannot be expanded much in the short term. In spite of this, it is possible for most airports, which operate using a slot system, to cope without significant additions to delays. In the short term, terminals will become more congested, especially if it is difficult to provide adequate facilities for security screening. While airports will cope, there may still be an underlying problem concerning the efficiency with which their scarce capacity is allocated between users. In the longer term, the expansion of capacity may not take the most efficient form. Airports are subject to strong environmental and political constraints on expansion, and in spite of new ownership and regulatory frameworks which many are operating within, investments in capacity expansion will often not be directed to the most cost effective solutions.

Airports are also facing changes in the patterns of demand they face, from new airline business models, such as LCCs, and from new aircraft types. The latter are not likely to have major impacts on the use of airports. The new business models, however, are making a difference. The increasing use of secondary airports, or major airports with spare capacity, is lessening the pressure arising from demand growth. However, with the proliferation of local airport subsidies, and cross subsidies within major airports and in airport systems, it is likely that a less than ideal allocation of traffic to airports will come about.

References

Air Transport Research Society, 2005. Airport Benchmarking Report—2005: Global Standards for Airport Excellence. Centre for Transport Studies, University of British Columbia, Vancouver.

Armstrong, M., Cowan, S., Vickers, J., 1994. Regulatory Reform: Economic Analysis and British Experience. MIT Press, Cambridge, MA.

Bass, T., 2003. The role of market forces in the allocation of airport slots. In: Boyfield, K. (Ed.), A Role Market Airport Slots. Institute of Economic Affairs, Readings 56, London pp. 21–50.

Bisignani, G., 2006. Regulate Europe's Airport Monopolies. International Air Transport Association.

Civil Aviation Authority, 2003. Economic Regulation of BAA London Airports (Heathrow, Gatwick and Stansted) 2003–2008. CAA Decision, London.

Civil Aviation Authority, 2006. Airports Review—Policy Update. CAA, London.

Doganis, R., 2006. The Airline Business. 2nd ed. Routledge, London.

Forsyth, P., 2005. Airport infrastructure for the Airbus A380: cost recovery and pricing. Journal of Transport Economics and Policy 39 (3), 341–362.

Forsyth, P., 2006. Estimating the Costs and benefits of regional airport subsidies: a computable general equilibrium approach. In: Paper to the German Aviation Research Society Conference, Amsterdam.

Gillen, D., Niemeier, H.-M., 2006. Airport Economics, Policy and Management: The European Union Paper Delivered at Fundacion Rafael del Pino Conference Comparative Political Economy and Infrastructure Performance: The Case of Airports, Madrid.

Graham, A., 2004. The regulation of US airports. In: Forsyth, P., Gillen, D., Knorr, A., Mayer, O., Niemeier, H-M., Starkie, D. (Eds.), The Economic Regulation of Airports: Recent Developments in Australasia, North America and Europe. Aldershot, Ashgate.

Helm, D., Thompson, D., 1991. Privatised transport infrastructure and incentives to invest. Journal of Transport Economics and Policy 35, 13–24.

Hendriks, N., Andrew, D., 2004. Airport regulation in the UK. In: Forsyth, P., Gillen, D., Knorr, A., Mayer, O., Niemeier, H.-M., Starkie, D. (Eds.), The Economic Regulation of Airports: Recent Developments in Australasia, North America and Europe. Aldershot, Ashgate.

Humphreys, B., 2003. Slot allocation: a radical solution. In: Boyfield, K. (Ed.), A Role Market Airport Slots. Institute of Economic Affairs Reading 56, London.

International Air Transport Association, 2000. Peak/off-peak charging. In: Paper to the Conference on the Economics of Airports and Air Navigation Services, Montreal.

Klenk, M., 2004. New Approaches in airlien/airport relations: the charges framework of Frankfurt Airport. In: Forsyth, P., Gillen, D., Knorr, A., Mayer, O., Niemeier, H-M., Starkie, D. (Eds.), The Economic Regulation of Airports: Recent Developments in Australasia, North America and Europe. Ashgate, Aldershot.

Lawton, T., 2002. Cleared for Take-Off: Structure and Strategy in the Low Fare Airline Business. Ashgate, Aldershot.

Morrison, S., 1982. The structure of landing fees at uncongested airports. Journal of Transport Economics and Policy 16, 151–159.

National Economic Research Associates, 2004. Study to Assess the Effects of Different Slot Allocation Schemes. A Final Report for the European Commission, D.G. Tren. NERA, London.

Productivity Commission (Australia), 2006. Review of price regulation of airport services. Draft Report, Canberra.

Starkie, D., 2003. The economics of secondary markets for airport slots. In: Boyfield, K. (Ed.), A Role Market Airport Slots. Institute of Economic Affairs, Readings 56, London.

Starkie, D., 2004. Testing the regulatory model: the expansion of Stansted Airport. Fiscal Studies 25, 389–413.

Part II:

Aircraft Design and Manufacturing

5

The international decentralisation of US commercial aircraft production: implications for US employment and trade

Alan MacPherson, David Pritchard

Abstract

This paper examines the role of industrial offset agreements in the global decentralisation of US commercial aircraft production. Particular attention is given to the manufacturing processes involved in the design and assembly of large passenger jets (100 seats or more). It is argued that the current geography of aircraft production at the global level has been shaped by a new international distribution of input costs and technological capability. Specifically, low-cost producers within several of the newly emerging markets (NEMs) have acquired front-end manufacturing expertise as a direct result of industrial offset contracts and/or other forms of technology transfer (e.g. international joint-ventures, imports of advanced machine tools). We find that the growth of international offset agreements portend the transformation of Boeing from an aircraft manufacturer to a systems integrator. The economic implications of this potential reconfiguration of the US commercial aircraft industry are discussed in the context of several techno-market futures, some of which look rather bleak for US workers in this industry. © 2003 Elsevier Science Ltd. All rights reserved.

1. Introduction

The commercial aircraft industry has long been the single most important sector of the US economy in terms of skilled production jobs, value-added, and exports [1]. Over the last decade, however, this sector has become increasingly import dependent, as evidenced by rising levels of intra-industry trade (IIT). Recent research suggests that part of this import thrust can be traced to industrial offset agreements that transfer significant portions of US aircraft production to foreign companies [2]. In order to sell Boeing 747s to Air China, for example, at least part of the final product must be manufactured or assembled inside China itself. Offset agreements within the aircraft industry have become increasingly complex, such that, by now, major producers like Boeing and Airbus operate with globally decentralised supply networks that are not wholly shaped by cost, quality, or logistical factors [3]. We argue that many of these subcontracting relationships have been configured in response to the industrial development priorities of foreign governments that control the purchasing decisions of their domestic airlines. If this argument is correct, then the geography of input supply for a global company like Boeing may not simply reflect issues such as unit costs, price-quality considerations, or input delivery speeds. More simply, our argument is that big buyers can impose purchasing conditions that aircraft suppliers cannot ignore.

This paper examines the role of industrial offset agreements in the global decentralisation of US commercial aircraft production. Three key arguments are advanced that point to a major restructuring of the industry over the near future. First, it is argued that industrial offset agreements act as conduits for international technology transfer. In simple terms, these agreements deliver new production methods to foreign manufacturers, some of whom are destined to become future competitors [4]. Ultimately, industrial offsets represent an international transfer of production skills from one nation to another [5,6]. A second and related argument is that offsets allow foreign competitors to build new production capability [7–9]. Specifically, we contend that US compensatory trade agreements with Russia and China have created the technological foundations required for market entry (i.e. both of these nations will soon have the ability to manufacture large passenger jets for global markets). Third, we argue that key segments of the US commercial aircraft industry are poised on the edge of market exit [10]. For example, evidence presented later shows that the only remaining US producer of large civil aircraft (Boeing) has invested little in new manufacturing technology over the last decade or so (the company's capital stock is close to obsolete). At the same time, Boeing has been following a systems-integration strategy (i.e. buy components from overseas, and assemble aircraft at home) [11]. Overall, our main thesis is that US commercial aircraft production faces an uncertain future in terms of employment, exports, and long-run survival. While our analysis is focused mainly upon the production of large passenger jets (i.e. aircraft that can seat at least 100 people), much of the discussion which follows is pertinent to the regional jet market as well. As we show later, moreover, other US sectors have moved toward systems integration and/or offset-related marketing over the last few years. In short, some of the arguments advanced in this paper can be applied to a variety of US high-technology activities outside the aerospace sector.

2. Direct and indirect offsets: an overview

Industrial offset can be defined as a form of compensatory or reciprocal trade where exporters (sellers) grant concessions to importers (buyers). A direct offset usually involves some form of production sharing (subcontracting), technology trans-

A. MacPherson, D. Pritchard / Futures 35 (2003) 221–238   223

fer, or worker training, whereas indirect offsets can include counterpurchase agreements or other forms of countertrade (e.g. barter) [2]. Industrial offset agreements are common in sectors where unit selling prices are high (e.g. aircraft, weapons systems, machine tools), and where buyers are either owned or heavily regulated by national governments (e.g. airlines, defense departments, public utilities). No exporter will enter into an offset agreement unless there are significant competitive pressures to do so. Conversely, no importer will attempt to negotiate an offset unless substantial bargaining power is present. Offsets are particularly prevalent in markets where unit costs are high, buyers are part of an oligopsony, and sellers are desperate to make a sale (competition is intense). Under these conditions, exporters can exploit offsets as a competitive tactic [2]. Other things being equal, export contracts are won by firms that offer the best offset conditions.

In the context of the commercial aircraft sector, the first industrial offsets that we are aware of started in the 1960s when Douglas first subcontracted the wing and fuselage assemblies for the DC-9 and DC-10 [12]. The wing assembly was outsourced to Dehavilland in Toronto, while the fuselage sections went to Alenia in Italy. These transactions resulted in substantial sales of Douglas aircraft to the national carriers of Canada and Italy. One of Boeing's early offsets was with Japan in 1974, when Mitsubishi was given contracts to produce inboard flaps for the 747 (resulting in major sales of 747s to Japan). In virtually every case that has been documented, the goal of an offset agreement is to secure a sale that would not take place in the absence of compensatory provisions. Although Douglas is credited with the first batch of offsets as we know them today, Douglas no longer exists as an independent aircraft company and Boeing has become the nation's single largest corporation in terms of offset-related commitments. As we write, there is no explicit US policy regarding offsets, and the US Department of Commerce has yet to issue guidelines regarding commercial best-practice in this sphere. The only regulatory requirement at present is that offsets valued at $5 million or more must be 'screened' to ensure that sensitive technologies are not delivered to potentially hostile nations [10]. In short, current US policy regarding commercial offsets has been framed with respect to military and/or national security issues rather than economic considerations (e.g. domestic job retention).

3. Recent trends in US commercial aircraft production

The commercial aircraft sector accounts for approximately 8% of the nation's industrial exports ($53 billion in 2000), almost 800,000 jobs, and close to 10% of US industrial output [1]. Despite strong export performance over the last 40 years, evidence is mounting that this sector is not nearly as healthy as it was in the 1960s or 70s. In 1960, for example, imports of aircraft and parts amounted to only 5% of exports by value, compared to 45% today. In terms of global market share for large passenger jets, the US moved from an almost complete monopoly (95%) in 1960 to a decidedly weaker position by 2001 (49%). Part of this shift can be explained by the emergence of Airbus, which moved from zero market share in 1970 to a 51%

224   *A. MacPherson, D. Pritchard / Futures 35 (2003) 221–238*

position by 2001 [8]. Faced with an increasingly competitive environment, the US commercial aircraft industry has responded via rationalisation, joint-ventures, mergers, and various types of international subcontracting agreements [9]. By now, there is only one major US producer and only two high-volume domestic parts manufacturers (contrast this with the 1970s, when there were three large producers and over ten major parts suppliers). Foreign content has increased dramatically over the past four decades. For example, the foreign content of a Boeing 727 was only 2% in the 1960s, compared to nearly 30% for the Boeing 777 in the 1990s [10]. In the case of the Boeing 777, there is no domestic production for the vertical and horizontal stabilisers, the center wing box, or the aft and forward fuselage sections (the only significant part of the airframe that is domestically manufactured is the wing assembly).

To an extent, of course, the falling domestic content of US-built aircraft reflects a cost-driven trend toward international sourcing [11]. Of the $23 billion import bill for 2000, roughly 55% consisted of airframe parts for Boeing's assembly plants in Seattle. Although this type of intra-industry trade (IIT) has been growing for some time, US revealed comparative advantage (RCA) in aircraft production remains strong (Table 1). Whether or not the RCA index will remain above unity over the long-run is far from assured (discussed later).

The rapid growth of IIT owes much to the nature of competition within the global aerospace sector. While Airbus and Boeing compete vigorously in terms of price, product quality, reputation, and delivery speed, the ability to offer and/or satisfy offset packages is important as well. Direct offset agreements between airlines and aircraft producers are designed to transfer a segment of the manufacturing work to the buyer. Thus, for example, Boeing 737s contain Chinese parts (tail assemblies) because Air China negotiated offset production as a condition of purchase. Not sur-

Table 1
US trade in commercial aircraft and parts (1970–2000)[d]

| Year | (US$ millions) | | Imports/Exports[a] | IIT[b] | RCA[c] |
	Exports	Imports			
1970	2286	271	11.8	0.21	4.08
1975	5644	81	1.4	0.03	5.20
1980	13494	2662	19.7	0.33	8.71
1985	5674	1894	33.3	0.50	3.25
1990	35770	10817	30.2	0.46	5.70
1995	29580	10739	36.3	0.53	3.60
2000	52920	23772	44.9	0.62	3.70

[a] Imports as a % of exports.
[b] Intra-industry trade index: IIT $= 1-[(x-m)/(x+m)]$ where: x = exports; m = imports.
[c] RCA = (US aircraft x/total US x)/(world aircraft x/total world x). RCA = revealed comparative advantage.
[d] Source: US Department of Commerce, 2001 [1].

A. MacPherson, D. Pritchard / Futures 35 (2003) 221–238   225

prisingly, the proliferation of offset agreements has cut the domestic supplier base for major aircraft companies such as Boeing. To an extent, then, part of the recent employment trajectory for the US aircraft industry can be traced to offset-induced imports (Table 2). For instance, many of the US airframe parts that were once manu-factured by domestic companies are now imported under offset agreements with companies from South Korea, Japan, China, and Russia. Significantly, several of the companies that were once prominent suppliers to Boeing are no longer in business (e.g. Fairchild, Douglas, Convair).

Perhaps a more disturbing feature of Table 2 is that employment levels for aeros-pace R&D scientists and engineers (S&Es) have been falling steadily for some time. Between 1970 and 2000, total aerospace S&E employment dropped from 573,000 to 120,000 (an 800% decrease). Over the same period, S&E employment as a pro-portion of total aerospace employment dropped from 30 to 15% (further cuts are widely anticipated in light of the post-September 11 slowdown in air travel and aircraft orders). Thirty years ago, the US aerospace sector held a 22% share of the nation's total S&E employment, compared to just over 6% today. When we factor in the fact that the aerospace workforce as a whole is aging, the steady drop in S&E employment suggests that the industry will soon face a major human capital shortage [12].

This said, the US aircraft industry has been driven by foreign competition to reduce unit costs as far as possible, and thus the growth of international subcontracting is not very surprising [13]. It would appear that this trend has been commercially suc-cessful for both Boeing and Airbus. Over the long-run, however, the financial inter-ests of the Airbus/Boeing duopoly may not be well served by this strategy. An issue of mounting concern is that offset agreements involve technology transfer (i.e. advanced production capability is delivered to potential competitors). A related con-cern is that most of the world's aircraft producers expect that future growth of rev-

Table 2
US employment in commercial aircraft production (1970–2000)[e]

Year	Jobs (000s)[a]	S&E Jobs (000s)[b]	S&E %[c]	S&E as % of all sectors[d]
1970	1900	573	30.2	22.5
1975	1870	390	20.9	21.4
1980	1690	341	20.2	17.7
1985	1235	264	21.4	20.2
1990	1200	238	19.9	16.3
1995	832	155	18.7	12.1
2000	798	120	15.1	6.2

[a] Production plus non-production workers (total employment).
[b] R&D scientists and engineers.
[c] R&D scientists and engineers as a % of aerospace employment.
[d] Aerospace R&D scientists and engineers as a % of total manufacturing employment.
[e] Sources: US Department of Commerce, 2001 [1]; Pritchard, 2002 [12].

226   *A. MacPherson, D. Pritchard / Futures 35 (2003) 221–238*

enue passenger miles (RPMs) will be concentrated in the Asia-Pacific region. According to Boeing, for instance, global air travel is expected to increase by 75% over the next ten years, suggesting a need for over 22,000 new aircraft [14]. Given that most of the RPM growth is forecast for the Asia-Pacific region (especially China), it is widely anticipated that aircraft orders among newly emerging markets (NEMs) will outstrip orders among the industrialised nations within the next few years. This implies that many of the Asian NEMs will soon be in a position to impose tougher offset requirements than at present. A more problematic scenario for the US industry (and for Airbus as well) is that several of the NEMs may eventually enter the market as highly competitive aircraft producers. How likely is this?

4. A new geography of commercial aircraft production

The evidence in support of a major shift in the geography of aircraft production at the global level comes from three interlinked processes that have already gained significant momentum. The first process concerns technology transfer via industrial offsets (which first started in the mid-1960s). The second process concerns the acquisition of advanced manufacturing equipment (machine tools) by the NEMs (often linked to offsets). The third process concerns the rapid economic growth of the NEMs. Simply stated, several NEMs are poised on the threshold of launching their own aircraft programs on the basis of production technologies gained via offsets and/or imports of advanced capital goods.

The transfer of strategic technology from western to non-western producers can be rapid. For example, a 1995 offset contract between Boeing (US) and Hyundai (South Korea) provided Hyundai with the engineering and technical specifications required to build wings for the Boeing 717. The wing is the most critical part of an airframe and the production procedures required for wing assembly can be described as 'core technology'. By 1997, Hyundai had purchased some of the world's most advanced machine tools for riveting and milling the wing components and is now successfully producing wing assemblies for Boeing. Over the space of only two years, a nation with no prior production capability in key areas of airframe construction became fully competitive as a result of two types of technology transfer (i.e. industrial offsets and machine tool imports). While the trade literature is replete with similar examples involving both Airbus and Boeing, the fundamental point is that offset agreements have increasingly involved the transfer of core production capabilities that were once exclusively controlled by the duopoly.

A second factor concerns the advanced manufacturing technology that NEMs can buy at arm's length from US, Japanese, or European machine tool (MT) companies. MT products are critical to aircraft assembly. Most of these products have lifespans of 20–30 years (e.g. CNC riveting machines, multi-axis workstations, etc). If a Chinese or Russian aircraft company were to invest in contemporary MT products for manufacturing purposes, then that company would be operating with state-of-the-art production equipment. Much of Boeing's capital stock consists of machines that were bought more than 20 years ago [10]. Other things being equal, a new foreign

A. MacPherson, D. Pritchard / Futures 35 (2003) 221–238 227

producer that invests in current manufacturing techology will hold a production advantage over most older companies (many of whom do not replace their machines until such machines depreciate beyond repair). Of course, other things are rarely equal. A further advantage for the NEMs is that labour costs are typically at least 50% lower than those that prevail in Europe or North America.

The third factor in our argument is that most of the world's RPM growth is forecast to take place within or between the NEMs of Asia. Aircraft producers that target airlines operating in this rapidly expanding region do not need to worry about US Federal Aviation Authority (FAA) or European Joint Aviation Authority (JAA) certi-fication standards (these standards must be met before a commercial aircraft can enter EU or US/Canadian airspace). Compliance with FAA/JAA standards increases costs for all producers [12]. In essence, then, any NEM that wants to build an aircraft industry to serve an essentially non-western market will enjoy an additional cost advantage over western producers (most of whom do not manufacture non-certified aircraft as a matter of principle). Taken together, these three factors portend a global restructuring of the commercial aircraft industry in terms of production locations, regional markets, and, ultimately, jobs. The question thus arises: how strong is the evidence for all this? And when can we expect to see signs of a global shift of this type?

The following section addresses these questions in terms of several strands of emerging evidence. The first strand of evidence comes from the growth of US indus-trial offset agreements and the widening technological gulf between Boeing and Airbus (Boeing trails). The second strand of evidence concerns the accumulation of production capability in China and Russia. Both of these nations already have the technological and production infrastructure to manufacture passenger aircraft that can take off, fly, land, and navigate just as efficiently as their western counterparts— and at half the cost. Having acquired important production skills via international offsets, new manufacturing technology via MT imports, and crucial avionics systems via joint-ventures and/or import contracts with western suppliers, it is curious that so few scholars have taken notice of the emerging capabilities of non-western producers.

5. Industrial offsets and aircraft manufacturing technology

A snapshot of the evolution of Boeing's industrial offset exposure is shown in Table 3, which collates the 700-level product family alongside the company's sourc-ing strategy for airframe components (foreign vs domestic). A striking feature of these data is that foreign sourcing has expanded dramatically over time (compare the 727 with newer models such as the 767 and 777). In the case of the 767, industrial offsets have been used to source a number of critical airframe components, including the inboard and outboard flaps, the front and centre fuselage, the aft fuselage, the stabiliser, the dorsal and vertical fin (including the rudder), the elevators, and all external doors. The foreign content of a Boeing 727 (which started production in the 1960s) was only 2%, whereas the foreign content of the 777 (1990s) is close to 30% [11,12]. The upshot of all this is that Boeing operates with only two major

228   *A. MacPherson, D. Pritchard / Futures 35 (2003) 221–238*

Table 3
Boeing's airframe production by source[a]

Launch year: Aircraft model	1963 727	1966 737	1969 747	1981 757	1982 767	1994 777
Wings	D	D	D	D	D	D
Inboard flaps	D	F	F	F	F	D
Outboard flaps	D	F	F	F	F	F
Engine nacelles	D	D	D	D	D	D
Nose	D	D	D	D	D	D
Engine strut	D	D	F	D	D	D
Front fuselage	D	D	D	F/D	F	F
Center fuselage	D	D	D	F/D	F	F
Center wing box	D	D	F	D	D	F
Keel beam	D	D	D	D	D	F
Aft fuselage	D	D	D	D	F	F
Stabiliser	D	F/D	D	D	F	D
Dorsal fin	D	D	D	F	F	F
Vertical fin	D	F/D	D	D	F	D
Elevators	D	F	D	F	F	F
Rudder	D	F	D	F	F	F
Passenger doors	D	D	D	D	F	F
Cargo doors	D	D	F	F	F	F
Section 48	D	F/D	F/D	D	F	F
# of major parts from foreign sources	0	7	6	8	13	12

[a] D = domestic production; F = foreign production; F/D = shared production. Source: Pritchard, 2002 [12].

domestic subcontractors today, compared with ten in the 1970s. Examples of formerly major US suppliers include Avco, Convair, Douglas, Fairchild, Grumman, Lockheed, Martin, Northrop, and Rockwell. As noted earlier, some of these suppliers have gone out of business altogether (e.g. Convair), while others have merged and/or exited the commercial aircraft business (e.g. Lockheed-Martin). All told, an estimated 125,000 domestic aerospace jobs were lost between 1975 and 2000 as a direct result of Boeing's international offset agreements [12]. Presumably even more jobs were lost via multiplier effects, especially among smaller subcontractors.

In contrast to Boeing, Airbus subcontracts internationally to support the production of its older models only (e.g. the A300). Newer models are close to 100% European content [8]. A further contrast is that Airbus more typically offers indirect offsets as a means of securing contracts. As an example, Airbus has the ability to offer foreign airlines landing rights to major EU airports such as Heathrow and Gatwick. Boeing cannot do this on the US side because regulatory and legal conditions are quite different. These are interesting distinctions for at least three reasons. First, direct offsets by Boeing involve production-sharing arrangements that allow the

A. MacPherson, D. Pritchard / Futures 35 (2003) 221–238   229

foreign partner to begin assembly work using brand new machine tools (the foreign partner thus becomes a state-of-the-art subcontractor that can produce at lower cost than either a US supplier or a production unit inside Boeing itself). Second, the fact that Airbus will only do this for older models suggests that the two companies are following radically different sourcing strategies. Third, it would appear that Airbus has wider scope for offering indirect offests than Boeing.

Another contrast between Boeing and Airbus concerns the vintage of the machine tools and manufacturing processes that are used to assemble commercial aircraft. Evidence from Pritchard [12] reveals that the wing and fuselage assembly riveters for the Boeing 747 and 767 models were delivered to Boeing in the 1960s and early 1970s. Although these machines have been electrically upgraded since then, the basic assembly procedures are based on machine tools that are nearing the end of their life cycles. Airbus, in contrast, has been moving away from riveting technologies to laser welding and composite materials (non-metallic), necessitating multi-billion dollar investments in new generations of tools and fixtures. Although Boeing's equipment for the assembly of 777s comes from the 1990s, the equivalent Airbus stock comes from the 2000s [11,12].

Unlike the flexible manufacturing systems (FMS) described in the engineering literature for use in sectors such as automobiles, the commercial aircraft industry requires machine tools that are designed to meet the unique specifications of particular models (e.g. the size and shape of aircraft panels dictates the dimensions of the machine tool). As an example, the wing riveting systems for the Boeing 737 cannot be used on the 777 because of the size and configuration of the 777's wing [12]. One consequence of this relative lack of flexibility is that the inherent design of an aircraft lends itself to the use of dedicated assembly equipment over the life cycle of the aircraft. For Boeing, this means that old systems are in place for the most part, if only because Boeing's product family is old. A major problem with old capital equipment is that rates of machine failure are high (downtime becomes an issue). A further problem is that machining speeds and accuracy levels are low when compared to the high-speed machines of the 2000s. With no new large aircraft programes in place to compete with the emerging Airbus line of products (including the A380), the technological gulf between Boeing and Airbus is expected to widen [8]. At present, Boeing does not have any commercial aircraft that operate with fly-by-wire navigational systems, nor does Boeing have a replacement for the ageing 747 (which is nearing the end of its life cycle). Although the Airbus/Boeing duopoly is likely to remain intact for some time (Boeing has order backlogs in excess of $31 billion), the stability of this duopoly is questionable in light of the growing technological advantage of Airbus. As shown in the following section, moreover, non-western producers are beginning to emerge as potential challengers as well.

6. Potential competition from outside the duopoly

It is sometimes forgotten that both China and Russia have long enjoyed substantial technological capability in aerospace production, notably on the military side. In

230   *A. MacPherson, D. Pritchard / Futures 35 (2003) 221–238*

recent years, however, both of these nations have developed an extensive manufacturing infrastructure for the production of commercial aircraft. The Russian capability is spread across multiple locations within the CIS (Commonwealth of Independent States), including major factories in Kazan, Ulyanovsk, Kiev and Voronezh. While China's civil capability is more modest, no less than ten factories produce major aircraft components (including aero engines) for 20 western manufacturers. The Chinese aerospace sector is controlled by Aviation Industries of China (AVIC), which is a large national corporation under the leadership of the State Council [15]. The Russian aerospace sector, in contrast, has moved toward a joint stock company structure, with shares held by the Russian government, the design bureaus (e.g. Tupelov and Ilyushin) and manufacturers (e.g. Aviastar). The Russian/CIS industry has produced several western adapted aircraft over the last ten years, while the Chinese industry is rapidly gaining launch capability as a result of western offsets. Significantly, a Chinese-built regional passenger jet (70 seats) is slated to enter service by 2007 [16]. Given that this jet is expected to include western components and avionics, FAA/JAA certification standards are likely to be met.

Much of the impetus behind these developments can be traced to joint-ventures that link China and Russia with the western duopoly (Boeing in particular). For example, Boeing currently has more than 30 joint projects in Russia, including a program with Ilyushin to redesign the Boeing 777 arch beam. In April of 2001, Boeing signed an agreement with the Russian agencies to develop several new initiatives, including the establishment of collaborative aircraft maintenance/modification facilities and the possible co-development of a new regional jet. At the same time, Boeing also has multiple joint ventures with Chinese producers, including offsets for the production of nose sections, vertical fins, tails, cargo doors, and fuselage panels [12]. It should be emphasised that many of these joint ventures have encouraged producers in Russia and China to invest in state-of-the-art manufacturing equipment. For instance, the CIS aircraft plants in Kazan and Ulyanovsk have invested heavily in automatic fastening equipment for wing and fuselage production. Significantly, this type of equipment is not currently in place in any of Boeing's factories.

At present, China's AVIC employs 560,000 workers, while the Russian/CIS employment base is estimated at around 600,000. There is widespread agreement that the employment trend is curving upward for both players, while the trend for the US is distinctly downward [11]. More important, perhaps, is the fact that S&E employment in the aerospace sectors of both nations recently surpassed 8% (compared to 6% in the US). Notwithstanding the fact that productivity gaps are likely to be present between the US and Russia/China, the general employment and occupational trends are suggestive of growth in both of these nations.

An interesting aspect of the emerging aerospace programmes of China and Russia is that they are both evolving with help from Boeing. In 1998, for instance, Boeing and Tupelov completed the initial phase of a US/Russian joint-venture for supersonic research, which included 19 flights of the TU-144. In China, moreover, Boeing has several FAA-approved subcontracting/offset links for the production of horizontal stabilisers and vertical fins for the 737, as well as cargo doors for the 757. Significantly, Russia now has a production model TU-204 (210 passenger jet) that is

A. MacPherson, D. Pritchard / Futures 35 (2003) 221–238 231

expected to receive JAA certification by 2003, while China recently acquired production rights to co-manufacture Canadair's Challenger jet. In sum, both of these NEMs now have the basic infrastructure to produce all of the major airframe components that are required to assemble large passenger jets, as well as regional jets.

7. Policy implications: the case for government intervention

There is little doubt that the US commercial aircraft sector is operating on borrowed time as far as the manufacturing side of the business is concerned. Boeing's Chief Executive Officer (Phil Condit) appears to agree [13]. Is there a case for government intervention to curtail the erosion of US manufacturing capability? Although Condit [13] regards new international joint-ventures as being critical to the commercial side of the company's aerospace interests, it would seem that Boeing has other concerns that are more important over the long-run (e.g. military markets, aircraft maintenance services). The question thus arises: would a commitment by the US government to protect or enhance Boeing's commercial aircraft divisions make any sense at this point in time?

The theory of strategic trade policy holds that a public subsidy can be economically justified if the ultimate social benefits exceed the costs of government assistance (as well as the extra costs that might face consumers during the subsidy period). For instance, the theory suggests that export subsidies can affect the underlying structure of an oligopolistic game, so as to allow domestic producers to achieve extra profits from exports that exceed the amount of the subsidy [17]. How might such a theory be applied to Boeing? On the plus side, Boeing meets all of the theoretical criteria that are required for strategic trade policy to work [18]. On the negative side, Boeing appears poised to exit the business of commercial and/or conventional aircraft manufacturing on its own volition [13]. To an extent, then, the case for government intervention is weakened by the strategic intentions of the company itself, as well as by the fact that intervention ought to have been considered during the initial rise of Airbus some 30 years ago [12].

This said, there is little doubt that Boeing has long met the industry-level criteria required for strategic intervention. According to Spencer [17], these criteria include: (1) the presence of major entry barriers to new competitors; (2) the existence of significant foreign competition; (3) high levels of industry concentration (both at home and abroad); (4) little chance that factor prices would increase in response to domestic targeting; (5) good prospects that the domestic industry would garner cost and/or learning economies via increased production; and (6) equally good prospects that targeting would minimise technological spillovers to competitors (or maximise domestic access to foreign technology). Interestingly, Spencer [17] notes that Airbus met most of these criteria during its rise as a challenger to Boeing, and that Airbus received substantial public subsidies whereas Boeing did not [12].

At this stage, however, at least four factors suggest that US government intervention would not be successful even if substantial export and/or R&D subsidies were granted. First, from a game-theoretic point of view, Airbus would probably interpret a new subsidy programe as an unfair increment to the implicit support that Boeing already receives with regard to US military contracts. If one accepts that the best strategy in a 'prisoner's dilemma' is 'tit-for-tat' [19], then Airbus would likely respond with additional subsidies. Second, Boeing has already started to shift its core business away from commercial aircraft manufacturing toward space vehicles, communications, technical services, and specialised defense applications. Given this shift, it might be more effective to target Boeing's emerging priority areas than its commercial aircraft interests. Third, Boeing's drift toward a systems integration mode for commercial aircraft production suggests that export subsidies would gener- ate windfall profits rather than long-run technological or cost advantages. Fourth, the much publicized concept of a Sonic Cruiser to capture the business class traveler segment has generated minimal interest among the world's major airlines. Will a prototype of this futuristic aircraft ever be built? We suspect not. Finally, the US has never engaged in strategic trade policy before, and has no experience in the design and/or implementation of subsidy programes to gain an international competi- tive advantage [12]. This is not to suggest that US trade subsidies are absent. Rather, the suggestion is that no Administration has attempted to target a specific sector with strategic trade policy objectives in mind. On balance, then, we would suggest that it is too late for the US government to do anything of significance to reorient the US commercial aircraft sector along a growth path.

8. Techno-market futures for the US aerospace industry

If Airbus becomes the dominant global supplier of large passenger jets in the 2000s (albeit facing emerging competition from China, Russia, and possibly India), then what will the US aerospace workforce do? Presumably there will be a reduced need for skilled machinests, R&D scientists, test engineers, and other talented people in fields such as MT maintenance (not to mention unskilled or semi-skilled workers). Boeing has already announced a 30,000 employee cutback in light of September 11, as well as a reduced commercial aircraft production schedule over the period 2001– 2007 (500 less aircraft than anticipated in 1999). At the same time, foreign producers of regional jets (e.g. BAe Industries, Canadair, Embraer) are starting to erode the US/Boeing share of the smaller jet market at a remarkably fast rate [12]. These circumstances point to a number of techno-market futures for the US commercial aircraft industry. We believe that the first and most likely future will involve a shift towards a mix of high-end military work (e.g. space vehicles, defense systems), high- end service activity (e.g. preventive aircraft maintenance and repair), and satellite communications. This is an interpretation that meshes closely with the strategic state- ments of Boeing itself. A second industrial future might involve a mix of the above, combined with a retained presence in the commercial aircraft market via complete systems integration (e.g. design at home, manufacture abroad). A third future, though an unlikely one, is that the Airbus A380 fails completely as a commercial venture, leaving Boeing an opportunity to introduce an updated 747 that might stretch the company's position within the global market for large passenger jets for another 20

A. MacPherson, D. Pritchard / Futures 35 (2003) 221–238 233

years or so. This scenario might also buy time for the development of a Sonic Cruiser that could be manufactured on a competitive basis.

We choose to focus on the first future because this is what the company's current CEO sees as the most likely path for Boeing [13]. Under this scenario, Boeing becomes a multinational services conglomerate with both military and commercial interests (but with only limited involvement in commercial aircraft production). While the military side of the company's long-range mission remains uncertain (Boeing does not advertise detailed aspects of its military programs), it seems unlikely that the production of 20-year-old designs for fighter aircraft or 40-year old designs for bombers will represent growth markets for the company over the next few years. In light of the fact that Lockheed-Martin won a $200 billion contract for the production of the USAF's next generation of fighter aircraft in November of 2001, it seems unlikely that Boeing will want to compete in this particular market (i.e. defensive military aircraft).

On the commercial side, however, it is evident that Boeing has identified a new set of futures for corporate growth (Table 4). These futures are based almost entirely upon aviation services such as the re-marketing of used airplanes, flight crew training, airport routing, airframe maintenance, and aircraft upgrades (e.g. engine replacement). All told, Boeing expects that these types of aviation services will generate an annual average of $87 billion in revenues over the next 20 years, compared to commercial aircraft sales of only $12 billion in 2000 [20]. Annual revenues of around $87 billion would represent a 65% share of the global market for commercial aviation services. Although Airbus currently holds a 51% market share for new orders of large passenger jets, close to 80% of the big jets that are currently in service are Boeing products. Looking at the maintenance and repair needs of this enormous fleet of US-built aircraft, it should come as no surprise that Boeing wants to dominate the global market for service and maintenance contracts.

All of this implies a new occupational structure for Boeing's workforce, as well as new skill requirements. After all, R&D scientists are not needed for flight crew

Table 4
Boeing's estimates of the size of the world market for commercial aviation services (2000–2019)[a]

Service	$ Billions
Used airplane remarketing	20
Airplane servicing	441
Heavy airplane maintenance	588
Engine repair	268
Airframe component repair	394
Major airplane modifications	43
Airframe and engine parts	257
Flight crew training	49
Airport and route services	622
20 year total	2682

[a] Source: Speednews, 2001 [20].

training; specialised machinests are not needed for route planning or air-traffic control systems design; semi-skilled manufacturing workers are hardly needed at all; and, who needs a production engineer to sell old aircraft under a used airplane re-marketing initiative? Given that annual revenues from aviation services are expected to exceed commercial aircraft sales by a factor of at least 4 over the period 2000–2019, it is not difficult to see why Boeing would want to exit and/or downscale the manufacturing side of its business.

To an extent, of course, the scenario described above mirrors a broader trend that has characterised the US economy since the 1970s. Specifically, there has been a structural shift toward non-production occupations, as well as a general shift toward information and/or knowledge-based services. Seen from this perspective, Boeing is evolving in tandem with the US economy as a whole. For example, US service exports have recently been growing faster than merchandise exports [1]. If Boeing becomes a service-based corporation along the lines described above, then the US current account will surely be given a boost. After all, projected revenues from aviation services are much higher than those for commercial aircraft [13]. The downside is that the US will lose much of its manufacturing capability in a critically important sector (i.e. skilled production jobs will disappear, and the existing supplier base will suffer further losses). Over the short-run, we are likely to see major employment decay in skilled production occupations such as machining, testing, and welding. Looking to the future, however, it is possible that these losses will be counterbalanced by new jobs spread across radically different skill categories (e.g. marketing, planning, software design, logistics). Overall, the net social benefits (or costs) are likely to depend upon the extent to which Boeing can capture a dominant share of the global market for aviation services over the 2000s. It was once said that Boeing 'bet the company' on the 747 [12]. Is Boeing doing the same again regarding aviation services?

9. Related trends in other industries

Lest one conclude that the commercial aircraft sector represents a special case, it should be mentioned that other US industries have been following similar trajectories in terms of industrial offset agreements and/or systems integration [21]. Compensatory trade provisions are now common across a wide range of product-markets, including construction equipment, machine tools, defense systems (e.g. armored vehicles), locomotives (e.g. subway systems), and industrial machinery (e.g. automated textile looms). A common denominator among these industries is that unit selling prices are high. A further commonality is that the US domestic market is not large enough to support US firms in these industries (i.e. export sales are critically important). Given the intensely competitive global market for high-technology goods in these types of sectors, industrial offset agreements have become increasingly important to the export-marketing process. Although such agreements are generally believed to involve higher dollar figures for the commercial aircraft sector than for any other sector, the fact remains that many of America's largest high-technology

A. MacPherson, D. Pritchard / Futures 35 (2003) 221–238   235

companies are offset-affected. Notable examples include Caterpillar (construction and earthmoving equipment), Cincinnati Machine (multi-axis CNC machine tools), and Lockheed-Martin (military aircraft). To date, however, it is fair to assert that very little empirical work has been conducted on the extent to which US high-technology companies have become dependent upon offset agreements. Although the 2001 Presidential Commission on Offsets [22] offers anecdotal evidence to support all of the claims stated above, we must concede that hard data are simply not available. This is because no US company is required to divulge the extent to which its commercial export contracts are offset-related. While the US Department of Commerce collects aggregate data by sector, these data are not published and are hard to obtain. Nevertheless, the latest available data suggest that direct military offsets over the period 1993–1998 cost US companies (suppliers) an estimated $2.3 billion in lost work [22]. If these estimates were to be spread across all US commercial sectors that are offset-affected, then presumably we are talking about a good deal more than $2.3 billion in lost work.

With regard to systems integration and the rise of international subcontracting (whether offset-related or not), many other US sectors have been following a path that is similar to the commercial aircraft industry. For example, the US personal computer industry is now organized on a systems integration basis, while the US automotive industry is beginning to move in the same direction [23]. Although Dell laptop computers are designed and assembled in the US, the critical components and modules are manufactured in Taiwan and South Korea. In a similar vein, US automotive companies have increasingly sourced key components from US-owned subsidiaries based in Mexico and Canada to take advantage of multilateral trade deals such as the North American Free Trade Agreement. The key point, however, is that systems integration is *not* the same phenomenon as international outsourcing (i.e. buy cheap parts from abroad). The primary difference is that systems integration implies an eventual elimination of the domestic manufacturing process altogether.

If the above argument is correct, then it would seem that the US economy is restructuring in a fashion that was not fully anticipated 10 or 20 years ago when the literature on the 'information age' first started to become popular. Specifically, US industrial exports in high-technology sectors such as aircraft and computers are not likely to diminish over the near future. Instead, it would appear that the import-content of these exports is slated to increase dramatically. One possible industrial future for the US might be an information-based economy that has no 'manufacturing' at all, but plenty of 'manufactured' exports. Another industrial future, and a less appealing one, is an economy based upon service activity alone (e.g. export designs, and do no assembly at home). One reason that we selected the US commercial aircraft industry for this paper is that Boeing appears to be the US corporate leader in terms of all of these possible futures. Sooner or later, industrial offset agreements are likely to endow foreign producers with the technological capability to perform both basic and advanced manufacturing tasks to suit any US company that wants to operate on a systems integration basis. The task remains to monitor and evaluate the diffusion of this mode of international business activity across different sectors, nations, and product-markets.

236   *A. MacPherson, D. Pritchard / Futures 35 (2003) 221–238*

10. Summary and conclusions

US exports of large passenger jets are likely to grow under a systems integration approach over the next few years. Even so, the task of manufacturing is destined to shrink inside the US itself. Industrial offset agreements have already transferred core production technologies to foreign producers, while limited domestic investment in new machine tools continues to undermine Boeing's capacity to manufacture in a competitive fashion. Airbus now holds a 51% share of the world market for large passenger jets, compared to a 0% share in 1970 when Airbus first started production. Further, it would appear that several low-cost NEMs have become viable challengers within the regional jet market (e.g. Russia, China, Brazil). Strategic trade policy might have prevented all this if the US government had intervened during the early rise of Airbus. At this stage in the game, however, it is probably too late for public intervention to arrest or reverse the decline of the US commercial aircraft sector. The fact that Boeing has not pressured the US government for strategic support suggests that a phased exit from commercial aircraft manufacturing was planned some time ago.

The shift toward a systems integration model implies that the import content of US commercial aircraft exports will continue to increase, especially in light of Boeing's offset-driven marketing strategy. To maintain a healthy RCA score, IIT will need to grow steadily over the 2000s. In short, US commercial aircraft production has become globalised, and the US must import in order to export. The fact that few domestic suppliers are still in business means that additional imports are almost inevitable. Contrast this with Airbus, which offers indirect offsets rather than production-sharing as a means of securing contracts. Recall also that Airbus subcontracts internationally for the production of older aircraft, whereas newer models are produced with close to 100% European content. We believe that Boeing intends to exit the market for large passenger jets as soon as current backlogs and/or new orders for aircraft within the existing product family have been filled. Recall that Boeing does not have any new civil aircraft programs (note that the Sonic Cruiser proposal is a concept, not a program). Contrast this with Airbus, which has invested heavily in advanced automation for a new generation of products (including the A380 superjumbo). On balance, we find it hard to believe that significant production activity on the civilian side of the aircraft industry will remain in the US beyond Boeing's 3–4 year backlog. The fact that the company recently moved its corporate headquarters from Seattle to Chicago means that strategic decision-making now takes place far away from Boeing's main production sites. One could be cynical about this, in that disgruntled or redundant production workers can no longer confront senior management face-to-face without hopping on a plane (at considerable expense). Perhaps a more realistic view is that most global companies prefer to locate their corporate headquarters in world cities. Seattle is an attractive place to live, but Chicago is a world city with a very large airport. Where better in the US to launch a new commercial trajectory based on aviation services?

Finally, it should be repeated that the commercial aircraft industry is not the only US sector that has been drifting toward systems integration. Other high-technology sectors have been following a similar path, including the machine tool industry, the electronics sector, and the automotive industry. In all three cases, rising intra-industry trade reflects an accelerating trend toward international subcontracting and domestic downsizing. This has profound implications for the future occupational structure of the US industrial workforce, as well as for the nation's merchandise trade balance. Although deindustrialisation is hardly a new theme in the literature on structural economic change, the rise of systems integration within strategic sectors such as aerospace and machine tools is hardly good news for US production workers with specialized industrial skills—nor is it good news for the US subcontractor base. On a more positive note, systems integration at least promises to ensure a continued US presence within such sectors (albeit in a design/assembly role rather than a manufacturing role).

References

[1] United States Department of Commerce. US industry and trade outlook, 2001, US Department of Commerce, International Trade Administration

[2] Wessner C. Trends and challenges in aerospace offsets. National Research Council. Washington DC: National Academy Press, 1999.

[3] Eriksson S. Global shift in the aircraft industry: a study of airframe manufacturing with special reference to the Asian NIEs. Publications edited by the Department of Geography, University of Gothenburg, Series B, No. 86, PO Box 3016, S-400 10 Gothenburg, Sweden, 1995.

[4] Markusen A. Offsets and US export controls. Statement of Commission Member Ann Markusen Regarding Offsets and US Export Controls, Statement Report of the Presidential Commission on Offsets in International Trade, Washington DC, January 18, 2001.

[5] Pinelli T. Knowledge Diffusion in the US Aerospace Industry: managing knowledge for competitive advantage. London: Alex Publishing Corporation, 1997.

[6] Udis B, Maskus KE. Offsets as industrial policy: lessons from aerospace. Defence Economics 1991;2:151–64.

[7] Turnipseed D, Rassuli A, Sardessai R, Park C. A history and evaluation of Boeing's coalition strategy with Japan in aircraft development and production. International Journal of Commerce and Management 1999;9:59–83.

[8] Smith DJ. European retrospective: the European aerospace industry 1970–2000. International Journal of Aerospace Management 2001;1:237–51.

[9] James AD. Defense industry consolidation and post-merger management: lessons from the USA. International Journal of Aerospace Management 2001;1:252–67.

[10] Pritchard D. The global decentralisation of commercial aircraft production: implications for US-based manufacturing activity. International Journal of Aerospace Management 2001;1:213–26.

[11] Mowery DC. Collaborative joint-ventures between US and foreign manufacturing firms: an overview. In: Mowery DC, editor. International collaborative ventures in US manufacturing. Cambridge, MA: Ballinger Publishing Company; 1988. p. 1–22.

[12] Pritchard D. The global decentralisation of US commercial aircraft production. PhD Dissertation, Department of Geography, University at Buffalo, Buffalo NY, 2002, USA.

[13] Condit P. Transforming Boeing: a view of the future. Speech to the Commercial Club of Chicago on September 25, 2001 (www.boeing.com/news/speeches/current/condit_010925.html).

[14] Boeing, 1999 Current Market Outlook (www.boeing.com).

[15] Chuan S. Survey of Chinese aviation industry. Beijing, China: Aviation Industry Press, 1997.

[16] Speednews, AVIC announces Chinese Regional Jet. Issue number 1109, November 10, 2000 (www.speednews.com).

[17] Spencer B. What should trade policy target? In: Krugman P, editor. Strategic trade policy and the new international economics. Cambridge MA: MIT Press; 1986. p. 69–90.

[18] Grossman GM. Strategic export promotion: a critique. In: Krugman P, editor. Strategic Trade Policy and the New International Economics. Cambridge MA: MIT Press; 1986. p. 47–68.

[19] Richardson JD. The new political economy of trade policy. In: Krugman P, editor. Strategic Trade Policy and the New International Economics. Cambridge MA: MIT Press; 1986. p. 257–82.

[20] Speednews, Quarter ended September 30th. Issue number 1160, November 2, 2001 (www.speednews.com).

[21] Kalafsky R, MacPherson A. Recent trends in the export performance of US machine tool companies. Technovation 2001;21:709–17.

[22] Presidential Commission on Offsets. Status report of the Presidential Commission on offsets in international trade. Executive Office of the President of the United States, January 18, 2001.

[23] Dicken P. Global Shift: Transforming the world economy, 3rd ed. London: Paul Chapman, 1998.

6

Aerospace Clusters: Local or Global Knowledge Spillovers?

JORGE NIOSI & MAJLINDA ZHEGU

ABSTRACT   The literature about regional innovation systems, clusters and industrial districts insists on the importance of local knowledge spillovers. Nevertheless, more recently a few authors have put in question the importance of local knowledge spillovers. This paper provides an analysis of some of the most dynamic aerospace clusters in the world, located in Montreal, Seattle, Toulouse and Toronto. We start by discussing theories of clustering, then provide research questions as well as empirical evidence on the international nature of knowledge spillovers. Local knowledge spillovers are less significant, of a different nature, and they may make a scanty contribution to explain the geographical agglomeration of firms. Conversely, international spillovers help to explain the relative dispersion of industry across nations. Resilient geographical clustering is related to the anchor tenant effects as creators of labour pools and owners of very large manufacturing plants creating regional inertia. We thus reject the local knowledge spillover explanation of aerospace clusters in favour of another one based on anchor firms and their effects on the local labour pool.

KEY WORDS: Aerospace, aircraft, industrial clusters, industrial districts, internationalization, regional innovation systems

The aerospace industry is one of the largest high-technology employers in advanced countries. By 2000, there were 1,220,000 aerospace employees in the world, of whom 49 per cent were in the USA, 35 per cent in the European Union, 7.5 per cent in Canada, 2.7 per cent in Japan and 5.7 per cent in the rest of the world (Table 1). Within this industry, the civil aviation manufacturing sector is the most important: in 2000, 66 per cent of European aviation manufacturing employees were in civil production and 33 per cent in the military sector. The figures in the USA were 59 and 41 per cent, respectively.

6   *Jorge Niosi & Majlinda Zhegu*

Table 1. Comparative aerospace industry employment, 2000

Country/region	Percentage of employment
USA	49.9
European Union	35.2
Canada	7.5
Japan	2.7
Rest of the world	5.7
Total	100
	(1,220,000)

In the last 10 years, civil aircraft original equipment manufacturers (OEMs) have been competing for orders from airline companies, whose revenues have been declining. The four major civil aircraft prime contractors are Airbus and Boeing (for planes over 100 seats) and Bombardier and Embraer for regional jets. To reduce costs, aerospace OEMs have increased their outsourcing to suppliers of subassemblies (such as engines, structures, landing gear and avionics) and concentrating on their core competencies of design, assembling and marketing aircraft. At the same time, they have made efforts to reduce, reorganize and rationalize their supply base. Thus, knowledge management in the supply chain has become critical (Bozdogan *et al.*, 1998; Gostic, 1998). Also, due to the increasing use of just-in-time and other supply chain methods, production has tended to concentrate in a few cities, or regional aircraft clusters, which include Montreal, Seattle, Toronto and Toulouse. However, international outsourcing has produced international spillovers[1] and created new poles of growth, mainly in South East Asia.

This paper is about the dynamics of the clusters and the nature of knowledge spillovers that occur within and among aerospace clusters. Section 1 recalls theories and presents the research questions. Section 2 recalls the characteristics of the aerospace industry and Section 3 presents data on clusters. Section 4 goes back to the theoretical discussion about regional and international knowledge spillovers. A conclusion puts the new data in a more general perspective.

1. Theory

Clustering and dispersion of industry are submitted to opposing forces. Centripetal forces tend to concentrate industry in a few geographical regions. Centrifugal forces push in the opposite direction and tend to

---

[1] In this paper we use the concept of spillover and externalities as synonymous. Both refer to unintended benefits or losses that some economic agents impose on others. "Flows" refer to both spillovers and also contractual, conscious exchange.

disperse industry across regions and nations. This section will review some of these forces, with an emphasis on the role of local versus international knowledge spillovers. We oppose the tenants of the dominance of centripetal forces, most prominent among them being local knowledge spillovers, and the followers of a more recent tradition suggesting that international externalities have become more conspicuous. This paper intends to examine how well these opposing theories explain geographical clustering in aerospace.

1.1. Centripetal Factors

Regional agglomerations of high-technology firms were analysed using different frameworks and different concepts. These concepts include industrial districts (the Marshall tradition), regional poles (the Perroux model), clusters and regional systems of innovation, to name just a few.

The industrial district tradition, based on Alfred Marshall's seminal studies in the late 1800s and early 1900s, is about agglomeration of small and medium-sized companies in the same or related industries (Meardon, 2001). Universities, government policies and public laboratories play a very small role in these districts. These are self-organized agglomerations of private firms competing in similar markets, together with specialized suppliers of equipment and services. This tradition has captured the imagination of Italian social scientists, who have produced a very rich set of studies using this framework. Marshallian externalities have been summarized as either economies of specialization, labour market economies (based on the local human capital pool) and/or knowledge spillovers.

Another tradition, based on François Perroux' work, is more about regional poles built around "industrializing industries", that is, sectors such as transportation equipment, that attract upstream manufacturers of parts and components, as well as metal, primary metals, rubber, plastic products and glass manufacturing attracting downstream producers using these materials. Such regional agglomerations do not require supporting institutions like universities or government laboratories. In the postwar period, European governments (particularly in France and Italy) applied this concept of Perroux poles in an effort to develop backward areas. Knowledge externalities, in this tradition, do not play a major role; agglomeration is more an input–output fact, based on demand created by prime contractors.

In the late 1980s and 1990s, two different major currents have developed in the USA and Western Europe. One, mostly based in the USA, emphasizes local knowledge spillovers, non-market scientific and technological leakages from research universities and public laboratories as major explanations for the clustering of high-technology firms. Authors like David Audretsch, Maryann Feldman, Rebecca Henderson, Adam Jaffe and Manuel Trajtenberg (see the chapter by Feldman, 2000 for an overview of the literature) tried to measure these spillovers with different levels of accuracy, but mostly through citations of patents and scientific literature.

8   *Jorge Niosi & Majlinda Zhegu*

Against this current, Krugman (1991) suggested that these spillovers, if they exist, do not leave any track, and thus, scientific attention should be devoted to other, more relevant issues.

The other current is about local and regional systems of innovation. Philip Cooke and Kevin Morgan (1998), based on the work of Bengt-Åke Lundvall, Chris Freeman and Richard Nelson, and later Charles Edquist and Jeremy Howells, emphasized the dynamics between several organizations and institutions such as innovative firms, research universities, public research institutions and government incentives. Regions which possess the full panoply of innovation organizations set in an institutional milieu, where systemic linkage and interactive communication among the innovation actors is normal, approach the designation of regional innovation systems (Cooke and Morgan, 1998).

Finally, Michael Porter has suggested that his famous diamond can be applied to innovative clusters as well. He defines clusters as geographical concentrations of interconnected companies and institutions in a particular field. The dynamic nature of clusters, he suggests, is based upon inter-firm local competition, the supply of equipment and services, input factor (human capital, research infrastructure, venture capital) and demand factor (sophisticated local users) (Porter, 1998, 2001). In Porter's view, like in Perroux, clusters are tightly linked input–output systems. Externalities do not play a role in his theory.

More recently, the concept of anchor firms, attracting human capital and specialized suppliers and providing knowledge spillovers has come to the forefront (Feldman, 2003). The anchor hypothesis has never been applied to aerospace, but it may provide some elements of explanation about geographical clustering in this industry.

1.2.   Centrifugal Factors

Even if a growing literature relates local knowledge spillovers and regional agglomeration of industry, another current tends to emphasize the international dispersion of industrial activity. The latter current links cross-border externalities with the increasing internationalization of economic activity. Through foreign direct investment (FDI), foreign patenting, international R&D collaboration and international trade, knowledge flows across borders have increased exponentially in the postwar period (Coe and Helpman, 1995; Baldwin *et al.*, 1999; Xu, 2000). The theory and measurement of these international externalities is as recent and unstable as the concepts and dimensions of regional spillovers (Branstetter, 2000). However, some of the mechanisms of these spillovers are already known, such as face-to-face meetings involved in both FDI and international alliances as well as the international transfer of blueprints, manuals and personnel.

International spillovers are not the only factors that disperse industry across nations. The product life cycle theory postulates that, as process technology becomes more standardized and non-proprietary, dominant designs appear, and markets become global, companies start competing on the basis of price. They tend to locate in nations where costs are lower and new markets for mature products are still open (Vernon, 1966). Thus, new products are normally launched in developed nations, where consumers are more affluent and ready to take risks in the acquisition of novel goods and services. As average costs decline, products are first exported to other affluent nations, and then to the more advanced new industrializing countries. Production follows markets, as the innovators create foreign facilities in order to restrain the entry of competitors from low cost regions. Alternatively, they can outsource parts and components in less developed nations, thus taking advantage of lower costs and being exposed to lower risks than through FDI.

Agglomerations of high-technology firms are not necessarily regional innovation systems. From the abundant theory and studies on multinational corporations, we know that advanced technology products may have been designed and developed in one area (or several geographic areas) and produced in other regions. These include pharmaceutical products that large multinational corporations develop in numerous expatriate laboratories located in different countries (Taggart *et al.*, 2001). Also, both aircraft and telecommunication equipment may be developed in one or several locations, offering advantages for R&D, and produced in other locations with comparative advantages for production. Thus, regional agglomerations of aircraft firms may exploit some local advantages (including cheap workforce, tax credits or government subsidies) without major interaction and learning processes going on within the region. Also, clustering may occur because of the existence of a specific advantage in a region, such as a labour pool or government incentives.

1.3. Research Questions

We developed two major research questions to explain aerospace clusters, on the basis of the theoretical literature on clusters and spillovers. The first one concerns knowledge production and associated spillovers.

1. Which activities within the aerospace industry cluster and which do not?
2. What may explain such clustering?

2. Aerospace Industry: Local or Global

2.1. Introduction

Strategically vital for the national economy and security, the aircraft industry has been observed by scholars mostly from a national or regional point of view (Eriksson, 1995). Diverse studies demonstrate some positive influence of clustering in the industry performance (Beaudry, 2001). But

10   *Jorge Niosi & Majlinda Zhegu*

others suggest that in the case of aerospace firms agglomerative advantages are operating weakly (Lublinski, 2003).

The dominant characteristics of the aircraft industry are helpful in explaining why traditional centralization factors do not apply. Aerospace is a high value-added sector, strongly affected by scale and timing. The industry success depends on rapid technological progress; government support for corporate R&D is essential. Their activity depends on components and parts which can be widely dispersed in terms of both industry and location. Transportation costs of these components are not relevant in overall aircraft costs. Also, demand (market) is not geographically bounded.

The analysis of recent developments in the aerospace sector reveals that the primary centripetal force has been the regional pool of skilled and semi-skilled labour. Less important factors have been the location to the original industries of the cluster (often engineering sectors close to aircraft such as railway manufacturing) and the entrepreneurial talent (Cunningham, 1951; Todd and Simpson, 1986). History offers numerous cases of government deciding industrial location or relocation. These decisions have combined national strategic interests with regional development policies, as appears in the history of the aircraft industry in Canada, France, Italy and the USA. The persistent increase of R&D costs has been the major centrifugal force for the aircraft global decentralization: in order to reduce R&D costs, the industry has been gradually implementing strategies of international cooperation.

Aerospace production is scattered throughout Western Europe and North America, suggesting major international and inter-regional knowledge flows. Table 2 gives an indication of the size of the top 12 aerospace clusters in North America. California dominates with two major clusters

Table 2. Top North American aerospace metropolitan areas, 2000

Rank	Metropolitan area	Number of aerospace jobs
1	Los Angeles, CA	107,500
2	Seattle, WA	95,500
3	Washington, DC	45,000
4	Wichita, KS	40,000
5	New York, NY	33,500
6	Montreal, Que.	26,000
7	Dallas, TX	24,500
8	Boston, MA	20,500
9	Philadelphia, PA	19,500
10	San Francisco, CA	19,500
11	Atlanta, GA	11,500
12	Toronto, ON	8,000

Note: Business establishments with 100 employees or more.
Source: Pricewater Cooper and or estimates.

which, together with Washington State, represent close to 50 per cent of US aerospace employment. Conversely, there is a much larger dispersion in European industry, where all 15 countries have some aerospace activity, due to historical reasons (Table 3). The UK, France and Germany, however, represent over 50 per cent of the 429,000 European aerospace employees. Toulouse is by far the most important cluster in Europe, with 25,000 aerospace employees. No study has compared the efficiency and effectiveness of such widely divergent arrangements. Krugman (1991) has suggested that the similar geographical dispersion of the European auto industry is inefficient and may be explained by political rather than economic reasons. However, aircraft are produced in short runs, and increased transportation costs due to geographic dispersion may not be as important in aerospace as they are in the auto industry.

Economic concentration in this industry is very high. For each sector (large civilian aircraft, regional aircraft, business jets, helicopters, etc.) there are only a few competitors. Barriers to entry are very high due to capital commitments required to design and produce aircraft. Competition among the few is however strong. The industry is hierarchically organized into "tiers". As summarized in Figure 1, at the top of the pyramid one finds the airframe assemblers (prime contractors or OEMs) such as Airbus, Bell Helicopter Textron, Boeing, Bombardier, Embraer and Eurocopter. These companies design planes and helicopters, prospect markets and order subassemblies from the second tier. At this second level, we find manufacturers of propulsion systems such as General Electric, Pratt & Whitney or Rolls-Royce. Producers of on-board avionics, such as Honeywell in the USA and Sextant Avionique in France, also belong to this category. Tier 2 also includes manufacturers of airframe structures and subassemblies such as landing gear, nacelles and hydraulic systems. Messier-Dowty (France) and Héroux-Devtek (Canada), both producers of

Table 3. European aerospace clusters, 2000

Country	Number of aerospace jobs	Main clusters
UK	150,000	Bristol, Lancashire, Farnborough
France	101,000	Toulouse, Bordeaux, Ile-de-France
Germany	70,000	Bavaria, Hamburg/Bremen
Italy	39,000	Turin, Milan, Naples
Spain	18,000	Madrid, Bilbao
Sweden	13,000	Linkoping, Göteborg
Netherlands	11,000	Amsterdam
Belgium	7,000	Sonaca
Ireland	4,000	Dublin
Portugal	4,000	Lisbon
Austria	4,000	Vienna
Greece	4,000	Athens

12 *Jorge Niosi & Majlinda Zhegu*

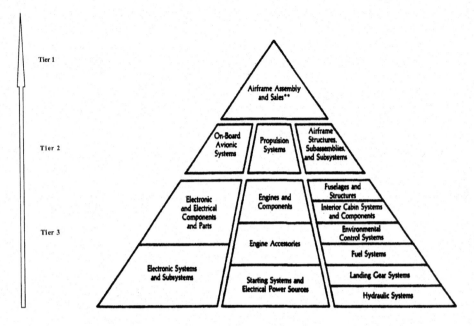

Figure 1. The producers' pyramid

landing gear, belong to this category. Tier 3, producers of electronic subassemblies, hydraulic systems and fuselage parts, is also a very concentrated group of producers at the global level with a handful of firms dominating each segment.

One other group of firms is usually added to the pyramid. Aerospace clusters always include hundreds of small and medium manufacturers offering parts and components assembled by tier 2, 3 and sometimes by tier 1 firms. Even if these firms often get most of their revenues from the aerospace industry, they are also offering their products and services to a large range of other industries.

Most large aerospace clusters thus consist of one or several OEMs surrounded by hundreds of small and medium-sized tier 4 suppliers of components and parts. In aerospace clusters, knowledge spillovers are technology based and centred on supply chain management linking the OEMs and their suppliers. Unlike biotechnology, in the study of aerospace spillovers, citations to patents and licensing are useless as measurement methods: these companies do not usually publish scientific papers, or license technology, and their processes are most often protected through secrecy rather than patents. *Supply chain management is the vehicle of knowledge spillovers in this industry. This chain is basically international.* Supply chain management includes such dimensions as technical specifications, concurrent engineering, strategic engineering alliances, quality control, product co-development, certification of suppliers, delivery time, risk-sharing, cost-sharing, production volumes and prices (Bozdogan *et al.*, 1998; Gostic, 1998). Aerospace prime contractors have moved from arm's length American-style procurement practices to more "Japanese" inspired supply chain collaboration with both OEMs of subassemblies and suppliers exchanging knowledge on products, processes and costs. Inter-firm teams and OEM training schemes aimed at the suppliers are major mechanisms to transfer knowledge from one organization to another, across borders and regions.

Aerospace regions are specialized. They manufacture high-value products, in batches from a few hundred to several thousand. Their major components (aircraft, fuselages, wings, engines, avionics, landing gear) can be shipped from one place to another, transportation costs being a small fraction of total costs. Thus, there are civil aircraft assembly clusters (such as Montreal, Seattle or Toulouse), engines clusters (around GE's engine plants in Cincinnati, Ohio and Lynn, Massachusetts). With Boeing as a major assembler, Seattle is specialized in engineering and production of large commercial aircraft. Toulouse (France) is the major production site of Airbus and ATR. All these aircraft regions have been active in the aerospace industry for as long as one century (Toulouse) or at least 50 years (Fort Worth, Texas). The specialization of regions in different nations reinforces the international spillovers in this industry, as the regions where systems integrators are based "import" engines or fuselages from regions of other nations where these are produced.

Aerospace clusters are characterized by major geographical inertia due to heavy sunk costs in large plants with costly and complex sophisticated equipment that cannot be easily moved from one location to another. Contrary to biotechnology and software, where human capital is dominant, large aerospace plants are used for decades. Also, the industry is characterized by increasing returns: successful companies tend to gain market share and thus increase the size of the existing plants, build new plants in the same region or absorb other companies' plants in the same region or in other ones. For these reasons, aerospace clusters are long-term phenomena. As regional agglomerations do not disappear but get more specialized, thus international flows are reinforced by the long-term trend.

2.2. Internationalization of the Aircraft Industry

Four periods of internationalization may be distinguished in the evolution of the aircraft industry: (1) the period of the USA's industrial supremacy; (2) the European catching up; (3) the duopolistic war between Airbus and Boeing; and (4) the worldwide diffusion of the industry.

From the end of World War II until the beginning of the 1960s, the USA's predominance was absolute, in terms both of production and market. During this period, the American aircraft supply chain remained dispersed but only in a national base. In the meantime, the USA protected its domestic aircraft market. The "Buy American Act" was the strong

14   *Jorge Niosi & Majlinda Zhegu*

protection mechanism, imposing penalties on US government agencies who preferred importing foreign over domestic equipment (Todd and Simpson, 1986). None of the European countries had by itself the technological and financial capabilities of the American aircraft industry. Thus, they had no other choice but to purposely initiate and develop international relationships, mostly through intra-European cooperation.

During the 1970s, the European countries reinforced this strategic industry and accelerated the creation of the Airbus consortium. The American aerospace sector was quickly involved in the new oligopolistic war. There were clear signals from the other side of Atlantic, announcing the end of American leadership.

By the end of the 1980s and during the 1990s, international cooperation between different members of the aircraft value chain became common-place for both American and European firms. With the "better, faster, cheaper" era of aircraft, time came when even the American giant industry could not afford either high technological and financial efforts, or market risks related to the new development programs. As Esposito (2004) demonstrates, the success of aircraft firms is based on the existence of a complex network of long-term relationships having an "evolutionary" nature where collaboration and competition exist hand in hand. Hagedoorn (2002) points out that international R&D partnering in aerospace and defence is well above the average compared to other high-tech industries. During the 1990–98 period this industry had the highest international partnering index of all sectors.

Nowadays, it is not anymore possible to overlook the global integration of the aircraft industry. The six big European and American groups emerging from an intensive industrial concentration process are pushing for more and stronger technological competition in their market segments, and at the same time are reinforcing their international R&D collaboration.

The emergence of the aerospace industry in other counties is evident. The geopolitical ambitions have strongly motivated governmental actions for the development of the aircraft industry. This will has nurtured a form of cooperation with advanced countries that have helped a few of them (Brazil, China, India, Korea) to accumulate the necessary capabilities for being successful in this sector. One of the most prominent mechanisms for technology transfers in aerospace has been the frequent use of offset agreements. Governments are usually owners of national airlines, thus they have been in a convenient position to impose their conditions on aircraft producers (Mowery, 1987; Pan, 1996; McGuire, 1997). In a first step, these countries have become part of the international aircraft supply chain. In a few years, they will acquire enough specialized technology, know-how and experience allowing them to be active players on a global scale. Few studies are concentrating on this potential competition from the outside of the three decades old USA–EU duopoly (Eriksson, 1995; Pritchard, 2002).

3. The Research

The study consists of a detailed examination of two aerospace clusters (Montreal and Toronto) and a summary comparison to two of the largest aircraft clusters during their growth and decline. The research was conducted through personal interviews with company officials and used secondary data from many different sources.

3.1. A Diversified Montreal Cluster

Montreal represents over 50 per cent of Canada's employment in the aerospace industry. It is the only city in Canada and one of the few in the world where an entire aircraft can be designed. The production of aircraft started in Montreal in the 1920s with several American, British and Canadian producers competing to produce small, regionally flown propeller aircraft. In 1944, a group of Canadian Vickers employees (the Canadian subsidiary of British Vickers, producing aircraft in Montreal) founded Canadair in Ville St-Laurent, in Montreal's north end. After World War II and the cold war, Canadair produced mostly military aircraft. Dozens of companies spun off from Canadair or were attracted to Montreal to supply parts and components for it (Pickler and Milberry, 1995). In 1976, the company acquired the exclusive rights to the blueprint of the Learjet 600, a business jet designed by William Lear, of Learjet Corporation, in Wichita, Kansas (Phillips *et al.*, 1994). With some local adjustments, the aircraft became the Challenger 600, whose first prototype flew in 1978. In 1986, Bombardier Corporation of Montreal bought Canadair and decided to enter the regional aircraft market with a modified version of the CL600. The development of the regional jet was decided in 1987 and the first prototype flew in 1991; it was the RJ100, accommodating 50 passengers; production was launched in 1993. Several subsequent versions enlarged the regional jet up to 90 seats. In the meantime, in 1992, Bombardier had bought de Havilland in Toronto. In 1989, with the acquisition of Short Brothers by Bombardier in the UK, and that of Learjet in Wichita, Kansas, Bombardier completed a range of aircraft with between 5 and 100 seats. The regional aircraft market is now dominated by turbofan technology; Bombardier was one of the few companies to introduce it. The world market for aircraft had changed radically when, in the late 1980s, the large airlines moved from point-to-point to hub-and-spoke networks requiring large aircraft only for the service of major airports, and regional aircraft for the feeding lines around the hub. The era of regional jets had arrived. In a decade, Bombardier Aerospace, with 15,000 employees in Montreal alone and 28,000 around the globe, became the world's third largest producer of aircraft, and Montreal became a thriving aerospace RSI. In the meantime, Bombardier transferred its aircraft design capabilities for new planes to Montreal. Since these capabilities originated from scattered sites, Bombardier benefited from a new wave of major international knowledge

16   *Jorge Niosi & Majlinda Zhegu*

spillovers. *Canadair, and now Bombardier have become the anchor firms that created the labour pool upon which most other companies have located in the metropolitan area.* Today all its families of business and regional jets are developed in Montreal. General Electric engines manufactured in the USA power most Canadian regional jets (CRJs), which use imported avionics and other major components.

In the 1920s, attracted by the first aircraft producers, Pratt & Whitney Canada (P&WC), a subsidiary of US-based United Technologies, started overhauling and repairing American designed and built aircraft engines. After World War II, P&WC started producing small turbines in Montreal, and incorporated local design capabilities for them (De Bresson *et al.*, 1991). Today, the family of P&WC products has expanded. Its engines are entirely designed and manufactured in Montreal, and protected through dozens of US patents (Table 4). These engines are found in some Bell Helicopter Canada (BHC) models manufactured in Montreal. P&WC engines are also powering some of Bombardier's models produced in several plants, including those made in Toronto (DHC-8) and Montreal (water bombers CL-215 and CL-415). P&WC has a total of 6,700 employees in its engineering and production facilities in Montreal's southern end. Over 90 per cent of their products are exported.

In 1984–85, with financial support from the Canadian government, BHC, the main American producer of helicopters, transferred its production capabilities for the manufacturing (but not the design) of its civilian helicopters to Montreal. Like Bombardier, BHC also produced incoming international knowledge spillovers. During the next 17 years, the new Mirabel facility of BHC produced over 2,500 copies of seven successful models that were exported throughout the world. Two of these models use

Table 4. Patents in Canadian aircraft (1976–2002)

Company	Montreal	Toronto	Winnipeg	Vancouver	Halifax	Ottawa	Calgary
Company 1	73	23	7	3	0	0	0
Company 2	12	10	0	0	0	0	0
Company 3	8	4	0	NA	NA	NA	0
Company 4	8	3	NA	NA	NA	NA	NA
Company 5	7	2					
Company 6	3	2					
Company 7	2	2					
Company 8	2	1					
Company 9	2	1					
All other	10	1					
NRC labs	NA	NA	NA	NA	NA	5	NA
Total patents	127	49	7	3	0	5	0

NA=not applicable.
Source: USPTO.

Aerospace Clusters 17

P&WC turbines designed and manufactured in Montreal. All others use US-made Allison engines. All models make use of US-designed and -manufactured shafts and other major parts. BHC employs 1,200 personnel in its plant in Montreal's north end. BHC was also attracted by Montreal's labour pool.

Bombardier Aerospace and P&WC represent over 40 per cent of Montreal aerospace employment. When BHC is added, these three companies employ well over 50 per cent of the total aerospace personnel of Montreal.

Other important companies are also prominent in the regional aerospace cluster. Honeywell Canada (a US subsidiary) is another major avionics manufacturer, with global mandates for several products, bringing highly valuable technological knowledge to Montreal. CMC Electronics (975 employees in Montreal), the former Canadian Marconi Corporation, since the late 1990s under Canadian ownership and control, is Canada's main avionics producer. Its products are not incorporated in Bombardier's planes, but exported to other major aircraft producers. Héroux-Devtek, with 650 employees in Montreal, is a producer of landing gear, used in Bombardier jets, among other (mostly foreign) aircraft. French companies Messier-Dowty (landing gear produced entirely for European customers) and Thales (avionics and a supplier of Bombardier) also deserve to be mentioned. Another major company in Montreal is CAE, the world's largest producer of flight simulators (4,000 employees in Montreal). In all, over 250 manufacturing small and medium-sized companies at different levels constitute the Montreal aerospace cluster (Figure 2). These small and medium-sized enterprises (SMEs), tier 4 firms, represent not more than 20 per cent of the regional cluster employment and produce parts and components for tier 1, 2 and 3 OEMs. A local network of knowledge flows of lesser proportions thus links the four tiers of the regional pyramid. Figure 2 summarizes the composition and dynamics of the Montreal aerospace cluster.

International knowledge spillovers are thus the norm for all the large manufacturers operating in the region. Montreal generates and receives from abroad major knowledge externalities through its tier 1 and 2 producers.

University research and training within the cluster. Some local spillovers are university–industry ones. In 1986, Bombardier funded the first Chair on aeronautical engineering at the École polytechnique, University of Montreal. In 2001, Concordia University hosted the newly created Concordia Institute for Aerospace Design and Innovation (CIADI). CIADI was an initiative of seven major aerospace firms of Montreal (BHC, Bombardier, CAE, CMC, EMS Technologies, PW&C and Héroux-Devtek). These companies wished to increase the inflow of graduates from local universities and increase academic research. Contrary to biotechnology, in which university incubated industry, in aerospace, industry stimulated university to supply ideas and graduates for their existing demand.

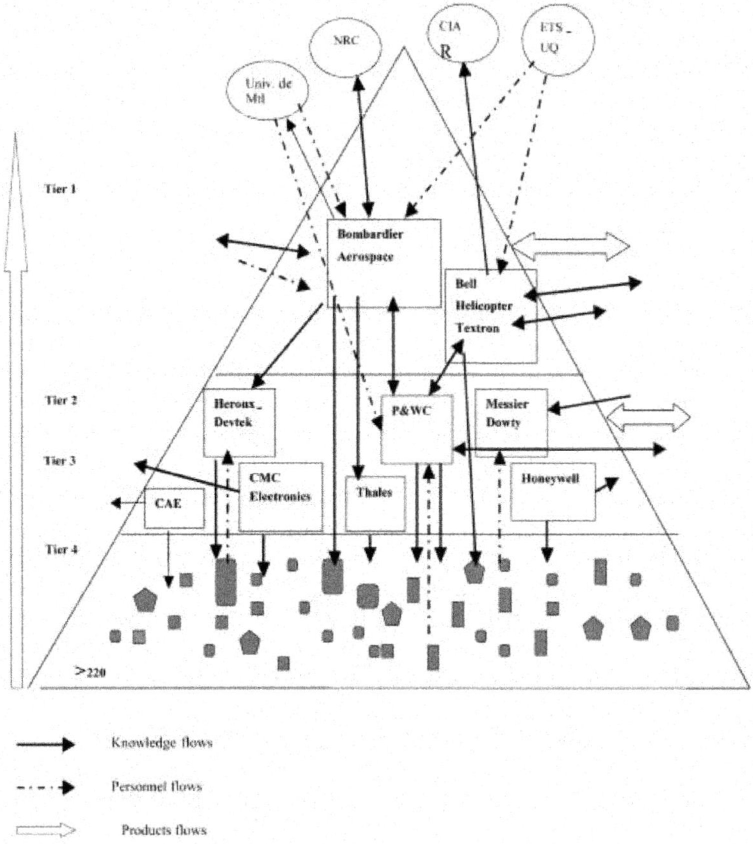

18   *Jorge Niosi & Majlinda Zhegu*

Figure 2. Montreal aerospace cluster

Consequently, the local network of knowledge increased, with technology moving from companies to universities.

Government laboratories. Public research institutes contributed, but not significantly, to cluster dynamics or its local spillovers. National Research Council of Canada (NRC) Institutes for Aerospace Research are located in Ottawa. In October 2000, the Canadian government announced the creation of a new NRC facility on aerospace research, this time to be located on the campus of the University of Montreal. The Aerospace Manufacturing Technology Center is now being built.

3.2.   Toronto: An Old and Specialized Cluster

Toronto represents one quarter of Canada's aerospace employment. One company, De Havilland Canada (DHC), now part of the Bombardier aerospace group, dominates Toronto's regional innovation system in aerospace. DHC was originally founded in 1928 as a subsidiary of the British de Havilland, and started assembling British-made aircraft in the late 1920s. These were small planes used for aerial surveillance and fire identification. Production increased continuously until World War II, when DHC manufactured military aircraft for the Allies' war effort. Over 200 companies clustered around DHC at that time. In 1946, the sudden interruption of government orders reduced employment from 7,000 in 1944 to 200 in 1946 and new companies spun off in the Toronto area. Later on, DHC started designing new aircraft including the very successful DHC-2 Beaver and DHC-3 Otter. New models kept the company afloat until the success of the DHC-6 Twin Otter raised the employment to 7,900 in 1965. However, the company lost ground to competitors and new models and subcontract orders did not materialize. In 1971, DHC employment had dropped below 2,000. In 1974, the Canadian government acquired DHC from its British parent, Hawker Siddeley (the 1966 merger of two British companies Avro and de Havilland). The following year, DHC launched its DHC-7 Dash airliner, and in 1983 it added the Dash-8, a turboprop regional airliner. In 1986, Boeing bought DHC and in 1992 sold it to the Montreal-based Bombardier group. In 1992, DHC had some 3,150 employees in Toronto. By 2002, it employed 5,420 people, and it was one of the largest employers in that metropolitan area. In Toronto, DHC has kept its ability to design entire regional aircraft. Its present models are powered by P&WC engines manufactured in Montreal. By the late 1990s, DHC started producing parts and final assembly of the Global Express, a large business jet designed by Bombardier. In the DHC-8 only the electrical system (Allied Signal) and the landing gear (Menasco Aerospace) were produced in the Toronto region. All the other major elements including avionics (from Sextant Avionique, France), the nacelles (Short Bombardier, Northern Ireland), flap system (Microtecnica, Italy), propellers (Messier-Dowty, France) and hydraulics (Abex, USA) come from abroad. Thus, the DHC supply chain is not particularly linked to other Toronto firms, reducing the potential for major regional knowledge spillovers. DHC needed to control costs and obtain high-quality products. Also, their production is confined to a few hundred copies of each model. As such, they adopt suppliers around the world on the basis of cost, quality and timely delivery, regardless of their location. Figure 3 summarizes DHC's major subassemblies and the location of its suppliers. The figure gives a good indication of the major knowledge spillovers involved in its supply chain. *Even if the regional input–output matrix of large subassemblies is almost empty in Toronto, DHC has served as an anchor firm, the presence of which has created a large labour pool in the region and attracted or spun off hundreds of firms thriving on this skilled labour supply.*

The second largest manufacturer in Toronto is Honeywell Canada, with 1,300 employees mostly in avionics and communications equipment. Even if this is mostly a production site, using imported designs from the USA,

20   *Jorge Niosi & Majlinda Zhegu*

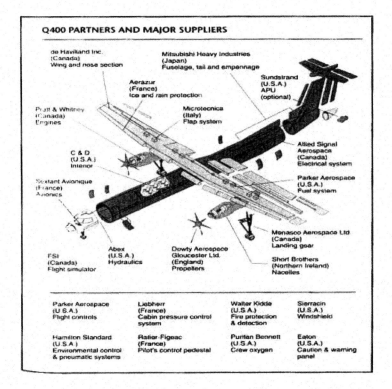

Figure 3. DHC suppliers for the Dash-8

Honeywell has kept some R&D capabilities as witnessed by its patented novelties invented in Toronto. Honeywell's avionics is not intended for local aircraft production. International knowledge spillovers are here overwhelming.

The third major company is Boeing Canada, a tier 2 subsidiary. The original plant belonged to Douglas Corporation that bought it from DHC in 1953. When MacDonnell Douglas became part of Boeing, that plant continued its production of aircraft subassemblies under the control of, and for assembling by, its new parent, which provides US-made designs. In 2002, Boeing had some 800 employees in Toronto.

University research. The University of Toronto provided many of the most skilled engineers working for DHC through the years. The Institute for Aerospace Studies is a 50-year-old institution devoted to research and teaching in areas such as flight simulation and dynamics, materials and structures, propulsion and combustion. It also runs programs and options at both undergraduate and graduate levels. Ryerson University in Toronto also offers an undergraduate program in aerospace engineering. Finally, York University offers an Honours Program in Space and

Communication Sciences in its Faculty of Pure and Applied Science. All these programs have contributed to replenish Toronto's pool of skilled manpower in aerospace. The university–industry link is a channel for some local spillovers.

Government laboratories.   Even if federal aerospace labs are located in Ottawa, some collaboration has existed between DHC and NRC laboratories. Reduced versions of the DHC-8 were tested in Ottawa's wind tunnel. Several parts of different aircraft were designed at NRC. The Aerospace Materials Institute has also contributed to different models of the DHC family (Hotson, 1998). On the whole, however, DHC was a very independent firm with few inter-regional spillovers from and to NRC government laboratories. There are no local spillovers between public labs and industry in Toronto aerospace.

3.3.   Other Major Aircraft Clusters

Toulouse.   Based in Toulouse, France, Airbus Industrie is a European consortium, founded in 1969 with a Franco-German lead, and later British and Spanish participation. Its first product, the A300, a 266 seat commercial plane, had British wings, mostly German fuselage, French nose section and lower part of the centre fuselage and Spanish tails. Both GE and P&W in the USA made the engines. Honeywell supplied US-made avionics and Messier-Hispano-Bugatti the landing gear. Toulouse is the main, but not the only, assembly location for Airbus; the second is Hamburg, Germany.

Today, Airbus has become the world's largest producer of commercial aircraft. In 2000, it produced 311 planes in Toulouse. Airbus assembles six different models of aircraft with parts and components coming from 1,500 contractors located in 30 countries. The largest single provider is the USA with over 800 suppliers located in 40 states. In the meantime, Toulouse has become a major aerospace cluster, with hundreds of firms.[2] These include ATR, the Franco–Italian manufacturer of turboprops, which produced 22 turboprops in 2000. Other firms present in the region are Turbomeca (turbines), Messier-Dowty (landing gear for 30 airframers both civil and military, including Airbus) and EADS Socata, the French member of the European consortium. EADS produces small aircraft and structures for Airbus in the region. Toulouse has attracted other aerospace producers not necessarily linked with civil aircraft, such as Matra and Alcatel (satellite telecommunications). In addition to Toulouse, Airbus Industrie has 12 other European production sites, in Breme, Hamburg, Munich and Stade (Germany), Chester (UK), Madrid and Seville (Spain), Amsterdam (Netherlands), Gosselles (Belgium), as well as Meaulte, Nantes and St Nazaire (France).

---

[2] According to INSEE, in 1997 there were 494 plants in the Toulouse region directly linked to aerospace (INSEE, 1997).

22   *Jorge Niosi & Majlinda Zhegu*

Seattle. In the USA, Boeing started producing aircraft in 1917. Boeing dominated the large commercial aircraft industry for over 50 years, from World War II to the end of the 20th century. It is still the world's largest producer of both military and civil aircraft, and the largest aerospace company in the world. Its main commercial production plants are located in Seattle (WA) and Long Beach (CA). The first location represented some 60,000 (or 75 per cent) of Boeing's commercial airplane division in 2001.

Boeing is somewhat different from other prime contractors, so far as, for decades, it internalized most of its main structural parts. One indication of the vertical integration of Boeing is the high percentage of aerospace employees in its two major locations. In each case, Boeing represents over 80 per cent. Engines from its six different models come from all producers: GE and P&W in the USA, but also Rolls-Royce in the UK and CFM-SNECMA in France. Avionics are supplied most often by Honeywell (USA) and BAE Systems (UK).

The fact is that Boeing has probably produced less international (as well as inter-regional and regional) spillovers than the other major aerospace producers. But the 2001 crisis forced Boeing to accelerate its vertical disintegration and look for foreign partners and foreign locations in order to increase market penetration, as well as to reduce design and production costs.

3.4.   *Knowledge Spillovers in Aerospace*

As the previous descriptions suggest, most prime contractors design products, then call for tenders among tier 2 suppliers across the world and send them their designs and requirements. These tier 2 producers make technical and commercial proposals to the OEM, and the latter proceeds to a selection of partners/suppliers. In many cases, detailed engineering is left to the tier 2 producers, but increasingly often international collaboration and associated massive knowledge flows occur between tier 1, 2 and 3 firms, while local spillovers are less important in quantity and strategic value and relate tier 4 firms with OEMs in the upper tiers. More often than not, final aircraft assembling occurs in one region (typically Hamburg and Toulouse for Airbus, Seattle for Boeing, and Montreal for Bombardier), engine assembly in another (Bristol for Rolls-Royce, Hartford, Connecticut and Montreal for P&W, Evendale, Ohio or Lynn, Massachusetts for GE), yet critical parts such as avionics, landing gear or nacelles are produced somewhere else. Four characteristics appear when these knowledge flows are examined. First, they are mostly international. Second, they are mostly constituted of explicit and codified knowledge. Third, they involve several independent companies. And finally, they are closely tied to markets for parts, components and subassemblies.

We studied Bombardier Engineering System in some detail. The prime contractor transmits its technical requirement documents for each new product to its supplying partners, and they in turn send back their technical and commercial proposals to respond to Bombardier's demands. Once Bombardier chooses its final partners, work starts often for co-development (detailed engineering) of the major subassemblies such as fuselage parts, wings, landing gear and avionics. Bombardier will decide the delivery schedules, quality requirements, performance and other characteristics of the different sections it buys, with the exception of engines. The large assembler is also responsible for the certification of the new aircraft, again with the exception of engines, which are certified independently by the producers (such as GE, P&W, Rolls-Royce, Honeywell or the smaller European producers such as SNECMA in France). The large assembler generates most knowledge and transmits it to its partners/suppliers. International knowledge spillovers and markets for components are created in this way. These spillovers may serve Bombardier's suppliers to address the demands of other aircraft producers.

As for Boeing, the comparison of the official list of over 400 suppliers with that of tier 2 and 3 manufacturers in the Seattle region shows that only a handful of Boeing suppliers have facilities in the area. Most major parts of Boeing's commercial aircrafts are acquired from other regions of the USA, and increasingly often, from abroad.

In Brazil, 95 per cent of Embraer's suppliers are located abroad. International suppliers are responsible for over 60 per cent of final cost (and 38 per cent of final cost is represented by Embraer), thus providing an indicator of the reduced importance of local knowledge flows (Cassiolato *et al.*, 2002).

In an in-depth analysis about the impact of offset agreements on the future development of US commercial aircraft production, MacPherson and Pritchard (2003) have revealed the extreme importance of this mechanism for the international transfer of technology and knowledge spillovers. Acting as an intensive conduit for technology transfer, this practice has created new competitors or/and reinforced old ones. The authors argue that key segments of the US commercial aircraft industry are facing the risk of quitting the market. Table 5 shows the progress of foreign producers' participation in the manufacturing of different Boeing airframes, during the period 1963–94.

4. Back to Theory

A substantial literature on regional innovation systems, clusters and local agglomeration of firms has emphasized the many factors that make face-to-face transmission of knowledge, thus local knowledge spillovers, preferable to international or even national ones. The tacit element of knowledge can be more easily transmitted without distortion in local communication. The transmission of knowledge is also cheaper within regions than between regions. Finally, more channels of local knowledge transfer (such as conferences, participation in local associations, face-to-face meetings, etc.) are available than between regions, where the transmission of papers, telephone and other electronic communication are pervasive.

24   *Jorge Niosi & Majlinda Zhegu*

Table 5. Boeing's airframe production by source

Launch year	1963	1966	1969	1981	1982	1994
Aircraft model	727	737	747	757	767	777
Wings	D	D	D	D	D	D
Inboard flaps	D	F	F	F	F	D
Outboard flaps	D	F	F	F	F	F
Engine nacelles	D	D	D	D	D	D
Nose	D	D	D	D	D	D
Engine strut	D	D	F	D	D	D
Front fuselage	D	D	D	F/D	F	F
Centre fuselage	D	D	D	F/D	F	F
Centre wing box	D	D	F	D	D	F
Keel beam	D	D	D	D	D	F
Aft fuselage	D	D	D	D	F	F
Stabilizer	D	F/D	D	D	F	D
Dorsal fin	D	D	D	F	F	F
Vertical fin	D	F/D	D	D	F	D
Elevators	D	F	D	F	F	F
Rudder	D	F	D	F	F	F
Passenger doors	D	D	D	D	F	F
Cargo doors	D	D	F	F	F	F
Section 48	D	F/D	F/D	D	F	F
No. of major parts from foreign sources	0	7	6	8	13	12

D=domestic production; F=foreign production; F/D=shared production.
Source: MacPherson and Pritchard (2003).

However, an important literature has also emphasized the existence and frequency of international knowledge spillovers (Gong and Keller, 2003). These externalities occur through international trade, international direct investment, international technology transfer, and alliances or acquisitions. We have observed all these types of channels at work in the aerospace industry, as Table 6 shows.

We hypothesize that the aerospace industry—even if it is a science-based one by any standard—is a century-old activity in which knowledge has become fairly codified and can be transmitted on electronic and printed support without difficulty. Most of the literature on local spillovers is based either on traditional industries in which tacit knowledge is pervasive (such as glass-making, shoe or ceramic manufacturing in Italy) or on high-technology new industries in which much knowledge is not yet codified (such as biotechnology) (Table 7).

International knowledge spillovers mostly occur between tier 1 and 2 manufacturers, usually large corporations. Conversely, local knowledge spillovers, and aerospace clusters, are based on geographically close

Table 6. Channels for international knowledge spillovers in aerospace

Type of channel	Authors	Hard evidence	Examples
Foreign direct investment and international consortia	Baldwin *et al.* (1999), Xu (2000), Girma and Watelin (2001), Gong and Keller (2003)	Close to 50 percent of Canadian industry assets are under foreign control. Increasing number of European aerospace consortia	Bell Helicopter Canada, Goodrich Canada, Honeywell Canada, Messier-Dowty, P&WC, Rolls-Royce Plc in Canada. Airbus, ATR and EADS in Europe
International trade of parts, supply chain management, international transfer of aircraft and parts design	Coe and Helpman (1995), Gostic (1998), Prudente (1999)	Exports represent well over 70 percent of Canadian aerospace industry revenue. Imports are in the 70 percent range	Bombardier through BES, Héroux-Devtek, Honeywell Canada, P&WC
International alliances for co-development, international acquisitions	Mowery (1987), Dussauge (1990), Dussauge and Garrette (1995)	Numerous major cases of co-development within and outside the supply chain	Bombardier/Mitsubishi for structures, P&WC/ MBU for engines, Bombardier/Learjet, Bombardier/Short Brothers

relationships between tier 2, 3 and 4 producers. The latter, usually SMEs, manufacture pieces and parts for the tier 2 and 3 subassemblers, the products of which may then be exported to other locations for final assembly in aircraft by tier 1 OEMs. Aerospace clusters are places where most knowledge transferred is not strategic (such as designs of aircraft metal parts, fasteners, seats, carpets and paints and their manufacturing techniques) but usually gathers hundreds of SMEs around one or several tier 1 and 2 assemblers into a specific metropolitan area.

5. Conclusion

Our two research questions, based on theoretical literatures, obtain clear responses. Aerospace clusters show many industry-specific characteristics when compared with automobile, biotechnology and information technology regional innovation systems. Specifically, aerospace clusters display strong international connections rather than local ones; also, the materials exchange within the cluster (often measured by input–output matrix) tends to disappear as international outsourcing of large subassemblies looms larger in the product life cycle strategy of firms. Also, anchor firms remain at the centre of the cluster, surrounded by scores of small and medium-sized

26   *Jorge Niosi & Majlinda Zhegu*

Table 7. Knowledge spillovers and flows in aerospace and biotechnology

Variable	Aerospace	Biotechnology
The main sources of knowledge spillovers	Large designers and final assemblers	Universities, venture capital firms and government labs
The main spillover beneficiaries	Tier 2 and 3 firms	Entrepreneurial SBFs
Nature of knowledge externalities	Codified knowledge on supply chain management: designs, tech specs, TQC, JIT, manufacturing blueprints	Codified (publication and patent) and personal knowledge on biotech products and processes, on financing and management
Most frequent geographical dimension of knowledge externalities	International (companies in different countries)	Local, regional and national (companies and institutions in the area)
Number of personnel involved in typical spillover	Thousands	Dozens
Duration of spillover processes	Years	Years
Level of organization of knowledge flows	Highly structured by major firms, and linked to markets	Spontaneous, and less structured with technology markets emerging
Hierarchy of flows	High	Low
Amount of knowledge flowing	Massive, due to complex products (thousands of documents per product)	Scattered (a few articles/ patents per flow)

producers of those parts and components used by the remaining OEMs within the region. The following conclusions may as well be drawn.

First, large firms dominate aerospace clusters and represent a magnet for suppliers. Originally these were Perroux clusters, but as markets for subassemblies became international, they are now Marshallian industrial districts more than anything else: today large successful assemblers "attract" scores of other firms to the clusters through the creation of a large labour pool of skilled workers. Porter's theories do not easily apply to this type of cluster. Dynamic factors in Porter's model do not correspond to these agglomerations: there is neither local inter-firm competition, nor local demand. Aircraft are world products, and inter-firm competition takes place around the globe, not within the cluster. These are anchor-firm industrial districts in one specific sense: large OEMs create some economies of specialization and more often labour market economies. In these former Perroux clusters, suppliers were attracted with the prospect of selling parts and components to the local OEM. Progressively, however, these suppliers may have diversified their markets in order to reduce their dependence on one major client.

Second, in aerospace production clusters and innovation clusters may not overlap. Products may be designed in one place and produced in other areas as is the case for Montreal's civil helicopters and Long Beach-produced Boeing 777 designed in Seattle. This other type of international and inter-regional knowledge spillover is frequent in aerospace.

Third, in aerospace the role of universities and government laboratories is secondary. They may appear late or not appear at all within the regional system. Aerospace corporations may attract these institutions (i.e. the new NRC laboratory being attracted to Montreal), or change them (i.e. new aerospace graduate programs and research in Montreal created decades after the establishment of the regional system), contrary to biotechnology, where universities often incubated the private firms.

Fourth, inertia due to large sunk costs in major manufacturing plants makes aerospace clusters long-term phenomena. Aerospace clusters are usually everlasting elements of the regional landscape. Thus most aerospace clusters are reconverted from the design and assembly of entire aircraft to the production of subassemblies for more successful producers (cases of Belfast for Bombardier, Lancashire for Airbus and Boeing, Long Beach for Boeing). These conversions also generate major international or inter-regional knowledge externalities.

Fifth, regional knowledge spillovers are variable, depending on the local importance of the supply chain. Most often, regional knowledge externalities are fairly reduced, due to the fact that most of the planes are assembled with components provided by overseas manufacturers. Also, university and government laboratories produce few regional spillovers in aerospace where the bulk of the new productive knowledge is produced within the firms. Thus, there is room for scepticism, as Breschi and Lissoni (2001) have suggested, about the ubiquity of regional knowledge spillovers in high-technology clusters.

Finally, clusters and regional innovation systems tend to be formed by one or two large tier 1 OEMs and/or tier 2 producers, surrounded by hundreds of small and medium-sized producers of parts and components. In spite of strong regional concentration, new poles are growing in the emerging markets of Latin America (Brazil) and South East Asia, based on increasing manufacturing capabilities and the use of market leverage to attract international production.

References

Baldwin, R., Braconier, H. and Forslid, R. (1999) Multinationals, endogenous growth and technological spillovers: theory and evidence. IUI Working Paper No. 519, Stockholm.

Beaudry, C. (2001) Entry, growth and patenting in industrial clusters: a study of the aerospace industry in the UK, *International Journal of Economics and Business*, 8(3), pp. 405–436.

28   *Jorge Niosi & Majlinda Zhegu*

Bozdogan, K., Deyst, J., Hoult, D. and Lucas, M. (1998) Architectural innovation in product development through early supplier integration, *R&D Management*, 28(3), pp. 163–173.

Branstetter, L. G. (2000) *Looking for International Knowledge Spillovers: A Review of the Literature with Suggestions for New Approaches* (Boston, MA: Kluwer).

Breschi, S. and Lissoni, F. (2001) Knowledge spillovers and local innovation systems: a critical survey, *Industrial and Corporate Change*, 10(4), pp. 975–1005.

Cassiolato, J., Bernardes, L. and Lastres, H. (2002) *Innovation Systems in the South: A Case Study of Embraer* (Geneva: UNCTAD).

Coe, D. T. and Helpman, E. (1995) International R&D spillovers, *European Economic Review*, 39(5), pp. 859–887.

Cooke, P. and Morgan, K. (1998) *The Associative Economy* (Oxford: Oxford University Press).

Cunningham, W. G. (1951) *The Aircraft Industry: A Study in Industrial Location* (Los Angeles, CA: Morrison).

De Bresson, C., Niosi, J. and Dalpé, R. (1991) Technological capability, linkages and externalities, in: D. McFetridge (Ed.) *Foreign Investment, Technology and Economic Growth*, pp. 385–439 (Calgary: University of Calgary Press).

Dussauge, P. (1990) Les alliances stratégiques entre firmes concurrentes. Le cas de l'industrie aérospatiale et de l'armement, *Revue française de gestion*, 80, pp. 5–16.

Dussauge, P. and Garrette, B. (1995) Determinants of success in international alliances: evidence from the global aerospace industry, *JIBS*, 3rd quarter, pp. 505–530.

Eriksson, S. (1995) Global shift in the aircraft industry: a study of airframe manufacturing with special reference to Asian NIEs. Publications Edited by Departments of Geography, University of Gothenburg, Series B, No. 86.

Esposito, E. (2004) Strategic alliances and internationalisation in the aircraft manufacturing industry, *Technological Forecasting & Social Change*, No. 71.

Feldman, M. (2000) Location and innovation: the new economic geography of innovation, spillovers and agglomeration, in: G. L. Clark, M. S. Gertler, M. P. Feldman & K. Williams (Eds) *The Oxford Handbook of Economic Geography*, pp. 559–579 (New York and Oxford: Oxford University Press).

Feldman, M. (2003) The locational dynamics of the US biotechnology industry: knowledge externalities and the anchor hypothesis, *Industry and Innovation*, 10(3), pp. 311–328.

Girma, S. and Wakelin, K. (2001) Regional underdevelopment: is FDI the solution? A semi-parametric analysis. GEP Research Paper, No. 2001/11, University of Nottingham, UK.

Gong, G. and Keller, W. (2003) Convergence and polarisation in global income levels: a review of recent results on the role of international technology diffusion, *Research Policy*, 32, pp. 1055–1079.

Gostic, W. J. (1998) Aerospace supply chain management. MBA Thesis, MIT Sloan School of Management, Boston.

Hagedoorn, J. (2002) Inter-firm R&D partnerships: an overview of major trends and patterns since 1960, *Research Policy*, 31(4), pp. 477–492.

Hotson, F. (1998) *de Havilland in Canada* (Toronto: Canav).

INSEE (Institut national de la statistique et des études économiques) (1997) *15 ans d'aéronautique et d'espace en Midi-Pyrénées* (Paris).

Krugman, P. (1991) *Geography and Trade* (Cambridge, MA: MIT Press).

Lublinski, A. E. (2003, July) Does geographic proximity matter? Evidence from clustered and non-clustered aeronautics firms in Germany, *Regional Studies*, 37(5), pp. 453–468.

MacPherson, A. and Pritchard, D. (2003) The international decentralisation of US commercial aircraft production: implications for US employment and trade, *Futures*, 35, pp. 221–238.

McGuire, S. (1997) *Airbus Industry: Conflict and Cooperation in US–EC Trade Relations* (New York: St Martin's Press).

Aerospace Clusters 29

Meardon, S. (2001, January) Modelling agglomeration and dispersion in city and country: G. Myrdal, F. Perroux and the new economic geography, *American Journal of Economics and Sociology*, 60(1), pp. 25–57.

Mowery, D. (1987) *Alliance Politics and Economics. Multinational Joint Ventures in Commercial Aircraft* (Cambridge, MA: Ballinger).

Pan, T. (1996) International technology transfer in the aircraft industry from the perspective of the newly industrialized countries. Doctoral Thesis, Rensselaer Polytechnic Institute.

Phillips, A., Cantwell, J., Gambardella, A. and Granstrand, O. (1994) The formation of the US market for business jets: a study in Schumpeterian rivalry, in: O. Granstrand (Ed.) *The Economics of Technology* (Amsterdam: Elsevier).

Pickler, R. and Milberry, L. (1995) *Canadair, the First Fifty Years* (Toronto: Canav).

Porter, M. (1998) Clusters and the new economics of competition, *Harvard Business Review*, November–December, pp. 77–90.

Porter, M. (2001) Innovation: location matters, *Sloan Management Review*, 42(4), pp. 28–36.

Pritchard, D. (2002) The global decentralisation of commercial aircraft production. PhD Dissertation, Department of Geography, University of Buffalo, Buffalo, NY.

Prudente, R. G. (1999) Strategic outsourcing and supplier integration in the helicopter sector. MSc Thesis, MIT, Cambridge, MA.

Taggart, J., Berry, M. and McDermott, M. (2001) *Multinationals in a New Era* (Basingstoke: Palgrave).

Todd, D. and Simpson, J. (1986) *The World Aircraft Industry* (Dover, MA: Auburn House).

Vernon, R. (1966) International investment and international trade in the product cycle, *Quarterly Journal of Economics*, 80, pp. 190–207.

Xu, B. (2000) Multinational enterprises, technology diffusion and host country productivity growth, *Journal of Development Economics*, 62, pp. 477–493.

7

The Airbus 380 and Boeing 787: A role in the recovery of the airline transport market

John M.C. King

Abstract

This paper focuses on the potential role of the new A380 and B787 aircraft in the evolving air transport market. It looks at the way these aircraft can fit into the overall operations of global market. It considers the alternative ways in which these aircraft designed primarily for super-long-range services may be deployed in other ways within a network context.
© 2006 Elsevier Ltd. All rights reserved.

1. Introduction

The paper considers whether the Airbus A380 and the Boeing B787, have a role in the continuing recovery of the air transport industry and in allowing airlines to develop new business and network models to meet emerging market demands. We examine these aircraft, which seemingly reflect two quite different views of the future of aviation markets, from the position of establishing their commonalities and differences and then considers these aircraft may be used within the broader framework of the airline market. The issues are relevant from a number of perspectives. The aircraft embrace new technologies—particularly the B787 and offer new levels of fuel efficiency with reduced environmental impacts. With unstable fuel prices and increasing alertness to broader environmental issues such as noise and emissions, the aircraft have considerable importance to airlines, consumers and the broader community. Second, the two aircraft appear to be aimed at different route structures but the technical design and the practical use in complex networks may mean they will be complementary yet create turbulence by adding excess capacity in some market segments.

Examples of intelligent misuse are shown by demonstrating how two of the world's most successful airlines, Cathay Pacific Airways of Hong Kong and Singapore Airlines of Singapore use specialised aircraft, the A340-600 and A340-500 designed for super-long-haul services on a mixture of the routes for which they were purchased but also other types of route, mediums or short-haul, for which they would not superficially seem suited. The paper looks at practical matters of scheduling, directional flight times and other issues in relation to aircraft use and concludes that the relative fuel efficiency of the two types means that while the aircraft are complementary to each other, each will have a role in traffic growth.

2. The continuing recovery

The advent of new aircraft types has an important impact on the current and future value of existing fleets. As well as interest rates, current prices and future values, anticipated residual values of hardware at lease expiration impacts on aircraft ownership cost and ultimately, on the fares paid by passengers.

The recession in the airline industry was clearly present by mid-2001, but September 11 was a cataclysmic event in terms of air transport markets. There has, however, been a significant recovery since then although almost 2 years of traffic growth was lost. The recovery is seen in passenger and cargo data and in aircraft orders. Aircraft are being ordered further into the future, with some deliveries more than 6 years away in 2013 and beyond, while other carriers are taking operating leases of up to 9 years. The orders and lease commitments have resulted in changes to used aircraft market values and lease rates. For a selection of 10-year-old aircraft both market values and lease rates have risen noticeably (Table 1).

J.M.C. King / Journal of Air Transport Management 13 (2007) 16–22   17

Table 1
Ten-year-old aircraft market values and lease rate (percent difference July 2006 vs. July 2005 and current base)

	MV CHG vs. 2005 (%)	CMV vs. BV (%)	CMLR CHG vs. 2005 (%)	CMLR vs. BLR (%)
A319	6	7	16	26
A320	2	7	20	21
A321-200	-2	6	9	2
A330-200	0	10	7	33
A340-300	2	-5	2	9
BB737-300	5	7	3	44
BB737-400	2	-10	9	23
BB737-700	9	23	10	28
BB737-800	8	16	14	23
B747-400	0	6	1	12
BB757-200	1	-15	26	10
B767-300ER	15	4	23	48
BB777-200ER	4	8	4	11
MD-11F	4	19	2	28

Note: MV = market value, CMV = current market value, BV = base value, CMLR = current market lease rate, BLR = base lease rate.
Source: Airclaims August 2006.

The October 2006 decision by Airbus Industrie that A380 deliveries would be delayed a further 12 months beyond initial delays has impacted on all fleets of aircraft of the B767-300ER type and higher capacities. Carriers must now retain aircraft they had planned to dispose of and this will force up the value of available aircraft. In the majority of cases, both market values and lease rates have improved over a year ago and are now positioned above their base equivalents. Among single-aisle aircraft, lease rates rose for all the newer generation A320 and B737 family, with the B737-NG running slightly ahead of its Airbus rivals. New aircraft rates have reached $400,000/month or higher. B737 classics rates have also risen, as have those for the B757 that have seen a renaissance in values after a decline.

Single-aisle aircraft asset values are mixed: the A319, B737-NG and B737-300 are rising, the A320 at a lesser rate and the A321-200 has remained stable, although late-2006 lease rate rises are likely to produce higher asset values. The B757 saw small increases in asset value.

Wide-body aircraft have had, in 2005, year on year lease rate rises for most types, led by the B767-300ER, which continues to be in strong demand as an interim type until the B787 is available. A330s and B777s rates also increased although the A340-300 lagged. And B767-300 values can be expected to decline. As B787 series aircraft are delivered to a large number of operators, B767-300s are likely to be sold, returned to lessor or parked. The 787, at least in its smaller variants, is a B767-300ER replacement with enhanced passenger comfort and range.

In value terms, wide-bodies have mostly seen small increases in rates, even for the B747-400 and MD-11, spurred by increasing demand for freighter conversions that have taking up surplus capacity from the passenger

fleet. The B767-300ER was again at the forefront of asset value improvement.

The resurgence of air travel and cargo demand continued into 2006 with traffic, both passenger and cargo, up. IATA passenger traffic rose 6.8% and freight 5.4% while carriers load factors rose by 1.4% in May. Until new, large aircraft orders flow into carriers' fleets, it may be expected that load factors will remain high and may further increase. The International Civil Aviation Organisation (ICAO) released its latest medium-term forecast in June 2006. World airline scheduled passenger traffic is expected to grow by 6.1% in 2006, 5.8% in 2007 and 5.6% in 2008. For the period 2006–2008, the Middle East will record an average annual growth rate of about 10.7% (12.0% in 2006, 10.5% in 2007 and 9.5% in 2008). Airlines operating in Asia/Pacific, Europe and Africa will experience increases above the average but those operating in North America, Latin America and the Caribbean will grow below it.

3. The A380 and the B787

The A380 and the B787 aircraft are yet to come into commercial service. (Technical specifications of the aircraft are given in Tables 2–4). The A380 has been subject to significant delays in delivery resulting in Airbus Industrie compensating customers. In the mid-size range, the Boeing B787 series is due for first delivery in 2008, however there are reports of delivery delays, a result of it is using a number of new technologies, particularly regarding composite materials and avionics. The aircraft is reportedly 'overweight' though Boeing, at the time of writing, has not confirmed this. The aircraft had not flown as of autumn 2006.

Qantas Airways, one of the A380 launch customers, reported in its 2005–2006 financial year results that it has brought to account $100 million (Australia—approx $76 million US) compensation from Airbus Industrie for delayed delivery of its initial and subsequent aircraft. Qantas was anticipating putting its first aircraft into service in northern winter 2007. The technology and fuselage width of the B787 has forced Airbus Industrie to relaunch its A350 as a new type with a wider fuselage and a greater use of advanced technologies. This aircraft, to be delayed until around 2012, is known as A350-XWB. The B787 aircraft was designed as a B767-300 replacement but the largest model crowds the space occupied by Boeing's well-established B777-200 and the B777-200 maybe preferred in its long-range version and regional (standard) versions will be less sought after.

The relevant question is not whether these aircraft are competitive with each other, but rather what is the level of complementarity. The aircraft do different things: they differ in size and capacity and consequently designed to serve very different markets. The B787 serves medium- to long-haul markets of low to medium density while the A380 is designed for long-haul, high-density markets. They also do one thing in common: they fly very long distances.

18 J.M.C. King / Journal of Air Transport Management 13 (2007) 16–22

Table 2
B787 AND B767 series—replacement comparison—technical specifications

	B787-3	B787-8	B787-9	B757-300	767-300	767-400
Length	55.5 m	55.5 m	63 m	54.5 m	55.0 m	61.4 m
Height	16.5 m	16.5 m	16.5 m	13.6 m	15.9 m	16.8 m
Wingspan	51.6 m	58.8 m	60.0 m	38 m	47.6 m	51.9 m
Cross-section	5.75 m	5.75 m	5.75 m	3.5 m	4.70 m	4.70 m
MTOW	163,500 kg	216,500 kg	244,940 kg	123,600 kg	156,500 kg	204,120 kg
Seats	290–330	210–250	250–290	243 (Two class)	218 (Three class)	245 (Three class)
Cargo	16 tons	16 tons	16 tons		10 tons	?

Table 3
A350-XWB-900 and B787-9—alternative comparison—technical specifications

	A350-XWB-900	B787-9
Seating	314 (3-class)	250 (3-class)
Range	8500 nm (15,700 km)	8800 nm (16,300 km)
Cross-section	233 in (591 cm)	226 in (574 cm)
Wingspan	210 ft (64 m)	197 ft (60 m)
Length	210 ft (64 m)	206 ft (63 m)
Height	56 ft (17 m)	56 ft (17 m)
Cruise speed	Mach 0.85	Mach 0.85
MTOW	584,200 lb (265,000 kg)	540,000 lb (244,940 kg)

Table 4
A380 and 747-8—alternative comparison—technical specifications

	A380	B747-8
Seating	550	400
Range	18,000	14,800 km
Width (cabin)	6.58	61 m
Length	73 m	74.2 m
Height	24.1 m	19.4 m
Wingspan	79.8 m	68.5 m
Cruise speed	900 km/h (0.84 mach)	910 km/h (0.85 mach)
Max. take-off weight	560,000 kg	435,450 kg

Source: Airbus Industrie web-site, Boeing Commercial Airplane website.

Both have a range above 15,000 km or about 17 h flight time. The aircraft have similar seat kilometre costs with advantage to the A380. Seat kilometre costs (SKM), however, depend on the number of seats installed. If an aircraft is required to operate a sector beyond its optimal range then the number of saleable seats is reduced—there is a trade off between distance flown and fuel burned thus weight, and inevitably passengers, carried. Singapore Airlines, for example, carries less than 190 passengers in its version of the A340-500 whereas the same body sized A340-300 is typically operated in configurations between 240 and 280 seats.

The two aircraft have similar range and similar available seat kilometre (ASK) cost but they have a dramatically different risk profile. The A380 has a higher capital cost, it requires more staff; not only onboard but for passenger check-in and ramp handling. Ground service costs will be higher—not only are more staff required, the ramp

equipment input (high lifts, tugs, etc.) is all bigger and more expensive than the equipment required for a Boeing B787.

Airport costs are also higher for the Airbus product, especially in those airports where weight-based landing fees are still charged. Those airports that charge extra for air bridge access will also add to the cost of A380 operations as dual level air bridge access is required. In 2005/2006 Sydney Airport spent AU$110 million converting two gates for A380 operations, the figure includes taxiway, and apron, expansion as well as the creation of three-level, three-point access aerobridges. The delay in delivery means that no benefit will accrue to the airport until 2007 when Singapore Airlines becomes the first operator at Sydney, followed by Qantas and Emirates later that year or early in 2008.

4. The A380 challenge

The first challenge for operators of the A380 is to reach a break-even load factor. This is eased by it having fewer seats, but only at a price of higher seat kilometre costs, consequently a higher yield is required. The result of too few seats in the A380 is that efficiency of size may be lost, and/or it may have a higher passenger kilometre cost than an optimised B787. This may require fares to remain at current levels, not the lower fares that consumers may expect. Airbus is reluctant to forecast fares because of inter alia, uncertainty over future fuel costs as well as market structure affects.

The optimal market sizes for the aircraft are different: Table 5 shows the market sizes required for a daily flight by

J.M.C. King / Journal of Air Transport Management 13 (2007) 16–22   19

Table 5
Seat configuration—market size—daily service—70% load factor

Aircraft	Seats	Market size
A380	500[a]	127,750
	550[b]	140,525
	700[c]	178,850
B787	240	61,320
	260	66,430
	280	71,540

[a] Qantas configuration.
[b] Airbus standard class configuration.
[c] Potential high density.

Table 6
Market size: A380 routes

City pair	Uplift/discharge PAX	Growth over previous year (%)
Sydney–Los Angeles	648, 205	4.1
Sydney–London	486,941	19.1
	Cargo (FTs)	Growth over previous year (%)
Sydney–Los Angeles	28,347	11.4
Sydney–London	12,032	19.9

Table 7
Passengers by uplift/discharge by country for Australia

	2005	Growth over previous year (%)
US	1,450,988	8.7
UK	752,587	22.6

each aircraft at 70% load factor for three on board seat numbers. There are a large number of city-pair markets where the B787 can be used and its role can be seen as either a long-distance hub busting aircraft or a frequency builder. Hub operators such as Singapore Airlines, and Cathay Pacific Airways need to operate in multiple time slots. It is not likely that the A380 will be operated with multiple services in many one-city pair markets but be supplemented with B777, B787, or A330 services.

Singapore Airlines plans to use its aircraft on the Sydney–Singapore–London sixth freedom routes; it is a Sydney–London service via its Singapore hub. The airline is a long established and effective operator of sixth freedom services in the Australia–Europe markets and has preferred supplier arrangements with Tourism Australia.[1] The carrier serves multiple capital cities in Europe, including Moscow and non-capitals such as Milan and Barcelona, that are linked on the one flight. Qantas, which will receive its aircraft later than Singapore Airlines in mid-2008, plans to operate it on its Sydney–Los Angeles route initially, but is expected to operate it between the two slot constrained airports of Sydney and London (via an intermediate point), when further deliveries have been made. Neither Sydney nor London, however, are necessarily sole destinations and it is useful to look at whole of country data for passengers to obtain a more accurate picture of market size.

These markets have the capacity to absorb the A380. Indeed, they have the capacity to absorb high-frequency operations by the aircraft. The Sydney–Los Angeles non-stop route, as an example, has 20 B747-400 flights a week by Qantas and seven by United Airlines. Air New Zealand, has one-stop services and Air Pacific and Air Tahiti Nui offer one-stop sixth freedom services as well (Tables 6 and 7 give 2005 based data). The number of one and non-stop services, including Qantas, which also operates via Auckland, is 55 B747 flights weekly. In addition, Hawaiian Airlines operates a daily B767-300 from Sydney, with connections at Honolulu, to Los Angeles, among other points in Western US (data from the August Official

Airlines Guide, 2006). There appears to be room for Qantas, United Airlines, and Singapore Airlines to operate its A380s without forcing a contraction in carriers or frequency.

4.1. Using the A380: seat configurations

How will the A380 be used? It is an open question as to whether it will be used optimally. Sir Richard Branson, the Virgin Group Chairman, among others, has talked of luxury and space. (The aircraft is to have everything except swimming pools!) Of course, the space is finite: the greater the non-saleable space and the fewer the saleable seats, the higher the fares must be to achieve a break-even load factor. Lower seat-mile costs and thus lower fares for a given aircraft come only with larger numbers of passengers through more seats or higher load factors. Although, at 80% year-round load factors, in the peak season, passengers will be turned away because of the directional and day of the week issues, many departures will be oversold and operate at 100% load factor. The limited aerobridges at Sydney and Melbourne, for example, equipped for A380 operations may also mean non-optimal slot times for some departures that could impact on load factor.

A look at the initial use of other new types shows that there were apparent luxury extras. If we look back in history, on the B747-100, and initially the B747-200, the upper deck was used as a lounge (Lufthansa had a bar with a wooden barrel of beer) but this was well before sleeper beds in the first class compartment. The area in the nose, forward of door L1 had between 24 and 28 seats in a typical B747, before sleeper beds today, the same space is occupied by 12–14 beds. It is arguable that first class passengers have more space than previously but the space is personal and the communal space has been eliminated. The saleable seats are reduced by 50%. The few B742-200s still operating as passenger aircraft have seats in the

---

[1] Tourism Australia is a statutory authority of the Australian Government with the remit to promote Australian domestic and international tourism.

20   *J.M.C. King / Journal of Air Transport Management 13 (2007) 16–22*

bubble, as do all B747-400s and 300s. A real customer service issue arises with super-long-haul flights. Passengers become restless through boredom. The cabin design issue is to decide whether, with fewer seats than the maximum, passengers should again be given communal space or personal space (e.g. greater pitch).

The same issues will develop with the A380—as time goes on the seats will increase in number and the luxuries shrink as the need to drive profits from the aircraft's operation will dominate marketing pressures.

It is arguable that the aircraft as planned by Qantas and Singapore Airlines has too few seats to achieve the 20% seat km cost advantage the aircraft is claimed to have over the B747 (Table 8). Qantas plans to have 501 seats in its A380, that is only 11.3% more than the 450 seats Qantas has in its B747-300 in two classes and only 9.4% more than the 458 seats that the Qantas affiliate Air Pacific has in its B747-400. It is however 40% above the lowest density Qantas aircraft, the B744—400ER that has only 343 seats. The aircraft, however, has a higher capital cost and greater fuel consumption than the B747-400 and it incurs higher other direct operating costs, for example, airspace use fees (air navigation charges) that are weight-based. Aircraft pilots have also traditionally had their remuneration based on aircraft size and speed. Thus productivity gains may be dissipated as other factors take their rents.

The use of a low-density B744ER with three-class services at 343 seats is optimised for the Los Angeles–Melbourne route. Melbourne generates reasonable levels of front end, high-yield traffic and can accept a lower seat number than predominantly leisure-focussed routes such as, Los Angeles–Brisbane; Melbourne is 12,793 km from Los Angeles whereas Sydney is 12,093 km. The additional 700 km (about 50 min at cruise speeds), has to be flown against prevailing head winds and so the weight trade-off is, once again, between passengers and fuel. The high-density B744 operated by Air Pacific has 458 seats and is operated in leisure markets, particularly, Sydney, Nadi, and when used 4 times per week to Los Angeles, flies only a distance of 8883 km. The payload/range/fuel issue is not present over this distance.

5. Using aircraft optimally: intelligent misuse

While the aircraft have the capacity to uplift the traffic that is available in the recovery phase in the aftermath of the September 11 shock, it is not clear that A380 fares will be low enough to create new demand. If the aircraft is to have a positive role in the recovery, it is desirable to understand how airlines use their aircraft. There is a concept known as intelligent misuse. Cathay Pacific Airways and Singapore Airlines have specialised aircraft optimal for one route and use them on such routes, but also use them in other ways and on other routes. The idea of intelligent misuse is that it avoids fleet-type enlargement and maintains higher annual flight hours.

As an example we look at a Cathay Pacific Airlines service. The airline has A340-600s obtained for its HKG–JFK (New York)–HKG route. The sector times on these routes are extremely long and reflect the distances involved (Table 9). The Cathay aircraft are used according to the schedule seen in Table 10 and on 2 routes: Hong Kong–New York and Hong Kong–Sydney. The turnaround time at JFK is acceptable at 1 h 45 min. but there are longer turnaround times at Hong Kong and Sydney. These latter times are chosen to optimise connections from London flights, southbound at Hong Kong, or northbound from Sydney, the connections are to London and Continental Europe. Cathay Pacific operates to Frankfurt, Paris, Amsterdam and Rome in European. Sixth freedom traffic is an important element in the Cathay schedule. Longer turnarounds at Sydney also enables the carrier to undertake minor maintenance, especially cabin repairs, though long turnarounds at Sydney all require an aircraft to be positioned away from the terminal because of restricted apron space at the international terminal.

This schedule cycle of over 50 h flight time requires 9 h 5 min ground time, hence to operate New York daily, three

Table 9
Sector times—ultra Long Haul Routes Cathay Pacific Airways

Route	Approx flight time (h, min)
Hong Kong–New York	15,50
New York–Hong Kong	16,20

Note: The directional difference is a reflection of the prevailing westerly winds. Flight times on such very long routes are significantly impacted by en-route winds. Tail winds provide shorter flight times, stronger head winds result in longer flight times. On key long sectors flight time can vary significantly over short periods. Generally, winter winds are stronger than summer winds.

Table 8
Qantas and Air Pacific seat numbers and variation

Aircraft	Total seats	% Variation
B744ER (Three class)	343	
Longreach	358	4.37
B744 (Two class)	432	20.67
B743 (Two class)	450	4.17
B744 (FJ—Two class)	458	1.77
A380 (QF)	501	9.39

Table 10
Cathay Pacific: Hong Kong–New York and Hong Kong–Sydney schedule

Route	Depart	Arrive
HKG–JFK	10.15	12.50
JFK–HKG	14.35	19.55 + 1
HKG–SYD	23.45	11.55 + 1
SYD–HKG	16.10	22.25

J.M.C. King / Journal of Air Transport Management 13 (2007) 16–22   21

aircraft are required i.e. Monday an aircraft departing to JFK from HKG returns Tuesday night and a Tuesday departure to JFK ex-HKG returns Wednesday night and so on. This continuous cycle requires only two aircraft however planes do require regular and unscheduled maintenance hence an additional aircraft.

To find sufficient utilisation for a fleet of three aircraft, one of the aircraft flies a daily night/day time rotation to Sydney. If one of the A340-600s requires unscheduled maintenance and is not available for the 10.15 am departure from Hong Kong to New York, then, the Sydney aircraft is used as the back up to operate the New York flight and another aircraft type is used to Sydney. The choice will be determined on the day—ideally it would be a three class A340-300 or a A330-300 (Table 11) however Cathay Pacific also operates both of those types as two class airplanes. Whatever aircraft is chosen, there will be disruption to the commercial product. Whichever aircraft is substituted there will be insufficient business class seats, and if there is a desire to protect first class passengers, there will be insufficient economy class seats, as the A340-600 has a greater number of economy class seats than the A340-300.

The alternative to this intelligent misuse of the super-long-haul A340-600 on the Sydney route is to acquire another A330-300, configure it in three classes for the Sydney route and significantly reduce the flying hours of the A340-600 fleet. The increased costs are the capital cost of the additional planes and the need to find additional flying for the aircraft beyond its Sydney schedule and the increased ownership cost per flight hour, through lower utilization of the A340-600 fleet. Cathay Pacific has no orders for A380s or B787s but has ordered 20 B777-300ERs for delivery commencing mid 2007.

We turn to Singapore Airlines' Sydney–Singapore–London route. This is, like the Cathay route, super-long. To operate a daily Sydney–Singapore–London service using A380s, three aircraft are required. Whilst return flight times are less than 24 h, the ground time at the points of origination/termination and the intermediate point—Singapore—means that a return trip cannot be completed in 48 h with the aircraft ready for a new cycle. Hence, daily operation between Sydney and London, assuming constant slot times, requires more than two aircraft but less than three. The challenge, for Singapore Airlines, is to find

sufficient viable use for the available hours on the third A380. As the fleet grows, the problem is reduced as either new points are added to the A380 network such as Melbourne, to where Singapore Airlines currently flies one B747-400 and two B777s each day, or Frankfurt to which it flies two B747-400s per day. These are strong markets and can easily accept a modest capacity increase of about 150 seats per day. But there are also short-haul routes where Singapore Airlines currently misuses its super-long-haul fleet that need consideration.

Singapore has been operating a small fleet of its A340-500s between Singapore and New York and the requirement of the New York schedule meant that there was surplus time available. The aircraft is scheduled to operate Singapore–New York–Singapore twice daily, a distance of 890 km, with a schedule time of 1.5 h, or just over 1 h flight time. The aircraft is smaller than the B777-300 that is the mainstay of the New York route and its cabin/class configuration is different, the commercial disruption to the operation is not significant. To operate the A380, an aircraft 2.5 times the size of the A340-500, may not be feasible, in at least one direction of the cycle, the departure times are sub-optimal for the market.

Intelligent misuse is an aircraft scheduling technique that allows maximum use of aircraft embracing routes other than those they are designed for has been successfully adopted by many airlines. The probability is though, that the sheer size of the A380 will militate against its misuse in this context to any great extent. The B787 is seen through its smaller size to have greater flexibility and thus its intelligent misuse is more likely than that of the A380.

6. The continuing revival

Do the new Airbus and Boeing aircraft have a role in the revival of the air transport market? Yes, they both will, but in different ways. Neither aircraft is right nor wrong, it depends on market size and growth rate. However, while both aircraft have similar range capability, there are consequences from making the wrong choice. If the aircraft is too big and the break-even load factor is not reached, then losses will occur or frequency will be lost in an attempt to maintain load factor that will also impact on yields. If the aircraft is too small, because the number of frequencies will rise, direct operating costs will rise, and in many markets competitive pressure may mean that yields cannot be increased. This is a particularly likely outcome for the Australia–UK market.

Dynamic fleet management provides a way to manage this problem. There are at least three commercial computerised systems available to achieve dynamic and real time fleet management, but airlines in the past have performed the function manually. This process is about matching aircraft and configuration to changing market patterns on a short-term basis. Dynamic fleet management works well in a domestic or short-haul international context where open skies, or at least capacity and type

Table 11
Cathay Pacific: possible Sydney Aircraft type options

Seat class	340–600	340–300		330–300	
	Three class	Three class	Two class	Three class	Two class
F	8	8	—	8	—
C	60	30	30	32	44
Y	218	205	257	211	267
Total	286	243	287	251	311

22   *J.M.C. King / Journal of Air Transport Management 13 (2007) 16–22*

flexibility, exist. In long-haul operations, however, there is also the need to consider:

- crewing problems when aircraft types are changed,
- directional market issues,
- bilateral issues,
- code-share and alliance issues.

There is a 'golden rule' of aircraft sizing: when a capacity shift is to take place, the revenue to be earned from the smaller aircraft must be equivalent to the break-even revenue point of the larger aircraft, otherwise, there is no point to the substitution. The challenge is to capture the market without generating over capacity by substitution. The context is one of temporal, seasonal and directional demand imbalances. Using either the B787 or the A380 as a substitute for the other is a real challenge and the A380 has, depending on the configuration adopted for either aircraft, twice the capacity.

7. Conclusion

The A380 and B787 aircraft are not alternatives, but complementary. They can be used and misused in markets than can absorb them. The further they are flown, the faster unit costs fall, the more often a market is served, the higher the yields, and, by flying intelligently, total fleet costs can be reduced. As both have lower fuel costs per passenger kilometre than existing aircraft types of the same broad size, they will help maintain markets in a time of high fuel costs and regional political instability that has produced new travel deterring security measures. The long delay in deliveries of A380 is having a significant impact on carriers, their fleets and their schedules. It was initially thought that the A380 would have been in service in 2006. In 2006, Airbus confirmed that Singapore Airlines will have its first delivery in the second half of 2007 and all other carriers are scheduled to receive their initial aircraft in 2008. It may be that the recovery will have plateaued, especially as the US economy remains uncertain. With major technical problems resulting in delayed delivery the end result may be that the A380 will have a short-term role in the recovery. The B787 will help carriers' costs but may not stimulate new traffic The benefits may go to the carriers rather than passengers.

There are no alternatives: Boeing has no orders for its developed and slightly larger version of the B747—the dash 8—and Airbus has yet to announce a firm commitment to its new mid-sized aircraft, the A350-XWB (extra wide body) that is slated for 2012 delivery. If the recovery is to continue until significant fleets of the two, perhaps three, new types become available, then it will be on the basis of aircraft now flying or enhanced variants such as versions of B777 and an allegedly improved A340-600.

8

The politics of airplane production: The emergence of two technological frames in the competition between Boeing and Airbus

Alexander Z. Ibsen

Keywords:
Airplanes
Boeing
Airbus
Two-party democracy
Frames
Technological philosophy

A B S T R A C T

Economic models of technological innovation, as well as modern sociological approaches to the study of organizations, predict that two-actor markets will eventually evolve into one dominant technological logic. Why is it, then, that the only two global manufacturers of large commercial airplanes have developed diametrically opposed technological philosophies? Based on secondary historical sources, this article employs a theory of two-party democracies from political science and the theory of sociotechnical frames to explain why Boeing pilots are allowed ultimate command of their aircraft whereas Airbus confers this authority to the flight computer.

1. Introduction

For anyone who has ever flown on a large airplane owned by an airline based in an affluent country, the chances are almost exactly 50% that the plane will be made by Boeing Commercial Airplanes, and 50% that it will be made by Airbus S.A.S. At the same time, it is 100% certain that it will not be made by anyone else. Most passengers probably cannot tell the difference, nor will they care about the type of aircraft they boarded; indeed, they are more interested in flight comfort, safety, and reliability, and it makes little difference whether the plane was manufactured by Boeing or Airbus.

The truth is, however, that there are significant differences in the cockpits of airliners built by the two companies. The Boeing pilot is in full command of the airplane and its flight computer, whereas in an Airbus airplane the computer has ultimate control over the pilot. The differences are both visual and technical, and highlight two very different technological philosophies that have gradually emerged in modern commercial aviation.

This paper utilizes the political theory of two-party democracies as well as social constructivist theories of sociotechnical change to explain the emergence of these two radically different technological philosophies. The two systems will be broadly introduced before the theoretical perspectives adopted here are presented. Relying on insider testimonies reproduced in published works, the paper attempts to reverse-engineer the two companies' trajectories that have led to such divergent technologies in contemporary aviation. Although the different technological philosophies have been widely commented on separately, no attempt has been made to analyze the two strategies within one overarching framework. Consequently, one of the most important high-tech industries has escaped academic attention with regretful loss of important insights.

2. Two technological philosophies

With the launch of Airbus's A-320 family of single-aisle aircraft in 1988, and with Boeing's introduction of the B-777 wide-body plane six years later, both companies divested themselves of decades of mechanical flight control systems in favor of

A.Z. Ibsen / Technology in Society 31 (2009) 342–349   343

fully computerized fly-by-wire technology. All ensuing types of aircraft from both producers did, and will in the foreseeable future, rely on this type of flight control. Functionally speaking, there are few differences between Boeing and Airbus. They both introduce computer interpretation and transformation of information between the pilot's commands and the aircraft's physical reactions.

In digital fly-by-wire, the pilot's motions on handles and levers in the cockpit are transmitted to the primary flight control computers via control surfaces, and are further introduced to the flight actuators only after the computers have assessed the command as compatible with the plane's design limits as well as its current course in the air. A curious principle of aviation is that systems of aircraft design and flight control must choose a position on a stability/control continuum. Less stable aircraft are more agile and capable of variable performance in the air. On the other hand, demands on pilots increase as the system approaches more control and less stability. With fly-by-wire, a plane is allowed to give up considerable stability in favor of performance and control due to relaxed pilot-work intensity by computers.

A NASA historian comments: "Aeronautical engineers employed computers in flight control systems not because they represented a new technology and were 'progress for progress' sake', but because they were part of a solution to the flight control problem" [1, p. 128]. This particular technology was first introduced by NASA in the Apollo program in an exercise module used to prepare astronauts for lunar landings. Thereafter fly-by-wire was used almost exclusively by American commercial and military pilots, culminating in the introduction of the first digital (as opposed to analog) computer system for the F-8 project at the Dryden Flight Research Center in the early 1970s [1, pp. 57–69]. The militaristic growth and development of American fly-by-wire evolved from the availability of U.S. government research funds for such projects.

European air travel also had an early introduction to fly-by-wire technology in the Anglo-French *Concorde*, which was fitted with an analog version of the computer system. On both sides of the Atlantic, therefore, the technology was well-known and pursued by researchers. And while it had a civil origin in Europe, Boeing has from the beginning maintained close connections with military aeronautics [2]. Table 1 provides an overview of the current flight control systems of Boeing and Airbus. Details will not be worked through here, except for those pertaining to the two technological philosophies.

As Table 1 illustrates, during normal flight, the computers in both systems interject between pilot and plane actuators to make sure the aircraft remains airborne. This is secured by flight control calculation, which prevents it from stalling, loosing load factor, being short of speed, or banking too strongly. Details differ between the two versions, but the basics are the same. The true difference appears when we move from normal control law to secondary or alternate law. In the Boeing system, there are no longer any restrictions on the pilot's input whereas some still apply for the Airbus pilot. A Boeing pilot is free to choose this control law at any time during flight; it only automatically activates when multiple systems in an Airbus machine fail. The same is true for the direct control law: both aircraft will under this law completely eliminate the computerized command interjection, and pilots will navigate in the same way they would have steered a fully mechanical plane—except, the Airbus pilot cannot initiate this control by him/herself whereas a Boeing pilot can. In the jargon of the airline industry, the Airbus version is said to employ 'hard' envelope protection, whereas the Boeing uses 'soft'.

In addition to computer differences, the cockpits of the two airliners also look distinctly different. By dispensing with certain mechanical elements, digital fly-by-wire aircraft have no need for the classical instruments and navigation equipment that was needed to maneuver older airplanes. This is obvious in Airbus cockpits in the A-320 family and later models, which are fitted with liquid crystal displays rather than analog control panels; also the aircraft is navigated by one-hand control sticks that look identical to the joysticks used in video games. In contrast, Boeing's 777 model has maintained the traditional

Table 1
Comparison of the two flight control systems.

AIRBUS			
Normal Law	Alternate Law	Direct Law	Mechanical Back-Up
		Conventional Airplane	No Computers Functioning, Sidestick Inoperative
Load Factor Limitation Pitch Attitude Protection High Angle of Attack Protection Speed Protection Bank Angle Protection Yaw Control	Load Factor Limitation Speed Protection Yaw Damping Only		

BOEING			
Normal Law		Secondary Law	Direct Law
		No Protections	Conventional Airplane
Pitch Attitude Protection High Angle of Attack Protection Thrust Asymmetry Compensation Speed Protection Bank Angle Protection Yaw Control			

Sources: A-320 flight manual. Flight controls. Denver, CO: Jeppesen; 1993. B-777 flight manual. Flight controls. Denver, CO: Jeppesen; 1996.

344   A.Z. Ibsen / Technology in Society 31 (2009) 342–349

steering yoke, which looks and even feels like the conventional stick on mechanical aircraft. This is because it includes sophisticated feedback machinery that makes it behave as if the pilot's input was directly transferred to the actuators. This function is called 'feel' in aviation. Therefore, the B-777 yoke is nothing more than a gigantic joystick that pretends to be a conventional steering yoke.

Hence, the two manufacturers offer different implementations of the same technology. Airbus makes pilots the handlers of flight computers. This is reflected in Northwest Captain Kenneth Waldrip's statement, made at the introduction of the A-320 to the American market: "It's a dream to fly—but you'd better make sure that the pilot flying it understands that computer" [3, p. 1534]. This does not mean that greater computer skill is required from Airbus pilots than from Boeing pilots; it simply means that Airbus pilots need to be aware that the flight control system will not permit them to exercise any command they want. By comparison, if there are warnings, or there is shaking in the yoke's 'feel' system, or other problems may arise, Boeing pilots can decide on and initiate any command freely. At the launch of the B-777, a brochure advertising the new aircraft stated Boeing's technological philosophy: "The pilot is the final authority for the operation of the airplane" [4]. The statement was, in all likelihood, meant to counter any anxiety on the part of potential purchasers about the new and highly computerized model.

Any system of automation, such as digital flight control, needs to balance numerous factors relating to both humans and machines. Fundamentally, the pre-set interpretation of human input by a machine must, in some way, be matched by a non-fixed interpretation of the machine's behavior by the human. There is an inherent asymmetry in this flow of information: whereas feedback must be enhanced to help the human, the automated technology does not need feedback [5]. In the air, feedback has to take into account not only the interplay between pilot and computer, but also the plane's actual physical behavior. It is this latter requirement—and its solution—that has caused the two companies to chose different paths.

3. A global duopoly

After Lockheed Martin pulled out of the airplane production business in the early 1980s and McDonnell Douglas was acquired by Boeing a decade later, only Boeing and Airbus were left to manufacture the largest commercial airplanes, resulting in one of only a few global duopolies. The industry of airplane manufacturing is highly capital intensive due to the great demand for expensive technology and the first-class expertise of the manpower involved, which helps to explain why there are no new market entrants.

In markets where perfect substitutes are available, economists assume that rational companies avoid direct price wars and try to use non-price methods to differentiate their products instead [6]. Such a situation is likely to occur in duopolistic markets. When duopolistic production involves technology-intensive manufacturing, economic theory further predicts that the competitors will engage in technological 'leapfrogging' by alternately supplanting each others' inventions [7]. Hence, economic models of duopolies expect only temporary differences in technological philosophies—essentially only for a brief period after a new innovation has taken place. This has not been true in modern aviation. Rather, aviation technology lasts for decades. For instance, except for some upgrading of software and flight display in the flight deck, the famous B-747 'jumbo jet' continues to rely on technology from the late 1960s. Therefore, manufacturers offer products that incorporate a decades-long spectrum of inventions. It has been documented that Airbus and Boeing respond to technological innovations from competitors with investment that yields price cuts, and vice versa, rather than following suit in technological adoptions [8]. In other words, the 'leapfrogging' phenomenon seen in other industries is not found in aviation.

Another theory comes from sociology. When organizations are subject to similar kinds of market pressure, New Institutional theory assumes that the broader environment influences contestants equally and simultaneously, with the result that all market actors adopt similar organizational strategies [9]. The market for commercial jets is a good example: although passengers are the ones who purchase air travels, the consumption of aircraft is really done by the airlines. With a few exceptions, mainly in the low-cost carriers, airlines operate with fleets of planes of different sizes and performance abilities. Therefore, Boeing and Airbus compete for the same buyers who keep their purchases for many years. The fact that the technological strategies are so different runs against the predictions of New Institutional theory.

It is possible that political factors distort the picture so that the market alone cannot be held responsible. Indeed, given the political importance of employment creation, export revenue, and national prestige of both Boeing and Airbus, it is not surprising that both companies have caused numerous headlines. At times the market in which the two giants function seems more politically than economically driven. Every few years, one or both companies are the focus of trade disputes from either side of the Atlantic [10–13]. A final agreement between the Americans and the Europeans might never be reached due to the highly complex politics involved.

The political involvement in aircraft manufacturing is not surprising. Economically speaking, attempts by governments to smooth out the competitive disadvantages facing their home company is expected when trade is international [14]. In fact, by studying the few cases of successful aircraft manufacture, commentators have reached the conclusion that only companies that have enjoyed extensive state sponsorship and domestic help internationally have prevailed [15]. Political involvement has direct economic consequences to the producers. For example, price hikes that occurred as a result of political disputes have been documented in the air jet market [16].

However, there is nothing in the political environment that explains the adoption of opposite technological philosophies. Essentially, the question as to whether to keep the pilot in ultimate command or remand this privilege to the computer is

A.Z. Ibsen / Technology in Society 31 (2009) 342–349   345

a question of strategy that does not rest on experience or on political pressure, since both Boeing and Airbus have access to the same technology. What is different is how the two companies have chosen it to function.

The technological developments in the aircraft industry cannot, therefore, be accounted for by either economists' models, sociological explanations, or simply by pointing to political rivalry. Surely all these factors matter for certain parts of the industry, but with regard to the question of the choice of man or machine, none offers a satisfactory answer. We shall have to look for it elsewhere.

4. The politics of airplane production

The claim here is that the duopoly of aircraft production resembles the political struggle within a two-party political system. In a classic model from political science, Anthony Downs [17] reversed the conventional relationship between elections and party ideologies. Instead of assuming that parties win elections based on the appropriateness of their agenda, his theory gives elections preeminence, with the implication that all party action is aimed at maximizing votes [p. 35]. Political ideology serves two roles for democratic parties in this theory. First, it serves the heuristic purpose of making the party appear consistent across different political actions. In order to be identified as an ideology in the first place, the alleged purpose motivating party activity must be stable and internally consistent: "ideologies are never internally contradictory" [p. 113]. The other purpose is to eliminate uncertainty. By adhering to certain principles of action, voters have grounds to predict the likelihood of the outcome of their choice during elections. On the other hand, voters will be divided in the degree to which they are uncertain of the results from election. Those most certain will also constitute the most fervent political interest group. Parties, therefore, chose ideological affiliation in alignment with those groups that have the strongest belief in the outcome from successful elections. In effect, "uncertainty forces rational governments to regard some voters as more important than others" [p. 95].

There is an important parallel to duopolies in this model. According to Downs, both parties in two-party democracies try to appeal to the majority of voters—or the average voter—in order to capture the largest base of support [p. 68]. Both parties will therefore go to great lengths to try to resemble each other as much as possible in political appeal. To distinguish one party's candidate from the other, the party will develop a systematic ideology that is only modestly different from its competitor's. It follows from the majority principle in politics that both the government and the voters are interested in only "marginal alterations in the structure of government activity" [p. 53]. This distribution of the majority principle is, however, only fulfilled as long as there is a large measure of political consensus in the population of voters [p. 114].

The market for mid- and large-size airplanes meets these theoretical requirements well. There is great consensus among market actors as to what constitutes an attractive product, namely, a safe and economically efficient aircraft. The majority opinion is that safety must never be compromised; a dictum adhered to with equal strength at both Airbus and Boeing. Lastly, although there are only two suppliers, there are several interest groups that have a stake in the product design, just as there are many potential interest groups within a democratic system.

Fig. 1 attempts to corroborate the claim that the basic two-party strategies of democracies applies to the duopoly of airplane manufacture. When considering seat capacity, the figure shows that neither company has tried to specialize in only one segment of the market. Both companies have, throughout their commercial duel, responded to every launch by the other by offering compatible, albeit slightly different alternatives. By using the jargon of political science, the attempt by both companies to offer aircraft for the entire seat capacity spectrum is equivalent to the fight for the 'average voter'.

5. Technological frames

In his exposition on sociotechnical change, Wiebe Bijker [18] offers as a demand for a theory of technological development that it situates the object of study within a social context of both users and producers [p. 47]. All existing technology is an accomplishment within a web of social actors who accept the claims to problem solving, goals, and assumptions of the invention. This accomplishment is what Bijker calls a 'technological frame' [pp. 124–25]. Neither one person nor even one side of the market alone is fully able to design this technological frame. Rather, the accomplishment of a viable technological frame is settled in relationship between several social groups, leaving no one fully in charge of the outcome.

Relevant groups in modern airplane manufacturing are the two producers (Boeing and Airbus), airline carriers, engine manufacturers, national governments, pilots, and air transportation agencies. All of these contribute to any technological choices and to developments from both Boeing and Airbus.

5.1. Airbus: technological frame of dependence

The adoption of digital fly-by-wire with hard envelope protection was certainly not a fad limited to one particular Airbus model, the A-320 family. In fact, all later Airbus models did, and will continue to use the same technological philosophy. Airbus affirms its system's adherence to the strictest safety requirements; above all, however, the economic benefits emerging from the new plane's better in-air performance, easier maintenance, lower weight, and better fuel consumption seem to have played an even greater role [19]. The economic benefits accrue to those who pay for manpower, maintenance, fuel, and repair—the airlines. This section will show how Airbus's flight control system is part of a technological frame that has been shaped to appeal to the airlines.

346

A.Z. Ibsen / Technology in Society 31 (2009) 342–349

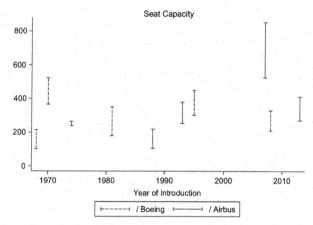

Fig. 1. Seat Capacity as an illustration of duopoly strategy.
Note: The Boeing families are, chronologically, B-737; B-747; B-757/B-767; B-777; B-787. The Airbus order is A-300/A-310; A-320; A-220/A-340; A-380; A-350.
Sources: www.boeing.com/commerical; www.airbus.com/en/aircraftfamilies/productcompare/

When introduced to American carriers, the A-320 was harshly attacked by flight crews. Pilots' unions on both sides of the Atlantic were opposed to Airbus's system, mainly because it reduced the number of jobs, but also due to initial suspicions regarding safety with the hard envelope protection [12, p. 163]. In the words of a United pilot at the time: "This sort of sophistication [hard envelope protection] should be left to the single-seat fighter, where it appropriately belongs and where the pilot can bail out in a hurry when the inevitable occurs—a privilege neither I nor my passengers enjoy" [20].

Regardless which decade one looks at, pilots and their associations constitute a strong interest group in aviation. For instance, Robert Crandall, former CEO of American Airlines, told Jean Pierson, then managing director of Airbus, that because American Airlines' pilots were opposed to the new cockpit, the company could not buy the A-320, despite American's interest [21, p. 98]. A survey of 132 pilots of advanced aircraft found that pilots endorsed a human-centered philosophy and saw fully automated flight control systems as creating a heavier mental workload. In particular, pilots expressed a desire to maintain control of the most complex parts of their job, such as communicating, managing, and planning, especially in high workload situations [22]. The so-called 'human-centered avionics' approach to pilot-work has maintained that automation has the unintended tendency to tune out small errors and create opportunities for large ones; to diminish the workload in the relaxed parts of the flight and add to it in the busiest phases; and to amplify the importance of ongoing communication between crew members even as the immediate incentives to communicate are muted [4].

It was apparent that Airbus could not rely on support from the people who would actually operate the new technology in the air. However, after the Airline Deregulation Act was adopted in 1978, the aviation industry in the United States changed dramatically, and competition between carriers suddenly became an important factor. With a growing number of potential purchasers, rather than a few large ones, the desires and needs of individual companies had to be reckoned with in order to successfully introduce new aviation technology. Although Airbus is a European company, as Gerard Blanc (Airbus's executive vice president for operations at the time of the A-320 launch) testified: "All of our big turning points were in the U.S. market" [21, p. 100]. And, those turning points were discovered with the airlines.

It is due to the airlines' desire for competition and lowered prices that they have pitched the two giants against one another [21, p. 224]. In the American market, much of the acceptance of the A-320 was not a matter of the plane's techno-logical achievements but due to Boeing's reluctance to comply with American carriers' desire for a modernized version of the B-737. According to Airbus spokesman Robert Alizart, "Boeing should have killed this upstart. If Boeing had produced a clean sheet of paper the A-320 would never have become Airbus's bread and butter" [21, p. 100]. However, competition alone would probably have resulted in nothing more than disappointment for Airbus had the company not had something to offer besides low sales prices.

The answer lies in the technological frame Airbus negotiated. First of all, the A-320's fly-by-wire with hard envelope protection was completely new to the market. This feature itself appealed to airlines interested in the technological prestige of having the first mover advantage with a new machine. Most important, though, was the fact that Airbus introduced its new technology with the promise that future aircraft would utilize the same flight control system and cockpit configuration. This principle of commonality, well-known in the airplane industry, offers carriers the advantage of focusing on one type of tech-nology throughout all their equipment. It gives airlines the advantage of buying multiple parts from the same supplier, the

A.Z. Ibsen / Technology in Society 31 (2009) 342–349   347

opportunity to engage with only one form of pilot training, with all the benefits that come from specialized know-how. In the words of an industry commentator: "Cockpit commonality has been the cornerstone of cockpit design in Airbus aircraft" [23].

Airbus's success at the American market was a direct result of their conscious strategy to establish fleet commonality. In interviews with Northwest Airlines representatives, John Newhouse [21] found that American carriers who purchased the A-320 did so because Airbus explicitly announced that future models—beginning with the A-330 and A-340—would be built with the same cockpit configuration. "This commonality in the Airbus family is known to have tilted a number of sales campaigns toward Airbus" [p. 102]. In fact, the A-380 Superjumbo, launched almost 20 years after the A-320, flies with almost the exact same technology as that of its predecessor. Not only does this signal the prescience of the A-320 technology, but also Airbus's persistence in adhering to its philosophy of fleet commonality, and the wisdom of this early strategy.

In real terms, the benefit to airlines of fleet commonality is clearly revealed in a February 15, 2008 press release, issued by EADS (Airbus's parent company). It explains that the European Aviation Agency and the Federal Aviation Authority jointly approved reduced training requirements for flying the Superjumbo for pilots who were certified for all of Airbus's digital fly-by-wire models (A-320 family, A-330, and A-340). In other words, within less than two weeks, pilots who used to fly planes carrying no more than 130 passengers could be certified to airplanes carrying as many as 850. EADS states that this gives airlines significant cost savings since training times can be halved compared to standard rating courses. How is this possible? EADS explains: "Reduced transition training is only possible due to the unique flight operational commonality between Airbus fly-by-wire aircraft... Commonality is a fundamental design criterion for Airbus as demonstrated by the fact that [reduced transition training] is available now for all combinations of Airbus fly-by-wire aircraft in service" [24].

Airbus's fleet commonality design is a technological frame that has fostered loyalty from many airlines. It is a technological frame because the technical details of the flight control system do more than simply facilitate the introduction of new models to the market. Instead, the technological frame actively shapes future company strategy and success. Even the choice of developing new models has been partially made with a view to preserving the technological frame. For instance, Hanko von Lachner, Airbus's general secretary, said: "An argument in favor of the A-380 was Boeing's 777. It was a better airplane than our A-340. But we calculated that the A-380 would help to protect the A-340. An airline that bought the A-380 would be unlikely to buy the Boeing airplane" [21, p. 155].

Airbus's technological frame is therefore one of dependence. The company anticipated possible future technological trends, developed a flight control system it would stick to without yielding, and thereby made airlines reliant on their products if they wanted to make money on the equipment already in their fleet. True, the hostile pilots had to be converted, but once several large airlines were swayed, their flight crew became specialized in the same technological frame of dependence as their employer. Today, half of the pilots in several countries are only able to operate an Airbus plane. And as a result, it is harder to find incendiary or negative remarks about digital fly-by-wire with hard envelope protection. As expected from candidates in a two-party democracy, Airbus chose to affiliate with the one group in the duopoly that was likely to appreciate the company's technological ideology, namely, the airlines.

5.2. Boeing: technological frame of accommodation

The reason Boeing chose a different technological philosophy lies in the company's decision to affiliate its technological frame with pilots. When digital fly-by-wire technology seemed inevitable, Boeing chose to implement its own version, even though it needed a technological frame that was different from the one Airbus had introduced. It took Boeing eight years to produce its response: the B-777. Karl Sabbagh [25] followed the B-777 project from within the company, and he related, "John Cashman, Boeing's chief test pilot on the 77, was instrumental right from the beginning in making sure that the fly-by-wire system reflected the views of pilots rather than relying on engineers". This led to the decision to "let the pilot make the final decision rather than the fly-by-wire computers" [p. 149].

'Softer' envelope protection, which can be overridden, reflects pilots' general attitude to the safety of digital fly-by-wire. For instance, the *Journal of the Airline Pilots Association* published a piece written by a member pilot in 2000 which instructed plane crash investigators to "first assume that the FCS [flight control system]—and not the pilot—induced it [the accident] until proven otherwise," when investigating accidents involving aircraft fitted with fly-by-wire [26].

Regarding the implementation of 'feel' feedback in instruments and retaining the traditional yoke, Sabbagh [25] reports that "Boeing pilots who worked on the system tried very had not to turn the 777 into a plane that is flown by *reading* things rather than feeling them" [p. 153]. Pilots' desires were also taken into account by Boeing in maintaining the traditional yoke. Sabbagh explains that the designers of the 777 fly-by-wire system wanted pilots to feel at home, and they built artificial feedback into the system that gave useful information to the pilot about how far s/he had pulled the lever. Apparently, there "was an almost religious fervor in the way the system's designers left a degree of freedom for the pilot in the system" [p. 153]. It is interesting to note that whereas today's pilots might favor a cockpit that resembles traditional aircraft, laboratory experiments suggest that individuals without any flight experience are more reliable when navigating with an untraditional sidestick [27].

Only two new models have been developed by Boeing that implement digital fly-by-wire flight control—the B-777 and the new B-787 *Dreamliner* (scheduled for operation sometime in 2010). The latter will contain virtually the same digital fly-by-wire as its predecessor, and the cockpit configurations will be almost identical. This includes 'feel' feedback in some instruments, as well as a yoke instead of a sidestick [28,29]. Neil Adams, manager of business development at Rockwell Collins Systems Division (the company that furnishes Boeing's cockpits on the 777 and 787), explained: "Boeing has tried to make the

348 A.Z. Ibsen / Technology in Society 31 (2009) 342–349

cockpit of the B-787 identical to that of the B-777, so a pilot can go in [to the cockpit] blindfolded, touch it, and it feels exactly the same" [29, p. 51]. As a result, B-777 pilots can obtain certification for the B-787 in five days or less. At first glance, it looks as if Boeing's technological frame is identical to that of Airbus in that Boeing, too, aims for airlines' loyalty through fleet commonality. Closer inspection reveals this is not the case.

Of course, the American company has to appeal to airlines just as its European competitor. The important thing to bear in mind, though, is that Boeing's technological frame was developed before the final product was introduced to the market. By allowing pilots into the development of their system, airlines were later presented with a technological solution that was furnished in accordance with the opinions of the pilots. This process resulted in a technological frame that did not attempt to introduce something radically new, but instead something that was compatible with what already existed. This is noteworthy because Boeing explicitly tried to set limitations on the technology they mastered. Here too, the testimony of the test pilot in the 777 project is illuminating. John Cashman explained: "We really want to keep the airplane flying just like he's [the pilot] always flown it. We don't want him to have to learn new techniques... We're trying to keep the airplane so the pilot, when he climbs into it, doesn't have to learn anything new" [25, p. 159].

Boeing's technological frame therefore means establishing commonality between its new models and older ones—and even with smaller aircraft made by other non-Airbus companies. Outside of the military, digital fly-by-wire does not exist in any of the smaller regional jets (as of 2009), or in any of the older larger models. In developing Boeing's fly-by-wire system and its cockpit design, Adams from Rockwell Collins stated: "What we are trying to do is create the 'feel' of a mechanical cable system. It allows the pilots to feel like they are flying a 1950 aircraft in 2007" [29, p. 50]. The direct benefits of this technological philosophy do not really get to the airlines. Airline management neither enjoy the right to override flight control systems nor are they the ones to feel the feedback in cockpit instruments that resemble older mechanical aircraft.

Boeing's technological frame is therefore one of 'accommodation.' Pilots' needs and desires are diligently implemented in the flight deck by the company, and pilots are allowed to command the plane fully as they see fit. Airlines are not forced into technological dependence, as they are by Airbus, but receive new aircraft that behave as close as possible to smaller regional jets and older large aircraft. Leaving aside all marketing strategies and tactics adopted by the company, we notice that Boeing's technological frame has been adjusted to meet the desires of the flight crew. The ideological alliance with this latter group distinguishes Boeing's policy from that of Airbus, and explains the choice to abandon strong envelope protection and the retention of more traditional flight deck instruments with tactile feedback built in. When the systems were launched, Airbus was looking ahead at what would be the future technological norm, whereas Boeing looked back at what already existed.

6. Conclusion

This paper has argued that marketing strategies and technical development alone cannot account for the emergence of different technological adoptions for commercial airplanes. Instead, attention has to be given to the ideological alignments of those who manufacture the aircraft. Politics in two-party democracies (insofar as voters share a general agreement of desirable outcomes from elections) often involve efforts to become as similar to the opponent as possible, while still striving to maintain a unique identity. This identity is secured by ideological commitments with certain groups of voters. Based on testimonies by some authors who have been privy to the technical planning processes of both Boeing and Airbus, this paper has shown that in today's duopoly of airplane manufacture, both companies forged ideological alliances, but each with a different social group. Boeing diligently maintained its commitment to the desires of pilots, whereas Airbus engaged in new alliances with the airlines. The idea of 'technological frames' was used to address the social context in which any technological application gets credibility and receives its final form. Boeing's frame was described as one of 'accommodation,' and Airbus's was characterized as a frame of 'dependence.'

After more than a decade of coexistence between these two philosophies of flight control, the initial debate as to the best way has calmed, which must surely be attributed to the fact that both systems have been proved to work safely. Also, the situation has yet to occur where it can undeniably be determined that either company's flight control system would have prevented an accident befalling a plane from the competitor. The technological frames have both managed to settle and exist side by side.

The question now is: is it possible that the debate will reappear? It seems likely that the next great restructuring of the airline business will again raise the issue of automation. Within the next decade, or so, air travel in the United States might be permitted to proceed at each pilot's discretion, which is called 'free flight' air traffic control. Today planes must follow certain fixed routes, more or less like cars on interstate highways. However, recent advances in global positioning satellites, new ground/air communication links, enhanced collision-avoidance systems onboard planes, and powerful automation could make it possible to let pilots fly the shortest route between two points. This, of course, has the potential of reducing fuel consumption and is therefore highly attractive to airline carriers.

As discussed, both of the manufacturing giants will have to participate in new politics if 'free flight' control is introduced. Air traffic controllers are likely to resist that idea, given the likelihood of some job losses. Pilots and airlines, on the other hand, might favor the arrangement, although probably for different reasons: pilots might tend to prefer arrangements that increase their decision power in the air, whereas airlines are most interested in ways to minimize expenses.

The decision for Boeing and Airbus is with whom they will collaborate for the next technological frame. Whatever the outcome of future decisions about 'free flight' and an onboard flight control system, the technological philosophy will undoubtedly again occupy center stage. In the words of one commentator: "Understanding what human/technology capabilities would exist in a free flight world is essential to evaluating its safety" [30, p. 845].

A.Z. Ibsen / Technology in Society 31 (2009) 342–349 349

Acknowledgements

The author is grateful to Doctor Theodore Beneigh at Embry-Riddle Aeronautical University for help to understand the technical aspects of modern flight control systems.

References

[1] Tomayk JE. Computers take flight: a history of NASA's pioneering digital fly-by-wire project. Washington, DC: National Aeronautics and Space Administration; 2000.
[2] Lawrence PK, Thornton DW. Deep stall: the turbulent story of Boeing commercial airplanes. Aldershot, UK/Burlington, VT: Ashgate; 2005.
[3] Mitchell W. Flying the electric skies. Science 1989;244:1532–4.
[4] Sweet W. The glass cockpit: pilots who work in glass cockpits throw no stones, despite some deep ambivalences. Institute of Electrical and Electronics Engineers (IEEE) Spectrum 1995;32:30–8.
[5] Norman DA. The 'problem' with automation: inappropriate feedback and interaction, not 'over automation'. Philosophical Transactions of the Royal Society of London. Series B, Biological Sciences 1990;327:585–93.
[6] Beckman SR. Cournot and Bertrand games. Journal of Economic Education 2003;34:27–35.
[7] Giovannetti E. Perpetual leapfrogging in Bertrand duopoly. International Economic Review 2001;42:671–96.
[8] Tombak MM. Strategic asymmetry. Journal of Economic Behavior and Organization 2006;61:339–50.
[9] DiMaggio PJ, Powell W. The iron cage revisited: institutional isomorphism and collective rationality in organizational fields. American Sociological Review 1983;48:147–60.
[10] Carbaugh RJ, Olienyk J. Boeing–Airbus subsidy dispute: a sequel. Global Economy Journal 2004;4:1–9.
[11] Carbaugh RJ, Olienyk J. Boeing–Airbus subsidy dispute: an economic and trade perspective. Global Economy Quarterly 2001;2:261–82.
[12] Lynn M. Birds of prey: Boeing vs. Airbus, a battle for the skies. New York: Four Walls Windows; 1998.
[13] Love W, Sandholtz W. David and Goliath: Airbus vs. Boeing in Asia. In: Aggarwal VK, editor. Winning in Asia, European style: market and nonmarket strategies for success. New York: Palgrave; 2001. p. 187–224.
[14] Garcia Pires AJ. Losers, winners and prisoner's dilemma in international subsidy wars. CEPR Discussion Papers 2006;5979.
[15] Hira A, de Oliveira LG. Take off and crash: lessons from the diverging fates of the Brazilian and Argentine aircraft industries. Competition and Change 2007;11:329–47.
[16] Irwin DA, Pavcnik N. Airbus versus Boeing revisited: international competition in the aircraft market. Journal of International Economics 2004;64: 223–45.
[17] Downs A. An economic theory of democracy. New York: Harper & Row; 1957.
[18] Bijker WE. Of bicycles, bakelites, and bulbs: towards a theory of sociotechnical change. Cambridge, MA: MIT Press; 1997.
[19] Briere D, Traverse P. Airbus A320/A330/A340 electrical flight controls: a family of fault-tolerant systems. Twenty-Third Annual International Symposium on Fault-Tolerant Computing. 1993: 616–623.
[20] Fulford GA. Letter. Science 1989;245:582–3.
[21] Newhouse J. Boeing versus Airbus: the inside story of the greatest international competition in business. New York: Vintage Books; 2008.
[22] Tenney YJ, Rogers WH, Pew RW. Pilot opinions on cockpit automation issues. International Journal of Aviation Psychology 1998;8:103–20.
[23] Ian P. Avionics for a colossus. Avionics Magazine 2000;24:20–2.
[24] European Aeronautic Defense and Space Co. (EADS). Reduced pilot training now approved for the A-380. Press Release, 2008.
[25] Sabbagh K. 21st century jet: the making and marketing of the Boeing 777. New York: Scribner; 1996.
[26] Stowe S. Fly-by-wire: a primer for aviation accident investigators. Air Line Pilot 2000;69:18–21.
[27] Beringer DB. Applying performance-controlled systems, fuzzy logic, and fly-by-wire controls to general aviation. DOT/FAA/AM-02/7, 2002: 1–8.
[28] Ramsey JW. Boeing 787: integration's next step. Avionics Magazine 2005;29:20–9.
[29] Ramsey JW. The Dreamliner, in control. Avionics Magazine 2007;31:46–55.
[30] Barnett A. Free-flight and en route air safety: a first-order analysis. Operations Research 2000;48:833–45.

Part III:

Alternative fuels

9

Aviation fuel and future oil production scenarios

Emma Nygren, Kjell Aleklett, Mikael Höök

ABSTRACT

Most aviation fuels are jet fuels originating from crude oil. Crude oil must be refined to be useful and jet fuel is only one of many products that can be derived from crude oil. Jet fuel is extracted from the middle distillates fraction and competes, for example, with the production of diesel.

Crude oil is a limited natural resource subject to depletion and several reports indicate that the world's crude oil production is close to the maximum level and that it will start to decrease after reaching this maximum. A post-Kyoto political agenda to reduce oil consumption will have the same effect on aviation fuel production as a natural decline in the crude oil production. On the other hand, it is predicted by the aviation industry that aviation traffic will keep on increasing.

The industry has put ambitious goals on increases in fuel efficiency for the aviation fleet. Traffic is predicted to grow by 5% per year to 2026, fuel demand by about 3% per year. At the same time, aviation fuel production is predicted to decrease by several percent each year after the crude oil production peak is reached resulting in a substantial shortage of jet fuel by 2026. The aviation industry will have a hard time replacing this with fuel from other sources, even if air traffic remains at current levels.

Keywords:
Aviation fuels
Peak oil
Future air traffic scenarios

1. Introduction

The basis for globalization is global transportation and a driving force has been the growth in global air traffic. Projections by the aviation industry predict a 'business as usual' (BAU) future with a growth of 5% per year. Currently, aviation fuel is almost exclusively extracted from the kerosene fraction of crude oil.

When future energy scenarios are discussed a BAU scenario is also normally included. The most well-known scenario for future oil production is the one delivered by the International Energy Agency (IEA) in its yearly publication World Energy Outlook (WEO). This scenario is based on a growing global economy and that growth needs more oil.

The nations of the world are now gathering to make decisions to reduce global emissions of carbon dioxide. On the agenda is a target for a reduction in oil use on the order of 20% by 2020 and even more in the future. The Peak Oil community also discusses such a decline, but the decline is not based on political decisions, rather it is based on the fact that oil production in the future will naturally decline. Peak Oil scenarios can be said to be consistent with the ambitions of politicians.

We will investigate whether the BAU scenario presented by the aviation industry is consistent with the BAU scenario given by the IEA. We will also examine how a peaking and decline of oil production – whether politically motivated or due to natural decline – will affect the production of aviation fuel.

2. Methodology

The air traffic data in the article originates from outlooks by Boeing (2007) and Airbus (2007), which are in good agreement compared to other forecasters, such as the International Air Transport Association (IATA). The effect air traffic forecasts could have on future aviation fuel demand, if fulfilled, is demonstrated as three aviation fuel demand scenarios. The scenarios are all based on air traffic forecasts, but differ in the projected fuel efficiency increase of the world aviation fleet.

Today global oil production is roughly 81.5 million barrels per day (Mb/d), which is equivalent to an annual output of 3905.9 million tonnes (Mt) (BP, 2008). There are many different methodologies for predicting future crude oil production, all relying on different assumptions and ideas (Bentley and Boyle, 2007). Some are more optimistic when it comes to the amount that can be produced than others.

In this study, oil production forecasts from IEA (2008a), Aleklett and Campbell (2003) and Robelius (2007) are taken as representative scenarios for future oil production. The three different future crude oil production forecasts are converted into three scenarios of future aviation fuel production. The aviation fuel part of crude oil production is assumed to be a fixed percentage in each scenario.

4004   E. Nygren et al. / Energy Policy 37 (2009) 4003–4010

These forecasts for future demand and supply of aviation fuel are finally compared to see how well the demand and supply forecasts match each other. This will illustrate how compatible the air traffic forecasts are with future supply of oil.

3. Historical air traffic trends and industry forecasts

Airbus and Boeing are leading manufacturers of aircraft with 100 seats or more. Both companies construct forecasts, built on market knowledge and trade data, to predict future air traffic demand and other parameters. What is most important for this study is their view of the air traffic development, and particularly their numbers for revenue passenger kilometre (RPK), but to some extent also the forecast of goods traffic growth.

Fig. 1 shows the historical RPK flown and the growth predicted by Boeing and Airbus out to 2026. The numbers of passengers carried have grown an average of 4.9% per year since 1970, and in 2006 more than two billion people travelled by air. Counted in RPK, the growth has been 6.1% per year.

The amount of goods transported by aviation has grown by 5.3% per year since 1970, from 6.1 to 37.7 Mt per year. Every tonne is transported an average of 3780 km. If calculated in tonne–kilometres, the growth since the 1970s was 6.7% per year according to the Swedish Institute for Transport and Communication Analyses (SIKA, 2008).

Airbus has predicted a yearly growth of 4.9% and Boeing a yearly growth of 5.0% (Airbus, 2007; Boeing, 2007). Cargo traffic is predicted to grow by 5.8%, according to Airbus (2007) and 6.1%, according to Boeing (2007). Boeing also predicts that 80% of those aeroplanes flying today will be replaced by the year 2026 and that the new aeroplanes will be more fuel-efficient and more comfortable (Boeing, 2007). In the Airbus forecast, the percentage of planes that are expected to be replaced or reconstructed is 95% (Airbus, 2007).

Both companies believe in a strong Asia-Pacific market, but that a lot of new aeroplanes will also be sold to North America and Europe. The European and American markets will grow at a slower rate than the Asia-Pacific market and some of the new aeroplanes will replace those being retired, whereas in Asia-Pacific a lot of new capacity will be added.

4. Fuel consumption trends

Jet fuel demand and aviation traffic growth are not strictly correlated, since the efficiency of aircraft and air traffic management are improving. The aviation industry actually has gone through a huge development since the first commercial aircraft in service. Since the 1960s aircraft are 75% quieter and have reduced fuel consumption by 70% (Airbus, 2007). The Association of European Airlines (2008) declares that the current average fuel consumption is less than 5 l/100 RPK, and that the modern aircraft consume approximately 3.5 l/100 RPK. Fig. 2 shows the historical trend for average fuel consumption of the global fleet of aircraft together with an exponential extrapolation to predict possible future fuel consumption.

Industry and politicians in Europe have as a goal an improvement in fuel efficiency of 50% per RPK before the year 2020 according to the Advisory Council for Aeronautics Research in Europe (2001). The goal is supposed to be met through replacement of old aircraft with new, which are more fuel-efficient, combined with better air traffic management. The aim is to reduce carbon dioxide emissions but will at the same time decrease fuel consumption. Airframe manufacturers are supposed to contribute 20–25% of efficiency gains, engine manufacturers 15–20%, and improved operation 5–10% (Airbus, 2007).

Load factor is a measure of aircraft occupancy and it is easy to understand that a high load factor is crucial for efficient transportation. The load factor has improved over the years and was on average 76% in 2006 (SIKA, 2008).

5. Aviation fuel

Aviation fuels include both jet fuel for turbine engines and aviation gasoline for piston engines. The dominant fuel is jet fuel originating from crude oil as it is used in all large aircraft. Jet fuel is almost exclusively extracted from the kerosene fraction of crude oil, which distills between the gasoline fraction and the diesel fraction.

The IEA has estimated that the world's total refinery production in 2006 at 3861 million tonnes. The aviation fuel part was 6.3%, implying an annual aviation fuel production of 243 Mt

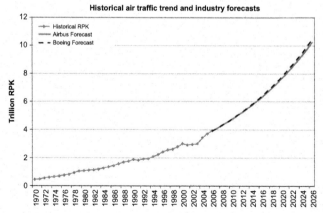

Fig. 1. Historical data of RPK and by Airbus and Boeing forecasted growth. The two forecasts from the aviation industry are virtually identical. *Source:* Boeing (2007), Airbus (2007) and SIKA (2008)

E. Nygren et al. / Energy Policy 37 (2009) 4003–4010   4005

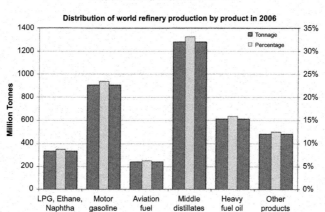

Fig. 2. Distribution of world refinery production in 2006. The total production was 3861 Mt. *Source:* IEA (2008b).

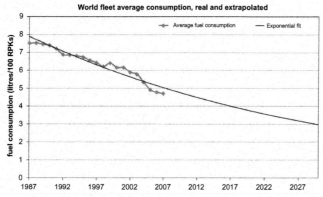

Fig. 3. The historical world fleet of aircrafts average fuel consumption together with an exponential extrapolation to predict possible future fuel consumption. *Source:* Airbus (2007).

(corresponding to about 5 Mb/d), including both jet fuel and aviation gasoline (IEA, 2008b). Fig. 3 shows how the world's refinery production is divided into different fractions.

The type of crude oil used in a refinery and the products manufactured are to some extent possible to vary: two Swedish refineries owned by Preem Petroleum AB are taken as examples of the effect this can have on jet fuel production.

The refinery Preemraff Gothenburg is situated on the west coast of Sweden. The atmospheric distillation process divides the crude oil into five different fractions. The second fraction of about 33% of the crude oil input contains the raw material for jet fuel production. This fraction is further processed in the distillate hydrotreater (DHT). About 14–15% of the feed to the DHT become kerosene (Åhman, 2008) and the kerosene fraction, of the initial crude oil used, can then be calculated to around 4–5%.

In 2007, crude oil input was 4.56 Mt, about 33 million barrels. Jet fuel production was about 12,000 cubic metres, corresponding to 75,500 barrels using conversion factors from BP (2008). A comparison, between the 33 million barrels crude oil input with 75,500 barrels jet fuel produced, gives jet fuel as only 0.2% of the crude input. That is, considerably less than the original kerosene fraction of 4–5% and kerosene that is not sold as jet fuel is primarily mixed into to the diesel fraction.

The size of jet fuel production at the Preem Gothenburg refinery is dependent on various parameters:

- the market situation at any given moment,
- the grade/quality of the crude oil processed,
- the logistic situation at the refinery.

If the refinery would like to increase jet fuel production, diesel production must decrease. This also implies that jet fuel production could be increased without large investments or time

4006   E. Nygren et al. / Energy Policy 37 (2009) 4003–4010

delays. During the year the proportion between diesel and jet fuel production changes and the fuel most profitable at that moment is produced (Åhman, 2008).

The other Preem petroleum AB refinery is Preemraff Lysekil, which is a refinery more adapted to heavy crude oil. Swedish Environmental class-1, ultra-low sulphur, diesel is a prioritized product, which has the consequence that no jet fuel at all is manufactured. The kerosene fraction is blended directly into the diesel fraction to provide the correct viscosity properties. Having fewer products is a way to increase the efficiency of the refinery (Preem, 2008).

The conclusion to be drawn is that aviation fuel production is not a fixed percentage of refinery output. In 2006, aviation fuel was 6.3% of world refinery production (Fig. 2), but in 1973 the aviation fuel part of refinery production was only 4.2%. Since 2001, production has varied been between 6.0% and 6.3% (IEA, 2008b). The volume of aviation fuel has changed a lot, from 114 Mt in 1973 to 243 Mt by 2006 according to IEA (2008a, b).

The kerosene fraction is an average of 8–10% of the crude oil, but all kerosene does not become jet fuel or diesel. Kerosene can also be used to decrease the viscosity of the heavy fractions of crude oil and is used as lamp oil in certain parts of the world.

Simple refinery process changes could increase jet fuel production and if the hydrocrackers were optimized to produce jet fuel the share could probably increase much more (Wernersson, 2008). To be able to produce even more jet fuel new hydrocrackers could be developed, but that would take time.

Production changes in the refinery can only change the yield of different products. If jet fuel production were to increase, obviously the production of other products would decrease (such as gasoline and diesel).

The environmental parameters that define the operating envelope for aviation fuels such as pressure, temperature and humidity vary dramatically both geographically and with altitude. Consequently, aviation fuel specifications have developed primarily on the basis of simulated performance tests rather than defined compositional requirements. Given the dependence on a single source of fuel on an aircraft and the flight safety implications, aviation fuels are subject to stringent testing and quality assurance procedures.

The fuel is tested in a number of certified ways to be sure of obtaining the right properties following a specification of the international standards from, for example, IATA guidance material, ASTM specifications and UK defence standards (Air BP, 2000). Tests are done several times before the fuel is finally used in an aeroplane.

6. Crude oil production forecasts

Attempts to forecast crude oil reserves and future production have been made over a long time period using a variety of different methods and approaches. There are forecasts by scientists, organisations and others.

Overviews of different forecasting methods have been done previously (Bentley and Boyle, 2007; Brandt, 2007; Carlson, 2007), and all of the models have their strengths and weaknesses. Bentley and Boyle concluded that the group of models that predict the peak in crude oil production before 2020 are the most realistic.

An industry task force, including aviation companies in the Virgin Group, has ranked peak oil as a larger threat to the UK than terrorism and climate change (UK Industry Task Force on Peak Oil & Energy Security, 2008). Even the IEA chief economist, Fatih Birol, has recently spoken of the proximity of oil peaking

(Birol, 2008). A growing awareness of peak oil and its imminence can be found.

In a discussion paper, prepared for OECD and International Transport Forum, the peak oil issue is summarized (Aleklett, 2007). The paper mostly concentrates on two oil production models, the depletion model and the giant field model.

The most well-known scenario for future oil production is the one delivered by the International Energy Agency in its yearly publication World Energy Outlook. This scenario is based on a growing global economy and that growth needs more oil. In WEO 2008 (IEA, 2008a), the increase in oil use till 2030 is divided between 1.3% for 2009 to 2020 and then 1% to the end of the period. The next step is to find production to fulfill demand. In this article this 'business as usual' is called Alternative 1.

Alternative 2 is a depletion model, called the 'Campbell depletion model'. The model and the results can be found in a peer-reviewed article (Aleklett and Campbell, 2003). The results have been updated later, the latest from 2008 (Campbell, 2008).

As Alternative 3, crude oil production forecast from the 'Uppsala giant field model' (Robelius, 2007) was chosen. It is the result of a doctoral thesis, meaning it has been reviewed and approved by a person chosen at Uppsala University and a grading committee of five persons.

Future aviation fuel production scenarios presented in this article are based on these three forecasts. Future oil production scenarios used in this study should not necessarily be seen as an example of how only supply constraints may influence future aviation. They can also be seen as a picture of how voluntary oil phase out and oil consumption reduction will impact the future. The cause of the decrease in oil supply is not important in this study, rather the size of future production flows.

The European Economic and Social Committee (2009) proclaimed that the oil demand for Europe must decrease by 50% by 2050, to meet the targets of the climate change and energy package. This would correspond to an approximate 2% annual decrease in oil consumption, which is virtually exactly what Campbell (2008) projects. Robelius (2007) and other peak oil forecasts agree with the climate change mitigation proposals and emission reduction scenarios.

Peaking of oil production or an oil consumption and emission reduction policy may, therefore, be seen as opposite sides of the same coin. In both cases, the flow of oil to the aviation fuel sector would decrease.

In numbers, the WEO 2008 forecasts an increase in world oil production (Alternative 1). The production is predicted to increase from 82.3 Mb/d in 2007 to 101.3 Mb/d in 2026 (IEA, 2008a). On the other hand, in the Campbell forecast (Alternative 2) crude oil production is expected to decrease from 84.4 Mb/d in 2008 to 61.5 Mb/d in 2026. This is the equivalent to an approximate 2% annual decrease in global oil production.

The Uppsala giant field model is based on production from the giant oil fields, fields with ultimate recoverable resources of at least 500 million barrels. Giant oil fields are the dominating contributors to world oil production, accounting for more than 50% of present output. The conclusion is that production in the giant fields determines the world peak in oil production (Robelius, 2007). Four different scenarios for future production were built and a peak in crude oil production was calculated to occur in a time span between 2008 and 2013 or as late as 2018 if adjusted to the IEA prediction for future oil demand. Oil production, as in the Campbell depletion model, is forecast to decrease and will in the year 2026 be 66 Mb/d in the worst-case scenario and 72 Mb/d in the best-case scenario (Robelius, 2007). The prognosis includes new field developments, deep-water production, tar sand, heavy oil and natural gas liquids (NGL).

E. Nygren et al. / Energy Policy 37 (2009) 4003–4010

4007

Table 1
Summary of future aviation fuel Scenario A, B and C.

Scenario	A	B	C
RPK growth/year	5%	5%	5%
Goods traffic growth/year	5%	5%	6.1%
Starting value aviation fuel consumption (2006)	243 Mt	243 Mt	243 Mt
Fuel consumption increase/year	5%	0.3% to 2020 then 4%	3%

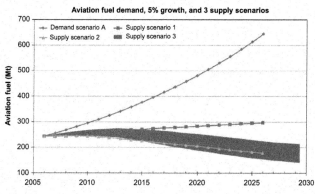

Fig. 4. Demand scenario A is the scenario where aviation fuel demand grows the most, at the same rate as the forecasted RPK growth. *Source*: Boeing (2007), Robelius (2007), Campbell (2008) and IEA (2008a).

7. Future scenarios of aviation fuel supply and demand

In this chapter, the scenarios of future aviation fuel demand and supply are presented, and the scenarios are the base for the calculations of the outlook on aviation fuel demand and supply. The time frame of the outlook was decided by the end date of the Boeing (2007) and Airbus (2007) forecasts. Consequently, the end date will be 2026 for this study.

Three scenarios have been constructed for future aviation fuel demand. The scenarios are based on industry forecasts, both when it comes to traffic growth and goals for fuel efficiency increase.

The forecast numbers for RPK growth is used as an indicator of the growth of jet fuel consumption. All the calculations of future aviation fuel demand have been calculated based on aviation fuel production in 2006 or normalized to that value, since that was the most recent aviation fuel production number published by the IEA. For closer discussion of the scenarios, see Nygren (2008). Demand scenarios 2006–2026:

A. traffic will continue to grow according to industry forecasts and average fuel consumption for the world aviation fleet will remain as it is today. Fuel consumption will increase at the same rate as the increase in traffic,

B. traffic will keep growing according to industry forecast but the average fuel consumption (litre/100 RPK) for the world aviation fleet will go down by 50% compared to 2005 by the year 2020. A decrease of 1% per year from 2020 to the year 2026 is assumed,

C. traffic will keep growing according to industry forecasts and average fuel consumption for the world aviation fleet will follow a curve (Fig. 2) extrapolated from the average fuel consumption of the years 1987–2007 (Table 1).

For each of the three scenarios, we use the three different crude oil production alternatives described in Section 6.

Aviation fuel is estimated to be 6.3% of total forecast crude oil production according to the three different crude oil production alternatives described in Section 6. The production is then normalized to the value of aviation fuel production in 2006, the real value for aviation fuel production in that year.

For the calculations in this article, aviation fuel production is fixed at 6.3% of crude oil production. Varying this number would give different outcomes for the available amount of jet fuel in the future and this will be discussed in the discussion section.

8. Future outlook

The result of the forecast is presented as three figures, each representing a demand scenario together with the three supply scenarios.

With a scenario of 5% fuel demand growth, and aviation fuel production fixed at 6.3% of crude oil production it can be seen (Fig. 4) that demand exceeds supply enormously in the three supply scenarios. The IEA production forecast would require aviation fuel to be about 13.7% of world crude oil production (i.e. refinery output) and the others an even bigger percentage.

In the case represented in Fig. 5, aviation fuel demand is much reduced in comparison to Fig. 4. It is a reduction by almost 5% a year to the year 2020, which almost reduces aviation fuel demand increase to zero compared to 2006.

The much steeper increase in fuel consumption 2020–2026 still keeps demand below the BAU supply scenario. The other three supply scenarios lead to a situation where demand exceeds supply. The lowest supply scenario, the worst-case scenario of the

4008   E. Nygren et al. / Energy Policy 37 (2009) 4003–4010

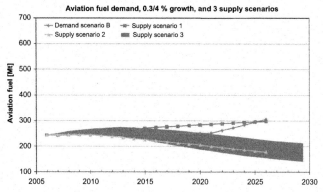

Fig. 5. The demand scenario B is where the aviation fuel consumption increases the least, despite a 5% growth of traffic. After 2020, a 4% growth is assumed and that dramatically changes the shape of the curve and makes it cross the line of the IEA supply forecast. *Source*: Boeing (2007), Robelius (2007), Campbell (2008) and IEA (2008a).

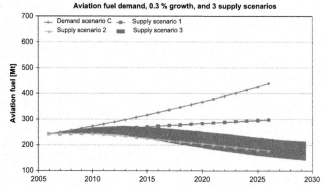

Fig. 6. The demand scenario C is following the current trend of aviation fuel consumption. *Source*: Boeing (2007), Robelius (2007), Campbell (2008) and IEA (2008a).

giant field model, would require aviation fuel to be 13.8%, which is almost the same as in the previous figure for the IEA supply case and the 5% demand scenario.

Fig. 6 represents a demand scenario that is an extrapolation of the current trend of efficiency improvements, and to some point may represent the most realistic development of aviation traffic. However, this trend does not look reasonable when compared to forecasts of future aviation fuel supply, since all supply scenarios end up below the demand scenario with the current division between refinery products.

9. Discussion

Maybe the most realistic scenario, of those proposed, is one where traffic grows by 5% and fuel consumption by 3% a year, following historic trends. That would require a growth for the aviation fuel part of refinery production from 6.3% of refinery output to about 9.3% in the BAU oil production scenario and 19.8%

of refinery output if the production follows the worst production case in the studied scenarios.

9.1. Biofuels

The aviation industry is actively searching for replacements for conventional jet fuel through the use of biofuels. Air New Zealand and Continental Airlines have recently performed two successful test flights (Air New Zealand, 2009; ATW, 2009). Furthermore, Virgin Atlantic (2008) reports successful test flights using biofuel. For the moment, biofuels is more of a problem for the aviation industry due to the issue with fatty acid methyl ester (FAME). Production of bio-jet fuels has so far only been for research purposes and far from on an industrial scale.

What would the effect be on the outlook of this article if the IATA goal of 10% biofuels in 2017 were fulfilled? For example, if consumption followed historic trends (Fig. 6), it can be seen that a 10% reduction of aviation fuel demand in 2017 would

E. Nygren et al. / Energy Policy 37 (2009) 4003–4010

4009

not take consumption down to the 'business as usual' production scenario.

Where should biofuels come from? If biofuels are to be 10% of aviation fuel by 2017, and consumption grows by 3% (Scenario C), 270 million barrels of bio-jet fuel will be required by 2017 (0.7 Mb/d). That is, more biofuels than is currently produced in total, when all transport biofuels counted for 0.6 Mb/d (219 million barrels in total for 2006), if adjusted for energy content (IEA, 2008b). Another thing to take into account is that about 83% of the biofuel produced was ethanol, which is not suitable for aviation traffic. The rest is biodiesel that theoretically could probably be further refined to jet fuel (Daggett et al., 2006). Aviation biofuel production is still in practice zero.

The IEA (2008a) believes a growth of biofuel consumption of 6.8% a year from 2006–2030, predicting a biofuel production of about 1.3 Mb/d in 2017. Around one-fifth of that is forecast to be biodiesel, which corresponds to less than 0.3 Mb/d. This value must be compared to the 0.7 Mb/d of bio-jet fuels needed. All of these numbers make it hard to believe that the aviation industry could achieve 10% biofuel by 2017 starting from zero in 2008.

The second highest ranked renewable energy company, according to Biofuel Digest, Sapphire Energy, state that they can produce 300–350 b/d of aviation fuel from algae in three years (ATW, 2009). However, this capacity is negligible compared to the aim of 10% bio-jet fuel utilization and would require a crash course development program to achieve the necessary production volumes.

Today, the increasing addition of biofuels to diesel is a problem for the aviation industry (Gallaher, 2008). One of the more common biodiesels is fatty acid methyl ester. FAME is not a hydrocarbon and no non-hydrocarbons are allowed in jet fuel, except for approved additives as defined in the various international specifications, such as DEF STAN 91-91 and ASTM D 1655. Consequently, biofuels-contaminated jet fuel cannot be utilized due to jet fuel standards (JIG, 2008a).

The problem with FAME is that it has the ability to be absorbed by metal surfaces (JIG, 2008a). Diesel and jet fuel are often transported in a joint transport system making it possible for FAME stuck in tanks, pipelines and pumps to desorb to the jet fuel. The limit for contamination of jet fuel with FAME is 5 ppm (JIG, 2008b). FAME can be picked up in any point of the supply chain, making 5 ppm a difficult limit and, therefore, the introduction of biofuels to the diesel fraction has had a negative impact upon jet fuel supply security (Gallaher, 2008).

Work is ongoing to be able to approve 100 ppm of FAME in jet fuel to ease the pressure on the oil product transport systems. Results from fuel analysis often arrive after delivery of fuel, meaning that airlines need to know how to act if the fuel is declared contaminated (Farmery, 2008). To help avoid FAME contamination there are several procedures that should be followed, for example, there should always be a buffer transport between biodiesel and jet fuel in pipeline systems and road tankers should be cleansed (JIG, 2008a).

9.2. Crude oil production outlook

Can the 'business as usual' scenario be too positive regarding future oil production? After the publication of World Energy Outlook 2008 (IEA, 2008a), some remarkable statements from IEA chief economist, Fatih Birol, have been made. Petroleum newspaper Upstream (2008) writes that IEA predict oil prices to rebound to around 100$ in 2010–2015. Furthermore, Birol (2008) has also stated that an oil peak could occur in 2020. The IEA (2008a) states that enough oil reserves are available for production, if the necessary investments are made. The recent

statements may probably be seen as a sign that the needed investments are not being made fast enough.

The European Union (EU) recognises that aviation contributes to about 2% of man-made CO_2 emissions, and therefore, aviation cannot be considered a major contributor to climate change (EU, 2009). Still a reduction of aviations impact on climate change is requested. The fuel consumption and, consequently, the CO_2 emissions are supposed to decrease by 50% by 2020 (demand scenario B in this article). The EU (2009) is discussing to include aviation in the EU emission trading scheme, as suggested by the International Civil Aviation Organization (2009). IATA (2009) would also like a scheme for reduction of emissions, but wishes it to be global so that country specific taxes could be avoided. Furthermore, IATA (2009) argues that aviation should be treated in proportion to its contribution to climate change and not unfairly punished economically.

9.3. Refinery production

Is there any room for a larger part of aviation fuel from crude oil? In the analysis, we have chosen 6.3%, the aviation fuel production fraction for 2006, to be a fixed aviation fuel fraction for the period 2008–2026. Historically, this number has increased from 4.2% to 6.3%. Technically, aviation fuel is part of the middle distillate fraction together with diesel. An increasingly strong global demand for diesel can make it hard to increase the aviation fraction and we could consequently expect that it will be less in the future.

Technically, it is possible to make aviation fuel a larger part of the petroleum product mix with proper investments, but there are no political visions or stimulus as there are no great awareness of the challenges to come.

9.4. Efficiency increases

Contrary to the car industry, the aviation industry has continually made improvement in aircraft efficiency. Between 1970 and 2007, efficiency has been improved by 70% roughly equivalent to 3% per year. Is it realistic to expect a subsequent 50%, or a 5% per year, reduction of aviation fuel consumption to be achieved by 2020? We believe that scenario B is unlikely to happen and that scenario C with an extrapolation of the trends during the last 20 years is the most probable scenario.

10. Conclusion

The most positive outlook for crude oil production in this study is still a very pessimistic scenario for the aviation industry. Only with a very successful development of fuel efficiency increases that more or less keeps the aviation fuel demand at current levels could it be possible for traffic to grow by 5% a year.

The aviation industry outlook on future traffic does not look realistic in the light of future crude oil production, taken that the aviation fuel percentage of refinery output cannot be increased hugely. The outlook of this article suggests that the aviation industry needs to rethink their position when it comes to future growth in air traffic, since it is dependent on the availability of conventional aviation fuel originating from crude oil. Even the 'business as usual' scenario of crude oil production requires big efficiency increases to the aviation fleet to maintain current rates of traffic growth.

The worst-case supply scenario creates a lack of aviation fuel in all of the demand scenarios discussed. The percentage of aviation fuel of produced oil products would need to increase from 6.3% up

4010   E. Nygren et al. / Energy Policy 37 (2009) 4003–4010

to 30% of crude oil production in the most diverse case (Fig. 4). Alternative fuels can play a role in increasing the amount of available fuel, but it seems unrealistic that it could provide a large contribution soon, taking into account the work still to be done in that area. The possibility of biofuels replacing conventional jet fuel is limited, considering the large amount that would be needed. However, the development of bio-jet fuel is still important for the future aviation industry.

A post-Kyoto political agenda to reduce oil consumption will have the same effect on aviation fuel production as a natural decline in the crude oil production. In the World Economic Outlook by the International Monetary Fund (IMF), the world real GDP growth will be back to be between 4% and 5% in 2011 (IMF, 2009). Political decisions or decline in aviation fuel production will affect future GDP growth, so it is advisable to revise economic outlooks and include a more holistic view of economic growth where fuel requirement and supply outlooks also are integrated.

Moriarty and Honnery (2008) speculate that the future of transportation is low-mobility, since transport is a derived demand. In a future world with decreasing supply of fuel, the current BAU-outlooks from within the aviation industry are unrealistic. The industry might be forced to adapt to a future with less aviation transport and the new challenges that would bring. Consequently, we conclude that *"when the winds of change are blowing, some seek shelter while others set sails for new oceans"*.

Acknowledgements

We would like to give our sincerest appreciation to Mike Farmery, global fuel technical and quality manager of Shell Aviation Limited, for his valuable comments and suggestions on fuel related material. We would also like to thank Robert Hirsch for constructive discussions. One of us, E.N., would like to thank Stena AB for support during part of the work. Finally, we would like to thank Simon Snowden of Liverpool University for proof-reading.

References

Advisory Council for Aeronautics Research in Europe, 2001. Meeting society's needs and winning global leadership, January 2001, see also: ⟨http://www.acare4europe.com/docs/Vision%202020.pdf⟩.
Air BP, 2000. Handbook of products, see also: ⟨http://www.bp.com/liveassets/bp_internet/aviation/air_bp/STAGING/local_assets/downloads_pdfs/a/air_bp_products_handbook_04004_1.pdf⟩ (accessed February 2008).
Air New Zealand, 2009. Biofuel Test Flight, ⟨http://www.airnewzealand.co.uk/aboutus/biofuel-test/default.htm⟩ (accessed 2009-01-16).
Airbus, 2007. Global Market Forecast 2007–2026, see also: ⟨http://www.airbus.com/en/corporate/gmf/⟩.
Aleklett, K., 2007. Peak Oil and the Evolving Strategies of Oil Importing and Exporting Countries, OECD Transport Forum discussion paper no. 2007-17, December 2007. See also: ⟨http://www.internationaltransportforum.org/jtrc/DiscussionPapers/DiscussionPaper17.pdf⟩.
Aleklett, K., Campbell, C., 2003. The peak and decline of world oil and gas production. Minerals & Energy—Raw Material Report 18, 5–20.
Association of European Airlines (AEA), 2008, Aviation and Environment: Facts, achievements, goals. See also: ⟨http://files.aea.be/Downloads/Avition_and_Environment.pdf⟩.
Åhman, C., 2008. Personal communication, Preemraff Göteborg.
ATW, 2009. Continental follows with algae, news article by Jerome Green Chandler, Eco-Aviation Today, January 12, 2009, Page 2, see also: ⟨http://www.atwonline.com/channels/eco/article.html?articleID=2613⟩.
Bentley, R., Boyle, G., 2007. Global oil production: forecasts and methodologies. Environment and Planning B: Planning and Design 34, 609–626.
Birol, F., 2008. Statements in an interview by George Monbiot, The Guardian, 15 December 2008, see also: ⟨http://www.guardian.co.uk/business/2008/dec/15/oil-peak-energy-iea⟩.
Boeing, 2007. Current Market Outlook 2007, Summary outlook, see also: ⟨http://www.boeing.com/commercial/cmo⟩ (accessed March 2008).
BP, 2008. Statistical Review of World Energy 2008, See also: ⟨http://www.bp.com⟩.
Brandt, A.R., 2007. Testing hubbert. Energy Policy 35, 3074–3088.
Campbell, C., 2008. Oil and gas production profiles 2008 base case, December 2008, see also: ⟨http://www.aspo-ireland.org/contentFiles/newsletterPDFs/newsletter96_200812.pdf⟩.
Carlson, W.B., 2007. Analysis of world oil production based on the fitting of the logistic function and its derivatives. Energy Sources, Part B: Economics, Planning, and Policy 2, 421–428.
Daggett D., Hadaller R., Hendricks R., Walther R., 2006. Alternative fuels and their potential impact on aviation, paper presented at the 25th Congress of the International Council of the Aeronautical Sciences (ICAS) hosted by the German Society for Aeronautics and Astronautics, Hamburg, Germany, September 3–8, 2006, NASA TM 2006-214365, see also: ⟨http://gltrs.grc.nasa.gov/reports/2006/TM-2006-214365.pdf⟩.
European Economic and Social Committee, 2009. European demand for oil must be reduced by over 50% by 2050! press release from 9 January 2009, CES/09/1, see also: ⟨http://europa.eu/rapid/pressReleasesAction.do?reference=CES/09/1⟩.
EU, 2009. Is civil aviation a major CO2 problem? See also: ⟨http://ec.europa.eu/transport/air/environment/environment_en.htm⟩.
Farmery, M., 2008. FAME contamination in jet fuel-action needed, Presentation at IATA, Shanghai, November 2008.
Gallaher, L., 2008. Supply Chain Study potential carryover of FAME into jet, Presentation at IATA, Shanghai November 2008.
IMF, 2009, April. World Economic Outlook, ⟨http://www.imf.org/external/pubs/ft/weo/2009/01/pdf/text.pdf⟩.
International Air Transport Association (IATA), 2009. Focus on Reducing Emissions-IATA Calls for Governments-Industry Alignment on Emissions, press release from 31 march 2009, see also: ⟨http://www.iata.org/pressroom/pr/2009-03-31-01.htm⟩.
International Civil Aviation Organization, 2009. Statements from the environment agenda, see also: ⟨http://www.icao.int/env/⟩.
International Energy Agency, 2008a. World Energy Outlook 2008.
International Energy Agency, 2008b. Key World Energy Statistics 2008 and previous editions, see also: ⟨http://www.iea.org/textbase/nppdf/free/2008/key_stats_2008.pdf⟩.
Joint Inspection Group, 2008a. Product Quality, Bulletin no. 21, November 2008.
Joint Inspection Group, 2008b. Product Quality, Bulletin no. 20, October 2008.
Moriarty, P., Honnery, D., 2008. Low-mobility: the future of transport. Futures 40, 865–872.
Nygren, E., 2008. Aviation Fuels and Peak Oil, diploma thesis from Uppsala University, see also: ⟨http://www.tsl.uu.se/uhdsg/Publications/Aviationfuels.pdf⟩.
Preem, 2008. About our refineries, see also: ⟨http://www.preem.se⟩ (accessed April 2008).
Robelius, F., 2007. Giant Oil Fields—The Highway to Oil: Giant Oil Fields and their Importance for Future Oil Production, doctoral thesis from the Faculty of Science and Technology, see also: ⟨http://publications.uu.se/abstract.xsql?dbid=7625⟩.
Swedish Institute for Transport and Communication Analyses (SIKA), 2008. Civil Aviation 2007, see also: ⟨http://www.sika-institute.se/Doclib/2008/Statistik/ss_2008_12.pdf⟩.
Upstream, 2008. IEA sees $100 in 2010 to 2015, see also: ⟨http://www.upstreamonline.com/live/article168774.ece⟩.
UK Industry Task Force on Peak Oil & Energy Security, 2008. The Oil Crunch-securing the UK's energy future, October 2008, see also: ⟨http://peakoil.solarcentury.com/wp-content/uploads/2008/10/oil-report-final.pdf⟩.
Virgin Atlantic, 2008. Biofuel demonstration, see also: ⟨http://www.virgin-atlantic.com/en/gb/allaboutus/environment/biofuel.jsp⟩ (accessed 2009-01-24).
Wernersson, C., 2008. Personal communication, Shell Raffinaderi AB.

10

The market development of aviation biofuel: Drivers and constraints

Per Gegg, Lucy Budd, Stephen Ison

ABSTRACT

Aviation biofuel is technically viable and nearing the commercial stage. In the last ten years, biofuels have moved from relative obscurity to a point where certain types of fuel have become fully certified for commercial use in up to 50% blends with standard jet fuel and commercial partnerships between airlines and biofuel producers are being established. Yet despite numerous successful test flights, aviation biofuels have yet to become widely commercialised. Drawing on the findings of in-depth interviews with leading global aviation biofuel stakeholders undertaken between October and December 2011, this paper identifies and examines the perceived factors that are affecting the market development of biofuels for aviation. The paper illustrates that market development is being driven by the combined effects of rising jet fuel prices, the potential future impact of emissions legislation and concerns about fuel (in)security. However, commercialisation is being constrained by high production costs, limited availability of suitable feedstocks, uncertainty surrounding the definition of the sustainability criteria, and a perceived lack of both national and international political and policy support for aviation biofuel. The implications of these findings for commercial aviation and the future development of global market for aviation biofuel market are discussed.

Keywords:
Aviation
Biofuel
Market development

1. Introduction

The need to develop commercially viable alternatives to traditional fossil-based liquid fuels for commercial aircraft is intensifying. The rising price of crude oil, potential new carbon emissions legislation, the negative environmental externality effects resulting from fossil-fuel consumption (including, but not limited to, atmospheric pollution and anthropogenic climate change), and growing global demand for air travel have collectively motivated research into sustainable fuel alternatives (Köhler et al., 2014; Nair and Paulose, 2014). Liquid biofuels are at the forefront of these developments as they have the potential to confer significant economic and environmental benefits and can be 'dropped in' to existing infrastructure. Worldwide, research and development into new types of alternative fuel has grown significantly during the last 10—20 years as a result of the use of mandates, tax breaks, subsidies and advantageous funding arrangements between biofuel producers and national governments (Panoutsou et al., 2013). This has resulted in commercial markets for liquid biofuels being established in Europe, North America, South America, Asia, Asia Pacific and Africa (Köhler et al., 2014).

Until recently, biofuels were predominantly used by the road transport sector as direct and more environmentally friendly substitutes for conventional petrol and diesel (see Freedman, 2014). Although the rail and maritime sectors have also begun to experiment with biofuels as a way to reduce the carbon intensity of their operations (Florentinus et al., 2012), some of the most dramatic developments have occurred within the commercial aviation sector. The aviation industry faces a unique and increasingly acute set of environmental and energy challenges and many airlines are currently pursuing biofuels as a means to reduce their oil dependency, lower their greenhouse gas emissions and improve their environmental performance. As the unprecedented high price of oil of $147USD a barrel in 2008 demonstrated, the air transport industry is particularly vulnerable to rising and volatile oil prices. Fuel constitutes a major component of an airline's operating cost. In the last 10 years, fuel costs have doubled to account for 28% of airline operating expenses in 2013 (PWC, 2013). As a result of the high oil price, a number of airlines worldwide were forced to declare bankruptcy during 2008 and hundreds of thousands of passengers had their travel plans disrupted. In addition to fuel price concerns, the air transport industry is also under increasing public and political pressure to address its environmental impacts (see Bows-Larkin and Anderson, 2013). In response, the industry is making a concerted effort to reduce greenhouse gas emissions (particularly of carbon dioxide) by investing in more fuel efficient technologies

P. Gegg et al. / Journal of Air Transport Management 39 (2014) 34–40
35

and environmentally friendly operating practices (Budd and Budd, 2013) as well as in alternative fuels sources to reduce emissions (Winchester et al., 2013a).

IATA has set a target for the global aviation industry to achieve carbon neutral growth by 2020 and reduce CO_2 emissions by 50% relative to 2005 levels by 2050 (IATA, 2009). In the US the Federal Aviation Administration (FAA) aims for 1 billion gallons of jet fuel to come from alternative renewable sources from 2018, representing 1.7% of predicted fuel consumption of US carriers (FAA, 2011; Winchester et al., 2013b). Moreover, alternative jet fuels can both qualify under the Renewable Fuels Standard in the US, and under the EU Renewable Energy Directive, although there is no specific mandate for jet fuel. Crucially, the industry has few short-term technological options at its disposal which would confer the required emissions reductions while simultaneously reducing oil dependency and protecting growth (Blakey et al., 2011; CCC, 2009). While some efficiency gains can be delivered through fleet renewal and enhanced air traffic management procedures such as continuous decent approaches and precision area navigation (P-RNAV) these measures will not, by themselves, be sufficient to deliver the drastic reductions in emissions which are required and additional interventions are required. At present, virtually all of the world's commercial aircraft are powered by engines that burn Jet A/A1 fuel and produce a range of pollution species as by-products of combustion and incomplete combustion. Although alternative propulsion technologies, such as hydrogen fuel cells and solar power, have been proposed and subjected to a degree of testing, and they are not yet certified for commercial use. Liquefied natural gas has also been produced as a future aviation fuel since it offers lower fuel burn and emissions and potential cost and availability benefits (Stephenson, 2012). One of the most attractive short-to-medium term options for the air transport industry is, however, to continue to operate existing engines and aircraft but use lower carbon fuels. As this will show, although certification for 50% blends of FT biofuels achieved in 2009 and HEFA fuels in 2011, many challenges to widespread commercialisation remain (IATA, 2013). The paper begins by reviewing the current state of aviation biofuel testing and research worldwide. This is followed by a description of the data collection method that was employed, an examination of the key findings, and a discussion surrounding their implications for commercial aviation and the continued development of aviation biofuels.

2. Developments in aviation biofuel

The term biofuel refers to any form of renewable energy that is derived from biomass.

Biofuels can be solid (e.g. wood), liquid or gas and can be produced from an array of feedstocks, wastes and production processes. There are two basic forms; primary biofuel and secondary biofuel. Primary biofuels, such as wood chippings and agricultural waste, are the most basic form of bioenergy and require no additional processing (see Naik et al., 2010). Secondary biofuels are made from biomass that has been processed to change its chemical composition. These processes include fermenting sugar crops to produce ethanol, pressing oil rich crops to produce vegetable oil, superheating biomass to create combustible gas and combining different types of liquid or gaseous biofuel together.

However, in order to produce biofuels that have the required chemical and flow characteristics for use in aircraft engines, advanced processing techniques have need to be developed (see Chuck and Donnelly, 2014). The main processes of producing aviation biofuel involve either hydrotreating vegetable oils to make hydrotreated renewable (HEFA) fuels or performing gasification of biomass feedstocks using the Fischer–Tropsch process (FT) (CCC,

2009). Both techniques produce a bio-derived paraffinic hydrocarbon known as Bio-SPK. Crucially, the resulting Bio-SPK not only has similar chemical properties and comparable flow characteristics at low temperatures to standard commercial Jet A/A1 fuel but it also does not contain Fatty Acid Methyl Esters (FAME), water, metal particles or other contaminants. To ensure the safety and performance of Bio-SPK fuels, a lengthy period of testing commenced. Trials on commercial aircraft followed from 2008 onwards and involved different airframe and engine combinations as well as a variety of different feedstocks and blend ratios.

As a result of extensive trials, ASTM (formerly known as the American Society for Testing and Materials, a global leader in the development of international voluntary standards) certification for BtL and HEFA fuels was granted for commercial purposes in up to 50% blends in 2009 and 2011 respectively (ASTM, 2011). The 50% blend limit was established to guarantee the presence of 'aromatics' in the fuel which are essential for the effective operation of engine fuel seals but which are not present in biofuels (Corporan et al., 2011). With ASTM certification achieved, major airlines began to source biofuels and operate scheduled commercial flights powered, in part, by biofuels. KLM operated one of the first revenue biofuel flights in July 2011 when it flew 171 passengers from Amsterdam to Paris in a Boeing 737 part-powered by biofuel derived from waste cooking oil (KLM, 2012). Later that year, Lufthansa conducted a six month trial using biofuel derived from a variety of plant and animal fats to power 1187 flights between Hamburg and Frankfurt (Lufthansa, 2012).

Although all of these trials involved short-term co-operation between airlines, airframe and engine manufactures, airports and biofuels suppliers, one of the main challenges airlines faced was sourcing sufficient supplies of biofuel. To overcome this challenge and reduce vulnerabilities in the supply chain, airlines and biofuel producers began establishing commercial partnerships. British Airways agreed to co-fund, with US firm Solena, the development of the UK's first commercial scale waste-to-biofuel aviation biofuel facility in east London which aims to convert 500,000 tonnes of domestic refuse into 50,000 tonnes of aviation biofuel a year (British Airways, 2013) while Virgin Atlantic entered into a partnership with Swedish biofuel company Lanza Tech (Enviro.aero, 2012). In June 2013 it was announced that United Airlines will purchase 15 million gallons of renewable jet fuel over a 3 year period (Lane, 2013). However, despite these (and other) commercial partnerships, barriers to market development remain. This paper reports on the findings of a series of in-depth interviews with major aviation biofuel stakeholders worldwide.

3. Method

25 Aviation biofuel stakeholders based in Europe and North America were identified from extensive literature and internet searches (Table 1). Respondents were drawn from sectors including airframe manufacturers, airlines, environmental consultants and (bio)fuel companies. Initial contact was made via email and interviews, which averaged 1 h in length, were conducted by telephone between October and December 2011. Whilst recognising the methodological limitations of the research undertaken, not least in terms of the limited sample of the stakeholders interviewed, the research presented here contributes to extant debates on the future commercial development of aviation biofuel by examining the perceptions of fuel producers, end users and policy makers.

The semi-structured interview schedule consisted of open-ended questions relating to four key areas that had been identified from the literature as representing gaps in the existing knowledge base. These areas were: the historical development of

Table 1
List of respondents.

Respondent	Sector	Job description
A	Airframe manufacturer	Senior VP of environment
B	Airframe manufacturer	Biofuel public relations officer
C	Airline	Environment manager
D	Airline	Environment director
E	Airline	Environment manager
F	Airline	Environment manager
G	Airline	Environment manager
H	Airline	Bioenergy and biofuels research
I	Airport operator	Operations director
J	Aviation biofuel producer	Director of corporate affairs
K	Aviation biofuel producer	Strategy director
L	Biofuel agency	Biofuel expert
M	Engine manufacturer	Director
N	Environmental consultancy	Consultant
O	Environmental consultancy	Consultant
P	Environmental consultancy	Director
Q	Fuel standards agency	Manager
R	International aviation body	Deputy director
S	Petrochemical company	Biofuel expert
T	Petrochemical company	Biofuel expert
U	Petrochemical company	Biofuel manager
V	Renewable energy assoc	Policy advisor
W	UK government	Aviation analyst
X	University academic	Professor energy
Y	US government	Aviation analyst

aviation biofuels, contemporary challenges facing commercialisation, stakeholders' views on policy and legislative support, and areas requiring further research. All of the interviews were recorded on a dicta-phone, transcribed and coded by the lead author. Anonymity was granted to safeguard personal privacy and to conform to the respondent organisation's confidentiality agreements. Consequently, individual respondents are identified by a letter and their generic job description.

4. Findings

The findings are organised under the headings of drivers and constraints. The section begins by highlighting the complexity and interdependency of key factors driving the development of aviation biofuels, followed by a discussion of the issues which are constraining the wide-spread commercial uptake and continued market development of aviation biofuels.

4.1. Drivers

The interviews identified six key drivers supporting the development and uptake of aviation biofuels. These drivers were either external economic factors (including high jet fuel prices and energy prices) or potential benefits associated with the fuels' eventual uptake (including job creation and economic growth). Although there is a high level of interdependency between individual factors, the single most important factor identified was the need to reduce carbon emissions.

4.1.1. Carbon reduction

All 25 respondents stated that the aviation industry needed to reduce its carbon emissions. This stems in part from political and public pressure as well as more stringent environmental targets. Although there was a general consensus among all respondents that carbon emissions were a significant driver, there were subtle differences between EU and US respondents. EU based respondents; which represented around two thirds of the interviewees, suggested that reducing emissions was motivated by

environmental legislation and voluntary industry targets. Non-EU respondents acknowledged the role played by environmental legislation, but suggested that other factors were also important. Interestingly, national environmental legislation within the US was deemed to be insignificant. US respondents were also much more open to discussing the threat that environmental legislation had for 'raising costs' rather than achieving a reduction in emissions. In fact, most non-EU respondents stated that the extra cost associated with carbon reductions was the primary driver for biofuels, not necessarily the emission reductions themselves. Airline D stated:

"Environmental legislation will increase our costs. This is the bottom line when we think about reducing emissions, and I know a lot of other airlines think exactly the same."

This view was shared by the majority of US respondents. This is not to say that EU respondents were unaware of the cost implications associated with reducing emissions since they appeared to be consciously factoring it into their future business strategies. EU airlines were also aware of the long-term implications of carbon pricing on profitability, but many had recognised there was potential to raise valuable revenue by reducing their emissions and selling permits that were surplus to requirements. According to Airline E, emissions reductions will play a larger role in the EU airline industry's business strategy in future years:

"Strategically we knew that emissions are a key issue to get right. We are looking therefore for long term solutions. We are not sure that biofuels will be the sole measure used but they will definitely be part of the mix."

In addition to the EU ETS, voluntary emission targets provide a strong motivation for EU airlines, engine and aircraft manufacturers to reduce their carbon emissions. One European airframe manufacturer focused on their own industry targets, asserting they are the most important driver in terms of aviation biofuels:

"Aviation is one of the few industries that have clear targets for reducing CO_2. [We want] carbon neutral growth by 2020 and 50% CO_2 reduction by 2050. That's a key target we have all committed to, along with all other airlines and manufacturers ... So this is the primary driver" [Airframe manufacturer A].

Industry led initiatives were also identified by Airline F as being important.

"The aviation industry is driving this more than anything else; more than investors, more than governments; even more than the fuel industry."

Despite there being a number of economic sectors involved in the development of aviation biofuels, around half of respondents agreed that the aviation industry is playing a leading role in developing aviation biofuels. It is doing this in three main ways. First, through initiatives such as the Sustainable Aviation Fuel Users Group (SAFUG) and the Commercial Aviation Alternative Fuels Initiative (CAAFI) which seek to encourage dialogue between stakeholders and governments, as well as encourage investment in the technology. The second is through airline producer partnerships; where certain airlines are planning to produce their own fuel by forming a co-funding agreement with biofuel producers; such as in the case of British Airways and Solena. Finally, by forming consortia of airlines, biofuel producers and feedstock growers that can streamline the development stages of new fuels and create sustainable supply chains. The importance of aviation led initiatives

P. Gegg et al. / Journal of Air Transport Management 39 (2014) 34–40   37

has strengthened considerably since the certification of BtL and HEFA biofuels in 2009 and 2011 respectively.

According to twelve respondents, the development of consortia created high profile interest in the fuel from investors, airlines and producers. Although the support is still limited, these initiatives appear to be creating a positive signal relating to the benefit of the fuel. Respondents stated that the predominant work that had been carried out had been organised by the aviation industry i.e. airlines, engine manufacturers and airframe manufactures. Indeed, Boeing and Airbus were cited as being particularly supportive of aviation biofuel development. One of the main reasons for this was the perceived lack of involvement of major oil companies.

"We were waiting for the big oil companies to come in and help us. However, I think what emerged was a fairly consistent feeling across the airline industry that we can't wait for big oil companies, so there are a number of airlines now that are getting involved in the manufacture of the fuels themselves." [Airline C]

Further evidence suggests that the airlines had a pioneering role in driving the initial interest in the fuel. Five respondents, all of which offer services to airlines, acknowledged that their initial interest in the fuel only came about after the airline industry approached them regarding advice or services. For example, one aviation biofuel producer stated that their initial venture into aviation fuels only came about after it was made apparent that a niche market existed for the fuels.

"...we already designed the technology so we had the possibility to also provide jet fuel, but we saw the road sector as the main user. The [aviation] market came to us.... they came to us pretty quickly after we announced our production capacity." [Biofuel Producer J]

4.1.2. Energy security

The issue of energy security was raised by all 25 respondents as a potential driver of aviation biofuels. It was acknowledged as being the most significant by U.S. and Brazilian respondents. The U.S. respondents spoke about the energy security benefits of the fuel and the ability to avoid oil imports. Energy security was also acknowledged to act as a major driver within the U.S. from a military perspective. Four respondents acknowledged that military demand for aviation biofuels within the U.S. may act as a catalyst for both the development and eventual uptake of the fuels in the commercial sector:

"From the military side, military customers are interested in the commercialisation of biofuels from a supply assurance perceptive, so fuel supply security. They don't want their fuel supply disturbed in the future." [Engine Manufacturer M]

Outside the U.S. securing energy supplies is attractive to governments both from an economic and a commercial perspective. Airframe manufacturer B acknowledged that the energy security benefit aviation biofuel could confer represents a significant benefit for national governments and policy makers. Reducing oil imports furthermore benefits national economies by creating additional labour demand for the production of domestic biofuel.

Despite the advantages, most respondents saw energy security as more of a long-term benefit that would manifest itself in ten to twenty years' time. Issues of oil supply and security were reflected in the discussion about oil prices and price volatility which were recognised as constituting another important driver.

4.1.3. Volatile oil prices

Oil price rises and oil price volatility were identified as long-term drivers by almost all of the respondents. Some respondents mentioned that the initial interest in biofuels followed the 2008 price spike, but this was denied by others. Oil prices were normally mentioned as a long-term driver in connection with carbon price rises. Indeed, the combined effect of oil price rises and carbon legislation was often cited as creating an important driving force. It was also suggested that oil price volatility will play a larger role than oil price in the short-term and long-term according to a quarter of the respondents. One possible explanation was expressed by an EU airline respondent. The airline stated that aviation biofuel producers will seek to match the price of jet kerosene, minus whatever carbon price is attached to the fuel in the future. This means that there will be no spot price incentive for using aviation biofuel compared to kerosene. The incentive instead comes from the fact that aviation biofuels may be more price stable.

4.1.4. Legislation

A significant number of respondents mentioned legislation as an important driver with mention made of the EU ETS and the ICAO resolution. The EU Emissions Trading System was by far the most discussed legislative driver. In total, twenty respondents mentioned the EU ETS as an important driver for aviation biofuel, either in combination with other drivers or exclusively. Most respondents stated that the legislation is predominantly a long-term driver because the price of carbon is currently too low. The EU ETS was described in two main ways: either a threat to the profitability of the aviation sector and/or as an opportunity to reduce the aviation industry's emissions. EU respondents tended to cite the environmental benefits of the system, whereas U.S respondents tended to cite the financial burden it will impose. All respondents however understood that the EU ETS will fundamentally affect the industry. Airport I stated:

"Emissions are going to start costing airlines money because of increased costs of carbon. I know for a fact that some airlines don't think about the EU ETS as an environmental issue, they think about the extra costs"

In contrast to EU airlines, North American respondents stated that US airlines are not subjected to significant environmental legislation nationally, and the main threat was perceived to be almost exclusively the EU ETS. Non-EU respondents also generally discussed their concerns about the possible introduction of an emissions trading system in other world markets. For example one major U.S. Engine manufacturer stated:

"...there is no domestic policy for reducing emissions that is being worked currently...but, the airlines are very worried about a spread of an ETS system globally that will increase the price of fuel..."

The second legislative measure mentioned were subsides for aviation biofuels. Three respondents mentioned the way the Dutch government had interpreted the renewable Fuel Directive was a potentially useful development. One respondent mentioned that is was an important driver locally for the industry, but not significant on a global scale. The third legislative driver related to ICAO's recent environmental resolution. One academic stated that ICAO had recently created a resolution that states that every member country must provide an action plan outlining the ways they intend to reduce aviation emissions. The UK academic spoke at length about how this is a positive move towards creating a global policy with respect to emission reductions. The respondent mentioned that up until now, ICAO's influence on environmental matters had been lacking and this is a significant indication that ICAO may begin ensuring countries are using appropriate measures to reduce emissions.

"This year it was for the "first" time that a resolution on the environment was made. So now every country must send an action

38   *P. Gegg et al. / Journal of Air Transport Management 39 (2014) 34–40*

plan for climate reduction to ICAO for them to review. This is a good start." [University academic, X]

4.1.5. Lack of alternative technology

Ten respondents acknowledged that the aviation industry has a lack of alternative technologies to de-carbonise. Respondents stated that the aviation industry has a serious long-term issue in that it does not have many replacement technologies that offer the same performance as the jet-airliner. It was stressed very clearly by two engine manufacturers and three airframe manufacturers that the industry needs to either diversify its propulsion technology or use a replacement low carbon fuel; with the latter being the most viable option. Although efficiency improvements are still the research focus for those companies, the long-term future of the industry points towards radical technologies such as biofuels which offer a step change in emissions. Other respondents expressed the same opinion by comparing the aviation industry to other transport sectors such as road and rail which have considerably better options for reducing emissions. Academic X stated:

"...if you look at the car industry they have several sources of emission reductions. Aviation does not. They can't rely on one type of fuel. For this reason biofuel is a potential solution"

Other respondents added that the only cost effective solution for the next 40 years will be to use aviation biofuels. The other technologies which are being looked at such as hydrogen and electric are too far away from feasibility and cost effectiveness. Aviation biofuels were therefore seen as an 'essential' intervention.

4.1.6. New business opportunities

Aviation biofuels create new business opportunities, although at present the economics of the fuel were still seen as undesirable and it will take several years before the fuel becomes economically viable. Nonetheless, the technology was championed by certain individuals with one airline stating that although the costs involved with producing the fuels today are high, in the long-run there is a clear economic case to support biofuels.

"We might lose money in the short term but in the long term the benefits are very large, we believe." [Airline E]

The academic respondent was also confident that the technology had clear economic advantages in the long-run, referring to their experience in researching the economics of the fuel in Europe. Other respondents described the need to support the technologies in their early stages in order to scale up production and reap greater benefits of economies of scale from the technology later. For example Airline F stated:

"...it takes a long time. But if we start the work now it will pay dividends in the future. First you've got to get the process right, and then you've got to get the network together for the raw product."

At present however the production volumes of the fuel remain small. Indeed, it appears that although the business opportunity that aviation biofuel presents is apparent considerably more effort and investment will be required to scale up production.

4.2. Constraints

Respondents acknowledged a number of constraints associated with the market development of aviation biofuels with the constraints often closely interlinked.

4.2.1. High production costs

High costs were mentioned by all respondents as a significant constraint to the development and uptake of aviation biofuels. All respondents acknowledged that the purchase price of aviation biofuels given current technology will be higher than the price of standard jet fuel. Biofuel producer K stated:

"The price of bio-kerosene is at least twice the price of fossil jet fuel alone. And the price is really a challenge. We are working hard to get the costs down but this is a major issue for everybody."

Estimates for price parity were given reluctantly, but most estimates were between 2015 and 2030. This large variation may be explained, in part, by the complexity of the cost issue. When respondents elaborated on the cost issue it was apparent that estimating the final cost of aviation biofuels can be difficult since the final price can be influenced by various factors such as: the production process, feedstock costs, the cost of infrastructure and legislative support. Each of these components will vary depending on the technology being used, the region, and the level of infrastructure available and legislative support.

4.2.2. Lack of investment

80% of the Respondents acknowledged that aviation biofuel technology was receiving insufficient investment. Most of these respondents believed that the main factors hindering the level of investment were: uncertainty about the technologies and legislative support and an inability to obtain credit given the global economic downturn. Further factors included an inability to de-risk investments and a lack of government investment. In terms of investment Airline C stated that:

"We had a hard time getting finance. Banks don't want to take a risk on a "first of a kind technology". Apart from the US, the UK hasn't got their heads around how they will de-risk these investments. The US on the other hand is doing much more than the EU."

When the airline mentioned de-risking, they were referring to the presence of government backed loans or guarantees that can be offered to insure against losses on the technology. Indeed, with the exception of the US, there are very few regions where 'de-risking' is occurring according to the respondents.

The other constraint relating to investment was acknowledged as a lack of government grant funds for new biofuel technologies and the way government funds are administered. Four respondents mentioned that the way grant funding is administered may be suppressing promising technologies before they have a chance to show their potential. The main issue being that funding is not being given out quickly enough. One respondent spoke passionately about the fact that very often in Australia and Europe the time required to administer funds could be up to a year. Referring to the Australian funding system specifically, respondent V stated:

"In almost all of cases, the political nature of the funding means that the time frames to allocate the funding are too long, if you have a start-up company that needs cash, 18 months is a ludicrous amount of time to wait — and it happens elsewhere. There is a need for quicker decision making."

4.2.3. Sustainable feedstock supply

A lack of sustainable feedstock supply is seen as an important constraint according to all the respondents. Respondents commonly described the aviation biofuel industry as being 'lacking

P. Gegg et al. / Journal of Air Transport Management 39 (2014) 34–40   39

in sufficient feedstocks to make existing technologies economically viable and sustainable'. The emphasis moreover was on a lack of 'sustainable feedstocks' which meet both economic and environmental criteria. The main reasons for a lack of sustainable feedstock supply that were acknowledged to include: the lack of a supply chain, feedstock research and a clear sustainability criteria.

A lack of supply chain was mentioned by ten respondents. Five respondents from the CAAFI initiative called this the 'agricultural vertical'. Respondents stated that at current levels, the agricultural vertical for sustainable feedstocks is almost non-existent in most regions. This means that the physical and monetary effort to obtain sustainable feedstocks is excessive. Respondents that had been involved in creating a supply chain for aviation biofuels in Brazil described the work required to source relatively small amounts of sustainable Jatropha feedstock as 'excessive' and 'non-economic'. The respondents described a situation in which the final feedstock delivery for a particular trial was amalgamated from numerous geographically scattered batches.

"...for one of the trials we sourced the Jatropha nuts ourselves. It was a big challenge because we had to squeeze every little bit we could find from all over the country just to get enough and there was no supply chain yet so the logistics were also a challenge." [Airline D]

The second issue acknowledged was a lack of feedstock research. Although major breakthroughs have been made surrounding new feedstocks and production methods, there is still a considerable amount of research required. One respondent stated that all too often attention is focused on the production side of the business i.e. on the processing technology, rather than on the feedstock bases. This was described as being highly counterproductive. The respondent elaborated on the views of other respondents in saying that more research effort and funding is required on the feedstock side to ensure that the processing technologies have sufficient raw materials to produce fuel. Respondent V stated:

"There's a tendency we focus on the production side of things because that is the attractive and interesting side of the business, whereas in reality there is so much work to be done on the feedstock side. The reality is that the plant you build once, while the biomass will be used for 30 or 40 years."

Related to a lack of feedstock research is a lack of sustainability criteria for aviation biofuel feedstocks. This was expressed by the same ten respondents from mixed sectors. Although there are various projects underway to tackle this issue, at present it is hindering the development of the industry. As well as creating uncertainty for investors, one respondent stated how farmers are not getting sufficient information about sustainability criteria. One US airline respondent described this sentiment for some U.S. farmers. Related to sustainability of feedstocks are the environmental effects of land use change and pressure on the food supply.

4.2.4. Inadequate legislation

Lack of legislation was a constraint which almost all of the respondents described as being a serious issue. Most respondents described this issue as a 'lack of level playing field' between road-based biofuels and aviation biofuels. Others discussed a lack of legislation more generally with respect to insufficient funding or supportive measures for the fuels.

The focus of many stakeholders was on the EU which, with the exception of the Netherlands, favoured the use of road-based biofuels over aviation biofuels in its use of legislation. Road-based

biofuels were described as being supported by a plethora of incentives and legislative support measures including: subsidies of feedstocks, mandates of biofuel blending and tax breaks. This was described as being 'unfair' for aviation biofuels.

Another common topic of discussion surrounding legislation was the EU ETS. Almost all of the respondents stated that that although the system has a zero carbon accounting procedure for aviation biofuels, this does not create any incentive to use aviation biofuels. This is because the price of carbon is too low.

An additional issue relating to legislation was the level of knowledge flows between legislators and the aviation biofuel community. The main area of focus related to the EU. It was expressed by over half of the EU respondents that there is inadequate knowledge flows between legislators and the industry, and this may be impacting on the industry's ability to develop. Airline C described their interaction with legislators as follows:

"We do try to talk a lot to legislators and make recommendation but there are so many issues to resolve. It's not all that encouraging that they are taking it all in from what we see."

In addition to the constraints above there were other issues which were mentioned by a few respondents. These include: applying too strict environmental criteria on aviation biofuels and a pipe-line infrastructure certification issue.

4.2.5. Strict environmental controls for biofuels

The issue of having strict environmental hurdles for aviation biofuels was flagged up as being a potentially overlooked constraint by three respondents. The issue surrounds the idea that legislators and NGO's are being too strict on setting environmental hurdles for aviation biofuels. Despite the fact that there are no formal environmental guidelines for aviation biofuels as yet, the respondents warned that the initial interest is too focused on overly optimistic technologies. The respondents explained that there may be a tendency to overlook slightly less environmentally beneficial technologies in favour of the 'Holy Grail' type technologies which seek to be almost perfect from the outset. Two respondents from the petrochemical industry stated that being 'too' strict on the technologies in their early stages was detrimental. They stated that the best opportunity was to develop technologies we know work well today and over time the sustainability will be improved. One respondent, from a major international petrochemical company, justified this suggestion based on experience with palm oil production:

"Biofuel production using Palm oil is the best one because it's an existing technology that we can scale up now, and we can get the yields up on those, rather than start with new technologies that are no good...the sustainability isn't as good today but if we put measures in place it can be."

4.2.6. Lack of supply chain certification

Although certification was a minor issue in the interviewees, one respondent spoke at length about a potentially overlooked issue surrounding the certification of the supply chains. The respondent, from a certification and testing company, explained that within the EU, aviation biofuel blends cannot be distributed through existing fossil-fuel pipe lines or mixed in with standard jet fuel mixing facilities. This is because of a lack of integration of ASTM with the UK's DEF-STAN and EU's AFQGS. This means that dedicated systems are still required for the fuel, despite it being fully certified in up to 50% HEFA and FT fuel blends with standard jet fuel. Although the volumes are quite low at present, it was acknowledged by one respondent that this is causing logistical constraints for trials.

40 P. Gegg et al. / Journal of Air Transport Management 39 (2014) 34–40

5. Conclusion

This paper has illustrated that the drivers and constraints for aviation biofuels are complex and there is no clear consensus about how to overcome the constraints. Certainly, respondents from all sectors agreed that developments in aviation biofuel are being driven by broad industry needs; namely the need to reduce emissions, the need to reduce vulnerability to oil price rises and exposure to future carbon pricing, energy security and the need to continue using existing engines and infrastructure. The opportunity created by new markets for biofuels was considered to be of lesser importance. However, as well as factors that are driving the development of the fuels, respondents identified a number of constraints that are conspiring to restrict the uptake and commercialisation of aviation biofuels. These constraints include a lack of feedstocks; high costs; low funding; sustainability concerns; a lack of policy incentives and fuel consistency and infrastructure. It is thus not unreasonable to assume that until concerns surrounding cost, sustainability and policy support are addressed, aviation biofuels will not form a significant share of the aviation fuel market.

Almost all the respondents suggested that further scientific research is required into new feedstocks and production technologies that utilise non-edible forms of biomass. The development of newer biofuel technologies is proceeding quickly, however cost and sustainability challenges remain. In the short-to-medium term it will be necessary for the industry to establish robust sustainability criteria and accounting procedures for aviation biofuels that can be agreed at a global level. In addition, the industry must work with other agencies so that any criteria that are agreed have credibility.

Acknowledgements

We would like to extend our thanks to the two anonymous referees for their very detailed and insightful comments which substantially improved the paper.

References

ASTM, 2011. Aviation fuel standard takes flight – D7566 revision adds bio derived components. Available online at: http://www.astm.org/SNEWS/SO_2011/enright_so11.html.

Blakey, S., Rye, L., Wilson, C.W., 2011. Aviation gas turbine alternative fuels: a review. Proc. Combust. Inst. 33, 2863–2885.

Bows-Larkin, A., Anderson, K., 2013. Carbon budgets for aviation or gamble with our future? In: Budd, L., Griggs, S., Howarth, D. (Eds.), Sustainable Aviation Futures. Emerald, Bingley, pp. 65–84.

British Airways, 2013. Solena – one destination. Available online at: www.onedestination.co.uk/environment/climate-change/biofuels/solena (accessed 22.07.13.).

Budd, L., Budd, T., 2013. Environmental technology and the future of flight. In: Budd, L., Griggs, S., Howarth, D. (Eds.), Sustainable Aviation Futures. Emerald, Bingley, pp. 87–107.

Chuck, C.J.O., Donnelly, J., 2014. The compatibility of potential bioderived fuels with Jet A-1 aviation kerosene. Appl. Energy 118 (1), 83–91.

Committee on Climate Change, 2009. Meeting the aviation target – options for reducing emissions to 2050. http://www.theccc.org.uk/reports/aviation-report (accessed 10.05.13.).

Corporan, E., Edwards, T., Shafer, L., DeWitt, M.J., Klingshirn, C., Zabarnick, S., West, A., Striebich, R., Graham, J., Klein, J., 2011. Chemical, thermal stability, seal swell, and emissions studies of alternative jet fuels. Energy Fuels 25 (3), 955–966.

Enviro.aero aviation biofuel flight tests. Available online at: http://www.enviro.aero/Testing-programme.aspx (accessed 12.05.13.).

FAA (Federal Aviation Administration), 2011. FAA destination 2025. Available online at: www.FAA.Gov/about/plans_reports/media/destination2025.pdf.

Florentinus, A., Hamelinck, C., van den Bos, A., Winkel, R., Cuijpers, M., 2012. Potential of Biofuels for Shipping. Final report. Ecofys Project number: BIO-NL11332. http://www.ecofys.com/files/files/ecofys_2012_potential_of_biofuels_in_shipping_02.pdf (accessed 12.05.13.).

Freedman, D., 2014. Market-driven considerations affecting the prospects of alternative road fuels. Philos. Trans. R. Soc. 372 (2006), 2–23.

IATA (International Air Transport Association), 2009. A global approach to reducing aviation emissions. Available online at: www.iata.org.

IATA (International Air Transport Association), 2013. IATA 2013 Report on Alternative Fuels, eighth ed. Available online at: www.iata.org/publications/documents/2013-report-alternative-fuels.pdf.

KLM, 2012. Sustainable biofuels – road to sustainable biofuels. http://www.klm.com/csr/en/climate/footprint/biofuels/index.html (accessed 12.05.13.).

Köhler, J., Walz, R., Marscheder-Weidemann, Thedieck, B., 2014. Lead markets in 2nd generation biofuels for aviation: a comparison of Germany, Brazil and the USA. Environ. Innov. Soc. Transit. 10, 59–76.

Lane, J., 2013. Fly the (environmentally) friendly skies: united to commence widescale aviation biofuel flights in 2014. Available at: www.biofuelsdigest.com/bdigest/2013/06/05/Fly-the-(environmentally)-friendly-skies:-Unitied-to-commence-widescale-aviation-biofuel-flights-in-2014/.

Lufthansa, 2012. Practical trial of biosynthetic fuel at Lufthansa successful. http://presse.lufthansa.com/en/news-releases/singleview/archive/2012/january/09/article/2061.html (accessed 10.05.13.).

Naik, S.N., Goud, V.V., Rout, P.K., Dalai, A.K., 2010. Production of first and second generation biofuels: a comprehensive review. Renew. Sustain. Energy Rev. 14, 578–597.

Nair, S., Paulose, H., 2014. Emergence of green business models: the case of algae biofuel for aviation. Energy Policy 65, 175–184.

Panoutsou, C., Bauen, A., Duffield, J., 2013. Policy regimes and funding schemes to support investment for next-generation biofuels in the USA and the EU-27. Biofuels Bioprod. Biorefining 7 (6), 685–701.

PricewaterhouseCoopers (PWC), 2013. Recovering airline industry on track for profitability in 2013, according to PwC. Available online at: www.pwc.com/us/en/press-releases/2013/recovering-airilne-industry-on-track.jhtml 24/06/2013 (accessed 07.03.14.).

Stephenson, D., 2012. Sweet ideas: options grow for possible power sources of future airplanes. Available online at: www.boeing.com/features/2012/05/corp_innovative_thinking_05_07_12.html.

Winchester, N., McConnachie, D., Wollersheim, C., Waitz, I., 2013a. Economic and emissions impacts of renewable fuel goals for aviation in the USA. Transp. Res. A: Policy Pract. 58, 116–128.

Winchester, N., McConnachie, D., Wollersheim, C., Waitz, I., 2013b. Market Cost of Renewable Jet Fuel Adoption in the United States. A Partner Project 31 report. Partner MIT.

11

Aviation biofuel from renewable resources: Routes, opportunities and challenges

Thushara Kandaramath Hari, Zahira Yaakob, Narayanan N. Binitha

ABSTRACT

Air transport describes an inevitable part in the day to day life of the modern world. It is highly responsible for the worldwide social contacts and business developments. The use of petroleum fuels as energy source for air transport is not sustainable. Aviation is one of the leading contributors to the total greenhouse gas emissions. Also, the fossil fuel prices are becoming more volatile day by day. So it is very essential to introduce and industrialize alternative aviation fuels generated from renewable resources, especially biomass. A number of industrial commitments and collaborations have emerged to find alternative ways to reach bio aviation fuels. Research on the conversion of biomass based sources to bio jet fuels is of current interest. The main concern is the production of biojet fuel, from renewable resources, with relatively low greenhouse gas life cycle and sustainability with affordable price. The present paper overviews the opportunities and challenges in the development of alternative fuels for aviation. The production process, feedstock used and the most promising global projects are also reviewed.

Keywords:
Bio jet fuel
Aviation
Feedstock
Production route
Challenge

Contents

T. Kandaramath Hari et al. / Renewable and Sustainable Energy Reviews 42 (2015) 1234–1244   1235

1. Introduction

Combustion of fossil fuels and human activities disturb the environment by the emission of greenhouse gases like nitrous oxide, carbon dioxide, methane etc. [1]. The requirement of oils for transport is growing day by day and it is expected to be increased by 1.3% per year up to 2030 [2]. There is no unique solution available for these complications and so alternative ways are to be found out such as modification in vehicle designs, development in public transport and replacement of conventional fuels with alternative advanced fuels and fuel technologies [3]. It is expected that by 2030, the carbon emission from the transport sector and the energy requirement will increase up to 80% [4]. Air transport acquired a significant role in the everyday life of modern world. The influence of air travel increased worldwide social contact, especially in improving business and marketing. The total diesel fuel and jet fuel consumption was in the range of 5 to 6 million barrels per day in between 2005 and 2010 [5]. The average cost of jet fuels was $320/t in 2004 which is increased to an average of $1005/t in 2011 [2]. Fig. 1 represents worldwide commercial jet fuel prize and usage, world market: 2011–2021 [6]. According to the report from U.S. Energy Information Administration (IEA), for the next thirty years, the jet fuel cost will increase gradually and the average price in the year of 2013 was ($2.82/gal) [7].

The production of alternative fuel for aviation is mainly inspired by increased petroleum costs and environmental concern [5]. Not only the increased cost and environmental effects, some other factors such as secured working of the aircraft engine, consistency etc. should also be considered [8]. Use of biofuels are attracted by the low greenhouse gas emissions while combustion, decrease in the dependence on fossil fuel sources and availability of renewable resources [9]. The aviation transport sector requires fuels with high energy density and so it depends mainly on liquid hydrocarbon fuels. Alternative aviation fuels must possess some specific qualities such as good cold flow properties, thermal stability and low freezing point [10]. The fuel must be well suited for the present design of the aircraft engine [11]. Sustainable aviation fuels must offer low carbon emission over their lifecycles. The energy crops used as the production source should not challenge the food production and ecosystem and also do not harm the environment and do not cause deforestation [12].

The feedstock used for the production of alternative aviation fuels are biological in origin and thus are renewable. Non edible oil crops such as camelina, jatropha, algae, halophytes, municipal and sewage wastes, forest residues etc are the major available resources for the energy production process [13]. Many technologies have emerged for the production of aviation bio fuel from the biomass resources. The conversion routes include thermochemical and biochemical approaches [14]. The bright future of alternative aviation fuel can be influenced by the co-operation between national and international organizations, states and countries [15]. International Air Transport Association (IATA) expects 30% contribution of Bio jet fuel for the jet fuel use by 2030 [16]. The annual universal production of biomass is about 100 trillion kilograms. So obviously, biomass is a potential feedstock having the ability to substitute fossil fuel resource [17,18].

In addition to the reduction in the emission of greenhouse gases, alternative aviation biofuels experiences several advantages

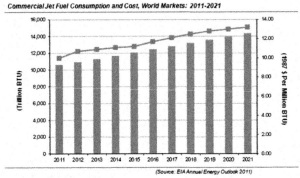

Commercial Jet Fuel Consumption and Cost, World Markets: 2011-2021

(Source: EIA Annual Energy Outlook 2011)

Fig. 1. Worldwide commercial jet fuel prize and usage, world market: 2011–2021 [6].

over conventional jet fuel. The fossil fuels are affected mainly by cost fluctuation [19]. Since the sources used for the production of bio aviation fuel are renewable and of low cost, a well suited production route can reduce the cost of the fuel. Bio aviation fuel production can offer economic profits, especially in developing countries where there is unusable land available for the cultivation of non-food crops and thus can support the supply chain process [20]. One of the major problems that related to fossil fuels is the difficulty in supply with increasing demand. Here the attraction of bio aviation fuels is that the feedstock is available worldwide and the production process is not location limited [21]. Bio aviation fuels can satisfy the fundamental properties of conventional aviation fuels such as low temperature performance, low flash point, good thermal stability etc. [22]. In brief the aviation biofuels are ecologically, economically and socially sustainable [23].

Daggett et al. gave a well outline of the alternative aviation fuels and their feasibility [24]. Bomani et al. provided a survey on biofuels as an alternative aviation energy source in which they included application of fuel produced from palm oil, algae, halophytes and biomass for aviation and road transport purposes [25]. Nygren et al. investigated the scenarios in aviation fuel and future oil production [26]. Liu et al. investigated various jet fuel production processes and discussed each process in detail [27]. A recent review by Kallio et al. analyzed the application of microbial biotechnology for the renewable production of jet fuel [28].

Even though bio jet fuels are excellent alternatives for conventional aviation fuels; there are many difficulties and challenges to overcome in order to achieve it. Collection of feedstock, the production route, characteristic of the produced fuel and its characterization are extremely challenging. The present paper deals with the opportunities and challenges in the production of aviation biofuel from renewable feedstock. Discussions on the characteristics of feedstock, the methods used in the production process, a comparison of renewable hydrocarbon fuel with biohydrogen, biodiesel, bioalcohol and biomethane as alternative fuels, the industry commitments and collaborations and future outlook and recommendations in this field are also included.

2. Renewable resources

Renewable feedstocks are better resources for the production of bio jet fuels. The important advantages of these feedstock are (1) sustainability (2) carbon dioxide recycling (3) renewability (4) eco-friendly technology and (5) less dependence on petroleum supplying countries [29]. The feedstocks generally favoured are non-food energy crops, algae, municipal and sewage wastes, waste wood, forest residues and halophytes. The characteristics of some of the renewable feedstock are mentioned below.

2.1. Camelina

Camelina is a non-food energy crop with high oil content. The average oil content of the plant is about 30–40% and the plant needs lesser amount of fertilizers for growth [30]. Camelina possesses many advantages. Camelina plant can grow on infertile soil or marginal land [31] and the plant is less susceptible to diseases and pets [20]. Camelina can be cultivated as a rotational crop for wheat and cereals and it needs minimum input [30]. The meal left after the extraction of oil can be used as animal feed. The cost of the camelina oil is very less ($0.40–$0.70/gal) and the current markets of the oil in US are Northwest US and Southern Canada; in 2012, 200 million gallons of camelina oil were produced only in US [22]. Since it can be cultivated as a rotational crop, it can solve the problems related to mono cropping which will help farmers to find additional profits from the land [32].

Otherwise the continuous mono cropping may cause decrease in the yield and can destroy the soil.

2.2. Jatropha

Jatropha is a non-edible energy crop which can grow in marginal land and so it does not compete with food crops. The jatropha plant is drought and pest resistant. The plant can grow even in unproductive soil under unfavourable climatic conditions and grows quickly [33]. The plant has a permanent pattern of high yield oil production [34]. Jatropha plant can continue yielding for 40 years once started when a small amount of moisture is available [35]. The meal left after the extraction of oil cannot be used since it is poisonous, but it is rich in N, K and P so can be used as organic manure [34]. Jatropha cultivation is currently occurring in South Africa, South and Central America and South East Asia [36]. The jatropha seed production also depends on location, management practices, varieties, etc. Information from current plantation reveals that the plant requires irrigation for better growing [37].

2.3. Algae

Algae is an attractive solution for the fuel scarcity issues because of their high lipid content, high rate of carbon dioxide absorption, low land use and faster rate of growth [38–40]. The most important benefit of algae is that algae do not affect crop cultivation since it does not require land or water to survive, which help to reduce the food-fuel competition [41]. Algae can produce large quantities of lipids and carbohydrate by using sunlight, waste water and carbon dioxide and thus can play a crucial role in wastewater treatment [42,43]. The biomass left after the extraction of algal oil can be used as animal feed, for preparing bio plastic and for nutrition and also the dried biomass can be further processed for energy production [31]. Microalgae are widely used for fuel purpose. It is easy to cultivate and can be harvested all the year [2]. Compared to other energy crops, algae can produce 30 times more yields per acre [21]. Algae can be processed into a variety of renewable fuels [44].

2.4. Wastes

Wastes from different sources are dependable feedstock for the production of alternative biofuels. Wastes of plant origin and animal origin, such as foodstuffs, wood products, paper, forest residues, industrial and agricultural residues, household wastes, bagasse, animal wastes and municipal wastes can be converted to biofuel through different potential routes [20]. These resources are of low cost and easily available. The use of waste materials for the production of energy will be an asset to the waste management technology without the generation of any harmful products. Municipal wastes and sewage sludge can contribute more since they are widely available and are rich in lipids [45]. The use of waste materials for the production of biofuels can overcome many difficulties such as need of fertilizer, irrigation, land and labour [46].

2.5. Halophytes

Halophytes are grasses that grow in salty water where plants could not grow usually [20]. Halophytes are mostly found in tropical and subtropical regions [47]. Halophytes are can grow in marshes, inland lakes, coastal shorelines, desert areas and in the sea [48]. The speciality of halophytes feedstock is that they will not compete with agricultural crops for fresh water supply and land [49].

T. Kandaramath Hari et al. / Renewable and Sustainable Energy Reviews 42 (2015) 1234–1244   1237

3. Alternative fuels for air transport

Alternative aviation fuels can be produced from all of the above renewable bioresources. The properties of alternative aviation fuels are (1) reduced greenhouse gas emission (2) renewable resources (3) compatibility with conventional fuel (4) sustainability and clean burning. The currently developing alternative fuels includes the following.

3.1. Hydroprocessed renewable jet fuels

Hydroprocessed renewable jet fuels (HRJs or hydroprocessed esters and fatty acids (HEFA) are generally paraffinic liquids having chemical formula C_nH_{2n+2}. HRJs are produced by the hydrodeoxygenation of vegetable oils, animal fats, waste grease, algal oil and bio oil and the major side products are water and propane [50]. The hydroprocessed renewable jet fuels are high energy biofuels that can be used as such as fuel even without blending. One of the major advantages of hydroprocessed renewable jet fuels is reduction in the emission of greenhouse gas such as carbon monoxide (CO), hydrocarbons (HC), nitrogen oxides (NO_x), and particulate matter (PM) [51]. The HRJs are free of aromatics and sulphur and possess high cetane number, high thermal stability and low tailpipe emissions [52]. These fuels are stable for storage and resistant to microbial growth [53].

The hydroprocessed renewable jet fuels are suitable for conventional aircraft engines without further engine modification and do not raise any fuel quality issues. These fuels avoid the chance of deposit formation in the engine and engine corrosion [54]. The fuel combustion is completely ash free. Because of the better cold flow properties, HRJs are highly fit for higher altitude flights [51]. Complete absence of oxygen and sulphur in the fuel decreases its lubricity [55]. The higher paraffin content in the fuel somehow adversely affects the cold flow properties like cold filter plugging point and cloud point which in turn depend on the type of feedstock used [56]. The difference in the cetane numbers of hydroprocessed renewable jet fuels and conventional petroleum fuels affects the fuel ignition in the engine. These problems are better solved by blending HRJs with conventional fuels [55].

The Nest Oil Company has established plants to produce hydrotreated renewable jet fuels. UOP Honeywell, ENI and Galp Energia have plans for to construct hydrotreating plants worldwide [57]. Aeroméxico, Air China, Air France, Finnair, Iberia and Air France KLM, Lufthansa have performed commercial passenger flights with hydroprocessed esters and fatty acids (HEFA) as fuels [58].

3.2. Fischer Tropsch fuels

Fischer Tropsch fuels (FT fuels) are hydrocarbon fuels, which are produced by catalytic conversion of syn gas (CO and H_2) [59]. A wide range of biomass feedstock can be used for the generation of syn gas [60]. The FT fuels are usually clean burning, high value fuels [61]. The FT fuels are characterized by non-toxicity, no emission of nitrogen oxides, high cetane number, reduced particulate emission, low sulphur and aromatic content etc. Also the fuel combustion is free of carbon dioxide and hydrocarbons [46]. Unlike many other alternative fuels, FT fuels does not need special distribution infrastructure and because of the quality of fuel and comfortable for distribution, FT fuels can be produced 2–3 million barrels per day [61]. The characteristics of FT fuels less depend on the nature of the feedstock used and the differences in fuel properties are mainly due to the operational conditions [62]. The FT process is expensive and the efficiency of the process ranges between 25 and 50% [59]. Due to less energy density, the Fischer Tropsch fuels offer low power and low fuel economy [61]. The

other problem with the fuel is low lubricity because of the absence of sulphur [62]. Solena is going to establish waste to bio jet fuel plants having a capacity of 50,000 t/year by 2017. StoraEnso and Neste Oil, UPM and Carbona have formed consortia to develop BTL plants in Europe [57]. The ASTM international standard, D7566, has approved specification for aviation fuels, FT fuels in 2009 and HRJs in 2011 [63].

3.3. Biodiesel

Biodiesel is alkyl esters of fatty acid, especially vegetable oils and animal fats and it is produced by the process of transesterification. Biodiesel fuel is biodegradable and possesses excellent lubricity [8]. Biodiesel as fuel shows the advantages of renewability in origin, high flash point, good energy balance and good miscibility with petroleum fuels. It contains no sulphur and show highly reduced greenhouse gas emissions [64]. It is also noted that the biodiesel fuels do not contain aromatic compounds, does not cause any water, soil or air pollution and it is non-toxic [65–67]. But the biodiesel fuel is not sufficient to use as an aviation fuel. The energy density of biodiesel is very low compared to conventional jet fuels [68].

Use of biodiesel as aviation fuel does not need further engine modification and infrastructure, but it does not show much efficiency [69]. The biodegradability of biodiesel may cause biological growth during storage which will affect the stability [8]. The freezing point of biodiesel is very high compared to petroleum based aviation fuel, which makes it insufficient for high altitude flights. The presence of polyunsaturated and unsaturated fatty acids decreases the stability of the biodiesel due to the oxidation of the unsaturated sites [46]. Because of the presence of ester groups, biodiesel is polar to some extent which will cause the formation of emulsion and therefore water separation will be difficult [8]. Inadequate feedstock supply and deprived economics are the other problems of biodiesel fuel [64].

3.4. Liquid biohydrogen and biomethane

Liquid hydrogen is being established as alternative jet fuel. Bio hydrogen is produced from a wide range of biomass resources by following both thermal and biochemical methods [70]. Liquid hydrogen possesses more energy per weight compared to conventional aviation fuel, but requires high storage volume [71,72]. The combustion of liquid hydrogen fuels causes low emission of greenhouse gases compared to petroleum based jet fuels [73]. The major problem is that the liquid hydrogen fuel cannot be used as such in the conventional aircraft engine so the engine has to be modified [74]. The production cost, formation of char and tar as side products are also to be faced [70]. The other problem associated with the use of liquid hydrogen is that upon mixing with air, it can burn in low concentration which will cause safety problems and the storage of hydrogen as liquid is also difficult since it need low temperature [75]. The emission of comparatively high amount of water vapour is a problem associated with hydrogen aircrafts [46]. Liquid methane can be used as fuel in cryogenic aircrafts. The use of carbon dioxide emission can be decreased about 25% by the use of liquid methane fuel. Engine design is a difficulty that has to be faced for the commercialization of the liquid methane fuels. The combustion of liquid methane fuel emits methane, which is a major greenhouse gas [46].

3.5. Bio alcohols

Bio alcohols are produced by the fermentation of starch and sugar or catalytic conversion of biogas. Ethanol and butanol are generally used as alternative fuels. Ethanol cannot be used for aviation purposes because of its high volatility, low flash point, and low energy density [52]. The case of butanol is almost similar. Alcohol as aviation fuel needs special delivery infrastructure and storage system [8]. Use of alcohol as jet fuel needs engine modifications [59]. The high volatility of ethanol causes safety problems during high altitude travels [52]. Blending of alcohol with conventional fuels is not feasible because of its poor fuel properties which will cause aviation issues.

4. Production routes

The fuel production routes have much importance in determining the fuel characters. The method adopted to produce the fuel will influence the product composition, fuel cost, fuel properties, availability and environmental impact. The generally used methods for the production of hydrocarbon fuels involve two types. One is thermochemical process and the other is biochemical process [14]. The other methods used for the production of alternative fuels are also discussed below.

4.1. Thermochemical process

Thermochemical process is the conversion of biomass to fuel by pyrolysis, gasification and upgrading. Pyrolysis is the process of thermal decomposition of biomass in the absence of air, which results in the formation of bio oil and methane with other side products [76]. Gasification involves the treatment of pyrolysis products with air or steam to produce syn gas, which is a mixture of hydrogen and carbon monoxide. Syngas can be upgraded by the FT process Instead gasification and the FT process bio oil can be subjected to hydroprocessing or hydrodeoxygenation which will result in hydrocarbon fuel same as that from the FT process [77].

4.1.1. Biomass to liquid process (BTL process)

Biomass to liquid process comprises the conversion of biomass to liquid hydrocarbon fuel. A wide range of feedstock can be subjected to this process, including municipal and agricultural wastes, cellulose, wood, and algae [23]. The process involves the following steps, namely pretreatment of biomass, gasification, syngas purification and FT synthesis or pyrolysis followed by hydroprocessing [78,79]. The method takes the advantages of sustainability, reduced greenhouse gas emissions and no food to fuel competition [80].

4.1.2. Fischer Tropsch process (FT process)

The Fischer Tropsch process comprises the catalytic conversion of syngas (CO and H_2) which is produced by the gasification of biomass to liquid straight chain hydrocarbon fuels [81]. The range of hydrocarbons produced depends on the catalyst, pressure and temperature conditions of the process [82]. Jet fuel produced by the FT process from different feedstock exhibits similar properties and they are characterized by zero sulphur and aromatics [52]. The resulted FT fuels show clean burning. FT fuels are now recommended to use in blending with conventional fuel to meet requirement of specific lubricity in the absence of sulphur [81]. The method takes the advantage of the production of total negative greenhouse gas fuels [62]. Since the fuel is free of aromatic compounds, it makes some fuel leakage problems in the engine due to shrinkage of the engine while blending and it can be better minimized by the use of additives [8]. Even though a wide range of feedstock like waste wood and agricultural residues can be upgraded using the FT process to fuel, the method is quite expensive [23,68].

4.2. Hydroprocessing

The method of hydroprocessing involves treatment of fats and oils (vegetable oils and bio oils) in the presence of hydrogen for the removal of oxygen from the feedstock. The hydrodeoxygenation step is followed by isomerization and cracking to get fuel of desired specifications like low temperature properties [83]. Hydroprocessing results in the formation of clean paraffinic fuels with high thermal stability, no aromatics and suphur and they are generally mentioned as hydroprocessed renewable jet fuels (HRJs) [84]. In the hydrodeoxygenation method, oxygen is most preferably removed as water and propane is one of the byproducts [85]. The most promising feedstock used for the production of HRJs are plant oils like jatropha oil, camelina oil, algal oil, bio oil, animal fats and waste grease that can be made available in plenty [52]. The method is efficient and it can produce hydrocarbon fuel with improved cold flow behaviours and high cetane number [78]. Hydroprocessed renewable jet fuels are comparatively economical [23]. The low lubricity of HRJs can be improved by blending with conventional jet fuel or by the use of additives [52].

4.3. Biochemical process

Biochemical process is the conversion of biomass to carbohydrates that can be further transformed into alcohol by the method of fermentation using enzymes or micro-organisms [86]. Studies are going on to decrease the cost of the pretreatment and hydrolysis process by enzymes, and also trying to develop new microorganisms to carry out the process. The current processes used are:

4.3.1. Direct sugar to hydrocarbon process (DHSC) and alcohol to jet process (ATJ)

The method includes biochemical fermentation or catalytic conversion of sugars from biomass hydrolysis or from direct sugar sources such as sugar cane to hydrocarbon fuels [87]. The process involves hydrolysis of biomass, carbohydrate fermentation, purification and hydroprocessing [88]. Direct Sugar to Hydrocarbon process does not involve the intermediacy of alcohol. The advantages of the use of this method are plentifully available cost-effective feedstocks that not directly cause food crisis, sustainability and fuel with the reduction in greenhouse gas emission up to 82% [89].

Alcohol formed by the biochemical or thermochemical fermentation of carbohydrates obtained from biomass or thermochemical and thermo biochemical combined conversion of syngas can be subjected to a series of steps to form hydrocarbon fuels [87]. The process mainly includes 4 steps-ethanol dehydration, oligomerization, distillation and hydrogenation [90]. A wide range of the potential feedstock can be used for the process, including starch, cellulose, sugar and waste [23]. The method is very economical since the feedstocks are not much expensive and the process does not need large amounts of energy [20]. Sugar and starch can be converted to alcohol by direct fermentation, but in the case of biomass it must be pretreated to get sugar, which is then directly fermented to alcohol or subjected to gasification followed by gas fermentation [91].

4.3.2. Bio alcohol production

Bio alcohols are produced by thermal and biochemical fermentation of carbohydrates resulted by the hydrolysis of biomass [52]. Biomass sources like corns and cellulose are first hydrolysed to extract sugars and then fermented followed by distillation to get bio alcohol. Direct sugar sources are subjected to fermentation to produce alcohol [92]. Bioalcohol can be produced from a wide

T. Kandaramath Hari et al. / Renewable and Sustainable Energy Reviews 42 (2015) 1234–1244   1239

range of biomass feedstock such as wood, agricultural wastes, forest residues and wastes [93]. Methanol, Ethanol and butanol have the potential to use as transportation fuels, but they are not suitable to use as aviation fuel alternatives. The low flash point, low energy density and pure low temperature properties limit its use as aviation biofuel [94].

5. Other alternative fuels production routes

5.1. Liquid hydrogen and liquid methane

Bio hydrogen can be generated from a variety of feedstock like municipal and sewage residues, cellulose forest waste materials and crops [95]. Bio hydrogen can be produced by biomass gasification. At higher temperatures and pressures, biomass is converted to hydrogen with CO and CO_2 as side products. From this hydrogen can be separated by membrane method or chemical methods. Hydrogen can also be produced from pyrolysed oil by catalytic steam reforming [96]. Another method is the biological route using algae and bacteria [97]. Introduction of liquid hydrogen for aviation decreases the greenhouse gas emissions [98]. Biomethane is produced by anaerobic digestion or fermentation of a large number of renewable feedstocks like waste materials, crops and biomass [99]. The major problem with the use of liquid gas fuels is the requirement of modification of aircraft engine which will make fuel system very complex [98].

5.2. Transesterification of oils/fats

Transesterification is the process of the catalytic conversion of fats and oils into fatty acids of alkyl esters which are well known as biodiesel [100]. The method biodiesel production is not much expensive and since it can be produced from non edible oils, it does not create a food-fuel crisis [101]. The biodiesel fuel produced by this method exhibits carbon neutrality, reduced emission of greenhouse gases, non-toxicity and biodegradability [9]. Biodiesel can be used in diesel engines without further engine modification,

but it is not a suitable alternative for aviation fuels. Biodiesel possesses low energy density and poor cold flow properties of the fuel causes freezing of fuel in the aircraft engine at higher altitudes [52]. Table 1 represents an overview of biojet fuel production routes, renewable sources and various alternative aviation fuels.

6. Industry commitments and collaborations

With the increasing need for alternative aviation fuels, there are many projects and collaborations developing worldwide. There are many public and private programmes including universities, institutes, companies and government organizations [102]. All the projects aim to commercialize renewable aviation fuels through different ways and from different sources. The important intentions behind the development of renewable aviation fuels are (1) decrease the dependence on non-renewable fossil fuel sources (2) reduce environmental impacts (3) use of cheaply available feedstocks (4) reduce the fuel cost. The current commitments and collaborations in this field are discussed here.

Private sector projects on aviation fuel developments are well emerged in United States, concentrating selection of feedstock, conversion routes and scaling up [102]. Commercial Aviation Alternative Fuels Initiative (CAAFI) is a confederation of airlines, airports, manufactures, fuel suppliers and government organizations Federal Aviation Administration (FAA) in the United States [103]. IATA, American Society for Testing and Materials (ASTM), Coordinating Research Council (CRC), Department of Conservation (DOC), Defense Advanced Research Projects Agency (DARPA), Defense Energy Support Center (DESC), International Civil Aviation Organization (ICAO), original equipment manufacturer (OEM) are some of the members in the group. The association stands for development, certification and verification of renewable jet fuel and to support energy safety, environmental security and aviation capitals [104]. Brazilian Alliance is a collaborative group formed by airlines, biomass producers, biofuel researchers and manufacturers. The purposes are (1) support the sustainable aviation fuel development (2) decrease the environmental impacts of aviation

Table 1
Overview of biojet fuel production routes, renewable sources and various alternative aviation fuels.

Renewable sources	Routes	Alternative aviation fuels
Jatropha Camelina Wastes Algae Halophytes	*Biomass to liquid process (BTL process) Pyrolysis+Gasification+ Fischer Tropsch process *Hydroprocessing *Biochemical process Alcohol to jet process Direct Sugar to Hydrocarbon process	Hydroprocessed Renewable Jet fuels (HRJs) Fischer Tropsch fuels (FT) Liquid Biohydrogen Liquid Biomethane Bioalcohols

industry and (3) commercialization and scaling up of bio jet fuels [2]. Defence Energy Support Centre and US Military Services work in co-operation for the development, commercialization and certification of alternative jet fuels. They plan to reduce the dependence on petroleum fuels, exploitation of renewable resources and to produce advanced fuel with decreased greenhouse gas emissions.

The US Air Force Research Laboratory is prepared to test the fuels produced by FT process and hydroprocessing of jatropha, camelina, algae oils and animal fats [105]. Biojet Corporation (USA) is a collaborative project including South Pole Carbon Asset Management Ltd. of Zurich, Switzerland, Abundant Biofuels Corporation of Monterey, California, Mitch Hawkins & Co. Inc., of Santa Ynez, California. Biojet Corporation makes an association with algae developers and also uses jatropha and camelina oils as resources [106]. Energy & Environmental Research Center(EERC), USA with DARPA has industrialised a process called catalytic hydrodeoxygenation and isomerization (CHI process). The method makes use of feedstocks such as camelina oil, algal oil, canola oil, corn, tallow and waste grease for the production of bio jet fuels that are highly compatible with conventional fuels [86]. Global Seawater Inc., (GSI) established in UK and USA is a project mainly concerned with the production of alternative aviation fuels from seawater crops like halophytes. The work is primarily based on Salicornia bigelovii, which is a native plant in Europe, United States, South Asia and South Africa [107].

Rentech, Inc. is a USA based company concentrated on the production of hydrocarbon fuels from biomass sources. The project works on Rentech Process the basic principle of which is FT process and it converts biomass, green waste, municipal and solid wastes to synthetic jet fuels. The hydrocarbon fuel produced by the company can be better blended with conventional fuel to use in military and commercial jet fuel [108]. UOP (USA) is a well-known company in the fields of petroleum refining and processing. They have resourcefully synthesized hydroprocessed renewable jet fuels from various natural sources such as camelina oil, algal oil, jatropha oil and tallow by the process of deoxygenation, isomerization and cracking [86]. Universal Oil Products, US mainly focused on hydrodeoxygenation of free fatty acids for fuel production [68]. Amyris, USA with Total Alternative Aviation Fuel aim to produce renewable hydrocarbon fuels by Direct Sugar to Hydrocarbon (DSHC) process with low greenhouse gas emissions and better fuel properties. They also plan to gain acceptance from OEM and to get ASTM and Def Stan authentication [88]. Tecbio, Brazil tries to upraise their crop Babassu palm for biokerosene production with NASA [68]. The Midwest Aviation Sustainable Biofuels Initiative (MASBI) established in 2012 focused to promote midwestern U.S. energy security. The Canadian company Applied Research Associates, Inc (ARA) used hydroprocessed vegetable oil on business jet flight [109].

International Air Transport Association (IATA) is an international trade industry. Their aviation plan is based on four main policies (1) development of fuel technology i.e., finding new energy sources, production of clean bio jet fuels and engine compatibility (2) Aircraft processing with good efficiency (3) Infrastructure (4) favourable aviation economy [110]. Boeing, a multinational American aerospace company that is highly dynamic in the field of development and testing of alternative aviation fuel with Airbus aim to initiate innovative fuel technologies, to improve life cycles, to advance international flight operations and reliable fuel distribution [111]. Aliança Brasileira para Biocombustiveis de Aviação, ABRABA (Brazilian Alliance for Aviation Biofuels), Brazil is collaboration project of institutes, industries and government for the generation of sustainable biojet fuels [112]. Many private companies and organizations are on the road from different countries all over the world mainly U.S, Japan, Qatar, Mexico,

Singapore, Brazil, China, Canada and Australia [102]. Airlines have signed agreements with fuel producing companies, Alaska Airlines with Hawai'i Bio Energy, United Airlines with Alt Air and Avianca Brasil with Byogy for the development of bio jet fuels. Alt Air plans for a hydroprocessing plant by 2014 having a capacity of 90 kt/year [109].

Dynamotive Energy Systems Corporation (DESC) in partnership with Tecna SA and IFPen/Axens produces 1 gal of jet fuel at cost between \$1.82 and \$3.25 from biomass by Dynamotive's fast pyrolysis and refining processes through two ways [59]. Imperium Renewables, Inc. (IRI) with Pacific Northwest National Laboratory (PNNL) follow Alcohol to Jet process for the jet fuel production using waste materials from forests, municipalities and agriculture [113]. Altair Fuels (US) targets to supply 75 million gal/year of bio jet fuels using potential oil crops like Camelina [114]. Solena (US) follows Fischer tropsch method for the conversion of agricultural and municipal wastes to biojet fuels and it also takes the advantages of a cleaning technology [115]. Virent (US) in partnership with Shell and Cargill uses sugar cane, cone starch and sugar beet as feedstock for the generation of biojet fuels [116]. They also plans to use corn stover, switch grass, wood and bagasse as potential feedstocks [117]. Air Force Certification Office (AFCO) is a fuel certifying agency which has legalized the use of FT fuel blends [118]. SkyNRG, Netherlands planned to start flights with Thomson airlines, Fin Air and Alaska airlines powered by biojet fuel produced from waste cooking oil [34]. Sapphire Energy aim to produce 300–500 b/d algal aviation biofuel within three years [26].

According to Solazyme Inc.USA, they will produce large amount of oil from microalgae which can be effectively converted to bio jet fuel [2]. European Aerospace Defence System in 2010 and US Navy in 2011 tested flight with microalgae bio aviation fuel. European airlines has invested 2.7 billion euro to achieve 4% development by 2020 and IATA plans for 6% development in biofuel production [34]. Alternative Fuels and Biofuels for Aircraft Development (ALFA-BIRD) is an assignment financed by European Union. The objectives of the projects are (1) production of new aviation bio fuels and their analysis, introduction of injection systems and modelling, testing the compatibility of the newly developed fuel [86]. Syntroleum Corporation produces FT fuels using natural gas as the feedstock and USAF (US Air Force) tried flight with 50:50 blend of the produced fuel with JP-8 [119]. Dynamic Fuels, USA is a joint mission of Syntroleum Corporation and Tyson Foods, Inc. aiming the development of advanced feasible routes for the production of high quality aviation fuels and fuel technologies.

Tyson foods supplies animal fats and it is hydroprocessed to clean jet fuels. Their project targets to produce 284 million liters of fuel per year [86]. Avantium Chemicals in Netherlands (Europe) has established the method of catalytic conversion of sugar to 5-hydroxymethylfurfural. It could be used as a component in aviation fuel with good stability and blending properties [120]. Neste Oil Corporation is a worldwide Finland (Europe) based marketing company focused on the production of good value transportation fuels. They use the biomass to fuel process which is well known as NExBTL process. The feedstocks used by them are vegetable oils mainly jatropha and algae as well as animal fats [54,121]. Swedish Biofuels AB (Sweden) company also makes efforts for the development and industrialization of renewable alternative jet fuels. They have secured patents in this field. With LanzaTech they produce jet fuel mainly from wood, forest residues, agricultural wastes and grains. The method of synthesis involves production of sugar from the biomass feedstock followed by fermentation. The resulted alcohols are then chemically converted into hydrocarbon [122].

Airbus is a European aircraft manufacturing company. They focus on the current situation of aviation fuels, development of sustainable biojet fuels, development of technology and certification of Bio SPK. They have also performed test flights with

T. Kandaramath Hari et al. / Renewable and Sustainable Energy Reviews 42 (2015) 1234–1244   1241

renewable aviation fuels [123]. GE Aviation a part of General Electric Company (GE) US uses bio oil hydroprocessing [68]. Aviation Initiative for Renewable Energy in Germany (AIREG) work for advanced research and development in aviation biofuels and combining experts in the field to achieve fuels with reduced emissions and sustainability [124]. The Sustainable Aviation Fuel Users Group (SAFUG) based in Europe involving Natural Resources Defence Council and the Roundtable for Sustainable Biofuels (RSB) concentrated on production of advanced aviation fuels from renewable sources with minimum impacts on the environment and ecosystems. They also decided to cultivate plants which can financially support undeveloped areas and communities [125].

Sustainable Way for Alternative Fuel and Energy in Aviation (SWAFEA) mainly concerns with lifecycle analysis, compatibility of alternative fuel, environmental influences and fuel economics [12]. The Nordic Initiative for Sustainable Aviation, NISA is founded by Nordic stakeholders for the development of a sustainable aviation fuel [109]. Lufthansa tested flights with biofuel in 2011 as a part of burnFAIR research project between Hamburg and Frankfurt [126]. Initiative Towards sustainable Kerosene for Aviation, ITAKA is a collaborative initiative that targets to connect feedstock cultivators, biofuel producers, distributors and users in developing a large scale camelina bio jet supply chain [57]. Air France-KLM has set a schedule for the development of next generation biofuels, new technologies, policies and legislation [127].

Sasol (SA) is marketing company which is now functioning in Qatar and establishing a new branch in Nigeria. They adopted the Gas to liquid process (GTL) fuels through Fischer Tropsch synthesis for the synthesis and scaling up of hydrocarbon. They have certified the use of 50:50 blend of FT fuel with JET-A for aviation purpose [68]. An Indo-Canadian programme involving Pratt, Universities of Laval, Ryerson, Queens, Whitney, HPCL, Indian Institute of Science Bangalore, IIP, Info Tech, Indian Oil, IIT (K) is signed for renewable fuel production, blending and applications [128]. Chinese Academy of Sciences in partnership with Boeing has started Joint Research Laboratory for Sustainable Aviation Biofuels for the production of algal biojet fuels [112]. Japan Airlines with Boeing produces bio jet fuel from algae, jatropha and camelina oils and uses in aircraft engines with 50:50 blends with Jet-A [129].

Virgin Australia, Australia's second largest airlines company joined with government and other industries work for the development of renewable aviation fuel, fuel technologies and commercialization of alternative aviation fuels for affordable price [130]. Sustainable Aviation Fuel Road Map (SAFRM), an enterprise of the SAFUG was launched targeting local supply chain development of bio jet fuels [112]. Queensland Sustainable Aviation Fuel Initiative in Australia focuses on the production and lifecycle assessment of bio jet fuels from oil crops, sucrose and algae. They plan to develop sugar to bio aviation fuel process by yeast fermentation [131]. The Global Bioenergy Partnership (GBEP), The Roundtable for Sustainable Biofuels (RSB), International Sustainability and Carbon Certification (ISCC), REDcert, The Renewable Transportation Fuel Obligation Sustainable Biofuel Meta Standard (RTFO), Sustainable Biodiesel Alliance are the existing sustainability evaluation programs [132].

7. Challenges

Even though the need of alternative aviation biofuels are exceeding, there are many challenges to overcome and to achieve the goals. The price gaps between bio and conventional jet fuels, sustainability and financial problems in commercialization are major concerns in the development of alternative jet fuels [127]. Economic and environmental issues including land-water usage, greenhouse gas (GHG) and particulate emissions, fuel-food

competition are the major obstacles come across. Sustainability is a big obstacle to overcome which depends mainly on the availability of feedstock and the fuel production route that bring out social, economic and environmental impacts [133].

7.1. Environmental challenges

One of the major issues that should be faced is the social and environmental impact of fuel production and management. 2.5% of man-made carbon dioxide was from aviation sector in 2005 and it is expected to become 4–4.7% by 2050 [134]. The uprising demand for bio jet fuels creates afforestation issues which will affect the fertility of soil and biodiversity and will cause increase in atmospheric CO_2 [72]. Use of agricultural land for crop cultivation for biofuel production will cause food scarcity and it will reduce soil quality and water availability in the soil. The use of fertilizers and insecticides will result in soil destruction and water pollution [135]. The fuel developed must not arise any human health issues [136].

7.2. Production issues

Cost effectiveness of the process and feedstock flexibility are major hurdles related to production process [137]. Even though there are projects developing on the basis of algae as feedstock, there are many problems and difficulties related to algae. The selection and production of useful algal species and lipid extraction is a puzzling process [138]. The production of bio jet fuel from algae needs optimization of the process, production cost, properties and its certification [139]. The suitable catalyst selection and right designing of the process are important tasks to be faced by the alternative fuel producers [140]. The production process is feedstock dependent and so varying [141]. Production process must be consistent, competent and highly efficient.

7.3. Distribution problems

Quality of product and suitable blending for effective functioning are problematic in the supply process [137]. The costs of HRJ and BTL fuels are now in a range of $0.80–$2.00/L which is 3 times higher than that for petroleum based jet fuels [12]. Fuel infrastructure, fuel marketing, storage of feedstock and fuel, byproducts marketing regulations and certifications are also major tasks to overcome [44]. The current production cost of biojet fuels should be reduced; otherwise it will not be feasible and the increasing prize will affect the production investments [102]. The coordination of investors and biomass suppliers is also highly essential [124].

7.4. Feedstock availability and sustainability

The feedstock which is cost effective that can grow with minimum water supply and fertilizers, with good yield, without affecting the food crops and thereby avoiding food to fuel issues, that possess low greenhouse gas emission and provides economical benefits are largely favoured for the production of aviation biofuels [20]. The challenges related to feedstock are availability of feedstock in bulk scale with comparatively low cost and restrictions for large scale applications [137]. The major problems associated with algae culture are temperature maintenance and energy requirement [139]. Large amount of fuel must be produced to test in aircrafts and need large amount of feedstock [141]. While producing alternative aviation fuels, the feedstocks must be selected such as to minimize impact on the land use and water intake [136]. Now the availability of biomass feedstock for the

1242 T. Kandaramath Hari et al. / Renewable and Sustainable Energy Reviews 42 (2015) 1234–1244

production of bio jet fuel is restricted due to competition with the current fuel requirements [142].

7.5. Compatibility with conventional fuel

Renewable jet fuels must be compatible with the conventional jet fuels. In contrast to conventional jet fuels; bioaviation fuels must not contain sulphur and aromatics, must possess low freezing point and high auto ignition temperature [136]. Separation of bio aviation fuels at large airports will not be easy and some airlines face problems while using the biofuels [143]. In addition there are other problems like introduction of renewable fuel into commercial aviation service, certification, engine and quality testing and application of the fuel in aircrafts [19]. The fuel developed must be resistant to a wide range of operational circumstances, must show good performance and safety guaranteed [21]. Thermal stability and storage stability are two important issues regarding aviation biofuels. Low temperature properties, combustion characteristics and presence of small impurities like metals and micronutrients also do matter [141].

8. Future outlook and recommendations

Defence Logistics Agency Energy (DLA Energy) is now targeted to link market scale production and certification of bio aviation fuels through partnerships with manufactures and government organizations [109]. Production and commercialization of bio jet fuels can influence land, water and food resources, biodiversity and can make economical and social impacts. Shortage of inducements and programmes to scale up sustainable production and distribution of feedstock, lack of cost effective technologies for production of bio jet fuels are the existing complications that slow down the research in this field. The future aviation fuel or the production process (1) must never raise food–fuel competition (2) must not make environmental issues and (3) must be sustainable with tolerable cost.

Considering the feedstock, non-edible oils, biomass and algae can contribute as potential feedstock, while algae can be used as raw material for the production of fuel in the regions such as Australia, Arabia, north-west Africa and deserts in the United States while evaluating their availability [127]. The production process can be improved by adopting new production technologies and by the use of locally available feedstock which will bring out regional development. Involvement of government and other investing organizations and industries, long term policies and other partnerships will provide more job opportunities and will help to maintain the sustainability of the fuel production and distribution.

9. Conclusion

The production of alternative aviation fuels from renewable bioresources is a highly promising technology which is expected to substitute the petroleum based fuels. Among the various processes and alternative fuels, hydroprocessed renewable jet fuel (HRJ) and Fisher Tropsch fuels (FT fuels) have the potential to replace the conventional jet fuels. The main problems with biodiesel and bioalcohols as aviation fuels are their poor fuel properties. The use of liquid hydrogen and liquid methane fuels are favoured, but their high production cost and less suitability to conventional aircraft engines make them less preferred. Many challenges arise including availability of feedstock, compatibility of alternative fuels with conventional fuels, environmental concern and production and distribution issues. The increasing interest of government

and international organizations can help the scaling up, commercialisation and supply chain infrastructure to large extent. The use of waste materials from different sources which are largely available as the feedstock can contribute to the issues related to feedstock costs.

References

[1] Solomon S, Qin D, Manning M, Chen Z, Marquis M, Averyt KB et al., editors. IPCC Climate change 2007: the physical science basis, Contribution of working group 1 to the fourth assessment report of the intergovernmental panel on climate change. Cambridge University Press: Cambridge, United Kingdom and New York, NY, USA; 2007.
[2] Bello BZ. Captured CO_2 to grow microalgae for bio-jet fuel production. UKCCSC Winter School University of Cambridge; 2012.
[3] IEA World energy outlook, Chapters 2, 3, 14. International Energy Agency: Paris; 2006.
[4] Metz B, Davidson OR, Bosch PR, Dave R, Meyer LA., editors., IPCC climate change 2007: mitigation, contribution of working group 3 to the fourth assessment report of the intergovernmental panel on climate change. Cambridge University Press: Cambridge, United Kingdom and New York, USA; 2007.
[5] Faaij A, van Dijk M. White paper on sustainable jet fuel. SkyNRG (SkyNRG) 2012.
[6] The bigger implications from the think bankruptcy. ⟨http://www.navigantresearch.com/2011/06⟩.
[7] U.S. Energy Information Administration, (2012): Annual Energy Outlook 2012.
[8] Hemighaus G, Boval T, Bosley C, Organ R, Lind J, Brouette R, et al. Alternative jet fuels, a supplement to Chevron's aviation fuels technical review. Chevron Corporation; 2006.
[9] Kubickova I, Kubicka D. Utilization of triglycerides and related feedstocks for production of clean hydrocarbon fuels and petrochemicals: a review. Waste Biomass Valor 2010;1:293–308.
[10] Mohammad M, Hari TK, Yaakob Z, Sharma YC, Sopian K. Overview on the production of paraffin based-biofuels via catalytic hydrodeoxygenation. Renewable Sustainable Energy Rev 2013;22:121–32.
[11] Future transport fuels. Report of the European expert group on the future transport fuels; 2011.
[12] Baljet M. Aviation biofuel. Global Media Day 2010.
[13] Bertran BL. Biodiesel cost analysis in Spain and Turkey. Istanbul Technical University, Institute of Science and Technology. MSc thesis; 2009.
[14] Growing America's energy future: renewable bioenergy, biomass program. Energy efficiency and renewable energy; 2010.
[15] ICAO review: sustainable alternative fuels for aviation. ICAO aviation and sustainable alternative fuels workshop; 2011.
[16] SINOPEC bio-jet fuel technology. In: The fifth China–Japan–Korea petroleum technology congress; 2012.
[17] Bridgwater AV. Review of fast pyrolysis of biomass and product upgrading. Biomass Bioenergy 2012;38:68–94.
[18] Murtala AM, Shawal NN, Usman HD. Biomass as a renewable source of chemicals for industrial applications. Int J Eng Sci Technol 2012;4:721–30.
[19] Pandey PK. Opportunities in bio-fuels for aviation. National Seminar on Bioenergy Solutions; 2011.
[20] Beginner's Guide to Aviation Biofuels. Air Transport Action Group. 2nd ed; 2011.
[21] Beginner's Guide to Aviation Biofuels. Air Transport Action Group; 2009.
[22] Rekoske J. Biofuels: challenges & opportunities. Asia Pacific Clean Energy Summit & Expo; 2010.
[23] Bio aviation fuel stock supply-challenges, strategies and recent developments. ICAO aviation and sustainable alternative fuels; 2011.
[24] Daggett D, Hendricks R, Walther R. Alternative fuels and their potential impact on aviation. NASA/TM—2006-214365; 2006. ⟨http://gltrs.grc.nasa.gov⟩.
[25] Bomani BMM, Bulzan DL, Centeno-Gomez DI, Hendricks RC. Biofuels as an alternative energy source for aviation–a survey. NASA/TM—2009-215587; 2009.
[26] Nygren E, Aleklett K, Hook M. Aviation fuel and future oil production scenarios. Energy Policy 2009;37:4003–10.
[27] Liu G, Yan B. Chen G. Technical review on jet fuel production. Renewable Sustainable Energy Rev 2013;25:59–70.
[28] Kallio P, Pasztor A, Akhtar MK, Jones PR. Renewable jet fuel. Curr Opin Biotechnol 2014;26:50–5.
[29] Bozell JJ. The use of renewable feedstocks for the production of chemicals and materials—a brief overview of concepts. ⟨http://www.nrel.gov/docs/gen/fy04/36831f.pdf⟩.
[30] Herreras Y, Stern V, Capuano A. Sustainable raw material production for the aviation industry. Environ Rep 2010:168–71.
[31] International air transport association report on alternative fuels. 5th ed; 2010.
[32] Shonnard DR, Williams L, Kalnes TN. Camelina-derived jet fuel and diesel: sustainable advanced biofuels. Environ Prog Sustainable Energy 2010;29:382–92.

[33] Jingura RM, Musademb D, Matengaif R. An evaluation of utility of *Jatropha curcas* L. as a source of multiple energy carriers. Int J Eng Sci Technol 2010;2:115–22.

[34] van der Hagen. The application of bio jet fuels until 2050 scenarios for future developments. Master thesis, Utrecht University; 2012.

[35] *Jatropha curcas*-derived biofuel industry in Africa. In: Conference proceedings, The Network of African Science Academies (NASAC); 2010.

[36] Sustainable biofuels: prospects and challenges. The Royal Society Sustainable biofuels, Policy document 01/08; 2008.

[37] Rosillo-Calle F, Teelucksingh S, Thrän D, Seiffert M. The potential role of biofuels in commercial air transport–Biojetfuel. IEA bioenergy task 40, Sustainable International Bioenergy Trade.

[38] Hu Q, Sommerfeld M, Jarvis E, Ghirardi M, Posewitz M, Seibert M, et al. Microalgal triacylglycerols as feedstocks for biofuel production: perspectives and advances. Plant J 2008;54:621–39.

[39] Singh A, Nigam PS, Murphy JD. Mechanism and challenges in commercialisation of algal biofuels. Bioresour Technol 2011;102:26–34.

[40] Jorquera O, Kiperstok A, Sales EA, Embirucu M, Ghirardi ML. Comparative energy life-cycle analyses of microalgal biomass production in open ponds and photobioreactors. Bioresour Technol 2010;101:1406–13.

[41] Maniatis K, Weitz M, Zschocke A. 2 Million tons per year: a performing biofuels supply chain for EU aviation. Bruxles: European Commission; 2011.

[42] Subhadra B, Edwards M. An integrated renewable energy park approach for algal biofuel production in United States. Energy Policy 2010;38:4897–902.

[43] Singh A, Olsen SI. A critical review of biochemical conversion, sustainability and life cycle assessment of algal biofuels. Appl Energy 2011;88:3548–55.

[44] Morello J, Pate R. The promise and challenge of algae as renewable source of biofuels. Biomass Program Webinar 2010.

[45] Kargbo DM. Biodiesel production from municipal sewage sludges. Energy Fuels 2010;24:2791–4.

[46] Saynor B, Bauen A, Leach M. The potential for renewable energy sources in aviation. PRESAV final report; 2003.

[47] Abideen Z, Ansari R, Gul B, Khan MA. The place of halophytes in Pakistan's biofuel industry. Biofuels 2012;3:211–20.

[48] Hendricks RC, Bushnell DM. Halophytes energy feedstocks: back to our roots. In: The 12th international symposium on transport phenomena and dynamics of rotating machinery; 2008.

[49] Ehel A, Zilberstein A, Alekparov C, Eilam T, Oren I, Sasson Y, et al. Biomass production by desert halophytes: alleviating the pressure on food production. Recent Adv Energy Environ 2010:362–7 isbn: 978-960-474-159-5.

[50] Arvidsson R, Persson S, Froling M, Svanstrom M. Life cycle assessment of hydrotreated vegetable oil from rape, oil palm and Jatropha. J Clean Prod 2011;19:129–37.

[51] Gong DY, Kaario O, Tilli A, Larmi M, Tanner FX. A computational investigation of hydrotreated vegetable oil sprays using RANS and a modified version of the RNG k−ε model in OpenFOAM. SAE World Congress; 2010.

[52] Hileman JI, Ortiz DS, Bartis JT, Wong HM, Donohoo PE, Weiss MA. Near-term feasibility of alternative jet fuels. RAND Infrastruct Saf Environ 2009.

[53] Aatola H, Larmi M, Sarjovaara T, Mikkonen S. Hydrotreated vegetable oil (HVO) as a renewable diesel fuel: trade-off between NOx, particulate emission and fuel consumption of a heavy duty engine. SAE International; 2008.

[54] Mikkonen S, Hartikka T, Kuronen M, Saikkonen PHVO. Hydrotreated vegetable oil–a premium renewable biofuel for diesel engines. Neste Oil Proprietary Publication; 2012.

[55] Lapuerta M, Villajos M, Agudelo JR, Boehman AL. Key properties and blending strategies of hydrotreated vegetable oil as biofuel for diesel engines. Fuel Process Technol 2011;92:2406–11.

[56] Simacek P, Kubicka D, Kubicková I, Homola F, Pospisil M, Chudoba J. Premium quality renewable diesel by hydroprocessed of sunflower oil. Fuel 2011:902473–9.

[57] Hamelinck C, Cuijpers M, Spoettle M, van den Bos A. Biofuels for aviation. ECOFYS Netherlands 2013.

[58] Winchester N, McConnachie D, Wollersheim C, Waitz IA. Economic and emissions impacts of renewable fuel goals for aviation in the US. Transp Res Part A 2013;58:116–28.

[59] Commercial case business evaluation of Dynamotive's fast pyrolysis & upgrading processes. Dynamotive energy systems corporation.

[60] Veringa HJ. Advanced techniques for generation of energy from biomass and waste. ECN biomass. 〈https://www.ecn.nl/fileadmin/ecn/units/bio/Overig/pdf/Biomassa_voordelen.pdf〉.

[61] Clean alternative fuels: Fischer–Tropsch, United States Environmental Protection Agency EPA420-F-00-036; 2002.

[62] Kreutz TG, Larson ED, Liu G, Williams RH. Fischer–Tropsch fuels from coal and biomass. In: 25th Annual international Pittsburgh coal conference 2008.

[63] Young NN. The future of biofuels: U.S. (and Global) airlines & aviation alternative fuels. In: EIA conference 2014.

[64] Moser BR. Camelina (*Camelina sativa* L.) oil as a biofuels feedstock: golden opportunity or false hope. Lipid Technol 2010;22:270–3.

[65] Biodegradability of biodiesel in the aquatic environment. Development of rapeseed biodiesel for use in high-speed diesel engines. Progress report; 1996, p. 96–116.

[66] Acute toxicity of biodiesel to freshwater and marine organisms. Development of rapeseed biodiesel for use in high speed diesel engines. Progress report; 1996, p. 117–31.

[67] Arkoudeas P, Kalligeros S, Zannikos F, Anastopoulos G, Karonis D, Lois E, et al. Study of using JP-8 aviation fuel and biodiesel in CI engines. Energy Convers Manage 2003;44:1013–25.

[68] Roberts WL. Bio jet fuels. In: The fifth international biofuels conference; 2008.

[69] Wardle DA. Global sale of green air travel supported using biodiesel. Renewable Sustainable Energy Rev 2003;7:64–71.

[70] Balat M, Balat M. Political, economic and environmental impacts of biomass-based hydrogen. Int J Hydrogen Energy 2009;34:3589–603.

[71] Faab R. Cryoplane: Flugzeuge mit Wasserstoffantrieb, 2001. / 〈http://www.haw-hamburg.de/pers/Scholz/dglr/hh/text_2001_12_06_Cryoplane.pdfS〉 (Accessed April 13, 2006).

[72] Charles MB, Barnes P, Ryan N, Clayton J. Airport futures: towards a critique of the aerotropolis model. Futures 2007;39:1009–28.

[73] Birkenstock W. Hydrogen aircraft fuel research plans. Flug Revue 1998:66 (September).

[74] Airbus Deutschland GmbH, liquid hydrogen fuelled aircraft–system analysis: final technical report (Publishable Version), 2003. / 〈http://www.aero-net.org/default.htmlS〉 (Accessed April 13, 2006).

[75] Midilli A, Aya M, Dincer I, Rosen MA. On hydrogen and hydrogen energy strategies I: current status and needs. Renewable Sustainable Energy Rev 2005;9:255–71.

[76] Probstein, Ronald F, Edwin HR. Synthetic fuels. Mineola, New York: Dover Publications Inc.; 2006.

[77] Horne PA, Williams PT. Influence of temperature on the products from the flash pyrolysis of biomass. Fuel 1996;75:1051–7.

[78] Fuels for the aviation industry, 〈http://www.ifpenergiesnouvelles.com〉.

[79] You F, Wang B. Multiobjective optimization of biomass-to-liquids processing networks. 〈http://focapo.cheme.cmu.edu/2012/proceedings/data/papers/013.pdf〉.

[80] Clauben M, Schindler M, Vodegel S, Caelowitz O. The biomass-to-liquid process at CUTEC: optimisation of the Fischer–Tropsch synthesis with carbon-dioxide rich synthesis gas; 2005.

[81] SWAFEA, State of the art on alternative fuels in aviation; 2011.

[82] Demirbas MF. Biorefineries for biofuel upgrading: a critical review. Appl Energy 2009;86:S151-61.

[83] Pearlon MN. A techno-economic and environmental assessment of hydro-processed renewable distillate fuels. Massachusetts Institute of Technology; 2011 Master thesis.

[84] Edwards JT, Shafer LM, Klein JK. U.S. Air Force hydroprocessed renewable jet (HRJ) fuel research. Interim report; 2012.

[85] Sotelo-Boyás R, Trejo-Zárraga F, Hernández-Loyo FJ. Hydroconversion of triglycerides into green liquid fuels. In: Karamé I. hydrogenation; 2012, isbn: 978-953-51-0785-9.

[86] Alternative fuels foreword. International Air Transport Association, IATA, report on alternative fuels; 2009.

[87] Freire G. Aviation biofuels development. ICAO aviation and sustainable alternative fuels workshop 2011.

[88] Amyris-total alternative aviation fuel partnership–direct sugar to hydro-carbon (DSHC) jet biofuel; 2013. 〈http://rezn8d.net/?attachment_id=3369〉.

[89] Airshow B. Breaking the barriers with breakthrough jet fuel solutions. Renewable aviation fuel joint development program 2012.

[90] Alcohol to Jet (ATJ) engineering though ASTM. ICAO aviation and sustainable alternative fuels workshop; 2011.

[91] IATA report on alternative fuels. International Air Transport Association. 6th ed.; 2011.

[92] Sugarcane-based bioethanol-energy for sustainable development. BNDES and CGEE. 1st ed.; 2008.

[93] Ethanol from biomass. Biofacts; 1995. 〈http://ntl.bts.gov/lib/000/700/715/ethanol.pdf〉.

[94] Serrano-Ruiz JC, Dumesic JA. In: Guczi L, Erdohelyi A, editors. Catalytic production of liquid hydrocarbon transportation fuels. Catalysis for Alternative Energy Generation; 2012. p. 29–56. http://dx.doi.org/10.1007/978-1-4614-03449_2.

[95] Kapdan IK, Kargi F. Bio-hydrogen production from waste materials. Enzyme Microb Technol 2006;38:569–82.

[96] van Zon N Liquid hydrogen powered commercial aircraft, analysis of the technical feasibility of sustainable liquid hydrogen powered commercial aircraft in 2040.

[97] Reith JH, Wijffels RH, Barten H. (Ed). Bio-methane & Bio-hydrogen, status and perspectives of biological methane and hydrogen production; 2003. isbn: 90-9017165-7.

[98] Cryoplane hydrogen fuelled aircraft. Submission for the Energy Globe Award 2001, Category "Transport", Hamburg; 2000.

[99] Molino A, Nanna F, Ding Y, Bikson B, Braccio G. Biomethane production by anaerobic digestion of organic waste. Fuel 2013;103:1003–9.

[100] Helwani Z, Othman MR, Aziz N, Kim J. Fernando WJN. Solid heterogeneous catalysts for transesterification of triglycerides with methanol: a review. Appl Catal A: Gen 2009;363:1–10.

[101] Alonso DM, Bond JQ, Dumesic JA. Catalytic conversion of biomass to biofuels. Green Chem 2010;12:1493–513.

[102] Green growth and the future of aviation. Paper prepared for the 27th Round Table on Sustainable Development to be held at OECD Headquarters; 2012.

[103] Schenk DP, Altman R. The CAAFI coalition, leading the quest for a new, sustainable jet fuel dynamic; 2009.

[104] Edwards T. AF Research lab activities supporting CAAFI, Alternative aviation fuels evaluation to support certification; 2011.

[105] Air Force Research Laboratory Alternative Fuels Team wins major prize for aviation biofuels work; 2011. ⟨http://www.biofuelsdigest.com/bdigest/2011/09/23/air-force-research-laboratory-alternative-fuels-team-wins-major-prize-for-aviation-biofuels-work/⟩.

[106] Biojet. ⟨http://www.biojetcorp.com⟩.

[107] Global sea water Inc. ⟨http://seawaterfoundation.org/gsi/news.html⟩.

[108] Integrated pilot project for fuel production by thermochemical conversion of wood waste. Clear fuels-Rentech pilot-scale bio refinery; 2011. ⟨http://www1.eere.energy.gov/bioenergy/pdfs/ibr_arra_clearfuelstechnology.pdf⟩.

[109] IATA. Report on alternative fuels. 8th ed.International Air Transport Association; 2013 8th ed. International Air Transport Association; 2013.

[110] Rötger T. Sustainable fuels from around the world. IATA; 2012.

[111] Aviation and the environment, demonstrating commitment with action. The Boeing company; 2009.

[112] Sustainable aviation fuels northwest: powering the next generation of flight, SAFN report; 2011.

[113] Plaza J. Innovating renewables for the future: WCTA. Imperium Renewables, Inc; 2011.

[114] Sustainable flying: biofuels as an economic and environmental salve for the airline industry. EQ² insight, managing the future today; 2010.

[115] Young NN. Buying and flying sustainable alternative aviation fuels. Deployment from an airline perspective. ICAO aviation and sustainable alternative fuels workshop; 2011.

[116] Virent is replacing crude oil. An introduction to Virent advanced biofuels and the RFS: the state of technology, investment and market outlook; 2012.

[117] Held A. Virent is replacing crude oil. Louisiana biofuels and bioprocessing summit 2012.

[118] Summary of IATA 2009 Report on Alternative Fuels. ⟨http://www.iata.org/SiteCollectionDocuments/2page2009ReportonAlternativeFuels_final_.pdf⟩.

[119] Albany OR, Fairbanks AK, Morgantown WV, Pittsburgh PA, Sugar Land TX. Fischer–Tropsch fuels. R&D FACTS clean fuels 2011.

[120] van Putten R-J, van der Waal JC, de Jong E, Rasrendra CB, Heeres HJ, de Vries JG. Hydroxymethylfurfural, a versatile platform chemical made from renewable resources. Chem Rev 2013;113:1499–597.

[121] NExBTL renewable diesel. ⟨http://www.nestejacobs.com/binary.asp?GUID=B4D4B9E2-966C-48D5⟩.

[122] Mitchell P. Aviation biofuels. All energy 2012.

[123] Nash P. Airbus alternative fuels. World biofuels market 2011.

[124] Buse J. Aviation initiative for renewable energy in Germany (Aireg) connecting know-how-propelling progress; 2012.

[125] Flight path to Sustainable Aviation, towards establishing a sustainable aviation fuels industry in Australia and New Zealand. Sustainable aviation fuel road map; 2010.

[126] Biofuel at Lufthansa. ⟨http://www.lufthansagroup.com/fileadmin/downloads/en/LH-Biofuel-Flyer.pdf⟩.

[127] Nair S, Paulose H. Emergence of green business models: the case of algae biofuel for aviation. Energy Policy 2014;65:175–84.

[128] Kumar A. Bio-Jet fuels: a step towards green aviation. DSDS 2010.

[129] Abe Y. JAL biofuel flight demonstration. The Boeing Company; 2009.

[130] Sustainable aviation biofuel development at Virgin Australia.

[131] Queensland sustainable jet fuel initiative ⟨http://ussc.edu.au/s/media/docs/other/110302_Avalon_McCarthy.pdf⟩.

[132] Alternative aviation jet fuel sustainability evaluation report, ⟨http://ntl.bts.gov/lib/43000/43100/43137/DOT-VNTSC-FAA-12-03.pdf⟩.

[133] The challenges for the development and deployment of sustainable alternative fuels in aviation, ⟨http://www.icao.int/environmentalprotection/GFAAF/Documents/ICAO%20SUSTAF%20experts%20group%20outcomes_release%20May2013.pdf⟩.

[134] Lee DS, Pitari G, Grewe V, Gierens K, Penner JE, Petzold A, et al. Transport impacts on atmosphere and climate: aviation. Atmos Environ 2010;44:4678–734.

[135] Cseke LJ, Podila GK, Kirakosyan A, Kaufman PB, Kirakosyan A, Kaufman PB. Plants as sources of energy. Recent advances in plant biotechnology, editor., chapter 9, 163–210.

[136] Duff B. The chemical sciences roundtable: opportunities and obstacles in large-scale biomass utilization, biomass utilization for fuels, products and power. DOE biomass program; 2012.

[137] Toro FA. Biofuels in aviation major challenges, potentials major R&D activities and needs. Joint IEA-GHG-TransPoRD workshop; 2010.

[138] Albrecht KO, Hallen RT. A brief literature overview of various routes to biorenewable fuels from lipids for the National Alliance for Advanced Biofuels and Bio-products (NAABB) Consortium; 2011.

[139] Carlson LS, Lee MY. Algae to alkanes. Department of Chemical & Biomolecular Engineering Senior Design Reports (CBE), University of Pennsylvania; 2010.

[140] Bloch M. First generation bio-diesel and bio-jet fuels production. IFP Sessions 2009.

[141] Holmgren J. Bio aviation fuel. In: World biofuels markets congress 2008.

[142] Ogden J, Anderson L. editors. Sustainable transportation energy pathways a research summary for decision makers; 2011.

[143] Lo J. Aviation alternative fuels, practical deployment hurdles. ICAO aviation and sustainable alternative fuels workshop 2011.

12

The impact of advanced biofuels on aviation emissions and operations in the U.S.

Niven Winchester, Robert Malina, Mark D. Staples, Steven R.H. Barrett

ABSTRACT

We analyze the economic and emissions impacts on U.S. commercial aviation of the Federal Aviation Administration's renewable jet fuel goal when met using advanced fermentation (AF) fuel from perennial grasses. These fuels have recently been certified for use in aircraft and could potentially provide greater environmental benefits than aviation biofuels approved previously. Due to uncertainties in the commercialization of AF technologies, we consider a range of assumptions concerning capital costs, energy conversion efficiencies and product slates. In 2030, estimates of the implicit subsidy required to induce consumption of AF jet fuel range from $0.45 to $20.85 per gallon. These correspond to a reference jet fuel price of $3.23 per gallon and AF jet fuel costs ranging from $4.01 to $24.41 per gallon. In all cases, as renewable jet fuel represents around 1.4% of total fuel consumed by commercial aviation, the goal has a small impact on aviation operations and emissions relative to a case without the renewable jet fuel target, and emissions continue to grow relative to those in 2005. Costs per metric ton of carbon dioxide equivalent abated by using biofuels range from $42 to $652.

JEL classification:
L93
Q42
Q54

Keywords:
Aviation
Biofuels
Climate Change
Emissions Abatement

1. Introduction

Recent estimates indicate that aviation currently accounts for approximately 5% of total anthropogenic radiative forcing (Dessens et al., 2014; Lee et al., 2009). Furthermore, the International Civil Aviation Organization (ICAO, 2013) predicts that in the absence of mitigation measures, driven by a sevenfold increase in air traffic, total greenhouse gas (GHG) emissions associated with aviation will be 400–600% higher in 2050 than in 2010.

To address these concerns, in 2009 the International Air Transport Association (IATA) announced that it aimed to achieve carbon-neutral growth in global airline operations from 2020 onward, and to reduce aviation GHG emissions in 2050 by 50% relative to 2005 (IATA, 2009). The industry's strategy for meeting these goals rests upon improvements in operations, airport and air traffic management, airframe and engine technologies, as well as large-scale introduction of aviation biofuels that have significantly lower GHG emissions on a lifecycle basis than petroleum-derived jet fuel (IATA, 2009). Hileman et al. (2013) quantify the reduction in lifecycle GHG emissions intensity required to achieve the 2050 IATA goal in the U.S. They find that, after accounting for predicted growth in airline operations and fuel-efficiency improvements, aviation GHG intensity would need to decrease from 1.37 g of carbon dioxide equivalent (CO_2e) per kilogram-kilometer in 2005 to 0.22 g in 2050; a decrease of 84%.

Motivated by energy security and climate concerns, the U.S. Federal Aviation Administration (FAA) has established a voluntary goal that one billion gallons (~3.8 billion liters) of alternative jet fuel is consumed annually from 2018 onward in the U.S. (FAA, 2011). This goal includes renewable fuel targets set by the U.S. Air Force and Navy, so the biofuel goal for commercial aviation is a fraction of this amount.

Operating concurrently with the FAA's biofuel goal, the National Renewable Fuel Standard (RFS2) regulates biofuels used in ground transportation in the U.S. RFS2 sets mandates for biomass-based diesel, cellulosic biofuel, undifferentiated advanced biofuels and the total quantity of biofuels. The U.S. Environmental Protection Agency ensures that the RFS2 mandates are met by issuing a renewable identification number (RIN) for each gallon of biofuel produced, and requiring refineries to purchase a certain amount of RINs for each gallon of fuel sold for ground transportation (U.S. GAO, 2014). Separate RINs and turn-in targets are issued for each biofuel category. Aviation biofuels qualify for RINs, which have a monetary value, and therefore reduce the cost of renewable jet fuel to airlines.

Almost all biofuel currently produced is ethanol or biodiesel which, due to contamination and safety concerns, cannot be used in aircraft engines (Hileman et al., 2009; Waterland et al., 2003). Therefore, additional biofuel technologies need to be developed that are compatible with existing infrastructure and aircraft (Hileman et al., 2009).

N. Winchester et al. / Energy Economics 49 (2015) 482–491   483

Large-scale deployment of aviation biofuels from pathways suited for aviation face significant challenges. These include high production costs and lack of integration of aviation biofuels into regulatory frameworks (Carriquiry et al., 2011; Carter et al., 2011; Gegg et al., 2014), limits in scale-up due to feedstock availability (Seber et al., 2014; U.S. DOE, 2011), environmental and socio-economic consequences of large-scale land-use change and competition with food and feed needs (Kretschmer et al., 2009; Searchinger et al., 2008; Serra and Zilberman, 2013), water consumption associated with biomass cultivation (Scown et al., 2011; Staples et al., 2013), and the time required for scaling-up biomass cultivation and conversion facilities (Richard, 2010).

This paper deals with the impact of large-scale deployment of advanced aviation biofuels from perennial grasses such as switchgrass or miscanthus using a set of technologies known as fermentation and advanced fermentation (AF). Our modeling approach relies on an economy-wide model of economic activity and energy systems to quantify the additional cost of advanced renewable jet relative to its conventional counterpart, and the impact of achieving the FAA's goal on aviation operations and emissions.

We focus on biofuels from AF technologies since they are commonly regarded as one class of next-generation biofuels that face smaller environmental and economic challenges compared to traditional biofuels from oily crops or grains (Tilman et al., 2009). AF technologies can not only use sugary crops (such as sugarcane) and starchy crops (such as corn grain), but also convert non-edible lignocellulosic biomass from agricultural residues or perennial grasses. Energy grasses have high water, light and nitrogen use efficiency (Somerville et al., 2010), are suited for a broad range of climatic and soil conditions, and can be grown on land not suitable for food crops (McLaughlin et al., 2002). This potentially reduces competition for scarce land with food or feed purposes compared to growing oily crops or grains for fuel production. Moreover, due to relatively high conversion efficiencies and low fossil fuel input requirements during processing, lifecycle GHG emissions can be significantly lower than emissions for other biofuels such as those from oily crops or grains (Staples et al., 2014). This increases the potential for emissions reductions from using aviation biofuels. Additionally, biofuels from lignocellulosic biomass that have associated lifecycle GHG emissions of at least 60% below those of their conventional counterpart qualify for the (currently) most stringent RFS2 biofuel sub-mandate and can therefore yield higher RIN prices, which makes production of these fuels, ceteris paribus, more viable from a business perspective compared to other biofuels.

While there is a wide body of literature that deals with CO_2 abatement in the airline industry through market-based measures (e.g., Hofer et al., 2010; Malina et al., 2012; Winchester et al., 2013b), only a few archival studies, as discussed below, have been published that quantify the environmental and economic impact of large-scale aviation biofuel adoption. Moreover, none of the existing papers on aviation biofuels examine the impact of advanced biofuels on aviation emissions and economic activity. In addition, no study to date has incorporated the interactions between an aviation-specific renewable fuel goal fulfilled with advanced biofuels and the corresponding biofuel RIN markets under RFS2 system for transportation fuels. Finally, most existing studies either do not address production costs of aviation biofuels, or simply assume that they will converge to the price of petroleum-derived jet fuel at some assumed point in time (e.g., Sgouridis et al., 2011).

Hileman et al. (2013) assess a portfolio of mitigation options in terms of their potential contribution to meeting the air transport industry's goal of a 50% reduction in absolute GHG emissions by 2050 relative to 2005 levels. Their results indicate that in order to achieve the industry goal, a relatively rapid adoption of new, more efficient aircraft designs would be necessary as well as the large-scale introduction of alternative fuels with low lifecycle GHG emissions compared to conventional jet fuel. In particular, in order to meet the IATA goal, they find that under the assumption that the aircraft fleet in 2050 is 116% more efficient in terms of fuel burn per kilogram-kilometer compared to current-

generation narrow body aircraft, 30% of jet fuel consumed would have to come from renewable sources at a lifecycle GHG footprint of 10% of that of conventional jet fuel per unit of energy consumed.

Sgouridis et al. (2011) also assess strategies for mitigating CO_2 emissions from air transportation. They find that if aviation biofuels can be offered at price parity to conventional jet fuel, between 15.5% and 30.5% of total jet fuel consumption in 2024 could be from renewable fuels, which would decrease cumulative CO_2 emissions from aviation between 2004 and 2024 by 5.5% to 9.5% relative to their reference case.

Krammer et al. (2013) use a systems model for the aviation industry to simulate aviation biofuel adoption under different socio-economic and policy assumptions. Like Sgouridis et al. (2011), they assume that biofuel usage does not incur a price premium compared to conventional jet fuel, and that market uptake is only limited by fuel availability. Under these assumptions, they find that 50% of global jet fuel burn could be satisfied by biofuels by 2041, and that global GHG emissions attributable to aviation would be 48–53% lower than in a baseline (no-biofuels) case.

Using a numerical general equilibrium approach, Winchester et al. (2013a) quantify the economy-wide and aviation-specific impact of using one class of aviation biofuels derived from oily crops. To our knowledge, this is the only study that models price differences between aviation biofuels and conventional jet fuel with the associated market impacts. Winchester et al. (2013a) find that if the aviation alternative fuels goal described above were to be met with these fuels exclusively, an implicit subsidy would have to be paid ranging from $0.35 to $2.69 per gallon of renewable jet fuel. The lower estimate assumes that all feedstock demand can be satisfied through rotation crops grown on fallow land that do not directly compete with food or feed crops, while the higher estimate assumes soybeans grown on existing agricultural land to be used as feedstock. Abatement costs are calculated at approximately $400 per metric ton of CO2e abated in the soybean case, and approximately $50 per metric ton for optimistic assumptions on the availability of oilseed rotation crops. Total abatement of GHG emissions due to the use of biofuels is calculated at approximately 1% compared to the baseline case in the year 2020.

The remainder of this paper proceeds as follows: In Section 2 we outline aviation biofuel pathways, focusing on the technology sets and feedstock considered in this paper. Section 3 presents a stylized analysis of the interaction between aviation biofuel goals and RFS2 mandates in a simplified setting. Our modeling framework and scenarios are explained in Section 4. We present results and discuss them in Section 5. The final section concludes.

2. Advanced fermentation biofuels

Jet fuels are certified for use in commercial aviation through ASTM, a global standard setting organization. The first two biofuels to be certified in 2009 and 2011, respectively, were synthetic paraffinic kerosene (SPK) from biomass using a Fischer-Tropsch process, and SPK consisting of Hydroprocessed Esters and Fatty Acids (HEFA) jet fuel, also known as Hydrotreated Renewable Jet fuel (ASTM, 2011). This certification allows these fuels to be used in existing aircraft engines and fuel infrastructure up to a blending percentage by volume of 50% (ASTM, 2011). While these fuels have not been deployed at large scale, some airlines are using blends on selected routes. For example, in summer 2013, United Airlines executed a purchasing agreement with Alt Air Fuels for 15 million gallons of HEFA jet fuel from animal fats and non-edible oils to use on routes from Los Angeles International Airport (United Airlines, 2013). In South Africa, Sasol is providing SPK jet fuel using a Fischer-Tropsch technology and coal as a feedstock to airlines operating at O.R. Tambo International Airport in Johannesburg (Sasol, 2011).

In June 2014, ASTM revised D7566, the aviation fuel standard concerning synthesized hydrocarbons, to include a type of biofuel called "Synthesized Iso-Paraffinic" (SIP) fuel from hydroprocessed fermented sugars. The SIP fuel is produced by the fermentation of biomass derived sugars into Farnesene, followed by hydrotreatment and fractionation of

Farnesene into Farnesane, and they may be blended at a maximum of 10% by volume with conventional jet fuel (ASTM, 2014). Currently only one company, Amyris, produces SIP fuels.

SIP fuels are a subset of a larger class of novel aviation biofuel production technologies referred to as fermentation and advanced fermentation. AF fuel production involves the mechanical, chemical or biological extraction of polymer sugars from biomass, and subsequent decomposition to monomer sugars. The monomer sugars are metabolized (fermented) by a microorganism to produce energy carrying platform molecules, which are then chemically upgraded to drop-in fuels or blendstock. In addition to Amyris, a number of private companies are in different stages of commercialization of technologies that can be categorized as AF, such as LS9, Solazyme, Byogy Renewables, and Gevo. Efforts are under way to certify additional AF fuels, produced using processes other than that used by Amyris, possibly at higher blending percentages (ASTM, 2013).

In this paper, we consider a technology set representative of a broad range of AF technologies that can produce jet fuel from perennial grasses. We choose switchgrass (Panicum virgatum) as a representative feedstock since its agro-economic properties are relatively well studied compared to other perennial grasses. In our analysis, conversion efficiencies, product slates (the mix of products produced), and material requirements for growing switchgrass and converting it into AF jet fuel follow a recent analysis by Staples et al. (2014).

By focusing on AF jet fuel production pathways, our analysis encompasses a wide-range of feedstock-to-fuel technologies. Specifically, AF jet fuel pathways may vary with respect to fermentation to different platform molecules (each with unique utility requirements for upgrading to jet fuel), feedstock pretreatment technologies, the overall efficiency of feedstock-to-fuel conversion, and the proportion of jet fuel in the final product slate. Additionally, significant uncertainties remain about the properties of AF processes as they are yet to be implemented at commercial scale. Building on results from Staples et al. (2014), we consider a range of capital costs, energy conversion efficiencies and product slate cases to capture uncertainties associated with fuel production costs using a nascent technology such as AF.

3. A stylized analysis of aviation biofuel goals and of RFS2 mandates

As the effect of the aviation renewable fuel goal will depend on interactions between this goal and RFS2 mandates, this section delineates these interactions in a stylized setting. Under RFS2, the RIN value for each fuel category will evolve so as to offset the higher production cost of renewable fuel compared to conventional fuel.

Although renewable jet fuel consumption is not mandated under RFS2, this fuel is eligible for RINs. AF jet fuel could qualify under the cellulosic, undifferentiated advanced and biomass-based diesel categories. However, as the cost of AF jet fuel is likely to be higher than costs for fuels that can be used for ground transportation, renewable jet fuel will not be produced without incentives in addition to those under RFS2. As there are no current plans to mandate the use of aviation biofuels, following Winchester et al. (2013a), we assume that the FAA's biofuel goal is met by commercial airlines and the military voluntarily purchasing a set quantity of renewable fuel each year, even though this fuel is more expensive than conventional jet fuel. From an economic perspective, an equivalent representation of this mechanism is a tax on purchases of conventional jet fuel and a subsidy to renewable jet fuel production, where the per-gallon subsidy is chosen to induce the desired level of production and the per-gallon tax is chosen so that total tax revenue is equal to the total cost of the subsidy. For these reasons, we refer to the additional costs that airlines pay to purchase renewable fuel relative to conventional fuel as an implicit subsidy.

To demonstrate how the RFS2 mandate for cellulosic fuel and the aviation biofuels goal interact to determine the implicit subsidy to renewable jet fuel, consider a 'regular' cellulosic technology that produces fuel that cannot be used to replace jet fuel, and an AF pathway that

Table 1
Renewable jet fuel policy cases considered in the stylized analysis.

Label	Description
Include	Renewable jet fuel goal included in RFS2 mandates
Additional	Renewable jet fuel goal specified as an additional target to RFS2 mandates
Exceed	Cellulosic biofuel production exceeds the RFS2 mandate for this fuel

produces renewable diesel and jet fuel.[1] Let c_R denote the production cost for the regular cellulosic technology, and c_A represent the production cost for AF fuel, both in jet fuel-equivalent gallons. Additionally, reflecting current costs, assume that the regular cellulosic pathway is less expensive than the AF technology and that both biofuels are more costly than petroleum-based fuel; that is, $p < c_R < c_A$, where p is the price per jet-equivalent gallon of petroleum-based fuel. Without specific incentives for renewable jet fuel, the RFS2 cellulosic mandate will be met using regular cellulosic fuels and, in perfectly competitive markets, the RIN price per jet-equivalent gallon (r) will evolve so that $c_R = p + r$. Within this setting, we consider three alternative policy cases, which are summarized in Table 1.

Our first case, referred to as *Include*, represents the current policy setting where renewable jet fuel is included within the RFS2 mandates and the aviation industry is not required to surrender RINs. Let $s^{Include}$ denote the implicit subsidy per gallon of renewable jet fuel in this case. If α gallons of renewable jet fuel are produced per gallon of total distillate ($0 < \alpha \leq 1$), for each gallon of (total) fuel produced, AF producers will receive $\alpha(p + r + s^{Include})$ from jet fuel sales and $(1 - \alpha)(p + r)$ from diesel sales. Solving for the value of $s^{Include}$ that equates AF revenue and costs results in:

$$s^{Include} = \frac{1}{\alpha}\{(c_A - p) - r\} = \frac{1}{\alpha}\{(c_A - p) - (c_R - p)\} = \frac{(c_A - c_R)}{\alpha} \qquad (1)$$

Eq. (1) illustrates that the implicit jet subsidy is independent of renewable jet production costs relative to the price of conventional fuel. That is, the RFS2 policy insulates airlines from high cellulosic fuel costs. If a pathway only produces jet fuel ($\alpha = 1$), the subsidy is equal to the difference between the cost of AF jet fuel relative to regular cellulosic fuel. If renewable jet fuel is produced jointly with renewable diesel ($\alpha < 1$), the subsidy is larger as it is only offered on a fraction of output and must compensate for losses on all gallons produced.

The relationship between the implicit jet subsidy and cellulosic-AF cost premiums for alternative values of α is shown in Fig. 1. As illustrated by this figure and Eq. (1), the implicit jet subsidy will be larger: (1) the smaller the proportion of jet fuel in total distillate (α), and (2) the larger the difference between the cost of AF and regular cellulosic fuel.

We further illuminate two outcomes that may arise under changes to the RFS2 policy. The first variation we consider, referred to as *Additional*, is an aviation renewable jet fuel goal specified as an additional mandate within RFS2. In this case, RINs associated with jet fuel production cannot be sold to ground transportation fuel providers and the implicit subsidy required to induce AF production would be:

$$s^{Additional} = (c_A - p) + \frac{(1-\alpha)}{\alpha}(c_A - c_R) > s^{Include} \ \forall \ \alpha, 0 < \alpha \leq 1 \qquad (2)$$

If the pathway only produces jet fuel, the subsidy must compensate for the difference between production costs and the price of conventional fuel. If less than 100% jet fuel is produced, the subsidy must compensate for the AF-regular cellulosic cost difference plus the per-gallon loss (net of RIN income) on renewable diesel production multiplied by

---

[1] Even though AF fuel qualifies for cellulosic, undifferentiated advanced, and biomass-based diesel RINs, we focus on interactions between the RFS2 mandate for cellulosic fuels and the aviation biofuel goal, as the cellulosic RIN price is currently higher than other RIN values.

N. Winchester et al. / Energy Economics 49 (2015) 482–491   485

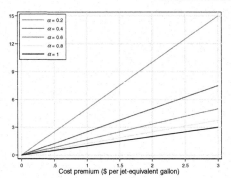

Fig. 1. The relationship between the implicit jet subsidy and the cellulosic-advanced fermentation cost premium.

the number of diesel gallons produced per gallon of jet, which is given by $(1 - \alpha)/\alpha$.

The second alternative we consider, referred to as *Exceed*, is an increase in the aviation biofuel goal relative to RFS2 mandates. This change is consistent with an increase in the renewable jet goal or a decrease in RFS2 mandates, as has occurred under the EPA's visa waiver credits for cellulosic fuels in recent years. Our analysis above assumed that the cellulosic RIN value is constant. If there is a large increase in the renewable jet goal relative to RFS2 mandates, inducing renewable jet fuel production may result in renewable diesel production exceeding the combined value of mandates for which this fuel is eligible. This would drive the RIN price to zero and the implicit jet subsidy would be:

$$s^{Exceed} = \frac{(c_A - p)}{\alpha} > s^{Additional} \; \forall \, \alpha, \; 0 < \alpha < 1 \qquad (3)$$

In this case, as the implicit jet subsidy only applies to α units of fuel and the RIN price is zero, s^{Exceed} is larger than the difference between unit production costs and the price of petroleum-based fuel.

To summarize and further compare the three policy cases, implicit jet subsidies for alternative values of α when $p = \$3$, $c_R = \$4$ and $c_A = \$6$ are shown in Fig. 2. If RINs associated with renewable jet fuel can be sold to providers of ground transport fuel, as currently legislated

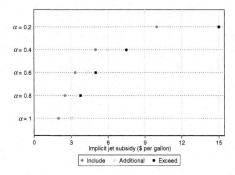

Fig. 2. The implicit jet subsidy for alternative aviation biofuel goal cases ($p = \$3$, $c_R = \$4$ and $c_A = \$6$).

and represented by the *Include* case, the implicit jet subsidy will depend on the cost premium between AF production and regular cellulosic fuels. If the aviation goal is specified as an additional RFS2 mandate, as in the *Additional* case, the jet fuel subsidy will be higher than the case where airlines are not required to purchase RINs. If the aviation goal relative to RFS2 mandates is such that RIN prices for cellulosic diesel are zero, as in the *Exceed* case, the implicit jet subsidy will have to compensate for the difference between AF costs and the price of conventional fuel. In all cases, the implicit subsidy to renewable jet fuel is negatively related to the proportion of advanced fermentation output that is jet fuel.

Our stylized framework can also be used to examine the marginal impact of changes in p. We focus on the *Include* case as this setting is consistent with current policies and goals. If $p < c_R < c_A$, Eq. (1) shows that $s^{Include}$ is invariant to changes in p. This is because any change in p within this range will be absorbed by the cellulosic RIN price. If $c_R \leq p < c_A$, the cellulosic RIN price will be zero, $s^{Include} = 1/\alpha(c_a - p)$ and the marginal impact of a change in $p = -1/\alpha$. That is, there is a negative relationship between the two variables and changes in $s^{Include}$ are larger than changes in p when $\alpha < 1$. This is because, say, an increase in p not only reduces the compensation required per gallon of jet fuel, but also decreases compensation needed for the diesel proportion of the product slate. Conversely, a decrease in p will require an increase in $s^{Include}$ that compensates for additional losses on both jet fuel and diesel production. Clearly, if $p \geq c_A$ renewable jet fuel is cost competitive with conventional fuel and $s^{Include} = 0$.

4. Modeling framework

To capture interactions among the aviation and agricultural industries and the broader economy, we develop and apply a bespoke version of the Economic Projection and Policy Analysis for Aviation (EPPA-A) model (Gillespie, 2011). The EPPA-A model is a global recursive dynamic numerical general equilibrium model of economic activity and energy production and is built on version five of the MIT EPPA model (Paltsev et al., 2005).[2] The model's aggregation is outlined in Table 2. Large economies such the U.S., China and Russia are identified as separate regions and most small economies are included in composite regions. The model's sectoral aggregation includes a detailed representation of energy production and transportation. Transportation options represented in the EPPA-A model include air transportation, other industrial transportation (road, rail and sea transportation) and household transportation, which is a composite of privately-owned vehicles and industrial (air and other) transportation. Energy sectors in the model include production of primary energy (coal, crude and natural gas) and secondary energy (aviation fuel, other refined oil and electricity). Primary energy can be produced from conventional resources and non-conventional sources, such as biomass (which is discussed in detail below), oil sands and shale gas. Additionally, several electricity technologies are represented, including traditional fossil, natural gas combined cycle, and large-scale wind and solar generation.

Production of each commodity assembles primary factors and intermediate inputs using constant elasticity of substitution (CES) functions under the assumption of perfect competition. International trade for all commodities except crude oil is modeled following the approach outlined by Armington (1969), which assumes that goods are differentiated by region of origin. Crude oil is considered to be a homogenous commodity and sells for the same price in all regions (net of transport costs). Final demand is captured by, in each region, a representative consumer that earns income from factor rewards and government transfers and allocates expenditure across goods and investment to maximize utility. The model is calibrated using economic data from the Global Trade Analysis Project database (Narayanan and Walmsley,

[2] A public release version of the EPPA model is available at http://globalchange.mit.edu/research/IGSM/eppadl.

Table 2
Aggregation in the EPPA-A model.

Regions	Sectors	Primary inputs
United States	*Energy sectors*	*Non-energy resources*
Canada	Coal	Capital
Mexico	Crude oil	Labor
Brazil	Natural gas	Crop land
Latin America	Aviation fuel	Pasture land
Australia-New Zealand	Other refined oil	Forest land
European Union	Electricity	*Energy resources*
Rest of Europe and C. Asia		Crude oil
Russia	*Non-energy sectors*	Shale oil
Japan	Crops	Conventional natural Gas
China	Livestock	Shale gas
East Asia	Forestry	Coal
Rest of Asia	Energy-intensive industry	
India	Other industry	
Africa	Services	
Middle East	Air transportation	
	Other industrial transportation	
	Household transport	

2008) and energy data from the International Energy Agency. The base year for the model is 2004 and it is solved through time for 2005 and in five-year increments thereafter.

We tailor the EPPA-A model to suit our needs by: (1) including conversion technologies and feedstock supplies for advanced fermentation and other biofuels, (2) including a mechanism to enforce the goal for renewable jet fuel, and (3) explicitly representing RFS2 biofuel mandates and RIN markets.

4.1. Advanced fermentation fuel in the EPPA-A model

We include an AF pathway in the EPPA-A model by adding production functions for switchgrass and conversion of this feedstock to liquid fuel. The nested CES-structure for switchgrass production is outlined in Fig. 3, where σ is used to indicate the elasticity of substitution between inputs in each nest. The production specification permits substitution between land and energy–materials, and between land–energy-materials and capital–labor. This structure allows endogenous yield improvements to changes in land prices by using more other inputs (e.g., machinery and fertilizer) and follows the structure used for agricultural production in Paltsev et al. (2005). Production costs for switchgrass are based on estimates from U.S. DOE (2011) and cost input shares are sourced from Duffy (2008).

The production structure for AF fuels is sketched in Fig. 4. This technology produces jet fuel and, in some cases, diesel and surplus electricity by combining switchgrass and other inputs. When applicable,

co-products are produced in fixed proportions with jet fuel and are specified exogenously in each specification. In the top level of the nest, switchgrass and other inputs are combined in a CES nest with $\sigma_{KLI-S} = 0.2$ to allow producers to extract more energy per ton of biomass than specified in the base case by using more other inputs. Due to uncertainty in the development of AF production, we consider alternative parameterizations of the production function for this technology. Staples et al. (2014) estimate AF costs under alternative assumptions regarding the product slate, the energy efficiency of biomass conversion, and capital costs. We capture the range of these estimates by representing six alternative specifications. Specifically, we consider separate low and high jet fuel product slate specifications for three cost cases: low-cost (high efficiency and low capital costs), medium-cost (medium efficiency and medium capital costs), and high-cost (low efficiency and high capital costs).

Revenue by product and costs by input per gallon of jet fuel produced for each of the six alternatives are presented in Table 3. In these calculations, revenues and costs by commodity are mapped to sectors identified in EPPA-A. As a result, diesel output is a perfect substitute for the other refined oil sector, and inputs of chemicals and enzymes are sourced from energy-intensive industry. Revenue from the sale of RINs and the implicit subsidy to renewable jet fuel are not included in this table, as they are derived endogenously in our modeling framework.

In low- and high-jet specifications, 62% and 100%, respectively, of total finished fuel output is jet fuel and the remainder is diesel. Revenue per gallon of jet fuel produced is higher in the low-jet case than the high-jet specification due to diesel sales, but costs are also greater, so Table 3 reports costs divided by revenue to facilitate comparison across alternative specifications. In low-cost cases, which assume high energy conversion efficiency, AF produces surplus electricity, while this process purchases electricity in other cost cases. Reflecting assumptions underpinning these cases, feedstock and capital costs are significantly higher in high-cost cases than low-cost cases. Other factors constant, production costs are higher for high-jet cases than low-jet alternatives as high-jet specifications employ fermentation to an alcohol platform molecule, which has a greater overall feedstock-to-fuel conversion efficiency than the platform molecules in low-jet cases. The cost and revenue numbers in Table 3 are at base prices and change in our simulations due to price changes, economy-wide productivity improvements, and substitution possibilities.

Table 3 also reports lifecycle CO_2 equivalent (CO_2e) emissions for each cost case, measured in grams of CO_2e (gCO_2e) per megajoule (MJ). Stratton et al. (2011) estimate that lifecycle CO_2 emissions from conventional jet fuel are 87.5 gCO_2e/MJ. Relative to this estimate, lifecycle emissions in low-cost (high energy conversion efficiency) cases are about 15% of those for conventional fuel and the corresponding number is around 60% in medium-cost cases. In high-cost cases, largely due to a relatively low energy conversion efficiency, lifecycle emissions for AF fuel are similar to those for conventional fuel.

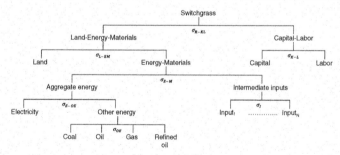

Fig. 3. Switchgrass production.

N. Winchester et al. / Energy Economics 49 (2015) 482–491   487

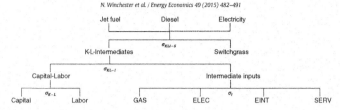

Fig. 4. Advanced fermentation production.

4.2. Other biofuel characteristics in the EPPA-A model

Other biofuels added to the EPPA-A model for our analysis include pathways for corn ethanol, soybean biodiesel, cellulosic ethanol, and undifferentiated advanced biofuel. These pathways are added to the model by including, for each pathway, production functions for biofuel crops and conversion of feedstocks to biofuels. Our representation of these production functions follows Winchester et al. (2013a), except the function for switchgrass cultivation, which follows that outlined in Fig. 3. Guided by Humbird et al. (2011), the production costs for cellulosic ethanol, in 2010 is $2.26/gal ($3.80 per jet-equivalent gallon) and is subject to input price changes and economy-wide productivity improvements.

We also augment the EPPA-A model to include RFS2 mandates and associated RIN markets for corn ethanol, biomass-based diesel, cellulosic biofuels, and undifferentiated advanced biofuels. These mandates and markets are modeled by including a separate permit system for each type of fuel, as detailed by Winchester et al. (2013a). AF fuel is eligible for biomass-based diesel, cellulosic and undifferentiated advanced RINs, which are allocated on an energy-equivalent basis. Similarly, we enforce the FAA's renewable fuel goal using a permit system that grants one permit for each gallon of renewable jet fuel produced and requires commercial aviation and the military to purchase, respectively, δ_C ($0 \leq \delta_C \leq 1$) and δ_M ($0 \leq \delta_M \leq 1$) permits per gallon of jet fuel consumed. The parameters δ_C and δ_M are determined endogenously in EPPA-A to meet the volumetric renewable fuel targets outlined in Section 4.3. This specification is equivalent to the revenue-neutral tax and subsidize system discussed in Section 3, where the commercial aviation permit value equals the implicit per-gallon subsidy from airlines to producers of renewable jet fuel.

Several interactions among AF outcomes and other biofuels are captured in our modeling framework. First, the cellulosic ethanol and AF pathways compete with each other for the same feedstock. Second, mandates for other biofuels will place upward pressure on land prices. Third, if AF processes produce diesel as a co-product with jet fuel, RIN prices for cellulosic (and possibly also biomass-based diesel and undifferentiated advanced fuels) will influence the implicit subsidy to renewable jet fuel, as highlighted in Section 3.

4.3. Scenarios

We assess the economic and environmental impacts of the U.S. goal for renewable jet fuel through 2030 under an AF pathway by defining eight scenarios. The first, *Reference*, simulates economic activity and aviation operations without any biofuel policies and is used as a benchmark for other scenarios. In the *Reference* case, we calibrate the EPPA-A model to jet fuel price forecast from EIA (2013) and aviation output, measured in revenue passenger miles (RPMs), and fuel consumption forecasts from the FAA (2013). Our next scenario, *RFS2*, simulates renewable fuel mandates set out in the Energy and Independency and Security Act of 2009. As the Act does not set targets beyond 2022, we extent the mandates by assuming that the target for each fuel relative to total transport fuel consumption is constant from 2022 onward.

Our remaining six scenarios impose the FAA's goal that one billion gallons of renewable fuel is consumed by U.S. aviation each year from 2018 onwards, in addition to the renewable fuel targets in the *RFS2* scenario. As noted in Section 1, the FAA one-billion gallon per year biofuel goal from 2018 includes targets for the U.S. Navy and Air Force. The Navy aims at procuring 50% of its energy consumption afloat (marine fuels and jet fuel) from alternative sources by 2020 (U.S. Navy, 2010), which would amount to approximately 280 million gallons of annual alternative fuel consumption in 2020 (U.S. GAO, 2014). The Air Force originally set a renewable jet fuel target for 2016 but has since moved its target date to 2020. Under the original target, 50% of the Air Force's total domestic aviation fuel use was to be met by fuel blends that included alternative fuels that are "greener"—presumably in terms of GHG emissions—than conventional counterparts (U.S. Air Force, 2010). Carter et al. (2011) calculate that this target equates to 370 million gallons of renewable fuel per year. Under the revised target, 50% of fuel used for non-contingency operations must be blended with alternative fuel (U.S. Air Force, 2013), but non-contingency is not specified. Due to this ambiguity, we consider an Air Force target consistent with the original specification (370 million gallons per year) starting from the revised implementation date (2020). Consequently, our analysis examines the economic and emissions impact of a commercial aviation biofuel consumption goal of 350 million gallons per year from 2020 onwards.

Reflecting uncertainties regarding the development of AF pathways, we simulate the renewable jet fuel goals for commercial aviation and military use separately for the six parameterizations of this technology outlined in Table 3. All renewable jet fuel scenarios are consistent with the *Include* policy case considered in Section 3, as this case follows current legislation.

Table 3
Revenues, costs and lifecycle emissions for advanced fermentation jet fuel pathways.

Product slate:	Low-cost		Medium-cost		High-cost	
	High-jet	Low-jet	High-jet	Low-jet	High-jet	Low-jet
Revenue per gallon of jet fuel produced (2010$)						
Jet fuel	2.71	2.71	2.71	2.71	2.71	2.71
Other refined oil	-	1.59	-	1.59	-	1.59
Electricity	0.05	0.08	-	-	-	-
Total revenue	2.76	4.37	2.71	4.29	2.71	4.30
Costs of total product slate per gallon of jet fuel produced (2010$)						
Switchgrass	0.88	1.42	1.35	2.20	2.26	3.62
Capital	2.29	3.70	4.49	7.53	9.34	15.01
Labor	0.09	0.14	0.25	0.42	0.52	0.84
Natural gas	0.05	0.07	0.06	0.10	0.05	0.08
Electricity	-	-	0.14	0.23	0.39	0.63
Energy-int. industry	0.75	1.20	1.14	1.86	1.91	3.06
Services	0.27	0.43	0.76	1.28	1.57	2.53
Total cost	4.32	6.96	8.20	13.62	16.04	25.76
Cost/Revenue	1.56	1.59	3.03	3.18	5.92	5.99
Lifecycle emissions (gCO2e/MJ)	11.70	13.50	33.20	37.40	80.70	89.80

Source: Authors' calculations based on estimates from Staples et al. (2014).

5. Results

We solve the model in five-year increments from 2005 out to 2030 for the Reference and RFS2 scenarios, and the six scenarios that impose the FAA's renewable jet fuel goal under alternative representations of the AF fuels discussed in Section 4. To illuminate important findings, our discussion of results focuses on 2030. Results for the U.S. in this year are reported in Table 4. In the *Reference* scenario, which does not include any biofuel mandates or goals, corn ethanol is the only biofuel produced, due to the higher cost of other biofuels relative to conventional fuel. In 2030, U.S. commercial aviation flies 1.3 billion RPMs and consumes 25,387 million gallons of jet fuel. Using the estimates reported in Section 4, lifecycle CO_2e emissions from this fuel are 295 million metric tons (Mt), which represents a 25% increase relative to the 2005 level.

When RFS2 renewable fuel mandates are simulated, the cellulosic target is met by fuel from the cellulosic ethanol technology, as production costs for this technology are lower than those for AF under all cost assumptions. The cellulosic RIN price, in 2010 dollars, is $0.35 per jet-equivalent gallon ($0.21 per gallon of ethanol). There is a small decrease in the price of jet fuel relative to the *Reference* scenario (from $3.23 to $3.21) as RIN prices passed on to consumers of ground transportation fuel reduce demand for these fuels, which ultimately depresses the (net of RIN value) price of refined oil products. Despite the decrease in the jet fuel price, aviation operations, fuel use and emissions decrease relative to the *Reference* scenario due to a GDP-induced decrease in demand for aviation services.

In the six scenarios that impose the U.S. goal for renewable jet fuel, AF pathways produce enough fuel to meet the aviation goal and the balance of the RFS2 mandate for cellulosic fuel is sourced from the cellulosic ethanol technology. AF fuel in all renewable jet scenarios are allocated cellulosic RINs, as the value of these RINs is greater than value of other applicable RINs.

In the medium-cost, high-jet case, the cost of renewable jet fuel is $8.21/gallon. For each gallon of jet fuel, renewable jet fuel producers receive $0.35 for cellulosic RINs, so the price of renewable jet fuel is $7.86 ($8.21 minus $0.35). As the price of conventional jet fuel is $3.21/gallon, this represents an implicit subsidy from airlines to renewable jet fuel producers of $4.65 ($7.86 minus $3.21) per gallon of renewable jet fuel. The average jet fuel price reported in Table 4 is the average price paid by commercial aviation when this industry purchases 25,065 million gallons of conventional fuel at $3.21/gal and 350 million gallons of AF fuel at a price of $7.86/gal. As renewable fuel represent only 1.4% of total commercial aviation consumption, the average jet price is very close to the price of conventional fuel. Relative to the *RFS2* scenario, the aviation renewable fuel goal reduces RPMs and fuel consumption by, respectively 0.80% and 0.88%. The larger reduction in fuel

consumption relative to RPMs reflects price-induced efficiency improvements. Combined, the substitution of conventional biofuels and reduced fuel use decrease lifecycle CO_2e emissions from 25,228 Mt to 25,065 Mt.

In the medium-cost, low-jet scenario, the implicit subsidy to renewable jet fuel ($11.36/gal) is higher than in the corresponding high-jet simulation ($8.25/gal). This is because, as highlighted in Section 3, the implicit jet subsidy must also compensate losses on the production of renewable diesel. This results in an average jet fuel price of $3.32/gal and, relative to the high-jet case, drives slightly larger reductions in RPMs and CO_2 emissions. There is no change in renewable jet fuel use across scenarios, as the consumption of this fuel is set by the goal.

In low-cost cases, the implicit jet subsidy is $0.45/gal and $0.50/gal when there are, respectively, high- and low-jet product slates. These subsidies result in, relative to the *RFS2* scenario, small changes in the average jet price and consequently small changes (<0.1%) in RPMs and fuel consumption. In high-cost cases, the implicit jet subsidy is $13.12 and $20.85/gal in, respectively, high- and low-jet product slate settings. Compared to other cases, there are relatively large decreases in GDP in high-cost settings, as more resources are diverted from other activities to meet the renewable jet fuel goal when capital costs are high and energy conversion efficiency is low. Relatively large increases in the average jet price and decreases in GDP reduce RPMs by, respectively, 2.3% and 3.6% for high- and low-jet cases, relative to the *RFS2* scenario. The corresponding decreases in fuel consumption are 2.5% and 3.8%.

5.1. CO_2 emissions and abatement costs

We further investigate the impact of the renewable jet fuel goal on emissions by reporting proportional changes in lifecycle emissions — due to biofuel consumption and reduced total fuel use — relative to the RFS2 scenario in Table 5. In low-cost cases, emissions fall by 1.3% relative to the RFS2 scenario, which is mostly due to the substitution of regular fuel for biofuel. In the medium- and high-cost cases, due to lower energy conversion efficiency, emissions reductions due to the replacement effect are smaller than in the low-cost case, but higher average fuel costs drive larger reductions in fuel use and ultimately larger emissions reductions. The net effect is that emissions reduction are larger in high-cost than low-cost cases. As a result, the largest total reduction in emissions is for the high-cost, low-jet case (which has the highest implicit jet subsidy), even though there is a small increase (0.02%) in emissions due to biofuel consumption owing to greater lifecycle emissions from renewable fuel than conventional fuel.

To examine the cost effectiveness of emissions reductions, Table 5 also reports CO_2e abatement costs, and the number of gallons of biofuel

Table 4
Summary of economic outcomes in 2030.

	Reference	RFS2	Low-cost		Medium-cost		High-cost	
			High-jet	Low-jet	High-jet	Low-jet	High-jet	Low-jet
Cellulosic RIN prices and implicit jet fuel subsidies (2010$/jet-equivalent gallon)								
Cellulosic	-	0.35	0.35	0.35	0.35	0.35	0.35	0.36
Renewable jet	-		0.45	0.50	4.65	7.73	13.12	20.85
Jet fuel costs and prices (2010$/gal.)								
Renewable jet fuel cost	-	-	4.01	4.05	8.21	11.30	16.68	24.41
Renewable jet price	-	-	3.66	3.71	7.86	10.94	16.33	24.06
Average jet fuel price	$3.23	$3.21	$3.22	$3.22	$3.28	$3.32	$3.40	$3.51
National metrics								
Switchgrass price (2010$/t)	-	$57.33	$57.33	$57.33	$57.32	$57.32	$57.32	$57.31
GDP (Δ relative to ref.)	-	-0.33	-0.34	-0.33	-0.36	-0.38	-0.42	-0.46
Aviation metrics								
Revenue passenger miles (billion)	1,347	1,342	1,341	1,341	1,331	1,324	1,311	1,294
Fuel consumption (gallons, million)	25,387	25,288	25,267	25,266	25,065	24,920	24,667	24,317
Lifecycle CO_2e emissions (Mt)	295.1	294.0	290.2	290.3	288.9	287.4	286.5	282.8

N. Winchester et al. / Energy Economics 49 (2015) 482–491   489

Table 5
Proportional reductions in lifecycle CO_2e emissions and abatement costs.

	Low-cost		Medium-cost		High-cost	
	High-jet	Low-jet	High-jet	Low-jet	High-jet	Low-jet
Proportional reduction in lifecycle CO_2e emissions relative to the RFS2 scenario						
Due to biofuel use	-1.2%	-1.2%	-0.9%	-0.8%	-0.1%	0.0%
Due to reduced fuel use	-0.1%	-0.1%	-0.9%	-1.5%	-2.5%	-3.8%
Total	-1.3%	-1.3%	-1.7%	-2.2%	-2.6%	-3.8%
Gallons of biofuel consumption required to abate one metric ton of CO_2e						
Biofuel per t of abatement[a]	99.3	101.7	138.6	150.2	1,106.8	-
CO_2e abatement cost (2010$/t) due to:						
Fuel replacement[b]	$45.0	$50.6	$645.1	$1,161.8	$14,515.7	-
Fuel replacement and changes in operations[c]	$42.1	$47.2	$318.4	$409.5	$609.1	$652.4

Note: [a] Number of gallons of conventional fuel that must be replaced by renewable fuel to abate one t of CO_2 emissions at constant operations; [b] Abatement costs due to the fuel replacement effect are calculated assuming that conventional fuel is replaced by biofuels at constant operations; [c] Abatement costs due to replacing conventional fuels with biofuels and changes in operations (including the impact of higher average jet fuel prices on fuel efficiency and aviation activity).

that need to be used in order to abate one metric ton of CO_2 at constant operations. These estimates include "well-to-wake" GHG emissions from fuel production, as well as CO_2 emissions from combustion, but do not include non-CO_2 combustion emissions such as soot or water vapor. In the low-cost, high-jet case, using the lifecycle CO_2e estimates discussed in Section 4, replacing conventional fuel with biofuel reduces emission by 75.8 gCO_2e (87.5 minus 11.7) per MJ of fuel, which equates to 10.07 kilograms per gallon of fuel. Consequently, 99.3 gallons of biofuel are required to abate one metric ton of CO_2e emissions.

Abatement costs due to the fuel replacement effect in Table 5 are calculated by multiplying the per-gallon renewable jet subsidy by the number of biofuel gallons required to reduce emission by one metric ton. As enforcing the goal also leads to price-induced changes in fuel efficiency and aviation activity (operational effects), we also report abatement costs due to the combined impact of the replacement and operation effects. These costs are calculated by dividing the additional fuel costs paid by airlines by the decrease in emissions (relative to the RFS2 scenario).[3] Operational effects have a small impact on abatement costs in low-cost cases, where abatement costs are $42.0/t$CO_2e$ and $46.9/t$CO_2e$, respectively, for high- and low-jet settings. In contrast, due to higher average jet fuel prices and larger income-induced changes in demand, operational effects significantly reduce abatement costs in other cases, but abatement costs are also higher. In the medium-cost case, abatement costs are between $318/t$CO_2e$ and $410/t$CO_2e$, and the corresponding numbers in the high-cost case are $609/t$CO_2e$ and $650/t$CO_2e$.

5.2. Alternative petroleum-based fuel prices

Our results were based on a reference fuel price of (in 2010 dollars) $3.23 per gallon of jet fuel in 2030. EIA (2014) consider a range of fuel prices bounded by 'low oil price' and 'high oil price' cases. The per-gallon price of jet fuel (in 2010 dollars) in 2030 for each EIA case is, respectively, $1.97 and $4.24. Using the insights from Section 3, we assess how fuel prices within this range affect results from our simulation exercises. A key finding from our stylized analysis was that the implicit subsidy to renewable jet fuel is independent of the price of petroleum-based fuel, providing the cost of 'regular cellulosic' fuel is

---

[3] As some of the additional cost of renewable jet fuel relative to convention fuel is absorbed by ground transportation providers through the purchase of cellulosic RINs, the economy-wide abatement cost is higher than the total abatement cost reported in Table 5.

greater than the cost of petroleum-based fuel (and the cost of renewable jet fuel is greater than the cost of regular cellulosic fuel). As the 2030 cost of cellulosic ethanol was $3.58 per jet-equivalent gallon in our simulation analysis, absent large general equilibrium effects, our results for petroleum-based fuel prices below $3.58 per jet-equivalent gallon would be similar to those reported in Tables 4 and 5. The price of conventional jet fuel in the EIA's high oil price scenario is higher than the cost of renewable jet fuel in the two low-cost cases in our simulations exercises. However, as the higher oil price would increase costs throughout the economy relative to those in our simulations, it is not possible to determine if renewable jet fuel in low-cost cases will be competitive with conventional jet fuel.

6. Conclusions

This paper considered the economic and emissions impacts on U.S. commercial aviation of the FAA's renewable jet fuel goal when this target is met using AF fuel from perennial grasses. As this fuel is more expensive than conventional fuel under our baseline petroleum price, we assumed that the goal would be met by commercial aviation voluntarily purchasing renewable fuel at a price premium, which is equivalent to airlines offering biofuel producers an implicit subsidy.

In a stylized analysis, we showed that RINs offered under RFS2 reduced the implicit subsidy required to induce production of AF jet fuel. This analysis also demonstrated that, as the jet fuel subsidy has to cover losses on all fuel produced, the implicit subsidy was higher when only a fraction of AF output was jet fuel than when 100% of distillate was jet fuel. We also showed that, under current policy conditions, the jet fuel subsidy is the same for all petroleum-based fuel prices below the cost of producing cellulosic fuel for ground transportation. However, if the price of petroleum based fuel is above the cost of cellulosic fuel for ground transportation, the jet fuel subsidy is negatively related to this price.

We also used the simplified setting to investigate how two possible policy changes may influence the subsidy to renewable jet fuel. First, specifying the goal for renewable jet fuel as an additional requirement to the mandates in RFS2 would increase the implicit subsidy. Second, under certain policy changes, the production of diesel as a co-product with renewable jet fuel may drive RFS2 RIN prices to zero. In this case, a higher implicit subsidy to renewable jet fuel is required than in our core policy case.

The paper quantified the impact of AF fuels from perennial grasses using an economy-wide model that included detailed engineering estimates of AF technologies assuming a reference jet fuel price of that reached $3.23 per gallon in 2030. Due to uncertainty surrounding the evolution of AF technologies, we considered a range of assumptions concerning capital costs, energy conversion efficiency and the product slate. The most favorable case assumed high energy conversion efficiency and low capital costs. Under these assumptions in 2030, the implicit subsidy to renewable jet fuel was $0.45 when all distillate was jet fuel and $0.50 when only ~60% of distillate was jet fuel. In a medium-cost case, the corresponding subsidies were $4.69 and $7.73, and in a high-cost case the numbers were $13.12 and $20.85.

Despite the large variation in subsidies across cases, the impact of the goal on the average jet fuel price was moderated by the small proportion of renewable fuel (~1.4%) in total fuel purchased by airlines. Consequently, there were small changes in aviation operations in all scenarios. Decreases in emissions from commercial aviation in 2030, relative to a case without renewable jet fuel, ranged from 1.3% to 3.8%, and 2030 emissions were more than 20% higher than 2005 emissions in all cases. Costs per metric ton of CO_2e abated ranged from $42 to $652. Interestingly, in high-cost cases, the high cost of abating emissions by replacing conventional fuel with renewable jet fuel had a positive feedback that reduced emissions by decreasing aviation operations (through higher airfares) and inducing improvements in fuel efficiency, which ultimately reduced abatement costs. Furthermore, due to low conversion efficiency and ultimately high biofuel lifecycle emissions, reduced fuel use accounted for 96% of total emissions reductions in the high-cost, high-jet case. These results correspond to a reference jet fuel price of $3.23 per gallon and AF jet fuel costs ranging from 4.01 to $24.41 per gallon.

We note that the calculated abatement costs for AF jet fuel of approximately $300 to $400 per tCO_2e in the year 2030 for the medium fuel costs assumptions are similar to the abatement costs for jet fuel from soybean oil using the HEFA process of around $400 per tCO_2e as quantified by Winchester et al. (2013a). As noted by Winchester et al. (2013a), there are opportunities to reduce this cost to $50 per tCO_2e, through the development of rotation crops that could be grown on otherwise fallow land and without the use of energy-intensive inputs. On top of reductions in feedstock costs, there are additional opportunities for reductions in abatement costs for AF jet fuels. These include engineering a product slate that solely consists of jet fuel, which reduces the overall fuel volume to be produced and correspondingly reduces the implicit subsidy that is needed to achieve the FAA goal. There are also additional prospects for efficiency improvements of the novel technology during commercialization. Combined, these developments could reduce abatement costs—as shown in our low-cost, high jet product slate simulation—to approximately $40 per tCO_2e, which is within the range of projected 2030 carbon prices under a cap-and-trade regime proposed by the U.S. government in 2009 (Winchester et al., 2013b). Other abatement options for the airline industry currently (as of March 2015) cost around $7.30 per tCO_2e in the case of emission allowances under the EU ETS and around $0.45 per tCO_2e for carbon offsets in the form of certified emission reductions – but have historically been as high as $40 and $20 per tCO_2e for emission allowances and offsets, respectively (European Energy Exchange, 2014; Quandl, 2014). These numbers suggest that the emissions offsetting scheme proposed by IATA is currently more cost-effective than using biofuels to abate aviation emissions, but biofuels may play a future role as the cost of these technologies decrease and global demand for emissions reduction credits increase the price of offsets.

Acknowledgements

The authors wish to thank James I. Hileman, Hakan Olcay and Carl Ma for helpful comments and suggestions. Remaining errors are our responsibility. This work is funded by the U.S. Federal Aviation Administration (FAA) and Defense Logistics Agency Energy (DLA Energy) through Project 47 of the Partnership for Air Transportation Noise and Emissions Reduction (PARTNER). The Joint Program on the Science and Policy of Global Change is funded by the U.S. Department of Energy and a consortium of government and industrial sponsors (for the complete list see http://globalchange.mit.edu/sponsors/all). Any opinions, findings, and conclusions or recommendations expressed in this material are those of the authors and do not necessarily reflect the views of the FAA or DLA Energy.

References

Armington, P.S., 1969. A theory of demand for products distinguished by place of production. IMF Staff. Pap. 16, 159–176.
ASTM, 2011. Standard Specification for Aviation Turbine Fuel Containing Synthesized Hydrocarbons. Designation D7566-12a. ASTM International, West Conshohocken, PA.
ASTM, 2013. New Specification for Research Report: Evaluation of Alcohol to Jet Synthetic Paraffinic Kerosenes (ATJ-SPKs). Work Item WK41378. ASTM International, West Conshohocken, PA.
ASTM, 2014. Standard Specification for Aviation Turbine Fuel Containing Synthesized Hydrocarbons. Designation D7566-14a. ASTM International, West Conshohocken, PA.
Carriquiry, M.A., Du, X., Timilsina, G.R., 2011. Second generation biofuels: Economics and policies. Energy Policy 39, 4222–4234.
Carter, N., Stratton, R., Bredehoeft, M., Hileman, J., 2011. Energy and environmental viability of select alternative jet fuel pathways. 47th AIAA Joint Propulsion Conference, San Diego, CA.
Dessens, O., Köhler, M.O., Rogers, H.L., Jones, R.L., Pyle, J.A., 2014. Aviation and climate change. Transp. Policy 34, 14–20.
Duffy, M., 2008. Estimated costs for production, storage and transportation of switchgrass. Ag Decision Maker, File A1-22. Department of Economics University Extension, Iowa State University (Available at: https://www.extension.iastate.edu/agdm/crops/html/a1-22.html).
Energy Information Administration, 2013. Annual energy outlook with projections to 2040. Energy Information Administration, Washington, DC (Available at: http://www.eia.gov/forecasts/aeo/, Accessed November 13, 2013).
Energy Information Administration, 2014. Annual energy outlook with projections to 2040. Energy Information Administration, Washington, DC (http://www.eia.gov/forecasts/aeo/, Accessed November 24, 2014).
European Energy Exchange, 2014. EU Emission Allowances, Secondary Market, Market data from July 2nd 2014. Available at:, http://www.eex.com (Accessed July 3, 2014).
FAA (Federal Aviation Administration), 2011. Destination, 2025. Available at:, http://www.faa.gov/about/plans_reports/media/destination2025.pdf (Accessed April 24, 2014).
FAA (Federal Aviation Administration), 2013. FAA aerospace forecasts FY 2013-2033. Federal Aviation Administration, Washington, DC (Available at: http://www.faa.gov/about/office_org/headquarters_offices/apl/aviation_forecasts/aerospace_forecasts/2013-2033/, Accessed November 13, 2013).
Gegg, P., Budd, L., Ison, S., 2014. The market development of aviation biofuel: Drivers and constraints. J. Air Transp. Manag. 39, 34–40.
Gillespie, C.W., 2011. A general equilibrium analysis of climate policy for aviation. (Masters Thesis). Massachusetts Institute of Technology, Cambridge, MA.
Hileman, J.I., Ortiz, D.S., Bartis, J.T., Wong, H.S., Donohoo, P.E., Weiss, M.A., Waitz, I.A., 2009. Final report of PARTNER Project 17. Report No. PARTNER-COE-2009-001 Cambridge, MA.
Hileman, J.I., De la Rosa Blanco, E., Bonnefoy, P.A., Carter, N.A., 2013. The carbon dioxide challenge facing aviation. Prog. Aerosp. Sci. 63, 84–95.
Hofer, C., Dresner, M.E., Windle, R.J., 2010. The environmental effects of airline carbon emissions taxation in the U.S. J. Transp. Res. Part D Transp. Environ. 15, 37–45.
Humbird, D., Davis, R., Tao, L., Kinchin, C., Hsu, D., Aden, A., Schoen, P., Lukas, J., Olthof, B., Worley, M., Sexton, D., Dudgeon, D., 2011. Process Design and Economics for Biochemical Conversion of Lignocellulosic Biomass to Ethanol. National Renewable Energy Laboratory, Golden, CO.
IATA (International Air Transport Association), 2009. A global approach to reducing aviation emissions. Available at:, http://www.iata.org/SiteCollectionDocuments/Documents/Global_Approach_Reducing_Emissions_251109web.pdf (Accessed April 12, 2013).
ICAO (International Civil Aviation Organization), 2013. Environmental report. Destination Green, Montreal.
Krammer, P., Dray, L., Köhler, M.O., 2013. Climate-neutrality versus carbon-neutrality for aviation biofuel policy. Transp. Res. Part D: Transp. Environ. 23, 64–72.
Kretschmer, B., Narita, D., Peterson, S., 2009. The economic effects of the EU biofuel target. Energy Econ. 31, S285–S294.
Lee, D.S., Fahey, D.W., Forster, P.M., Newton, P.J., Wit, R.C., Lim. L.L., Owen, B., Sausen, R., 2009. Aviation and global climate change in the 21st century. Atmos. Environ. 43 (22), 3520–3537.
Malina, R., McConnachie, D., Winchester, N., Wollersheim, C., Paltsev, S., Waitz, I.A., 2012. The impact of the European Union emissions trading scheme on U.S. aviation. J. Air Transp. Manag. 19, 36–41.
McLaughlin, S.B., De La Torre Ugarte, D.G., Garten, C.T., Lynd, L.R., Sanderson, M.A., Tolbert, V.R., Wolf, D.D., 2002. High-value renewable energy from prairie grasses. Environ. Sci. Technol. 36, 2122–2129.
Narayanan, B.G., Walmsley, T.L., 2008. Global Trade, Assistance, and Production: The GTAP 7 database. Center for Global Trade Analysis, Purdue University, West Lafayette, IN.
Paltsev, S., Reilly, J., Jacoby, H.D., Eckaus, R.S., McFarland, J., Sarofim, M., Asadooria, M., Babiker, M., 2005. The MIT Emissions Prediction and Policy Analysis (EPPA) model: Version 4. Joint Program on the Science and Policy of Global Change, Report No. 125. Massachusetts Institute of Technology, Cambridge, MA.
Quandl, 2014. Available at:, http://www.quandl.com/futures/ice-cer-emissions-futures (Accessed July 1st, 2014).
Richard, T.L., 2010. Challenges in scaling up biofuels infrastructure. Science 329, 793–796.
Sasol, 2011. Sasol Facts, Johannesburg, South Africa. Available at, http://www.sasol.com/sasol_internet/downloads/11029_Sasol_Facts_2011_1309786765289.pdf (Accessed April 8, 2012).
Scown, C.D., Horvath, A., McKone, T.E., 2011. Water footprint of U.S. transportation fuels. Environ. Sci. Technol. 45 (7), 2541–2553.
Searchinger, T., Heimlich, R., Houghton, R.A., Dong, F., Elobeid, A., Fabiosa, J., Tokgoz, S., Hayes, D., Yu, T.H., 2008. Use of U.S. croplands for biofuels increases greenhouse gases through emissions from land-use change. Science 319, 1238–1240.
Seber, G., Malina, R., Pearlson, M.N., Olcay, H., Hileman, J.I., Barrett, S.R., 2014. Environmental and economic assessment of producing hydroprocessed jet and diesel fuel from waste oils and tallow. Biomass Bioenergy 67, 108–118.
Serra, T., Zilberman, D., 2013. Biofuel-related price transmission literature: A review. Energy Econ. 37, 141–151.
Sgouridis, S., Bonnefoy, P., Hansman, R.J., 2011. Air transportation for a carbon constrained world: long-term dynamics of policies and strategies for mitigating the carbon footprint of commercial aviation. Transp. Res. A Policy Pract. 45 (10), 1077–1091.
Somerville, C., Youngs, H., Taylor, C., Davis, S.C., Long, S.P., 2010. Feedstocks for lignocellulosic biofuels. Science 329, 790–792.
Staples, M.D., Olcay, H., Malina, R., Trivedi, P., Pearlson, M.N., Strzepek, K., Paltsev, S., Wollersheim, C., Barrett, S.R., 2013. Water consumption footprint and land requirements of large-scale alternative diesel and jet fuel production. Environ. Sci. Technol. 47, 12557–12565.

N. Winchester et al. / Energy Economics 49 (2015) 482–491   491

Staples, M.D., Malina, R., Olcay, H., Pearlson, M.N., Hileman, J.I., Boies, A., Barrett, S.R.H., 2014. Lifecycle greenhouse gas footprint and minimum selling price of renewable diesel and jet fuel from advanced fermentation production technologies. Energy Environ. Sci. 7, 1545–1554.

Stratton, R., Wong, H.M., Hileman, J., 2011. Quantifying variability in life cycle greenhouse gas inventories of alternative middle distillate transportation fuels. Environ. Sci. Technol. 45 (10), 4637–4644.

Tilman, D., Socolow, R., Foley, J.A., Hill, J., Larson, E., Lynd, L., Pacala, S., Reilly, J., Searchinger, T., Somerville, C., Williams, R., 2009. Beneficial biofuels - the food, energy, and environment trilemma. Science 325, 270–271.

U.S. Air Force, 2010. U.S. Air Force energy plan.

U.S. Air Force, 2013. U.S. Air Force energy strategic plan: 2013.

U.S. DOE (Department of Energy), 2011. U.S. billion-ton update: Biomass supply for a bioenergy and bioproducts industry. R.D. Perlack and B.J. Stokes (Leads), ORNL/TM-2011/224. Oak Ridge National Laboratory, Oak Ridge, TN.

U.S. GAO (Government Accountability Office), 2014. Alternative Jet Fuels: Federal Activities Support Development and Usage, but Long-term Commercial Viability Hinges on Market Factors. GAO report GAO-14-407.

U.S. Navy, 2010. A Navy energy vision for the 21st century.

United Airlines, 2013. United Airlines and AltAir Fuels to Bring Commercial-Scale, Cost-Competitive Biofuels to Aviation Industry. Press release, June 4 2013, Chicago, IL.

Waterland, L.R., Venkatesh, S., Unnasch, S., 2003. Safety and performance assessment of ethanol/diesel blends (e-diesel). NREL/SR-540-34817. National Renewable Energy Laboratory technical report.

Winchester, N., McConnachie, D., Wollersheim, C., Waitz, I.A., 2013a. Economic and emissions impacts of renewable fuel goals for aviation in the U.S. Transp. Res. A Policy Pract. 58, 116–128.

Winchester, N., Wollersheim, C., Clewlow, R., Jost, N.C., Paltsev, S., Reilly, J., Waitz, I.A., 2013b. The impact of climate policy on U.S. aviation. J. Transp. Econ. Policy 47, 1–15.

13

Biofuels in aviation: Fuel demand and CO_2 emissions evolution in Europe toward 2030

Marina Kousoulidou, Laura Lonza

ABSTRACT

Keywords:
Air transport sector
Sustainable fuels
Biofuels
European policy
CO_2 and fuel projections
European Advanced Biofuels Flightpath
Emission trading scheme-ETS

This article presents the results of a scenario-based study carried out at the European Commission's Joint Research Centre aimed at analyzing the future growth of aviation, the resulting fuel demand and the deployment of biofuels in the aviation sector in Europe. Three scenarios have been produced based on different input assumptions and leading to different underlying patterns of growth and resulting volumes of traffic. Data for aviation growth and hence fuel demand have been projected on a year by year basis up to 2030, using 2010 as the baseline. Data sources are Eurostat statistics and actual flight information from EUROCONTROL. Relevant variables such as the number of flights, the type of aircrafts, passengers or cargo tonnes and production indicators (RPKs) are used together with fuel consumption and CO_2 emissions data. The target of the European Advanced Biofuels Flightpath to ensure the commercialization and consumption of 2 million tons of sustainably produced paraffinic biofuels in the aviation sector by 2020, has also been taken into account. Results regarding CO_2 emission projections to 2030, reveal a steady annual increase in the order of 3%, 1% and 4% on average, for the three different scenarios, providing also a good correlation compared to the annual traffic growth rates that are indicated in the three corresponding scenarios. In absolute values, these ratios correspond to the central, the pessimistic and the optimistic scenarios respectively, corresponding to 360 million tonnes CO_2 emissions in 2030, ranging from 271 to 401 million tonnes for the pessimistic and optimistic scenarios, respectively. This article also reports on the supply potential of aviation biofuels (clustered in HEFA/HVOs and biojet) based on the production capacity of facilities around the world and provides an insight on the current and future trends in aviation based on the European and national policies, innovations and state-of-the art technologies that will influence the future of sustainable fuels in aviation.

© 2016 Elsevier Ltd. All rights reserved.

Introduction

World air traffic is on a steady growth path establishing the air transport sector as one of the most rapidly growing transport sectors, moving more than 3 billion passengers and 670 billion revenue tonne kilometres (RTKs) in 2012 (Airbus, 2012). According to ATAG (2014a,b), every day 8.6 million passengers are being transferred, 99,700 flights are being performed and $17.5 billion worth of goods are being carried, constituting air transport a major contributor to global economic prosperity. According to Boeing (2013), despite uncertainties, passenger traffic rose by over 5% globally compared to 2011 levels and this trend is expected to continue over the next 20 years (Boeing, 2013).

M. Kousoulidou, L. Lonza / Transportation Research Part D 46 (2016) 166–181   167

Along with the rapid growth in air transport activity and hence, in energy consumption, the increased environmental impacts must also be taken into account. The aviation industry is currently pursuing alternative fuels as a means to reduce oil dependency, lower greenhouse gas emissions and improve environmental performance (Gegg et al., 2014). Until recently, biofuels were predominantly used by the road transport sector as a means to tackle climate change, diversify energy sources, and secure energy supply (Kousoulidou et al., 2012). Although the rail and maritime sectors have also begun to experiment with biofuels as a way to reduce the carbon intensity of their operations (Florentinus et al., 2012), some of the most dramatic developments have occurred within the commercial aviation sector.

According to Gegg et al. (2014), fuel constitutes a major component of an airline's operating cost. In the last 10 years, fuel costs have doubled to account for 28% of airline operating expenses in 2013 (PWC, 2013). Aviation biofuels are not expected to be competitive with fossil jet prices at least in the short term (before 2020). Therefore, the main driver for industry is that of responding to increasing public and political pressure to address its environmental impacts (Bows-Larkin and Anderson, 2013) through investments in more fuel efficient technologies and environmentally friendly operating practices (Gegg et al., 2014) as well as in alternative fuel sources (Winchester et al., 2013). According to Krammer et al. (2013) and ATAG (2011): the implementation of sustainable, advanced-generation aviation biofuels will be expected to play a large role in reducing CO_2 emissions. According to the Air Transport Action Group (ATAG, 2011), an essential component of the overall strategy to carbon-neutral growth of the aviation sector is low-carbon, sustainable aviation fuels, namely alternative drop-in fuels with bio-based components.

So far, over 1500 passenger flights with biofuels have taken place and the consensus is that the lifecycle carbon saving from moving to biofuels could be up to 80% over that of the traditional jet fuel (ATAG, 2014a,b). Several sources report the number of flights that take place with the use of biofuels such as the "Passenger flights database" of ATAG, ATAG (2014a,b) or the data provided in the BioJetMap project. The BioJetMap is a biokerosene flight database and web application initiated in 2012 (BioJetMap, 2012), and further developed under the HBBA study project and the scope is global and historical. Its time-enabling traces the evolution of the aviation biofuels sector through successive demonstration, test and commercial flights. More specific, according to the aforementionted databases, at EU level, KLM was the first airline company that flew commercially using bio-jet blends produced from used cooking oil (supplier: SkyNRG/Dynamic Fuels), on the route Amsterdam-Paris in June 2011, on a B737. After that, 200 flights followed. KLM is also executing the Amsterdam-New York JFK route using a blend of used cooking oil and camelina oil biofuels, on 26 weekly routes and the Amsterdam-Paris route with four daily flights.

On the same track, Lufthansa became the first airline worldwide to use a blend of biofuel mix from jatropha, camelina and animal fats (supplier: Neste Oil), in scheduled daily operations when it conducted a six-month test run with an Airbus A321 on the Frankfurt–Hamburg route. More than 1187 flights have been conducted over a six month period. Finnair, Iberia, Thomson Airways, Air France, Norwegian and SAS are the European airline companies that performed commercial flights with alternative fuels.

Outside the EU, efforts have been made toward the promotion of biofuels on commercial flights. For example, Alaska Airline/Horizon Air executes the route Seattle – Washington D.C on a A737s, Q400s, using a blend from Used Cooking Oil (supplier: SkyNRG/Dynamic Fuels). Gol Airline executed flights to multiple destinations in Brazil, on a B737 using biofuel blends from inedible corn oil and used cooking oil (supplier: UOP). 200 flights on biofuel were executed during the FIFA World Cup 2014. Quite recently China entered the game, with Hainan Airlines conducting China's first commercial biofuel flight from Shanghai to Beijing with biofuel supplied by Sinopec.

Sgouridis et al. (2011) suggest that the proportion of biofuels in total fuel consumption by commercial aviation was 0.5% in 2009 and will rise to 15.5% in 2024 in a "moderate" scenario, and to 30.5% in an "ambitious" scenario. In the EU, the European Commission, in close coordination with aircraft manufacturers, operators and European biofuel producers, have endorsed the "European Advanced Biofuels Flightpath", an industry-wide initiative to speed up the market uptake of aviation biofuels in Europe. It provides a roadmap to achieve an annual production of two million tonnes of sustainably produced biofuel for aviation by 2020 (EC, 2011a,b).

According to ATAG (2011), the supply of fuel to the commercial aviation industry is on a smaller scale and less complex than for other forms of transport. For this reason, it is anticipated that it will be easier to fully implement the use of sustainable biofuels in aviation than in other transport systems. It is also important to note that aviation is not looking at just one source of biofuel and can benefit from the most suitable feedstock in any given location and thus spreading the sources for better security of supply.

This article presents the results of a study carried out at the European Commission's Joint Research Centre aimed at analyzing the growth of European aviation toward 2030, the resulting fuel demand and the deployment of biofuels in the aviation sector in Europe reporting also on the supply potential of aviation biofuels on the production capacity of facilities around the world.

Overview of the current status

Aviation growth

The air transport sector is one of the most rapidly growing transport sectors, moving more than 3 billion passengers and 670 billion revenue tonne kilometres (RTKs) in 2013 (ATAG, 2014a,b).

The recent traffic growth is not uniform and has been driven by the acceleration of demand in emerging countries like Brazil, Russia, India and China (Alonso et al., 2014). Future growth projections made by international organizations and aircraft manufacturers converge at 4–5% annual rates of air traffic growth (Airbus, 2012; IATA, 2012, 2013; ICAO, 2012, ACI, 2013a,b; Airbus, 2013; Boeing, 2013; EUROCONTROL, 2013).

2012 was one of the best years the airline industry since the economic downturn with airlines making $7.6 billion profit (Boeing, 2013). According to IATA forecasts 2014 has been even more profitable, with traffic following the trend of at least 5.0% annual growth. Regarding freight aviation transport, today, there are nearly 1650 dedicated freighter aircraft worldwide with a cargo hold of at least 10 tonnes and more than 200 airliners. According to Airbus (2013), despite the impact of economic crisis, competition from other modes and the resulting difficulties for the air cargo market, the total number of Freight Tonnes Kilometres (FTKs) in 2012 was 4% above the pre- crisis high in 2007 and 20% higher than the low in 2009, while for the period 2012–2032, worldwide air freight is expected to grow at 4.8% per year. According to Airbus (2013), over the same forecast period, there is demand for 1859 converted aircraft and 871 new aircraft. Evidently, the domestic and intraregional markets were surprisingly resilient in the face of weak economic and trade growth, helping to spur demand for standard-body freighter airplanes (Boeing, 2014). The biggest market for freighter aircraft will remain North America, with Asia Pacific is expected to grow its fleet three times in the forecast period. This could be explained by the fact that the evolution of air cargo demand is inevitably associated to world trade and business confidence and both of these factors are on an ascending path.

Projections to 2031 from the Airbus Global Market Forecast show an increase in aircraft demand to 28,200 new-build passenger and freighter aircrafts, underlining the long term growth prospects for the industry. There is no doubt that much of this new demand will come from the emerging markets, regions including Asia, South America and Africa. However, there is equally no doubt that more mature markets in Europe and North America will continue to grow and benefit from the emerging regions' strong air transportation growth (Airbus, 2012). In any case, the expected growth of aviation will expose the sector to additional policy risk due to the related environmental impacts.

Environmental impact

Along with the rapid growth in air transport activity and in energy consumption offsetting efficiency gains of new aircrafts, the increased environmental impacts must also be taken into account. Emissions from aircraft engines affect the radiative balance of the atmosphere, and therefore the climate system, through various mechanisms (Dessens et al., 2014b). These include direct emissions of the greenhouse gas carbon dioxide (CO_2) (Sausen and Schumann, 2000; Sausen et al., 2005; Lee et al., 2009; Benito et al., 2010), and emissions of nitrogen oxides (NOx) (Stevenson et al., 2000, 2004; Köhler et al., 2008), which influence atmospheric chemistry and result in changes of the abundance of ozone (O_3) (Zeng and Pyle, 2003) and methane (CH_4), Stevenson et al. (2000). Water vapor from aviation transported or directly emitted within the stratosphere is assumed to have a negligible effect on climate (Wilcox et al., 2012). Fuel sulfur is converted to gaseous H_2SO_4, an important aerosol precursor in the atmosphere. In the case of aviation, emissions of particulates (Herndon et al., 2005; Agrawal et al., 2008; Onasch et al., 2009; Gettelman and Chen, 2013) can both directly scatter and absorb incoming solar radiation and indirectly affect the microphysical and thus the optical properties of clouds (Dessens et al., 2014a,b).

Overall, CO_2 is considered the most important greenhouse gas (GHG) emitted by aircrafts and is included in the EU Emissions Trading Scheme (EU ETS). Airline operations worldwide produced 689 million tonnes of CO_2 in 2012 (and 705 million tonnes in 2013), 2% of the total human carbon emissions of over 36 billion tonnes. Around 80% of all aviation emissions are from flights over 1,500 kilometres, for which there is no practical alternative transport mode (ATAG, 2014a,b).

ICAO (2009) forecasts that by 2050 aviation emissions could grow by a further 300–700% compared to 2005, while according to Berghof et al. (2005), Horton (2006) and Kelly and Allan (2006), aviation CO_2 emissions are likely to experience a greater than three-fold increase between 2000 and 2050. It is clear that the benefits from the expected growth in the air transport sector will come at a cost, most notably a significant increase in aviation greenhouse gas emissions (Kurniawan and Khardi, 2011).

Aviation is striving to reduce its environmental footprint in the short and mid-term while at the same time aiming for lower fuel cost burdens over the long term (fuel accounts for 28% of an airline's operating cost), ATAG (2014a,b).

While efficiency gains can be delivered through fleet renewal and enhanced air traffic management procedures, such as continuous descent approaches and precision area navigation (P-RNAV) (Gegg et al., 2014), these measures will not deliver targeted reductions in emissions making additional interventions a requirement. At present, virtually all of the world's commercial aircraft are powered by engines that burn Jet A/A1 fuel and produce a range of pollution species as by-products of combustion and incomplete combustion. Although alternative propulsion technologies, such as hydrogen fuel cells and solar power, have been proposed, they are not yet certified for commercial use. Liquefied natural gas has also been produced as a future aviation fuel since it offers lower fuel burn and emissions and potential cost and availability benefits (Stephenson, 2012). One of the most attractive options for the air transport industry is, however, to continue to operate existing engines and aircrafts but use lower carbon fuels. As this article reports, although certification schemes are in place and other under way for blends of biofuels, many challenges to widespread commercialization remain (IATA, 2013).

M. Kousoulidou, L. Lonza / Transportation Research Part D 46 (2016) 166–181   169

Regulatory targets and goals

Taking into account the growth projections, there is a need to reduce emissions and especially CO_2 related to aviation, despite its currently relatively small contribution to total CO_2 emissions (Anger and Köhler, 2010). In response to this matter, the aviation industry worldwide has developed a set of ambitious targets aimed at limiting its climate impact, while enabling it to continue contributing to economic growth. The targets include: improving fleet fuel efficiency by 1.5% per year until 2020, capping net aviation emissions from 2020 and most ambitiously, to halve aviation CO2 emissions by 2050, compared to 2005 (ATAG, 2011). These voluntary targets adopted by industry were set after careful analysis and follow the industry's track record of measured progress, while also being far-reaching. Since 2012, aviation emissions have been included in the EU ETS (EC, 2008) and the International Air Transport Association (IATA) in 2009 set out goals aimed at achieving stable carbon emissions from 2020 onwards despite further growth in air traffic, to be achieved by a combination of different parameters such as fleet renewal, operational and infrastructure measures, retrofits, offset mechanisms and the use of alternative fuels (Krammer et al., 2013).

At its 37th session in October 2010, the ICAO Assembly decided to develop a certification standard for CO_2 emissions. The standard will be used to ensure that new aircrafts meet a baseline for CO_2 emissions. With IATA's full support, an important milestone was reached in July 2012 when ICAO's Committee on Aviation Environmental Protection (CAEP) agreed on a metric for the new CO_2 standard and the Certification procedures were adopted in February 2013. Beyond IATA's target for the global aviation industry to achieve carbon neutral growth by 2020 and reduce CO_2 emissions by 50% relative to 2005 levels by 2050 (IATA, 2009), in the US, the Environmental Protection Agency (EPA) announced the collaboration with the International Civil Aviation Organization (ICAO) to develop regulations for the greenhouse gas emissions from aviation. The agency will hold a public hearing on the issue and will open a 60-day public comment period. According to EPA, a new standard could only be ready as soon as 2017 with implementation for 2018.

Regarding the measures on intensifying the use of alternative fuels in aviation, as already mentioned, the European Commission, in close coordination with aircraft manufacturers, operators and European biofuel producers, have launched the "European Advanced Biofuels Flightpath", an industry-wide initiative to speed up the market uptake of aviation biofuels in Europe to achieve an annual production of two million tonnes of sustainably produced biofuel for aviation by 2020 (EC, 2011a,b). At a non-EU scale, Boeing, Embraer and the Fundacao de Amparo a Pesquisa of the State of Sao Paulo (FAPESP) completed an action plan – Flightpath to Aviation Biofuels in Brazil – that identified gaps in a potential biofuel supply chain. Under a memorandum of understanding, Boeing and Embraer will perform a joint biofuel research, as well as fund and coordinate research with Brazilian universities and other institutions. The research will focus on technologies that address gaps in a supply chain for sustainable aviation biofuel in Brazil, such as feedstock production and processing technologies. Indonesia has introduced a biojet fuel mandate of 2% commencing in 2016, rising to 5% by 2025.

Aviation fuels

Jet fuels

The generic name for aviation fuels used in gas-turbine engine powered aircrafts is "Jet fuel". Traditionally jet fuel (or 'kerosene') corresponds to the kerosene distillation fraction of crude oil with a typical carbon chain-length comprised between C11–C13 (Maurice et al., 2001). According to Maurice et al. (2001), since the development of the first jet-powered aircrafts in the late 1930s, the two main operational standards are Jet A used in the US and Jet A1 used widely elsewhere in the world. The composition of jet fuels has always been a compromise between the cost (availability of suitable raw material and the requirement for processing) and performance (propulsion properties, safety, and engine-friendliness), with very little emphasis on the environmental impact (Kallio et al., 2014).

Jet fuels are optimized to engine-specific technical requirements and operational conditions. The relative proportion of the various hydrocarbon constituents determines the so-called bulk properties of the jet fuel including energy content, combustibility, density 775–840 kg/m^3 for Jet A1) and fluidity. According to Kallio et al. (2014), other important factors such as fuel stability, lubricity, corrosivity and cold flow behavior (for Jet A1 the technical specification for freezing point is $-47\,°C$) are influenced by minor components in the fuel such as sulfur (in Europe, the sulfur level specification for Jet A1 is 3000 ppm weight), oxygen and nitrogen hetero-compounds which are minimized to enhance the combustion properties and reduce the environmental impact.

Alternative drop-in fuels in aviation

Sustainable fuels can reduce life cycle CO_2 emissions by up to 80% (IATA, 2013). Such savings are entirely achieved in the feedstock production and conversion process into biofuels whereas no relevant savings are obtained in the actual combustion of the biofuel blended into fossil jet fuel. This is due to the asstrict fuel specifications which lead to an entirely comparable physiochemical composition of the bio-based component and the fossil component and thus leading to an entirely comparable behavior in the fuel combustion phase. According to IATA (2013), biofuels derived from sustainable oil crops such as jatropha, camelina and algae or from wood and waste biomass can reduce the overall carbon footprint by around 80% over their full lifecycle. According to ICAO (2015), there is a potential for significant emissions reductions which depends on the feedstock type, the cultivation and of course the conversion process. In any case, aviation biofuels need to be

170 *M. Kousoulidou, L. Lonza / Transportation Research Part D 46 (2016) 166–181*

evaluated considering the full life cycle of the fuel. Potential benefits in terms of carbon emissions resulting from the use of biofuels use occur from feedstock production and fuel conversion and not from fuel combustion.

Non-biogenic emissions associated with biofuels result from the cultivation, harvesting and transport of biomass as well as its conversion into biofuel. For that reason, pathway-specific calculations would result in emission values ranging from emissions reduction potentials of up to 80% compared to jet fuel of fossil origin to emissions several times larger than that of fossil jet fuel.

According to literature data, the use of alternative fuel blends with Jet A-1 leads to significant reduction in engine soot and SOx emissions due to the reduced content of aromatics and sulfur (Knörzer and Szodruch, 2012). Other species are less affected and their emissions changes may depend on the combustion chamber technology (NOx, CO, UHC) while the lower consumption associated to higher energy content of SPK is a factor for NOx and CO_2 emissions reduction.

Test flights using biofuels have been carried out by numerous airlines and have proven that biofuels work and can be mixed with existing jet fuel. Challenges ahead involve decreasing the production costs, expanding supply potential, investing in feedstock production and conversion facilities, and ensuring efficiency over the entire supply chain, in order to provide the opportunity to alternative jet fuels to play a dynamic role in aviation fuel supply.

Developments in aviation biofuel and production pathways

There is a variety of pathways that have been defined to produce alternative jet fuels from bio-based and waste materials with several options for conversion technologies, although in principle four are the main ones. A pathway can be defined based on the feedstock(s) used, the conversion process(es), and the resulting fuel(s). Alternative jet fuels vary substantially in their chemical composition: some pathways can generate synthetic paraffinic kerosene (SPK) without aromatics, while others can generate aromatic compounds as well. This has important consequences on blending grades with fossil-based, conventional jet fuel.

Three of the aforementioned routes, the Hydrogenated Vegetable Oil (HVO also known as HEFA, Hydro-processed Esters and Fatty Acids) and the Fischer–Tropsch (FT) have been certified (ASTM D7566 standard specification) to be used in blending of up to 50% with fossil jet fuel while the Synthesized Iso-Paraffinic (SIP) was approved by the ASTM International in 2014 and it may be blended at up to 10% (by volume) with conventional jet fuel. Hydrogenated Pyrolysis Oils (HPO) and other biomass/sugar based biojet fuel which include Alcohol-to-Jet, pyrolysis and catalytic cracking (Hydroprocessed Depolymerized Cellulosic Jet), catalytic hydrothermolysis and catalytic conversion of sugars plus the Boeing proposal to use green diesel at a low blending ratio are progressively becoming certified and therefore have the potential to become commercially available (Hamelinck et al., 2013; IATA, 2014).

HEFA fuels are produced by hydroprocessing esters and fatty acids, such as edible (soybean, canola) and non-edible (camelina, jatropha) plant oils, algal oil, yellow grease (rendered used cooking oil), and tallow. Under a HEFA process, the renewable oil is processed using hydrogen treatment (hydroprocessing) to yield a fuel in the distillation range of jet fuel, diesel and naphtha (UOP, 2005; Pearlson, 2011; Knörzer and Szodruch, 2012; Pearlson et al., 2013). Hydrogen demand for hydrogenation of different feedstock qualities varies, resulting in conversion cost advantages for certain raw materials like palm oil and animal fats (Hamelinck et al., 2013). In absence of technical restraints, market forces and legislation are the main forces for raw material selection. HEFA production processes using plant oils such as palm oil have been heavily criticized as being unsustainable. According to Hamelinck et al. (2013) HEFA/HVO processes using plant oils can be sustainable, but clear sustainability criteria are needed as a prerequisite. On July 1, 2011, ASTM approved the jet fuel product slate of HEFA under alternative fuel specification D7566 (ASTM 2011). HEFA fuel that meets this specification can be mixed with conventional jet fuel, up to a blend ratio of 50%.

HEFA/HVO production is already on a full commercial scale and is currently the leading process for producing renewable jet fuel and several airlines (including Air France, Finnair, Iberia, KLM, Lufthansa) have performed commercial passenger flights with blends of up to 50% renewable fuel produced using this technology (IATA, 2012).. Neste Oil operates two 190,000 tonne/year HEFA/HVO plants in Finland, an 800,000 tonne/year plant in Singapore and another 800,000 tonne/year HEFA/HVO plant in Rotterdam. UOP Honeywell and its customers have announced several HVO projects worldwide. In Europe both ENI and Galp Energia have plans for HEFA/HVO plants each with a capacity of 330,000 tonne/year but these are yet to be constructed (Hamelinck et al., 2013). Algal oils can also replace vegetable oils in HEFA/HVO or similar processes but these are not expected to be commercially available in the short term. Due to high infrastructure cost for industrial algal cultivation and conversion as well as dubious competitiveness perspectives for algae-based biofuels compared to other high-value products produced from the same feedstocks (such as production for the cosmetics or nutraceuticals industries), it is unclear when competitiveness vs. conventional plant oil or other advanced biofuels cost will be achieved. However, due to the fact that in principle there are no issues related to land use, algal oils have attracted significant interest by the aviation sector.

Synthetic Fischer–Tropsch fuels, also called BtL fuels (biomass-to-liquids), is produced by a two-step process in which biomass is converted to a syngas rich in hydrogen and carbon monoxide. After cleaning, the syngas is catalytically converted through Fischer–Tropsch (FT) process into a wide range of hydrocarbon liquids, including bio jet. Fuel produced using the FT process was certified for aviation by ASTM International Standard D7566 in September 2009. Today, according to the ASTM D7566 standard, FT-fuel is approved for a 50% blend with Jet-A1 fuel (http://www.astm.org/Standards/D7566.htm). The 50% blend limit is established to guarantee the presence of 'aromatics' in the fuel which are essential for the effective and proper operation of engine fuel seals but which are not present in biofuels (Corporan et al., 2011). With ASTM certification achieved,

M. Kousoulidou, L. Lonza / Transportation Research Part D 46 (2016) 166–181   171

major airlines have started sourcing biofuels and operating scheduled commercial flights powered, in part, by biofuels, Gegg et al. (2014).

Considering availability of alternative bio-based alternative jet fuel which can be expected from available conversion processes, an aggregate estimation indicates that approximately 140 k tonnes of Fischer–Tropsch fuel per year – with the addition of approximately maximum 50 tonnes from municipal waste treatment – could be made available to the European aviation industry considering domestic production (but not domestic feedstocks). The prospects for FT jet fuels depend of course to a great extent on the construction of pilot plants in the next few years.

Hydrogenated Pyrolysis Oil, referred to as HPO kerosene, is based on pyrolysis oils from lignocellulosic biomass. Pyrolysis oils can be hydrotreated either in dedicated facilities or co-processed with petroleum oils in refineries. Today pyrolysis oil is at the edge of research toward demonstration level.

Globally, there have been several attempts for the development of fast pyrolysis processes. For example, Ensyn/Envergent Technologies, which is a joint venture between UOP Honeywell and Ensyn Corp from Canada and BTG in the Netherlands are implementing the pyrolysis process on a commercial scale to produce crude pyrolysis oil (Hamelinck et al., 2013). In Pennsylvania, ARS scientists recently filed a patent application for a new system that removes much of the oxygen from bio-oils without introducing catalysts, thus producing a final product with considerably higher energy content than those produced by conventional fast pyrolysis. Contrary to vegetable oils, pyrolysis oil contains a few hundred different chemical components. For application in the transport sector the crude pyrolysis oil needs further upgrading to produce HPO, however one or more hydrogenation steps are required to achieve the desired product quality. Contrary to FT and HEFA/HVO fuels, HPO will still contain a certain amount of aromatic compounds which are currently needed in jet fuel to avoid engine sealing problems. Therefore, HPO may complement HEFA/HVO and FT (EC, 2011a).

Apart from the aforementioned conversion routes, several novel routes have also been announced and are currently being researched (Stratton et al., 2011). These include the use of micro-organisms such as yeast, algae or cyanobacteria that turn sugar into alkanes, which is the basic hydrocarbons for gasoline, diesel and jet fuel, the transformation of a variety of sugars into hydrogen and chemical intermediates using aqueous phase reforming, and then into alkanes via a catalytic process and the use of modified yeasts to convert sugars into hydrocarbons that can be hydrogenated to synthetic diesel (Hamelinck et al., 2013). None of the above processes has been demonstrated on a commercial scale so far, however, following recent announcements and the progress made by US biofuel start-ups such as Virent, Amyris and Gevo whose fuels are now considered by ASTM, these pathways are certain to be included in future studies and projects. In France, a project subsidy was recently granted to the ProBio3 project that investigates microbial conversions on specific fatty acids of carbon substrates from renewable non-food resources and industrial by-products (LISBP, 2012). In the Netherlands, the University of Wageningen researches algae cultivation and biorefinery. In the AlgaeParc the University of Wageningen aims to develop cost-effective and sustainable microalgae production methods outdoors (Hamelinck et al., 2013). From a longer term perspective, and with a view to the emergence of innovative technologies, it is worth noting that in 2014 the first ever "solar" jet fuel was produced, made from CO_2, water and solar energy, under the European SOLAR-JET project. The technology is currently at lab-scale, but could open the way to large-scale sustainable production of alternative fuels (IATA, 2014).

Despite the effervescent research and innovation scene when it comes to sustainable aviation biofuel production, one of the main challenges airlines face is clearly sourcing sufficient supplies of biofuel. To overcome this challenge and reduce vulnerabilities in the supply chain, airlines and biofuel producers have begun establishing commercial partnerships. As examples, according to Gegg et al. (2014), British Airways agreed to co-fund, with US firm Solena, the development of the UK's first commercial scale waste-to-liquid aviation biofuel facility in east London which aims to convert 500,000 tonnes of domestic refuse into 50,000 tonnes of aviation biofuel a year (British Airways, 2013) while Virgin Atlantic entered into a partnership with Swedish biofuel company Lanza Tech (Gegg et al., 2014). In January 2016 it was announced that United Airlines will purchase 15 million gallons of renewable jet fuel over a 3 year period (Lane, 2016).

Methodology

Having as clear an understanding as possible of how today's fuel demand volumes generated by the aviation sector are expected to evolve in Europe is the rationale behind the creation of a database considering traffic fleet and activity, including fuel efficiency and related GHG emissions. The methodology and the data sources used to build that database are described in Section 3.1.

The supply baseline and projections is described in Section 3.3. Demand and supply volumes are then analyzed jointly in Section 4.

Traffic data

Air transport traffic data have been collected from European Commission's Eurostat Air Transport Statistics (Eurostat) databases. Eurostat's task is to provide the European Union with statistics at European level that enable comparisons between countries and regions. For the purpose of this paper, the following data have been extracted by the Eurostat database and have been handled accordingly. More information on Eurostat databases on http://ec.europa.eu/eurostat/statistics-explained/index.php/Air_transport_statistics#Database.

- Air passenger transport between the main airports of xx and their main partner airports (routes data), whereas the name in Eurostat database is "avia_par_xx database"and it includes total commercial passenger air flights, total passengers on board and total passenger seats available.
- Freight and mail air transport between the main airports of xx and their main partner airports (routes data), whereas the name in Eurostat database is "avia_gor_xx database" and it includes all-freight and mail total commercial air flights and total freight and mail on board in tons.

Where xx stands for each one of the 29 EU countries (EU+2).
For each country the following information has been extracted:

- Air passenger transport between the main airports of xx and their main partner airports (routes data)
  o Total commercial passenger air flights
  o Total passengers on board
  o Total passenger seats available
- Freight and mail air transport between the main airports of xx and their main partner airports (routes data)
  o All-freight and mail total commercial air flights
  o Total freight and mail on board in tons

All the above mentioned information is given for each airport pair, between the main airports of country xx and their main partner airports.
Data have been segmented and presented, for each country, giving the above mentioned parameters between the reference country and the EU+2 countries plus the NO-EU countries.
Therefore, for each country an Excel file exists with five Sheets:

- Passengers flights
- Passengers & RPKs
- Seats & ASKs
- Freight flights
- Freight & RTKs

Data are given yearly from 2000 to 2010. This range may vary depending on data availability for each individual country. Baseline year to project data is 2010.
Data are also segmented per distance bands:

- Less than 500 km
- From 500 km to 1000 km
- From 1000 km to 1500 km
- From 1500 km to 2000 km
- From 2000 km to 2500 km
- More than 2500 km

Cross-checks have been performed to assess the quality of processed data.
Based on the expected growth of the aviation sector as calculated from the traffic data, a detailed calculation of the fuel demand and the CO_2 emissions has been performed.

Fuel demand data and CO_2 emissions

Air transport source of data to quantify fuel demand is EUROCONTROL Data Demand Repository (DDR), where information on all flights in EUROCONTROL countries is stored (with information from the flights plans). In particular, it is possible to retrieve data an all flights of a specific day. The amount of flights makes retrieving data for the 365 days of a year unfeasible. Therefore a sample of data is downloaded and then averaged in line with standard practice in the airline industry.
Reference year for the database is 2010. Data extracted consists of, for each flight, the following information:

- Departure airport
- Arrival airport
- Type of aircraft
- Type of flight

Data collected have been processed and segmented. First, the distance between airports pairs have been evaluated using a distance calculator, from the airports geographical coordinates. Flights have been then filtered per type.

M. Kousoulidou, L. Lonza / Transportation Research Part D 46 (2016) 166–181   173

Secondly, the fuel consumption for every flight has been evaluated. To do that, the Corinair database has been used. From the fuel consumption the CO_2 emissions are calculated in accordance with prescriptions of the EU Emissions Trade Scheme (ETS) Directive (EC, 2008) (multiplied by 3.15: the value of 3.16 is used by others, i.e. ICAO (2013).

Therefore, the information for each flight is:

- Departure airport
- Arrival airport
- Type of aircraft
- Fuel consumption in LTO cycle (approach, landing, taxiing, take-off and climb, below 3000 feet over the airport)
- Fuel consumption in climb/cruise/descent
- Total flight fuel consumption
- Total flight CO_2 emissions

Finally data have been segmented giving the above mentioned quantities for the EU+2 countries plus the non-EU countries and presented by pairs among every country (departure) and the rest of the countries (destination).

Data are segmented per aircraft type, taking into account the MTOW (Maximum Certified Takeoff Weight) and the propulsion type.

Data are also segmented per the same distance bands as the activity data collection.

This data source has permitted evaluating the number of flights per country pairs segmented per aircraft type and distance band. The number of flights thus obtained from EUROCONTROL data compares relatively well with the number of flights obtained from Eurostat data.

Regarding CO_2 emissions, the figure obtained for 2010 is 216 Mtons which compares well with the reference value used by the European Commission in the inventory performed to implement the ETS in the aviation sector.

Supply

Increased efficiency in aircraft performance and responsible growth are key components to reduce energy use, however, global growth in demand is expected to lead to substantial increases in fuel demand.

For the projection of future supply of aviation biofuels, the study of Hart Energy (2013), NER300 projects and working documents of the IEA Task 37 as well as the recent revision of the JEC Biofuels Programme (2014) and data from Neste Oil have all been taken into account. All plants that are currently working or have announced their annual capacity to 2020 have been included and there has been a clustering between biojet, biokerosene and HEFA/HVOs both in an EU and global supply scale. Data regarding HEFA/HVO production include the published information on annual capacity from the following plants: Neste Oil Porvoo, Neste Oil Rotterdam, Neste Oil Singapore, ENI/UOP Venice, ENI/UOP Venice, Diamond Green Diesel, US Emerald Biofuels, US Galp Energia (Portugal), Cepsa Spain Huelva and Cadiz, PREEM Oil Pitea (Sweden), UPM Lappeenranta (Finland). In order to evaluate the capacity of the current alternative aviation fuel plants to meet the future fuel demands, a comparison between the estimated capacity of the plants and the central scenario (BaU) regarding future fuel demands has been made.

According to JEC 2014, the main increase in non-conventional biofuels is indeed caused by HEFA/HVO co-processing projects. Some Biomass-to-Liquid (BtL) projects have also been announced most of them located outside of Europe and still projected to reach a total production of 0.1 Mtoe by 2020. It is therefore assumed that the biofuel supply used in aviation will be in competition with the road transport sector, which may mean a shift of available supply volumes form one sector to the other.

Results and discussion

Fuel demand projections

Looking at twenty years ahead, it is safer to consider a range of potential scenarios instead of just a single forecast, on how air transport in Europe might evolve. Each scenario in this study is based on different assumptions, including economic growth, fuel prices, load factors etc. This leads to different volumes of traffic, and different underlying patterns of growth.

Data for aviation growth and hence fuel demand have been projected on a year by year basis up to 2030, using 2010 as the baseline and overall and three different growth scenarios have been defined. Since the reference year is 2010, but 2011, and 2012 data are already available, actual growth rates for these years are included in all scenarios with projections starting from the year 2013 onwards. Evolution patterns of world regions recommend using different growth scenarios for the traffic growth within European borders and the flights beyond them (Alonso et al., 2014). This is the philosophy adopted in this study in order to evaluate the evolution of air transport in the European Union. Scenarios, covering the period 2013–2030, have been developed. A "Business as Usual-BaU" or most-likely scenario is followed by two additional ones, the "Crisis Scenario" and the "Optimistic Scenario", the first assuming a number of credible negative trends that may appear during that period and the second following the hypothesis of more optimistic conditions. Table 1 shows the average annual growth rates that have been estimated based on various parameters, for each scenario.

BaU scenario

A collection and survey of available studies by specialized bodies has been performed, including international organizations and industry (ICAO, 2007; Airbus, 2012, 2013; IATA, 2012; Boeing, 2012; ACI, 2013a,b; EUROCONTROL, 2013; Alonso et al., 2014; Boeing, 2014). As the intention of the paper is to take as the baseline the most likely scenario, the previous nine sources have been evaluated and then the highest and lowest values were excluded and the statistical mode of the other six was adopted. However, the highest and lowest values were set equal to the next lower and maximum values identified in the database, in order to avoid excluding entirely a whole set of values. It has also been taken into account that the latest 20-year forecast updated report from EUROCONTROL (2013), starts lower than the previous one published in 2010, due to the economic downturn leading to slower traffic growth rates than expected. In the same report, the baseline economic growth is also expected to be slower from 2020, and airport expansion plans have been sharply reduced compared to the previous forecast (EUROCONTROL, 2013).

The BaU scenario considers an initial period (2013–2016) of slow economic growth within the European Union countries in the order of 2.5% annual growth, followed by a slightly gradual recuperation in the 2017–2020 and the 2021–2025 period, in the order of 2.7% and 2.8%, respectively (Fig. 1).

During the last 5 years of the scenario, which cover the period 2026–2030, the growth falls back to the 2013–2016 period values. This is due to the fact that the aviation traffic growth is expected to slow down from 2025 as markets mature, economic growth decelerates and as the capacity limits at airports increasingly become an important issue (EUROCONTROL, 2013).

Traffic growth is not immediately translated to fuel consumption since several factors play a role in the improvement of the energy efficiency of air transport, such as the fleet replacement, the substituting of specific aircraft models with new, more efficient ones as they enter into the market, the use of larger aircrafts as the average commercial aircraft size is continuously increasing, and the improvements in air traffic control and navigation procedures (Alonso et al., 2014). In any case, the calculation of the practical consequences of all those elements is rather complicated. According to the study of Alonso et al. (2014), during the last 15 years IATA has been comparing the values of the RTKs with fuel consumption and the results show an average annual improved efficiency, measured in tonnes of fuel per RTK, of around 1.9% (IATA, 2013) for the IATA members.. Moreover, according to the ICAO's climate change mitigation program, an aspirational goal of a 2% annual improvement for the world air transport sector by 2020 has been set (ICAO, 2011). Furthermore, according to IATA, an annual efficiency improvement in the order of 1.5% has been adopted as a voluntary commitment. Taking into account the above information, the annual figure of 1.5% efficiency improvement has been used in the BaU Scenario for the full 2013–2030 period (IATA, 2013)

Regarding the implementation of biofuels in aviation, in this study, the assumption has been made that starting from 2017, the introduction of biokerosene is 1% of the total fuel usage, with this percentage progressively increasing, achieving the 2 million tonnes in 2020 and remaining constant at this level until 2030, consistently with the European Commission's "Advanced Biofuels Flight Path" ambition level (http://ec.europa.eu/energy/renewables/biofuels/flight_path_en.htm).

Alternative scenarios

The Crisis (or pessimistic) Scenario starts from a rather low-growth 7-year forecast, with an average annual growth in the order of 0.8% for the period 2013–2016 and 0.9% for the period 2017–2020 (Fig. 2).

This is based on the hypothesis of a spin out of the EU economic crisis until the end of 2020, described by high oil prices, fragile economic growth, no population migration, no free trade agreements with extra-European partners, high price of travel etc. The accumulation of these factors described in other studies as well (EUROCONTROL, 2013; Alonso et al., 2014; IATA, 2013), form a rather negative picture that leads toward an expected lower demand for international flights but also for intra-European ones. In the Crisis Scenario, this negative forecast is expected to slightly improve at a slow pace from 2020 to 2030, reaching a slow growth rate in the order of 1.1% by the end of 2030.

The Optimistic Scenario starts from a high-growth scenario of the 7-year forecast (2013–2016 and 2017–2020) as it assumes a fast and robust recovery of the EU economy, returning to pre-crisis growth rates in the middle of the present decade, with average annual growth rates in the order of 3.3% (Fig. 3).

Table 1
Average annual growth rates for each scenario implemented in the study.

Scenarios	Average annual growth scenario				
	2013–2016 (%)	2017–2020 (%)	2021–2025 (%)	2026–2030 (%)	Average (%)
BaU	2.5	2.7	2.8	2.5	2.6
Crisis	0.8	0.9	1.1	1.2	1.0
Optimistic	3.2	3.5	3.3	3.1	3.25

M. Kousoulidou, L. Lonza / Transportation Research Part D 46 (2016) 166–181   175

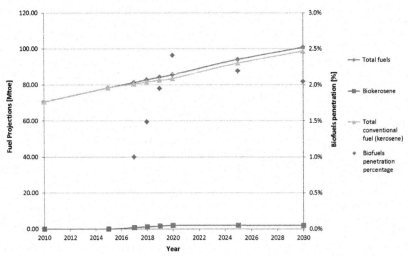

Fig. 1. Fuel projections to 2030 expressed in Mtoe and biofuels percentage penetration for the same period, according to the baseline scenario.

This scenario presents the most challenging traffic situation for Europe supported by quite strong economic growth, stable fuel prices, wide range of open skies agreement where international markets would gain from a high consumer expenditure increase in the United States and a soft landing of the overheated Chinese economy. Overall, the expected average annual growth is in the order of 3.3% (ranging from 3.2% to 3.5%) for the 2013–2030 period and it is the highest of all scenarios. The growth rates do not increase on a period per period basis since it is assumed that in the last five years period (2026–2030) the growth rates will slow down to less rapid ones in the order of 3.1%, due to a mix of factors such as the market saturation and the capacity constraints at airports. According to EUROCONTROL (EUROCONTROL, 2013), one of the major challenges of future air traffic growth identified by the previous updates of the long-term forecast is the capacity at the airports available for accommodating increasing number of flights. In the EUROCONTROL report in 2010 (EUROCONTROL, 2010), the 20-year forecast estimated the number of flights lost to insufficient airport capacity to be over

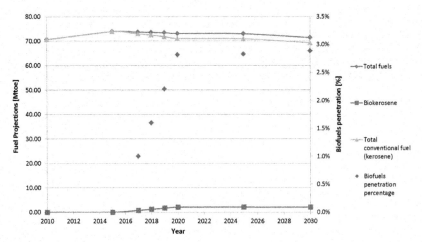

Fig. 2. Fuel projections to 2030 expressed in Mtoe and biofuels percentage penetration for the same period, according to the crisis scenario.

2 million by 2025 in its strongest-growth scenario. In both alternative scenarios, the efficiency improvement and the percentage of bio-kerosene usage are kept at the same levels than in the BaU Scenario.

The projections for CO_2 emissions in all three scenarios are shown in Fig. 4.

Regarding the BaU scenario, CO_2 emission projections to 2030 result in a baseline value of 360 million tonnes of CO_2, ranging between 271 and 401 million tonnes respectively for the Crisis and Optimistic scenarios. These projections correspond to average annual growth rates of CO_2 emissions in the order of 3% for the BaU scenario, 1% for the Crisis scenario and 4% for the Optimistic Scenario, based on the assumptions made for the average annual growth of aviation. Although aviation is a relatively small industry, it has a disproportionately large impact on the climate system. It accounts for 4–9% of the total climate change impact of human activity and even though there is an urgent need to reduce this impact, greenhouse gas emissions from aviation continue to grow. For example, since 1990, CO_2 emissions from international aviation have increased 83%, while by 2020, global international aviation emissions are projected to be around 70% higher than in 2005 even if fuel efficiency improves by 2% per year (EC, 2013). ICAO forecasts that by 2050 they could grow by a further 300–700% (ICAO, 2012).

Supply projections of aviation alternative fuels

Fig. 5 shows the demand and supply projections for aviation alternative fuels to 2030, clustered in HEFA/HVOs and biojet, expressed in Mtoe. The study of Hart Energy (2013), NER300 projects and working documents of the IEA Task 37 as well as the recent revision of the JEC Biofuels Programme (2014) and data from Neste Oil have been taken into account in order to quantify the fuel demand and supply of aviation alternative fuels. In order to identify the gaps in future supply, a clustering between biojet, biokerosene and HEFA/HVOs both in an EU and global supply scale has been made.

According to Fig. 5 shows that the biokerosene demand regarding 2020 to reach 2.06 Mtoe will be met from the HEFA/ HVO production at an EU level, leaving for the moments no doubts regarding of EU production on alternative aviation biofuels. According to the calculation based on the supply data provided by the various alternative fuels plants, the HEFA/HVO supply on an EU level will be in the order of 2.31 Mtoe (in 2020), while at a non EU level it will be around 1.53 Mtoe, providing a total of 3.84 Mtoe of HEFA/HVO fuels at a global level. Regarding biojet supply at an EU and global level, this is in the order of 0.15 Mtoe by 2020, indicating the hesitation of the industry toward dedicated production of biojet fuel. Limited availability of production facilities is one reason. Another reason includes costs. According to Hamelinck et al. (2013) there are many factors influencing feedstock costs, but competition for arable land at the beginning of the process chain, as well as competition with alternative energy supply concepts at the end of the process chain, will characterize the future biojet fuel role significantly. The evolution in the demand for biojet fuel is driven by many factors but the following are particularly important: (i) growth in demand for air travel, (ii) overall availability on biojet fuels based on sustainable feedstock and infrastructure adopted for provision, (iii) issues relating to environmental, sustainability, social, political, and regulatory, (iv) market developmental considerations driven by fossil fuel and feedstock prices, incentives, mandates and other fiscal instruments, and (v) technical and sustainability standards for international trade.

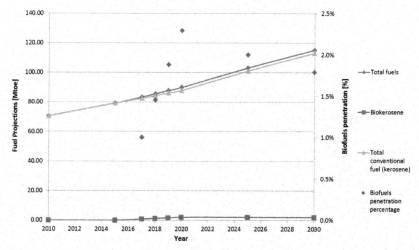

Fig. 3. Fuel projections to 2030 expressed in Mtoe and biofuels percentage penetration for the same period, according to the optimistic scenario.

M. Kousoulidou, L. Lonza / Transportation Research Part D 46 (2016) 166–181   177

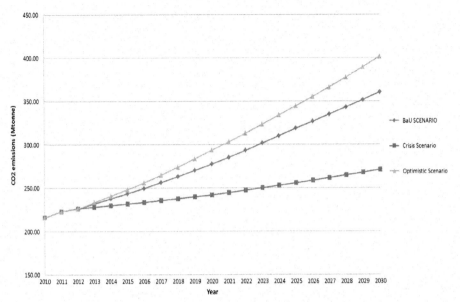

Fig. 4. CO$_2$ emission projections to 2030 for the three different scenarios, expressed in million tonnes.

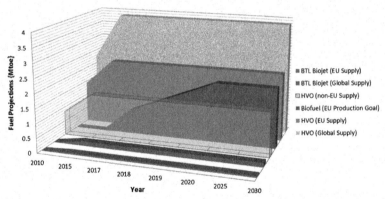

Fig. 5. Demand and supply projections for aviation alternative fuels to 2030, clustered in HVOs and biojet, expressed in Mtoe.

At the moment, one of the most important barriers for biojet fuels is the price gap that exists with fossil jet fuel. At current volumes prices for bio jet fuel are 2–4 times higher than the prices for fossil jet fuel. The price gap has already decreased significantly since the first test with bio jet fuel, at which time the costs were about 30 times higher than the costs for fossil fuel. Co-production across different sectors (e.g. pulp and paper, sugar beet) may be another promising way forward especially in the first steps of the alternative aviation fuel industry: technology-specific integration of process units, material and energy flows is indeed expected to push costs downwards. In any case, mechanisms to cover price differentials with fossil fuels are essential. In Europe the RED provides a mechanism that helps to partially overcome the price gap. The value for supplying a certain amount of renewable energy in transport is shaped by the price gap between fossil fuels and biofuels in road transport, the sector in which most of the renewable energy is supplied. Because the price gap in road transport is smaller than for aviation the RED mechanism does not provide sufficient financial incentive to overcome the difference in price between jet fuel and biojet fuel (Hamelinck et al., 2013).

HEFA/HVOs appear to be the most promising alternative to supply significant amounts of biofuel for aviation, however, this picture might change with an intense penetration of Fischer–Tropsch fuels in the aviation market. The FT process is highly relevant to aviation fuels, where the high energy density requirements of efficient flight restrict the energy storage options available to aircraft. Due to the uncertainty of the actual future supply values, the calculations in this study did not include any potential production of FT fuels.

In order to meet the 2 million ton target set in the Flightpath 2050 (EC, 2011b), a very important share of HEFA/HVO produced in Europe could be absorbed by the aviation sector in competition to demand for diesel fuel generated by the road transport segment. As mandatory targets for renewable fuels uptake are imposed by EU regulation on the road transport segment but not on aviation, whereas the aviation segment (EU domestic flights for the time being and subject to revision of ICAO's position in 2016) is subject to the Emissions' Trading Scheme (ETS), it is reasonable to expect fierce competition between the two modes.

Uncertainties

Evidently, any conclusions drawn from projections into the future are bound to uncertainties inherent in the assumptions and tools used in the process. In this work, uncertainties occur both in the initial planning and estimation of the growth of aviation and hence having a direct impact on the three assumed growth rate scenarios, as well as from the evaluation of the fuel consumption based on the EUROCONTROL data which were processed and segmented. The calculation of fuel consumption for every flight was performed using the Activities 080501–080504 of the Corinair database (EEA, 2007), which gives the fuel consumption (as a function of the distance flown) per aircraft type and per flight phase. Although the LTO cycle was used, this is, as already described in Section 2, a simplified procedure, as it does not fully capture the dependence of fuel consumption of a given flight on the flight actual data such as take-off weight, trajectory, altitude, speed, and meteorological conditions. Moreover, it was not possible to include all aircraft types and therefore assumptions were made in order to estimate the fuel consumption of certain aircraft types based on the Corinair fuel consumption given data of similar types. Within the framework of the Corinair – CORe INventory AIR emissions, the European Environment Agency (EEA) and its European Topic Centre on Air and Climate Change (ETC-ACC) have developed a set of software tools to support European countries in compiling annual air emission inventories. These tools allow for a transparent and standardized, hence consistent and comparable, data collecting and emissions reporting procedure in accordance with the requirements of international conventions and protocols and EU legislation. The EMEP/CORINAIR Atmospheric Emissions Inventory Guidebook (AEIG) is used by several European Member States (over 20) in their official reporting of national emission inventories and estimates or values given in the guidebook are considered to have a good degree of accuracy compared to other available tools. More specific, according to the EMEP/CORINAIR Atmospheric Emissions Inventory Guidebook (AEIG), the use of 'representative' emission factors may contribute significantly to the uncertainty. In terms of the factors relating to the landing and take-off (LTO) activities, the accuracy is better than for cruise (due to the origin of the factors from which the average values are derived from). It would be hard to calculate a quantitative uncertainty estimate. The uncertainty may however lie between 20% and 30% for LTO factors and 20–45% for the cruise factors, according to the EMEP/CORINAIR Atmospheric Emissions Inventory Guidebook. Moreover, uncertainties lie in emission factors for the engines. ICAO estimates that the uncertainties of the different LTO factors are about 5–10%. For cruise, the uncertainties are assumed to vary between 15% and 40%. In any case, the impact of the simplifications performed in this study could be relevant in the evaluation of the fuel consumption of a single particular flight, but are far less important when we are estimating aggregated data involving thousands of flights, and furthermore if we are using this data for comparative purposes.

The economic forecasts used here were updated in May 2014, taking into account latest revision of forecasts from the study of Alonso et al., 2014 and the EUROCONTROL (2013) which was updated in January 2013, apart from six more studies (ICAO, 2007; IATA, 2012; Airbus, 2012, 2013; Boeing, 2014 and Airport Council International, 2013). According to the latest report from EUROCONTROL (2013), we could even still see further downward revisions in growth, and further delay of the recovery. However, assuming that the economic recovery and hence the future of aviation is far less optimistic than expected, the "Crisis" scenario presented in this study covers the assumptions of further growth delays.

Other sources of uncertainty include:

(a) The changes in oil prices which have an immediate and direct impact on the growth of aviation, since the fares and cost of travel are influenced immediately., as well as on the attractiveness of investments in the alternative fuel sector due to price differentials. While there is considerable uncertainty about the future price of conventional jet fuel, prices are generally expected to increase in the coming decades.

(b) The participation of aviation in Emission Trading Scheme (ETS). The EU Emissions Trading Scheme (EU ETS) is a cornerstone of the European Union's policy to combat climate change and its key tool for reducing industrial greenhouse gas emissions cost-effectively.

Since the start of 2012, emissions from all flights from, to and within the European Economic Area (EEA) – the 28 EU Member States, plus Iceland, Liechtenstein and Norway – are included in the EU Emissions Trading Scheme (EU ETS). The legislation, adopted in 2008, applies to EU and non-EU airlines alike. To allow time for negotiations on a global

M. Kousoulidou, L. Lonza / Transportation Research Part D 46 (2016) 166–181   179

market-based measure applying to aviation emissions, the EU ETS requirements were suspended for flights in 2012 to and from non-European countries. For the period 2013–2016, the legislation has also been amended so that only emissions from flights within the EEA fall under the EU ETS. Exemptions for operators with low emissions have also been introduced. There is no doubt however that such regulatory measures contribute to the uncertainty of air transport industry as well as to the projections on the uptake of alternative fuels by the aviation sector.

(c) "The Policy framework for climate and energy in the period from 2020 to 2030" (COM(2014) 15 of 22 January 2014) proposed by the European Commission recommends that the EU seeks to get 27% of its energy from renewable sources by 2030. It does not set specific targets at the national level and therefore does not require specific countries to adjust their policies to meet the goal. The role of energy efficiency policies will be clarified when the European Commission adopts its Energy Efficiency Directive later this year. The policy framework for 2030 does not include specific sub-targets for the transportation sector neither for the uptake of renewable fuels in the transport sector nor specific reductions of GHG emissions. At the time of writing, the position of European Member States is fragmented with no clear and unique signal as to whether carbon intensity of transportation fuels can be expected beyond 2020 or advanced biofuel production incentivised in a 2030 framework.

(d) Political instability in specific regions, wars or pandemic diseases which pose an on-going threat to global security can in turn influence either on a short-term or long-term the future of aviation growth. In this study, none of the scenarios considers or takes into account a severe threat of this kind. For example, in order to evaluate the direct impact of the political stability and the absence of violence/terrorism in the projections related to aviation growth, data from the 2009 update of the Worldwide Governance Indicators (WGI) research project, covering 212 countries and territories between 1996 and 2008 should be taken into account. These aggregate indicators are based on hundreds of specific and disaggregated individual variables measuring various dimensions of governance, taken from 35 data sources provided by 33 different organizations. However, the "Crisis" scenario does consider a rather fragile economic growth, no population migration and a slightly unstable political background.

Conclusions

In spite of the economic crisis, world air traffic continues to grow establishing the air transport sector as one of the most rapidly growing transport sectors. Along with the rapid growth in air transport activity, the increased environmental impacts become a pressing concern. This article presents the results of a study carried out at the European Commission's Joint Research Centre aimed at analyzing the future growth of aviation, the resulting fuel demand and the deployment of biofuels in the aviation sector in Europe, in order to assess the future sustainability of European aviation. Three scenarios have been defined using different input assumptions such as the economic growth, the fuel prices, the load factors etc. This leads to different volumes of projected traffic, and different underlying patterns of growth. Data for aviation growth and hence fuel demand have been projected on a year by year basis up to 2030, using 2010 as the baseline. Data sources are Eurostat statistics and actual flight information from EUROCONTROL. Relevant variables such as the number of flights, passengers or cargo tonnes and production indicators (RPKs) are used together with fuel consumption and CO_2 emissions data. The target of the European Advanced Biofuels Flightpath to ensure the commercialization and consumption of 2 million tons of sustainably produced paraffinic biofuels in the aviation sector by 2020, has also been taken into account. Projections to 2030 show that in the central scenario, an initial period of slow economic growth within the European Union is expected, followed by a slightly gradual recuperation in the 2017–2020 and the 2021–2025 period, in the order of 2.7% and 2.8%, respectively. During the last 5 years of the scenario, the aviation traffic growth is expected to slow down as markets mature, economic growth decelerates and as the capacity limits at airports increasingly become an important issue, as indicated also by EUROCONTROL.

Results regarding CO_2 emission projections to 2030 reveal a steady annual increase in the order of 3%, 1% and 4% on average, for the three different scenarios, providing also a good correlation compared to the annual traffic growth rates that are indicated in the corresponding scenarios. In absolute values, these ratios correspond to the central, the pessimistic and the optimistic scenarios respectively, corresponding to 360 million tonnes CO_2 emissions in 2030, ranging from 271 to 401 million tonnes for the pessimistic and optimistic scenarios, respectively.

Results regarding fuel demand projections to 2030 reveal an annual increase in the order of 2.6% for the most "likely to happen" scenario. In absolute values, this results into a projected total demand of 118 Mtoes in 2030 ranging from 89 to 131 Mtoes for the pessimistic and optimistic scenarios, respectively.

Results regarding aviation biofuels supply projections to 2030 show that the biokerosene demand regarding 2020 to reach 2.06 Mtoe will be met from the HEFA/HVO production at an EU level, leaving for the moments no doubts regarding the strength of EU production on alternative aviation biofuels. HEFA/HVOs appear to be the most promising alternative to supply significant amounts of biofuel for aviation. However, this picture might change with the penetration of Fischer–Tropsch fuels in the aviation market. It is expected that in order to meet the 2 million ton target set in the Flightpath 2020 2050, a very important share of HEFA/HVO produced in Europe would be absorbed by the aviation sector in competition to demand for diesel fuel generated by the road transport segment. Given the fact that at the moment aviation has no alternative options other than the liquid drop-in fuels, while the road transport sector has already turned to electricity and fuel cells, as well as natural gas (both compressed and liquefied) for a broader range of options, this means that on a European and a national level, policies should harmonize the incentives for road biofuels with those for alternative jet fuel. Regarding the effect of biofuels in CO_2 emissions, it is beyond any doubt that aviation biofuels need to be evaluated considering the full life cycle of the fuel. Potential benefits in terms of carbon emissions resulting from the use of biofuels use occur from feedstock production and fuel conversion and not from fuel combustion.

Evidently, any conclusions drawn from projections into the future are bound to uncertainties inherent in the assumptions and tools used in the process. In this work, uncertainties occur both in the initial planning and estimation of the growth of aviation and hence having a direct impact on the three assumed growth rate scenarios, as well as from the evaluation of the fuel consumption based on the EUROCONTROL data which were processed and segmented.

This article also reports on the demand and supply of aviation biofuels (clustered in HEFA/HVOs and biojet) based on the production capacity of production facilities around the world.

Comparing projected demand volumes for alternative aviation fuels with currently available projections in terms of supply projections available in Europe, it becomes apparent that dedicated bio-jet production will not be sufficient to meet demand and that the capacity of the aviation sector to absorb HVO production capacity at the burden of the road transport mode will be based on price considerations and – inherently – mandatory targets to reduce emissions on the different transportation modes. Factoring in uncertainties regarding additional sub-targets for the transportation sector beyond 2020, it can reasonably be expected that competition for available HVO supply will be price-based. The uncertainty surrounding implementation of market based mechanisms comparable to the EU ETS and the full implementation of the latter as of 2017 make scenario-based projections of possible costs for HEFA/HVO broadly unreliable.

The slower than expected pace of development of other advanced biofuels due to industrial scaling problems (e.g. Chloren example) but also to regulatory uncertainty leading to limited investments in the sector indicate that the availability of sufficient supply to meet the voluntary targets set by the aviation industry at competitive costs with fossil fuels is difficult to predict.

This paper does not present results on other non bio-based pathways for alternative aviation fuels: the Gas-to-Liquid option could indeed impact the overall balance both for volumes and costs of FT-based alternative aviation fuels.

Further research needs

In order to evolve our current knowledge in the fuel demand projections in the aviation sector and provide more detailed information there are some necessary steps that need to be included in future work. More precisely, there is the need to:

- Add revisions/update as data become available and technology readiness of identified pathways matures.
- Provide further refinement of analysis for other world regions.
- Provide specific analysis on the role of political instability factors on growth patterns of the aviation sector.
- Once the EU regulatory framework after 2030 becomes clearer, cost competitiveness with (a) other transportation modes; and (b) alternative uses of available primary energy sources and overall balance on GHG emissions beyond the aviation sector (ref. WTW Report Ch.6 alternative uses of biomass).
- Perform country-specific projections, according to two indicators which are directly correlated to the growth in aviation: the political stability environment and the absence of violence/terrorism. This enables to create realistic scenarios for each country, apart from the aggregated ones for the whole of Europe.

Acknowledgements

The authors would like to thank Professor Gustavo Alonso from the Department of Aeronautics in the Polytechnic of Madrid (E.T.S.I. Aeronáuticos, Universidad Politécnica de Madrid, E-28040 Madrid, Spain) for his valuable help and contribution.

References

ACI, 2013a. ACI Airport Economic Survey 2013.
ACI, 2013b. Airport Council International, Global Traffic Forecast 2012–2031.
Agrawal, H. et al, 2008. Characterization of chemical and particulate emissions from aircraft engines. Atmos. Environ. 42 (18), 4380–4392.
Airbus, 2012. Global Market Forecast 2012–2031.
Airbus, 2013. Global Market Forecast Future Journeys 2013 to 2032. <http://www.airbus.com/company/market/forecast/?eID=dam_frontend_push&docID=33752>.
Alonso, G. et al, 2014. Investigations on the distribution of air transport traffic and CO_2 emissions within the European Union. J. Air Trans. Manage. 36, 85–93.
Anger, A., Köhler, J., 2010. Including aviation emissions in the EU ETS: much ado about nothing? A review. Transp. Policy 17 (1), 38–46.
ATAG, 2011. Powering the future of flight: The six easy steps to growing a viable aviation biofuels industry. <http://www.cphcleantech.com/media/2450701/poweringthefuture.pdf>.
ATAG, 2014a. Aviation Benefits Beyond Borders. <http://aviationbenefits.org/media/26786/ATAG__AviationBenefits2014_FULL_LowRes.pdf>.
ATAG, 2014b. Passenger Biofuels Flights Data. <http://aviationbenefits.org/environmental-efficiency/sustainable-fuels/passenger-biofuel-flights/>.
Benito, A., et al., 2010. Estimation of historical CO_2 emissions. In: 12th World Conference on Transport Research, Lisbon.
Berghof, R., et al., 2005. Constrained scenarios on aviation and emissions. CONSAVE.

M. Kousoulidou, L. Lonza / Transportation Research Part D 46 (2016) 166–181　　　　　181

BioJetMap, 2012. <http://www.biojetmap.eu/#31080>.
Boeing, 2012. Boeing, Current Market Outlook 2012. Boeing Commercial Airplanes, Seattle.
Boeing, 2013. Boeing Annual Report. <http://www.boeing.com/assets/pdf/companyoffices/financial/finreports/annual/2014/annual_report.pdf>.
Boeing, 2014. World Air Cargo Forecast 2014–2015. <http://www.boeing.com/resources/boeingdotcom/commercial/about-our-market/cargo-market-detail-wacf/download-report/assets/pdfs/wacf.pdf>.
Bows-Larkin, A., Anderson, K., 2013. Carbon budgets for aviation or gamble with our future? In: Budd, L., Griggs, S., Howarth, D. (Eds.), Sustainable Aviation Futures Bingley. Emerald, pp. 65–84.
British Airways, 2013. Annual Report.
Corporan, E., Edwards, T., Shafer, L., DeWitt, M.J., Klingshirn, C., Zabarnick, S., West, Z., Striebich, R., Graham, J., Klein, J., 2011. Chemical, thermal stability, seal swell, and emissions studies of alternative jet fuels. Energ. Fuels 22, 955–966.
Dessens, O. et al, 2014a. Effects of decarbonising international shipping and aviation on climate mitigation and air pollution. Environ. Sci. Policy 44, 1–10.
Dessens, O. et al, 2014b. Aviation and climate change. Transp. Policy 34, 14–20. http://dx.doi.org/10.1016/j.tranpol.2014.02.014.
EC, 2008. European Commission, Directive 2008/101/EC of 19 November 2008 Amending Directive 2003/87/EC so as to Include Aviation Activities In the Scheme For Greenhouse Gas Emission Allowance Trading Within the Community.
EC, 2011a. 2 Million Tons Per Year: a Performing Biofuels Supply Chain For EU Aviation, Technical Paper.
EC, 2011b. Flight Path 2050. Europe's Vision for Aviation.
EC, 2013. European Advanced Biofuels Flight path Initiative. [Online] Available at <http://ec.europa.eu/energy/renewables/biofuels/doc/20130911_a_performing_biofuels_supply_chain.pdf> (Accessed: 30-01-2014).
EEA, 2007. EMEP/CORINAIR Emission Inventory Guidebook, Eurostat statistics (2007) <ec.europa.eu/eurostat>.
EUROCONTROL, 2010. Long Term Forecast – Flight Movements 2010–2030, EUROCONTROL Data Demand Repository (DDR) (2010). <www.eurocontrol.int>.
EUROCONTROL, 2013. Challenges of Growth 2013 Task 4: European Air Traffic in 2035, <www.eurocontrol.int>.
Florentinus, A., et al., 2012. Potential of biofuels for shipping Final Report. Ecofys Project number: BIONL11332. <http://www.ecofys.com/files/files/ecofys_2012_potential_of_biofuels_in_shipping_02.pdf>.
Gegg, P.K. et al, 2014. The market development of aviation biofuel: drivers and constraints. J. Air Trans. Manage. 39, 34–40.
Gettelman, A., Chen, C., 2013. The climate impact of aviation aerosols. Geophys. Res. Lett. 40 (11), 2785–2789.
Hamelinck, C., et al., 2013. Biofuels for Aviation.
Herndon, S.C. et al, 2005. Particulate emissions from in-use commercial aircraft. Aerosol Sci. Technol. 39 (8), 799–809.
Horton, G.R., 2006. Forecasts of CO_2 emissions from civil aircraft for IPCC. DTI.
IATA, 2009. Annual Report. <http://www.iata.org/pressroom/Documents/IATAAnnualReport2009.pdf>.
IATA, 2012. Annual Report.
IATA, 2013. IATA 2013 Report on Alternative Fuels, eighth ed. <www.iata.org/publications/documents/2013-report-alternative-fuels.pdf>.
IATA, 2014. The Alternative Fuels Report. <http://www.iata.org/publications/Documents/2014-report-alternative-fuels.pdf>.
ICAO, 2007. Outlook for Air Transport to the Year 2025.
ICAO, 2009. Information Paper, Global Aviation CO_2 Emissions Projections to 2050.
ICAO, 2011. Annual Report of the Council. <http://www.icao.int/publications/Documents/9975_en.pdf>.
ICAO, 2012. Global Aviation CO_2 Emission Projections to 2050.
ICAO, 2013. Environment Report. <http://www.icao.int/environmental-protection/Pages/EnvReport13.aspx>.
ICAO, 2015. An overview on international discussions on Aviation Biofuels.
Kallio, P. et al, 2014. Renewable jet fuel. Curr. Opin. Biotechnol. 26, 50–55.
Kelly, T., Allan, J., 2006. Ecological effects of aviation. The Ecology of Transportation: Managing Mobility for the Environment. Springer, pp. 5–24.
Knörzer, D., Szodruch, J., 2012. Innovation for Sustainable Aviation in a Global Environment: Proceedings of the Sixth European Aeronautics Days. IOS Press.
Köhler, M.O. et al, 2008. Impact of perturbations to nitrogen oxide emissions from global aviation. J. Geophys. Res.: Atmos. (1984–2012) 113 (D11).
Kousoulidou, M. et al, 2012. Impact of biodiesel application at various blending ratios on passenger cars of different fueling technologies. Fuel 98, 88–94.
Krammer, P. et al, 2013. Climate-neutrality versus carbon-neutrality for aviation biofuel policy. Transport. Res. Part D: Trans. Environ. 23, 64–72.
Kurniawan, J.S., Khardi, S., 2011. Comparison of methodologies estimating emissions of aircraft pollutants, environmental impact assessment around airports. Environ. Impact Assess. Rev. 31 (3), 240–252.
Lane, 2016. Sustainable aviation biofuel: The Digest's 2016 8-Slide Guide to United Airlines. <http://www.biofuelsdigest.com/bdigest/2016/01/24/sustainable-aviation-biofuel-the-digests-2016-8-slide-guide-to-united-airlines/>.
Lee, D.S. et al, 2009. Aviation and global climate change in the 21st century. Atmos. Environ. 43 (22), 3520–3537.
LISBP, 2012. Probio3 project, winner of the"Investissement d'Avenir – news item at <www.lisbp.insa-toulouse.fr>.
Maurice, L.Q. et al, 2001. Advanced aviation fuels: a look ahead via a historical perspective. Fuel 80 (5), 747–756.
Onasch, T.B. et al, 2009. Chemical properties of aircraft engine particulate exhaust emissions. J. Propul. Power 25 (5), 1121–1137.
Pearlson, M., 2011. Economic and environmental assessment of hydroprocessed renewable distillate fuels Masters Thesis. Massachusetts Institute of Technology, Cambridge, MA.
Pearlson, M. et al, 2013. A techno-economic review of hydroprocessed renewable esters and fatty acids for jet fuel production. Biofuels, Bioprod. Biorefin. 7 (1), 89–96.
PWC, 2013. PriceWaterhouseCoopers, Recovering airline industry on track for profitability in 2013, according to PwC. <www.pwc.com/us/en/press-releases/2013/recovering-airilne-industry-on-track.jhtml>.
Sgouridis, S. et al, 2011. Air transportation for a carbon constrained world: long-term dynamics of policies and strategies for mitigating the carbon footprint of commercial aviation. Transport. Res. Part A: Policy Practice 45 (10), 1077–1091.
Sausen, R. et al, 2005. Aviation radiative forcing in 2000: An update on IPCC (1999). Meteorol. Z. 14 (4), 555–561.
Sausen, R., Schumann, U., 2000. Estimates of the climate response to aircraft CO_2 and NOx emissions scenarios. Clim. Change 44 (1–2), 27–58.
Stephenson, D., 2012. Sweet ideas: options grow for possible power sources of future airplanes. <www.boeing.com/features/2012/05/corp_innovative_thinking_05_07_12.html>.
Stevenson, D. et al, 2000. Future estimates of tropospheric ozone radiative forcing and methane turnover- the impact of climate change. Geophys. Res. Lett. 27 (14), 2073–2076.
Stevenson, D.S. et al, 2004. Radiative forcing from aircraft NOx emissions: mechanisms and seasonal dependence. J. Geophys. Res.: Atmos. (1984–2012) 109 (D17).
Stratton, K., et al., 2011. Life Cycle Greenhouse Gas Emissions from Alternative Jet Fuels, PARTNER Project 28 report.
UOP, 2005. Universal Oil Products, Opportunities for Biorenewables in Oil Refineries, Des Plaines, IL. <http://www.osti.gov/bridge/servlets/purl/861458-Wv5uum/861458.pdf>.
Wilcox, L. et al, 2012. Radiative forcing due to aviation water vapour emissions. Atmos. Environ. 63, 1–13.
Winchester, Niven, McConnachie, Dominic, Wollersheim, Christoph, Waitz, Ian A., 2013. Economic and emissions impacts of renewable fuel goals for aviation in the US. Transport. Res. Part A: Policy Practice 58, 116–128.
Zeng, G., Pyle, J.A., 2003. Changes in tropospheric ozone between 2000 and 2100 modeled in a chemistry-climate model. Geophys. Res. Lett. 30 (7).

Part IV:

Business Model Innovation

14

Where next for low cost airlines?
A spatial and temporal comparative study

Graham Francis, Ian Humphreys, Stephen Ison, Michelle Aicken

Abstract

The purpose of this paper is to analyze the international development of the low cost airline model. The paper examines and seeks to characterize the factors which have encouraged and inhibited the spatial and temporal spread of low cost carriers. A typology of low cost carriers is developed to illustrate the diversity of practices identifiable under the generic low cost banner. The authors of this paper identify stages of development with respect to time and compare the development of low cost operations in different countries of the world. The economic and political impacts of the spread of the low cost model are examined and the sustainability and future patterns of growth considered.
© 2005 Elsevier Ltd. All rights reserved.

Keywords: Low cost airlines; Growth; International development

1. Introduction

Low cost airlines have had a widely publicised and dramatic impact on particular air transport markets but to date the nature and extent of this 'revolution' has been regionalized with operations being influenced by a variety of different international contexts. The low cost revolution had its origins in the US and the concept has proved to be financially and operationally robust for a number of short haul airline operations around the world. This paper seeks to address the question as to why low cost carriers have to date only established themselves in certain geographical localities? Low cost airlines would appear to have been shielded from the full impact of systematic and asymmetrical shocks in the airline industry and have grown while traditional airlines have experienced a declining market. It is the contention of this paper that certain factors have combined to either inhibit or facilitate the growth of low cost airlines in various locations.

Whilst there is a diverse academic literature in terms of low cost carriers (see for example Doganis, 2001), there is a dearth of academic papers mapping the international development of the low cost model (with the possible exception of Lawton, 2002).

The purpose of this paper is to address this gap in the low cost literature by aiming to:

(a) trace the development and life cycle of low cost airline markets world-wide;
(b) develop a typology of different low cost carriers;
(c) identify those factors that have contributed to or inhibited the growth of low cost airlines; and from this analysis;
(d) speculate about future international trends and the consequences for the aviation industry and its stakeholders.

To achieve these aims the paper draws on both the aviation business and academic literature in order to

84   G. Francis et al. / Journal of Transport Geography 14 (2006) 83-94

assess global patterns of low cost growth and development. It is important to note that a paper of this nature can only represent developments up to and including a particular point in time. Clearly the low cost sector is highly dynamic and any attempt to capture its true identity is a highly problematic activity.

This paper begins by defining the low cost concept and developing a typology of different approaches, then describes the geographical pattern of the development of low cost operations through time. It continues by examining if the developments to date allow us to predict future growth patterns and finally draws conclusions regarding the prospects for the model over time and space.

2. Characterising low cost models

Although the term 'low cost airlines' is frequently used as if they are homogeneous, observations of airline operations and management reveal that there are many variations of the model and a great diversity between airlines (Calder, 2002; Lawton, 2002; Gillen and Morrison, 2003; Francis et al., 2004). It is more appropriate therefore to refer to low cost airline *models*. The general concept is that costs are reduced compared to traditional scheduled airline operations in a number of ways. The core characteristics common to the majority of low cost airlines are: high aircraft utilization, internet booking, use of secondary airports, minimum cabin crew, lower wage scales, lower rates of unionisation among employees, one class of seating thus allowing more seats per aircraft than traditional airlines (who offer alternative seat pitches for different classes of travel), short 'on the ground' turn around times, no cargo carried to slow down turn around times, a simple fare structure and pricing strategy, e-ticketing, no seat allocation, passengers having to pay for food and drink, flexible working terms and conditions for employees relative to traditional airlines, point to point services and no connections offered (Doganis, 2001; Williams, 2001; Mason et al., 2000). Combined these factors have enabled airlines to reduce their costs and offer lower fares relative to prices traditionally charged for a route.

Low cost carriers have developed a variety of modifications to the above in order to gain and maintain their competitive and cost advantages over traditional or so called 'legacy' airlines. It should be noted that many of the characteristics common to low cost airlines are also now being adopted by 'legacy' airlines. In order to characterize and trace the spread of low cost carriers the authors have developed a typology of low cost carriers under which it is possible to conceptually categorise five broad types of low cost carriers:

1. *Southwest copy-cats*;
2. *Subsidiaries*;
3. *Cost cutters*;
4. *Diversified charter carriers*;
5. *State subsidised competing on price*.

Southwest copy-cats. This category comprises airlines that have been set up from scratch or those that have been remodelled by independent entrepreneurs. These airlines are closest to the 'Southwest model' (Doganis, 2001) and they minimise costs through operating mainly point to point services, a single type of aircraft and high aircraft utilisation. Airlines such as Southwest Airlines, WestJet, Ryanair, SkyEurope or easyJet fall into this category, although it is important to note that there is still diversity within this category. Some airlines fall short of implementing all of the features of the 'Southwest model' whereas others have extended it. For example Ryanair operating to underused airports, easyJet operating to main airports and Southwest operating to both. Sunair extended the 'Southwest model' with the use of older aircraft. Debonair failed by offering frills at a fare below long run average costs.

Subsidiaries. Typically comprise low cost carriers that have been set up as subsidiaries of long established major airlines to compete and gain a share of the low fare sector. These carriers frequently try to operate in a similar manner to the airlines identified in the 'Southwest copy-cats' category. Although the degree of cost minimisation varies depending on what costs and assets are inherited from the legacy airline, in terms of mixed fleet types, union agreements that prevent work conditions, flexibility and pay falling to levels possible if the airline was not a subsidiary. Such agreements can restrict cost reductions. Although supposedly autonomous there are often elements of cross-subsidisation. Such airlines would include Ted by United, Song by Delta, Snowflake by SAS, MetroJet (US Airways), Tiger Air by Singapore airlines, Freedom Air by Air New Zealand, bmibaby by bmi and originally Go by British Airways. These airlines often encounter issues of competing with their parent airline on certain routes. Virgin Atlantic has set up Virgin Blue, Pacific Blue and Virgin Express with routes that do not compete because they serve distinct geographic markets. Such 'subsidiaries' are frequently formed in response to market entry by 'Southwest copy-cats'. There can also be a tacit threat of their introduction in response to potential market entry.

Cost cutters. These are typically long established legacy airlines that are now attempting to cut their operating costs. In many cases by simply not offering all the frills they once did, such as free in-flight food. These airlines continue to operate to a hub and spoke pattern, they might try and rationalise the number of aircraft types but essentially these airlines continue to operate a short and long haul network to major airports, but have introduced low fares, one way fares and internet booking in order to compete for the low fares market. Airlines such as BA and Aer Lingus have both shed large numbers of staff and begun to rationalise their fleets in order to compete. Airlines such as Air France, Air New Zealand (express class as distinct from their low cost subsidiary Freedom Air) and Iberia have begun to offer cheap one way fares and make passengers pay for their food or have reduced food to a minimum on certain routes.

Diversified charter carriers. These are low cost subsidiaries developed by charter airlines in order to operate low cost scheduled services. Some charter airlines have begun to operate scheduled services using subsidiary airlines which imitate the characteristics of the airlines set up from scratch ('Southwest copy-cats'). Adopting a single fleet type, high aircraft utilisation, charging for food, one way fares and internet booking. A distinct feature of these airlines is that the costs associated with their subsidiary status are low because their parent airlines have long been considered to have the lowest costs within the airline industry (Doganis, 2001). Many of the routes link existing European holiday destination airports that are already served by their charter arm, but on a scheduled seat only basis. Such airlines include Thomson by Britannia, Hapag-Lloyd express by Hapag-Lloyd and MyTravelLite by MyTravel.

State subsidised competing on price. These airlines are not true low cost carriers as such. They are financially supported by Government ownership or subsidy allowing them to offer low fares without the need to cover their long run average costs. These airlines offer low fares on their scheduled services as part of a national strategy to develop tourism or to promote a particular airport as a hub for a region. Emirates is a current example of this but historically many airlines have only survived through government support.

Whilst we have attempted to categorise low cost carriers within the authors' typology it is important to recognise that there is still variability within each category presented. This paper now considers the international development of different low cost airline models.

3. The international development of low cost carriers

This section traces the international development of the low cost model, categorising the stages of development of low cost services in different geographical markets. Table 1 illustrates the market penetration of the low cost operators around the world. It also indicates the timing of the main elements of deregulation which has frequently been a catalyst for the development of low cost operations. The main geographical areas are also detailed in the order in which low cost operations began.

Table 1
Low cost market shares around the world

Region (country)	Year low cost operations began	Year(s) in which market de-regulation took place	Share of overall market (%)
North America			
USA	1978	1978	24–25[a]
Canada	1996[b]	1996	30
Europe			
UK/Ireland	1995	1993	40
EU	1999	1995	20
EU expansion	2002	2004	<1
Australia/NZ			
Australia	1990	1990	30+[c]
New Zealand	1996	1984	..
Asia			
Malaysia	2001	2001	2
Singapore	2001	2001	<1
Japan	1998	1998[d]	1[e]
China[f]	–	Ongoing	–
Thailand	2004	2003	<1
India		2003[g]	<1
Rest of world			
Brazil	2001[h]	1998	3
S. Africa	2001[i]	1999	1
Gulf States	2004	2003	<1

[a] de Neufville (2004) 12 Jan '04 Transportation Research Board Annual Meeting "not a real stretch for low cost US market to expand from 20–25% to 50% in the next 20 years".
[b] WestJet, see Lawton (2002).
[c] Virgin Blue has 30% of the Australia market and Qantas has responded with a new low cost carrier in order to protect its market share Airliner World (2003, vol. 12(12). p. 23). It is hard to calculate the market share in NZ which is dominated by Air NZ subsidiaries many of which have remodelled themselves with elements of the low cost model.
[d] *Source*: Thomas (2002).
[e] *Source*: Thomas (2002).
[f] Lawton (2002, p. 181) says China has begun to remove restrictions.
[g] Air Deccan.
[h] Gol, see Lawton (2002, p. 184).
[i] Kulula.com see Lawton (2002, p. 184).

3.1. North America

3.1.1. USA
3.1.1.1. Southwest and the birth of the low cost concept.
Pacific Southwest pioneered the low cost model in the US, but it was Southwest Airlines who operated the model, subsequently developing into the sixth largest airline in the US serving 63 million passengers and operating 377 aircraft (Air Transport World, 2003).

In the US the low cost sector has grown and currently represents approximately 25% of the US domestic market in terms of passengers carried (Field, 2003). de Neufville (2004) states that it is "not a real stretch for the low cost US market to expand from 25% to 50% in the next 20 years". Studies of the impact of low cost carriers on

86   *G. Francis et al. / Journal of Transport Geography 14 (2006) 83–94*

communities have revealed that where low cost services operate, fares are reduced, not only on the specific city pair, but also on neighbouring city pairs, a phenomenon referred to as the 'Southwest effect' (Windle et al., 1996). Low cost carriers have led to a step change in the air-port–airline relationship (Graham, 2003; Francis et al., 2004). In particular at any one time over 50 communities are reported to be trying to persuade Southwest airlines to introduce services to their regions (Calder, 2002).

Whilst the general pattern of low cost development in the US is one of growth, it can be categorized in *six* stages.

3.1.1.2. Innovation 1971–1978. Low cost airlines have their origins in certain US states most notably Texas and California which comprised densely populated metro-politan regions separated by distances making them suit-able for air travel. The competitive stance of the state regulators in the early 1970s allowed low cost air services to develop, compete and charge competitive fares for intra-state services. US intrastate carriers were exempt from most federal (CAB) regulation regarding fares and service. It was not until 1978, under the US Deregulation Act that airlines were allowed to enter the previously restricted inter-state domestic US airline market and to operate routes, frequencies and to set fares related to what the market could bear. Although the Act was intro-duced in 1978, it took several years for new airline ser-vices to develop. The introduction and development of services was dependent on entrepreneurs such as Herb Kelleher and Rollin King of Southwest who took the ini-tiative to expand low cost services in the US domestic market (Calder, 2002; Doganis, 2001).

3.1.1.3. Proliferation of the low cost model 1979–1985. This period was characterised by intense price competition. Encouraged by the initial success of Southwest a large number of new airlines entered the market and began to compete with major established scheduled carriers. Several other former intrastate, former charter, and brand new airlines entered service during this period using various elements of the low cost model. People's Express was the highest profile of many early 'no-frills' airlines that were ultimately unsustainable. Other carri-ers that grew significantly at this time were Pacific Southwest, New York Air, Jet America and Midway Airlines. In response a number of the major airlines introduced their own low cost subsidiary airlines such as Delta Express, Continental Lite and Shuttle by United Airlines. These were the first examples of those airlines that typify those under the 'subsidiaries' category of the authors low cost typology, subsidiaries born out of com-petition.

3.1.1.4. Consolidation 1985–1992. Over this period a large number of new entrant airlines failed, went bank-

rupt or merged with the major airlines as they sought scale economies and enhanced market coverage. Even Southwest airlines purchased smaller local operators as a means of expanding their operation. Few new entrant airlines lasted longer than five years. A number of the low cost subsidiaries launched by major carriers to com-pete with new and established low cost airlines were abandoned (such as United Shuttle and Continental lite). The main problem was that they inherited high costs from their parent companies and inhibitive work-ing practices under union agreements.

3.1.1.5. 1992–1996 second wave of new entrants and 1997–2000, a second round of consolidation. During the period 1992–1996 a second wave of independent new entrants emerged that copied elements of the Southwest model, but were not complete 'copy-cats'. Operators such as Vanguard Airlines, Kiwi Air and Western Pacific Air-lines entered the market to compete with the major carri-ers but the majority of these carriers either went bankrupt or were taken over. A catalyst for this was the downturn in low cost airline traffic that was experienced across the US in response to the ValuJet crash in May 1996. The media in its coverage raised consumer concern in relation to the safety aspects of low cost airlines (Cobb and Primo, 2003).

3.1.1.6. Market maturity. The current situation in the US is that of one established low cost airline with several medium-sized players such as AirTran Airways and Jet-Blue Airways operating in certain geographic localities. Post-9/11 the depletion of yields in the US market has raised the profile of the low cost model, particularly as low cost services appear to be those that are able to make a financial return in low yield market conditions. In response to this, major airlines introduced a second wave of 'subsidiaries' such as Delta re-introducing low cost carrier operations under the Song brand and United having introduced a low cost subsidiary 'Ted'. In the future low cost growth could be further facilitated if there are corporate failures amongst the 'legacy' airlines. The question is how much further can low cost services grow?

3.1.2. Canada

The Canadian market further illustrates how 'copy-cat' and 'subsidiary' low cost airlines can emerge and offers some cautionary tales. Perhaps the best known Canadian low cost airline is WestJet, which started oper-ations with three planes in 1996. WestJet has grown revealing the capacity for low cost operations in the Canadian market not facing direct competition from Southwest who have so far only operated domestically in the US. WestJet is cited as a "successful" low cost airline (Calder, 2002, p. 153; Lawton, 2002, p. 169). However, there have been a number of unsuccessful Canadian

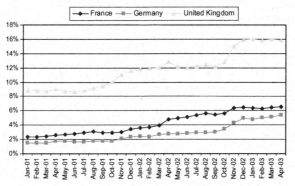

Fig. 1. Market share of European low cost airline operations. *Source*: Adapted from Eurocontrol Statistics (2003).

cases, most notably CanJet, Roots Air, Canadian Shuttle and Greyhound Airlines (Lawton, 2002). Until its demise Canada 3000 was Canada's second largest carrier. Canada 3000 had a background as a charter airline (and is therefore an example of the fourth category in our typology detailed in Section 2) but was keen to establish international routes and even airline alliances (Knibb, 2001; Lawton, 2002). The pressure on low cost airlines in contested markets was illustrated when the dominant carrier Air Canada[1] launched Tango and Zip as its low cost subsidiaries and Canada 3000 (that held 13% of the domestic market) was forced into bankruptcy in late 2001. Consequently, in 2003 WestJet accounted for 14% of the domestic market (Lawton, 2002, p. 172) while Air Canada's low fares subsidiaries were reported to account for 16.8% of the domestic market (Flint, 2003, pp. 22–26). Subsequently Air Canada withdrew its low cost subsidiaries Tango and Zip in late 2004. So in Canada for the moment the 'subsidiary' model has come and gone.

3.2. Europe

Since 1995, low cost carriers in Europe have experienced a significant growth in their market share. This trend is expected to continue (see Fig. 1).

3.2.1. UK and Ireland take the initiative
The European low cost phenomenon originated in the UK and Ireland led by 'Southwest copy-cats' easyJet and Ryanair in 1995. There are a number of reasons for the growth in the market share of low cost airlines in the UK and Ireland. The economic regulatory framework was conducive to the development of low cost airline operations

and the UK and Ireland had a liberal bilateral agreement and Governments that encouraged airline competition. Deregulation of the European market allowed these airlines to offer services throughout that market from 1995 and to serve domestic routes within other European countries from 1997. The low fares from these island nations were extremely attractive compared to the cost (including travel time) of alternative surface transport modes. Entrepreneurial leadership, exploiting the new market opportunities was also crucial to the development of low cost services. In this respect the role of Stelios Haji-Ioannou (easyJet) and the Ryan family/Michael O'Leary (Ryanair) were central. Overall the importance of the appropriate business strategy at a competitive price was emphasised by the failure of Debonair, an airline that attempted to offer 'frills' within a low fares market.

A further factor that aided the low cost growth in UK and Ireland was underused airport capacity and the managers of privatised/commercialized airports willingness to offer reduced airport charges to low cost airlines in order to raise passenger throughput and reap the benefits of increased passenger spending in airport retail outlets (Francis et al., 2003).

A major difference from the development of the low cost model in the US was the aggressive direct sales approach of Ryanair and easyJet. By 2001 both airlines were reporting over 80% of their sales direct via the Internet and the remainder through call centres. The Internet allowed consumers to compare prices and by the use of friendly web design, the purchase of air tickets became simple and no longer the domain of the travel agents who had previously exerted a strong influence on ticket sales (Dumazel and Humphreys, 1999). The Internet removed a barrier since selling direct to the market enabled the airlines to make savings in terms of distribution costs and establish detailed market information with respect to their customers.

---

[1] In 2004 Air Canada had about an 80% market share following its takeover of Canadian Airlines and the demise of Canada 3000.

The major airlines have responded in two ways, namely, by establishing subsidiaries and/or becoming 'cost cutters'. For example in 1998 British Airways established its own low cost airline, Go, KLM transformed part of their UK subsidiary into Buzz airlines and in 2002 bmi set up a subsidiary bmibaby. By 2002, however, a degree of consolidation had taken place in the UK market with Go purchased by easyJet and Buzz by Ryanair. In terms of cost cutting the traditional scheduled airlines, most notably, BA and Aer Lingus have also responded to low cost competition by reducing their workforce costs, offering Internet sales and one way fares. As such, if purchased in advance, fares have often been competitive with those of low cost operators. British Airways having managed to achieve this to such an extent that in 2003 it was voted Guardian/Observer low cost airline of the year! (Dennis, 2004).

The charter airlines have introduced scheduled low cost subsidiaries to serve and protect core markets to Southern European destinations with the introduction of services from MyTravelLite (MyTravel), and Thompsonfly (from TUI/Britannia), the latter taking the bold step of buying an airport in the UK Midlands (Coventry) in order to facilitate its operation. By 2003 the low cost airlines accounted for 40% of all passengers travelling from the UK and Ireland to European destinations.

3.2.2. European Union (EU): innovation and proliferation

Low cost growth in mainland Europe began to become possible with the EU's so called 'third package' deregulation in 1993, although this did not come fully into effect in terms of fifth freedom rights until 1995, has only recently entered the proliferation stage and initially generated few serious players, other than Virgin Express from Brussels. In 1999, however, Ryanair and easyJet began to develop European operating bases. Growth on the Continent continued with new operating bases for Ryanair and easyJet based in Germany, Switzerland and Italy. In addition, after initial resistance from the French authorities easyJet and Ryanair began to operate from bases in France. Ryanair in a number of cases have redefined airport economics by getting airports in effect to pay them to use their facilities (see Francis et al., 2003). Although in 2004 an agreement with Charleroi airport was ruled by the European Commission to be in part anti-competitive many of the arrangements entered into by low cost airlines can be argued to be transparent and therefore are unlikely to be altered as a consequence of this agreement.

In a move similar to that of other major airlines several European airlines have established low cost subsidiaries. Lufthansa for example have responded by reworking their Germanwings subsidiary into the low cost formula. SAS have introduced Snowflake and KLM Basiq Air.

Overall a variety of low cost airlines have emerged representing the first four categories of our typology. The European airline market has demonstrated a volatility and fragility in terms of service provision with an analysis of OAG data revealing that 28% of the low cost airline services which started between 1997 and 2002 were withdrawn, compared to an average of 2% for full fare scheduled operations. In total low cost services have grown to represent in the region of 10% of the total European passenger market and 20% of the short haul European market, a total that looks set to expand given the fact that easyJet and Ryanair the two main low cost protagonists have, both ordered over 100 new aircraft.

3.2.3. EU expansion: innovation

Innovation of low cost services was facilitated in 2002 by the Czech and Slovak Governments who both liberalised their bilateral agreements allowing low cost air services with the UK. This enabled them to take advantage of the inbound tourism market for the benefit of the economy and to prepare for joining the single European aviation market, along with eight other states in May 2004. Low cost operations to Prague were established by UK airlines and the Slovak's became the first country in Eastern Europe to operate the 'Southwest copy-cat' Sky-Europe, that by 2003 served Amsterdam, Paris and London. In order to capitalise on the lucrative market around Vienna, on their web site the airline has renamed their Bratislava base as Bratislava/Vienna West.

Full membership of the single European aviation market has led to the proliferation of air services. The relative success of SkyEurope and low cost services in Prague and Budapest has led Austrian Airways and Czech Airlines to establish low cost subsidiaries and in 2004 for Malév (Hungarian Airlines) to introduce low fare services. Polish low cost services have started with Whizz Air and Air Polonia, whilst Citrad Airlines have begun services from Bulgaria. The availability of runway capacity in Eastern Europe and fares that are attractive for Western European tourists as low cost destinations, suggest that there is potential for growth in this market and that moves to date are in their infancy.

3.3. Australia and New Zealand

In this section the developments in Australia and New Zealand are examined. Many of the developments have been interlinked particularly in relation to Trans-Tasman low cost routes.

3.3.1. Australia

3.3.1.1. Deregulation and entrant activity 1990–1999. "The Australian domestic aviation industry was deregulated in 1990. Prior to this, two incumbent airlines dominated the

G. Francis et al. / Journal of Transport Geography 14 (2006) 83–94 89

market" (Forsyth, 2003, p. 277). The duopoly existed, whereby Qantas and Ansett both had equal access to the market. Several features existed which where favourable to low cost carrier entry, namely, a number of dense routes, for example between Sydney–Melbourne, and access to a large leisure market. These were offset, however, by carriers facing problems gaining access to terminals, obtaining capital and competition.

A number of new start-ups did enter the Australian market but most attempts at securing a share of the market and being profitable have failed. Compass Airlines started low cost operations in 1990, but experienced financial difficulties a year later as a result of a price war (Nyathi et al., 1993). In 1992, Compass Mark II began operations which lasted only six months, followed by Impulse which also experienced cash flow problems prior to becoming part of Qantas. Innovation in the low cost sector that has survived (to date) arrived in the form of Virgin Blue Airlines in 2000 driven by the entrepreneurial backing of Sir Richard Branson (Airliner World, 2003). Virgin Blue differed from other low cost airlines by offering connecting services, code shares with major airlines and direct competition with Qantas at fares often around half the price. Significantly the collapse of Ansett in 2001 left a potential gap in the market for low cost airlines which Qantas and Virgin Blue exploited by operating routes previously serviced by Ansett which originally had 40% of the market.

3.3.1.2. Consolidation: contesting market share 2001–2004.

There has been no clear evidence of a proliferation of low cost services in the Australian market, beyond the innovation stage. Although the Australian market was only fully deregulated in 1990, it was the collapse in 2001 of Ansett airlines, a major player with 40% of the domestic market, that allowed Virgin Blue to capture a significant market share with more than 30% of the domestic market (Easdown and Wilms, 2002; Forsyth, 2003). In 2002, in response to low cost competition, Qantas introduced its own low cost subsidiaries JetStar and Australian Airlines for international services (Australian Aviation, 2004).

Virgin Blue is now operating international services to New Zealand, Fiji and Vanuatu through a separate Virgin subsidiary known as Pacific Blue (Airliner World, 2003). Spirit Airlines a 'no frills' airline was proposed to begin operations in 2001 with five MD-80s but were yet to secure approval from the licensing authorities (Airliner World, 2003).

3.3.2. New Zealand

Whilst New Zealand was at the forefront of deregulation (Kissling, 1998) domestically the 'low cost revolution' has been slow to develop. The situation is different for international Trans-Tasman services where by 2004 low cost competition was beginning to intensify.

3.3.2.1. First new entrants.

The domestic aviation market in New Zealand was deregulated in 1984 (Collier, 1999). Despite this early deregulation low cost services did not develop until 1995, and these were limited in size and scope. In 1995, Kiwi Airlines started low cost Trans-Tasman operations between New Zealand and Australia, initially operating as a charter airline, but then subsequently becoming a scheduled carrier. Air New Zealand responded by launching its own low cost subsidiary Freedom Air which combined with competition from Qantas forced Kiwi Airlines out of business (Wilson, 1996; Airliner World, 2003; Forsyth, 2003). However, the New Zealand Competition Commission accepted the establishment of Freedom Air on the premise that it would need to exist for a minimum period of 10 years. The failure of Kiwi to survive in the face of Air New Zealand's low cost subsidiary Freedom Air and Qantas may be indicative of the difficulties facing start up 'Southwest copy-cat' low cost airlines. There is also a tacit threat from Air New Zealand's low cost subsidiary Freedom Air against any other would-be start-up airlines. Certainly Freedom Air fares increased after the demise of Kiwi International until, restrained by the emergence of new low cost carriers and scheduled carriers like Emirates on the Trans-Tasman route who commenced operations with subsidised fares.

3.3.2.2. A second wave of new entrants.

The potential for new entrants appears to be gathering momentum. K2000 was launched late in 2000 by the former management of the now defunct Central Pacific Airlines and Kiwi Air to take advantage of an expected increase in passenger traffic prior to the dawn of the new millennium, but lasted all of 6 weeks. (Airliner World, 2003).

Deregulation, within New Zealand has meant that new entrants and particularly large airlines with substantial capital are seeing New Zealand as an attractive market to enter and are viewing the domestic and Trans-Tasman routes as possible revenue earners. Pacific Blue, a New Zealand registered subsidiary of Australian Virgin Blue is seeking access to the market and looking to serve Australia with Trans-Tasman services in 2004. It was established as a New Zealand subsidiary in order to save money on staff costs due to different regulations in New Zealand. Domestically Air New Zealand has remodelled itself with its 'express class' adopting many of the low cost airline practices on all flights of 6 hours or less (in addition to running its low cost subsidiary Freedom Air). Despite the 'supposed' liberalisation of the international aviation policy in New Zealand, the industry is still characterised by one dominant carrier Air New Zealand and a series of bilateral air service agreements that regulate the industry. Jump Airlines had intended to inaugurate operations to Fiji and begin operating low cost services early in 2004 but has postponed its start up.

3.4. Asia

3.4.1. Innovation

A number of industry commentators have claimed that the low cost model would not work in Asia owing to regulatory restrictions, long sector distances and low costs of operation among incumbent airlines (Thomas, 2002; Pinkham, 2003). This view has in part been based on the limited expansion of the low cost model in the Japanese market subsequent to domestic deregulation in 1997 shortly after which Skymark airlines (a 'Southwest copy-cat') began offering domestic services. In 2001 the low cost model began to be adopted in other Asian countries despite regulatory restrictions.

According to the Centre for Aviation in the Asia Pacific Region there are opportunities for low cost services, namely; "… rapid demographic and economic progress in many countries; congested and high cost hub airports alongside underutilized regional airports; broader government policy objectives to stimulate tourism and trade outside capital cities; opportunities for "soft liberalization", allowing international access to smaller airports behind national gateways, with limited risk to national flag carriers" (www.centreforaviation.com).

Encouraged by results of low cost services in Europe and the US, Malaysian carrier Air Asia began domestic operations in December 2001 based on the Southwest model, and in 2004 was seeking approval for a range of international services. In order to circumvent regulatory restrictions Air Asia has established an airline registered in Thailand and has inaugurated low cost international services between the two countries. The adoption of the 'Southwest copy-cat' model has begun to gather momentum with the entry into the market of Singaporean carriers ValuAir and Tiger Airways (49% owned by main carrier Singapore Airlines and Ryanair founder Tony Ryan 16%). The launch of three low cost airlines in Thailand (2004) has stimulated momentum in terms of low cost growth in the region. In addition to the Air Asia joint venture, Orient Thai subsidiary 'one two go' and Thai Airways new low fares carrier, 'Sky Asia' have launched domestic services with a view to expanding into international markets. The relaxation of air service regulations in order to allow the development of low cost services from and within Thailand has been supported by the Thai Prime Minister who sees low cost services as the key to developing Thailand's tourism and low cost markets (Ionides, 2004). In India, Air Deccan begun regional operations in 2003 with the aim of offering an air service that is cheaper than rail. Vietnam Airways re-branded VN Express to operate as a low cost feeder subsidiary and Indonesian (Lion Air) has operated services in Indonesia since 2000 and is seeking to serve Singapore alongside an existing route to Malaysia.

The benefits of low cost services to tourism bodies, municipal authorities and secondary airports will increase the pressure on Governments to liberalise air service regulation in Asia. As such the forecast made by Tony Ryan (founder of Ryanair) for 10% of the market to be low cost by 2014–2019 appears achievable (Ionides, 2004).

3.5. Rest of the world

3.5.1. Innovation

Low cost airlines have emerged in a number of countries throughout the rest of the world. These were led by Brazil and South Africa. In both cases liberalisation of domestic markets was closely followed by low cost airline activity, with competition that forced certain airlines to cease operations after only a short period of time. The large distances between densely populated cities and the relative speed of airlines with respect to surface modes of transport provided a favourable context for domestic low cost activity. The first low cost carrier ViaBrasil was formed in 1998 but like other initial entrants to the Brazilian market it only adopted certain elements of the Southwest model. ViaBrasil withdraw its services by 2003 and Nacional Transportes Aeros ceased operations in 2002 after only one year. Areafly have maintained low cost services since 1999 but the most successful low cost airline has been GOL that began to serve the Brazilian domestic market in 2001. GOL has adopted many features of the 'Southwest copy-cat' model and has subsequently grown to serve twenty destinations. Elsewhere within the continent low cost services were introduced to Costa Rica in 2004. In Mexico low cost services were prevented by government regulation when in 2001 Vuelamex leased three aircraft but were refused an operating license for reasons that are still unclear.

In South Africa, Intensive Air operated as a low cost carrier between 2000–2002, and the 'Southwest copy-cat' Kulula established services in 2001 and has succeeded to the extent that there are reports that in 2004 South African Airways are considering setting up their own low cost subsidiary. "1 time", a new low cost airline also entered the market in 2004. Elsewhere within the African continent, Kenya Airways established Flamingo Airlines in 2002. Flamingo is a low cost subsidiary that operates short haul feeder services. The only other recorded instance of low cost operations is a single route established on a trial basis in 2003 within the CIS, by Sibir airlines with fares one third of the competing airlines. It is unclear how the regulatory authorities will respond if the airline is successful and wishes to adopt the model for other routes.

In the Middle East the degree of deregulation within the Gulf Co-operative Council area allows for the development of low cost airlines. Two 'Southwest copy-cat' airlines Menajet and Transgulf Express were reported to be starting operations in the first half of 2004, both based at Sharjah in the UAE both operating to Gulf and North African destinations.

G. Francis et al. / Journal of Transport Geography 14 (2006) 83–94   91

4. What factors have influenced or impeded the spread of low cost operators?

The previous section has highlighted the varied pattern of the spatial, temporal and nature of low cost airline growth. Although the growth does not follow a uniform life cycle in all cases a number of stages in the growth of low cost carriers are clearly evident. Table 2 seeks to compare market developments of low cost airlines around the world with low cost development in the US (see Section 3.1).

From an examination of the low cost model the spread seems to have been affected by the complex interaction of a number of factors (See Table 3). The mere presence of deregulated markets seems to be insufficient in itself. Deregulation may therefore be described as a necessary but not sufficient condition for the growth of low cost activity. Certain countries such as New Zealand experienced early deregulation but relatively little low cost growth until 2004, while in mainland Europe low cost activity gained momentum at least four years after full deregulation. In some Asian countries, such as Malaysia, Singapore and Thailand, market deregulation appears to have been driven by the respective Governments trying to create favourable market conditions for low cost services the aim being economic growth from lower priced travel and increased tourism.

The entrepreneurial flair of a key individual appears to be highly significant in terms of the success of low cost operators. 'Champions' are central to the success of any new initiative and the low cost revolution is no exception with notable personalities heading the main low cost airline activities. In the US experience it was Herb Kelleher and Rollin King (Southwest), in Europe Tony Ryan (Ryanair) and Stelios Haji-Ioannou (easyJet), while in Australia, Richard Branson has played an important role with Virgin Blue airlines. In Thailand, the support of the Thai PM has been pivotal as has Tony Ryan in Singapore and Tony Fernandes at Air Asia. Richard Branson's entry into the New Zealand low cost market with Pacific Blue illustrates that even though a market may exhibit

Table 3
Catalyst for the spread of low costs

- Deregulated markets
- Entrepreneurs
- Population and relative wealth
- Airport availability/capacity sold cheap and free of congestion to allow intensive operations
- Internet—sales ease, simple tariff, price transparency, circumnavigation of travel agent control of distribution channel

Source: Authors.

the conditions necessary for the development of low cost carriers, without the entrepreneurial drive deregulated markets may still lack low cost operations.

Population growth and economic wealth should not be underestimated. Latent demand in many parts of the world has been exploited by the low cost carriers. Europe has a critical population mass and the enlargement of the EU will only fuel this growth. There are also dense routes, for example between Sydney and Melbourne in Australia and in Asia high traffic volumes are ripe for low cost operators.

The availability of cheap and underutilised airport capacity at secondary airports able to facilitate swift aircraft turnaround has facilitated the low cost model of operation. The growth in the use of the Internet has acted as a catalyst for the spread of low cost operators, allowing them to cut distribution costs and to circumvent the use of travel agents in many cases that previously controlled ticket sales. Linked to this has been the simplification of the pricing structure and with it price transparency.

One of the research questions the authors wished to address at the start of the research for this project was: "if low cost airlines are such a good idea why is not everybody doing it?" During the life of this project the answer to this question has increasingly become they are! There is still an uneven spread, however, with areas of low and high uptake of the low cost model. The authors' explanation for this is that in certain instances there are a number of impediments (see Table 4).

Table 2
Market developments of low cost airlines compared to the US

Stages	USA	Canada	Europe			Asia	Australia	New Zealand	Rest of World
			UK	Mainland	East Europe				
1. Innovation	✔	✔	✔	✔	✔	✔	✔	✔	✔
2. Proliferation	✔	✔	✔	✔					✔
3. Consolidation	✔	✔	✔				✔	✔	
4. Second phase of new entrants	✔								
5. Consolidation	✔								
6. Market maturity	✔								

Source: Authors.

Table 4
Impediments to spread of low costs

- Regulation preventing low cost entrants into markets, in particular on international routes
- Availability of airport capacity to allow market entry and swift turnaround times
- Demand for air travel

Source: Authors.

A number of these impediments simply represent the 'flip side' of the factors which have been advanced as a catalyst for growth. In terms of the regulated market it would appear from the experience of Asia that it is possible for the potential of low cost services to act as a spur for the introduction of more favourable market conditions. Without freedom to enter routes and to charge what fares an operator wishes, the low cost model is impeded in its development. Markets such as China may clearly have huge potential for low cost services yet while market access remains restricted so is the development of low cost carriers.

The availability of airport capacity and route access, particularly at secondary airports is likely to become more of a constraint on the growth of low cost operators over time. Success will breed its own problems at certain airports where spare capacity will be fully utilised and airport management will face strategic decisions regarding how to expand facilities, a move that may not be 'economic' based on the low aeronautical charges generated by low cost services.

While some low cost carriers have undoubtedly been successful not all have enjoyed longevity. There are clearly first-mover advantages but the sector is littered with failed attempts at low cost operation, such as Kiwi Airlines in New Zealand, United Shuttle and Continental Lite in the US, Flying Finn and Debonair in Europe. Some times due to inappropriate business models which only included some elements of the so called 'Southwest Model' and others which failed due to competitive responses from incumbent airline operators.

Start-up 'Southwest copy-cat' airlines have had a particularly high failure rate[2] even Southwest and Ryanair started from existing airlines. A critical mass would appear important for success not least in terms of economies of scale and market penetration. Entrepreneurs also require financial backing to deter aggressive price and capacity behaviour by major airlines that can have the effect of putting less well resourced carriers out of business in a very short space of time. Southwest, Ryanair, Virgin Express, Virgin Blue and Freedom Air, were all developed from existing airlines and easyJet had significant financial resources.[3]

[2] Although not all have simply failed many have been subject to market consolidation (merger/takeover).
[3] Albeit from shipping operations not airline operations.

5. Implications of the spread of low cost carriers

There are a number of significant implications stemming from the spread of low cost operations. In terms of regional development, there have and will be winners and losers as not all airport/regions will attract low cost services and they may not last. For example Fiji is currently enjoying a tourism boom as a result of low fares being offered from New Zealand. The traditional scheduled 'legacy' airlines have frequently responded by cutting costs and/or setting up subsidiaries.

As far as airports are concerned low cost airlines offer opportunities and threats (see Francis et al., 2004). The apparent panacea of increased passenger numbers needs to be viewed in light of the commercial reality of low aeronautical charges and not all airports being able to generate sufficient non aeronautical revenues from passengers. This depends in no small part on the retail capability available at individual airports. There are many cases of low cost services being sought by communities for their tourism benefits, though the benefits are not always confined to the locality of the airport as passengers may travel onwards by ground transport. Customers are the apparent 'winners' in the short term. Will fares gradually increase without corresponding changes to the level of service? The experience of 30 years from the US would suggest not, although the market 'barriers to entry' and the number of competitor airlines capable of providing competition is a key factor. There is also likely to be a change in the available choice of destinations. Customers who could once book onto a 'spoke service' from a secondary airport and have their bags checked through a hub and onto a final destination may lose that level of service. At a number of airports that low cost service means that when a passenger needs to make a connection they have to queue up and check in once more at the hub airport.

There are environmental impacts of the low cost model and more research is required in relation to its lack of sustainability. The use of efficient full aircraft by low cost airlines is to be commended (particularly if they are simply capturing existing market share), however, they are increasingly stimulating a growth in demand that is not (environmentally) sustainable. The very low fares being offered can make more sustainable forms of surface transport less attractive and have been responsible for generating travel for 'the sake of travel', making previously unattainable weekend breaks possible.

6. Speculating on the future of low cost airlines

The success of the low cost model seems likely to continue to put pressure on the traditional 'legacy' airlines. The future is likely to see consolidation of the low cost

G. Francis et al. / Journal of Transport Geography 14 (2006) 83–94 93

market with legacy airlines responding by cutting costs and offering lower advance purchase fares or setting up their own low cost subsidiaries.

6.1. Long haul low cost operations

Low cost airlines have predominantly been short haul operations, partly because of the regulatory context of long haul services and partly because some facets associated with low cost operations are less compatible with long haul flights such as the need for food, seat pitch and in-flight entertainment. There is already evidence of a long-haul low cost model since currently one-fifth of Southwest airline flights are long haul (over 4 hours flight time) trans-US (Flint, 2003). Historically the relaxation of fare regulation on the transatlantic market has led to extremely competitive pricing, so much so that low cost ventures such as Laker's Skytrain in the 1980s have struggled to compete against aggressive pricing from established airlines (see Calder, 2002; Lawton, 2002). The European inclusive tour airline, Mytravel currently offers a low cost transatlantic service where passengers pay for their seat but pay extra for frills such as food and entertainment. A low cost long haul service to Australia from Manchester (UK) and Munich (Germany) has been started by Traveldirect.com and another proposed by Backpackers Express, however, the success of such services remains to be seen.

6.2. Continued adoption aspects of the low cost model by the main scheduled 'legacy' airlines

Low cost or low fare? It is important to distinguish between price competition based on a loss leader mentality with that of a more sustainable operating cost advantage. However, many airlines (Air New Zealand, SAS, Lufthansa, KLM, BA) have become 'cost cutters' adopting more cost efficient practices such as Internet sales, pricing (one way fares), rationalisation of fleets and operating stations. Cost consciousness appears to be impacting even at the other end of the spectrum with BA citing cost awareness amongst Concorde's traditional passengers/customers as being a reason for the cessation of Concorde flights. Yet many traditional 'legacy' airlines still have substantial 'locked-in costs', which will need to be removed by value engineering.

6.3. Growth of the low cost model

It is likely that the low cost market will continue to grow in both absolute and relative terms. It is predicted (de Neufville, 2004) that the market share will increase in established markets such as the US and EU. New operations can also be expected to emerge in areas of the world not currently served. History would have us believe that by no means all of the operators will survive but those that do can achieve a significant market-share and impact on the pricing level of an even larger part of the market.

7. Conclusions

The spatial and temporal spread of low cost airlines has varied depending on geographical context but it is clearly inextricably linked to airline market deregulation that allows the low cost carriers the freedom to develop their operations. Entrepreneurial drive and resources have been a key factor in exploiting market opportunities and enabling growth.

The typology developed in this paper has allowed the authors to not only trace the spread of low cost airlines but also to examine the different characteristics of these airlines. Frequently the trend is for start-up 'Southwest copy-cats' to be the first low cost movers into markets. The initial response to this has often been for the main legacy airline(s) in the market to establish their own low cost subsidiaries. With the continued success of some low cost carriers many legacy airlines have gone on to become cost-cutters removing frills and inefficiencies from their operations. Attracted by the apparent success of the low cost concept in some markets there has been a second wave of 'Southwest copy-cats'. Additionally Charter carriers have been tempted into diversifying into low cost operations.

The uneven spread and speed of the low cost model around the world, however, cannot be attributed to deregulation alone. The authors believe that there are significant 'first-mover' advantages for airlines establishing themselves in the new areas of global expansion. There is a noticeable power of the low cost incumbents in the market. In this respect entrepreneurial ability of key individuals appears to have played a significant part in the success of the most successful low cost airlines.

Whilst the low cost concept is portrayed as successful it is important to note that many low cost airlines have failed particularly those starting from scratch. Those who have only adopted some of the low cost features of the 'Southwest model' seem to have a greater propensity to fail. The authors predict the continued success of the low cost concept but the turbulence of the airline industry is such that it is much more difficult to forecast for individual low cost airlines.

Deregulation has been a necessary precursor to the introduction of low cost airlines but not sufficient in itself to foster their success. Whilst the spread of low cost carriers has frequently followed liberalisation, in some cases the economic impetus of low cost airlines is pressurising governments to consider deregulation. Asia and EU expansion appear likely to lead to the next wave of low cost operations.

Acknowledgements

The authors wish to thank Professor Chris Ryan and Alessandro Fidato for their assistance with this project. The authors are also grateful for the constructive comments of the two anonymous referees.

References

Airliner World (anonymous), 2003. Low- cost airlines, Airliner World, Supplement.

Air Transport World, 2003. World airline report. Air Transport World 40 (7), 28–44.

Australian Aviation (anonymous), 2004. Jetstar Rising, Australian Aviation, No. 202, p. 16.

Calder, S., 2002. No Frills: The Truth Behind the Low-cost Revolution in the Skies. Virgin Books, London.

Centre for Asia Pacific Aviation, 2002. Key findings of the new low cost airline report, November 2002, Available from: <http://www.centreforaviation.com/infobank/publish/article_263.shtml> accessed on 11th June 2003.

Cobb, R., Primo, D., 2003. Plane Truth. Brookings Institute, Washington, DC.

Collier, A., 1999. Principles of Tourism. New Zealand. Addison Wesley Longman Ltd., Auckland.

de Neufville, R., 2004. Current design challenges for airports worldwide, Transportation Research Board, Washington, DC. 11–15 January.

Dennis, N., 2004. An easy ride so far? How sustainable is the low cost airline business model in Europe. In: Proceedings of the Universities Transport Studies Group 36th Annual Meeting, Newcastle Upon Tyne, 9. 9.12.

Doganis, R., 2001. The Airline Business in the 21st Century. Routledge, London.

Dumazel, R., Humphreys, I., 1999. Travel agent monitoring and management. Journal of Air Transport Management 5 (2), 63–72.

Easdown, G., Wilms, P., 2002. Ansett the Collapse. Lothian Books, Melbourne.

Field, D., 2003. Low fare carriers sustain growth path. Airline Business 19 (8), 13.

Flint, P., 2003. The world has changed forever. Air Transport World 40 (3), 22–26.

Forsyth, P., 2003. Low-cost carriers in Australia: experiences and impacts. Journal of Air Transport Management 9, 277–284.

Francis, G.A.J., Fidato, A., Humphreys, I., 2003. Airport airline interaction: the impact of low cost carriers on two European airports. Journal of Air Transport Management 9 (4), 267–273.

Francis, G.A.J., Humphreys, I., Ison, S., 2004. Airports' perspectives on the growth of low-cost airlines and the remodelling of the airport–airline relationship. Tourism Management 25, 507–514.

Gillen, D., Morrison, W., 2003. Bundling, integration and the delivered price of air travel: are low cost carriers full service competitors? Journal of Air Transport Management 9 (1), 15–23.

Graham, A., 2003. Managing Airports: An International Perspective, second ed. Butterworth Heinemann, Oxford.

Ionides, N., 2004. Three Thai carriers sound no-frills fanfare for Asia. Airline Business 20 (1), 19.

Kissling, C., 1998. Liberal aviation agreements—New Zealand. Journal of Air Transport Management 4, 177–180.

Knibb, D., 2001. Canadian challengers. Airline Business(September), 1–101.

Lawton, T.C., 2002. Cleared for Take Off: Structure and Strategy in Low Fare Airline Business. Ashgate, Aldershot.

Mason, K., Whelan, C., Williams, G., 2000. Europe's Low Cost Airlines. Cranfield University Air Transport Group, Cranfield.

Nyathi, M., Hooper, P., Hensher, D., 1993. Compass Airlines 1 December 1990 to 20 December 1991. What went wrong? Transport Reviews 13 (2), 119–149 and 13 (3), 185–206.

Pinkham, R., 2003. The low cost question. Airline Business 19 (12), 29.

Thomas, G., 2002. Asia's absent revolution. Air Transport World (September), 42–47.

Williams, G., 2001. Will Europe's charter carriers be replaced by "no frills" scheduled airlines? Journal of Air Transport Management 7 (5), 277–286.

Wilson, E., 1996. Dogfight: The Story of Kiwi Airlines' Collapse. Howling at the Moon Productions, Auckland.

Windle, R., Lin, J., Dresner, M., 1996. The impact of low-cost carriers on airport and route competition. Journal of Transport Economics and Policy 30 (3), 309–328.

15

Airlines within airlines: Assessing the vulnerabilities of mixing business models

David Gillen, Alicja Gados

A B S T R A C T

In this paper we examine two questions; what is it that makes some cases of airlines within airlines apparently successful while in many other cases it is just the opposite? And second, why would a carrier attempt such a strategy, is there a common set of circumstances or is each case unique? In the US, Canada and Europe a number of legacy carriers have sought to respond to LCC entry by creating an LCC within the legacy carriers; most have failed but some have succeeded, most notably in Australia and Germany. We first examine the evolution of the LCC business model and illustrate the different forms it takes today. Following this we provide a discussion of the underlying sources of cost advantage of the LCC and assess which sources are sustainable in the longer term. Finally we examine the conditions under which these apparent successes have occurred and look for common threads. We find market dominance, judicious network planning and co-ordination are necessary conditions for success.

© 2009 Elsevier Ltd. All rights reserved.

Keywords:
LCC
New business models
Legacy carrier
Airline within airline

1. Introduction

In June 2008 United Airlines made the decision to shut down 'Ted' the airline within an airline it had started in an attempt to compete with the LCC sector in the US; Ted mainly served such tourist destinations as Las Vegas and Cancun, and lots of points in Florida, and was aimed at stopping Southwest in those markets. This venture followed the ill-fated Shuttle by United airline within an airline that was started in hopes of staving off Southwest's entry into the California market. Ted was the last of the US carriers to abandon this business model; others that had been discarded in the US included Shuttle by United, CALite (Continental), Metrojet (US Airways), Delta Express (Delta), Song (Delta). All had been put in place to compete with the low cost carrier business model (LCC) – Southwest, JetBlue and AirTran in most cases in specific markets. In Canada, Air Canada finally abandon Zip, an attempt to compete with Westjet in the latter's primary western Canadian markets. This after having previously had a try with Tango, which was more of a fighting brand designed to focus primarily on one carrier, Canada 3000.

Although best known in the airline industry as 'a firm within a firm' strategy, there are other industries, not many, that have also tried (unsuccessfully) to use this strategy generally targeted at a specific product or geographic market. A good example is the Saturn by GM which was and is a car company within a car

company. The motivation for GM was to produce a car that could compete with foreign imports while GM would continue competing with other North American producers particularly in the North American market. Neither Saturn, nor GM for that matter, has been a success story with continual erosion of market share and spiralling losses.

There are numerous examples in North America that the airline within an airline business model does not work and a few examples in Europe but many fewer; an example is Hapag Lloyd Express, an LCC which despite appearing successful was folded back into the mother airline. But we also see apparent successes of the firm within firm approach such as Jetstar with Qantas and Tiger with Singapore and German Wings with Lufthansa. In this paper we explore two questions. What is it that makes these cases apparently successful while in many others it was just the opposite? And second, why would a carrier attempt a strategy, is there a common set of circumstances or is each case unique?

In the following section we describe those factors that led to the adoption of the airline within an airline strategy. We include changes in the regulatory structure as well as the development of new technologies such as the Internet. Section 3 looks at the history of the low cost carrier and describes how the business model differs from legacy carriers; where the cost advantages lie. In Section 4 we ask why a firm (airline) would pursue a strategy of a firm within a firm; why can hotels seemingly pursue this strategy successfully while others cannot. Finally in Section 5 we explore what the future might look like and the potential successes of Tiger, Jetstar and German Wings. We also provide a summary and conclusions in this section.

26   *D. Gillen, A. Gados / Research in Transportation Economics 24 (2008) 25–35*

2. What changed to lead to such a strategy?

2.1. Deregulation

The first low cost carrier (LCC) appeared in the US in the early 1970s before deregulation in domestic aviation in 1978. The low cost evolution spread to Europe in the 1990s and is a more recent, but fast-growing development in Asia.[1] In the US, the states of California and Texas were large enough to support intrastate carriers. Western Pacific Airlines in California and Southwest Airlines in Texas operated as low cost–low fare unregulated carriers. These carriers provided the empirical justification that based the motive to deregulate the domestic market in the US. After US deregulation by Congress in 1978, new entrant LCC airlines emerged. A large number of carriers emerged with low fare, low frills or no frills, however many collapsed in a few years proving that low fares were not sufficient to succeed in the market (Taweelertkunthon, 2006). The airline People Express expanded aggressively using its low-fare, no frills concept. It over-extended itself during expansion and eventually began to incur massive losses, and survived only until full service carriers (FSC) began innovations, with hub and spoke systems (H&S), frequent flyer programs, and yield management. In 1987 Texas International acquired the airline.

After deregulation, most LCC entrants were not successful in establishing a niche market, and dropped out quickly after operating in a short period. The advantage of lower costs in many cases stemmed from low factor prices[2] rather than from superior business strategies. The strategy was not well understood; LCC business models were not studied thoroughly in the economics literature in the 1980s. However Southwest Airlines, the Dallas airline has been continuously profitable since the early 1970s, and is one of the two remaining. Their successful business model has been emulated by many aspiring airlines (Taweelertkunthon, 2006). Some unsuccessful network carriers have transformed to be successful LCC airlines by basing their strategy on the Southwest model. Ryanair has become the cost leader in Europe from using the strategy. In addition, AirTrans has become profitable by using both its established hub and spoke system with a point-to-point service. The model has been modified in different ways, for example JetBlue has appealed to higher-end business passengers with cabin upgrades, such as satellite TV and leather seats. In the UK, easyJet operates without a travel agent and is positioned to attract leisure and business traffic, by serving both primary and secondary airports in Europe.

In a regulated industry, there is little incentive to plan or identify successful markets or market failures, or keep costs under control and be responsive to consumer demands. When the airline industry was deregulated, there was a fundamental change in the way firms conducted business. Firms must be driven by market opportunities and financial needs, and not by regulatory considerations. Prices need to be based on cost, operations must be efficient, and consumer oriented niches must be exploited. Emerging competition from low fare carriers arose at this time, with lower ticket prices and higher frequency of service. Empirical cost drivers are significant, and during the transition period following deregulation, carriers adopted a diverse variety of strategies to improve productivity, reduce costs, and increase market share, involving both operations and volume based cost drivers (Banker & Johnston, 1993). The deregulated market allowed LCCs to pick up price-sensitive market share.

When planning, a carrier must consider both the demand and supply side. The demand side has two key features: price and market access. Fare sensitivity is widely understood and variability between customers, coupled with a detailed information base from computer reservations systems (CRS) has allowed extensive price discrimination to be possible. Knowledge of willingness to pay plus the airline practice of yield management means fares vary with time of day, week, year, and destination. Fare setting reflects the variety of travellers ranging from the business traveller with considerably less fare elasticity that the visiting friends and relatives (VFR) passenger with high fare elasticity. Within each generic passenger group there are varying degrees of sensitivity. Within the business category, there can be client or company paid, fare insensitive travellers to the self-employed fare sensitive traveller, to a time-constrained conference participant, who will search for the lowest fare possible given time constraints.

2.2. Targeting unsatisfied demand

LCCs became unique with the strategy that pursued potential passenger's "discretionary entertainment dollars" and not necessarily "travel dollars", that is, initially they were not luring passengers away from legacy carriers. Instead, they were targeting customers 'off the couch' – passengers looking to spend leisure dollars. Initially, LCC passengers were customers that would initially not have flown; they were a previously ignored market. LCCs, with lower fares for travel were able to target this untouched market and facilitate demand. Within this market, LCCs practice a form of yield management (but not nearly to the same extent as FSCs). LCCs may have three fare classes while FSCs can have ten or more. An array of fare discrimination reflects the broad range of willingness to pay (WTP) and the airlines' ability to distinguish and exploit these differences. A key difference is that legacy carriers have a complex array of products which lead to complex pricing practices while LCCs have simple products and hence simple pricing strategies.

2.3. Coalition of passenger groups was finally broken

The proportion of US travellers subject to price premiums has decreased due to increasing share of LCC traffic (Hofer, Windle, & Dresner, 2008). LCCs were able to modify passenger groups and create a new market segment. With heavily segmented customer groups, legacy carriers are no longer able to cover all customer and market segments with a single network model. They need to preserve core business with intercontinental connections and the required feeder platform, around which a variety of business segments can emerge. Success in segments must be competitive on a stand-alone basis, in terms of cost and quality. Cross subsidizing among segments (the old network paradigm) is no longer feasible.

In response to LCC threat, among many strategic competition challenges, an airline can adopt one of three strategies: (1) become a premium carrier, such as Emirates, (2) transform to a LCC, like Aer Lingus, or (3) become a superior network carrier, such as Qantas or Lufthansa. A premium strategy requires a lot of new expertise and transformation to an LCC demands a new company culture; both strategies require considerable investments at high risk. A more differentiated approach to key customer segments will make the biggest difference when an airline is faced with a failing strategy, since turning to premium and LCC strategies leads to considerable uncertainty. This suggests that spinning off an LCC is not optimum to restructuring the network, hence becoming a 'better' network carrier.[3] Qantas realigned its customer segmentation and

---

[1] The development in Asia is unique where the economics and aviation environment are unlike that of the US or the EU.
[2] This concept is explored in some detail later in the paper.

[3] For instance, Qantas, after experiencing falling yields like many other legacy carriers due to LCC growth, discovered their customers can be segmented into not only domestic versus intercontinental travellers and leisure versus business travellers but also into two additional dimensions: loyal versus opportunistic clients and outbound versus inbound clients.

D. Gillen, A. Gados / Research in Transportation Economics 24 (2008) 25–35
27

reshuffled both its brand and platform portfolio. The main success factor for this new model was the right balance between front-end differentiation and back-end synergies. Although the client perceives a more customized service offering than before, a dedicated governance model ensures as many network and operations synergies as possible (Franke, 2007).

2.4. Internet booking and fare search engines

In the beginning, LCCs leveraged the power of e-commerce to enhance sales of their product offering. The LCC simplified product and pricing is ideally suited to internet purchase, with credit card fees passed on to the passenger. Distribution costs played a major role in the success of LCCs, but today are easy to duplicate and are a declining cost advantage. In the long run, it is difficult for firms competing with information technology (as a competitive advantage) to gain sustainable advantage because these resources are easy to imitate and substitutes are readily available. Airlines have installed CSR systems in travel agencies to appropriate returns from investments in IT, and expect a number of benefits to accrue from the strategy, including increased efficiency, bias, and fees from other airlines (Duliba, Kauffman, & Lucas, 2001). Home websites and third party agencies were eventually spawned by the internet and offer a distinct cost advantage by predominantly selling directly to the consumer (Boyd & Bilegan, 2003). For example, easyJet attains 86% of its bookings via the internet (Williams, 2001). This allows for more competitive fare pricing. The advent of LCCs into the short-haul market led to dramatic restructuring of pricing strategies of many major airlines (Anjos, Cheng, & Currie, 2004). Tickets are increasingly sold on a one-way basis, rather than as a return trip, which has allowed many restrictions to be removed that were associated with lower priced airline tickets.[4]

2.5. The LCC model

The LCC model is strategically different from the traditional, full service airline model. Overall, there exist three main sustainable airline strategies:[5] a full service broad geographic coverage carrier, a short haul LCC, and a charter carrier which focuses on longer haul low cost traffic. Each strategy involves different demand-side exploitation. An FSC exploits the full range of the demand curve with yield management, a short haul carrier is focusing on more price sensitive traffic,[6] and a charter carrier focuses on longer haul VFR traffic and a lower portion of the demand function. Both LCCs and charter strategies require a high load factor to break even since margins are relatively small compared to FSC, which has a lower break even due to the variety of fare classes served.

Market access is a particularly important characteristic of airline demand and competition. Passengers favour an airline with broad geographic coverage and available capacity. Business passengers favour high frequency. Thus, market access has two dimensions: geographic coverage and capacity in terms of frequency. The objective is to maximize flight revenue. As the departure date of the flight approaches, the airline through its yield management system will adjust the number of seats assigned to lower fare classes to try and sell off inventory and not have it go to waste, given the perishability of the product.

LCCs exhibit common product and process design characteristics that enable them to operate at a much lower unit cost per unit of output. Important cost savings are also derived from organization design and culture. Successful LCCs focus on one fleet type, mostly the Boeing 737. The advantages of a common fleet are numerous; everything is purchased in one model for the entire fleet.[7] Training costs are reduced; with only one type of fleet, employees focus on one aircraft and become specialists, and economies of density are achieved in training. Economies of density occur for all startup airlines once each aircraft type reaches a certain number, but LCCs reach that point sooner, and have a much more scalable training system. Further savings are garnered through higher productivity through specialization in all airline departments.

Source of airports is another basis of savings; low cost airlines focus on secondary airports that have excess capacity, and are willing to forego airside revenues in exchange for non-airside revenues that are developed as a result of the traffic stimulated from low cost airlines.[8] These less congested airports offer faster turn times and more efficient use of staff and aircraft. These advantages are not specific to secondary airports, as primary airports can also achieve operation efficiencies. Another important cost component is seat density. Per flight costs are similar, yet LCCs reduce the cost per seat, allowing them to charge less per seat to make a profit. Passenger retainment strategies, such as frequent flyer programs are revenue draining and require administration, and are foregone in favour of offering the passenger better pricing. Studies have shown passengers have a high fare elasticity (Botimer & Belobaba, 1999; Weatherford & Belobaba, 2002) and a survey by Gillen, Morrison, and Stewart (2007) reports how the demand elasticity varies by length of haul and market type.

Essentially LCCs have attempted to reduce the complexity and resulting cost of product by 'unbundling' those services that are not absolutely necessary; this extends to airport facilities as well. While savings in product design are obvious to the passenger, the process charges are what in fact have produced the great cost savings for the airline. In addition, the accounting and marketing functions of the airline become easier to manage. This is because simpler business models require less analysis for decision-making.

Although the description "low cost" carrier is for the most part representative of success of LCCs, it is certainly not exclusively so. It is not just the low costs that produce the unique strategy. Controlling demand is as important as controlling supply, or cost. The innovative pricing technique of yield management can make high cost airlines profitable and low cost airlines less profitable. Airlines with ineffective yield management systems will fail to exploit either cost effectiveness or added customer value. Airlines with longer hauls will price lower as will those with larger proportions of freight and incidental output. The reason is that yield reflects the ability of an airline to generate revenue within a market or set of markets. This depends on market characteristics, level and nature of competition, the airline strategy and the general macro economic conditions (even poor airlines can generate revenue in a boom economy). A carrier that is able to generate sufficient yield will be able to extract more than sufficient rent to compensate for the higher costs (Gillen, 2006).

Ability to price above costs reflects market power but this can occur by adding more customer value than competitors due to limited competition in the market. Cost competitiveness is important but a profit maximizing firm is not necessarily cost minimizing

---

[4] Restrictions such as Saturday night overnight stay, or duration of round trip.

[5] There is actually a fourth strategy, which is to provide traffic to a larger FSC but this is a highly focused strategy and is dependent on the growth of the mainline carrier into which passenger traffic is fed.

[6] However, LCC strategy can include walk-on business traffic, which is less frequency sensitive.

---

[7] Heavy maintenance, parts, supplies, even safety cards.

[8] Secondary airports charge less for landing and terminal fees, and make up the difference in commercial activity created by additional passengers.

28 D. Gillen, A. Gados / Research in Transportation Economics 24 (2008) 25–35

(Gillen, 2006). The economics define the range of potentially successful strategies. Large carriers do not have cost advantage from scale, but from density economies. Cost differences among carriers arise from a number of sources including input prices, however sustainable cost advantage is a result of efficiencies from operation and organization. LCCs achieve advantage creating low costs from an accumulation of integrated activities.

3. Evolution of the LCC: how the LCC and traditional business models differ?

LCCs have enjoyed continued profitability and gradual growth during their 35 years of operations. They have specific cost advantages that make them credible competitors to network carriers, based on low fares. Operational efficiency is a source of cost advantage and a factor in their success, although operational efficiency is not strategy (Porter, 1996). Competitive strategy is about being different, meaning deliberately choosing a different set of activities to deliver a unique value mix. Southwest Airline's success stems from a deliberate choice to undertake activities differently or to perform activities differently than competitors. They offer short haul, point-to-point service between midsize cities and secondary airports in large cities, trading off with the economies of hub and spoke dynamics. No meals, no assigned seats, or interlining transfers, allow them to be free of activities that slow down other airlines. Strategic fit, the way activities fit and reinforce one another, creates a sustainable competitive advantage. The activities in Southwest's strategy involve a whole system of activities not a collection of pieces, and this is maintained by simplicity: that is, simplicity in product, process, and organization (Porter, 1996).

Two key aspects differentiating the LCCs from the network carriers are point-to-point services and single class flights with few frills, and from these differences flow the differences in productivity. Many other advantages of lower input prices do not depend on these factors. Morrell (2005) exhibits important cost categories for success, such as labour, aircraft rentals and depreciation, fuel, the largest differences in several instances being 'other' costs, which include marketing costs, outside services, handling and overheads.

LCCs deviate from the hub and spoke (H&S) model, which since 1978, has emerged as the most effective logistical system for moving passengers, and effectively contributed immensely to the success of many full service carriers (FSCs). Dominant hubs can channel traffic from a very large number of cities to a particular hub–city pair flight segment. By creating hubs, dominant carriers can therefore increase schedule frequency, which significantly reduces schedule wait for passengers and allows them to add many origin and destination pairs to the network. The addition of one spoke station to the hub network results in the economy of traffic density because of the traffic stimulation at hubs (Oum & Zhang, 1990).

Costs can vary considerably between carriers. There are many reasons for this to be the case. Underlying production technology exhibits minimal scale economies but sizable density economies. Carriers with a large network, although they have demand advantage, do not have cost advantage, while those that build the market *within* a given network do have cost advantages. Hub and spoke strategies are the method for exploiting density economies. Economies of scope are limited but do exist between scheduled services and freight, and marginally between scheduled and charter. A broad network with high density, or a mix of scheduled and charter are sustainable strategies given the demand side of the market.

Major carriers also rely on established frequent flyer programs, which have been successful at creating brand loyalty. These programs are a type of entry barrier because of start up and operating costs, and providing reward redemption for customers (Gillen, 1988). It is much cheaper and simpler for large network airlines to provide these programs rather than entrants, because network size and power of hub and spoke systems induces passengers to fly the incumbent so rewards can be redeemed on the many city pairs available. Using yield management, carriers can sell empty seats at low prices to passengers who may not otherwise have flown, and are therefore able to compete with lower prices relative to those offered by LCCs themselves. In order for a yield management system to be successful, an airline must attach sufficient and appropriate restrictions to discount fares and therefore lower flight revenue, where inexpensive seats are sold to passengers who otherwise may not have flown.

Low frills and lower wages marginally account for this gap in costs, and a lean production model underpinned by quick, streamlined processes is the root basis of success. At least one-third of the cost gap comes from the typical LCC production pattern with high frequency commuter flights between major destinations, such as with easyJet, or one aircraft serving a few destinations from a given base, such as Ryanair, resulting in substantially higher productivity of aircraft and crew (Franke, 2004).

By identifying strategic choices and sources of operational efficiency, the real advantage stems from appropriate team organization leading to successful relationship coordination (Gillen & Lall, 2004). The choice of a low cost business model with point-to-point service provides the strategic advantage, and is complemented by operational effectiveness. The result is simplicity of processes and organization. System coordination is a major factor proving the uniqueness of Southwest's strategy because it is difficult to duplicate.

The viability of the all-premium business model is being questioned after the airline Eos filed for bankruptcy and ceased operations at the end of April. Low cost carriers are increasingly overcoming border restrictions and spreading their reach through offshore bases and cross-border joint ventures. A growing number of low cost carriers, particularly in Southeast Asia, are entering into cross-border joint ventures as a way of expanding their operations and brands internationally. For European Union carriers, which can operate to anywhere from anywhere within the EU, borders hardly matter anymore. Beyond Europe, however, borders and the rules that go with them still restrict airlines to bases within their own countries unless they can find a foreign partner willing to help them create an offshore base. This involves more than interlining or codesharing; it requires shared ownership, control, operations, and more. The growth in long haul, low cost carriers contributes to cross-border ventures by encouraging long haul airlines to form feeder hubs at the ends of their long routes, and is a new trend (Knibb, 2008a).

The severe crisis of the entire global airline industry has threatened the financial sustainability of many airlines. Particularly in North America, network carriers have suffered tremendous losses, while LCCs have enjoyed profitability and rapid growth. In Australasia and Europe, FSCs have fared better. Simple and efficient business models, with a lean cost structure, with up to 60% lower unit costs in comparison to incumbent carriers have created substantial cost advantage for LCCs (Franke, 2004) and may explain why LCCs were not only spared from the harsh effects of the downturn, but boosted by it. In fact, the LCC model can sustainably operate at 40–50% of the stage length adjusted unit cost of the average network carrier (Doganis, 2001). Cost advantage arises from the nature of the operation: higher seating density and higher daily aircraft utilization. The cost gap could be up to 5–8 cents US per ASK for the LCC compared to 10–15 cents per ASK for the FSC (Hansson, Ringbeck, & Franke, 2002). The LCC strategy appears to be more resilient.

D. Gillen, A. Gados / Research in Transportation Economics 24 (2008) 25–35   29

4. Airline within an airline

4.1. Why pursue such a strategy?

The competitive response of operating various business models within the same grouping or holding company simultaneously based on a low cost and full service bundling, and delivering the same basic product, has been applied to retailing, car rental, railroad, banking, insurance, news, power supplying, tour operator, consulting and airport businesses. In some industries, the business within a business model could be implemented successfully (Graf, 2005). This strategy appears to be an intermediate competitive response, for the protection of markets, acceleration of changes in the existing organization, and profiting from the final sale of the LCC. For example, British Airways was successful in creating stock market value for Go, but could not influence the growth of Ryanair and easyJet. After it sold Go for a considerable price, it enforced the transformation of its own business model (Graf, 2005).

Network airlines have overall delivered good market growth, at times modest profits, increased productivity and declining average fares over the past 20 or more years. However, even before September 11, 2001, for some time viability has been worsening. Some analysts suggest that hubs can be bypassed and point-to-point operations take a much greater share of the market. Can full service carriers even compete with LCCs?

LCCs have enjoyed high, profitable growth. These airlines have been spurred by the declining attractiveness of congested hub airports and high last minute fares of FSCs. Increased security at airports has further exacerbated hub airport delays (Morrell, 2005). Simplicity is the main focus of LCCs, which have been able to get their costs down to about half of legacy carriers (Doganis, 2001). With higher load factors and a marked labour cost advantage, the corresponding 60% drop in fares has resulted in traffic growth of three to four times previous levels on some routes, and there is increasing overlap with network carrier markets.[9] FSCs have responded to LCCs in two major ways:

- Establishment of low cost, no frills divisions, 'airlines within airlines,' attempting to apply elements of the LCC business model
- Removing significant sources of cost from their own business model, without extensive restructuring of their own business model, or reducing service levels to business class passengers

Therefore, establishing an LCC subsidiary has three possible objectives:

1. Spin off profitable business and segment markets:
- Qantas, Lufthansa, Singapore
- Introduces greater efficiency and lower overall costs
- Hard to achieve in the competitive climate
2. To respond to LCC competition in key markets:
- American, Northwest, America West, Air Canada, Continental, United and Delta
3. Establishing a test for adapting the low cost concept to mainline operations and entering markets:
    Singapore, Cathay Pacific

Although there is evidence of the importance of networks in reducing costs (Brueckner, Dyer, & Spiller, 1992), research also shows that increasing aircraft size (to meet denser traffic flows

---

[9] For instance, Southwest began transcontinental flights in the US using Philadelphia, a network carrier hub, as a base for expansion.

across networks), particularly over shorter stage distances, does not reduce unit costs as much as expected (Wei & Hansen, 2003). The decreasing success of the hub approach is due in part to gained popularity of point-to-point discount carriers, serving non-stop passengers, making connections a by-product of the system.

New operations of an LCC within a network carrier are channelled through divisions of the company, rather than stand-alone subsidiaries. This made it difficult to achieve low cost work practices and approaches to suppliers, since it was perceived they were supported by their parent company (Morrell, 2005). Union resistance is also a major obstacle, and a cap on operations. For example United Shuttle and Metrojet (the US Airways LCC) were limited to 25% of total US Airways block hours and 130 of B737 size aircraft (which was around 20% of United's 1998 fleet) due to scope clauses in pilot contracts. Costs are reduced by:

- Substantial reductions in in-flight catering
- Single aircraft type (Delta, US Airways)
- Higher aircraft and other asset utilization
- Improved crew utilization, some reduced salaries
- Reduced distribution costs

Most carriers were not able to get their unit costs down to "Southwest" levels; as a result their breakeven load factors were much higher. An airline within an airline tends to cause a lot of brand confusion. LCC offshoots in the US are very difficult to operate successfully. They are unlikely to meet any of the three objectives (Morrell, 2005). There are many inconsistencies in the way network carriers apply the LCC business model to a subsidiary discussed in this paper, and Graf (2005) suggests correcting these may improve chances, at least for LCC subsidiaries in the EU. This implies the need for the establishment of entirely separate subsidiary companies that are totally insulated from parent labour practices, which may not be possible in the US.

LCCs do not gain strong cost advantages simply from lower factor prices (Gillen, 2006). Low factor prices are neither necessary nor sufficient for least cost competitiveness. Analysis shows that airlines such as Jet Blue, Southwest and Westjet have not gained strong cost advantages simply from lower factor prices. The bundling of factors, the way they extract productivity and organize their production process is very important. Airline costs can be expressed in a number of different ways.

US legacy carriers pay their staff significantly higher salaries than recent startup airlines and indeed are saddled with substantial legacy costs built up over a period of years. LCCs achieve higher aircraft and crew productivity than network carriers, possible in part because of a single type fleet, shorter turnaround times through less catering, little or no cargo and no seat allocation. Pilot contracts encourage high productivity by reducing the fixed salary element of pay, and increasing the variable part related to flight hours. LCCs produce much higher overall labour productivity than the network carriers. Network to connecting passengers lowers the productivity airlines can achieve.

Fuel is the second largest cost item for Southwest. Volume is important in achieving lower prices, economies of scale can be achieved on the transport and service elements of the overall price: large requirements at a hub airport will help reduce this. Hedging will also have a significant influence on the net price paid, after allowing for gains or losses on derivatives trading.

LCCs also achieve lower aircraft capital operating costs than network carriers, including depreciation and rentals for owned and leased aircraft. Perhaps the large aircraft that network carriers use would be expected to give lower per unit costs through economies of scale. However this advantage is offset by aircraft manufacturers marking up the price of larger aircraft, which is what they can do as there is less competition between suppliers of larger aircraft. LCCs go for standard versions, with less expensive buyer furnished equipment. Also, often they time purchases strategically to coincide with the low parts of the industry cycle, and get attractive prices. Southwest was the launch customer for 737s, at a time when aircraft prices were relatively depressed (1994).

Network carriers and LCCs face similar input prices for outsourced maintenance and handling, and ATC charges. LCC costs for maintenance are usually artificially low based on circumstance – a large part of their fleet is very new and still benefits from manufacturers' warranties. Landing charges are much lower at underused airports, and LCCs are more aggressive when negotiating with suppliers, building in bonus and penalty payments. LCCs also do not incur some costs such as in-flight catering, airport lounges, drinks and meals for delayed passengers.

The largest cost discrepancy[10] is staff costs, due to LCC high productivity and lower wage salary rates. Offshoots give little help with the latter, and the higher productivity levels that can be achieved are difficult to replicate system-wide, due to both business model and union arrangements (Morrell, 2005). The second largest difference is selling costs, and again in this instance, LCC subsidiaries are neither necessary nor helpful. Progress towards e-ticketing and internet sales can be achieved regardless of whether an LCC has been initiated. Another gap is aircraft capital costs, where network carriers need to move towards greater standardization and higher utilization to adequately lower costs, but in both cases their business model will prevent them from this. Other costs differences, such as in-flight food, can be easily replicated over shorter haul sectors without building an LCC subsidiary. Overall these subsidiaries contribute little to help network carriers reduce system wide unit costs; most optimistically are an attempt to compete away LCC threats on selected routes (Morrell, 2005).

Instead of setting up a subsidiary, network carriers can reduce the cost gap via reductions in input prices, particularly labour, and productivity improvements. Morrell (2005) examines the cost reductions of US network airlines,[11] two of which did not set up LCC subsidiaries.[12] The data shows no indication that those network carriers with offshoots had made any more progress on narrowing the cost gap than the network carriers who did not establish an LCC within themselves. Employee productivity, measured in seat kilometres divided by average staff available, shows that Southwest performs better than the selected majors, in spite of its shorter average sectors.

Aircraft ownership costs for the US majors and nationals increased by 24% between 1995 and 2002 (Air Transport Association, 2003). Increasing aircraft utilization allows the schedule to be flown with fewer aircraft, therefore mitigates the impact of such increases. Large hubs used by network carriers are oriented towards making connecting flights and do not attempt to maximize aircraft productivity. On the other hand, LCCs try to achieve high aircraft utilization and a large number of daily rotations. None of the major US airlines have experienced much change in average hours per aircraft per day (in the period 1995–2000). From 2000 to 2002, capacity and schedules have been cut back, such that efficiency could not be raised.

US legacy carriers have done little to reduce the gap in unit costs with Southwest. Average salaries remain higher and productivity has hardly improved. Southwest has allowed pay to grow faster than the inflation rate, yet has achieved productivity gains. This has widened the gap in productivity with legacy airlines although some

of this has been achieved by operating over longer sectors, which is an anecdotal observation. There was no evidence that those carriers that operated their own LCC had more success in closing the cost/productivity gap with the LCCs than those who did not. Apart from aircraft utilization, there is little evidence that having an LCC offshoot made it harder to achieve savings in mainline operations.

A few offshoots in the US conformed strictly to the Southwest model, and those that did suffered from brand confusion and union restrictions on operations. None were completely segregated in separate subsidiary companies with their own accounts and financial and operating autonomy, therefore it is not surprising their cost levels remained well above true LCC levels. The LCCs have been able to offer such low fares that they have created new markets that the network carriers could never capture, but as they grew significantly in size, entering larger (trans-continental) markets, network carriers had to respond.

Subsidiaries are mainly a means of targeting LCC competition in key markets, and could never be spun off as profitable businesses. LCCs have significant cost advantages over network airlines, and the cost gap (with labour and other costs) has not narrowed significantly relative to Southwest, and LCC startups exhibit even larger differences. Having an LCC subsidiary does not improve the chances of unit cost reductions in mainline operations. Direct competition with LCCs is not optimal, since the cost gap cannot be closed, and using an offshoot to achieve this is likely to be ineffective, nor is it necessary, since the total market is large enough for both models to co-exist, with fewer players in each, particularly for network models. Perhaps a better airline to compete with would be ones like AirTran and Frontier, which compete more directly for flows of traffic, often from small cities, over the networks.

4.2. What does the strategy involve?

We provide a few examples to illustrate the airline within an airline where failures have resulted; the major causes have been discrepancies in business models, large differences in cost, and not careful separation thus cannibalization of the LCC by the parent FSC (competition).

Air Canada has attempted a couple LCC experiments:

- Tango, 2001. No frills service to reduce operating costs. Flew major longer distance Canadian routes, and some holiday destinations. Lower fares, few in-flight services. Hoped to serve southern winter destinations: the name is short for Tan and Go. In early 2001, airlines like Canada 3000 and Air Transat found these markets very lucrative.
- Zip, 2002, totally separate airline with own staff and management.

Tango was initiated to compete with Canada 3000; their route maps were nearly identical. This competitive 'fighting brand' in combination with a series of managerial blunders at Canada 3000 led to the latter's demise. Air Canada now was faced with an orphan that did not fit the Air Canada business model and attempts to run Tango as an airline within an airline presented mounting difficulties. Zip was established to compete with WestJet in the western Canadian routes, WestJet's home turf. It was never a credible threat.

Tango and Zip were both dissolved by 2004 for numerous reasons including issues with fuel surcharges on sub-economical flights. Tango was requiring customers to pay more than double their fare rate in these additional fuel surcharges, which drew criticisms, because charges were not made known to customers until the time of boarding. Air Canada filed for CCAA, similar to Chapter 11 in the US and was able to reduce its mainline labour costs to levels similar to those at Tango and Zip.

---

[10] Between FSCs and LCCs.
[11] Delta, Continental and United, compared with costs of Southwest airlines.
[12] American and Northwest.

D. Gillen, A. Gados / Research in Transportation Economics 24 (2008) 25–35   31

Both Japan and Dubai are setting up low cost airlines. Japans All Nippon Airways (ANA) and the government of Dubai (who started Emirates) will initiate the low cost startup. The Emirate LCC will not be part of the Emirates group. ANA will include the LCC subsidiary in its business model (Airline Business, April 23, 2008). This comes as a surprise as Emirates had earlier expressed no interest in a low cost model, planning to commit to the full service network model and widebody fleet (Airline Business, March 20, 2008). However, recent announcements by potential LCC startups in the Middle East combined with the planned growth of competitors to Emirates may have stimulated Emirates management to reconsider.

Continental Lite was started up in 1993 after Continental Airlines emerged from bankruptcy. The subsidiary lasted until 1995, after losing $120 million in 1994. At its peak, approximately 35% of Continental Lite flying consisted of point-to-point, linear services not integrated with the company's hubs. Linear trips proved to be exceptionally unprofitable and responsible for 70% of all losses in 1994.

US Airways started MetroJet in 1998 which ran until elimination in 2001, citing cut capacity by more than 20% due to the aftermath of 9/11, and a substantial reduction in point-to-point flights (non-hub flights). Delta's LCC Delta Express was created as their no-frills brand in 1996. It was based out of Orlando International Airport and primarily competed with Continental Lite, MetroJet, Southwest and JetBlue. The fleet consisted of one aircraft type, a Boeing 737-200 with no in-flight entertainment or meal service. It ceased operations in 2003, after the airline Song was established. Song was a single class airline designed to compete directly with JetBlue. Although considered as a successful addition to the Northeast to Florida market, the airline suffered financially, and as a result was folded into the main brand in 2006. Song differentiated itself by providing leather seats, free personal entertainment in every seat, audio MP3 programmable selections, satellite television, and sung flight safety instructions. Fashion designer Kate Spade designed the flight crew uniforms; the flight featured customized cocktails, and an in-flight exercise program. The airline created its own distinct mark on the industry. The airline engaged in a long-term branding strategy that identified a set of style conscious professional women as target customers. The airline strived to meet not only travel needs but social needs too. Absorbing the airline back into mainline operations was seen as a move to reduce costs and emerge from bankruptcy.

Shuttle was launched by United in 1994, as a cost-competitive service on routes under 750 miles. It was aimed initially at Southwest's expansion in the California market and this became the modus operandi in other US markets; stop Southwest. Lower costs were achieved through special work rules and wage rates for pilots, high station and aircraft utilization and minimal add-on service. Shuttle was shut down in 2001.

In order to compete with the LCC model, subsidiaries need to create a similar low cost employment system and human resources management policies to support the system, which will be very different from the parent company. How the staff respond to the management practices will have a crucial influence on the airline. New entrant low cost airlines operate on average at 43–65% of FSC's operating costs (Harvey & Turnbull, 2006). The particular difficulties of this carrier within a carrier model have to do with brand confusion, employment issues and practices. If FSC wage rates and other employment conditions were adopted, there would be little cost advantage, and the challenges of adopting a unique management style to support the LCC strategy. Harvey and Turnbull contrast the employment management differences between two low cost subsidiaries, Go (British Airways) and bmibaby (bmi), illustrating the far-reaching influence that empowering management can have on the success of the airline when it comes to employee relations.

The extent to which authority is devolved to units within the divisional firm and the extent of subsidiary autonomy is an important determinant of employee relations and organizational performance. The nature and extent of any devolution will be influenced by a large number of structural factors, the size of the subsidiary relative to the parent, import of the subsidiary to the performance of the parent, age of subsidiary, and a host of strategic factors that are either centripetal or centrifugal pressures (or tendencies) on employee relations. Centripetal pressures include the desire to exclude trade unions from business strategy decisions, by limiting local union influence, allowing greater upper management autonomy, the need to control several employee related costs, such as pensions which have a direct influence throughout the organization, and the need to ensure some kind of consistency of practice to avoid anomalies within different divisions or subsidiaries.

For FSCs establishing an LCC, there will be a tendency to localize trade union influence to isolate rather than integrate the trade union. The initiative to obtaining significantly lower labour costs puts a premium on centrifugal rather than centripetal forces (Harvey & Turnbull, 2006). Centrifugal forces may be beneficial to allow local management to affect those policies of which they have greater awareness. In order to ensure institutional separation, local managers should be seen as autonomous. It will reinforce the perception that local management have discretion in other strategic decision-making areas.

Management style may be assessed in terms of degrees of individualism and collectivism. Individualism is the extent to which the firm acknowledges the sentiments of the individual employee and seeks to develop and encourage them, and collectivism is the extent to which the organization recognizes the collective rights and interests of employees. Although collectivism is often associated with unionization, high levels of collectivism in management style can be present in non-union structures. Within the subsidiaries of multi-divisional firms, distinctive management styles often prevail, and divergence from the parent approach depends on the type of product and markets, also technology and skill level of the dominant groups are also important variables. This is well illustrated in the management of flight crews at LCC subsidiaries of network carriers.

The pilot is an atypical employee who poses a particular HR challenge due to two professional features: substantial bargaining power and disincentive to leave an airline. Pilots possess strategic skills and exhibit low substitutability due to general and specific skills (examinations, commercial pilots' license acquisitions). Pilots have little or no transferability, and experience the binding effect of seniority rights.

High quality relationships are more likely where centrifugal rather than centripetal forces prevail. Management at LCC subsidiaries have a greater scope to forge a new and distinctive management style, divorced from adversarial relationships, such as with Go, which was separated from the adversarial relationships that have characterized management–labour relations at BA. Where centripetal forces prevail, as in bmibaby, the culture of conflict continues.

In both cases, management sought to combine a low cost operating system and higher quality product. Both carriers succeeded, but in bmibaby this was at the expense of flight crew commitment and job satisfaction. At Go the management team was too successful for BA, competing for passengers on short-haul routes with the BA brand behind them, but at much lower fares, with exceptional service, and excellent, happy and helpful flight crew. Acquisition by easyJet will imply further changes to management style, and may well spell the end of its distinctive and successful management style.

32   D. Gillen, A. Gados / Research in Transportation Economics 24 (2008) 25–35

4.3. Compatibilities, incompatibilities and characteristics

LCCs have two generally universal source of success: asset productivity and people productivity (Field, 2008a). The notions of success stemming from internet-only distribution, single fleet type, or secondary airports do not hold anymore; rather, it is the productivity of people and assets that are the mainstays of the business model.

The LCC airline within a network airline model has prompted suggestions that it is an intermediate competitive response (Graf, 2005). Graf finds two major incompatibilities in operating two business models: the contrary and conflicting configuration in two business models; and the inconsistencies in the way the business model of a low cost unit has been applied to the new unit. While operating the LCC within their model, carriers attempt to shed a significant amount of costs from their own operations, without changing business models or reducing service levels to business passengers. However analysis shows that the unit cost gap compared with Southwest has narrowed only very slightly between 1995 and 2002 for Northwest, Continental and Delta, but for United and American it has varied moderately. Overall having an LCC subsidiary airline does not improve the chances of cost reduction in the incumbent's operations (Morrell, 2005).

In addition, even though some LCC subsidiaries conformed strictly to the Southwest model, they suffer from brand confusion and labour restrictions on their operations[13] due to unionization of the workforce. The new LCC carrier Ted by United is likely to suffer from brand confusion, since Ted's flights are bookable through the reservation system showing both Ted's and United's markets, Ted's passengers can accumulate miles from United's frequent flyer program, and because Ted flights are operated by United. Graf (2005) and Morrell (2005) have raised concerns whether launching LCCs within their business is a reactionary short or medium strategy for coping with the LCC threat. The strategy may not be viable when taking into account the risk of cannibalization and the incompatibilities associated with two distinct business models.

The running of two different and conflicting airline business models can result in poor quality, dissatisfied customers, and discouraged employees (Porter, 1996). The move in Continental airlines, with Continental Lite, almost forced the parent into bankruptcy. The subsidiary LCC reportedly was responsible for 70% of the $55 million Continental lost each month. The large number of attempts exhibits the spread of this strategy in the airline industry as one of the options for incumbents to participate in the growing market for budget air travel, and reaction to the popularity of LCCs. Management of the incumbent airlines is not completely aware of the negative impacts of running these subsidiaries in their companies, and think that incompatibilities of the business models are the causal reasons for failure. There is rationale for companies to operate various business models with the same output; theory of generic strategies and the concept of business modelling offer insights into the incompatibilities and why such structures often fail, particularly if certain rules are not observed.

Evolutionary theory considers evolutionary processes within organizations. The ongoing process of adjustment and change inside organizations is driven by social and economic imperatives. The reasons behind evolution can be exogenous factors, such as changes in the market, technology or endogenous changes such as organizational structure that encourage autonomous strategic behaviour by business units. Variations emerge through an evolutionary process, where the most appropriate are retained. An organization is a collection of strategic initiatives which compete for limited organizational resources to enhance their relative importance within the organization (Burgelman, 1991). If an organization encourages autonomous behaviour, frequently, overlapping products are produced. Competing activities and behaviour are sometimes intended to ensure that market opportunities are taken up.

It appears that the motivation for a network carrier to establish an LCC subsidiary is rational. Several business units are founded offering similar products due to economies of scale and scope. Certain markets are heterogeneous enough that they allow distinct offerings for different segments. Product variety ensures that each product gets closer to the segment's ideal set of attributes (Sorenson, 2000). Firms respond to the demand by creating business units with overlapping activities and offerings, which increases the potential for revenue since it satisfies each of customers' needs, and by enabling growth opportunities. Costs can also be reduced through sharing and transferring of resources between units, or higher batch production. The costs of this model can range from cannibalization, cost of duplication, and strategic incoherence. Overall the costs and benefits of overlapping activities and product offerings have to be carefully balanced, as tradeoffs are pervasive (Markides, 1999).

Porter analyzed the issue of incompatible strategies. He defines strategy as the creation of a unique and valuable position involving a different set of activities. Generic strategies of cost leadership, differentiation, or focus can be used as alternative directions of the strategy process to attain competitive advantage. An organization must decide on its strategic position, which cannot be combined in one grouping, because each strategy requires a different set of resources and capabilities, different organizational structures, control and incentive mechanisms. These in turn lead to different management styles, corporate cultures, and highlight the need to make a choice, in order to avoid the difficult situation of being caught between inherent contradictions of different strategies (Porter, 1980).

The business model is the way a company, corporate system or industry creates value on the market. Elements of a business model are execution and configuration of the activities of the value chain, by the mechanism of generating returns, by the combination of the products offered and markets served. This is different from a corporate system, which offers only various products or brands; the combination of products offered and markets served differ but not the construct of the value chain or returns mechanism.[14] There are five different business models in the airline industry. The basic output of all the models is the same, transporting passengers between two destinations; the value chain configuration is different, and the way that they create value in the marketplace. Their main strategic success factors are also different.

Table 1, taken from Graf (2005), shows the disjuncture between the two business models. Graf (2005) looks at five airlines[15] that have housed LCCs within their company, as part of their strategy. Graf finds that incumbent airlines have taken different approaches in configuring the dimensions of the business model of the LCC. Also, the implementation differs in the way business models have been positioned and linked in the grouping.

Specifically, the differences arise from the following dimensions:

1. The product and service concept
2. Communication concept

---

[13] As was the case with MetroJet by US Airways, Delta Express by Delta and Shuttle by United.

[14] This strategy of distinctive offerings has been applied in different industries, such as hotels, textile, tour operators, consumer goods, cellular phones and cars.
[15] British Airways with Go, KLM with Buzz, KLM also with Transavia (Basiq Air), Lufthansa with Germanwings, and Swiss International with Swiss in Europe.

D. Gillen, A. Gados / Research in Transportation Economics 24 (2008) 25–35

33

Table 1
Distinctions between the network and LCC business models (Graf, 2005).

	Network carrier	Low cost carrier
Product/service concept: What is the benefit to which customers?	Comprehensive and differentiated	Simple offer
	Several customer segments addressed	One customer segment addressed
Communication concept: How is the benefit attributed to the market?	Complex communication	Simple communication
Revenue concept: Revenue sources	Complex pricing	Simple pricing
	One revenue source	Various revenue sources
Growth concept	Hybrid	Simple
	Market shares	Efficiency gains
Competence configuration: Necessary core competencies	Network management	Market presence
	Revenue management	
	Product offer and quality	Process and cost management
	Marketing	
Organizational form: Features of the organization	Complex	Simple
	Outsourcing operations	Outsourcing services
	Static corporate value	Dynamic corporate value
Cooperation concept: Cooperation partners	Extensive horizontal cooperation	Restricted horizontal cooperation
	Extensive vertical cooperation	Some vertical cooperation
	Complex linkages	Simple linkages
Coordination concept: What coordination model in networks is used?	Application of various and complex models	Application of one single and simple model

3. Revenue concept
4. Competence configuration
5. Organizational form

Different configurations exist with respect to destinations served, customer segments addressed, branding and price systems chosen, means of production (aircraft type), emphasis on distribution channels (go-to market mechanism), the organization and staff assigned, the corporate context settled and the competencies conceded. Elements are either identical, related or separated for the business models of the network and low cost carrier. Overall, incumbent airlines have each time attributed a different level of independence and autonomy to the LCC unit.[16] The level of independence granted will also influence the number and extent of the negative impacts within the grouping.

Incumbent airlines have four possibilities: exploiting economies of scale and scope, taking advantage of growth opportunities, and considering market and organizational dynamics. Motives for establishing a low cost unit can be identified in these terms. There are two reasons why incompatibilities arise. They arise due to contrary and conflicting configurations, which on one hand are determined by the definitions and requirements of the business models themselves, and cannot be controlled by management. They can also be the result of the management approach regarding positioning and linking the two business models. They also arise due to inconsistencies in the way the business model of an LCC is applied to the new unit. The incumbent airlines differ from the ideal configuration of how to set up an LCC. Both reasons for the incompatibilities can be illustrated within the concept of business modelling. The contrary and conflicting configurations of the two business models become clear when gradually comparing the eight dimensions of the two business models. Most definitions and requirements of the two models are incompatible (see Table 1).

However, the extent and number of incompatibilities and negative impacts depends on the management approach, whether it has decided to integrate or separate the branding and communication concept, markets and segments served and the means of production and organization deployed. Incompatibilities in setting up a parallel LCC also occur due to the inconsistent application of

the business model definitions. Configuration of the low cost unit has to take into consideration, and the main strategic success factors shown in the competence configuration of the LCC business model, market presence and process and cost management. A low cost carrier implementing service amenities, such as differentiated products, baggage transfer, connections, free meals, travel agency bookings, or operation to primary airports will not be as cost efficient as is necessary. If the complexity of the system is increased, the productivity of the aircraft and staff is reduced, the product and service concept is no longer compatible with competence configuration and organizational form. Offering more service amenities will cause passengers to less associate the carrier with low fares. In this respect, the communication and revenue concept are not compatible with the competence configuration. The same kind of incongruence arises if the LCC decides to cater to other customer segments or to set up cooperation with other airlines, whereby complexity and cost levels also build up (Graf, 2005).

Certain negative impacts of establishing a low cost unit are controllable and others are not. Incompatibilities can arise as the definitions and requirements of the business models lead to contrary and conflicting configurations, and cannot be influenced by management. If the incompatibilities result from approach taken by management in positioning and linking the business model in the grouping, there are leverages. The extent of incompatibilities depends on the consistent application of the LCC business model to the new unit.

Graf (2005) offers ten propositions of potentially how to control the incompatibilities.

1. Consistency in the application of the business models.
2. Conflicts will be minimized if the markets are clearly divided by segments and regions.
3. If attributes of the product and service components and the revenue components are clearly communicated, product transparency into the product offerings and requirements is increased.
4. There should be clearly set boundaries in terms of branding and resources.
5. The LCC should have high autonomy to act in the market, in decision making concerning operational issues.
6. Begin from ground-up for the LCC rather than taking significant capital from the incumbent to start the subsidiary.
7. The number and extent of negative impacts grow with the size of the LCC.

---

[16] Germanwings, for example, has the highest independence, and Swiss in Europe has the lowest. The paper identifies that only Germanwings and Go can be classified as true subsidiaries, while Basiq Air, Buzz and Swiss in Europe are within-carrier LCCs.

8. Establishment of the business model raises complexity in the grouping, as the firm gets more diversified.
9. The more important co-operations and the resulting network effects are for the value proposition of the case under consideration, the higher the number of potential incompatibilities with other partners.
10. The more mature the market, the smaller the segments, and the more concentrated the demand is, the higher the negative impacts.

The separation of the LCC concerning most of the eight dimensions of the business modelling concept discussed is important. The operation of different business models in separate entities or organizations while maintaining a certain level of control is an efficient strategy. It is important to keep markets apart. Transferring decentralized traffic flows to LCC and deploying the aircraft of the network carrier just to hub operations could be an efficient work sharing strategy for the business units. But separating the unit in various dimensions will not guarantee long term success unless established firms also employ the appropriate managerial policies that will support the co-existence of both business models. The key is how well the management is able to manage incompatibilities and limit negative impacts. Cost benefit analysis could be valuable here. If issues do not apply or cannot be managed, incumbent airlines should focus instead on strategic response options. One option is to embrace the disruptive strategic innovation of the LCC by adapting or transforming the network carrier business model. Aer Lingus is an example of where the original dimensions of the network carrier business model have been changed to those of an LCC.

4.4. Have we seen successes?

Earlier we noted that three carriers seem to have found the right formula form operating what appear to be airlines within airlines. Qantas owns the subsidiary Jetstar, which it originally opened in response to the threat posed by Virgin Blue; Jetstar has evolved into more than a fighting brand. It operates an extensive domestic regional network and provides some international services. Jetstar offers a limited number of connecting flights. In 2004 Jetstar entered the Asian low cost market with its flights to Hong Kong, and in direct competition with Singapore Airlines. It has been said that Qantas is the only airline in the world to have successfully run a full service premium carrier and low cost airline in parallel (Creedy, 2008). Qantas focuses on service for business class passengers while Jetstar focuses on competitive economy segments; the airlines are not in direct competition.

Singapore Airlines International (SIA), the sixth largest airline in the world based on passengers carried and the largest based on market capitalization, established Tiger Airways, modelled after Ryanair. It complements Singapore's premium service. In essence, the target market is different. Notably, SIA, like Qantas with Jetstar, owns 49% of its LCC subsidiary instead of a wholly owned subsidiary.

Lufthansa's Germanwings is their successful LCC subsidiary, which operates short haul on point-to-point flights for a number of bases in Germany. It is the first LCC in Germany to offer connecting flights. Germanwings is not hampered by Lufthansa's expensive wage agreements and restrictive scope clauses (upper limit capacity agreements with unions). Lufthansa claims it practices a hands-off approach with the subsidiary, while retaining whole ownership.

In Malaysia, the flag carrier Malaysia Airlines, impaired by the entry of AirAsia into its home market, has proved that a legacy carrier can reinvent itself to compete with a low cost upstart, and indeed thrive in a market where air travel has boomed and continues to flourish (Pilling, 2008b).

The success of Singapore, Qantas and Lufthansa appears to depend on a number of factors. First, these airlines dominate their domestic markets partly due to historical factors, partly due to government complicity in indirectly protecting them and partly due to their dominance in international markets through the bilateral process; Lufthansa will no longer have this exclusive right under new EU rules and certainly not with the new EU–US Open Skies Agreement which came into operation in 2008.

A second success factor is a complete separation of operations except at the strategic level; the 'other' carriers are completely separate and do not enter into the primary carrier's business model; for example providing feed. Having said this Tiger, the Singapore subsidiary may be used to open up the Australian market for feeding and distributing passengers in the domestic Australian market. It could be Singapore is using Tiger as a bargaining chip for better 5th freedom rights in Australia; it is not clear.

A third success factor is the lack of integration with the primary carrier in any way; the airline within an airline can focus on those factors that provide LCCs with their cost advantage and achieve them.

Fourth, there has been an evolution in the LCC model and legacy models. Many LCCs now offer a broader array of services, albeit monetizing all of them while the legacy carriers have managed to reduce their costs and to some degree unbundled their complex products. Therefore there is less of a difference in cost or product design; we get specialized route development, domestic versus long haul, and fleet specialization.

Fifth, these carriers have better network management to reduce their own competition; Qantas, Singapore and Lufthansa who have been careful to not cannibalize or confuse the products, keeping them separate and serving a different market; also these airlines dominate their domestic market and have strong positions in their long haul (due to bilaterals) which means they have captive feed in a way.

However, things are changing, Australian and South-East Asian airlines are moving in on each other's markets. On the strength of trade and traffic growth, they are adding routes and launching cross-border operations that will merge the two regions, as already seen between Australia and New Zealand, and in Europe. Paradoxically, it is not the legacy airlines such as Qantas or Singapore Airlines that are making these moves. Instead it is the low cost carriers that are bridging the divides that traditionally separated Australia and South-East Asia (Knibb, 2008b).

5. Summary and conclusion

Firms within firms arise because management wishes to focus resources on a specific competitor or geographic market. The target has to be clearly identifiable and the primary firm must have a clear competitive advantage, otherwise the secondary (firm within the firm) will not be a successful strategy. In the airline business the fighting brand and focused firm is a dying strategy mostly because the LCC business model and legacy business model have moved from one of vertical[17] differentiation to one of horizontal[18] differentiation. Some consumers prefer to fly an LCC for various reasons, mainly their price elasticity, but also schedule, reliability, on-time

---

[17] This differentiation occurs in a market where the several goods that are present can be ordered according to their objective quality from the highest to the lowest; one good is better than another. It can be obtained along one decisive feature, along a few features each of which has a wide possible range of (continuous or discreet) variables, and across several features, each of which has only a presence or absence of the attribute.
[18] Horizontal differentiation emerges when products are different according to features that cannot be ordered, no product can be said to be "better" or superior to the other. For example, flying an LCC is not inferior to flying FSC.

performance, etc. One of the shifts has been the increased use of LCCs by business travellers. Traditionally, those business class travellers have been a major business source for FSCs, however a study by Mason (2000) revealed and gauged the propensity of business travellers to use short haul, low cost carriers for trips. Company size influences the price elasticity of business passengers and on the value placed on those purchase factors. Small and medium businesses are more likely to use LCCs (Mason, 2000).

Where we have seen greater use of firms within firms such as with Qantas, Singapore, Cathay Pacific and Lufthansa, they have been used for differing purposes. Cathay and Singapore have used their secondary firms to meet some competition but more so to enter markets. Lufthansa and Qantas developed their secondary carriers, German Wings and Jetstar respectively, to meet LCC competition. They have been successful not in eliminating competitors but at holding their market share to about 30%. Both carriers have been disciplined in using their secondary carriers to avoid cannibalizing their primary product and to not create brand confusion, something which many others have been guilty of. All four carriers have a sustainable, at least for the moment for Lufthansa, competitive advantage because of their domestic market dominance and the implicit protection by their respective governments.

In the present economic climate of mid-2008 and with oil prices unlikely to go below $100 again, there will be some rationalization in the industry. Some are calling for massive consolidation, Jeff Dixon of Qantas, for example, but it is not clear how any efficiencies are to be had by such a strategy; where do the cost savings lie? Yet a number of carriers most notably in the US are in desperate financial shape, have very weak fuel hedging strategies (except Southwest) and have a domestic economy which is near recession. In the near term fewer carriers, but in the mid to longer term technology, will provide some relief. It is unlikely that firms within firms will be a popular or successful strategy in the future as we will see greater alliance competition; the LCCs are and will remain more cost efficient but not by the margins they enjoyed in the past and greater liberalization of international bilaterals through more open skies agreements, changing conditions on foreign ownership restrictions and having broader use of rights of establishment all make the firm within a firm strategy non-workable.

References

Air Transport Association (2003). US airline cost index: major and national passenger carriers, second quarter. http://www.airlines.org\econ, 14 November.
Airline Business (2008). News focus: Dubai to launch low-cost carrier, 20 March.
Airline Business (2008). ANA looks to set up low-cost carrier, 23 April.
Anjos, M. F., Cheng, R. C. H., & Currie, C. S. M. (2004). Maximizing revenue in the airline industry under one-way pricing. Journal of the Operational Research Society, 55(5), 535–541, 2005.
Banker, R. D., & Johnston, H. H. (1993). An empirical study of cost drivers in the U.S. airline industry. Accounting Review, 68(3), 576–601.
Botimer, T. C., & Belobaba, P. P. (1999). Airline pricing and fare product differentiation: a new theoretical framework. Journal of the Operational Research Society, Yield Management, 50(11), 1085–1097.
Boyd, E. A., & Bilegan, I. C. (2003). Revenue management and e-commerce. Management Science, 49(10), 1363–1386, (special issue on E-Business and Management Science).
Brueckner, J. K., Dyer, N. J., & Spiller, P. T. (1992). Fare determination in airline hub-and-spoke network. Rand Journal of Economics, 23, 309–333.
Burgelman, R. A. (1991). Intraorganizational ecology of strategy making and organizational adaptation: theory and field research. Organizational Science, 2, 239–262.
Creedy, S. (2008). Qantas's new chief Alan Joyce supports Jetstar. Australian Business.
Doganis, R. (2001). The airline business in the 21st century. London: Routledge.
Duliba, K. A., Kauffman, R. J., & Lucas, H. C. (2001). Appropriating value from computerized reservation system ownership in the airline industry. Organizational Science, 12(6), 702–728.
Field, D. (2008a). Low-cost carriers tweak their models. Airline Business, May.
Franke, M. (2004). Competition between network carriers and low-cost carriers – retreat battle or breakthrough to a new level of efficiency? Journal of Air Transport Management, 10(1), 15–21.
Franke, M. (2007). Innovation: the winning formula to regain profitability in aviation? Journal of Air Transport Management, 13(1), 23–30.
Gillen, D. (1988). Duopoly in Canada's airline industry: consequences and policy issues. Canadian Public Policy, 15(1), 15–31.
Gillen, D. (2006). The evolution and future of aviation in Canada: winners and losers in the new market reality. The Evolution and Future of Canadian Aviation, Draft Manuscript January. Sauder School, University of British Columbia and the Van Horne Institute, University of Calgary.
Gillen, D., & Lall, A. (2004). Competitive advantage of low-cost carriers: some implications for airports. Journal of Air Transport Management, 10(1), 41–50.
Gillen, D., Morrison, W. G., & Stewart, C. (2007). Air travel demand elasticities: concepts, issues and measurement. In D. Lee (Ed.), Advances in airline economics. The economics of airline institutions, operations and marketing, vol. 2. Amsterdam: Elsevier.
Graf, L. (2005). Incompatibilities of the low-cost and network carrier business models within the same airline group. Journal of Air Transport Management, 11(5), 313–327.
Hansson, T., Ringbeck, J., & Franke, M. (2002). Airlines: a new operating model. McLean, VA: Booz Allen Hamilton.
Harvey, G., & Turnbull, P. (2006). Employment relations, management style and flight crew attitudes at low cost airline subsidiaries: the cases of British Airways/Go and bmi/bmibaby. European Management Journal, 24(5), 330–337.
Hofer, C., Windle, R. J., & Dresner, M. E. (2008). Price premiums and low cost carrier competition. Transportation Research Part E: Logistics and Transportation Review, 44(5), 864–882.
Knibb, D. (2008a). Low-cost carriers expand reach through cross-border deals. Airline Business, April 24.
Knibb, D. (2008b). Bridge building: airlines bridge the divide between southeast Asia and Australia. Airline Business, 21 August.
Markides, C. C. (1999). All the right moves: a guide to crafting breakthrough strategy. Boston, MA: Harvard Business School Publishing.
Mason, K. J. (2000). The propensity of business travellers to use low cost airlines. Journal of Transport Geography, 8(2), 107–119.
Morrell, P. (2005). Airlines within airlines: an analysis of US network airline responses to low cost carriers. Journal of Air Transport Management, 11(5), 303–312.
Oum, T., & Zhang, Y. (1990). Airport pricing: congestion tolls, lumpy investment, and cost recovery. Journal of Public Economics, 43(3), 353–374.
Pilling, M. (2008b). Distribution 2008: flying off the shelf. Airline Business, 20 May.
Porter, M. E. (1980). Competitive strategy: techniques for analyzing industries and competitors. New York: The Free Press.
Porter, M.E. (1996). What is strategy? Harvard Business Review November/December, 61–78.
Sorenson, O. (2000). Letting the market work for you: an evolutionary perspective on product strategy. Strategic Management Journal, 21, 577–592.
Taweelertkunthon, N. (2006). The empirical valuation of the potential success in low cost business model in Asian aviation market (Master of Science in Business Administration, Transportation and Logistics, University of British Columbia, Vancouver), 174 pp.
Weatherford, L. R., & Belobaba, P. P. (2002). Revenue impacts of fare input and demand forecast accuracy in airline yield management. Journal of the Operational Research Society, 53(8), 811–821.
Wei, W., & Hansen, M. (2003). Cost economics of aircraft size. Journal of Transportation Economics and Policy, 37, 279–296.
Williams, G. (2001). Will Europe's charter carriers be replaced by "no frills" scheduled airlines? Journal of Air Transport Management, 7(5), 277–286.

16

Low cost carriers going hybrid: Evidence from Europe ☆

Richard Klophaus, Roland Conrady, Frank Fichert

ABSTRACT

Keywords:
Airline industry dynamics
Airline strategies
Low-cost airlines
Hybrid airlines

This paper reports the findings of a survey on European airlines often categorized as low-cost carriers to see to which extent they have changed their business model towards a hybrid strategy, adopting features of full service network airlines. Data is provided on relative frequencies of attributes of the low-cost business model retained and modified respectively. The survey concludes that short-haul airline business models in Europe converge. A large percentage of low-cost carriers has evolved into hybrid carriers which blend low-cost traits with those of full service network carriers.

1. Introduction

The market share of low-cost carriers (LCCs) grew rapidly following their entry into the European market in the mid-1990s, forcing traditional full service network carriers (FSNCs) to review and adjust their short-haul market strategy. Today, LCCs carry more than one third of the scheduled passenger traffic within Europe and their market share even exceeds 50% on some large intra-European markets. Passenger growth, however, is slowing down as the European LCC market appears to mature.

The archetypical LCC configures resources and practices that enable the airline to operate with lower costs than traditional FSNCs. The LCC business model is generally seen to be based on the following features (Doganis, 2010; Sterzenbach et al., 2009):

- point-to-point traffic,
- single aircraft type (usually Airbus 320 or Boeing 737 family),
- predominant use of so-called secondary airports,
- direct sales of tickets, especially over airline's own website,
- only one one-way fare per flight available at each point in time,
- single class cabin and
- no frills such as complimentary in-flight services or frequent flyer programs.

In practice, the LCC business model is blurring (Franke and John, 2011; Taneja, 2010). Diverging market strategies can be observed

among the group of airlines usually categorized as LCCs. The notion of hybrid airlines, however, lacks a comprehensive assessment of their key characteristics.

We present a methodology for assessing and comparing airline business models and apply it to the 20 largest European LCCs according to a capacity ranking published twice a year by the German Aerospace Center (Deutsches Zentrum für Luft- und Raumfahrt, 2010) as well as to four major European FSNCs that serve as a control group. We examine the extent to which LCCs blend low-cost characteristics with the features of FSNCs, which characteristics remain distinct between LCCs and FSNCs, and which tend to be common for all carriers. Mason and Morrison (2008, updated in Mason et al., 2011) also provide a methodology for comparing airline business models. They use a product and organizational architecture approach, apply it to six European airlines and calculate scores per airline based on 'best in class' performance by carriers for each of the individual items benchmarked, i.e., each airline's business strategy is represented relative to other benchmarked LCCs. In contrast, we assess whether a carrier follows the archetypical LCC business model. Furthermore, Mason and Morrison use cost and revenue data that is only published by few airlines. The approach presented in this paper is based on publicly available data, allowing also the assessment of smaller carriers' business models.

2. Carriers included in the survey

To facilitate data acquisition, our analysis is limited to the four largest LCC markets in Europe, i.e., UK, Spain (ES), Italy (IT) and Germany (DE). They account for two thirds of all seats and departures as well as for more than half of the number of routes offered by LCCs in Europe (Deutsches Zentrum für Luft- und Raumfahrt, 2010). Between 2009 and 2010 the growth in seat capacity in

☆ A previous version of this study was presented at the 16th Hong Kong Society for Transportation Studies (HKSTS) International Conference, 17–20 December 2011, Hong Kong.

R. Klophaus et al. / Journal of Air Transport Management 23 (2012) 54–58   55

these four markets was 1.8% in comparison to 4.5% in Europe indicating their more mature status. The number of routes offered in the four largest markets increased by 9.4%. This strong route expansion combined with a small capacity growth reflects a network strategy of many European LCCs, especially Ryanair and easyJet, to develop new routes rather than to increase frequency of flights on existing routes.

Table 1 provides basic information on the 20 LCCs. The carriers are ranked according to seat capacity during a week in July 2010. Four airlines (Air Berlin, Aer Lingus, Meridiana, and Air Italy) also operate several long-haul routes. However, the following survey focuses on their short-haul operations. The number of airports served refers to the carrier's destinations in the four selected countries. The operational statistics were obtained from several sources. Data for some carriers is not completely consistent across differing sources which may reflect the dynamic nature of the low-cost segment within the European aviation market. In some cases only the carriers' websites provided data on passenger numbers.

Except Sverigeflyg all current members of the European Low Fares Airline Association (ELFAA) are included in the survey. Sverigeflyg is the main brand for a group of local Swedish airlines totalizing less than one million passengers in 2010. Compared to a recently published compilation of the world's 70 largest low-cost carriers in the magazine Airline Business (Dunn, 2011), Table 1 excludes three European airlines: Thomson Airways (UK), Monarch (UK) and Cimber Sterling (Denmark). Based on their passenger numbers these carriers would have to be included in the survey. Deutsches Zentrum für Luft- und Raumfahrt (2010) appears not to view these carriers as LCCs but rather as leisure carriers offering flights primarily to holiday destinations such as the Balearic Islands, the Canaries, and Turkey. However, some carriers (e.g. Air Berlin, Meridiana which purchased Air Italy in fall 2011, Transavia and Corendon) are included in the German Aerospace Center ranking despite of the fact that apart from scheduled services they also operate charter flights.

Seat capacity and the number of passengers transported by Ryanair and easyJet exceed several times those of the smaller carriers. Nevertheless, even the smallest carrier has more than one million annual passengers that may already allow for economies of scale to qualify as LCC. In addition, all carriers operate aircraft with a capacity of more than 100 seats.

Besides the 20 largest European LCCs we analyze a control group of FSNCs, consisting of Alitalia (AZ), British Airways (BA), Iberia (IB) and Lufthansa (LH), i.e., carriers traditionally considered to be the 'national' carriers in the four selected markets.

3. Criteria for the LCC business model

Archetypical LCCs are characterized by practices that enable them to reduce costs in comparison to traditional carriers. Table 2 depicts the selected criteria to assess whether a carrier follows the LCC business model. These features of an airline's business model refer to fleet composition, airport and route choice as well as to the carrier's service and pricing policy. However, no criterion relates directly to labor productivity or costs per available seat kilometer due to the lack of reliable and comparable data. Some criteria like in-flight service, checked baggage, frequent flyer program and code sharing are self-explaining. Point-to-point service means that a carrier does not offer connecting flights including transfer of passengers and baggage.

Fleet size and fleet structure have a significant impact on an airline's operating costs. Operators of large fleets might benefit from economies of scale. The homogeneity of a fleet can be

Table 1
Low-cost airlines in the survey.

Carrier	IATA airline code	Weekly seat capacity (2010)	Home country	Passengers (million) 2010	Destinations UK, ES, IT, DE (2011)
Ryanair	FR	1,903,041	Ireland	72.1	70
easyJet	U2	1,263,888	UK	48.8	56
Air Berlin	AB	463,301	Germany	33.6[a]	57
Norwegian	DY	359,715	Norway	13.0	19
Vueling	VY	356,940	Spain	11.0	30
Aer Lingus	EI	283,919	Ireland	9.3[a]	33
Flybe	BE	264,052	UK	6.7	41
Wizz Air	W6	244,800	Hungary	9.6	27
Germanwings	4U	238,954	Germany	7.7	28
Meridiana fly	IG	166,087	Italy	4.6[a]	21
Jet2	LS	128,621	UK	3.3	26
Air Baltic	BT	120,030	Latvia	3.2	12
Bmibaby	WW	85,566	UK	2.3	20
Transavia	HV	81,692	Netherlands	5.1	25
Niki	HG	80,210	Austria	3.4	21
Wind Jet	IV	71,348	Italy	3.0	14
Blu Express	BV	69,730	Italy	2.2	14
Corendon	7H	56,374	Netherlands	n/a	3
Blue Air	OB	42,584	Romania	1.4	12
Air Italy	I9	39,502	Italy	1.2[a]	10

Source: Deutsches Zentrum für Luft- und Raumfahrt (2010), Dunn (2011).
[a] Including long-haul operations.

measured on different levels reaching from aircraft manufacturers (e.g., Airbus, Boeing) via aircraft families (A320 family, B737 family) to aircraft types and versions within one family. For example, the single-aisle A320 family comprises the A318, A319, A320 and A321. They share the same pilot type rating, enabling crews to fly any of them with a single license endorsement. Whereas several airlines in the survey have a completely homogenous fleet, consisting of one aircraft type - Ryanair operates only B737-800, other carriers operate two or even more aircraft families.

The fleet homogeneity index is calculated as the number of aircraft of the family with largest fleet share divided by fleet size. Hence, the maximum value is 1 like in the case of Ryanair. The value of the index is influenced by the number of aircraft families but also the spread of the fleet across aircraft families. The fleet homogeneity index value of a carrier operating a fleet consisting of nine aircraft of the same type and one from another type is 0.9 whereas a carrier operating two families each with five aircraft

Table 2
Criteria for the LCC business model.

Business model practice	Criterion	Value
Single aircraft type	Fleet homogeneity index	>0.75
Predominant use of secondary airports	Secondary airport index	>0.5
Point-to-point traffic	Point-to-point services only	Yes
No code sharing	No code sharing	Yes
Only one one-way fare per flight available at each point in time	One-way fares only	Yes
	No more than one fare at any time	Yes
	No more than two fares at any time	Yes
Single class cabin	Single class cabin	Yes
No frills	No complimentary in-flight service with lowest fare category	Yes
	No complimentary in-flight service with highest fare category	Yes
	No free checked baggage with lowest fare category	Yes
	No free checked baggage with highest fare category	Yes
	No frequent flyer program	Yes

56   R. Klophaus et al. / Journal of Air Transport Management 23 (2012) 54–58

has a homogeneity index value of 0.5. Hence, the fleet homogeneity index does not only reflect the number of types of aircraft operated but also their even or uneven distribution in the fleet. We define a value of the fleet homogeneity index above 0.75 as sufficient for a LCC business model. Lower values shall indicate a hybrid business model. Heterogeneity, however, may result from fleet renewals, mergers and acquisitions or from payload-range considerations in the context of network design and scheduling.

According to the textbooks, LCCs only serve secondary airports offering lower landing fees and quicker turnaround times. There, however, is no generally accepted definition of a secondary airport in dissociation from a primary airport. Here, secondary airports in our four markets are defined as those not served by the 'national' carrier with aircraft having at least 100 seats. Services only based on code sharing are excluded. The minimum seat requirement prevents airports from being classified as primary just because they are served by one of the main carriers with small aircraft.

The secondary airport index is defined as the weighted percentage of secondary airports based on all airports served by a carrier in the four selected countries. The weights are assigned according to the number of destinations served from the airports by the respective carrier. We define a value above 0.5 as sufficient to satisfy this criterion.

An archetypical LCC does not rely on intermediaries like travel agencies and global distribution systems to sell its tickets. Most LCCs, though, show their fares in such systems, with Ryanair being a prominent exception. Although some travel agencies do book customers on Ryanair flights via the airline's website for a fee, we do not consider these offerings to be a deviation from the direct sales principle; the airline is not actively involved in the process. Furthermore, some websites collect flight offers and forward customers to the LCC home page for the booking process. To avoid the opacity of multiple distribution channels we limit our pricing analysis to fare information publicly accessible via the LCCs' websites.

If the LCC's fares offered via the internet do not include return tariffs at a lower price than the sum of the two one-way fares the criterion 'one-way fares only' is considered to be fulfilled. LCCs like Ryanair do not offer more than one fare at any time during the booking period of a specific flight. For them the value of the criterion 'no more than one fare at any time' is 'Yes'. Despite a simple structure based on one-way sectors some LCCs offer more than one fare. The higher fare category offers additional services, for example, free checked baggage, seat selection or changing a booking without a surcharge. Finally, we checked whether some LCCs offer more than two fares at any time.

If the seats are the same for all passengers travelling on short-haul flights, this is considered to be a single class cabin. Seating with more legroom for passengers in the front row or exit row of an aircraft, as well as the opportunity to board first and to reserve exit row seats for a fee, is compatible with this criterion. In contrast, we consider Germanwings as a carrier offering two classes of service, economy and premium economy, because extra legroom is provided in the 'Best Seat' zone (first ten rows) for a surcharge. The carrier deliberately reduces seating capacity to sell some seats at higher prices.

4. Results

Most airlines included in the survey operate a homogenous short-haul fleet. The fleet homogeneity index ranges from 0.41 (Air Baltic) to one. The average value is as high as 0.92. Fleet homogeneity of the four FSNCs in the control group ranges from 0.67 (LH) to

one (IB). LCCs as well as FSNCs today tend to operate homogenous short-haul fleets. Hence, fleet homogeneity or heterogeneity seems to be no valid indicator to differentiate between these two carrier segments.

In contrast to the textbook model, the average value of the secondary airport index among the 20 carriers is rather low (0.21). Many airlines hardly use airports defined as secondary in the four selected countries. Only three airlines reach a degree of secondary airport use sufficient to meet the LCC criterion; Wizz Air (0.58), Flybe (0.53) and Ryanair (0.50).

One approach to classify airline business models is to establish a simple LCC index by counting how many of the 13 dichotomous criteria are fulfilled. For a pure LCC all criteria should be 'Yes' or exceed the defined threshold values. If the value of one is assigned to all fulfilled criteria, the maximum value of the simple LCC index is 13. On the other hand, for a typical FSNC the index value should be zero.

Table 3 shows the values of the simple LCC index for the analyzed airlines. Whereas Ryanair is strictly following the textbook model, the mean of 7.65 indicates that the market strategy of many other airlines included in the survey qualifies as hybrid. Moreover, one fourth of the airlines in the survey only fulfill two or three out of 13 criteria, seriously questioning their status as LCC or even hybrids. We apply a classification with an index minimum of 11 to qualify as a 'pure low-cost carrier' (Type I). Airlines with an index value between eight and ten might be called 'hybrid carriers with dominating low-cost characteristics' (Type II), whereas airlines with an index value between four and seven qualify as 'hybrid carriers with dominating full service airline characteristics' (Type III). Finally, airlines of Type IV may not even be classified as hybrids. With the exception of Air Berlin these airlines do not operate hub-and-spoke systems; we refer to them as full service airlines.

The FSNCs in our control group have an index value of one (IB) or zero (AZ, BA, LH). All European LCCs – with the exception of the small carrier Air Italy – offer only one-way fares on their websites, i.e., no price discount is given on round trips. This is the single common feature that distinguishes them from FSNCs. On the other hand, all larger LCCs besides Ryanair offer incentive schemes for frequent travelers. Furthermore, the secondary airport index

Table 3
Simple LCC index.

Type	Airline	Value
I	Pure LCC	
	Ryanair	13
	Wizz Air	12
	Blu Express	12
	bmibaby	11
	Blue Air	11
II	Hybrid carrier with dominating LCC characteristics	
	easyJet	10
	Jet2	10
	Corendon	10
	Transavia	9
	Vueling	8
	Aer Lingus	8
	Wind Jet	8
III	Hybrid carrier with dominating full service airline characteristics	
	Norwegian	7
	Flybe	6
	Germanwings	5
IV	Full service airline	
	Air Berlin	3
	Air Baltic	3
	Niki	3
	Meridiana fly	2
	Air Italy	2

R. Klophaus et al. / Journal of Air Transport Management 23 (2012) 54–58   57

Table 4
Sub-indices to describe airline business models.

Sub-index	Components
Fleet homogeneity	Fleet homogeneity index
Secondary airport	Secondary airport index
Pricing	One-way fares only
	No more than one fare at any time
	No more than two fares at any time
Network	Point-to-point services only
	No code sharing
Service	Single class cabin
	No complimentary in-flight service with lowest fare category
	No complimentary in-flight service with highest fare category
	No free checked baggage with lowest fare category
	No free checked baggage with highest fare category
	No frequent flyer program

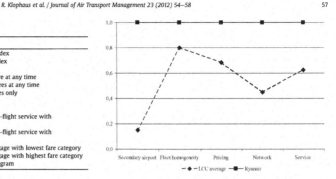

Fig. 1. Values of sub-indices for Ryanair and LCC average.

suggests that the vast majority of LCC serve the same airports as FSNC.

Some of the criteria used for the simple LCC index are related, i.e., several basic properties of an airline business model are covered with two or even more criteria. Therefore, the number of observed criteria can be consolidated to a smaller number of sub-indices. We differentiate five sub-indices as shown in Table 4 with the associated components. Each of these sub-indices describes one crucial property such as the carrier's fleet structure, airport choice, pricing policy, network strategy and its service offering. Three of the five sub-indices consolidate criteria.

Based on the value zero or one assigned to each criterion the five sub-indices are calculated as the average value. For example, if an airline offers only point-to-point services but code shares with some other airline, the network index for the airline is 0.5. Giving equal weight to each of the sub-indices, an overall index is calculated; a consolidated LCC index. The index value ranges from zero to one, with the latter representing the archetypical LCC.

Table 5 shows the airline ranking according to the consolidated LCC index. With values of one and 0.97, Ryanair and Wizz Air follow the LCC textbook model. In contrast, Air Italy, Meridiana, Air Berlin, Niki and Air Baltic with values of 0.27 or even less should not be called LCCs based on the underlying criteria. The mean value of the

Table 5
Consolidated LCC index.

Airline	Value
Ryanair	1.00
Wizz Air	0.97
Blu Express	0.80
bmibaby	0.77
Blue Air	0.73
easyJet	0.70
Corendon	0.67
Flybe	0.60
Aer Lingus	0.57
Jet2	0.57
Transavia	0.57
LCC average	0.54
Vueling	0.50
Wind Jet	0.50
Norwegian	0.47
Germanwings	0.43
Air Italy	0.27
Meridiana fly	0.27
Air Berlin	0.17
Niki	0.17
Air Baltic	0.13

consolidated LCC index is 0.54 indicating a high degree of hybridization among the selected carriers.

The simple and the consolidated LCC index lead to a similar airline ranking. More specifically, the ranking of the airlines previously categorized as pure LCCs remains unchanged. This is an indication that the combination of the 13 criteria into five sub-indices does not cause a substantial loss in information. Flybe shows the biggest change by moving up from position 14 to eight because it is one of only three carriers fulfilling the secondary airport criterion. This criterion receives a relatively high weight in the consolidated LCC index because it is not combined with other criteria.

Fig. 1 shows the mean values of the five sub-indices and compares them with those for Ryanair. Many airlines deviate from the pure LCC business model, especially with respect to airport choice and network strategy.

All sub-indices are zero for FSNCs like British Airways or Lufthansa. Most notably, the fleet structure differs between the two carrier segments. However, even if carriers like BA or LH operate a heterogeneous fleet on short-haul routes, each sub-fleet is sufficiently large to obtain scale economies. For example, LH operates a heterogeneous fleet with 123 aircraft of the Airbus 320 family and 61 Boeing 737. Among the LCCs, only Ryanair and easyJet operate homogenous fleets with more 100 aircraft.

Based on the five sub-indices it is also possible to identify areas in which airlines follow the LCC model and in which they

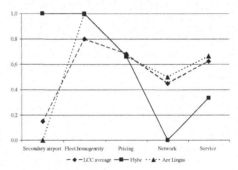

Fig. 2. Comparison of selected LCCs.

58 R. Klophaus et al. / Journal of Air Transport Management 23 (2012) 54–58

act like FSNCs. As an example, Fig. 2 shows the values of the sub-indices for Flybe and Aer Lingus. Whereas both carriers have similar values with regard to the consolidated LCC index, they differ in terms of airport choice, network strategy and service offering. Flybe is one of the few carriers in the survey with a secondary airport index of one, pointing at Flybe's roots as regional airline.

5. Conclusions

In Europe, FSNCs have joined the battle for cost-conscious short-haul passengers thereby forcing many LCCs to change or enhance their business strategy. Hence, most European LCCs are adopting a hybrid market strategy modifying key elements of their basic business model.

References

Deutsches Zentrum für Luft- und Raumfahrt, 2010. Low-cost Monitor 2/2010, Köln-Porz.
Doganis, R., 2010. Flying off Course: Airline Economics and Marketing. Routledge, London.
Dunn, G., 2011. Growth Expectations. In: Airline Business, pp. 28–36.
Franke, M., John, F., 2011. What comes next after recession? Airline industry scenarios and potential end games. Journal of Air Transport Management 17, 19–26.
Mason, K.J., Morrison, W.G., 2008. Towards a means of consistently comparing airline business models with an application to the low cost airline sector. Research in Transportation Economics 24, 75–84.
Mason, K.J., Morrison, W.G., Stockman, J., 2011. Liberalisation of air transport in Europe and the evolution of low cost airlines, working paper.
Sterzenbach, R., Conrady, R., Fichert, F., 2009. Luftverkehr – Betriebswirtschaftliches Lehr- und Handbuch. Oldenbourg, München.
Taneja, N.K., 2010. Looking beyond the Runway: Airlines Innovating with Best Practices while Facing Realities. Ashgate, Farnham.

17

Strategic alliances between airlines and airports—theoretical assessment and practical evidence

Sascha Albers, Benjamin Koch, Christine Ruff

Abstract

Strategic alliances are now widespread. This paper shifts the focus from alliances among airlines toward strategic alliances involving passenger airlines and airports. Following a conceptual path analyzing motives, potential benefits and problems, potential fields of cooperation are identified along with three basic classes of airline–airport alliances. Capacity-based, marketing-based, and security based cooperation models are assessed with regard to benefits for the participating airline and airport partners. This expands the existing literature that has largely neglected the airline–airport relationship and its potential for developing their respective competitive strategies. The case of the alliance between Lufthansa and Munich airport serves as an illustration. © 2004 Elsevier Ltd. All rights reserved.

Keywords: Airlines; Airports; Strategic alliances; Business strategy

1. Introduction

Strategic alliances among airlines are now common in the aviation industry and are frequently seen as a response of airlines to changing economic and regulatory conditions. These conditions, however, change for airports as well, and airport companies have been confronted with profound governance changes over the last decade (Carney and Mew, 2003). Theory and practice debate thus centers around questions regarding models and potential benefits of alliances among airport companies on the one hand and between airports and airlines on the other.[1] Although horizontal alliances between airlines have been extensively addressed in the literature (Agusdinata and de Klein, 2002; Brueckner, 2003; Pels, 2001; Oum et al., 2000) vertical alliances between airline and airport companies have attracted only marginal attention.[2]

From a strategic perspective, the basic motive for forming an alliance is gaining and sustaining competitive advantage for the participating companies (Das and Teng, 1999). This over-riding objective can be differentiated into a variety of sub-motives, inter alia cost and risk reduction and the access to new markets (Albers, 2000; Ebers, 1997).

This paper explores the neglected relationship between airlines and airports from a strategic management perspective. Especially, it seeks to explain the potential benefits of alliances between passenger airlines and their hub-airports.

---

[1]We define an alliance as any voluntarily formed, contractual collaborative arrangement between two or more independent companies with the declared intention of improving long-term competitiveness and thereby enhancing overall performance (Albers, forthcoming; Knoblich, 1969; Das and Teng, 2000).

[2]Regarding alliances between airport companies, *Pantares*, the strategic alliance between Fraport of Germany and Schiphol Airport of the Netherlands, has been the only airport alliance so far. Regardless of the ambitious expectations the partners had before entering into this partnership, this alliance has mainly shown the limits of this kind of inter-airport cooperation. For various reasons, the expected benefits have largely not been realized.

50   S. Albers et al. / Journal of Air Transport Management 11 (2005) 49–58

Infrastructure	Financial system	Accounting	Legal affairs	Management	
Human Resource Management	Personnel recruiting	Pilot-/Crew- and Security- training	Luggage dispatching training	Sales training	In-flight training
Technological Development	Computer Reservation System, Yield Management System, Costumer Relationship Management System			Product development, market studies	Fly Net (Internet on board)
Procurement		Fleet, fuel, information and communication technologies			
Exemplary activities	- Slot allocation - Yield Management - Fuel calculation - Crew planning and assignment - Scheduling - Supply of production resources (aircraft, fuel, ...)	- Ticket offices - Ground Handling / dispatching (passengers, luggage, freight, mail, aircraft) - Flight operations - Service on board - Security checks - Catering - Hub Management Network Management	- Transfer - Maintenance	- Advertisement - Frequent Flyer Programs - E-Tickets - Route planning - Fleet assignment	- Reservation service - Lost and found offices - Complaints management - Lounges
	Inbound Logistics	Operations	Outbound Logistics	Marketing & Sales	Service

Fig. 1. Value chain of the airline.

2. Conceptualization of airline and airport business processes

In producing air transport services, airports act as providers of the on-ground infrastructure for flight operations while airlines offer the transportation services per se. Regardless of the division of labor within the production of their product air transport services, airlines and airports focus on the same targets with quality of service being a defining variable. In aviation, quality is mainly a function of punctuality, reliability and service. International passenger airlines tend to be rather homogenous in terms of sales, service and transportation quality in the air. Competition is more likely to be seen in terms of ground services and in this sense airports are partners in their activities.

The concept of the value chain developed by Michael Porter (1985) offers a useful way to grasp the strategically relevant activities that are important to successful partnerships involving airline and airport companies.

In the value chain, companies' primary activities are distinguished from support activities. Primary activities are those that involve the creation, sale transfer and after-sales assistance of the product, whereas support activities are those that enable the performance of the primary activities. The generic primary activities identified by Porter are inbound logistics, operations, out-

bound logistics, marketing and sales, and service. The support activities are not distinct for different industries and cover the functions of procurement, human resource management, technological development, and infrastructure.

Cooperation among firms is not restricted to specific elements or forms of activities; primary, as well as support, activities can involve cooperation by firms. Major strategic benefits, however, are normally reaped by cooperating in primary activities that are distinctive for the industry under consideration. The focus, therefore, is on primary activities of airport and airline companies, and on the passenger side of the aviation industry.

The generic value chain of an airline is illustrated in Fig. 1. Within each airline category specific activities are presented to provide a basic understanding of the underlying complexity and requirements of the various processes.

Within the airline's value chain, special attention should be set onto the primary activity of operations since this includes the hub management function. If an airline configures its route network as hub-and-spoke-system, hub management (as part of its network management) is of special importance (Doganis, 1991). It affects all conceptual, coordinating and operational tasks for optimizing the quality of hub services. The most important factors influencing hub quality are

S. Albers et al. / Journal of Air Transport Management 11 (2005) 49–58   51

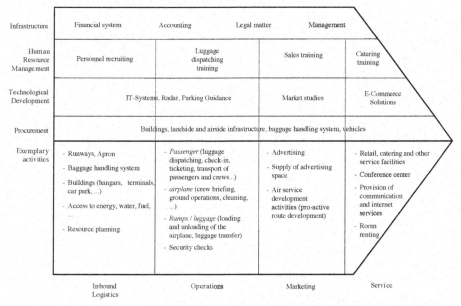

Infrastructure	Financial system	Accounting	Legal matter	Management	
Human Resource Management	Personnel recruiting	Luggage dispatching training	Sales training	Catering training	
Technological Development	IT-Systems, Radar, Parking Guidance		Market studies	E-Commerce Solutions	
Procurement	Buildings, landside and airside infrastructure, baggage handling system, vehicles				
Exemplary activities	- Runways, Apron - Baggage handling system - Buildings (hangars, terminals, car park, ...) - Access to energy, water, fuel, ... - Resource planning	- *Passenger* (luggage dispatching, check-in, ticketing, transport of passengers and crews...) - *airplane* (crew briefing, ground operations, cleaning, ...) - *Ramps / luggage* (loading and unloading of the airplane, luggage transfer) - Security checks	- Advertising - Supply of advertising space - Air service development activities (pro-active route development)	- Retail, catering and other service facilities - Conference center - Provision of communication and internet services - Room renting	
	Inbound Logistics	Operations	Marketing	Service	

Fig. 2. Value chain of the airport.

transfer reliability and punctuality. These influence both the airline's operations as well as the passenger's perception of the airline. Hub management thus includes developing and implementing concepts for optimizing the use of central resources such as gates and aircraft positions, as well as optimizing and securing minimum connection times.[3] Hub management (along with decentralized station/spoke management) is one of the core functions vital for ensurance of ongoing operations. It also concerns the organizing and monitoring of many of the services and activities that are provided by third parties, significantly increasing the complexity and number of interfaces of this core activity.

Primary and supporting activities for a generic airport company are illustrated in Fig. 2.

In its narrow engineering sense, the core tasks of an airport are the supply, maintenance and protection of the infrastructure that is necessary for landing, starting, taxiing and parking of airplanes. In its full social and commercial sense, its role is to facilitate the link between passengers arriving by car, taxi and other modes and

their access to aircraft. Additionally, and to support these primary tasks, the airport provides facilities such as terminals, gates and maintenance facilities which are essential for the completion of flight operations, and which facilitate the access to energy, water or fuel for the aircraft. These activities are the inbound logistics activities of airports.

Underdeveloped until the 1980s, the primary activity marketing has finally turned out as an integral part of the value chain of an airport as well, reflecting its importance as the core activity of a commercially run enterprise also for the airport business (Graham, 2001). Traditional economics distinguishes horizontal and vertical relationships among firms (Tirole, 1989). Airlines and airports involve vertical relationships if the airport is seen providing infrastructure and general services with the airline as its customer. The airline, however, is only one customer of the airport—passengers and other businesses also buy services from airport companies; the interests of passengers, airlines and airports thus overlap. It is in these areas of overlap where coordination of airports' and airlines' efforts can potentially generate the greatest benefits for their customers. Such coordination can be more complex for airports than for airlines. While airports regard both airlines and passengers as their key customers, airlines only view passengers as their customer group and

---

[3]Some airlines have started to alter their traditional hub-and-spoke systems from connecting banks to rolling or continuous hubs to lower costs for the carriers, but usually increasing connection times for passengers. (Dennis, 2000; Goedeking and Sala, 2003).

Table 1
Factors affecting the choice of airports

Passengers	Airlines
Destinations of flights	Slot availability
Image of airport	Network compatibility
Flight fare	Airport fees and availability of discounts
Frequency of service	Other airport costs (e.g. fuel, handling).
Flight availability and timings	Competition
Image and reliability of the airline	Marketing support
Airline alliance policy and frequent-flyer programs	Range and quality of facilities
	Ease of transfer connections
Range and quality of shops, catering and other commercial facilities	Maintenance facilities
	Environmental restrictions
Surface access cost and ease of access to airport/car parking costs	

Source: Graham (2001).

consider themselves as customers of the airports (Graham, 2001).

Choosing an airport is a complex decision for a passenger. In general, a passenger is mobile and looks for the most attractive airline connection and, within geographic limits they often have the choice between several airports. As the available destinations are the predominant decision criteria for passengers, it is important for airports to attract airlines that offer attractive destinations to the passengers. Table 1 provides an overview of key decision criteria for the choice of airports from passenger as well as airline perspectives. For an airline continuing to fly to an airport there must be sufficient profitable traffic.[4] Airports therefore also need to be attractive for passengers. In other words, airports have to satisfy the demands of passengers and airlines simultaneously, and to offer sufficient incentives to keep them as customers.

Both objectives are potentially more likely to be realized if airlines and airports form strategic alliances focused around their consolidated common goals of retaining and attracting passengers. From the airline's perspective, their value for the customer (the passenger), and thus their unique selling proposition, is determined by other factors. Beyond the choice of the most preferable flight connection, additional factors influence passengers' choice of airlines (Table 2).

3. Structuring the airline–airport relationship

3.1. Traditional airline–airport relationships and strategic alliances

Strategic alliances have been characterized as institutionalized cooperation among firms, as contractual arrangements aiming at providing a competitive advan-

---
[4]This argument applies less to distinct hub airports in large hub-and-spoke networks.

Table 2
Factors affecting the choice of airlines

Passengers
Service and/or price
Punctuality of flights
Security
High number of flight destinations
High frequency of flights
Fast and easy transfer connections
Airline Alliance Policy
Reservation Service (e-ticketing, seat reservation, car renting, etc.)

Source: Wiezorek (1998); Tretheway and Oum (1992); Diegruber (1991).

tage for the partners. Reductions in uncertainty ranks high among sub-motives provided for alliance formation (Albers, forthcoming; Sengupta and Perry, 1997) that can be seen as the coordination of the partner firms' long-term, strategic decision-making processes (Delfmann, 1989). Essentially, partners commit to longer-term business relationships and enabling relation-specific investments that, in the absence of such cooperation, would not have taken place. Furthermore, it allows partners to combine their distinct, but complementary, resources and capabilities through a variety of organizational interfaces, potentially allowing creation of innovative products and solutions for their customers. This contrasts to the separable technological and functional systems that are only marginally combined in traditional, arm's length relationships. The combination of resources, as well as relationship specific investments, enable partners to extract relational rents from their cooperation and to gain competitive advantage in their industry (Dyer and Singh, 1998).

Traditionally, airlines and airports have worked together in a more or less stable customer–supplier relationship. So why should an airport and an airline decide to engage into a strategic alliance? Such a decision should not be taken to respond to the alliance

S. Albers et al. / Journal of Air Transport Management 11 (2005) 49–58   53

Table 3
Typical relationships between airlines and airports in key countries

Country	Airline–airport relationship
USA	Airport as landlord and coordinator of services Airlines build their own terminals and facilities
Spain	One central, public airport operator company, owning and developing all (or most) airports of the country Airlines as customers to the airports
France, United Kingdom	Mixture of private and public airport companies, owning and developing their airports Airlines as customers to the airports

formation trend among airlines; the major drivers of airline alliances do not apply for the airport sector (Pal and Weil, forthcoming). It appears that the primary benefit for the formation of airline/airport alliances is the reduction of uncertainty for both partners. While this shift from market-like relations to cooperative links could already be observed in countries like the US, European airports generally lag behind (Table 3).

Sharing investment costs can reduce financial risk. This can involve lower capital expenditure per partner in a project, and also lowers risk if partners show a full commitment to the project. On the other hand, alliance formation expresses a long-term commitment of the airline to the airport and vice versa. The airport offers a safeguard for long-term traffic development and the airline can benefit from preferred treatment. Furthermore, strategic alliances represent a rather flexible governance form between market and hierarchy (Nohria, 1992; Williamson, 1991; Zajac and Olsen, 1993). Strategic alliances thus combine the advantages of flexible, long-term collaboration at a reasonable and foreseeable risk level while promising long-term benefits for both partners. They can be seen as commitment to coordinate strategic decisions by the partners for their mutual benefit.

3.2. Interfaces of airline and airport activities

An activity matrix is used to illustrate potential interfaces of airline and airport activities. The matrix represents the primary activities of airports and airlines on the vertical and the associated goals derived from customer satisfactions on the horizontal axis. Other factors, e.g. the compatibility of an airport with regard to the network of the airline or location-specific environmental regulations—are taken as given and are not considered. The analysis is performed for each sub-goal for the airport and airline companies. If one activity is identified to impact on an objective, the respective cell in the matrix is marked with a cross. If the influence is only limited, a cross in brackets appears (Fig. 3). Mutually beneficial cooperation among airlines and airports is assumed if a specific goal can be

influenced by both airlines and airports; if a column exhibits at least one cross in the airline and one in the airport line.

3.3. Analysis

Regardless of the customer group, each customer is sensitive to travel time considerations, and thus, to the punctuality of flights. While a punctual departure is influenced by the actions of both the airline and the airport, airlines generally regard the arrival punctuality as beyond their control due to its dependence on weather and air traffic control authorities. In contrast, the time between a landing and a take-off is dependent on the quality of airport-related services (inbound logistics and operations). Dispatching of airplanes and passengers depends on the quality of planning and controlling of the infrastructure and related process flows, and to the coordination of relevant ground-handling dispatching processes. Furthermore, an airline coordinates the punctuality of their operations through its hub management by optimizing the use of central resources and the timely enactment of relevant processes. Harmonization and integration of technical infrastructure, as well as closer coordination of operative procedures, can reduce irregularities and improve punctual departures. These measures, however, represent relationship-specific investments that are not costless and will not be borne by a partner unless continued commitment can be assured. A strategic alliance covering such areas can provide the necessary commitment.[5]

The objective of good connections is to enable seamless travel: a fast and easy transfer to connecting flights, high-quality connections to flights of alliance partners, and appropriate intermodal transfers (for example the transfer from airplane to rail). Through coordination of tasks within a hub, the operational processes (primary activity operations) of an airline can influence transfer quality. An airport in turn can adjust

---
[5]Punctuality of arrivals may also possibly be improved if air traffic authorities were integrated into the alliance.

54

S. Albers et al. / Journal of Air Transport Management 11 (2005) 49–58

Objectives / Primary Activities	Punctuality	Quality of transfer connections	Accessibility of the airport	Prices and charges	Service	Security	Variety of destinations, frequency and flight times	Image of the airport and the airline	Slot availability	Marketing activities	Access, quality and availability of facilities	Frequent Flyer Programs and airline alliance policy
Airport												
Inbound Logistics	X	X	X	X				X	(X)		X	
Operations	X				X	X		X	(X)			
Marketing			(X)					X		X		
Service				X				X				
Airline												
Inbound Logistics			X				X	X				
Operations		X	X			X		X				
Outbound Logistics								X				
Network Management & Marketing & Sales	X	X						X		X		X
Service				X				X				

Fig. 3. Activity Matrix.

the planning and controlling processes of its terminals, gates and apron and provide an adequate basis for an efficient process design and traffic flow. As this most likely involves changes in the layout of buildings and aprons, the adjustments made by an airport represents relationship-specific investments influenced by airline needs.

The accessibility of the airport plays an important role in the decision making of passengers. In this context, accessibility takes into account the entire time period between starting point (office, home) and reaching the gate at the airport. This embraces the time spent in the journey to the airport, dispatching, check-in, security and waiting until the airplane's departure (Tretheway and Oum, 1992). The aim here is to offer short and comfortable access for the passenger. Airlines are responsible for procedures at the check-in counters, although they may also offer remote check-in facilities at major hotels or city centers. Airports focus on the provision of on-site infrastructure, e.g. car parking (Sterzenbach, 1996)—and also engage in measures to improve their accessibility, e.g. special bus services and railway stations. Regarding this interface, a clear division of labor between airlines and airports seems to apply. The airport takes on necessary processes on the ground to allow the airline to offer its basic transportation services. Coordinated actions can be beneficial to both; however, the accessibility of the airport is generally the airport's domain and responsibility.[6]

Charges are often key determinants in customers' decisions. While deregulation and increasing competition have led to falling prices for many aspects of air transport, their impact on alliances between airlines and airports is limited. This is partly due to the strict international regulatory framework that does not normally allow airports to give discounts to selected carriers.[7] Only in the field of additional, non-standard international services can special agreements between the two partners be arranged that would create benefits for a potential alliance.

Services comprise all service related offers by the airline and the airport along the transportation chain, ranging from the check-in and the waiting and shopping areas at the origin airport to the in-flight services onboard and the handling of the passengers and their luggage at the destination. Since all the services as a whole determine the passengers' perception of the

---

[6]Although Lufthansa and Virgin Atlantic do have involvement in rail services to some of their airports, and in many countries airlines operate limmozine services for their customers.

[7]This is an ICAO rule that applies to international air services. Domestic services are free from this rule and here it often does not apply. Internally countries have sovereign rights to do as they please. In some cases, as with European Union, the right may be abdicated but this is uncommon.

S. Albers et al. / Journal of Air Transport Management 11 (2005) 49–58   55

product and travel experience, this field opens significant potentials for joint efforts of airlines and airports. These allow to actively and effectively address single customer groups.[8]

Security considerations can influence demand patterns, and this seems especially so following the events of September 11, 2001. The perceived need to protect passengers and buildings has risen significantly. Airlines as well as airports treat safety arrangements within their primary activity operations. Consequently an interface can be identified. An alliance between airlines and airports could be formed aimed at improving security before, during and after flights.

Other factors influencing airport choice include the variety and the frequency of destinations offered and the timetable of flights. Passengers favor advantageous flight times as well as a wide and differentiated spectrum of destinations to choose from. For airlines a dense network offers lower costs and thus allows for lower prices. An extensive network fosters loyalty for an entire, multiple-legged journey. Airports and airlines both benefit from this behavior. To increase their competitive advantage airport and airline seek to offer appropriate services that satisfy customers' demands but there are often capacity restrictions—i.e. the limited number of available slots—and constraints of national regulations. An airport can only marginally influence the airlines network planning activities. It is the domain of the airline to set-up and manage its network of routes, even though the airport certainly benefits from a greater variety of destinations. The major lever an airport possesses is to offer an airline an appropriate level of capacity to conform to its network ambitions.

Furthermore, the image, or reputation, of the airport and the airline can influence passenger behavior, although these effects are difficult to quantify. The reputation of an airline, for example, seems to be determined by a view of its price–performance ratio, including the in-flight service, confidence in the reliability of the airplanes, advertisement and sales as well as the quality of the value-added services provided before and after the flight. Similarly, the architecture and atmosphere of the airport infrastructure and services, efforts in sales activities, and the attractiveness of service enterprises seem to impact on the image of an airport. Nevertheless, these factors tend to have only a short-term effect on customers, who take advantage of the fierce price competition between airlines—both within the same market segment and increasingly involving low-cost carriers (Sigala et al., 2002; Lawton, 2002; Morrison, 2001). In particular, established airlines have

started to establish major global alliances with the aim of improving their attractiveness for passengers by extending their networks through partnering and realizing consistent service quality based on the idea of a seamless travel experience throughout the entire alliance network. Sustainable customer loyalty is being promoted through combined frequent flyer programs. Airports use the number of carriers and their quality of service from their facilities for marketing purposes. Airlines, however, have not yet built heavily on the quality characteristics of airports, even though short portraits of relevant airports are usually included in in-flight magazines. Corporate reputations are usually hard to establish and easily fade if not caressed. Long-term, strategic cooperation models therefore appear relevant if airline and airport decide to benefit from the partner's reputation.

By means of an alliance it may be possible to transfer the attitudes of one enterprise to its partner. Consequently within an alliance one partner can profit from the image of the other (image transfer) (Lewis, 1990). Therefore, one may assume that an alliance of firms with well-perceived images can lead to a combined competitive advantages in both the existing and new markets.

The availability of slots affects the decisions of airlines on whether to use a certain airport. To obtain entitlement to specific slots at an airport can be crucial for market access and the competitive position of an airline. Capacity at an airport often determines the availability of slots. An airline, however, cannot influence the overall slot capacity; this is determined by technical and by administrative factors (Pompl, 1998). The technical environment comprises infrastructural components, such as the number of runways, availability of dispatch facilities and air traffic control capacity. These are partially influenced by the airport but are mostly determined by political and environmental factors. Furthermore, administrative factors cover regulations governing the maximum number of flights or night flights. Thus, even though the availability of slots is an issue of special relevance at congested airports, cooperative efforts of airlines and airports may have limited effectiveness in changing the situation. Joint lobbying for changes in regulations or more capacity is often all that can be done.

An airline considers the marketing activities of an airport as an important element for its attractiveness for its own business. This does not only relate to financial incentives, but also includes market studies and advertising (Graham, 2001). Because of the interdependencies in their operations and overlaps in their customer bases, however, an airline/airport alliance that embraces cooperative advertisement may be appropriate to relate to the information needs of passengers.

Access, quality and availability of facilities are factors that affect both airports and airlines. Judging by the amounts they spend, passengers consider the quality and

---

[8]Examples for these group-specific services range from the provision of only a limited range of services for low-cost airlines and their passengers to dedicated terminals for major clients as in Dubai for Emirates or in Frankfurt for Lufthansa and Star Alliance partners.

56　　　　　　　S. Albers et al. / Journal of Air Transport Management 11 (2005) 49–58

Table 4
Development of scheduled services at Munich (2002–2004)

Area	Number of destinations				Number of frequencies				Star Alliance share	
	Star Alliance		Other airlines		Star Alliance		Other airlines		Frequencies	
	2002	2004	2002	2004	2002	2004	2002	2004	2002	2004
Europe	79	83	73	71	1.861	2.085	972	1.107	65.7%	65.3%
Inter-cont.	19	25	26	26	48	90	53	53	47.5%	62.9%
Total	98	108	99	97	1.909	2.175	1.025	1.160	65.1%	65.2%

Source: OAG data for January 2002 and January 2004.

the variety of retailing, catering and other services in an airport as important. In contrast, airlines value ground facilities, e.g. check-in desks, gates, parking possibilities for airplanes, and maintenance facilities. It is the task of the airport as part of the inbound logistics functions to provide the required infrastructural facilities.

3.4. A typology of airline–airport alliances

The potential fields of cooperation among airline and airports seem to fall into three major categories: capacity, marketing, and security.

Capacity-oriented cooperations appear to be the most promising area for strategic alliances between airports and airlines. The associated goals include purely operational issues (such as the optimization of processes through improved process design, interface reduction and communication improvement), although to achieve associated benefits these need to be redesigned and coordinated on a longer-term basis of collaborative agreements that ensures that partners are willing to engage in specific investments, and in infrastructure-related tasks. There is a broad bandwidth of possible joint activities ranging from inexpensive, easy to implement process and communication changes to capital-intensive infrastructure investments. While these activities, and their effects, can be planned and foreseen relatively easily, marketing-oriented cooperation focuses mainly on image transfer between airline and airport and is highly dependent on a number of external influences. Security-oriented cooperation between airlines and airports are important, but do not require long-term commitment and are thus, not of a strategic nature.

There are thus a broad variety of potentials for strategic alliances between airlines and airports. To put more flesh on the bones, we move to look at an example from German aviation that relates to partners investments in the construction of a joint terminal by Lufthansa and Munich Airport.

4. Lufthansa and Munich Airport

In most countries, an airport operating company runs terminals and other facilities, although in the US terminals

are rented or built and operated mainly by airlines or other enterprises. Each airline with sufficient traffic volume tries to operate its own terminal or at least its own gates. In Europe, the relationship between airlines and airports has started to change. Usually, the home base carrier and its partners exclusively use the best and most modern part of a terminal. With their cooperation at Munich airport, the airport operator Flughafen München GmbH and Lufthansa German Airlines have gone a step further. For the first time in Germany an airline has financially participated in the construction of an airport terminal. This came into service on June 29, 2003.

The importance of Lufthansa and the Star Alliance partners for Munich airport is illustrated in Table 4.

The financial participation of the airline in the terminal construction entitles Lufthansa to significantly influence and determine the planning and realization of the terminal. The activity is carried out considering the airline's requirements and with the engagement of its personnel as well as the integration of the airline's alliance partners. The activities in this alliance are the hub management and other aspects of operations activities.

From Flughafen München GmbH's point of view this alliance means a reduction in their royalties and in the operation of dispatching capacities, and may appear disadvantageous. However, through the airline's financial participation the airport's financial expenditure and responsibility as supplier of infrastructure is reduced. On the airport's side, the collaboration integrates its primary activities of inbound logistics. The alliance therefore helps both partners to attain their goals of ensuring and improving the transfer connection quality as well as providing easy access to, and a high quality of, airport facilities.

4.1. Airline—strategic benefits

Advantages for Lufthansa can be realized by enhancing processes in the dispatching and transfer area, or by supplying sufficient capacity to secure new market access. By participating in the construction of a terminal, the airline can influence the planning and building phases. Operating its own terminal, the airline has the possibility of determining and controlling the

S. Albers et al. / Journal of Air Transport Management 11 (2005) 49–58   57

organization and personnel for the new facility. It can realize the organization gains as regard to design (e.g. wall decoration in corporate colors) and facilities. The latter includes gates aimed at facilitating faster and more comfortable transfers. Supported by a corresponding flight schedule, the attractiveness of connections at the airport can be considerably improved to increase the transfer acceptance of the passengers.

Furthermore, long-term rights connected with the alliance create important barriers of entry to the market especially for airlines that were previously not represented at the airport. Due to its financial participation, the airline can use the terminal exclusively with its alliance partners and secure the scarce resources involved. Overall, the system reduces the intensity of airline competition.

Apart from the general advantages of an alliance for Lufthansa, a specific strategic benefit exists at Munich. The airport, contrary to most other international airports, does not yet have the limitations found at most other European airports. This gives Lufthansa the opportunity to develop Munich further as its second hub within a long-term strategic business plan.

4.2. Airport—strategic benefits

For Flughafen München GmbH the alliance produces cost-saving potential and risk reduction. The reduction of costs is achieved by lower investments in airport expansion because the airline pays a share, but there are also savings in human resource management. Mainly non-airport employees, causing the personnel costs to be lower than for an independently constructed and operated facility, operate the jointly constructed terminal.

While a runway has an economic life of at least a decade, the terminal's life is longer. If an airport enlarges or improves its facilities to meet the needs of Lufthansa, providing the carrier survives, this becomes a strategic instrument in reducing uncertainty concerning the viability of the investment concerned. Effectively the airline covers part of the risk concerning the committed capital.

4.3. Problems

Infrastructure extension at Munich is limited by the available air space at the airport, but the ground area can be extended as needed. In contrast, problems may arise concerning the alliance's contractual arrangement, especially regarding adequate divisions of decision rights, the distribution of shares, or the regulation of future competencies (Albers, forthcoming; Reuer et al., 2002).

Additional problems can stem from potentially adverse effects of the business cycle on Lufthansa's finances. While with the alliance Lufthansa secures market access, but is still susceptible to demand fluctuations. Capacity expansions involve large investments but airlines have traditionally raised capital only for fleet development. Lufthansa has now also invested in airport infrastructure. In contrast to fleet size, infrastructure cannot be easily adapted to changing conditions. Nevertheless, system shocks caused by sudden economic fluctuations, terrorist attacks or wars can immediately reduce demand for air transport services. This poses potential financial problems in an industry where airlines have not been commercially very astute in the past.

For Flughafen München GmbH, problems can arise from having a strong dependence on one airline. An alliance increases the power of Lufthansa and thus its influence. Due to its dominance the airline may be able to attain its goals not in dispatching and other areas but in doing so, the autonomy of the airport is reduced. Besides the increased bargaining power on Lufthansa's side, Flughafen München GmbH is also confronted with an increasing risk as regard to the economic well-being of its major customer. A bankruptcy of Lufthansa would translate into severe consequences for the airport. Another major problem for the airport is to attract business to its older facility. The alliance with Lufthansa may well make this even less attractive for other airlines. While it may open the chance for modernization of the terminal, at the same time it means substantial short-term losses for Flughafen München GmbH.

5. Conclusion

This paper has looked at the potential for cooperation between airlines and airports and identified the fields of capacity, marketing and security as having some potential. Realizable and beneficial areas of cooperation in the form of strategic alliances have been proposed and related to the reduction of uncertainty and allowing the extraction of relational rent for the partners. The most promising alliance type (capacity oriented alliance) has been exemplified by the case of Lufthansa and Munich airport.

This, however, is only a first step in the conceptualization of airline–airport relationships, the opportunities to be explored and the benefits that can be achieved by its re-evaluation. The proposals offer suggestions and starting-points for a further investigation of alliance possibilities. We submit, however, that a variety of additional forms exist regarding the specific parameter values of capacity and marketing-oriented alliances. The strategy of transferring traffic to other carriers in the short-distance sector or to nearby regional airports, for example, may be useful in facilitating traffic growth.

58 S. Albers et al. / Journal of Air Transport Management 11 (2005) 49–58

A variety of factors regarding competitors and other customers are also missed; for example, it may be expected that a preferred treatment of one specific airline would lead to a perceived discrimination of other airlines as customers of the airport in focus. The issues raised here, however, provide a valid and interesting platform for these interesting and relevant research questions as regard to airport–airline relations.

Strategic alliances between airlines and airports will likely be of increasing importance in the future, caused by the continuous growth of air traffic and the progressive opening of the markets. The indications are that the tendency for liberalization and globalization will continue intensifying. In the face of increasing competition, alliances between airports and airlines offer convenient instruments for developing a long-term competitive advantage.

Acknowledgements

The authors wish to thank JATM editor Ken Button for invaluable, constructive suggestions and comments on previous drafts of this paper.

References

Agusdinata, B., de Klein, W., 2002. The dynamics of airline alliances. Journal of Air Transport Management 8, 201–211.

Albers, S., 2000. Nutzenallokation in Strategischen Allianzen von Linienluftfrachtgesellschaften. Working Paper No. 101, Department of Business Policy and Logistics. University of Cologne, Cologne.

Albers, S., The Design of Alliance Governance Systems. Kölner Wissenschaftsverlag, Cologne (forthcoming).

Brueckner, J.K., 2003. International airfares in the age of alliances: the effects of codesharing and antitrust immunity. The Review of Economics and Statistics 85 (1), 105–118.

Carney, M., Mew, K., 2003. Airport governance reform: a strategic management perspective. Journal of Air Transport Management 9, 221–232.

Das, T.K., Teng, B.-S., 1999. Managing risks in strategic alliances. Academy of Management Executive 13 (4), 50–62.

Das, T.K., Teng, B.-S., 2000. A resource-based theory of strategic alliances. Journal of Management 26, 31–61.

Delfmann, W., 1989. Das Netzwerkprinzip als Grundlage integrierter Unternehmensführung. In: Delfmann, W. (Ed.), Der Integrationsgedanke in der Betriebswirtschaftslehre. Gabler, Wiesbaden.

Dennis, N., 2000. Scheduling issues and network strategies for international airline alliances. Journal of Air Transport Management 6 (2), 75–85.

Diegruber, J., 1991. Erfolgsfaktoren Nationaler Europäischer Linienluftverkehrsgesellschaften im Markt der 90er Jahre. Universitätsverlag, Konstanz.

Doganis, R., 1991. Flying Off Course—The Economics of International Airlines, second ed. Routledge, London, New York.

Dyer, J., Singh, H., 1998. The relational view: cooperative strategies and sources of interorganizational competitive advantage. Academy of Management Review 23, 660–679.

Ebers, M., 1997. Explaining Inter-organizational network formation. In: Ebers, M. (Ed.), The Formation of Inter-Organizational Networks. Oxford University Press, Oxford, New York.

Goedeking, P., Sala, S., 2003. Breaking the bank. Airline Business 19 (9), 93–97.

Graham, A., 2001. Managing Airports—An International Perspective. Butterworth-Heinemann, Oxford.

Knoblich, H., 1969. Zwischenbetriebliche Kooperation—Wesen, Formen und Ziele. Zeitschrift für Betriebswirtschaft (ZfB) 39, 497–514.

Lawton, T.C., 2002. Cleared for Take-Off. Ashgate, Aldershot.

Lewis, J.D., 1990. Partnerships for Profit. Structuring and Managing Strategic Alliances. Free Press, New York.

Morrison, S., 2001. Actual, adjacent and potential competition: estimating the full effect of southwest airlines. Journal of Transport Economics and Policy 35, 239–256.

Nohria, N., 1992. Is a network perspective a useful way of studying organizations? In: Nohria, N., Eccles, R.G. (Eds.), Networks and Organizations: Structure, Form, and Action. Harvard Business School Press, Boston.

Oum, T.H., Park, J.-H., Zhang, A., 2000. Globalization and Strategic Alliances. The Case of the Airline Industry. Pergamon, Amsterdam.

Pal, A., Weil, W., Evaluating airport cooperation and acquisition strategies. In: Delfmann, W., Baum, H., Auerbach, S. (Eds.), Strategic Management in the Aviation Industry. Kölner Wissenschaftsverlag, Cologne (forthcoming).

Pels, E., 2001. A note on airline alliances. Journal of Air Transport Management 7, 3–7.

Pompl, W., 1998. Luftverkehr—Eine ökonomische und politische Einführung, third ed. Springer, Berlin.

Porter, M.E., 1985. Competitive Advantage. Creating and Sustaining Superior Performance. Free Press, New York.

Reuer, J.J., Zollo, M., Singh, H., 2002. Post-formation dynamics in strategic alliances. Strategic Management Journal 23, 135–151.

Sengupta, S., Perry, M., 1997. Some antecedents of global strategic alliance formation. Journal of International Marketing 5, 31–50.

Sigala, M., Christou, E., Baum, T., 2002. The impact of low cost airlines on business travel. In: Keller, P., Bieger, T. (Eds.), Air Transport and Tourism. 52nd Congress 2002 of the Association Internationale d'Experts Scientifique du Tourisme. Editions AIEST, St. Gall.

Sterzenbach, R., 1996. Luftverkehr, second ed. Oldenbourg, Munich, Vienna.

Tirole, J., 1989. The Theory of Industrial Organization. MIT Press, Cambridge, London.

Tretheway, M.W., Oum, T.H., 1992. Airline Economics: Foundations for Strategy and Policy. University of British Columbia, Vancouver.

Wiezorek, B., 1998. Strategien europäischer Fluggesellschaften in einem liberalisierten Weltluftverkehr. Universitäts-Verlag, Dortmund.

Williamson, O.E., 1991. Comparative economic organization: the analysis of discrete structural alternatives. Administrative Science Quarterly 36, 269–296.

Zajac, E.J., Olsen, C.P., 1993. From transaction cost to transactional value analysis: implications for the study of interorganizational strategies. Journal of Management Studies 30, 132–145.

18

Airport alliances and mergers − Structural change in the airport industry?

Peter Forsyth, Hans-Martin Niemeier, Hartmut Wolf

ABSTRACT

Keywords:
Airport economics
Mergers and alliances
Airport competition

Recent years have seen a global trend towards the emergence of multi-airport companies operating at a global scale. This paper employs industrial and transaction costs economics to identify the main drivers that shape the patterns of international cross-ownership structures that have emerged in the airport industry. In addition, implications for competition and competition policy are drawn.

© 2010 Published by Elsevier Ltd.

1. Introduction

For decades airports were either operated as single entities or as part of national airport systems. Since the mid-1990s, however, in parallel with the global wave of airport privatizations, private investors entered the scene who often, in cooperation with already established airport companies, collected equity shares of airports across national borders. The result was the creation of airport holding companies that now operate on an international scale. One of the first to do so were Hochtief AG, a major private German construction company, and Aer Rianta, a division of the publicly owned Dublin Airport Authority, which together joined forces to create a consortium that now holds a variety of equity shares in European airports under the name Airport Partners. Later on equity investment funds entered the market for airport shares like, e.g. Macquarie Airports which now holds equity shares of airports in Australia, Belgium, Denmark and the UK. In some cases airports formed strategic alliances, with the former Pantares Alliance between Shiphol and Frankfurt formed in 2001 being one of the early examples of an airport alliance.

Initially it may seem that the appearance of mergers and alliances between airports simply replicates a trend already observed in the airline industry. Some observers of the industry had already stated that the formation of a few large airport groups would be an inevitable result of airline deregulation (Doganis, 2001). It still remains unclear, however, whether the trend is being driven by systematic considerations that will trigger structural change in the markets for airport services and, thus, affect competition and efficiency of the international airport system, or whether it reflects the *ad hoc* acquisition of assets by investors as the airport markets has

opened to private capital. In case of the former a competition authority may have to think of the possible anti-competitive effects of airport mergers and alliances, whereas latter they do not need to do so.

2. The drivers of consolidation: some lessons from the airline industry

To understand whether the trend to consolidation of the airport industry only reflects the search of private capital for new profit opportunities or whether it may be driven by strategic industry-specific considerations of investors, it may be worthwhile to turn to the airline industry to search for the rationales of consolidation there. Both the airline and airport industries are network industries, which means that the production of air transport and complementary infrastructure services can be characterized by considerable economies of density and scope. Both industries together − by providing complementary services to each other − serve the need to link places by air transport.

With regards to the airline industry, we note two things: first, opportunities for airline mergers are still limited because most countries and international air service agreements stick to. Consolidation in the global airline industry has mainly been through the forming of strategic alliances, although mergers have also taken place. Second, alliances between network carriers have become common, while alliances between low cost airlines and/or charter airlines remain rare. These type of airline differ in that the first operate integrated route networks centered around one or multiple hubs offering passengers a dense network of flight connections, while low cost and charter airlines typically focus on point-to-point networks. Integration of networks may, therefore, be the most powerful force behind consolidation in the airline industry.

50   *P. Forsyth et al. / Journal of Air Transport Management 17 (2011) 49–56*

Several general rationales exist for consolidation.[1]

- *Improving technical efficiency*: Joint production and distribution allows partners to realize economics of scale and density; e.g. code sharing allows airlines to offer passengers higher flight frequencies.
- *Reducing transaction costs to customers*: Airlines that offer connecting services to passengers and freight forwarders may increase profits by joint marketing of their services on the basis of "one stop shopping". This may save on transaction costs if customers making connecting flights only need to contact one partner, if joint branding of services makes it easier for customers to assess the quality of complementary service, and if airlines can coordinate flight schedules and adjust their networks to offer passengers seamless travel.
- *Eliminating market imperfections* adversely affect airlines serving only parts of an air transport network but many customers demand connecting flights and complementary services. If carriers only provide legs of a network where carriers have considerable market power with respect to their own services, then uncoordinated price setting by each carrier generates multiple price mark-ups on marginal costs reducing profit for airline. Joint pricing by airlines offering complementary services reduces price mark-ups to one, thus potentially increasing profit opportunities for all carriers. Joint pricing of complementary services also benefits customers, as prices are lower than they would be if each carrier sets its own prices, not taking the double price mark up effect for the entirety of the journeys that customers make (Tirole, 1992).
- *Overcoming regulatory restrictions* that prevent airlines from entering new markets or expanding in markets they already serve may take a number of forms, e.g. circumventing restrictions on traffic rights laid down in international air service agreements or foreign ownership limitations.
- *Getting access to resources* is a challenge when there is scarce take off and landing slots at airports.
- *Lessening of competitive pressures by price collusion* allows air carriers to earn supernormal profits. To be effective, however, this strategy needs barriers to market entry by potential rivals. Regulatory restrictions, as well as strategies by the industry, such as frequent flyer programs, may make it hard for newcomers to enter established markets.

3. The drivers of consolidation in the airport services industry

The airport industry may be described by the following characteristics with regard to

- *Market structures*: The airport industry is characterized by horizontal as well as vertical market structures. The former refers to competition between airports serving the same, or overlapping, catchment areas, and the latter to flight services linking airports. Linked airports provide air traffic to each other as point of origins and also receive traffic from each other as points of destination, thus, the economics of each airport's activities does not only depend on its own actions but also those of other airports to which airlines offer flight connections.

- *The range of services airports provide to customers*: Airports are multi-service industries providing infrastructure, ground handling and non-aviation services.
- *The institutional framework within which providers of airport services operate*: While the provision of infrastructure services of major airports worldwide is typically subject to some form of economic regulation, non-aviation and ground-handling services are usually not regulated.[2]

We analyse whether the same rationales identified as drivers for consolidation in the airline industry may also work in the airport industry. To do this, we distinguish between the services that airports provide to customers.

3.1. Non-aviation services

The non-aviation business of airports comprises a diverse range of services that are not directly related to air transportation. They include the leasing of terminal facilities for commercial offerings by specialised firms and the operation of shops, conference and parking facilities, etc. by the airport company. Non-aviation services are local services by nature. They are not complementary across airports. Service providers compete against similar services offered by rivals off airport and against services offered at competing airports. Thus, providers of non-aviation services operate within horizontal market structures, but not within vertical ones. What may be the potential drivers of consolidation in the non-aviation business?

- *Improving technical efficiency*: There may be some – however probably limited – scope for realizing cost economies by joint purchase of goods and services that airport companies offer directly to flight passengers, visitors to the airport and employees working at the airport site. There may also be some opportunities for improving marketing by the transfer of know-how between airports on how to allocate terminal capacity to different commercial offerings and how to design best contracts for the lease of terminal and other non-aviation facilities as well as the operation of commercial services offered by airport companies themselves. However, transferring knowledge about best practice in these areas does not need consolidation across airports, but can also be acquired by buying consultancy services by other airports or independent consultants.
- *Reducing transaction costs to customers*: As non-aviation services are not complementary across airports, potential for joint marketing seem to be limited. Customers do not need opportunities for one stop shopping of services provided at airports. There might be, however, some gains of joint branding across airports with regards to the quality of special services offered to customers who, e.g. search for office space to organize business meetings.
- *Eliminating market imperfections*: Because non-aviation services are not complementary across airports, there is no need for joint marketing strategies that aim at preventing the loss of profit opportunities within a vertical market structure.
- *Overcoming regulatory restrictions*: Non-aviation services are typically not subject to regulatory restrictions that prevent suppliers to enter new markets or expand their services in already established ones.

---

[1] For example, see Brueckner and Pels (2005), Li (2000), and Iatrou (2007).

[2] Entry to the ground-handling market may be restricted by legal restrictions.

P. Forsyth et al. / Journal of Air Transport Management 17 (2011) 49–56 51

- *Getting access to resources*: The provision of non-aviation services needs space on airport, which, however, is under control of the local airport company. Thus, mergers and alliances may help airport companies to expand their non-aviation business by offering these services at other airports.
- *Lessening of competitive pressures by price collusion*: In principle, mergers and alliances between airports serving the same, or considerably overlapping, catchment areas may be an appropriate means to make price collusion sustainable which would help these airports to sustain high profits in the non-aviation business. To be successful, however, such a strategy would control of the aviation part of infrastructure services, as revenues in the non-aviation business not only depends on the supply of non-aviation services, but also on airport choices by air travelers. Airport choices mainly depend on airport location as well as the price and quality of air transport and infrastructure services offered at that airport.

3.2. Ground handling

Ground handling comprises a diverse set of services, among them catering, cleaning, freight loading and fuelling of aircraft, the pushing off of aircraft from terminal piers, passenger transport on the apron, etc. At most airports only a small number of ground-handling firms compete for local contracts with airlines; specific services are often provided by just one firm. The provision of these services is highly work intensive while it needs only small irreversible investment into equipment and marketing. Different services are easily technical separable. Thus, economic barriers to market entry by potential rivals are low suggesting that, in the absence of legal barriers to market entry, even if only one firm is providing ground handling at a specific airport *de facto* contestability may exist (Wolf, 2003). Thus, service providers operate within horizontal market structures not only with respect to inter-airport, but also to on-airport competition.

The provision of ground handling differs from providing non-aviation services in that it is needed at both ends of a flight. Thus, services at both airports are complementary with costs and quality of handling at both potentially affecting the airlines' flight schedules and costs and, ultimately, its willingness-to-pay for these services. Therefore, providers of ground handling operate within a vertical market structure with the efficiency of services at one airport potentially impacting on efficiency at other airports. Given these features there are a number of potential drivers for consolidation of ground handling across airports

- *Improving technical efficiency*: Ground handling is a labour intensive business in which different kinds of services are easily separable. Thus, the efficient size of many firms is small implying that there are few opportunities for improving efficiency through mergers, although there may be some potential for cost savings with respect to joint purchasing of equipment. The labour intensity of the activity, however, means most costs are local, generated at the airport where the ground handling takes place. Even potential gains from joint purchase of equipment seem to be limited. Finally, with regards to potential transfers of know-how on managing ground-handling services, there are a number of opportunities to facilitate such transfer other than via mergers and alliances.
- *Reducing transaction costs to customers*: One stop shopping may help customers save on transaction costs, but such savings are often limited because of uncertainty about the quality of service offered. Airlines may react to this by learning which ground-handling provider are superior and adjust contracts

accordingly. Further, as barriers to enter ground-handling markets are low, potential quality competition may push up service quality. Finally, where allowed, airlines can opt for self-handling.
- *Eliminating market imperfections*: As ground handling is highly labour intensive and most of the equipment employed can be transferred between airports, ground-handling providers only need to make small irreversible investments. Thus, ground-handling markets are highly competitive by nature. Therefore market imperfections that may drive consolidation across airports for strategic reasons do almost not exist.
- *Overcoming regulatory restrictions*: In many countries there are few explicit regulations on market entry.
- *Getting access to resources*: Providers of ground handling need infrastructure on airports to park vehicles and access the apron to handle planes. Consolidation of ground handling across airports does little to help providers gain access to new markets, and if infrastructure is subject to competitive access, as in the EU, there is no need for strategic consolidation.
- *Lessening of competitive pressures by price collusion*: Because providing ground-handling services needs little irreversible investments, barriers to market entry by newcomers are low. Thus, collusion between incumbents may not help to generate supernormal profits.

3.3. Infrastructure

Infrastructure largely comprises facilities that are directly related to air transport; aprons, runways, terminals and baggage handling systems. They are provided by airport companies that either operate their own facilities or manage the operation of facilities owned by another. As the providers of infrastructure facilities compete across airports that serve the same regional markets, while offering complementary services to airlines across airports that serve the same O&D markets, infrastructure provision is characterized by horizontal as well as vertical market structures. In contrast to ground handling, however, the provision of infrastructure services is characterized by economies of density and involves large sunk costs. Potential entrants to the market, therefore, are confronted with economic barriers. In many cases, planning restrictions make it difficult to build new airport facilities close to an existing airport. In this context, there are numerous strategic considerations to take into account when examining consolidation.

- *Improving technical efficiency*: Most of the costs of infrastructure provision are local and, therefore, the potential for improving technical efficiency by forming an airport group is generally limited. Alliances may, though, offer some transfer of know-how.
- *Reducing transaction costs to customers*: The potential for lower transaction cost to customers is also limited because the most important determinants of airlines' airport choices are the traffic volumes that can be generated and the airlines' costs of serving the airport.
- *Eliminating market imperfections*: One rationale for the formation of an airport group may be the elimination, through cooperation on service offerings and the setting of airport charges, of market imperfections. By eliminating multiple price mark-ups on marginal costs, airport groups may improve their profits while making their services more attractive to airlines. However, as the airports' infrastructure services are typically subject to economic regulation the efficiency of both strategies depends on the effectiveness of regulation.

52　　　　　　　　*P. Forsyth et al. / Journal of Air Transport Management 17 (2011) 49–56*

- *Overcoming regulatory restrictions*: Compared to the airline industry there are hardly any explicit barriers similar to the restrictions on foreign ownership in air service agreements.
- *Getting access to resources*: While there may be few regulations restrictions, there may be a variety of other barriers to enter into markets where public authorities envisage airports as strategic assets for regional policy. In Australia and the UK, for example, while there are fully privatized airports, the majority of airports in Continental Europe are partially privatized with a minority share for the private investors. North American airports are primarily publicly owned.
- *Lessening of competitive pressures by price collusion*: Investments in infrastructure are large sunk, and land scarcity and environmental protection typically prevent newcomers entering established markets collusion between airports serving largely overlapping markets may help protect their quasi rents. This may be important if airports compete and an empty core problem arises that would, without some form of collusion, leads to market instability.

In summary, while transfer of know-how can play a temporary role in all services, the analysis has derived drivers for consolidation of airport services. In the non-aviation business, the need to get access to infrastructure seems to be the major potential driver for consolidation. Although complementarities of ground service offerings across airports exist, they cannot be major drivers for consolidation because markets are competitive by nature, forming strategic alliances of service providers across airports or mergers can do little to reduce transaction costs for customers or to lessen market imperfections. This is different for infrastructure services. Moves towards more consolidation may be driven by market imperfections either to eliminate double marginalization in vertical related markets or by monopolizing horizontal related markets.

4. Types of consolidation in the airport industry

Consolidation in the airport industry may take place either by forming strategic alliances or entering into mergers. We identify the rationales of airport companies to either become a member of an alliance or to merge with each other. We begin with a brief general discussion about the pro's and con's for each alternative. Next we present some stylized facts about a number of airport alliances as well as multi-airport companies.

4.1. Strategic alliances and multiple-airport ownership as governance structures

Strategic airport alliances and multi-airport companies differ in that they represent different governance structures. In case of an alliance, partners coordinate their strategies while staying independent. Thus decision making within an alliance is decentralized in the sense that all partners decide on their operations but promise each other to take the effects of their decisions on alliance partners into account. In contrast, the creation of a multi-airport company generates a centralized governance structure within which hierarchical decision making for all of the merged firms takes place.

Whether an alliance or merger is the preferred mode of consolidation depends on the transaction costs associated with each.[3] In case of complex transactions, market transaction costs

might become large if partners stay independent while relying on the legal system to enforce each other's obligations. If so, a merger might be preferred as it allows to solve conflicts of interest by central decision of the head of the multi-airport company. On the contrary, the enforcement of even complex contracts may incur little costs if no legal or economic obstacles prevent partners to leave an actual agreement and to enter into a market contract with another partner. This exit option creates pressure for each of the partners to fulfill their obligations efficiently. It is much harder to set efficient incentives by internal rules for those working within a merged company than for independent firms that together join forces while facing the threat of exit by partners in case they do not fulfill their obligations.

If the threat of exit is the more credible the less partners have to make major irreversible investments into the partnership which will be lost if the partnership is terminated (Williamson, 1985). From this we might conclude that consolidation in the airport industry will take place via the formation of airport alliances if partners join forces in areas that do not need considerable transaction-specific investments. In contrast, while the formation of multi-airport companies will be the preferred mode of consolidation in case such investments are needed to make the partnership workable. The first one refers especially to joint branding, purchase and marketing especially in the non-aviation and the ground handling business, while the latter one mainly refers to coordinated investments across airports into infrastructure facilities and also to partnerships that aim to lessen competition in the infrastructure business by price collusion.

4.2. Stylized facts about airport alliances

To understand what drove the formation of airport alliances it is useful to expand on the stated objectives of cooperations.

GICA, was established by Washington Dulles International and Chateroux-Doels Airports in 1999 and grew to 21 members by 2001 (Sunnucks, 2002).[4] It still operates today. The aim of GICA was "to create a worldwide organization of airports joining together for the purpose of promoting and developing the air cargo and logistics business" (Gateway, 2000). Its stated goals are the promotion of a global brand for cargo, an improvement of the airports' image in the cargo business, joint international marketing, the raising of the attractiveness of member airports for freight alliances, the establishment of an agreement on common operational standards, the operation of a common internet site, and the establishment of a common internship program. The alliance was mainly formed to foster joint marketing by establishing a common brand for member airports. However, according to Tretheway (2001) its success was limited.

Members of the AHS-alliance, which was established in the year 2000 as a joint venture of three German airports and grew up in terms of number of members in the following years,[5] provide common quality standards for ground-handling services at airports, enabling customers one stop shopping (Aviation Handling Systems). One might conclude, that the rationale for the establishing of the alliance was – as in the case of GICA – to improve on the marketing side. In addition, another rationale might be potential benefits from intra-alliance transfer of know-how on best operational practices within the alliance.

---

[3] Transaction costs comprise market as well as managerial costs, with the former representing costs generated by the writing and enforcement of contracts between independent partners and the latter to the costs of arranging and managing transactions that take place within a single firm (Williamson, 1985).

[4] Other members were the airports of Accra, Avalon, Bucharest, Casablanca, Cologne-Bonn, Dublin, Fairbanks, Hamilton, Houston, Kuala Lumpur, Manchester, Milan, Sharjah, Shenzen, and Stockholm (Sunnucks, 2002).

[5] The founding members of AHS were the airports of Bremen, Hamburg and Hannover. Later Muenster/Osnabrueck, Nuremberg and Stuttgart joined the alliance.

P. Forsyth et al. / Journal of Air Transport Management 17 (2011) 49–56   53

Pantares, established in 2000 by Fraport and Schiphol Group, represents an effort of two airport companies to join in a number of airport operational activities. It aims to produce co-operation in terminal and retail management, handling of aircraft and cargo, facility management, information technology, and international joint ventures. Initially, financial analysts expected Pantares to reap significant value because of the complementary skill sets of the companies. While Fraport was successful in ground handling, it was weak in retailing, Schiphol had the reverse portfolio of strengths (Morgan Stanley, 2001). One might, therefore, conclude that the formation of Pantares was largely driven by an attempt to exchange know-how amongst partners with regard to improve each partner's performance in complementary business areas. However, the performance of this alliance failed to fulfill its expectations. The initial plan to partner with Areoporti di Roma and the operator of Milan's Linate and Malpensa airports was never pursued, and Pantares was not mentioned by analysts again.

Given the negative experience with Panteras, Schiphol never-theless engaged in a new alliance this time with Aerporto De Paris (ADP). The objectives of the ADP–Schiphol alliances are

- *Aviation*: Improve competitiveness through dual hub and best-in-class service levels.
- *Non-aviation*: Retail, real estate and telecom activities through exchange of best practices.
- *International airport developments* with a key focus on strengthening the dual hub within SkyTeam network (ADP and Schiphol, 2008).

Each partner acquired an 8% stake in the other, although Schiphol is government owned and ADP is partially privatized and listed at the stock exchange. The French government will reduce its share from 68% to 60%. The alliance was implemented stepwise by steering groups and reciprocal membership in the supervisory board of each airport. The alliance is expected to generate revenue and cost synergies of €71 million per annum on a fully phased basis by 2013 and reduce capital expenditure by €18 million per annum thereafter; the savings coming 45–50% from aviation, 30–35% from retail, and 20–25% from other activities.

While it is early to evaluate the performance of this alliance, it is confronted by undoubted challenges. As with other alliances, know-how transfer and cost savings through standardization of processes, common new developments and joint purchasing are motivation but the potential synergies for ADP, equal to 6 % of earnings before interest, taxes, depreciation and amortization forecasts for 2012 (Morgan Stanley, 2008), had no impact on share price of ADP. The projected operating cost savings of €69 million relative to $1.538 million in operating costs for ADP and €20 million

relative to $841 million for Schiphol amount to 4.5% and to 2.5% are relative small compared to alliances and mergers in other industries where proponents usually claim double-digit savings. In addition the forecast synergies stemming from the pooling of purchases of specific equipment could be reaped without joint shares holdings. In general the specific cost savings from alliances may be smaller than claimed (Hüschelrath, 2009).

Further, ADP–Schiphol state that they will change their investment policy in foreign airports "to focus on opportunities that will the support dual hub concept within the international SkyTeam network in particular, and adopt an opportunistic approach in non-SkyTeam zones" (ADP and Schiphol Group, 2008). This could be interpreted as strategic rationale to overcome market imperfections which so far has not been a source of alliances or multi-airport companies.

"Strengthening the development of the dual hub strategy" is another strategic motive as it tries to change market structure by reducing hub competition. The merger between KLM and Air France, together with liberalization of bilateral air service agreements, has increased competition between the two hubs. De Wit (2009) shows that KLM and AF serve 52 unique destinations from Charles De Gaulle and 35 unique destinations from Amsterdam; 28 destinations are served from both hubs. As the hubs are currently not capacity constrained, and they are in a position to compete or cooperate for additional traffic; the latter strategy has been chosen.

In summary, with the exception of the ADP–Schiphol alliance, it is unlikely that possible consolidation of the airport industry will take place by airport companies forming strategic alliances to cooperate in the provision of infrastructure services. There might be limited scope to enter into alliance agreements in the areas of ground handling and the non-aviation business. However, if such moves would occur, there would probably be driven mainly by efforts to join forces on marketing to create a common branding for member's services and to allow customers for one stop shopping and to transfer know-how between members to improve performance in specific market segments. As barriers to market entry are low in the areas of ground handling and non-aviation business, strategic alliances between airports that are limited to these airport functions would not hamper competition in these markets seriously.

4.3. Stylized facts on the formation of multi-airport companies

By multi-airport companies we mean companies which involve common ownership of a number of airports, or cases in which an airport has a majority holding, or at least a strategic minority holding, in other airports. There are several types of airport companies:

Table 1
Airport companies: shareholdings and competition.

Airport company	Majority interest in more than an airport	Strategic holdings in airports	Ownership of potentially competitive airports	Operating concessions for other airports
Abertis (TBI)	Y	Y	N	Y
AENA	Y	Y	Y	Y
Aeroports de Paris	Y	Y	Y	Y
Dublin Airport Authority	N	Y	N	N
Ferrovial/BAA	Y	Y	Y	N
Fraport	Y	Y	N	Y
Hochtief (HTA)	Y	Y	N	N
Infratil	Y	Y	N	N
Macquarie	Y	Y	N	N
Peel	Y	Y	Y	N
Schiphol	Y	Y	Y	N

Key: Y – Yes; N – No.Source: Carter and Ezard (2007), Company websites.

Table 2

Links between airports that constitute an airport group in 2008.

	Abertis[b]		AENA[b]		Dublin airport authority		Ferrovial		Fraport		Hochtief		Macquarie		Schiphol	
	Airport	Aircraft seats to airport group relative to seats (%)	Airport	Aircraft seats to airport group relative to seats (%)	Airport	Aircraft seats to airport group relative to seats (%)	Airport	Aircraft seats to airport group relative to seats (%)	Airport	Aircraft seats to airport group relative to seats (%)	Airport	Aircraft seats to airport group relative to seats (%)	Airport	Aircraft seats to airport group relative to seats (%)	Airport	Aircraft seats to airport group relative to seats (%)
	Belfast International	7.9	Cartagena (Colombia)	3.6	Cork	23.6	Aberdeen	n.a.	Frankfurt	2.3	Athens International	1.5	Copenhagen	2.8	Amsterdam	4.1
	Bogotá	16.3	Barranquilla (Colombia)	6.2	Dublin	8.4	Edinburgh	30.3	Hahn	0.0	Düsseldorf International	5.2	Brussels	4.0	New York	1.8
	Burbank	0.0	Cali (Colombia)	3.3	Shannon	15.3	Glasgow International	22.5	Delhi	1.0	Hamburg	6.8	Bristol	2.7	Vienna	4.4
	Cochabamba	3.6			Düsseldorf	6.4	London Gatwick	5.5	Hannover	8.8	Budapest	3.9	Sidney	n.a.	Queen Beatrix Aruba	19.6
	Cali	65.9			Hamburg	6.7	London Heathrow	4.2	Burgos	3.1	Tirana International	11.4			Stockholm	4.4
	Cardiff International	6.1					London Stansted	6.3	Varna	3.8						
	London Luton	3.3					Southampton	14.7	Antalya	8.1						
	Montego Bay	11.4					Melbourne	37.3	Cairo	2.5						
	Middle Georgia Regional	0.0					Perth	32.7	Dakar	0.0						
	Miami International	4.2					Launceston	94.3								
	Stockholm Skavsta	0.0					Naples	6.1								
	Orlando Sanford	2.2					Sidney	23.5								
	Santiago de Chile	4.5					Belfast City[c]	51.5								
	Santa Cruz	56.4					Alice Springs Airport	63.6								
							Darwin International Airport	37.3								

[a] Without Mexican airports.

[b] Without Spanish airports.

[c] Sold in 2008. Source: Official Airline Data, 2008.

P. Forsyth et al. / Journal of Air Transport Management 17 (2011) 49–56   55

- National or regional state-owned airport corporations with (e.g. ADP) or without (e.g. AENA) minor private shareholdings.
- Companies that have been formed as a result of the sale of a group of airports by the government such as BAA.
- Major airports that own regional subsidiaries; e.g. Fraport owned the Frankfurt hub airport and the low cost airport Hahn until 2009.
- Cross-ownership between airports with airports holding minor shares in each other (e.g. Amsterdam Schiphol's interest in Brisbane airport).
- Private Airport Holdings owning a diverse portfolio of airports that they operate (such as Infratil which owns a number of small airports).
- Specialist investors, such as infrastructure funds, which are not directly involved into the operation of airports; e.g. Colonial First State.
- Facility owners and operators, such as companies that own terminals, for example, in a range of airports.

Table 1 presents some details of multi-airport companies. The list is selective, but it includes most of the groups that are functioning as companies which are investing in and owning a number of airports. Most of the main private and also some state-owned airport groups are included, and some government owned groups, such as Amsterdam Schiphol, are listed.

All but one of the groups listed above hold majority shares in more than one airport. All of them also have invested into strategic stakes in each other airports that allows influence of the management of other airports, though Macquarie Airports is moving to concentrate on majority ownership. Several groups, particularly those which are largely owned by governments, have investments in airports which are potentially competitive.

The formation of these groups came about in several ways. In some instances, state-owned airports had been consolidated into a single corporation, while in others, private investors bought a number of state-owned airports from governments at time of privatization (BAA) or bought airports, or strategic holdings in them, as shares became available in the market (Macquarie Airports). There are also several distinct types of owners; some airport groups are owned by government (ADP, AENA), some are owned by private investors (Ferrovial/BAA; Macquarie), others have mixed private–public ownership (Fraport), and there are airports in public ownership but are operated by private airport companies through a management contract.

With regard to types of private investors forming multi-airport companies, some investors have developed as specialist airport operator. Such corporations may seek to develop expertise in operating complete airports, as does Macquarie, or in some facets of airport operation, including ground handling and terminals. General investors, such as infrastructure funds, may be important in that they may have a say in airport management. Finally, another model where a successful major airport seeks to extend its expertise to manage other airports.

We define the formation of an airport group as driven by a strategic rationale if it aims at altering horizontal market structures within which those airports, that together form a group; or if it aims at overcoming market imperfections to avoid multiple price mark-ups on marginal costs of service provision.

Horizontal market structures can alter if a company owns more than one airport serving the same markets. The rationale may be to reduce competition to earn monopoly rents; BAA is an oft cited example. Starkie and Thompson (1985) argue that Stansted, Heathrow and Gatwick should have been privatized separately, but this was not done. Twenty years later the UK Competition Commission took up the issue and recommended a break up in

2008–2009 (Forsyth and Niemeier, 2010). Other examples include the privatization of ADP in 2006, in which a separation of Orly and Charles De Gaulle was not discussed (Forsyth et al., 2009), and the attempt of Vienna airport to take over the adjacent airport of Bratislava. The Austrian Competition Authority approved the take over with some actions to limit market power, but the Slowakian Anti Monopoly Commission rejected it (Forsyth et al., 2010).

A rationale for horizontal integration may also be to gain economies through coordinated operations. This is most likely to be the case for close-by airports, serving the same or overlapping markets. Some airport groups do coordinate flight services by allocating types of flight services to airports. Privately owned airport groups may not wish to refuse service to an airline at an airport, but they can develop specific airports to appeal to specific traffic types. Thus, Hahn airport targeted low cost carriers, while Frankfurt sought to attract full service carriers. Single owned airport groups may also be able to coordinate investment more effectively than separately. A single owner could avoid duplication of capacity increases and subsequent underutilization of new capacity. Investment in airport facilities is a slow process, and it is not likely that separate airports would over or under-invest because they are unaware of theinvestments planned for their competitor airports. As the construction of new infrastructure facilities usually requires formal planning approval, it is not clear that investment decisions made for independently owned airports would be uncoordinated, or that wasteful duplication would develop.

Majority interests and minority shareholdings, as well as operating concessions, may offer appropriate strategic means to allow cooperation within a vertical market structure. Cross-ownership, however only eliminates market imperfections and will only normally offer higher returns if there are strong vertical linkages within a grouping. As Table 2 shows, the links between airports that constitute an airport group is generally not very strong. The share of available seats from one airport to another within a group, relatively to the overall supply of seats if usually under 10%; Macquarie has acquired airports where this share is well below 5%. Higher values like that for Ferrovial exist because the BAA airports (Glasgow and Edinburgh along with Heathrow and Gatwick) and the Australian airports are closely linked. Abertis has acquired four European airports. Luton, Cardiff and Belfast are connected with cross shareholding of between 3% and 8%. Stansted, but not Luton, is connected with Stockholm Skavsta. None of the airport companies have so far developed a network structure aimed at eliminating market imperfections within vertical market structures, and this motivation does not seem to be a dominant rationale for consolidation.

5. Conclusions

The recent wave of airport privatizations has brought some consolidation to the industry leading some analysts to conclude that the outcome will be similar to that in the airline sector where alliances are playing a dominant role. We argued that this analogy is misleading because airport consolidation is not driven by network economies, and restrictive air service agreements do not forbid cross-country mergers. Rationales for airport consolidation differ between the services airports provide to airlines, passengers and freight forwarders. With regard to the non-aviation as well as the ground-handling business, there are no strong incentives for consolidation.

With regard to infrastructure services, consolidation takes place horizontally as well as vertically and may have negative effects on competition with uncertain social welfare implications. Vertical consolidation however can eliminate market imperfections and has the potential to be beneficial to society. Our analysis shows airports often cooperate to transfer know-how, but this is an unlikely force for permanent consolidation. Furthermore, while multi-airport companies have been formed, there are few airport alliances, although there are few regulatory constraints on to stop them. Where they have been formed, they have not been successful and it remains to be seen if that between ADP and Schiphol will succeed. As in the airline and other industries, horizontal consolidation often aims at limiting competition between suppliers serving the same markets, but this has not happened on a large scale with airports, and has been limited in the case of Vienna and Bratislava by the competition authorities. Cross-airport ownership has instead mainly been driven by new investment opportunities.

Acknowledgements

We are indebted to Johanna Arlinghausen, Karsten Fröhlich, Eric Njoya and Falko Weiser for excellent research assistance. Geert Boosten, Wolfgang Grimme, Hans Mohrmann and Jaap De Wit have helped us with the empirical research. Jürgen Müller has extensively commented on earlier versions of this paper. We are grateful to helpful comments from two anonymous referees.

References

ADP and Schiphol, 2008. Aéroports de Paris and Schiphol Group to Create a Leading Global Alliance in the Airport Industry. Press notice, Paris, Amsterdam. 21 October.
Aviation Handling Systems (AHS), Homepage, www.ahs-de.com/en/about_us/company_structure.html
Brueckner, J.K., Pels, E., 2005. European airline mergers, alliance consolidation, and consumer welfare. Journal of Air Transport Management 11, 27–41.
Carter, C., Ezard, K., December 2007. Global airport groupings. Airline Business, 58–59.
De Wit, J., 2009. Airports in recession. Presentation at the Hamburg Aviation Conference, Hamburg. http://www.hamburg-aviation-conference.de.
Doganis, R., 2001. The Airline Business in the 21st Century. Routledge, London.
Forsyth, P., Müller, J., Niemeier, H.M., Wiese, H.a.r.a.l.d., 2009. Regulating ADP Airports – An Economic Assessment. Paper to the 13th Annual World Conference. Air Transport Research Society, Abu Dhabi.
Forsyth, P., Niemeier, H.M., Wolf, H., 2010. International airport companies and airport alliances – The implications for competition. In: Forsyth, P., Gillen, D., Müller, J., Niemeier, H.M. (Eds.), Competition in European Airports. Ashgate, Aldershot.
Forsyth, P., Niemeier, H.`M., 2010. Competition and the London airports: how effective will it be? In: Forsyth, P., Gillen, D., Müller, J., Niemeier, H.M. (Eds.), Competition in European Airports. Ashgate, Aldershot.
Gateway, 2000. A Publication of the Metropolitan Washington Airports Authority, vol. 3. Spring. www.metwashairports.com.
Hüschelrath, K., 2009. Competition Policy Analysis – An Integrated Approach. ZEW Economic Studies, Heidelberg.
Iatrou, K., 2007. Airline Choices for the Future – From Alliances to Mergers. Ashgate, Aldershot.
Li, M.Z.F., 2000. Distinct features of lasting and non-lasting airline alliances. Journal of Transport Management 6, 65–73.
Morgan Stanley, 2001. Fraport, a Good F-rap(p)ort. Equity Research, London.
Morgan Stanley, 2008. ADP (Aeroports de Paris). Quick Comment: Strategic Alliance with Schiphol. Equity Research, London.
Starkie, D., Thompson, D., 1985. Privatising London's Airports. IFS Report Series No 16. Institute for Fiscal Studies, London.
Sunnucks, M., 2002. Dulles looks to load up on cargo. Washington Business Journal June 10, 2002. www.washington/bizjournals.com.
Tirole, J., 1992. The Theory of Industrial Organization (5th printing). MIT Press, Cambridge, MA.
Tretheway, M. 2001. Alliances and Partnerships Among Airports. In: 4th Hamburg Aviation Conference, Hamburg.
Williamson, O.E., 1985. The Economic Institutions of Capitalism. Firms, Markets, Relational Contracting. The Free Press, New York.
Wolf, H., 2003. Privatisierung im Flughafensektor. Eine ordnungspolitische Analyse. Springer, Berlin.

19

THE AIRPORT HOTEL AS BUSINESS SPACE

by

Donald McNeill

McNEILL, D. (2009): 'The airport hotel as business space', *Geografiska Annaler: Series B, Human Geography* 91 (3): 219–228.

ABSTRACT. This article seeks to contribute to debates about the mobile nature of contemporary economic practice, through a discussion of some key themes in the evolution of airport hotels as business spaces. It argues that despite being emblematic of a hypermobile business elite, the nature of hotels as business spaces requires careful unpacking. The article begins by discussing the evolution of the airport hotel, charting the shift from basic lodging standards to recent developments of five star airport hotels. It then seeks to explain the locational geographies of airport hotel development, in response to these new trends. Finally, the article describes how the business traveller is conceived of and (speculatively) catered for by airport hotel operators and designers within a discourse of connectivity, before providing some counter-examples of how such claims fail to address the hotel's place within the complexity of airport spatial organization.

Key words: business travel, airport hotels, property development, design, CBD, edge cities

Introduction

This article examines the changing nature of the hotel as a business space. It does so in the context of a growing interest in the constitutive nature of physical space for the conduct of contemporary capitalism (Thrift 2005). This has come from a number of directions, but many theorists are now exploring the grounded nature of the globalized economy, where some of the more monolithic institutions of social science enquiry – firms, cities, the state – are arguably best understood as in motion, as 'circulatory networks' (Amin and Thrift 2002, p. 63). This in many ways reflects a growing knowledge economy, which firms have tried to harness. As a result, the 'tools of corporate knowledge management have expanded enormously, involving a varied geography, from one-off locations chosen to build consensus, to the movement of knowledge-bearers and the wired transmission of digitised information' (Amin and Thrift 2002, p. 65). As William Mitchell (2003, p. 153) notes, 'the emerging, characteristic pattern of twenty-first-century work is not that of telecommuting, as many futurists had once confidently predicted; it is that of the mobile worker who appropriates multiple, diverse sites as workplaces'. These sites could be mo-

bile in themselves – on trains or planes, for example – or they could be temporary places of repose, such as airport lounges, cafes and hotels (Cresswell 2006).

At the same time, and ever conscious of the competitive nature of guest demand, there is a growing awareness in hotel management of these new ways of working. Recent years have seen a far-reaching transformation in the nature of hotel design and development. Hotels have long been important sites where, and through which, the business of cities is organized (McNeill 2008). Central institutions in the evolution of central business districts, they followed the decentralization of business activity that occurred in many post-war societies, often locating close to major road interchanges. Major chains such as Starwood or Marriott will now have a portfolio of hotel properties of different functional types, both in the older downtowns and in the new growth areas. The major chains have undertaken far-reaching refurbishment programmes that aim to upgrade everything from room quality, to information technology provision, to improved conference facilities, to the data management systems that log their customers. There is a shift towards customizing services towards clients, in many ways taking a cue from the explosion in boutique hotels (generally defined as individual, design-conscious, small-scale operations which many business travellers have embraced).

Airports have also attracted increasing attention as key sites of business activity. Airports are obvious successors of that earlier mode of propelling bodies through long distances across space, the railway. Geographers are increasingly interested in conceptualizing airspace, understood as 'an incredibly complex and differentiated terrain produced by uneven mobilities and immobilities which are continuously intermingling and synchronizing with one another' (Adey *et al.* 2007, p. 786). They are fundamental reference points in the governance and regulation of movement through space. However, while scholars have begun to take airports seriously as complex spatial phenomena in their own right, and particularly as hubs of mobility within a globalizing world economy these have only recently been exposed to more detailed micro-analysis (e.g. Fuller and Harley 2003; Adey 2007).

This article works through the significance of an urban space that combines these two microcosmic institutions: the airport hotel. Often disparaged as the most extreme form of non-place, a site of fleeting stopovers and rapid passenger churn, these institutions are some of the least known, yet most visited, institutions in the contemporary city. Their existence reflects the prevailing patterns of business travel, and their proliferation – in turn – gives an insight to the nature of the regional economy within which they are located. Certainly, they ease the process of 'synchronization' noted above as being fundamental to air travel. Yet they also have unpredictable connections with the airport and urban settlements that surround and abut it, as I will discuss. As airports are often seen as being key to the practice of rapid bodily mobility, it is interesting to consider how hotels also fulfil that function.

The evolution of the airport hotel

In 1953, Hyatt Von Dehn opened the first airport hotel in the US, at Los Angeles International, building an 80 room hotel that was full to capacity from the start. Adding 70 rooms in the first year, he is reputed to have run at 98 per cent capacity over the following eight years, a record for the hotel industry (Friedlander 1954). He would sell his hotel in 1957 to the Pritzker real estate family, who would name their hotel chain after him (Friedlander 1971). The growing desirability of airport hotels was reflected in the longer hours worked by air crew, as well as the need to deal with adverse weather conditions, lodging stranded passengers (Anon. 1954, 1958).

By the 1960s and 1970s, the arrival of the jet age had tripled air passenger numbers in the US. As commentators at the time noted, this would have a far-reaching impact on hotel service standards (Hammer 1968). The increasing remoteness of airports such as Dallas-Fort Worth, Dulles International of Washington, DC, and Montreal's Mirabel – placed in open countryside to cope with the rapid expansion in air travellers – meant that hotels became even more important, given the increasing time taken to commute downtown (Bruegmann 1996, p. 200). However, property developments associated with the new highways that serviced these airports tended to be speculative, both for office parks and hotels, with little attention paid to creating a quality product. Most of them would be extensions of standard highway motels, although the development of sound-proofing technology enhanced their desirability for travellers.

By 1971, the travel press was proclaiming 'the fanciest airport hotel so far', the Regency Hyatt at Chicago's O'Hare airport, designed by John Portman. As Friedlander (1971) describes:

> The Regency is an all-service hotel, with many of the de luxe facilities of a big-city, downtown pleasure palace. There is a handsome, expensive dining room described as semi-gourmet; a coffee shop expansively tucked into a corner of the lobby; an almost midnight-black, rectangular room in which one can barely make out a piano and a great many thirsty people; a large night-club booking big name acts from the East and West coasts; a rolling bar from which comely waitresses in hot pants serve drinks to lobby sitters in the best European hotel tradition; a glass-enclosed roof bar and restaurant rotating for a view of the planes and planes; a full range of meeting rooms all the way up to a ballroom that can seat more than 1000 or 850 diners; and an indoor circular swimming pool and health club.

This was seen as being the moment in which downtown came to the airport, and was a response to the huge rise in land costs which were seen as preventing new hotel construction in Manhattan.

Unsurprisingly, critics saw these new developments with barely disguised disdain: 'most of the O'Hare Airport hotels and motels look like what they and their ancestors are – simply designed and built boxes enclosing row after row of rooms to contain people temporarily' (Friedlander 1971). William Safire, in his 1978 essay for *The New York Times* entitled 'The airport world', made a plaintive plea for independent businesses to be allowed to survive:

> Airport 'authorities' concerned with the character of their communities should make an effort to bring in local private enterprise: a Hurley's bar, a friendly *bodega*, a kosher deli or a Mom-and-Pop massage parlor would be worth attracting to the spaces now allocated to the multinational concessionaires of Sameness, Inc.

While Bouman (1996) spotted a second-hand bookshop at Milwaukee, airports were increasingly

THE AIRPORT HOTEL AS BUSINESS SPACE

being driven by a commercial agenda, rather than one based on such ideals of public service. By the mid-1980s, non-aeronautical revenues were overtaking income from landing and passenger fees, with airport operators increasingly interested in marketing and market research, and to seek out a customer base (Graham 2003, p. 11), particularly in areas with a choice of airports. By the late 1990s, it was clear that running airport hotels could be big business. In 1997, the O'Hare Hilton and the Hyatt Regency O'Hare were averaging occupancy rates of 85 per cent and 76 per cent, respectively, putting them well ahead of the 72.5 per cent average for Chicago hotels (McDowell 1998b).

Unsurprisingly, hotel developments are one of the principal areas of value adding that airport operators can realize. They not only add to the attractiveness of their airports (given the synergies that hotels bring to business activities), they continue to serve as crucial stopgaps for passengers suffering from cancelled flights, and also provide a constant and reasonably predictable revenue stream. Urban planners emphasize the importance of 'airport cities', or aerotropolis planning models (Kasarda 2004, 2006), which are now increasingly popular in Southeast Asia. Here, airport development is placed within a strategic regional plan, which will integrate passenger travel with freight processing and service areas, as well as business parks, mall developments, and – of course – hotels. Indeed, in the context of the European Union, where national functional boundaries are dissolving, airports are shifting towards becoming 'multimodal interchange nodes', complex territorial forms where travellers may change between air and high speed rail networks, or step onto light rail connections within regions (Güller and Güller 2003). The release of platform territory (as opposed to land abutting the airport) for integrated hotel development is now an important strategy, as seen, for example, in Hong Kong International Airport's 1000 room Marriott hotel at their SkyCity development. This hotel is a key element in Hong Kong's Global TransPark model, where the airport acts as an important logistical centre for air cargo, telecommunications, flexible manufacturing, and logistics, particularly where the goods involved are high-value, but low weight (Kasarda 1998; Sit 2004). In this context, airport hotels will play an important role as a meeting place for the multiple agents involved in these new economic zones, which aims to integrate the Pearl River Delta with mainland China.

So, it is now the case that airport hotels are being constructed which are of comparable quality and design to city centre designs (Wade 1998). Examples include Sofitel's new hotel at Heathrow Terminal Five, complete with 'a fine dining restaurant, a brasserie with open theatre cooking and a library cocktail bar where white-jacketed waiters will mollycoddle guests with a wide range of champagnes, wines and cocktails'; London Stansted's Radisson SAS with its Vegas-style 13 metre-high, 4000 bottle wine tower, replete with 'wine angel' barmaids who fly to collect bottles on cables; and Munich's Kempinski, designed by renowned Chicago architect Helmut Jahn (Heydari 2007). Airport hotels in the US were predicted to have the second highest capital outlay in 2007 after five-star hotels, due primarily to high occupancy rates, but also to the fact that a high proportion of the guests are frequent travellers, registered under hotel loyalty schemes. Airport hotels can now act as brand leaders.

This is often closely related to the competitive nature of airport management, with new terminal designs usually incorporating entirely new hotels within their master plans. This is particularly the case in airports that seek to sustain a strong hub status, in other words acting as an inter-continental central point that deals with high volumes of transfer passengers. Singapore Changi's new Terminal Three building, for example, includes a four star Crowne Plaza, designed by noted Singaporean architects Woha Designs. The hotel was integrated within Changi's terminal master plan, allowing for strong connectivity with departure gates and inter-terminal transfers, as well as a pleasing formal integration within the terminal (rather than the box-like structures common to many airport hotel structures). Entrances to the hotel are located adjacent to the Singaporean metro rail system, as well as within a few paces of the check-in counters. A five star hotel was seen as unnecessary given the proximity of many luxury hotels within a 20 minute transfer from the airport, but a 3 star option was seen as not fitting with the image of the new terminal that the Civil Aviation Authority of Singapore sought to project (Lim 2008, p. 140). It should be borne in mind that not all hotels located within the airport platform are within the terminal (Schiphol's Citizen M design hotel is approximately five minutes walk from terminal), and the provision of direct access via covered walkways can add to the hotel's nightly rate, given the greater accessibility offered. By contrast, the Yotel chain – which has opened in a small number of terminals such as London Heathrow and Gatwick, and Schiphol – offers very small, high design cabin-style

DONALD McNEILL

rooms within the terminal for short blocks of time (typically four hours), an enhancement of the long-established transit hotel model. While a four-hourly rate is much cheaper than a full rate, the hotel operator can effectively sell the same room four or five times a day, given the unusual routines of the long distance air traveller.

However, most airport hotel developments are still archetypes of standardized urban hotels. As McDowell (1998b) notes:

> Because there is no effective way to prevent hotels from adding 'airport' to their name, and since most lie outside airports proper, plenty of dowdy, down-at-the-heels properties carry that designation. But many independent hotels and most major chains require that airport hotels be within 3 miles, or 10 minutes, of terminals.

In part, this reflects the changing nature of business travel market segments. There has been a general bifurcation in the hotel market between private travel (where service and luxury may be a driving factor) and middle management business travel (driven by cost and value to the company). Both coexist, but the middle management sector is served by a new breed of comfortable, well-designed hotels (such as Marriott's recent Courtyard brand), with stripped down facilities (no pool, for example, and a single restaurant option) (McDowell 1998a). Ultimately, and despite the growing number of five star hotels at airports, most airport hotel development companies will engage a standard hotel management company with a star branding that is measured against projected guest demographics. This in turn depends on the nature of the city, and the airport, itself.

Airport hotels and locational geography

As with every aspect of the property development process, hotels have their own set of rules regarding location, yields, guest demand, and pricing. In addition, most planning authorities have a stance on whether new hotels are to be encouraged, or limited due to potential oversupply. It is not always easy to assess the nature of airport land markets. Egan and Nield (2000) seek to explain hotel location through a model based around hierarchy, corresponding closely to neo-classical locational models. However, in the contemporary metropolis, the development of multiple nodes of decentred economic activity means that locational decision-making is

now far more complex than before. So while some kind of bid-rent reasoning is important, this no longer corresponds to proximity to existing city centres in any simple way. A recent report on London's hotel development market draws attention to this (GLA 2002, p. 203):

> Gross development value (GDV) is a measure of the value of the best use of a particular site. Although in theory, land will attract the use which generates the highest gross development value, in reality the existence of planning consents which limit options for development, the competing uses themselves, and the developer's assumptions about investment returns and risk will determine the overall site value and hence its price.

It would appear that while GDV might appear to rule out hotel development in many locations, at least according to oversimplified locational models, the final decision about a project's viability lies with the developer. Importantly, the hotel market is distinct in offering potential premiums for good management (GLA 2002, p. 203):

> One of the principal factors affecting the ability of hotel developers and operators to compete is their general acceptance of lower development margins to cover financing, sales and marketing and development profit. This reflects the industry's long term view of the operational performance and profitability of hotel assets rather than the focus on short term development profit found elsewhere in the commercial property world.

Given the rapidly rising number of air travellers during the last ten years, developers would be justified in predicting increased returns and RevPar (i.e. revenue per available room) in airports with a strong growth potential. For example, London Heathrow passenger numbers rose rapidly during the 2000s, which in turn markedly increased demand for available rooms. In addition, central government remains bullish about expanding capacity, perhaps through the approval of an additional runway. The potential expansion may make the hotel development a risk worth taking. For developers and investors, the airport is thus a dynamic market with strong prospects for future growth, notwithstanding fears of rises in aviation fuel and other demand constraints.

THE AIRPORT HOTEL AS BUSINESS SPACE

An important element of the attractiveness of airport property was the intensification of urban sprawl, certainly in the North American context. From the 1960s, processes of suburbanization were beginning to leapfrog airports, breaking the down-town-airport linkage (Bruegmann 1996), and cre-ating an edge city geography illustrated in David Birch's 'rubber band' locational analogy, a varia-tion on the Varignon Frame, as explained to Joel Garreau in *Edge City* (1991). Here, a firm's CEO uses a pegboard with a map of one's desired region drawn on it. For every facility important to the busi-ness, such as a university, an airport, or an area of affordable housing for employees, you put a peg in the board. You take a metal ring, with rubber bands of varying thicknesses attached to it, and hook the thickest band around the most important facility, and so on. This creates a tension in the ring, and when it is let go, it eventually settles over the most desirable 'central' place. For Garreau (1991, p. 76), the airport will be an important aspect of location:

> If, in the 1980s, you wanted relatively low land costs, attractive housing, good roads, and proximity to O'Hare International Airport, the metal ring would have settled for you in the Chicago metropolitan area somewhere around Schaumburg or Oakbrook, well west of down-town Chicago.

For the hotel industry, this served to redefine the traditional hotel – centrality variables that saw land prices feeding into the final room charge paid by visitors. Locational factors such as proximity to downtown, the quality and cost of public transport, the design and lay-out of hotel (again a reflection of location), and the availability of large meeting fa-cilities were reflected in the price offer. Major air-ports such as Dallas-Fort Worth, located between two significant settlements, became regional cen-tral points, meaning that the old downtowns of the two cities have reoriented themselves towards cer-tain government and tourism tasks, with major commercial developments now taking place closer to the airport (Bruegmann 1996, p. 203).

Along with this growing awareness of airports as central points in regional economies, developers began to buy up parcels of land along major road corridors. With Heathrow, for example, this would be the M4 corridor; for San Francisco Internation-al, it would be Interstate 280. The 'SFO' market – the area immediately around San Francisco Inter-national Airport was for a period one of the strong-est performing hotel markets in the US (McDowell 1998b; Tate 2004). However, by the end of the 1990s, it was beginning to stagnate. There were multiple reasons for this, however, as noted by Elgonemy (1999), which included weaker rates of demand growth in the San Francisco convention market (which has mopped up excess demand dur-ing periods of low vacancy rates in downtown ho-tels), greater supply within the airport market itself (an increase of 696 rooms since 1998, with an ad-ditional 1100 planned), very high room rates, and generalized national downturns in leisure and busi-ness travel. In addition, Elgonemy (1999) notes:

– Companies have been leaving San Mateo Coun-ty to the more affordable East Bay and Sacra-mento markets due to steep rents; and
– The lingering economic crisis in Asia has damp-ened both leisure and business travel to San Francisco, shifting demand to cheaper destina-tions such as Las Vegas and Los Angeles.

So, major international airports have generated clusters of decentralized hotel markets. This is not entirely driven by air transport, but may also be a function of restricted supply of hotel rooms in downtown markets (certainly the case in San Fran-cisco), and important regional corridor effects, giv-en SFO's relationship to Silicon Valley. The form taken by the airport hotel is increasingly influenced by changing organizational thinking about the na-ture of the 'distributed' workplace, which in turn drives guest demand for a wider range of services than has hitherto been demanded in airport hotels.

Hotels, 'meetingness', and the distributed workplace

Hotels have long played a significant role in tem-porarily 'fixing' mobile bodies, whether distressed or not. Ellsworth Statler's early 20th century hotel chain offered the latest standards of plumbing and design for the travelling salesman, at hitherto un-heard of prices (Davidson 2005). So despite talk of a 'new mobilities paradigm' (Sheller and Urry 2006), hotels have a long history as central agents in urban commercial culture. The hotel has operat-ed as a fixed point for the visiting traveller, both of-fering shelter and refreshment on their journey, but also allowing a reliable point of contact to business associates. This highlights the fact that despite the emphasis given to movement in studies of business travel, the nature of temporary fixity and immobil-

DONALD McNEILL

ity is as important as the mode of transport (Sheller and Urry 2006, p. 213). Furthermore, for Urry (2003), hotels allow moments of physical co-presence which are crucial to patterns of social life that occur at-a-distance, whether for business, leisure, family life, politics, pleasure or friendship. This is precisely because networked business cultures do not require constant face-to-face meetings, but instead 'intermittent occasioned meetings' (Urry 2003, p. 156):

> So life is networked but it also involves specific co-present encounters within certain times and places. 'Meetingness', and thus different forms and modes of travel, are central to much social life, a life involving strange combinations of increasing distance and intermittent co-presence.

The activities that take place at airport hotels can reflect, albeit anecdotally, something of their place within a city. Faludi (1982) drops a couple of examples. First, she talks about the 'Venezuelan export-importer [who] booked a room in the Holiday Inn airport hotel, ordered his audiovisual equipment and proceeded to strike a deal with an American executive in his "office". He flew out the next day, without setting foot in the city itself'. Second, she describes how a Ford Motor Company officer 'broke off a Florida vacation and flew to Detroit's Host International airport hotel to negotiate with the United Auto Workers. After the session, he napped and caught an early flight back to the beach'. The anonymity of airport hotels may also be an advantage. For example, the US's second largest cartelization trial concerning price-fixing of graphite electrodes (used for heating scrap metal into steel) found that the initial 'clandestine' meeting among the primary manufacturers from the US, France, Germany and Japan was at a London airport hotel (Labaton 2001).

Within the excited discourse of hotel management, there is an awareness of the role of the hotel in providing facilities for such 'meetingness', and of the need to guarantee a seamless continuation of business practice in an economy increasingly based upon mobile technologies, such as wireless computing and Blackberries (Dawe 2005). The success of the Hilton expansion around the world in the post-war period was premised upon the sustenance of such networks in the likes of Cairo, Istanbul, and Budapest, removing the disorientations of haggling, using modern design and engineering to

guarantee effective communication (Wharton 2001). The Wi-Fi hotspots that many hotels have constructed are the latest manifestation of this, a kind of 'electronic nomadicity' (Mitchell 2003, pp. 57–58). For Mitchell, 'other types of networks – transportation, energy supply, water supply and waste disposal – cannot operate wirelessly (or pipelessly) … but by providing efficient summoning and locating capabilities, wireless connectivity links our mobile bodies much more effectively to these more traditional resource systems' (Mitchell 2003, p. 57). Large, multi-office corporations organized around principles of horizontal (rather than the more traditional vertical) integration are now highly conscious of the need to manage distributed workplaces, where economic success may involve the co-ordination of a large number of specialized workers, many of whom may be on the road for a significant portion of time.

Above all, however, airport hotels have evolved in response to the changing nature of the labour force, as well as the increasing transnationalization of business activity. Lassen's (2006) case study of Hewlett-Packard employees located in Denmark reveals some interesting points, including the fact that 93 per cent of international trips are done by air, and that these often involve a sequence of meetings with different clients or contacts which can blur the distinction between places. This Lassen calls a 'life in corridors', where the working day consists of car or taxi rides between offices, airports and hotels, allowing little time for the appreciation of particular places. Travel thus becomes a routine, with hotels (not always at the airport, of course) providing a key structuring mechanism of time-compressed travel. As one respondent describes his experience of travel (quoted in Lassen 2006, p. 306):

> Brussels on Monday evening directly to the hotel, a meeting with the European executive, dinner with them, a beer in the bar, and then to bed. The next day in Belgium at a strategic meeting that lasts all day till five o'clock; then we drove in a car to Amsterdam … spent the night in a hotel and had dinner there, a beer in the bar and then to bed. Next a strategic meeting in Holland; this lasted till five o'clock, after which one goes to the airport in Amsterdam and then by plane to London, then to a hotel, a meeting with a German colleague at a hotel, dinner with this colleague, you know, a beer in the bar and up to the hotel.

These rhythms of business life are, as Lassen recognizes, softened by various modes of 'escape' from the predictability of business travel, which may include the consumption of design difference and technological innovation offered by some hotels.

The notion of the business traveller is now carefully deconstructed by hotel companies, designing brands that suit different demographic groups: the fashion industry buyer or media executive may have a very different set of tastes (and status requirements) than the legal team or accountancy delegation. A key aspect of a successful chain is the return guest, as they represent a stable market share. To sustain this, many chains run loyalty schemes, with offers of free nights, discounts in restaurants, and so on. However, there is a growing interest in using the data held against customer records in customizing the entire stay. Such customer service management techniques can include a smart card, where reception automatically checks in a guest through reading a remote chip in their bag or pocket, is allocated a room by computer, and the doorman or woman will directly them straight to their door: 'Once at the door to her room, she waves her "smart card" over a sensor in the latch. Click. The door opens, lights come on automatically, and her favourite music fills the room, which is now precisely acclimated to her preferred temperature' (Gregory 2001, p. 10).

However, there is an emerging debate about the psychological state of the business traveller, given the increasing difficulties to escape from 'the office' (Cohen 2005). The availability of mobile phones, Blackberries, and suchlike have – it is argued – exposed business people to increased stress, as they are almost literally unable to switch off from work. Here, the hotel room as mobile office is softened and smoothed in room design: there is a need for flexible lighting to read the small print on a contract, high speed room service to fit in with meeting timetables, and large uncluttered desks. Some hotels go further: W follows through the concept of escape by personalizing pillow types (Knight 2005). Such innovations certainly impinge upon life-work (im)balance, couched somewhere between stress removal and a totalizing work environment.

So, by stitching together a seamless contactability from home to office via physical transport to hotel 'office', the business traveller is always at work. The well-equipped hotel room acts as an exoskeleton. However, the experiential nature of such

spaces is not always so smooth. I want to illustrate this with a single example, that of the Sheraton Skyline hotel at London Heathrow. The Skyline's website is certainly aware of the importance of catering to a networked clientele, as the following excerpt from their website suggests (Sheraton 2007):

Connect You to Your Business

Recently renovated with state-of-the-art technology and less than two miles from Heathrow Airport, the Sheraton Skyline makes life and business easier with frequent public transport to the airport, fine dining and superb business services on site.

Power Up Your Meetings

Our 18 meeting spaces include a boardroom with videoconferencing, plasma screen, and leather seating. A 24-hour business centre handles any need while our flexible spaces – all with High Speed Internet Access – set up for large or small groups.

Work Right – Sleep Tight

We know how hard you work, so our Club rooms have the space and facilities you need to get it all done. We've also added Sheraton's Sweet Sleeper™ bed so your downtime will be just as productive as your work time.

However, the claims of hotels have been challenged by the emergence of review websites, particularly TripAdvisor which by 2008 was holding over 10 million, immediately accessible, user reviews of hotels and holidays. Some of these reviews disrupt the good intentions of the Skyline. I use two examples here. The first (Danglebone 2007) challenges the hotel's claim that guests can 'Work right, sleep tight':

Got a good rate of £99 including 31 days of car parking. Arrived 7.30pm and got virtually the last parking space. Asked for a quiet room (had no idea what was coming) and was allocated a good and comfortable room on the outside of the building rather than on the inner courtyard.

So far so good. However I then discovered that all bars and restaurants were closed as they had

DONALD McNEILL

functions going on in them, the only option for food and drink was room service. So I took myself off the the [sic] very nice Marriott next door and had a pleasant drink and some food.

On returning to the Sheraton, all hell had been let loose, there were around 30 cars queuing in the street to get to the (full) car park and cars had been parked/abandoned on every single bit of grass/flower bed. The central courtyard had been turned into the loudest disco you could imagine the entire building was throbbing with the vibrations and had been invaded by around 1000 people. I cannot imagine what it must be like to stay in a courtyard bedroom on a Friday night.

It was impossible to get some sleep as people from the functions were running around the corridors shouting loudly. And then when I finally got to sleep, the fire alarm was activated at 2am by a drunken idiot and the hotel was evacuated. Finally got to bed at 3am only to have to get up for my flight at 6am completely knackered.

Never again on a Friday night – is this a hotel or a nightclub?

The second example I use to contrast with the notion that airport hotels are woven into 'premium network infrastructures' (Graham 2000). This thesis suggests that business travellers are able to pay for priority access to portals such as airport terminals (through toll roads or dedicated transit routes, for example) that have seceded from the usual channels of public provision. Yet this is to ignore the fact that for many business travellers, even at the high end of the market, contemporary airports can still pose significant challenges to the traveller. The anonymity of airport governance, and the apparent lack of logic in intra-airport transit, is illustrated in this reviewer's attempt to reach a terminal from the Skyline using the Hoppa bus service (SFtraveler8 2006):

The Hoppa bus is another story. It's operated by the city or the airport or something, and has nothing to do with the hotel, other than the hotel does sell passes for 4 pounds. Don't do it. The last two times I took it, I waited 30–40 minutes (it's supposed to come every 10–15?). The Skyline is the last stop on the Hoppa's H3

route before proceeding to the airport, and both times the bus was full and could only take '3 people'. They supposedly call another bus, but how long would that take? … I avoid the Hoppa now on principal [sic]. It's messed up my schedule too many times, and it's way overpriced. If you MUST take the Hoppa, and you're leaving at a prime time (and what isn't a prime tiem [sic] at Heathrow), then I offer one tip. After you buy your ticket, exit the Skyline, turn right, and walk the short distance to the neighboring Marriot [sic]. You can catch the H3 there one stop earlier, and reduce the likelihood of being left out in the cold at the Skyline. But, unless you get lucky with timing, you still may have to wait 30 minutes.

These examples are, of course, anecdotal. Yet they flag the importance of the specificity of each hotel's biography, which cannot be assumed by mere location. Furthermore, despite the growing attention paid to 'connection' and relaxation, the hotel's revenue-generating activities (particularly its nightlife, and its role as a venue for local weddings, for example) can undermine its 'headline' claims. And the seeming randomness of the public transport linkage challenges evidence that the airport hotel plays a role as an efficient exoskeleton for the business traveller. Instead, mobility is limited by the apparent failure in the provision – public or private – of an efficient, time-saving, 'last mile' transit mechanism.

Conclusions

In conclusion, this article has argued that the business hotel plays a highly significant role as a business space, both within global and national circuits of knowledge, corporeal movement, and 'light' institutional activity (Amin and Thrift 2002). It is suggested that the hotel acts as an exoskeleton for the business traveller, in a manner that fits recent theorizations of cyborg urbanism. Recent developments in hotel technology would seem to bear this out, with hotel spaces and bedrooms being increasingly tailored or customized to fit the individual needs of the traveller.

In a similar way, the airport has played an important role in urban development, and it is argued that hotels play a fundamental role in anchoring the space-times of business travellers in these zones. The airport itself has shifted from being a lay-over to a new central place. However, this is

THE AIRPORT HOTEL AS BUSINESS SPACE

not a particularly new phenomenon, with considerable evidence to suggest that this process was well-enshrined in the 1970s and 1980s, where corporations with multiple branches saw the airport hotel – as a stripped down business meeting place –as an appropriate response to belt-tightening recession. Yet it now seems clear that with growing numbers of air travellers, there is a market for an increasing level of sophistication in airport hotel design. It is clear that alongside these conscious trends to finance large, business-oriented, hotels, there is the danger that such plans sustain the 'secessionary streetscapes' of recent megaprojects, part of a trend to plug in 'premium networked spaces' that prioritize time-poor, cash-rich travellers (Graham and Marvin 2001, pp. 262, 249). In this scenario, the hotel features as a node in such a network, a meeting point for 'cherry picked' broadband location, in some contexts – particularly in the developing world – located adjacent to premium toll roads, and with an urban design configuration that turns its back on the established urban form of the city.

Of course, it is easy to be dazzled by the high end hotel developments in global city airports. Although it is beyond the scope of this article, it is important to recognize that a lot of business travel takes place at the non-executive level, and may involve fairly routine work (small suppliers, for example, who may have to travel regularly within a regional market to sell specialized goods, or family-run import-export businesses, or conference attendees, who are often on restricted or minimal budgets). As business travel continues to evolve into multiple segments, there will therefore continue to be a broad range of airport hotels on offer, from budget brands through to luxury spaces. These reflect the wide range of business activities and mobilities that make up contemporary travel (as well as catering for leisure travellers, of course). The parallel development of more integrated airport complexes will increasingly seek to marshal advantages to be gained from new economic centrality, and in turn the airport hotel may come to reprise its historic role within downtown central business districts.

Acknowledgements

I am grateful to the special issue editors, the anonymous referees and the journal editors for their detailed and helpful feedback and suggestions for further reading.

References

ADEY, P. (2007): ' "May I have your attention": airport geographies of spectatorship, position and (im)mobility', *Environment and Planning D: Society and Space* 25 (3): 515–536.

ADEY, P., BUDD, L. and HUBBARD, P. (2007): 'Flying lessons: exploring the social and cultural geographies of global air travel', *Progress in Human Geography* 31 (6): 773–791.

AMIN, A. and THRIFT, N. (2002): *Cities: Reimagining the Urban*. Polity, Cambridge.

ANON. (1954): 'Big rise forecast in airport hotels', *The New York Times* 2 January [online archive]. URL www.nytimes.com [accessed 5 April 2007].

ANON. (1958): 'Airport hotel to open: international at Idlewild will greet public May 8', *The New York Times* 13 April [online archive]. URL www.nytimes.com [accessed 5 April 2007].

BOUMAN, M. J. (1996): 'Cities of the plane: airports in the networked city', in ZUKOWSKY, J. (ed.): *Building for Air Travel: Architecture and Design for Commercial Aviation*. Prestel/Art Institute of Chicago, Munich/Chicago, pp. 177–193.

BRUEGMANN, R. (1996): 'Airport city', in ZUKOWSKY, J. (ed.): *Building for Air Travel: Architecture and Design for Commercial Aviation*. Prestel/Art Institute of Chicago, Munich/Chicago, pp. 195–211.

COHEN, A. (2005): 'Virtual office can destroy the point of an hotel room', *The Times Focus Report: Hotels and the Business Traveller* 27 June: 4.

DAWE, T. (2005): 'Business hotels come into the 21ˢᵗ century', *The Times Focus Report: Hotels and the Business Traveller* 27 June: 2.

CRESSWELL, T. (2006): *On the Move: Mobility in the Modern Western World*. Routledge, London.

DANGLEBONE (2007): ' "Don't stay Fridays": Sheraton Skyline Hotel & Conference Centre', *TripAdvisor* 21 March [online document]. URL www.tripadvisor.com [accessed 26 May 2009].

DAVIDSON, L. P. (2005): 'Early twentieth-century hotel architects and the origins of standardization', *Journal of Decorative and Propaganda Arts* 25: 72–103.

EGAN, D. J. and NIELD, K. (2000): 'Towards a theory of intraurban hotel location', *Urban Studies* 37 (3): 611–621.

ELGONEMY, A. R. (1999): 'San Francisco international airport hotel market experiencing post-boom market correction', *Hotel Online* [online document]. URL http://www.hotel-online.com/Trends/PKF/Special/Aug99_SFOMarket.html [accessed 26 January 2007].

FALUDI, S. (1982): 'Airport hotels shedding stopover image', *The New York Times* 14 June [online archive]. URL www.nytimes.com [accessed 5 April 2007].

FRIEDLANDER, P. J. C. (1954): 'New York's first airport hotel', *The New York Times* 19 December [online archive]. URL www.nytimes.com [accessed 5 April 2007].

FRIEDLANDER, P. J. C. (1971): 'The fanciest airport hotel so far', *The New York Times* 1 August [online archive]. URL www.nytimes.com [accessed 5 April 2007].

DONALD McNEILL

FULLER, G. and HARLEY, R. (2004): *Aviopolis: A Book about Airports*. Black Dog, London.

GARREAU, J. (1991): *Edge City: Life on the New Frontier*. Doubleday, New York.

GRAHAM, A. (2003): *Managing Airports: An International Perspective*. 2nd edn. Butterworth-Heinemann, Oxford.

GRAHAM, S. (2000): 'Constructing premium network spaces: reflections on infrastructure networks and contemporary urban development', *International Journal of Urban and Regional Research* 24 (1): 183–200.

GRAHAM, S. and MARVIN, S. (2001): *Splintering Urbanism: Networked Infrastructures, Technological Mobilities and the Urban Condition*. Routledge, London.

GLA (2002): *Demand and Capacity for Hotels and Conference Centres in London*. Spatial Development Strategy Technical Report 13, PricewaterhouseCoopers for Greater London Authority, London [online document]. URL from http://www.london.gov.uk/mayor/planning/docs/tr13_hotels.pdf [accessed 1 June 2009].

GREGORY, S. (2001): 'The hotel of the future', *The Chicago Tribune* 24 April: 10.

GRIMES, P. (1982): 'Practical traveller; airport hotels', *The New York Times* 7 March [online archive]. URL www.nytimes.com [accessed 5 April 2007].

GÜLLER, M. and GÜLLER, M. (2001): *From Airport to Airport City*. Gustavo Gili, Barcelona.

HAMMER, A. (1968): 'Jumbo jets to create problem for hotels', *The New York Times* 3 November [online archive]. URL www.nytimes.com [accessed 5 April 2007].

HEYDARI, F. (2007): 'World's best airport hotels. Go ahead, miss that connection!', *ForbesTraveler.com* 13 December [online document]. URL http://www.msnbc.msn.com/id/22220098/ [accessed 22 January 2008].

JAKLE, J. A., SCULLE, K. A. and ROGERS, J. S. (1996): *The Motel in America*. Johns Hopkins University Press, Baltimore, MD.

KASARDA, J. D. (1998): 'The global TransPark: logistical infrastructure for industrial advantages', *Urban Land* 57 (4): 107–113.

KASARDA, J. D. (2004): 'Asia's emerging airport cities', in *Urban Land Asia*. Urban Institute, Washington, DC, pp. 18–21.

KASARDA, J. D. (2006): 'The rise of the Aerotropolis', *The Next American City* 10: 35–37.

KLEINFELD, N. R. (1980): 'O'Hare airport: bustling hub', *The New York Times* 19 August [online archive]. URL www.nytimes.com [accessed 5 April 2007].

KNIGHT, J. (2005): 'Room of the future may be inspired by class of the past', *The Times Focus Report: Hotels and the Business Traveller* 27 June: 3.

LABATON, J. (2001): 'The world gets tough on fixing prices', *The New York Times* 3 June [online archive]. URL www.nytimes.com [accessed 26 January 2008].

LASSEN, C. (2006): 'Aeromobility and work', *Environment and Planning A* 38 (2): 301–312.

LIM, V. (2008): *Creating Paradise: Singapore Changi Airport T3*. Civil Aviation Authority of Singapore/ SNP International, Singapore.

McDOWELL, E. (1998a): 'McRooms no more. Holiday Inn finds predictability isn't enough today', *The New York Times* 27 March [online archive]. URL www.nytimes.com [accessed 9 November, 2005].

McDOWELL, E. (1998b), 'Who needs sidewalks? Many road warriors prefer airport hotels to Downtown', *The New York Times* 14 January [online archive]. URL www.nytimes.com [accessed 9 November, 2005)

McNEILL, D. (2008): 'The hotel and the city', *Progress in Human Geography* 32 (3): 383–398.

MITCHELL, W. J. (2003): *Me++: The Cyborg Self and the Networked City*. MIT Press, Cambridge, MA.

O'NEILL, P. M. and McGUIRRK, P. (2003): 'Reconfiguring the CBD: work and discourses of design in Sydney's office space', *Urban Studies* 40 (9): 1751–1767.

RUTHEISER, C. (1996): *Imagineering Atlanta: The Politics of Place in the City of Dreams*. Verso, London.

SAFIRE, W. (1978): 'The airport world', *The New York Times* 20 November [online archive]. URL www.nytimes.com [accessed 5 April 2007].

SFTRAVELER8 (2006): ' "Great hotel, but be wary of the Hoppa": Sheraton Skyline Hotel & Conference Centre', *TripAdvisor* 2 September [online document]. URL www.tripadvisor.com [accessed 26 May 2009].

SHELLER, M. and URRY, J. (2006): 'The new mobilities paradigm', *Environment and Planning A* 38 (2): 207–226.

SHERATON (2007): 'Sheraton Skyline Hotel & Conference Centre', *Sheraton Hotels and Resorts* [online document]. URL http://www.starwoodhotels.com/sheraton/property/overview/index.html?propertyID=268 [accessed 2 April 2007].

SIT, V. F. S. (2004): 'Global TransPark: new competitiveness for Hong Kong and South China based on air logistics', *Geografiska Annaler: Series B, Human Geography* 86 (3): 145–163.

TATE, R. (2004): 'Airport hotels take off', *San Francisco Business News* 26 March [online document]. URL http://www.bizjournals.com/sanfrancisco/stories/2004/03/29/story6.html [accessed 26 January 2007].

THRIFT, N. (2005): *Knowing Capitalism*. Sage, London.

WHARTON, A. J. (2001): *Building the Cold War: Hilton International Hotels and Modern Architecture*. University of Chicago Press, Chicago.

URRY, J. (2003): 'Social networks, travel and talk', *British Journal of Sociology* 54 (2): 155–175.

WADE, B. (1998): 'Hotels at J.F.K. buff their image', *The New York Times* 6 December [online archive]. URL www.nytimes.com [accessed 26 January 2008].

20

Airport futures: Towards a critique of the aerotropolis model

Michael B. Charles, Paul Barnes, Neal Ryan, Julia Clayton

Abstract

It is predicted that the twenty-first century will be dominated by air transport, both for domestic and international carriage of passengers and cargo. Thus the airport, as a driver of regional growth, is expected to become more than merely a regional gateway. Rather, it will function as city in itself, with living spaces for workers and their families, factories relying on airborne inputs and service industries located around the airport, with major road and rail infrastructure connected to it. However, the 'aerotropolis', as this hub for industry and driver of economic development has been called, has not yet been critiqued adequately, especially from a long-term public policy and planning perspective. This article raises concerns about three different dimensions to the aerotropolis regarding its long-term sustainability, viz., energy provision, the security of critical infrastructure and export pathways. In particular, this article argues that air transport will not replace existing components of international economic development. The authors contend that the three dimensions need to be explored in order to arrive at a more balanced view of the aerotropolis and its place in an increasingly complex global future.
© 2007 Elsevier Ltd. All rights reserved.

1. Introduction

The concept of the aerotropolis, or 'airport city', has been promoted in recent academic and commercial literature, most notably by Kasarda [1–3]. Central to his vision is the ever-increasing importance of the airport, not only as a hub for human movement and its

1010   *M.B. Charles et al. / Futures 39 (2007) 1009–1028*

immediate ancillaries, but also as an industrial focus around which massive conurbations and concomitant support services will be located. Despite these prognostications, longer-term predictions relating to some aerotropolis inputs suggest a more uncertain future. In short, this paper seeks to identify some of the longer-term factors likely to impact on the aerotropolis, especially from a policy and planning perspective. In particular, this article focuses on three important areas, viz., energy, security and export pathways. The rationale for focussing on these areas is as follows.

First, air travel, in its current form, relies on the relative abundance of oil [4]. Indeed, the use of fossil fuels currently represents around 15% of aircraft operating costs [5]. Yet hydrocarbon-based fuel sources in our increasingly energy-hungry and globalized world are limited [6,7]. Moreover, the transition from hydrocarbon-based fuel to its eventual replacement is likely to be difficult, with great economic, social and environmental cost [8]. Even before the expected transition to another form of fuel is made, rising oil prices will surely impact upon the aerotropolis, at least as it is presently envisaged. It will also affect the industries and urban environments that will have become attached to it. In addition, it is not understood whether future aircraft power sources will take the same form as those used by contemporary aircraft. Thus the current aerotropolis is an economic 'focus' based on a non-renewable resource.

Second, in a world dominated by security concerns, it has become increasingly clear that commercial aircraft, critical infrastructure and important economic centres are subject to terrorist attack, in addition to natural phenomena [9]. In the wake of the 9/11 attacks on the World Trade Center and the Pentagon, in addition to the suicide bombing of the London Underground and Madrid's Metro, various studies have been undertaken in order to establish the best means to prevent catastrophic damage to a nation's economy as a result of asymmetric warfare, or, at least, mitigate the effects of a critical event of this nature [10]. In particular, concerns have emerged with regard to the wisdom of concentrating critical infrastructure in one location. Yet the very concept of the aerotropolis calls for even greater geographic concentration of critical infrastructure around a central transport hub. Indeed, the very *raison d'être* of the aerotropolis is the airport itself, without which the interconnected facilities cannot function in their intended manner.

Third, the aerotropolis concept presupposes that airports will become more important as commercial interest in seaports and rail hubs steadily decreases. This assumption raises some important questions from a logistics and international business perspective. The aerotropolis concept posits that, in an ever-increasing fashion, more of the items now transported by sea, road and rail will be transported by air as gateway airports become increasingly crucial to logistics and distribution [11]. In an era when modular and virtual businesses are now commonplace and components must be shipped from all parts of the globe to an assembly location, it is easy to see why air transport plays such an important part in driving efficiency and reducing lead times [12]. Indeed, it is now regarded as an essential element of just-in-time (JIT) logistics strategies [13]. Thus North Carolina has initiated a public–private partnership (PPP) development of a Global TransPark (GTP). The GTP enables more efficient logistics for manufacturing operations and includes air cargo facilities together with road and sea transport access, all inside a foreign trade zone [14].

However, it also seems clear that certain items, most notably bulk commodities such as grain, minerals and livestock, in addition to assembled value-added products such as cars,

M.B. Charles et al. / Futures 39 (2007) 1009–1028   1011

tractors and whitegoods, will still be cheaper to transport by means of sea or rail, as will the fuel that powers modern transport aircraft. In view of this, the aerotropolis as a universal JIT solution may need considerable refinement. Moreover, its relationship to other main ports needs to be ascertained in order to promote greater synergies between transport hubs.

2. Defining the aerotropolis

Kasarda [15] sees transportation developments as the driving force behind urban and economic development. With respect to transportation, he contends that the dominance of air transport took place as a result of five overlapping waves of transport development [16,17]. The first wave came as cities were built up around seaports, the second as rivers and canals provided networks of transportation, the third stemmed from the laying of railroads, while the fourth was derived from our shift to vehicular transport (which expanded cities into outer suburbs with separate business districts). Finally, we have entered the fifth wave, where airports will be the drivers of modern urban development [17].

Waves of growth are also found in neo-Schumpeterian theory, which holds that modern economies are determined by five interacting subsystems, viz., science, technology, economy, politics and culture [5]. The interactions of these subsystems form Kondratiev waves of growth and structural change [18,19], such as the 'railway wave' and 'automotive wave' discussed by Kasarda, who now envisages an 'aviation wave'. With respect to this theoretical framework, Geels [20], in his investigation into the dynamics of technological transition, dealt with the subsystem interactions that led to the transition from sail to steam in shipping, horses to trams in urban transport, railways to motor cars in land transport and piston-engined aircraft to those powered by jets in air transport. Geels also looked at the way in which these transitions were facilitated by investment in niches that eventually drove mainstream technological change. In the case of the 'aviation wave', the growth of international JIT for specialized industries (such as the semiconductor industry) might be posited as a niche catalyst for more widespread adoption of air transport for logistics needs.

The aerotropolis has increasingly become a portal to national and regional economic growth [49,107]. The changing role and criticality of the airport to a nation's economy is highly significant. In Australia, for example, international passenger movements have increased annually by 5.9% [24]. This is relatively consonant with the figures provided by the Intergovernmental Panel on Climate Change (IPCC), which prognosticates a rough figure of 5% annual growth until 2015 [22]. Between 1995 and 2005, domestic traffic increased by an annual average of 4.6% [23]. With respect to freight transport, while only 0.1% of Australia's international freight was transported by air in 2003/2004, this had a net value of AUD65.5 billion, which represented 26.4% of total freight value [24]. According to present models of freight traffic growth, airfreight will increase to 40% of the value of manufactured goods traded inter-regionally [25]. On a global level, air travel is expected to grow "between 200% and 300% between 2000 and 2030" [26].

Major airports being planned and built (or even re-built) at present are generally conforming to Kasarda's model. This is largely on account of the network of logistics centres for freight, business centres, shopping and entertainment facilities, accommodation and service providers that are located within and around the airport. Supporting this

1012   *M.B. Charles et al. / Futures 39 (2007) 1009–1028*

concentration of infrastructure are roads (or "aerolanes") and rail lines (or "aerotrains") [3,27]. Examples of the rise in aerotropolis-like airports include Dallas-Fort Worth and Washington Dulles International in the United States, São Paulo's Viracopas International Airport in Brazil, Amsterdam's Schiphol and London's Heathrow in Europe and, in Asia, Singapore's Changi, Hong Kong International and South Korea's Inch'on [1], in addition to Kuala Lumpur's International Airport, to which Kasarda links Malaysia's new Multimedia Super Corridor [2].

The attraction of the aerotropolis will result in changes with respect to demand for commercial rent space, which will ultimately result in the re-centring of demand away from the central business district (CBD) and more towards urban development based around the airport [17]. According to Kasarda, the most valuable attribute for land and rental space will be accessibility to an airport, rather than mere location [17]. Amsterdam's Schiphol airport is a current example of the commercial value of land being higher in the vicinity of the airport in comparison with the CBD or suburban areas [1]. This is further supported by evidence that Kasarda cites of airports having a causal link to economic and job growth within their vicinity [28].

2.1. Drivers of the aerotropolis

Kasarda [3,17] maintains that the aerotropolis accords with futurist Alvin Toffler's prognostication that, by the beginning of the twenty-first century, competitive success would be a function of one law: *survival of the fastest*. Kasarda [2] argues that most successful companies throughout the 1990s were those that employed high-speed transportation for inventory and sophisticated information technology. He cites the widespread use of JIT and the concomitant reduction in inventory, the commitment to source components globally and the desire to become faster and more flexible [28], all of which coheres with the concept of an intelligent transportation node [29]. The ability to transport by air has also opened up new and distant markets for highly perishable goods, such as cut flowers [30].

Kasarda [28] argues that air transport is the only feasible means to transfer goods across vast distances with the requite speed and efficiency, especially with respect to the business-to-business (B2B) transactions upon which the so-called new economy is based. Kasarda [17, p. 35] even describes air commerce as the "logistical backbone" of the new economy. It has also become a source of competitive advantage and differentiation [31–33]. As a result, distribution centres have proliferated around major airports, in addition to reverse logistics facilities for the "repair and upgrade of high tech products" [28, p. 44].

The rise of the Internet and the advent of e-commerce are also cited as important factors in the time-based competition model [28]. As other researchers have pointed out, not even the growing use of the Internet and other advanced telecommunication technologies will reduce the demand for air travel—unless, as May and Hill [34] moot, "concerns about oil depletion or global warming intensify". Global mobility is increasing. According to the notion of "compulsion to proximity", electronic communications—at least for the time being—do not seem to be an effective substitute for "physical travel" [35, p. 13]. Moreover, as Boden and Molotch [36, pp. 101–102] contend, human beings have a clear preference for "co-presence" over ICT-mediated communication. This is because co-presence is "so information rich that we feel a need to have it to know what is really going on" [36, p. 102], a view also supported by Meyrowitz [37]. Indeed, Kasarda [17] claims that improved

M.B. Charles et al. / Futures 39 (2007) 1009–1028   1013

telecommunication has actually *increased* demand for air travel by opening up long-distance business networks and opportunities.

In this context, tourism as a driver of the airport city also needs to be considered. According to May and Hill [34], the boundaries between transport, leisure and accommodation have now become overlapped, while interests groups are lobbying governments to increase airport capacity and economic compass in order to take advantage of aviation-related growth. In addition, long-haul business travel and tourism is now often entwined. This has led to the increasing collocation of airports and world-class hotels that allow the business and/or leisure traveller to rest between legs of a long and arduous journey and take advantage of leisure activities offered in adjacent facilities. The airport's function as a regional gateway is now no longer exclusively transport specific, which makes the aerotropolis a logical progression. All this activity places a great strain on the capacity of sustainable mobility and has led to growing concerns about noise pollution, local air pollution and other impacts on the region [34].

2.2. Economic considerations

As an economic concept, the aerotropolis is not dependent on resource location, yet it clearly adheres to the notion of agglomeration economies. This theory, according to Fujita et al. [38, p. 3], posits that "spatial concentration itself creates the favourable economic environment that supports further or continued concentration". Where agglomeration economies function, skilled workers may be plentiful, there may be ready access to large markets for the goods or services, or there may be ready access to production inputs [38–40]. This, in turn, influences community preferences, for members of the public may desire to live closer to where they work, i.e., within the bounds of the aerotropolis. However, Campbell [41] points out that there is no planning allowance within the aerotropolis model for dwellings that could house the working poor, i.e., those who perform the mundane and low-paid jobs that support the white-collar workers within it.

In addition, scale economies may be at play. Parfomak [42, p. 10] suggests that critical infrastructure "may become geographically concentrated in pursuit of 'scale economies'". While economies of scale are most readily associated with manufacturing, it has been noted that, in the United States, the concentration of container traffic at several 'megaports', rather than dispersal through a greater number of ports, is partly the result of economies of scale derived from warehousing and terminal operations [6]. By extension, comparable economies of scale should conceivably exist at aerotropolises, especially with respect to the provision of maintenance, cargo-handling arrangements, fuel provision and customs and security. Kasarda [2,15,43] argues that the aerotropolis is an unavoidable and even desirable outcome of a world driven by speed.

However, as a model for future economic and social development, there are some important issues that need to be considered. The following analysis focuses on three of these issues.

3. Energy and sustainability

In 1998, a report published by the European Commission [44] contended that the indefinite continuation of current aviation trends was inherently unsustainable. Even tourism, as May and Hill [34, p. 53] point out, can no longer be seen as a "smokeless industry". This was especially in view of the fact that "aircraft propulsion will remain dependent on fossil fuel (kerosene) for the foreseeable future" [4, p. 724]. In a world characterized by spiralling oil costs and increasingly compelling evidence of accelerated (i.e., human-induced) global warming, this strikes an even deeper resonance than it once did, more so since transport is responsible for 25% of the world's carbon emissions, in addition to the consumption, according to the IEA, of over 50% of the world's oil [45].

The new Boeing 787 Dreamliner is a response to the current situation. Incorporating more non-metal composite materials than previous airliners, and with more fuel-efficient turbofans, the light and exceptionally aerodynamic 787 uses around 20% less fuel than its predecessors [46]. Yet this, and further refinements on the theme, such as efficient blended-body/flying-wing designs that could reduce fuel consumption by up to 65%, represent merely stop-gap measures designed to stretch conventional aeronautical technology as far as possible [47,48]. This section of the paper will not deal specifically with environmental sustainability and air transport—a topic previously covered in some detail by Upham [4]. Rather, it will look at the question of fuel supply.

Building an aerotropolis, i.e., an industrial complex and urban community based around the central hub of an airport, necessitates the continued existence of the one thing that makes it all possible [22]. Ships can operate by means of sail power or oars, or even by means of a coal- or timber-fired combustion engine. It has also been demonstrated that ships can be powered by nuclear reactors. Many military vessels, such as aircraft carriers, naval cruisers and submarines, employ such propulsion systems (or hybrid nuclear/conventional propulsion systems) on a day-to-day basis with great success. Perhaps solar power might eventually be used. On the other hand, human beings have found it difficult to develop an effective and economically efficient heavier-than-air craft that can do without a hydrocarbon-based fuel source. Even the early Zeppelin airships, whose vast bulk was filled with hydrogen gas, required internal combustion engines that ran on oil-based fuel.

In short, hydrocarbon-based fuel is integral to our present concept of air travel. Thus a future for maritime transport without oil-based fuel is readily conceivable, but such a future for air travel is somewhat more problematic. At present, no economically viable long-term alternative has emerged [22].

Despite these prognostications, it is certainly not beyond the bounds of human endeavour and resourcefulness to develop a fuel that will directly replace current oil-based fuels. Indeed, the best-case scenario is that a fuel will be developed that can be used in existing types of turbofan engine in the not-too-distant future. Of course, it is likely that entirely non-oil-based fuels will be used in existing automobiles without the need to modify their engines [49]. In the future, hydrogen-powered vehicles and a greater reliance on hybrid automobiles are also possibilities [35,50]. However, the current generation of jet engines requires highly refined petroleum-based fuel to operate and appears to be far more problematic with regard to alternative fuels [8].

3.1. The prognosis for peak oil

Estimates of when the world will reach peak oil, i.e., the year in which half the planet's oil reserves are exhausted [51], are complicated by the different approaches taken by forecasters with respect to defining conventional and non-conventional oil, disagreement on the levels of reserves held by OPEC members, and uncertainty regarding the future

M.B. Charles et al. / Futures 39 (2007) 1009–1028 1015

demand for oil and production capabilities [12,59,52]. Production uncertainties raise questions about present technological capabilities in the context of obtaining unconventional oil such as heavy oil, oil sands and oil shale, whether their extraction and production may lead to negative net oil, and the effects that price will have on demand [52,53]. There is thus the potential for oil shocks as experienced in 1951 and the 1970s [53]. With the advent of research in alternatives to hydrocarbon-based fuels, such as cellulosic ethanol and hydrogen [54,55], and calls, such as that of US President George W. Bush, for massive reductions (75%) in the reliance on imports of Middle-Eastern oil by 2025 [56], the date for reaching peak oil may be extended beyond current estimates. The undeniable fact, however, is that this resource is non-renewable [57].

A general consensus sees peak oil production being reached between 2004 and 2061. This is regardless of the modelling used to forecast the date for reaching peak oil, reserve estimates and refinements based on price and cost [57,58]. Greene et al. [53]. qualify their prognostications with the view that the Middle East controls when peak oil is reached. Despite this, it seems likely that we *will* reach peak oil in the not too distant future. Campbell [59] warns of peak oil not being in evidence until after the event, and that governments need to look at ways of managing the transition from producing conventional oil to producing unconventional oil, in addition to adopting replacements for hydrocarbon-based fuels.

Since price may not respond immediately to achieving peak production [57], it is possible that the development of alternative technologies and fuel sources might not be initiated early enough for these replacements to reach a mature level before the end of oil production—or even a point where high prices would make the use of hydrocarbon fuels cost ineffective. Economic growth in the industrialized world has coincided with the greater production of hydrocarbons, which means that, as the world draws nearer to the end of conventional oil production, there is the potential for socio-economic disruption and international tension [8,52,57,59]. What effect this might have on the aerotropolis is debatable and probably depends on the extent to which a seamless transition between current fuel sources and those of the future can be achieved.

3.2. Alternative fuel supplies for air transport

Alternatives to hydrocarbon-based fuels are being investigated. One area of concentrated research is on fuels derived from biomass. There is cause to believe that, in the short term, ethanol fuels might be used to power General Aviation (GA) craft [55], i.e., aircraft powered by conventional piston engines. Brazil has had an ethanol programme for automotive use since 1975 [49] and is leading the world in sugar-based ethanol for GA, while the United States and Europe have developed biofuels based largely on corn (maize) and sugar-beet, respectively [108]. Biodiesel blended with conventional fuel has even been used in promising trials with turbine-engined aircraft [60], but more work is clearly needed.

Yet concerns exist as to whether biofuel production leads to negative net energy [61]. For example, Patzek et al. [62]. have determined that converting corn to ethanol results in an energy loss of 65%. Still, it is expected that, before 2020, synthetic kerosene suitable for use in turbine-engined aircraft will be widely available, with synthetic kerosene from natural gas (another unsustainable energy source) providing additional supplies [48]. Biomass-derived fuels (biofuels) are in themselves inherently unsustainable. Increased

1016   *M.B. Charles et al. / Futures 39 (2007) 1009–1028*

demand for biofuels would lead to greater deforestation, further degradation of low-fertility tropical soils and a concomitant rise in CO_2 output (from burn-offs, net reduction in global vegetation and the power needed to process the fuel) [53]. As arable land becomes increasingly devoted to producing crops destined for fuel production, an adverse social impact could be reduced global food supplies [63].

Hydrogen is another source of fuel being developed as a possible replacement for current aviation fuels. Aware of the necessity to reduce aviation's environmental impact, and the need to find replacements for current fuels, the European Union has funded, in partnership with a consortium of 35 businesses led by Airbus Deutschland, a comprehensive study that aims to determine the viability of the cryoplane, i.e., an aircraft fuelled by liquid hydrogen (LH_2) [64]. The resulting view is that the turbofan and turboprop engines of current aircraft *can* be modified to operate with LH_2 [54]. Unfortunately, the *minimum* lead time for development of the related technologies to support such a modification is in the order of 15–20 years [54]. Furthermore, there is pressure on airline manufactures to recoup development costs and gain maximum return on investment for new aircraft. For recently launched airliners such as the Boeing 777 and the Airbus A380, this process will take place over a period of 20–30 years, a factor which will militate against the short-term promotion of alternative aviation technologies [48].

There are considerable benefits associated with using hydrogen as a fuel source [65]. Hydrogen can be produced through electrolysis of water using electricity derived from many sources of renewable energy such as wind, wave or tidal generators [66]. Emissions are reportedly in the range of 20%–30% less than those produced by current kerosene fuels, with nitrogen oxide (NO_x) emissions reduced by as much as 80% [106]. Compared with kerosene, less LH_2 by weight needs to be burned in order to produce the same energy output [68].

However, there are problems to be overcome before hydrogen-powered aircraft become commercially viable. Although LH_2 has nearly three times the energy output of kerosene fuel, it requires four times the storage volume [68]. Thus the adoption of hydrogen technology for air transport use would necessitate a major rethinking in aircraft design and airport fuel storage methods, in addition to safety considerations. What is more, LH_2 needs to be stored pressurized in its liquid state at $-253\,°C$ (20 K) [106]. This would mean considerable investment in infrastructure to support the fuel's availability. Of importance, too, is that, despite the significant reduction in some harmful emissions, the production of water at altitudes of 11–12 km results in radiative forcing—something already recognized as a significant problem with conventionally powered subsonic aircraft that form cirrus clouds and contrails when cruising at altitude [4,22,34,48]. Of course, this can be controlled through flight altitude, but this would *increase* fuel consumption owing to the increase in drag at lower altitudes.

3.3. Sustainability futures

The issue of whether the airline industry (and related industries) has the capacity to anticipate the complexities of relevant technological issues and other market and global variables is important. This is especially so within the context of medium- to longer term planning. An approach that seems unreported in much of the aerotropolis material, at least to date, is the application of Foresight methods in order to examine the implications of the concept, in addition to its overall viability. An example of such an analytical approach is

M.B. Charles et al. / Futures 39 (2007) 1009–1028   1017

offered by May and Hill [34]. These researchers apply a dual methodology of Causal Layered and Scenario Analysis with a view to establishing an overview of tourism-related air travel into the future.

Although this research is not completely focussed on the trade and commerce interfaces embodied in the notion of the aerotropolis (as discussed in this paper), May and Hill's work does have useful analytical rigour. Generic scenarios posited include "Growth Forever"; "Sustainable Development"; "Ecological re-design"; "Cyber-revolution"; and "Crash". These are contrasted with the standard analytical components of Causal Layered Analysis, these being (a) open-sourced and sanctioned descriptions of issues; (b) social science analyses; (c) consideration of discourse analysis; and (d) meaning derived from aspects of myth and metaphor (after Inayatullah [69]). The factors are detailed in Table 1. Based on current assumptions, the aerotropolis concept would appear to be in the "growth forever" scenario. If this is so, then acceptance of only one scenario as more likely than the other possibilities might indicate incompleteness in the assumptions and planning applied to the aerotropolis concept, as least in its present state.

In short, the oil-fuelled aerotropolis of today and the immediate future, as presently envisaged according to Kasarda's [70, p. 363] "business as usual" (BAU) scenario for future aviation (which, as pointed out above, largely corresponds with May and Hill's [34] "growth forever" scenario) ostensibly represents an investment in an unsustainable mode of transport, powered by an unsustainable fuel source, transporting unsustainable components (many low-weight, high-value components are petroleum derived). Thus the increased emphasis on air transport vis-à-vis terrestrial forms of bulk transportation, especially shipping, carries with it the threat of focussing too much of our energy on a transport system that may not necessarily survive in its present form. There was

Table 1
Causal layer and scenario analysis—air travel (after May and Hill [34])

Causal layers	Growth forever	Sustainable development	Ecological redesign	Cyber-revolution	Crash
Open	Mass movement of people	Sustainable and responsible tourism	Questions of the scale of hyper-mobility	Virtual reality	Societal chaos
Social science	Reliance on free market forces—extrapolation of individual variables into the future	Restructuring capitalism; green-tech; hydrogen-powered aircraft	Recognition of global limits; complexity of human/nature links; redesign of societal systems	Ubiquity of embedded ICT systems	Ecological limits exceeded; oil reserves used; terrorism
Discourse	Expanding economic globalization	Steady-state; gradual progress	Eco-centric redesign, enhanced spirituality (group and self)	Linked minds via virtual realities and travel	Limits to growth
Myth	Faster, further away, bigger, more; the sky is the limit	Reassurance, progress is available; environment is benign	Gaia; expanded consciousness	World Wide Web; instant communication	Good versus evil; societal collapse

undoubtedly a time when the thought of steam-powered vessels entirely replacing those propelled by sail would have been unthinkable to some, just as there was once a time when the thought of air transport taking the place of ships would have been unimaginable. Thus, while the day when fossil-fuel-powered jets no longer rule the skies seems relatively distant, the possibility—or rather near certainty—must be considered with some gravity.

In addition, the concept of the aerotropolis could come under attack owing to environmental considerations, especially if these become encapsulated in future public policy initiatives. For example, a recent report produced by the Foresight Project on Intelligent Infrastructure Systems (IIS) of the UK proposed that "taxing aircraft fuel" could increase the demand for "fuel-efficient high-speed ... long-distance trains" [35, p. 10]. This would be carried out as a means, not to prolong conventional fuel supplies, but to mitigate climate change. Of particular interest is that, in the UK alone, 15–20% of the nation's greenhouse gas emissions could be aviation related by 2030 [5]. It is believed that these gases, being emitted in the troposphere, have even greater environmental impact than those released at ground level [5]. Thus, aside from the fuel sustainability issues outlined in this section, it is becoming very clear that air transport is having an increasingly significant impact on the planet with regard to global warming, especially since one trans-Atlantic return trip is roughly equivalent, with respect to global warming impact, to driving an automobile for more than 2 years [34].

The Foresight Project report also considers the possibility of "more coastal shipping", and even the need for "new canal routes", especially in view of the possibility of "reduced air travel" [35, p. 10]. Another of the Foresight reports contends that increasing energy footprints could be mitigated in the future by means of "reducing airfreight" [8, p. 27]. Among the four futures scenarios put forward by the Foresight Project, two of them entail retreating from the current reliance on air transport [51]. In addition, the IPCC has called for "environmental levies" in order to "reduce demand for air travel" [22, p. 11], something which reflects Elliot's belief that energy consumption patterns must change if a sustainable future is to ensue [21]. A reduction or at least stabilization in the growth of air transport, then, is being seriously looked at as a means to mitigate global climate change. Still, the measures signalled above, as May and Hill [34] suggest, will inevitably meet with considerable opposition from various interests groups, including the aviation industry, business groups, the tourism industry (such as the World Tourism Organization) and even trade unions.

4. Securing critical infrastructure: Dispersion vs. concentration

There are inherent security and resilience problems associated with the agglomeration of economic and associated infrastructure. For example, Johnson and Kasarda [71,72] make mention of the concentration of employment and buildings that could represent potential targets in the post-9/11 world. Yet this assertion is made in the context of central city locations rather than the airport and its immediate surrounds. Kasarda, it seems, has little to say about human- and naturally-induced threats to the aerotropolis. This section of the paper aims to address that gap.

4.1. Threats to the aerotropolis

Airports have been identified as potential targets for terrorists or other criminal activity [34,73]. They are also susceptible to military incursions [74]. As seen in the retaliation attacks by Israel on Hezbollah forces in Lebanon in July 2006, Beirut International Airport was one of the first targets to be taken out by coordinated air strikes. Along with the destruction of major roads and the blockading of the port, Lebanon's transportation system was brought to a standstill. It was only the lifting of the port blockade that allowed movements out of the country. This clearly displays the parlous nature of concentrating transportation predominantly in one form. From a risk and crisis management perspective, the growing complexity of the airport and surrounding landside facilities, in the form of adjacent industry and commercial enterprises, thus increases the potential for critical events to occur. This added complexity also expands the impact of such events should foreseen or unforeseen threat scenarios eventuate [34,75].

It has been recognized that, as networks expand in size and grow with respect to interactive complexity and interdependence, they become increasingly vulnerable to catastrophic failure [10,76–78]. In light of the evolution of the modern airport from a mere transport facility to a critical commercial, industrial and logistical hub, it is clear that the expanded nature of the airport opens itself to a proportionally expanded variety of threat scenarios. Indeed, the airport is emerging as a crucial sub-regional activity centre characterized by growing complexity in land use, infrastructure, transport and stakeholder relations, in addition to greater interconnectivity and interdependence of systems [4,79,80]. A growing trend among the burgeoning aerotropolises is for cybercities to emerge within the aerotropolis. Asia has two of the largest such ventures, with Korea's Inch'on having, as part of its broader agglomeration of infrastructure,an Asian version of Silicon Valley denominated Media Valley [28]. With cybercities linked to a potentially targeted airport, this could have serious ramifications, particularly with respect to the breakdown of communications and computer systems for companies located within the aerotropolis. This could conceivably have a flow-on effect on financial markets.

On the one hand, the concentration of critical infrastructure makes the aerotropolis a target for terrorist groups. On the other, the growing systems complexity of the airport increases its vulnerability to small and seemingly insignificant disturbances that can eventually manifest themselves as a critical event, with highly detrimental repercussions from an economic and social perspective [81,82]. Even a threat resulting in a temporary closure of an airport or carriageways linked to the airport can potentially have a significant impact and initiate a cascading sequence of effects with serious economic repercussions, as demonstrated by the costly delays at the end of 2005 when Adelaide's new airport (in Australia) commenced operations [83].

The notion of geographic concentration of critical infrastructure is of parti- cular importance, especially since it embodies questions of assurance of continuity and resilience, i.e., the generic capacity of a system to withstand disturbance, be it internally or externally sourced, and remains functional. The concentration and indeed collocation of critical infrastructure, which is thought to provide "substantial economic and social benefits", are thus relevant to the continued functionality of a system deemed vital to a nation's economic well-being, especially since these concentrations of infrastructure may be especially vulnerable, as Parfomak [42, p. 20] points out, to "catastrophic geographic disruption". It is important to define what is meant by the term "critical infrastructure" in order to see how it relates to the aerotropolis model described herein.

As defined in the USA Patriot Act of 2001 (P.L. 107-56 Section 1016e), "critical infrastructure" refers to

> systems and assets, whether physical or virtual, so vital ... that the incapacity or destruction of such systems would have a debilitating impact on security, national economic security, national public health or safety, or any combination of those matters [42, p. 2].

This definition was adopted in the Homeland Security Act of 2002 (P.L. 107-296, Section 2.4) [42]. The Bush Administration's *National Strategy for the Physical Protection of Critical Infrastructures and Key Assets* (NSPP) adds further defining information. Indeed, it lists the following as critical infrastructures and assets of national importance:

> information technology; telecommunications; chemicals; transportation; emergency services; postal and shipping services; agriculture and food; public health and healthcare; drinking water/water treatment; energy; banking and finance; national monuments and icons; defense industrial base; key industry/technology sites; large gathering sites [42, p. 3].

It is important to note that several of these rubrics, especially "transportation", "postal [and shipping] services", "drinking water/water treatment" and "key industry/technology sites" and perhaps even "defense industrial sites", might be associated with the aerotropolis.

The advent of the aerotropolis will obviously mean an even greater concentration of critical infrastructure than ever before. The provision of appropriate levels of cost-effective infrastructure, as well as the protection of that infrastructure [42], is seen as vital to a nation's economic sustainability and long-term growth [84–86]. The provisioning, maintenance and improvement of suitable infrastructure are also deemed essential to creating a more competitive industrial environment. This is particularly relevant to attracting greater levels of foreign direct investment (FDI), something which can obviously boost a nation's economy and employment levels [87]. Thus, a more intrinsically responsive and streamlined infrastructure environment, which is what the aerotropolis concept promises, should be able to reduce transport costs, decrease lead times and make a nation's goods and services more competitive [88].

In view of the above, it appears that nations need to secure their critical infrastructure and protect it from attacks emanating from both within and without. This is especially significant given that infrastructure is often geographically concentrated [42,89,90]. In effect, the aerotropolis represents the extreme end of critical infrastructure concentration. Apart from asymmetric threat scenarios, the devastating effects of adverse meteorological and seismic phenomena must also be taken into consideration [9,91]. The increasing interconnectedness of critical infrastructure systems also compounds the importance of protecting critical infrastructure [92,93].

In a report compiled by the Congressional Research Service in 2005, it was argued that geographic concentration of critical infrastructure is of great concern to policy makers and planners. Geographic concentration of critical infrastructure, according to Parfomak [42, p. 3], constitutes "the physical location of critical assets in sufficient proximity to each other that are vulnerable to disruption by the same, or successive, regional events". The hazards mentioned include not only "terrorism", but also "meteorological events" (such as cyclonic activity, severe storms, floods and ice storms), "earthquakes and tsunamis", and .

M.B. Charles et al. / Futures 39 (2007) 1009–1028 1021

"infectious diseases" [42, pp. 5–7]. Lichterman [94, p. 604] even signals the danger posed by "astronomical events" such as large meteor strikes. With reference to infectious diseases, a pandemic may remove essential personnel for weeks or months, cause such workers to be placed in quarantine, or restrict access to critical facilities [95]. Thus, in the context of the aerotropolis, an incoming flight reporting a number of sick passengers, all exhibiting influenza-like symptoms, could conceivably cause the aerotropolis to be closed down for a period of time, or at least become severely constrained in its activity, with passengers potentially having to be quarantined [96]. Such actions are likely to have far-reaching economic and societal repercussions. In fact, if a global influenza pandemic emerged, there is strong possibility that passenger air travel, particularly to and from international locations where the disease is clearly evident, would be very limited or cease altogether.

With regard to policy options that might reduce infrastructure vulnerability, it has been argued that little government intervention is necessary, especially since the private sector will "appropriately adjust its infrastructure practices out of its own financial interest" [42, p. 16]. This will presumably be the result of in-house risk management that will highlight the dangers of a cascading sequence of events within a specific region. While this theory may have value with respect to certain forms of critical infrastructure, it is difficult to see how business will be discouraged, for example, from setting up production or assembly facilities close to key process inputs.

As a result, there is a need to ascertain and further define the means by which innovative and leading-practice policy relating to critical infrastructure protection can be transferred and embedded into a nation's operating environments in order to enhance resilience. From studies already undertaken, it emerges that the establishment of more effective partnerships between governmental organizations and key stakeholder groups will help to decrease the probability of critical events and, in the case of such an event occurring, help to mitigate the impacts [42,67,92,97].

4.2. Air cargo and security

A further concern with respect to security is the growth in airports configured predominately, if not exclusively, for cargo. This is consistent with the "decoupling of tourism and transport" driver identified by the Foresight Project on Intelligent Infrastructure Systems [35, p. 39].

A recent study by al Chalabi and Kasarda [13] has demonstrated that, while larger hub airports have experienced low or even negative rates of growth, medium-sized and smaller airports have grown. This is predominately the result of space restrictions for storage and cross-docking at larger established airports, the tailing off of belly-cargo (mainly owing to passenger security concerns), the shift towards all-freight and the rationalization of passenger routes and ever-increasing congestion that incurs delays—something which, of course, defeats the purpose of JIT logistics [13]. In addition, al Chalabi and Kasarda [13, p. 83] point out that many medium-sized airports "often provide truckers the potential for direct speed-limit access to interstate highways". As a result, some airports have become specialist freight transportation hubs, such as Detroit's Willow Run, a facility which supplements Metro Airport. In the United States, this has resulted in the *diffusion* rather than the *concentration* of the air cargo industry [13]. These trends suggest that market forces, in many cases, will dictate the location, capacity and type of airports in the future, especially with respect to airfreight, rather than top-down strategic planning initiatives.

This also has security and planning implications. According to al Chalabi and Kasarda [13, p. 84], the 9/11 attacks "have reinforced and expanded the need for both secure facilities and segregation of cargo from passenger operations". Thus, the rise of cargo-centric airport hubs, or even separate cargo airports collocated with airports, has significantly reduced the threat of terrorist or related activity to airline passengers—but not to cargo-carrying aircraft and their crews [98]. Indeed, passenger terminals have witnessed an ever-increasing security presence, including mandatory baggage screening and other activities, in addition to a concomitant augmentation of airborne security in the form of sky marshals. Still, air-cargo aircraft and operators are required by law to be covered by transport security plans [99]. In addition, land- and airside transfer areas contain customs-controlled areas with defined levels of security applied, including access control systems [100]. Still, the degree to which these systems compare with passenger movements at airports is open to conjecture. What is more, increased customs and security would incur cost and time delays that would reduce the attractiveness of air cargo and thereby negate some of the benefits of air transportation as a cargo delivery option for JIT logistics [40].

Since airport security is very much visible to travellers and those working in passenger-oriented airport terminals, it arguably serves as an *assurance* of protection rather than an iron-clad guarantee. Just as the main purpose of armour is to make the wearer *feel* protected, so, too, does highly-visible airport security make the traveller feel protected, something which obviously serves a political purpose beneficial to the economy of the region. It follows, therefore, that there may be less emphasis on the physical prevention of asymmetric threat in specialist cargo facilities (and perhaps less means for public accountability). As reported in a variety of literature, maritime cargo transportation is highly problematic with regard to security [101]. Steps have recently been taken in order to minimize the potential for harm to occur, such as the International Ship & Port Security Code (ISSC), the Container Security Initiative (CSI) and the Customs & Trade Partnership against Terrorism (C-TPAT), all of which aim to "reduce the likelihood of maritime-vectored terrorism" [101, p. 519].

What seems clear from the above, as Georghe suggests, is that, in a world of increasing systemic complexity, new modes of governance need to be conceived, implemented and embedded in order to deal with the constantly changing decision-making environment [10]. The aerotropolis serves as a case in point and will require considerable research.

5. Airport as the most important port

In addition to the clustering of commercial activities and human resources, the 'airport city' is considered a strong contributor to the growth of exports. Moreover, there is an assumption embedded in the aerotropolis model that air transport will replace sea transport as the dominant mode of transportation. Circa 2003, international maritime cargo movements were estimated to be in the order of 250 million each year, with up to 90% of world cargo movement occurring in shipping containers [102].

Ocean ports generate large revenues and remain a gateway for imports and exports of both finished and intermediate goods. In 2004, nearly USD1.5 trillion worth of containerized goods were imported to the United States, and USD0.8 trillion of US goods were exported to other countries [103]. Almost half the imported goods arrived by

M.B. Charles et al. / Futures 39 (2007) 1009–1028   1023

sea. For example, the largest three ports, viz., Los Angeles, New York and Long Beach, handled about 40% of US maritime imports in 2004 [103].

Container ships tend to carry items that are relatively high in value per unit. That many businesses currently rely on the efficiencies of maritime trade in order to transport relatively low-weight/high-value goods, in addition to high-weight/low-value commodities, may be overlooked in discussions that suggest a preference for airfreight over maritime transport. In 2004, containerized imports arriving at US ports were valued at a total of USD423 billion [103], a figure which represents almost one-quarter of the value of all US imports. In the same year, maritime exports for a range of low-weight/high-value items amounted to significant revenues. Electric machinery, sound and television equipment and parts amounted to USD7.6 billion, while optic, photographic and medical instruments amounted to USD3.7 billion [103]. Given that only 7% of the world trading fleet comprises container ships, this export quantum is not only significant when extrapolated to global movements, but also emphasizes the extreme importance of maritime trade to the world economy. What is more, the Lloyds Register (January, 2005) broke up the world trading fleet in the following way: 25% tankers; 13% bulk carriers; 7% container ships; 12% passenger ships; 39% general cargo, with 4% miscellaneous [104].

Riverine and lake-based trade is also a significant focus of commercial activity. For example, a 2002 US Department of Transportation study on regional economic impacts of the St. Lawrence Seaway detailed the way in which the presence of an efficient maritime trading system enhances regional competitiveness. The study included the St. Lawrence Seaway and related waterways and ports, in addition to their inter-modal connections, vessels, vehicles and wider commercial users. The report indicated that a total of 152,508 jobs were in some way related to the 192 million tonnes of cargo moving on the US side of the Great Lakes seaway system in 2000. In addition, firms providing transportation services and cargo handling services made USD1.3 billion of purchases in the Great Lakes region—activity which supported 26,757 indirect jobs.

Maritime activity on the US side of the Great Lakes seaway system generated USD3.4 billion of business revenues for firms providing transportation and cargo handling services. This *excludes* the value of the commodities moved on the Great Lakes seaway system. Maritime undertakings on the US side of the seaway system created USD1.3 billion in federal, state and local tax revenue in 2000. In addition, firms providing the cargo handling and transportation services spent USD1.3 billion on purchases for a range of service-related deliverables (i.e., diesel fuel, utilities, maintenance and repair services) [105].

There is a tendency in the work supporting the ascendency of the aerotropolis as a generator of value and human capital to pay insufficient attention to the economic roles of modern maritime ports, in particular the so-called major hub-ports, e.g., Rotterdam, Hamburg and Singapore, among many others. While it cannot be presumed that proponents of the aerotropolis concept ignore the historical and current importance of maritime ports as generators of wealth, there is a possibility of isolationist thought, especially with respect to retaining a focus on passenger and freight movement by air as an attractant for expansion.

A number of notable international instances of the juxtaposition of both an international airport and a marine port exist. Examples of this include the Port of Rotterdam and Schiphol Airport (the Netherlands), as well as Haneda International Airport (Tokyo), and the many port locations close by in Tokyo Bay. Options for examining the interfaces between air and marine ports may be useful for consideration in the future and may make the notion of the aerotropolis more viable to regional planners, governments and commercials interests in general.

6. Conclusion

There is little doubt that the aerotropolis has emerged as an important component of regional and international economic development. The purpose of this paper has been to analyse some of fundamental underlying assumptions that might challenge an expanded role for 'airport cities'. The first assumption relates to the sustainability of air transport in its present form, especially since it is currently so dependent on hydrocarbon-based fuels. Here, the implication is that large investments in the business-as-usual aerotropolis assume the ongoing viability of current air transport technology and are thus likely to be misguided in the long term. Current aerotropolis development needs to be informed by the knowledge that, to survive, air transport will require a radical change in technology over the next 50 years [48].

The issue of the concentration of infrastructure around the aerotropolis is not unique to air transport. Indeed, the same observation applies to any conglomerations of infrastructure that are equally exposed to security threats. However, the aerotropolis concept does propose an amalgam of high-value assets. In addition, the aerotropolis will become a hub for other critical infrastructure such as rail and road transport. The aerotropolis thus becomes an area of vulnerability for activities much broader than air transport. In view of this, further analysis of the extent to which an aerotropolis should be allowed to become the focus of activity within a region is obviously required.

Finally, this article has sought to temper claims regarding the extent to which air transport has become a driver of economic activity and trade, and thereby will replace other components of international economic development. It is more likely to be the case that the aerotropolis will be a major partner in these developments rather than a substitute for other inputs into these systems, such as maritime transport, road transport and rail.

References

[1] J.D. Kasarda, Amsterdam airport Schiphol: the airport city, in: A. Frej (Ed.), Just-in-Time Real Estate, Urban Land Institute, Washington, DC, 2004, pp. 96–104.

[2] J.D. Kasarda, Gateway airports, speed and the rise of the aerotropolis, in: D.V. Gibson, M.V. Heitor, A. Ibarra-Yunez (Eds.), Learning and Knowledge for the Network Society, Perdue University Press, West Lafayette, IN, 2005, pp. 99–108.

[3] J.D. Kasarda, The rise of the aerotropolis, The Next American City 10 (2006) 35–37.

[4] P. Upham, Environmental capacity of aviation: theoretical issues and basic research directions, Journal of Environmental Planning and Management 44 (5) (2001) 721–734.

[5] J. Köhler, Transport and the Environment: Policy and Economic Consideration, Foresight Intelligent Infrastructure Systems Project, 2006. ⟨http://www.foresight.gov.uk/Intelligent%20Infrastructure%20Systems/ Reports%20and%20Publications/Intelligent_Infrastructure_Futures/Reviews/Transport_and_the_environment. pdf⟩ (Accessed May 22, 2006).

[6] M. Miozzo, P. Dewick, K. Green, Globalisation and the environment: the long-term effects of technology on the international division of labour and energy demand, Futures 37 (6) (2005) 521–546.

[7] R.K. Pachauri, The future of India's economic growth: the natural resources and energy dimension, Futures 36 (6/7) (2004) 703–713.

[8] B. Sharpe, T. Hodgson, Intelligent Infrastructure Futures: Technology Forward Look—Towards a Cyber-Urban Ecology. Foresight Programme of the Office of Science and Technology, Project on Intelligent Infrastructure Systems, 2006. ⟨http://www.foresight.gov.uk/Intelligent%20Infrastructure%20Systems/

M.B. Charles et al. / Futures 39 (2007) 1009–1028 1025

Reports%20and%20Publications/Intelligent_Infrastructure_Futures/Technology_Forward_Look.pdf⟩ (Accessed May 22, 2006).

[9] A.W. Shearer, Whether the weather: comments on 'An abrupt climate change scenario and its implications for United States national security', Futures 37 (6) (2005) 445–463.

[10] A.V. Georghe, Risks, vulnerability, sustainability and governance: a new landscape for critical infrastructure, International Journal of Critical Infrastructures 1 (1) (2004) 118–124.

[11] J.D. Kasarda, Airport-related industrial development, Urban, Land, June (1996) 54–55.

[12] N.P. Greis, J.D. Kasarda, Enterprise logistics in the information era, California Management Review 39 (4) (1997) 55–78.

[13] M. Al Chalabi, J.D. Kasarda, Airports: short- and long-term trends, in: A. Frej (Ed.), Just-in-Time Real Estate, Urban Land Institute, Washington, DC, 2004, pp. 81–85.

[14] J.D. Kasarda, D. Rondinelli, Innovative infrastructure for agile manufacturers, Sloan Management Review, Winter (1998) 73–82.

[15] J.D. Kasarda, The fifth wave: the air cargo-industrial complex, Portfolio: A Quarterly Review of Trade and Transportation 4 (1) (1991) 2–10.

[16] J.D. Kasarda, An industrial/aviation complex for the future, Urban Land, August (1991) 16–20.

[17] J.D. Kasarda, Aerotropolis: airport-driven urban development, in: R. Fishman (Ed.), The Future of Cities, Urban Land Institute, Washington, DC, 2000, pp. 32–41.

[18] C. Freeman, F. Louçã, As Time Goes By: From the Industrial Revolutions to the Information Revolution, Oxford University Press, Oxford, 2001.

[19] J. Köhler, Making (Kondratiev) waves: simulating long run technical change, in: K. Green, M. Miozzo, P. Dewick (Eds.), Technology, Knowledge and the Firm: Implications for Strategy and Industrial Change, Edward Elgar, Cheltenham, 2005, pp. 404–426.

[20] F.W. Geels, Understanding the Dynamics of Technological Transitions: A Co-Evolutionary and Socio-Technical Analysis, Twente University Press, Enschede, 2002.

[21] D. Elliot, Renewable energy and sustainable futures, Futures 32 (3/4) (2000) 261–274.

[22] IPCC, Aviation and the Global Atmosphere. A Special Report of IPCC Working Groups I and III in Collaboration with the Scientific Assessment Panel to the Montreal Protocol on Substances that Deplete the Ozone Layer, International Panel on Climate Change, 1999.

[23] Department of Transport and Regional Services, Aviation Statistics, Airport Traffic Data 1994–1995 to 2004–2005, Australian Government, Canberra, 2006.

[24] Department of Transport and Regional Services, Australian Transport Statistics—June 2005, Australian Government, Canberra, 2005.

[25] Air Transport Action Group, The Economic & Social Benefits of Air Transport, 2005. ⟨http://www.atag.org/files/Soceconomic-121116A.pdf⟩ (Accessed April 21, 2006).

[26] UK Department for Transport, The Future of Air Transport—White Paper and Civil Aviation Bill, 2003. ⟨http://www.dft.gov.uk/stellent/groups/dft_aviation/documents/divisionhomepage/029650.hcsp⟩ (Accessed May 22, 2006).

[27] J.D. Kasarda, New logistics technologies and infrastructure for the digitized economy, 2000. ⟨http://in3.dem.ist.utl.pt/downloads/cur2000/papers/S19P01.pdf⟩ (Accessed July 14, 2006).

[28] J.D. Kasarda, Logistics and the rise of the aerotropolis, Real Estate Issues 25 (4) (2000/2001) 43–48.

[29] N.P. Greis, J.G. Olin, J.D. Kasarda, The intelligent future, Supply Chain Management Review May/June (2003) 18–25.

[30] J.D. Kasarda, Global air cargo—industrial complexes as development tools, Economic Development Quarterly 5 (3) (1991) 187–196.

[31] N.P. Greis, J.D. Kasarda, Agile logistics, in: P.M. Swamidass (Ed.), Encyclopedia of Production and Manufacturing Management, Kluwer Academic Publishers, Boston, MA, 2002, pp. 31–36.

[32] G.N. Stock, N.P. Greis, J.A. Kasarda, Logistics strategy and structure: a conceptual framework, International Journal of Operations and Production Management 18 (1) (1998) 37–52.

[33] G. Vastag, J.D. Kasarda, T. Boone, Logistical support for manufacturing agility in global markets, International Journal of Operations and Production Management 14 (11) (1994) 73–85.

[34] M. May, S.B. Hill, Unpacking aviation travel futures and air transport, Journal of Futures Studies 7 (1) (2002) 41–65.

[35] Foresight, Intelligent Infrastructure Futures: Scenarios Toward 2055—Perspective and Process. Foresight Programme of the Office of Science and Technology, 2006. ⟨http://www.foresight.gov.uk/Intelligent%

20Infrastructure%20Systems/Reports%20and%20Publications/Intelligent_Infrastructure_Futures/2055_
Perspective_Process.pdf⟩ (Accessed May 22, 2006).

[36] D. Boden, H. Molotch, Cyberspace meets the compulsion of proximity, in: S. Graham (Ed.), The
Cybercities Reader, Routledge, New York/London, 2004, pp. 101–105.

[37] J. Meyrowitz, The rise of glocality: new senses of place and identity in the global village, Paper Presented at
The Global and the Local in Mobile Communication: Places, People, Images, Connection, Hungarian
Academy of Sciences, Budapest, 10–12 June, 2004. ⟨http://www.fil.hu/mobil/2004/meyrowitz_webversion.
doc⟩ (Accessed May 22, 2006).

[38] M. Fujita, P. Krugman, A. Venables, The Spatial Economy, MIT Press, Cambridge, MA, 1999.

[39] J.K. Brueckner, Airline traffic and urban economic development, Urban Studies 40 (8) (2003)
1455–1469.

[40] J.D. Kasarda, J.D. Green, Air cargo as an economic development engine: a note on opportunities and
constraints, Journal of Air Transport Management 11 (6) (2005) 459–462.

[41] S. Campbell, Metropolis from scratch: South Korea's New Songdo City, The Next American City 8 (2005)
9–11.

[42] P.W. Parfomak, Vulnerability of Concentrated Critical Infrastructure: Background and Policy Options,
CRC Report for Congress, Congressional Research Service, 2005. ⟨http://www.fas.org/sgp/crs/homesec/
RL33206.pdf⟩ (Accessed February 6, 2006).

[43] J.D. Kasarda, Time-based competition and industrial location in the fast century, Real Estate Issues 23 (4)
(1998/1999) 24–29.

[44] European Commission, The Common Transport Policy. Sustainable Mobility: Perspectives for the Future.
Communication from the Commission to the Council, the European Parliament, the Economic and Social
Committee and the Committee of the Regions, DG VII, European Commission, Brussels, 1998.

[45] IEA, Findings of Recent IEA Work, International Energy Agency, 2005. ⟨http://www.iea.org/findings⟩
(Accessed May 22, 2006).

[46] Boeing, Boeing 787 Dreamliner, 2006. ⟨http://newairplane.com/enUS/787Dreamliner/Efficient.html⟩.
(Accessed May 22, 2006).

[47] J. Akerman, Sustainable air transportation in 2050, Transportation Research Part D 10 (2005) 111–126.

[48] J.E. Green, Greener by design—the technology challenge, The Aeronautical Journal, February (2002)
57–113.

[49] E.L. Lèbre La Rovere, The Brazilian ethanol program: biofuels for transport, Paper Presented at
International Conference for Renewable Energies, Bonn, June 1–4, 2004. ⟨http://www.renewables2004.de/
ppt/Presentation4-SessionIVB(11-12.30h)-LaRovere.pdf⟩ (Accessed May 11, 2006).

[50] A. Taylor, The birth of the Prius, Fortune 153 (4) (2006) 65–72.

[51] A. Curry, T. Hodgson, R. Kelnar, A. Wilson, Intelligent Infrastructure Futures: The Scenarios—Toward
2055. Foresight Programme of the Office of Science and Technology, Project on Intelligent Infrastructure
Systems, 2006. ⟨http://www.foresight.gov.uk/Intelligent%20Infrastructure%20Systems/Reports%20and%
20Publications/Intelligent_Infrastructure_Futures/the_scenarios_2055.pdf⟩ (Accessed May 22, 2006).

[52] R.W. Bentley, Global oil and gas depletion: an overview, Energy Policy 30 (3) (2002) 189–205.

[53] D.L. Greene, J.L. Hopson, J. Li, Have we run out of oil yet? Oil peaking analysis from an optimist's
perspective, Energy Policy 34 (5) (2006) 515–531.

[54] Airbus Deutschland GmbH, Liquid Hydrogen Fuelled Aircraft—System Analysis: Final Technical Report
(Publishable Version), 2003. ⟨http://www.aero-net.org/default.html⟩ (Accessed April 13, 2006).

[55] S.L. Alvarez, S.R. Pascual, M.C. Suffern, M.E. Shauck, M.G. Zanin, Transitioning to Biomass Fuels in
General Aviation, n.d. ⟨http://www3.Baylor.edu/bias/publications/transitiontobiomass.pdf⟩ (Accessed
April 7, 2006).

[56] White House: President George W. Bush, State of the Union Address, 2006. ⟨http://www.whitehouse.gov/
stateoftheunion/2006/⟩ (Accessed March 24, 2006).

[57] J.L. Hallock Jr., P.J. Tharakan, C.A.S. Hall, M. Jefferson, W. Wu, Forecasting the limits to the availability
and diversity of global conventional oil supply, Energy 29 (11) (2004) 1673–1696.

[58] R. Guseo, A. Dalla Valle, M. Guidolin, World oil depletion models: price effects compared with strategic or
technological interventions, Technological Forecasting and Social Change, 2006, pp. 1–18.

[59] C. Campbell, The Rimini protocol an oil depletion protocol: heading off economic chaos and political
conflict during the second half of the age of oil, Energy Policy 34 (12) (2006) 1319–1325.

[60] D. Lopp, D. Stanley, Soy–Diesel Blends in Aviation Turbine Engines, Aviation Technology Department,
Purdue University, West Lafayette, IN, 1995.

[61] D.R. Keeney, T.H. DeLuca, Biomass as an energy source for the Midwestern US, American Journal of Alternative Agriculture 7 (1992) 137–143.

[62] T.W. Patzek, S.-A. Anti, R. Campos, K.W. Ha, J. Lee, B. Li, et al., Ethanol from corn: clean renewable fuel for the future, or drain on our resources and pockets?, Environment, Development and Sustainability 7 (2005) 319–336.

[63] G.Q.A. Anderson, M.J. Fergusson, Energy from biomass in the UK: sources, processes and biodiversity implications, Ibis 148 (2006) 180–183.

[64] European Union, H2aircraft—Cryoplane and the future of flight, Fuel Cell Today, 28 June, 2004. ⟨http://www.fuelcelltoday.com/FuelCellToday/IndustryInformation/IndustryInformationExternal/IndustryInformationDisplayArticle/0,1588,817,00.html⟩ (Accessed April 13, 2006).

[65] P. Nijkamp, A.R. Sytze, J.M. Vleugel, Transportation Planning and the Future, Wiley, Chichester, 1998.

[66] C. Koroneos, A. Dompros, G. Roumbas, N. Moussiopoulos, Advantages of the use of hydrogen fuel compared to kerosene, Resources, Conservation and Recycling 44 (2005) 99–113.

[67] H. Blear, The Tools to Combat Terrorism—Speech to the Royal United Services Institute, 2005. ⟨http://press.homeoffice.gov.uk/Speeches/02-05-sp-tools-combat-terrorism?version=1⟩ (Accessed July 27, 2006).

[68] R. Faaβ, Cryoplane: Flugzeuge mit Wasserstoffantrieb, 2001. ⟨http://www.haw-hamburg.de/pers/Scholz/dglr/hh/text_2001_12_06_Cryoplane.pdf⟩ (Accessed April 13, 2006).

[69] S. Inayatullah, Causal layered analysis: poststructuralism as method, Futures 30 (8) (1998) 815–829.

[70] P. Harper, The end in sight? Some speculations on environmental trends in the twenty-first century, Futures 32 (3/4) (2000) 361–384.

[71] J.H. Johnson Jr., J.D. Kasarda, 9/11 and the economic prospects of major US cities, Planning and Markets 6 (2003) 1–41.

[72] J.H. Johnson Jr., J.D. Kasarda, 9/11 reassessments of urban location costs and risks, Real Estate Issues 28 (2) (2003) 28–35.

[73] Commonwealth of Australia, Airport Security & Policing Review: An Independent Review of Airport Security and Policing for the Government of Australia (Review Team Leader: The Rt. Hon Sir John Wheeler DL), 2005.

[74] E.L. Glaeser, J.M. Shapiro, Cities and warfare: the impact of terrorism on urban form, Journal of Urban Economics 51 (2002) 205–224.

[75] Y.Y. Haimes, T. Longstaff, The role of risk analysis in the protection of critical infrastructures against terrorism, Risk Analysis 22 (3) (2002) 439–444.

[76] P. Lagadec, Crisis: a watershed from local, specific turbulences, to global, inconceivable crises in unstable and torn environments, Paper Presented at Future Crises, Future Agendas: An Assessment of International Crisis Research International Workshop, November 24–26, Sophia-Antipolis (Nice), France, 2004.

[77] Public Safety and Emergency Preparedness Canada, Joint Infrastructure Interdependencies Research Program, 2006. ⟨http://www.psepc-sppcc.gc.ca/prg/em/jiirp/index-en.asp⟩ (Accessed July 27, 2006).

[78] U. Rosenthal, R.A. Boin, L.K. Comfort (Eds.), Managing Crises: Threats, Dilemmas, Opportunities, Charles C. Thomas, Springfield, 2001.

[79] J. Hakfoort, T. Poot, P. Rietveld, The regional economic impact of an airport: the case of Amsterdam Schiphol airport, Regional Studies 35 (7) (2001) 595–604.

[80] York Consulting, The Economic Impacts of Airports, Report for ACI Europe, York Consulting, Leeds, 2001.

[81] C. Perrow, Normal Accidents: Living with High-Risk Technologies, Basic Books, New York, 1984.

[82] B.A. Turner, Man-Made Disasters, Wykeham, London, 1978.

[83] ABC World Today, Airport delays embarrassing Adelaide: Business, ABC World Today, 2005. ⟨http://www.abc.net.au/worldtoday/content/2005/s1535976.htm⟩ (Accessed August 4, 2006).

[84] P.M. Herder, W.A.H. Thissen, Critical infrastructures: a new and challenging research field, in: P.M. Herder, W.A.H. Thissen (Eds.), Critical Infrastructures: State of the Art in Research and Application, Kluwer Academic Publishers, Boston/Dordrecht/London, 2001, pp. 1–8.

[85] Å. Holmgren, S. Molin, T. Thedéen, Vulnerability of Complex Infrastructure: Power Systems and Supporting Digital Communication Systems, 2001. ⟨http://www.delft2001.tudelft.nl/paper%20files/paper1089.doc⟩ (Accessed February 8, 2006).

[86] A.J. Smith, Privatized Infrastructure: The Role of Government, Thomas Telford, London, 1999.

[87] T. Makin, The changing public–private infrastructure mix, Australian Journal of Public Administration 62 (3) (2003) 32–39.

[88] L.D. Nielsen, H. Gudmundsson, T.U. Thomsen, Mobility research—a growing field of social inquiry, in: L.D. Nielsen, H. Gudmundsson, T.U. Thomsen (Eds.), Social Perspectives on Mobility, Ashgate, Aldershot/Burlington, VT, 2005, pp. 1–10.

[89] J.H. Lambert, P. Sarda, Terrorism scenario identification by superposition of infrastructure networks, Journal of Infrastructure Systems 11 (4) (2005) 211–220.

[90] I.M. Pikus, Critical infrastructure protection: are we there yet?, Journal of Infrastructure Systems 9 (1) (2003) 1–5.

[91] J.K. Levy, C. Gopalakrishnan, Promoting disaster-resilient communities: the great Sumatra-Andaman earthquake of 26 December 2004 and the resulting Indian Ocean tsunami, International Journal of Water Resources Development 21 (4) (2005) 543–559.

[92] S.M. Rinaldi, J.P. Peerenboom, T.K. Kelly, Identifying, understanding, and analyzing critical infrastructure interdependencies, IEEE Control Systems Magazine December (2001) 11–25.

[93] C.P. Robinson, J.B. Woodard, S.G. Varnado, Critical infrastructure: interlinked and vulnerable, Issues in Science and Technology, Fall, 1998. ⟨http://205.130.85.236/issues/15.1/robins.htm⟩ (Accessed February 6, 2006).

[94] J.D. Lichterman, Disasters to come, Futures 31 (6) (1999) 593–607.

[95] Office of the President, Homeland Security Council, National Strategy for Pandemic Influenza. November 1, 2005.

[96] Commonwealth of Australia, National Action Plan for Human Influenza Pandemic, 2006. ⟨http://www.pmc.gov.au/publications/pandemic/docs/national_action_plan.pdf⟩ (Accessed August 22, 2006).

[97] J. Lembke, EU critical infrastructure and security policy: capabilities, securities and vulnerabilities, Current Politics and Economics of Europe 11 (2) (2002) 99–129.

[98] P. Adey, Secured and sorted mobilities: examples from the airport, Surveillance and Society 1 (4) (2004) 500–519.

[99] Commonwealth of Australia, The Aviation Transport Security Act 2004, 2006.

[100] Commonwealth of Australia, Export Control—Manual 12, Australian Customs Service, 2006. ⟨http://www.customs.gov.au/webdata/resources/files/ACSmanual_vol12.pdf⟩ (Accessed August 22, 2006).

[101] P. Barnes, R. Oloruntoba, Assurance of security in maritime supply chains: conceptual issues of vulnerability and crisis management, Journal of International Management 11 (2005) 519–540.

[102] OECD, Security in Maritime Transport: Risk Factors and Economic Impact, Maritime Transport Committee, Directorate for Science, Technology and Industry, July 2003. ⟨http://www.oecd.org/dataoecd/19/61/18521672.pdf⟩ (Accessed August 22, 2006).

[103] Congressional Budget Office, The Economic Costs of Disruptions in Container Shipments, The Congress of the United States, March 29, 2006. ⟨http://www.cbo.gov/ftpdocs/71xx/doc7106/03-29-Container_Shipments.pdf⟩ (Accessed August 22, 2006).

[104] ShippingFacts, Shipping and World Trade: Number of Ships by Total (and Trade), The Round Table of International Shipping Associations, 2005. ⟨http://www.marisec.org/shippingfacts/keyfactsnoofships.htm⟩ (Accessed August 22, 2006).

[105] US Department of Transportation, Maritime Trade and Transportation, SLSDC EIS, Bureau of Transportation Statistics, 2002. ⟨http://www.bts.gov/publications/maritime_trade_and_transportation/2002/index/html⟩ (Accessed August 22, 2006).

[106] W. Birkenstock, Hydrogen aircraft fuel research plans, Flug Revue September (1998) 66.

[107] H. Canaday, Planning the 'Aerotropolis': Henry Canaday talks to John Kasarda, Airport World 5 (5) (2000) 52–53.

[108] R. Hammerschlag, Ethanol's energy return on investment: a survey of the literature 1990–present, Environmental Science and Technology 40 (6) (2006) 1744–1750.

Index